POLITICAL SCIENCE
RESEARCH METHODS

FOURTH EDITION

Janet Buttolph Johnson
University of Delaware

Richard A. Joslyn
Temple University

H.T. Reynolds
University of Delaware

CQ PRESS

A Division of Congressional Quarterly Inc.

Washington, D.C.

CQ Press
A Division of Congressional Quarterly Inc.
1414 22nd St., N.W.
Washington, D.C. 20037

(202) 822-1475; (800) 638-1710

www.cqpress.com
Copyright © 2001 Congressional Quarterly Inc.

Printed in the United States of America

05 04 03 02 01   5 4 3 2 1

Cover and text design: Gerry Quinn

⊗ The paper used in this publication meets the minimum requirements of the American National Standard for Information Sciences—Permanence of Paper for Printed Library Materials, ANSI Z39.48-1992.

Library of Congress Cataloging-in-Publication Data

Johnson, Janet Buttolph, 1950–
  Political science research methods / Janet Buttolph Johnson,
Richard A. Joslyn, H. T. Reynolds.—4th ed.
     p. cm.
  Includes bibliographical references and index.
  ISBN 1-56802-329-4 (cloth : alk. paper)
  1. Political science—Methodology.   I. Joslyn, Richard.   II. Reynolds, H. T.
III. Title.

  JA71 .J55 2001
  320′.072—dc21   2001028447

To my friends and family
H. T. R.

To the instructors and students
who have used this book over the years
J. B. J.

Contents

Tables, Figures, and Helpful Hints

Tables

Figures

Helpful Hints

Preface

This book had its beginnings many years ago when Joanne Daniels, an editor at CQ Press, approached Henry Reynolds about writing a research methods book. Because he was busy with other projects at the time, he suggested that Joanne consider Jan and Rich, who were both regularly teaching research methods. Their experiences with teaching the course convinced them of the need for a book that presented the basic steps of the research process in a way that was relevant to students in political science, a book that demystified the research process but that also conveyed the excitement and care that go into conducting political science research.

For this fourth edition, we are very pleased that Henry Reynolds has joined the effort. His many years of experience in teaching social science statistics and research methods, and his considerable knowledge of the Internet as a research tool, are reflected in substantial changes to portions of the book, particularly those dealing with data sources, background research, and new statistical methods.

This fourth edition of *Political Science Research Methods* continues to meet the three primary objectives that guided us in the earlier editions. The first objective is to illustrate important aspects of the research process and to demonstrate that the research methods we describe here have been used by political scientists to produce worthwhile knowledge about significant political phenomena. To that end, we have extended our discussion of examples of research on political unrest and judicial decisionmaking, and we have added new case studies of political science research that investigate government abuse of human rights, the influence of economic development on democracy, and the effect of campaign advertising on voters. Fulfilling our other two objectives—giving readers the tools necessary not only to conduct empirical research projects of their own but also to evaluate others' research, and helping students with modest mathematical backgrounds to understand statistical calculations that are part of social science research—also required changes. Particularly important are references to Internet resources for conducting research and a discussion of logistic regression.

The book is organized to show that research starts with ideas—we call these hypotheses—and then follows a series of logical steps. Chapter 1 introduces a number of case studies, which are integrated into our discussion of the research process in the subsequent chapters. These cases, which form the backbone of the book, have been chosen to demonstrate a wide range of research topics within the discipline of political science:

American politics, public administration, the courts, international relations, comparative politics, and public policy. We refer to these cases again and again to demonstrate the issues, choices, decisions, and obstacles that political scientists typically confront while doing research. We want to show what takes place "behind the scenes" in the production of research, and the best way to do this is to refer to actual articles. The advantage to this approach, which we feel has been borne out by the book's success over the years, is that it helps students relate substance to methods. The cases demonstrate and make more immediate the relevance of the methods and statistical topics. Chapter 2 examines the definition of scientific research and the development of empirical political science. We discuss the role of theory in the research process and review some of the debates in modern political science.

In Chapters 3 and 4 we introduce the building blocks of scientific research. Chapter 3 explores concepts, hypotheses, variables, units of analysis, and the relationship between social theories and hypotheses. Chapter 4 includes some new examples that illustrate a variety of decisions and difficulties about conceptualization and the measurement of abstract political phenomena, including the measurement of different meanings of "democracy," attitudes toward political change in the former Soviet Union, and attitudes in selected European countries toward feminism. Also new to the chapter is a discussion of the use of factor analysis for exploring dimensionality of measures and for constructing multi-item scales.

Chapter 5 addresses research design and alerts readers to some of the important decisions that should be made before a research project reaches an advanced stage. This edition includes new examples of research designs and an expanded discussion of the types of nonexperimental research designs used by political scientists.

In Chapter 6 we discuss how and why to conduct background research. We have updated our lists of political science resources, and in this edition we describe ways to search the Internet for articles and data. We have also put a series of links on an accompanying web site (http://psrm. cqpress.com). An important part of the chapter helps students assess the quality of that information. Sampling is the topic of Chapter 7. We discuss how a sample is selected and define the limits to extrapolation; we have also added more discussion of sample size decisions.

Data collection is discussed in Chapters 8–10; our focus is on the research methods that political scientists frequently employ and that students are likely to find useful in conducting or evaluating empirical research. We discuss the principles of ethical research and the role of human subjects review boards and note the ethical issues related to methods of data collection. We start with a discussion of observation in Chapter 8, move to document analysis in Chapter 9, and continue with survey research and elite interviewing in Chapter 10. In Chapters 9 and 10 we include updated and web-based sources of aggregate statistics and survey questions and data.

The subject of Chapters 11, 12, and 13 is data analysis: how do we interpret data and present them to others? All three chapters contain updated examples and discussion. We include calculations and plenty of figures and tables to illustrate the various data analysis techniques. We have also tried to strengthen our discussion of significance tests. Chapter 13 includes material on logistic regression, a relatively new and increasingly important statistical tool in social research. Finally, in Chapter 14, we present a research report, using a published journal article that investigates the impact of variation in states' policies restricting access to abortions on variation in the rate of abortions among the states. We have added a new table, areas under the standard normal curve, to the appendixes, which contain tables for chi-square values and critical values from t distribution, F distribution, and Pearson r.

Among some of the book's new features are the helpful hint boxes, highlighted by the light bulb icon, which give students practical tips. They are easy for students to find and review. A glossary at the end of the book, with more than 250 definitions, lists important terms and provides a convenient study guide. In addition, a large number of new exercises has been added to the book. Each chapter has suggested reading lists and lists of terms introduced. The new design is open and readable, allowing for bigger and bolder graphics. Finally, a solutions manual is available to instructors who adopt the book.

Acknowledgments

We would like to thank several people who have contributed to this edition: Charisse Kiino, who demonstrated great patience while waiting for our revisions; Tracy Villano and Ann O'Malley, who edited the manuscript and produced the book; and Gerry Quinn, who created beautiful new designs for the cover and interior of the book. We are grateful to the reviewers: Paul Johnson, University of Kansas; Paul J. Wahlbeck, George Washington University; Michael C. Gizzi, Mesa State College; Franco Mattei, State University of New York at Buffalo; David Houston, University of Tennessee, Knoxville; Bryan W. Marshall, University of Missouri, St. Louis; Nicholas Alozie, Arizona State University; and Michael Lewis-Beck, University of Iowa. Special thanks to Laurie Rhodebeck at the University of Louisville for her technical review of the manuscript in the later stages of production. We would also like to thank Ramona Wilson, Mary McGlynn, and Cindy

Waksmonski from the Department of Political Science and International Relations for all their help and support—from express mailing of chapters to pots of hot coffee to their sunny dispositions when things were getting us down.

Janet Buttolph Johnson
Richard A. Joslyn
H. T. Reynolds

Chapter 1

Introduction

Political scientists are interested in acquiring knowledge about and an understanding of a variety of important political phenomena. Some of us are interested, for example, in the conditions that lead to stable and secure political regimes without civil unrest, rebellion, or governmental repression. Some are interested in the relationships and interactions between nations and how some nations exercise power over other nations. Other political scientists are more interested in the relationship between the populace and public officials in democratic countries, and in particular in the question of whether or not public opinion influences the policy decisions of public officials. Still others are concerned with how particular political institutions function; they conduct research on questions such as, Does Congress serve the interests of organized groups rather than of the general populace? Do judicial decisions depend upon the personal values of individual judges and the group dynamics of judicial groups or on the relative power of the litigants? To what extent can American presidents influence the behavior of members of the federal bureaucracy? Does the use of nonprofit service organizations to deliver public services change government control of and accountability for those services? Do political parties enhance or retard democratic processes? How much do the policy outputs of states vary and why do they vary?

This book is an introduction to the process and methods of using **empirical research**—research based on the actual, "objective" observation of phenomena—to achieve scientific knowledge about political phenomena. Scientific knowledge, which will be discussed in more detail in Chapter 2, differs from other types of knowledge, such as intuition, common sense, superstition, or mystical knowledge. One difference stems from the way in which scientific knowledge is acquired. In conducting empirical research the researcher adheres to certain well-defined principles for collecting, analyzing, and evaluating information. **Political science**, then, is simply the application of these principles to the study of phenomena that are political in nature.

There are two major reasons why students should learn about how political scientists conduct empirical research. First, citizens in contemporary American society are often called upon to evaluate empirical research about political phenomena. Debates about the wisdom of the death penalty, for example, frequently hinge on whether or not it is an effective deterrent to crime, and debates about term limits for elected officials involve whether or not such limits increase the competitiveness of elections. Similarly, evaluating current developments in Eastern Europe, Southeast Asia, Central America, and South Africa requires an understanding of the role of competitive elections, rights of expression, religious tolerance, and the ownership of private property in the development of democratic institutions and beliefs. In these and many other cases, thoughtful and concerned citizens find that they must evaluate the accuracy and adequacy of the theories and research of political (and other social) scientists.

A second reason for learning about political science research methods is that students often need to acquire scientific knowledge of their own, whether for a term paper for an introductory course on American government, a research project for an upper-level seminar, or a series of assignments in a course devoted to learning empirical research methods. Familiarity with empirical research methods is generally a prerequisite to making this a profitable endeavor.

The prospect of learning empirical research methods is often intimidating to students. Sometimes students dislike this type of inquiry because it involves numbers and statistics. Although to understand research well one must have a basic knowledge of statistics and how to use statistics in analyzing and reporting research findings, the empirical research process that we will describe here is first and foremost a way of thinking and a prescription for disciplined reasoning. Statistics will be introduced only after an understanding of the thought process involved in scientific inquiry is established, and then in a nontechnical way that should be understandable to any student familiar with basic algebra.

Students are also sometimes uneasy about taking a course in social science research methods because they view it as unrelated to other courses in their political science curriculum. But an understanding of the concepts normally included in a course in social science research methods is integrally related to a student's assimilation, evaluation, and production of knowledge in other courses. An important result of understanding the scientific research process is that a student may begin to think more independently about concepts and theories presented in other courses and readings. For example, a student might say, "That may be true under the given conditions, but I believe it won't remain true under the following conditions. . . ." Or, "If this theory is correct, I would expect to be able to observe the following. . . ." Or, "Before I'm going to accept that interpretation, I'd like to have this additional information. . . ." Students who can specify what information is needed and what relationships between phenomena must be observed in support of an idea are more likely to develop an understanding of the subjects they study.

Researchers conduct empirical research studies for two primary reasons. One reason is to accumulate knowledge that will apply to a particular problem in need of solution or to a condition in need of improvement. Research on the causes of crime, for example, may be useful for reducing crime rates, and research on the reasons for poverty may aid governments in devising successful income maintenance and social welfare policies. Such research is often referred to as **applied research** because it has a fairly direct, immediate application to a real-world situation.

Researchers also conduct empirical research to satisfy their intellectual curiosity about a subject, regardless of whether the research will lead to changes in governmental policy or private behavior. Many political scientists, for example, study the decision-making processes of voters not because they are interested in giving practical advice to political candidates but because they want to know if elections give the populace some measure of influence over the behavior of elected public officials. Such research is sometimes referred to as **pure, theoretical,** or **recreational research** to indicate that it is not concerned primarily with practical applications.[1]

Ordinarily political scientists report the results of their research in books or articles published in political research journals (see Chapter 6 for some examples of these journals). Research reported in academic journals typically contains data and information from which to draw conclusions. It also undergoes peer review, a process in which other scholars evaluate the soundness of the research before it is published. Occasionally, however, political science research questions and analyses appear in newspapers and magazines, which have a wider audience. Such popularly presented investigations can utilize empirical political science methods and techniques as well.

In this chapter we will describe several political science research projects that were designed to produce scientific knowledge about significant political phenomena. We will be referring to these examples throughout this book to illustrate many aspects of the research process. We present them in some detail now so that you will find the later discussions easier to understand. We do not expect you to master all the details at this point, rather, you should read these examples keeping in mind that their purpose is to illustrate a variety of actual research topics and methods of investigation. They also show how decisions about various aspects of the research process affect the conclusions that may be drawn about the phenomena under study. And they represent attempts by political scientists to acquire knowledge by building on the research of others to arrive at increasingly complete explanations of political behavior and processes.

Research on Regime Stability

One of the most interesting political phenomena in the world today is the variation in stability of political regimes. We live in a time of rapid change around the globe, with governmental shifts and civil unrest prevalent in Central

America, Eastern Europe, Southern Africa, and Southeast Asia. In contrast, the United States has embarked on its third century of relatively stable politics, and many other nation-states have also experienced long periods of political calm and continuity. It is only natural, then, for political scientists and others to wonder why some governments are more stable than others and to attempt to provide systematic explanations for the observed variation in regime stability.

Attempts to discover the factors leading to civil unrest and governmental change have been made for decades. One of the first such attempts to use empirical research methods may be found in *Why Men Rebel* by Ted Robert Gurr.[2] Gurr developed the concept of relative deprivation to explain and predict the amount of political violence in different countries. The concept is based on the belief that frustration leads to aggression. Gurr states that a gap may exist between the goods and conditions to which people believe they are rightfully entitled (people's *expectations*) and those that they think they are capable of attaining or maintaining (people's *capabilities*). The larger this gap, or relative deprivation, Gurr theorizes, the greater the frustration and the greater the chances of political violence. Increases in relative deprivation can result from (1) a decline in capabilities while expectations increase, (2) a decline in capabilities while expectations remain the same, or (3) an increase in expectations with no perceived accompanying change in capabilities. Thus absolute deprivation in objective terms does not lead to frustration if expectations are equally low; it is relative deprivation that is important.

To test his theory Gurr produced a measure of relative deprivation in thirteen nations based on the responses of individuals to opinion polls administered from 1957 to 1963. The polls asked respondents how they compared their past, present, and future position with their ideal of a good life. When this measure of relative deprivation was related to the magnitude of turmoil in the countries between 1961 and 1965, a fairly strong relationship was found, supporting the theory that the greater the relative deprivation, the greater the internal violence.

Gurr went on to suggest that relative deprivation is influenced by a number of factors, including economic well-being; power values, such as physical security and ability to participate in politics; and interpersonal values, such as social status, family happiness, and moral and ethical standards. Whether or not relative deprivation leads to political violence (defined by Gurr as violent political strikes, riots, coups d'état, civil wars, and revolutions) depends upon the extent and intensity of shared discontent by members of a society and the degree to which the political system and political actors are blamed. Moral and social attitudes toward violence and the expression of aggression, the use of alternative methods of redress, the expected utility of violence, and the extent of coercive measures practiced by the ruling regime also affect the likelihood of political violence.

Group expectations are related to the greatest gains experienced by other groups perceived to be socioeconomically similar, Gurr suggests. For instance, wage and benefit demands by one set of municipal workers are related to the gains of similar sets of municipal workers more than they are related to similar or dissimilar groups of workers in the private sector. Gurr also takes note of the theory that exposure to Western ways of life makes non-Westerners discontented with their own way of life and that migration to urban areas raises expectations unreasonably and hence leads to violence.

Although Gurr was able to find some empirical evidence in support of his relative deprivation hypothesis, his research did not result in a definitive or complete explanation of civil unrest or regime instability. Consequently many other political scientists have attempted to provide their own explanations for these phenomena. Let us take a look at three interesting attempts to account for violent political change in Latin America, Africa, and other parts of the world.

Explanations of political violence in Latin America often center on the unequal distribution of land.[3] To date, however, research on the topic has failed to produce a consensus about how political violence relates to land ownership inequalities. One problem is that it is unclear what kind of land ownership pattern is likely to lead to political violence. Some believe the most salient pattern occurs when a few people own most of the land and most people own little land; others focus on the pattern in which many people are without land. Clearly, how one measures land ownership is crucial to developing any explanation of political violence in Latin America.

Another challenge for research in this area is whether land inequality leads directly to political rebellion or whether other factors exist that either inhibit or exacerbate this connection. Land inequality may lead to political violence, for example, only when governmental authorities are disliked or viewed with suspicion. As a result, researchers are constantly reexamining the theories that lead them to expect relationships between such phenomena as land inequality and political violence to develop more complete explanations for such complicated behaviors.

Political scientists have also been interested in attempting to explain regime instability on the African continent. Over the past thirty-five years in many African nations changes in regime, often effected by military coups, have been common while in several other nations a single leader has retained power over many years. This situation has attracted the interest of scholars curious about the factors that distinguish stable from unstable regimes.

It is common to explain regime change in African systems of personal rule with factors such as the social, economic, and political characteristics of the countries and the leadership styles and personal characteristics of the leaders. Therefore such phenomena as a country's colonial experience, rate of economic growth, income level, and degree of ethnic conflict and a leader's means of achieving power, military background, and age have been measured and investigated by researchers.

One analysis of regime stability in Africa found that one of the best predictors of a ruler's persistence is the length of time he has been in power. Generally, the longer a ruler has been in power the more apt he is to continue in power regardless of other characteristics of the country and leader. The researchers believe that the length of time a ruler has been in power captures phenomena that are difficult to observe directly, such as a leader's ability to build and wield "networks of information, repression, and patronage."[4]

Another team of researchers sought an explanation of regime stability by extending their study beyond the African continent. Bruce Bueno de Mesquita, Randolph Siverson, and Gary Woller investigated the impact of foreign policy, including participation in an international war, on the probability of violent changes within a regime using information on international wars that occurred around the world between 1816 and 1975.[5] After exploring the relationships between regime change and that regime's role in a preceding war (Was the regime the initiator, target, or something else during the war?), the outcome of the war, and the costs of war participation, they discovered that of the 177 war-participating nations studied, 32 experienced violent regime change within three years of the war's end. Furthermore, they determined that regime changes are far more likely when a nation has lost a war and when there are a large number of battle deaths, and are less likely when a nation is a victorious initiator of a war.

Political scientists investigate the causes of civil unrest and regime instability primarily out of curiosity or the desire to promote better understanding of events of great consequence to humans. Although corporations and investment groups that must decide where to locate plants or invest overseas sometimes hire specialists to predict whether particular foreign countries are apt to experience political unrest and economic disruption, more often researchers work in this area not for money but because they are intrigued by governmental change, political unrest, and the transfer of political authority.

No doubt understanding the causes of civil unrest and regime instability will be an enduring topic of interest for decades to come. Similarly, other political scientists are interested in the consequences of civil unrest, particularly in the reactions of regimes to unrest. Our next two examples look at governmental reaction to civil unrest.

Repression of Human Rights

In recent years there has been increased public and scholarly interest in the human rights practices of governments. Several organizations (Amnesty International, the U.S. Department of State, and Freedom House, for example) publish annual reports on the human rights performance of nations worldwide. Researchers Stephen Poe and C. Neal Tate investigated the causes of state terrorism, which involves violations of personal integrity rights and includes such acts as murder, torture, forced disappearance, and imprisonment of persons for their political views.[6] Poe and Tate sought to explain variation of government or regime performance in human rights in 153 countries during the 1980s. Most of the previous studies on human rights abuses compared the practices of a more limited set of nations at a single point in time. Poe and Tate built upon the earlier research by examining change that occurred within a given country across a specified period of time.

Poe and Tate considered the following as possible explanations of variations in state terrorism:

- Presence of democratic procedures and protections (democracy). Because they offer an alternative method of settling conflicts, and because they provide citizens with the tools to oust potentially abusive leaders from office, democratic procedures and protections minimize serious threats to human rights. In fact, some definitions of human rights include wording that notes the need for access to democratic procedures and protections. (By focusing on variation in state coercion, the authors made sure that their measures of democracy were distinct from their measures of human rights abuses.)

- Population size and growth. A large population increases the number of opportunities for government coercion and creates stress on available resources. Rapid population growth creates even greater stress. In addition, rapid population growth results in an increase in the proportion of the population that is young, an age cohort that is more likely to engage in criminal behavior and threaten public order.

- Level of economic development and economic growth. Following Gurr's theory, rapid economic growth creates resentment within those classes that are not benefiting from the new wealth. Such resentment could destabilize a regime and thereby promote repression. However, higher levels of economic development will result in less repression as highly developed countries are able to meet the needs of their people.

- Establishment of leftist regime. States governed by a socialist party or coalition that does not permit effective electoral competition with nonsocialist opposition and removal from office of abusive leaders are predicted to have higher levels of state terrorism.

- Establishment of military regime. Military regimes are expected to be more coercive than other types of regimes, but this hypothesis needs to be tested because some military regimes take power claiming that the previous regime was violating the rights of citizens.

- British cultural influence. A colonial tie to British political and cultural influences is more favorable to protection of human rights than is a tie to other colonial influences.

- International and civil war experience. A state's experiences with both international and civil war influence a government's use of repression to control its citizens.

Poe and Tate found that governments with established democratic procedures and protections were unlikely to engage in human rights abuses. They also found that governments in more populous countries were more likely to engage in human rights abuses than were governments in less populous countries. However, population growth in and of itself did not affect levels of government repression. Neither did a history of British cultural influence nor the presence of an established military regime. Economic development had only a weak impact on reducing human rights abuses, while the impact of leftist governments was mixed. Poe and Tate found that national experience in international and civil wars had "statistically significant and substantively important impacts on national respect for the personal integrity of citizens . . . with civil war participation having a somewhat larger impact than participation in international war."[7] Experience with civil war appeared less likely to provoke human rights abuses in countries with democratic governments. Poe and Tate concluded that "basic rights can be enhanced by actors who would encourage countries to solve their political conflicts short of war, and use whatever means are at their disposal to assist them in doing so."[8]

Welfare: A Reaction to Civil Unrest?

The development and expansion of the modern welfare state in the United States is associated with the Great Depression of the 1930s and the War on Poverty in the 1960s. While welfare programs may be seen as simply a response to need, Frances Fox Piven and Richard Cloward offered a more political interpretation in their book, *Regulating the Poor.*[9] Piven and Cloward argue that modern capitalist states respond to civil unrest within the ranks of the economically disadvantaged by expanding relief rolls in order to maintain social control. Specifically, they contend that the rapid growth of the Aid to Families with Dependent Children (AFDC) program was a response to racial insurgency and the many incidents of black-related violence in the late 1960s. If their argument is correct, expansion of AFDC programs should vary systematically with unrest, not just in relationship to variation in need. Piven and Cloward's theory of welfare expansion is called the "insurgency thesis" and has been tested by numerous social scientists over the years.

A recent article by Richard Fording reviewed the results of previous studies, some of which supported the insurgency thesis and some of which did not.[10] Fording argues that previous research was flawed in a variety of ways. For example, many of the previous studies looked at variation in economic need as a cause of changes in welfare programs, but they used measures of overall poverty to gauge need rather than the number of female-headed families below poverty (AFDC was a program targeted at female-headed families). As trends in overall need and the prevalence of female-headed families differed (between 1959 and 1975, the number of families below poverty decreased 35 percent, while the number of female-headed families below poverty increased by 48 percent), tests for economic need as an alternative explanation could have been affected. Fording's research looked at the relationship between the level of civil unrest and growth in AFDC recipient rates for states on a year to year basis over a period of years, taking into account the level of state unemployment and presence of female-headed households.

In addition, Fording investigated a line of theoretical reasoning suggested by Piven and Cloward but never tested in previous research. Social control of threatening groups can take two forms: beneficent control or repressive control. Expanding welfare rolls is an example of beneficent controls. Piven and Cloward suggest that black insurgency in the 1960s met with a beneficent response because of the critical role black votes were expected to play in future elections. Fording observes, however, that the electoral power of blacks varied among the states. In the South blacks did not possess any significant electoral power until the passage and implementation of the Voting Rights Act of 1965. Outside the South, malapportioned electoral districts severely underrepresented urban areas where black communities were heavily concentrated. Fording argues that any model of the effect of civil unrest has to take into account access to electoral institutions. Furthermore, where blacks have access to electoral institutions, the relative size of the black population must be taken into account. Responsiveness to insurgency can be high in communities with relatively few blacks since white resistance is likely to be low. As the black population increases, Fording predicts that responsiveness will decline until the bloc of black voters is sufficiently large to overcome white resistance.[11]

Fording found that the relief explosion between 1962 and 1980 did not appear to be related to increasing economic capacity to pay for social welfare, nor to unemployment or female poverty. Rather, expansion of the rolls was related to population-based electoral systems, the abolition by the Supreme Court of state residency requirements governing the receipt of welfare, increasing party competition in state politics, the extension of medical coverage to AFDC recipients, and mass insurgency. Fording concluded that his analysis demonstrated that political violence can bring benefits to insurgent groups in the United States, benefits that are often more substantial than those brought about by more conventional means. Significant benefits are not guaranteed, however, and appear to be contingent upon several factors, including the existence of democratic institutions, the extension of the franchise to members of the insurgent population, the numerical strength of the insurgent groups, and the relationship between the insurgent group and the rest of society.[12]

Thus mass insurgency during the 1930s resulted in significant change due to the size of the insurgent group (labor); political violence was more severe during the 1960s, but its effectiveness was more limited due to the relatively small size of the black electorate. Fording suggests that success in eliciting a beneficent response by other groups employing political violence such as farm labor and the antiabortion movement may also vary across the states due to significant differences in the size of the insurgent population and opposition groups.[13]

Does Economic Development Promote Democracy?

Much political science research asks questions about the causes of differences in political practices among nations and the impact of those differences on politics and policies within nations. This type of research generally is subsumed under the label of comparative politics. The research on the causes of human rights abuses discussed above is an example of comparative politics research. Another example of comparative politics research concerns the relationship between countries' economic development and their mode of government. Democracy has long been linked to economic development, and numerous studies have demonstrated that the state of economic development influences the state of political development. Then, two studies conducted in the late 1980s challenged this conclusion, which in turn prompted a more recent analysis reevaluating the effect of economic development on the presence of democratic political systems.[14]

In their research Ross Burkhart and Michael Lewis-Beck used different measures of democracy that they argue are more accurate than previous measures and different statistical procedures that allowed them to look at the impact of economic development on democracy in nations over time, rather than simply looking at the association of economic development and democracy for a group of nations at one point in time. Burkhart and Lewis-Beck found that economic development has a significant effect on democracy, although the magnitude of the effect depends on a nation's position in the world economy. Nations with core economies (high wages, high profits, capital-intensive) experience improved democracy in the wake of heightened economic development to a greater extent than do nations with periphery economies (low wages, low profits, labor-intensive). However, even in periphery nations economic development fosters democracy. Burkhart and Lewis-Beck also found that "democratic reform by itself cannot be counted on to bring about the needed economic development. . . . [However] democracy, while not apparently a direct cause of economic development, certainly does it no harm."[15]

It is typical of research in political science that new data and new statistical procedures allow more complicated and precise analysis of existing data, resulting in the reexamination of knowledge and revision of conventional wisdom about political matters. In the next section we offer an example of new research on a topic that previously had been difficult to investigate.

Investigating Popular Influence on Public Policy

Researchers have long been interested in determining the extent to which public opinion influences the policy decisions of public officials. Most versions of democratic theory incorporate the idea that public officials should take the preferences of the populace into consideration when making policy decisions and that a democratic political system should give the populace an opportunity to express its preferences and constrain the behavior of public officials.

Investigating the relationship between public opinion and public policy decisions, though, is a difficult enterprise. Measuring what the public desires or prefers on any public policy question is challenging, especially when we attempt to compare the public's views with the types of legislative and administrative decisions made by public officials. Policy decisions are usually too complicated to ask the populace to approve or disapprove, and most public opinion surveys do not ask the public about the policy choices and priorities faced by public officials. Even if we could measure both public opinion and public policy in comparable ways, however, we would also face the difficult job of determining when and why they are congruent.

Yet the question of the relationship between public opinion and public policy is so important for evaluating democratic theory that measurement difficulties have not discouraged researchers. Benjamin Page and Robert Shapiro investigated the relationship between changes in public opinion and changes in public policy.[16] After sorting through thousands of public opinion questions asked of nationwide samples of adults between 1935 and 1979, Page and Shapiro found 357 instances in which opinion changed significantly (that is, by 6 percentage points or more from one time to the next). They then developed measures of public policy to evaluate the same 357 items in the period from two years before through four years after the measures of public opinion. Their framework allowed them to compare the amount of policy change that coincided with opinion change, to tell whether opinion change preceded policy change, and to measure the length of time that usually elapsed between opinion change and policy change.

Page and Shapiro found significant congruence between the direction of opinion change and the direction of policy change. In the 231 cases in which some policy change occurred, they found that 66 percent of those changes were in the same direction as the opinion change. Furthermore, by taking into consideration opinion changes that were relatively small, policy measures that were less than ideal, and time lags that were longer than one year, they were able to increase the proportion of opinion/policy changes that were congruent to 87 percent.

In a later study two researchers investigated the relationship between public opinion and public policy on military spending in the United States.[17] Using the results of public opinion surveys amassed between 1965 and 1990, Thomas Hartley and Bruce Russett looked for a relationship between popular support for military spending and the amount of actual spending over those twenty-five years. Even after they took into consideration the effects of other factors, such as levels of Soviet military spending, changes in the U.S. federal budget deficit, and general levels of U.S.-Soviet hostility, the researchers found a noticeable relationship between popular opinion about the level of military spending and actual expenditures on the military.

These findings are important, for they suggest that public officials do respond to changes in public opinion, at least when those changes are large and stable. Although this research does not reveal why or how policy changes are related to opinion changes, it does suggest that public opinion is a significant influence in the American political process and that democratic processes may be at work.

A Look into Judicial Decision Making

When the decisions of public officials clearly and visibly affect the lives of the populace, political scientists are interested in the process by which those decisions are reached. The decision-making behavior of the nine justices of the U.S. Supreme Court is especially intriguing because they are not elected officials, their deliberations are secret, they serve for life, and their decisions constrain other judges and public officials. As a result, political scientists have been curious for some time about how Supreme Court justices reach their decisions.

One school of thought concerning judicial decision making holds that decisions are shaped primarily by legal doctrine and precedent. Since most Supreme Court judges have spent many years rendering judicial decisions while serving on lower courts, and since judges in general are thought to respect the decisions made by previous courts, this approach posits that the decisions of Supreme Court justices depend on a search for, and discovery of, relevant legal precedent.

Another view of judicial decision making proposes that judges, like other politicians, make decisions in part based on personal political beliefs and values. Furthermore, because Supreme Court judges are not elected, serve for life, seldom seek any other office, and are not expected to justify their decisions to the public, they are in an ideal position to act in accord with their personal value systems.

One of the obstacles to discovering the relationship between the personal attitudes of justices and the decisions handed down by the Court is the difficulty of measuring judicial attitudes. Supreme Court justices do not often consent to give interviews to researchers while they are on the bench, nor do they fill out attitudinal surveys. Their deliberations are secret, they seldom make public speeches during their terms, and their written publications consist mainly of their case decisions. Consequently, about all we can observe of the political attitudes of Supreme Court justices during their terms are the written decisions they offer, which are precisely what researchers are seeking to explain.

An inventive attempt to overcome this obstacle is contained within Jeffrey Segal and Albert Cover's "Ideological Values and the Votes of U.S. Supreme Court Justices."[18] Segal and Cover decided that an appropriate way in which to measure the attitudes of judges, independent of the decisions they make, would be to analyze the editorial columns written about them in four major U.S. daily newspapers after their nomination by the president but before their confirmation by the Senate. This data source, the researchers argue, provides a comparable measure of attitudes for all justices studied, independent of the judicial decisions rendered and free of systematic errors. Here, too, though, the researchers had to accept a measure that was not ideal, for the editorial columns reflected journalists' perceptions of judicial attitudes rather than the attitudes themselves.

Despite this limitation, the editorial columns did provide an independent measure of the attitudes of the eighteen Supreme Court justices who served between 1953 and 1987. Segal and Cover found a strong relationship between the justices' decisions on cases dealing with civil liberties and the justices' personal attitudes as evinced in editorial columns. Those justices who were perceived to be liberal *before* their term on the Supreme Court voted in a manner consistent with this perception once they got on the Court. Judicial attitudes, then, do seem to be an important component of judicial decision making.

Other researchers have investigated the influence of so-called "extra-legal" factors on the decisions of Supreme Court justices. Are there factors in addition to ideology but outside of legal precedent that influence judicial decision making? Conventional wisdom suggests that the office of the solicitor general (the representative of the federal government before the Supreme Court) enjoys a special advantage over other parties. Some research has shown that the presence or absence of the solicitor general is a powerful predictor of how the Court will rule. However, this research has been criticized because it doesn't actually specify what it is about the office of the solicitor general that accounts for its success.[19] Kevin McGuire argues that it is important to specify the reasons for the office of the solicitor general's success so that its impact in support of or in opposition to another party before the Court can be measured adequately. The source of the solicitor general's advantage may be simply experience; the solicitor general appears before the Court regularly, whereas other parties appear less frequently. McGuire's research shows that when faced with a party of equal experience, the solicitor general enjoys no advantage. McGuire concluded that his findings fit well with the attitudinal model of judicial decision making; experienced parties are on equal footing in confronting the ideological predilections of the Supreme Court justices.

Research by Jeff Yates and Andrew Whitford provides even more insight into the relative influence of the rule of law, judicial attitudes, and extra-legal factors.[20] Yates and Whitford investigated explanations of Supreme Court rulings that were handed down between 1949 and 1993 in support of the president in cases involving the formal constitutional and statutory powers of the executive. They patterned their study after earlier research that had examined support for presidential power among federal district courts.[21] That research had found that presidential prestige, as measured by a president's average rating in Gallup presidential approval polls conducted in the three months preceding the date of a district court's decision on a case, and judges' loyalty to the president who appointed them were significant determinants of presidential success in federal district courts. An additional factor concerned whether the case dealt with presidential power in foreign/military affairs or in domestic matters.

Yates and Whitford identified six factors that might affect a justice's decision: 1) the policy area of the case; 2) whether or not the justice had been appointed by the president involved in the case; 3) whether or not the justice and the president shared party affiliation; 4) the party affiliation of the justice; 5) whether or not the justice had served in the executive branch; and 6) average presidential approval ratings. They found that the justices were more likely to support the president in cases involving foreign/military matters than in those concerning domestic policy. They also found that Republican justices were more likely than Democratic justices to support the president. Democratic justices tended to be more skeptical of presidential claims of power. In contrast to earlier findings, presidential appointment did not help to predict justices' votes. Perhaps when justices attain a seat on the highest court in the land they lose any incentive that federal district judges may have to favor their appointing president. Presidential approval ratings appeared to have no effect on justices' decision making.

In a second analysis, Yates and Whitford also investigated the impact of ideology using Segal and Cover's ideology scores and measure of the *trend* (rather than the average) in presidential approval ratings. Yates and Whitford hypothesized that a positive trend would influence justices to support the president. The type of case at issue, executive experience, appointing president, and shared party affiliation with the president were considered as well. Using these six factors, Yates and Whitford were able to predict correctly the justices' votes in 61.1 percent of the cases under study. Justices' ideology, presidential approval trend, and type of case were significant predictive factors. When they analyzed foreign/military cases and domestic policy cases separately, they found that their factors were better at predicting votes in domestic policy cases than in foreign policy cases. This suggests that extra-legal factors are more important in influencing justices' decisions in domestic policy cases while rules or strong norms (i.e., legal precedent) regarding presidential powers in foreign policy and military affairs are more apt to influence justices' decisions in foreign/military cases. However, in both types of cases ideology played a role in judicial decision making.

Influencing Bureaucracies

Political control of the bureaucracy is an ongoing topic of discussion and investigation by political scientists. A variety of theories about political influence on bureaucratic activities have ascended, only to be superseded by new theories based on yet more research. Theories have evolved from the politics-administration dichotomy, which strictly separates politics and administration, to the iron triangle, or capture, theory, which views agencies as responsive to a narrow range of advantaged and special interests assisted by a few strategically located members of Congress, leaving the president with relatively little influence. A more recent theory, the agency theory, suggests that presidents and Congress do have ways to control bureaucratic activities. According to this theory, policy makers use rewards or sanctions to bring agency activities back in line when they stray too far from the policy preferences of elected politicians. Control mechanisms include budgeting, political appointments, structure and reorganization, personnel power, and oversight.[22]

Research shows that agency outputs vary with political changes. The emergence of a new presidential administration, the seating of new personnel on the courts, and change in the ideological stances of congressional oversight committees all will exert influence on agency outputs. B. Dan Wood and

Richard Waterman tried to find out more about political control of bureaucracies. They studied a broad range of agencies to identify how agencies are controlled and to assess the relative effectiveness of the different control mechanisms.[23] They were also interested in determining whether Congress or the president is more effective at influencing bureaucratic outputs.

Wood and Waterman selected seven federal agencies, each representing a different organizational design. Using archives and interviews of high-ranking agency officials, they identified events that should have caused change in bureaucratic outputs. They then gathered information on agency outputs of regulatory enforcement activities, such as litigations, sanctions, and administrative decisions. In contrast to previous researchers, they obtained information on outputs on a monthly or quarterly basis. They then looked to see whether agency outputs had changed in the ways predicted based on the political changes that had occurred at the political level. Wood and Waterman found evidence that political controls did cause changes in outputs in all seven agencies. Political appointment had a very important impact on political control; reorganization, congressional oversight, and budgeting were also important factors in accounting for change in agency activities. These findings, indicating that agency outputs do respond to political manipulation, led Wood and Waterman to suggest that policy monitoring should become routine for federal agencies. Information on outputs could make politicians and bureaucrats more accountable and informed and help all participants in the policy process have access to information. The information could also aid scholars in further research on the behavior and decisions of public bureaucracies.

Effects of Campaign Advertising on Voters

Enormous sums of money are spent on campaign advertising by candidates vying for political office. Over $93 million was spent by the two major presidential candidates, Bob Dole and Bill Clinton, in the 1996 presidential general election.[24] Two recent studies on the effects of campaign advertising on the electorate reexamine conventional wisdom about the effects of political campaigns.

Stephen Ansolabehere, Shanto Iyengar, Adam Simon, and Nicholas Valentino, in their 1994 study on so-called "attack advertising," note, "It is generally taken for granted that political campaigns boost citizens' involvement—their interest in the election, awareness of and information about current issues, and sense that individual opinions matter. . . . [It] has been thought that campaign activity in connection with recurring elections enables parties and candidates to mobilize their likely constituents and 'recharge' their partisan sentiments."[25] Furthermore, voter turnout is thought to be stimulated by campaigns. But the authors of this study question whether campaigns in the age of television necessarily stimulate voter turnout. Indeed, they argue that contemporary campaigns value rhetoric over substance and private lives able to withstand media scrutiny over party ties, policy positions, and governmental experience. These campaigns frequently feature negative advertising. "More often than not, candidates criticize, discredit, or belittle their opponents rather than providing their own ideas."[26]

The researchers devised a controlled experiment in which groups of prospective voters were exposed to one of three advertisement treatments: positive political advertisements, no political advertisements, or negative political advertisements. After taking into account other factors likely to affect a person's intention to vote, Ansolabehere and his colleagues found that exposure to negative (as opposed to positive) advertisements depressed intention to vote by 5 percent.

Recognizing that the size of the experimental effect might not match the size of the real-world effect, the researchers also devised a strategy for measuring the effect of negative advertising in real campaigns. They measured the tone of the campaigns in the thirty-four states that held a Senate election in 1992. They calculated the turnout rate and something called the "roll-off" rate for each Senate race. The roll-off rate measures the extent to which people who were sufficiently motivated to vote in the presidential election chose not to vote in the Senate race. The researchers found that both the turnout rate and the roll-off rate were affected by campaign tone. Turnout in states with a positive campaign tone was 4 percent higher than in states where the tone was negative. The difference in roll-off rates was 2.4 percent, with roll-off rates higher in those states with more negative campaign advertising. These results confirmed the team's earlier results and demonstrate that campaigns may in fact depress voter turnout.

Ansolabehere and his colleagues suggest that the decline in presidential and midterm voter turnout since 1960 may be due in part to the increasingly negative tone of national campaigns. They also raise some interesting questions, asking whether or not candidates should "be free to use advertising techniques that have the effect of reducing voter turnout?" and whether or not, "in the case of publicly financed presidential campaigns, [it is] . . . legitimate for candidates to use public funds in ways that are likely to discourage voting?"[27]

In a research article also related to the impact of media use in political campaigns, Daron Shaw took on another piece of conventional wisdom: despite all the attention paid to presidential election campaigns, the campaigns do not seem to have much impact on the outcome.[28] Rather, research has shown that party identification and economic conditions seem to explain the outcomes of presidential races and that campaigns may do "little more than . . . activate latent candidate preferences."[29]

Shaw argues that previous studies have been flawed in their attempts to measure the impact of campaign activities on the electorate. For example, much of the research on campaign effects relies on national surveys in which survey respondents are asked to report exposure to the campaign. Such self-reporting may not give accurate information about actual campaign exposure. Another problem is that an individual's campaign exposure to one candidate or view may be offset by exposure to a competing candidate or view. In addition, campaign effects in one direction in some parts of the country may be offset by opposite campaign effects in other parts of the country.

To obtain a clearer picture of the possible effects of campaign activity, Shaw used state-level data on the number of candidate appearances and the amount of candidate television advertising purchases. Advertising purchases were measured in terms of gross rating points (GRPs) that indicate audience exposure instead of dollar amounts, which could vary greatly in the amount of air time purchased given cost differences in media markets across the country. Shaw focused on battleground states because weekly statewide polling data between September 1 and Election Day were available in these states. He found that an increase of 500 GRPs in a candidate's advertising purchasing advantage would directly increase a candidate's share of a state's vote by 2.2 points and that an extra day in personal campaign appearances would improve a candidate's showing by 0.8 points. Shaw also was able to examine the dynamic nature of campaigning. He found that differences in a week's advertising and appearances between the candidates were reflected in the polls the following week. The relationship between campaigning and voter preferences was strongest in the last two weeks of the campaign before the election, contradicting the popular wisdom that voters make up their minds early in a campaign.[30]

Conclusion

Political scientists are constantly adding to and revising our understanding of politics and government. As the several examples above illustrate, empirical research in political science is useful for satisfying intellectual curiosity and for evaluating real-world political conditions. New ways of designing investigations, the availability of new types of data, and new statistical techniques all contribute to the ever changing body of political science knowledge. Conducting empirical research is not a simple process, however. The information a researcher chooses to use, the method that he or she follows to investigate a research question, and the statistics used to report research findings may affect the conclusions that are drawn. For instance, some of these examples used sample surveys to measure important phenomena such as relative deprivation and public opinion on a variety of public policy issues. Yet surveys are not always an accurate reflection of people's beliefs and attitudes. In addition, how a researcher measures the phenomena of interest can affect the conclusions that are reached. Researchers studying the effect of land inequality on civil unrest in Latin America have disagreed about whether to measure landlessness, discrepancies in land ownership between the smallest and largest land owners, or land inequality across the entire range of land ownership. To some extent conclusions about the importance of land inequality have depended on how it was measured. Finally, some researchers conducted experiments in which they were able to control the application of the experimental or test factor, while others relied on comparing naturally occurring cases in which the factors of interest varied.

Several researchers in our examples were also unable to measure political phenomena themselves and had to rely on information collected by others, particularly government agencies. Can we always find readily available data to investigate a topic? If not, do we choose a different topic or collect our own data? How do we collect data firsthand? How can we be sure when we are trying to measure cause and effect in the real world of politics, rather than in a carefully controlled laboratory setting, that we have identified all the factors that could be affecting the phenomena we are trying to explain? Finally, do research findings based on the study of particular people, agencies, courts, communities, or countries have general applications to all people, agencies, courts, communities, or countries? To develop answers to these questions we need to understand the process of scientific research, the subject of this book.

Notes

1. *Recreational research* is a term used by W. Phillips Shively in *The Craft of Political Research,* 2d ed. (Englewood Cliffs, N.J.: Prentice-Hall, 1980), chap. 1.

2. Ted Robert Gurr, *Why Men Rebel* (Princeton: Princeton University Press, 1970).

3. See Manus I. Midlarsky, "Rulers and the Ruled: Patterned Inequality and the Onset of Mass Political Violence," *American Political Science Review* 82 (June 1988): 491–509, and the exchange between Edward Muller, Mitchell Seligson, Hung-der Fu, and Midlarsky in the June 1989 *American Political Science Review,* 577–595.

4. Henry Bienen and Nicolas van de Walle, "Time and Power in Africa," *American Political Science Review* 83 (March 1989): 19–34.

5. Bruce Bueno de Mesquita, Randolph M. Siverson, and Gary Woller, "War and the Fate of Regimes: A Comparative Analysis," *American Political Science Review* 86 (September 1992): 638–646.

6. Steven C. Poe and C. Neal Tate, "Repression of Human Rights to Personal Integrity in the 1980s: A Global Analysis," *American Political Science Review* (December 1994): 853–872.

7. Ibid., 866.

8. Ibid.

9. Frances Fox Piven and Richard Cloward, *Regulating the Poor: The Functions of Public Welfare* (New York: Vintage, 1971).

10. Richard C. Fording, "The Conditional Effect of Violence as a Political Tactic: Mass Insurgency, Welfare Generosity, and Electoral Context in the American States," *American Journal of Political Science* 41 (January 1997): 1–29.

11. Ibid., 9.

12. Ibid., 22–23.

13. Ibid., 24.

14. Ross E. Burkhart and Michael S. Lewis-Beck, "Comparative Democracy: The Economic Development Thesis," *American Political Science Review* 88 (December 1994): 903–910.

15. Ibid., 907.

16. Benjamin I. Page and Robert Y. Shapiro, "Effects of Public Opinion on Policy," *American Political Science Review* 77 (March 1983): 175–190.

17. Thomas Hartley and Bruce Russett, "Public Opinion and the Common Defense: Who Governs Military Spending in the United States?" *American Political Science Review* 86 (December 1992): 905–915.

18. Jeffrey A. Segal and Albert D. Cover, "Ideological Values and the Votes of U.S. Supreme Court Justices," *American Political Science Review* 83 (June 1989): 557–565.

19. Kevin T. McGuire, "Explaining Executive Success in the U.S. Supreme Court," *Political Research Quarterly* 51 (June 1998): 505–526.

20. Jeff Yates and Andrew Whitford, "Presidential Power and the United States Supreme Court," *Political Research Quarterly* 51 (June 1998): 539–550.

21. See Craig R. Ducat and Robert L. Dudley, "Federal District Judges and Presidential Power During the Postwar Era," *Journal of Politics* 51 (February 1989): 98–118.

22. This discussion is based on B. Dan Wood and Richard W. Waterman, "The Dynamics of Political Control of the Bureaucracy," *American Political Science Review* 85 (September 1991): 801–828.

23. Ibid.

24. Stephen J. Wayne, *The Road to the White House 2000* (Boston: Bedford/St. Martin's, 2000), 57.

25. Stephen Ansolabehere, Shanto Iyengar, Adam Simon, and Nicholas Valentino, "Does Attack Advertising Demobilize the Electorate?" *American Political Science Review* 88 (December 1994): 829–838.

26. Ibid., 829.

27. Ibid., 835.

28. Daron R. Shaw, "The Effect of TV Ads and Candidate Appearances on Statewide Presidential Votes, 1988–96," *American Political Science Review* 93 (June 1999): 345–362.

29. Ibid., 345.

30. Ibid., 356.

Terms introduced

APPLIED RESEARCH. Research designed to produce knowledge useful in altering a real-world condition or situation.

EMPIRICAL RESEARCH. Research based on actual, "objective" observation of phenomena.

POLITICAL SCIENCE. The application of the methods of acquiring scientific knowledge to the study of political phenomena.

PURE, THEORETICAL, OR RECREATIONAL RESEARCH. Research designed to satisfy one's intellectual curiosity about some phenomenon.

Exercises

1. Go to the library at your school and locate the following major political science journals: the *American Political Science Review,* the *American Journal of Political Science,* the *Journal of Politics, Public Administration Review,* and *Comparative Politics.* Browse through the table of contents of several back issues of these journals to get an idea of what the articles are about. Then read several of the abstracts that appear at the beginning of the articles. What are some of the major topics of concern in these journals?

2. Ask to speak with several of the political/social scientists at your school about the research they are conducting. What political phenomena are they interested in understanding? What questions are they trying to answer? Do they employ empirical research methods in their research?

Chapter 2
Studying Politics Scientifically

Why have modern industrial democracies like the United States, Britain, France, and Japan established far-reaching and generous welfare programs? An obvious answer is that these societies have humanitarian values and the resources to implement them. Welfare might be viewed as simply a form of public altruism. Yet, as the case study about welfare and civil unrest presented in Chapter 1 indicates, some scholars have developed an alternative view: they argue that welfare springs from the need to control discontent by alleviating suffering and deprivation. Frances Fox Piven and Richard Cloward make this claim in their provocatively titled book, *Regulating the Poor.* Their argument is at once counter-intuitive and contentious; counter-intuitive because it runs against popular or commonsense belief that governments help citizens for altruistic reasons, not to discourage or suppress actual or potential civil unrest, and contentious because it contradicts a number of historical and political studies. Thus, a number of questions arise: why should we accept Piven and Cloward's argument? How did they arrive at their conclusion? Was their method sound? What sorts of evidence support their thesis? Should we take their word simply because the authors are well-known policy analysts? If someone else examined the problem, would he or she come to the same conclusions?

These questions, in turn, fall under a broader one. In studying this type of political phenomena—which seems to involve not only matters of fact but also claims about how the world *is*, not about how it *should be*—is one method or approach superior to all others? In Chapter 1 we implicitly argued that the answer is, "Yes." There we emphasized empirical research methods, a set of procedures that employs *scientific* principles and techniques. Since science is just one way that humans acquire knowledge, we will in this chapter explore the ways in which scientific knowledge differs from other types of knowledge. We will also discuss important features of the scientific research process as they relate to the scientific study of politics and evaluate arguments against using scientific method in the study of political behavior and institutions. We will conclude the chapter with a brief history of political science as a discipline.

Characteristics of Scientific Knowledge

In our daily lives we "know" things in many different ways. We know, for example, that water boils at 212 degrees Fahrenheit and that a virus called HIV causes AIDS. We also may "know" that liberals are softer on crime than conservatives or that there is life after death. In some cases we know something because we believe what we read in the newspaper or hear on the radio. In others, we know something through personal experience or because it appears to be consistent with common sense or what someone we view as reliable has told us.

One way in which humans obtain knowledge is through the scientific process. Scientific knowledge differs from information derived from myth, casual observation, intuition, belief, or common sense. It has certain characteristics that these other types of knowledge do not share completely. Scientists believe that their findings are based on objective, systematic observation and that their claims can and must in principle be verified or falsified by a shared set of standards and procedures. For knowledge to be considered scientifically valid, it must exhibit several characteristics. First, scientific knowledge calls for **empirical verification.** That is, a statement must be proved true by means of objective observation. *Empirical* means "relying or based on observation or experience."[1] A political scientist uses senses to observe and record phenomena such as political protests, votes cast in the U.S. Senate, invasions of the territory of one nation by another and then describes and explains the observations as accurately as possible. In the examples in Chapter 1, for example, researchers recorded actual occurrences of land ownership, political disorder, and violence; human rights abuses; policy changes; and negative campaign advertising.

By *verified* we mean that our acceptance or rejection of a statement regarding something "known" must be influenced by observation.[2] Thus, if we say that people in the upper classes vote more frequently than members of lower strata, we must be able to provide tangible evidence, such as census or poll data, in support of this statement. Similarly, as Chapters 3 and 5 will make clear, an **explanation**, or systematic, empirically verified understanding of why a phenomenon occurs as it does, must be supported by observation and not simply asserted or assumed to be true without evidence.

The empirical nature of scientific knowledge distinguishes it from mystical knowledge. In the latter case, only "true believers" are able to observe the phenomena that support their beliefs, and observations that would disprove their beliefs are impossible to specify. Knowledge derived from superstition and prejudice is usually not subjected to empirical verification either. Superstitious or prejudiced persons are likely to note only phenomena that reinforce their beliefs while ignoring or dismissing those that do not. Thus, their knowledge is based on selective and biased experience and observation. Superstitious people are often fearful of empirically testing their superstitions and resist doing so.

Note that commonsense knowledge as well as knowledge derived from casual observation may be valid. Yet they do not constitute scientific knowledge until they have been empirically verified in a systematic and unbiased way. Alan Isaak notes that commonsense knowledge is often accepted "without question, as a matter of faith," which means that facts are accepted without being established by commonly accepted rules and procedures.[3]

Sometimes efforts to investigate commonsense knowledge have surprising results. Our intuition, for example, might lead us to predict that domestic violence or unrest will occur under conditions of severe economic deprivation or hardship. Evidence accumulated in Ted Gurr's study of civil strife, however, indicates that civil violence is likely to occur under conditions of what he terms relative deprivation.[4] If citizens' do not attain what their expectations dictate, then unrest is likely to ensue. It is citizens' perceptions—that is, the *relative* level of deprivation rather than the absolute level—that are key. In contradiction to our commonsense belief, Gurr found that economic conditions can be quite bad and yet a society will remain relatively peaceful if its citizens have come to expect and accept their situation.

Or consider the discussion of welfare and civil strife in Chapter 1. Richard Fording argued that even in a democratic system like the United States violence might bring more benefits to a disadvantaged group than conventional political participation. Such a claim runs counter to intuition that tells us that democratic procedures such as voting provide sufficient means for groups to express and redress their grievances.

The studies described in Chapter 1 showed that each of the researchers subjected their claims and explanations to empirical verification. They observed the phenomena they were trying to understand, recorded instances of the occurrence of these phenomena, and looked for patterns in their observations that were consistent with their expectations. In other words, they accumulated a body of evidence that gave other social scientists an empirical basis for further study of the phenomenon.

Scientific knowledge is also distinctive in terms of its scope and immediate purpose. The empirical research used to acquire scientific knowledge addresses what is, why, and what might be in the future. It does not typically address whether what is is good or bad or what ought to be, although it may be useful in making these types of determinations. Political scientists use the words *normative* and *nonnormative* to express the distinction. Knowledge that is evaluative, value-laden, and concerned with prescribing what ought to be is known as **normative knowledge**. Knowledge that is concerned not with evaluation or prescription but with factual or objective determinations is known as **nonnormative knowledge**. Most scientists would agree that science is (or should attempt to be) a nonnormative enterprise.

This is not to say that empirical research proceeds in a valueless vacuum. A researcher's values and interests, which are indeed subjective, affect the selection of research topics, time periods, populations, and the like. A criminologist, for example, may feel that crime is a serious problem and that long prison sentences for those who commit crimes will deter would-be criminals. He or she may therefore advocate stiff mandatory sentences as a way to reduce crime. But the test of the proposition that stiffer penalties will reduce the crime rate should be conducted in such a way that the researcher's values and predilections do not bias the results of the study. And it is the responsibility of other social scientists to evaluate whether or not the research meets the criteria of empirical verification. Scientific principles and methods of observation thus help both researchers and those who must evaluate and use their findings. Note, however, that within the discipline of political science, as well as in other disciplines, the relationship between values and scientific research is frequently debated. We shall have more to say about this subject later in this chapter.

Even though political scientists may strive to minimize the impact of biases when conducting their research, it is difficult, if not impossible, to achieve total objectivity. An additional characteristic of scientific knowledge helps to identify and weed out prejudices (inadvertent or otherwise) that may creep into research activities.[5] Scientific knowledge must be **transmissible**—that is, the methods used in making scientific discoveries must be made explicit so that others can analyze and replicate findings. The transmissiblity of scientific knowledge suggests that "science is a social activity in that it takes several scientists, analyzing and criticizing each other, to produce more reliable knowledge."[6] In order to accept results people must know what data were collected and how they were analyzed. A clear description of research procedures allows this independent evaluation. It also permits other scientists to collect the same information and test the original propositions themselves. If the original results are not replicated using the same procedures, they may be incorrect.

This does not mean that scientific knowledge is accumulated only or primarily through the exact repetition of earlier studies. Often research procedures are changed intentionally to see whether similar results are obtained under different conditions. Consider, for example, two studies concerning the connection between television violence and antisocial behavior among children.[7] In the first study researchers compared aggressive behavior among children in two Canadian towns. One of the towns had TV reception, the other did not. Surprisingly, the researchers found that younger children (ages eleven and twelve) living in the town with access to television were less, not more, aggressive. (Among older children—ages fifteen and sixteen—there was no difference.) This research was subsequently criticized because the two towns were not closely matched socioeconomically and because other factors related to aggressiveness among children, such as differences in school discipline, were not considered. A second study then followed involving children in a single town. The children were divided into "high" and "low" TV viewers. The "high" viewers were found to be slightly more aggressive than the "low" viewers. Yet even this study was flawed since no attempt was made to assess the amount of violence actually seen on TV by the high viewers. Low viewers could have watched particularly violent programs, so that the difference between the groups would have been minimized. The method of measuring aggressiveness was also suspect. But the point is that these supposed deficiencies could be detected because the research procedures were clearly described.

Thus shortcomings in a research design often lead others to doubt the results, prompting them to devise their own tests. This would not be possible, however, if researchers did not specify their research strategy and methods. Such descriptions permit a better assessment of results and allow others to make adjustments in design and measurement when pursuing further study.

THE USES OF REPLICATION

When picking a research topic, keep in mind a basic premise of scientific investigation: independent verification. If you come across a claim based on research that you find interesting or provocative or contrary to common sense, you might attempt to replicate at least part of the study. Suppose, for example, that a newspaper reports that the public generally favors a certain policy, but you suspect that the results are misleading because of the way the questions were worded or the circumstances in which they were asked. You might be able to replicate the study by using a different set of data. (In Chapter 6 you will find suggestions on places to find public opinion data that are relatively easy to analyze.) In other words, don't hesitate to study a problem that has already been well researched.

The results of these new studies can then be compared with the earlier results. This process produces an accumulated body of knowledge about the phenomena in question. In each of the examples in Chapter 1, the researchers revealed enough information about their methods so that others could evaluate the strengths and weaknesses of their measurements, explanations, and findings. In this way knowledge about these particular aspects of social and political life became increasingly informative.

Another important characteristic of scientific knowledge is that it is **general**, or applicable to many rather than just a few cases. Advocates of the scientific method argue that knowledge that describes, explains, and predicts many phenomena or a set of similar occurrences is more valuable than knowledge that addresses a single phenomenon.[8] For example, the knowledge that states with easier voter registration systems have higher election turnout rates than states with more difficult systems is preferable to the knowledge that Wisconsin has a higher turnout rate than Alabama. Knowing that party affiliation strongly influences many voters' choices among candidates is more useful knowledge to someone seeking to understand elections than is the simple fact that John Doe, a Democrat, voted for a Democratic candidate for Congress in 2000. The knowledge that a state, which has a safety inspection program, has a lower automobile fatality rate than another state, which does not, is less useful information to a legislator considering the worth of mandatory inspection programs than is the knowledge that states that require automobile inspections experience lower average fatality rates than those that do not.

A statement that communicates general knowledge is called an **empirical generalization**. An empirical generalization summarizes relationships between individual facts.[9] For example, the statement that states with easier voter registration systems have higher turnout rates than states with more burdensome systems connects information about voter registration systems and voter turnout rates in individual states and summarizes that information in a broad proposition that can be used as the basis of policy debate or further investigation.

Another characteristic of scientific knowledge is that it is **explanatory**. In scientific discourse the term *explanation* has various meanings, but when we say that knowledge is explanatory we are saying that a conclusion can be derived (logically) from a set of general propositions and specific initial conditions. The general propositions assert that when things of type X occur, they will be followed by things of type Y. An initial condition might specify that X has in fact occurred. The observation of Y is then explained by the conjunction of the condition and the proposition. The goal of explanation is sometimes to account for a particular event—the demise of the Soviet Union, for example—but more often to explain general classes of phenomena such as wars or revolutions or voting behavior.

Previously, we described Gurr's theory of civil violence. His general proposition is that when the gap between what people expect and want society to provide and what it actually supplies (relative deprivation) goes beyond a certain point, citizens will become frustrated, then angry, and then susceptible to acts of violence. As an example, in 1967 relative deprivation among African Americans in large cities was historically high because their *hopes* for a higher standard of living had outpaced their *actual* economic gains. These two factors—the generalization about deprivation and the specific conditions in American cities—account for or explain the outbreak of civil disorder that actually took place in the United States in the summer of 1967.

Explanation then answers "why" kinds of questions. The questions may be specific, as, for instance, "Why did a particular event take place?" or more general, as, for example, "Why do strong party identifiers tend to vote more regularly than independents?" Observing and describing facts is of course important. But most political scientists want more than mere facts. They are usually interested in identifying the factors that account for or explain human behavior. Gurr's theory of relative deprivation is valuable because it does more than simply describe particular civil conflicts. More important, it offers an explanation of why such violence occurs, which is more than a description of when and where it occurs.

Hence, accurate description is a prerequisite of explanation because one must have as accurate a picture as possible of *what is* before one can determine *why it is so*. History is replete with examples of erroneous explanations that were developed on the basis of inadequate observation. These explanations have been rejected and new ones have taken their place, often as the result of better descriptions. As an example, recent space exploration has made it possible to observe many more phenomena in astronomy than ever before and has led to the reappraisal of many theories regarding Saturn's rings, Jupiter's moons, and Mars's canals. In political science the development of sample surveys has allowed political scientists to study a wide range of human attitudes that previously had been virtually impossible to observe. It is important to remember, though, that all scientists believe that the real goal of their disciplines is explanation, not description.

Explanatory knowledge is also important because it is **predictive**, offering systematic, reasoned anticipation of future events. Note that prediction based on explanation is not the same as forecasting or soothsaying or astrology, which do not rest on empirically verified explanations. An explanation gives a scientific **reason**—that is, a justification of an action or behavior based on beliefs and desires—why a certain outcome is to be expected. In fact, many consider the ultimate test of an explanation to be its usefulness in prediction. Prediction is an extremely valuable type of knowledge since it may be used to avoid undesirable and costly events and to achieve desired outcomes. Of course, whether or not a prediction is "useful" is a normative question. Consider, for example, a government that uses scientific research to predict the outbreak of domestic violence but uses the knowledge not to alleviate the underlying conditions but to suppress the discontented with force.

In political science, explanations rarely account for all of the variation observed in attributes or behavior. So exactly how accurate, then, do scientific explanations have to be? Do they have to account for or predict phenomena 100 percent of the time? Most political scientists, like scientists in other disciplines, accept **probabilistic explanation**, in which it is not necessary to explain or predict a phenomenon with 100-percent accuracy. Some believe, however, that an explanation is acceptable only if it explains or predicts what it purports to explain or predict 100 percent of the time.

At this point we should acknowledge that many predictions in political science and the explanations that underlie them turn out to be weak or even false. Some have so many counter instances that they do not seem worthy of the designation "scientific." For this reason some scholars maintain that social scientists cannot achieve the exactitude and precision of the natural scientists and that instead they should attempt not to explain behavior but to understand it.[10] Needless to say, we do not entirely agree with this view; we will briefly explain our position later in the chapter.

The accumulation of related explanations sometimes leads to the creation of a **theory**—that is, a statement or series of statements that organize, explain, and predict knowledge. A theory in political science consists of broad generalizations together with a set of assumptions or axioms, definitions of concepts, and a commitment to a particular methodological approach. A "theory's major function is . . . to explain singular facts and occurrences, but perhaps more importantly to explain empirical generalizations."[11] Theories go beyond simply explaining collections of empirical findings because they are more powerful and abstract. As Isaak states, "A theory can explain empirical generalizations because it is more general, more inclusive than they are."[12] Theories also have two other functions: "to organize, systematize, and coordinate existing knowledge in a field" and to "predict an empirical generalization—predict what a particular relationship holds."[13] A theory of voting may explain voter turnout by proposing a number of factors that affect people's perceptions of the costs and benefits of voting: socioeconomic class, political efficacy, the ease of registration and voting laws, choices among candidates, availability of election news in the media, and so forth.[14] The more generalizations a theory systematizes and organizes, and the more of them it suggests or predicts, the stronger it is.

Theories of politics generate excitement in political science research and stimulate study. In our quest to understand our lives and the world around us, to create order out of complexity, we turn to theories. Not all of us turn to the same theories, however, and that too contributes to the excitement of studying politics. Each theory offers a different view of politics or focuses our attention on a different set of political phenomena.

We can see the excitement and value of theory-building in the work of Bruce A. Williams and Albert R. Matheny, who evaluated several competing theories in their examination of variation in state regulation of hazardous waste disposal.[15] Regulation of hazardous waste disposal is an example of social regulation, regulation that imposes costs on a specific group in order to benefit the public or some segment of it. Improper waste disposal imposes costs on the environment and human health. These costs, known as negative externalities, are not reflected in the price of a product. Put somewhat differently, the people who produce and use the products that generate hazardous waste do not pay the costs that arise when improper storage of that waste threatens the community. Avoiding or preventing negative externalities by requiring safe disposal of hazardous waste means imposing substantial costs on industry. There are at least three theories to explain and predict the amount or nature of waste disposal regulation enacted by the states.

According to economic theory, negative externalities are a type of market failure, since the market fails to deal with the problem. When this happens, government regulation of the market becomes justified and necessary. The market failure theory of government regulation predicts that social regulation is related to the severity of the market failure and that the costs to regulated industries should be equal to the costs or harms created by unsafe hazardous waste disposal.

Others argue that social regulation corresponds to more than just the presence or magnitude of market failures. They claim that social regulation is the result of political behavior. This theory predicts that exaggerated claims about dangers imposed by market failures must be made in order to generate public awareness and thence support for regulation and that, consequently, the resulting regulations impose unnecessarily high costs on industry. The flip side of this theory has industry opposing regulation and dominating the regulatory process by threatening economic slowdown, unemployment, even change of location. The political strength of an industry is related to its importance to the economy and to the level of government considering the regulation. Threats to relocate have a greater impact at the local or state level than at the national level. Thus regulation may be related to conditions of industry dominance, not the extent of market failure or actual pollution.

A third theory states that, while industry dominates the regulatory process, it does not necessarily oppose all regulation. According to this view, industry supports regulation as long as the costs of regulation can be shifted to government and away from industry. This regulatory outcome is called the socialization of the costs of production and is predicted by neo-Marxists, who maintain that many private industries could not make a profit without evading actual production costs. They also argue that effective regulation and avoidance of negative externalities is not possible without fundamental institutional reform of both government and the economy. We have then three quite different theories of why and how much government regulation of hazardous waste disposal occurs. Each theory has something different to say about the power of public interest groups and industry groups and the outcome of social regulatory efforts. The conflicting beliefs about politics they represent fuel many a debate about environmental regulations and the performance of government and the economy. Researchers investigating examples of social regulation may be far more interested in determining which of these theories seems to fit with the observed data than in the actual amount and consequence of a specific regulatory program. In fact, researchers may become quite attached to a particular theory and be convinced that it is the correct theory. But a researcher must never forget our final characteristic of scientific knowledge. This characteristic states that scientific knowledge is **provisional**, meaning that it is subject to revision and change. Future research may demonstrate that what we think we know scientifically is in fact partly or wholly wrong. New observations, more accurate measurements, improved research design, and the testing of alternative explanations may reveal the limitations or empirical inadequacies of an existing body of scientific knowledge.[16]

Scientists should always remain open to the alteration and improvement of their understanding of phenomena. To say that scientific knowledge is provisional does not mean that the evidence accumulated to date can be ignored or is worthless. It does mean, however, that future research could always significantly alter what we currently believe. In a word, scientific knowledge is tentative. Often when people think of science and scientific knowledge they think of scientific "laws." A scientific law is a "generalization that was tested and confirmed through empirical verification."[17] But these laws often have to be modified or discarded in the light of new evidence. So even though political scientists strive to develop law-like generalizations, they understand and accept the fact that such statements are subject to revision.

Acquiring Scientific Knowledge: Induction and Deduction

Induction is the process of reasoning from specific observation to general principle or theory. In induction, observation precedes theory. The researcher observes and records the phenomena and then attempts to derive or define a pattern or regularity from which an explanatory theory can be developed. This theory may also offer an explanation for patterns in other related observations. For example, imagine that you have made the following three observations. First, the Bemba of South Central Africa live a life of marginal subsistence consisting of nine months of abundance and three months of hunger. Despite deplorable conditions, there is no outbreak of violence or protest within the tribe during the three-month hunger period.[18] Second, the income of African Americans compared with that of whites of equal education rose rapidly during the 1940s and early 1950s but then declined precipitously so that half the relative gains were lost by 1960. Subsequently, violence broke out among blacks living in U.S. urban areas in the 1960s.[19] Third, political violence in Europe occurred during the growth of industrial and commercial centers, despite the fact that at the same time alternatives to the peasant's hard life emerged.[20]

In the first and third case studies the objective well-being of the population declined, but only in the third did violence break out. In the second case study there was no decline in the objective well-being of the population, yet violence occurred. Let's assume that in seeking an explanation in the first case, you reason that the cycle of the seasons and its ensuing periods of feast and famine had been experienced for many years and was unlikely to change. In the second case you reason that African Americans expected to maintain the economic gains they had made in the previous decade. And in the third case you reason that during the period of emerging industrialization all people expected to improve their living conditions, yet some members of society actually gained much more from the increased industry and commerce than others. Based on this reasoning, you could conclude that the second and third cases were similar because there was a discrepancy between *expected* and *actual* conditions, while in the first there was no discrepancy. From this you might develop the general theory that a large discrepancy or gap between expected and actual economic gains causes discontent, which in turn leads to violence. Thus you might "induce" the theory of relative deprivation from a few observations of specific cases of deprivation and violence. Generally speaking, it is difficult to point to examples of pure induction since often a researcher starts with a hunch and then collects information that he or she expects will show certain patterns in line with that hunch. While not a full-blown theory, a hunch places the researcher further along in his or her investigation than does observation alone.

Deduction, the second mode of scientific inquiry, is the process of proceeding from general principle or theory to specific observations. On the basis of theory certain phenomena are predicted. Then events are observed and measured to see if they occur as predicted. The definition of explanation given earlier in this chapter is an example of deduction. For example, to test the theory that the earth is flat, it should be possible to find the earth's edge and to sail in a straight line directly from a starting point to the edge of the earth and back. Or, as another example, take the theory of imitation, which claims that new behavior is partly acquired by copying others. If this theory is correct, an increase in the portrayal of sex and violence on TV could be expected to lead to an increase in such behavior among viewers.[21] To test this theory one might take two groups with similar sexual habits or levels of aggression and expose one group but not the other to TV programs with sex and violence. If the group that is exposed to television sex and violence exhibits an increase in sexual arousal and aggressive or violent behavior, but the group unexposed does not, then one could conclude that TV did affect viewer behavior in accordance with the theory of imitation.

Scientific research typically involves both deduction and induction. Thus a researcher may start with a theory and deduce certain phenomena that he or she will attempt to observe. If the observations are not quite what was expected, some modification of the theory will be made and the revised theory subjected to further testing. Sometimes the theory may have to be discarded and, on the basis of observations, a new theory induced.

For example, Ptolemy's theory that the heavens revolved around the earth was developed two centuries before Christ.[22] It was quite successful at predicting the changing positions of planets and stars, but not as successful at predicting other astronomical phenomena. There were many discrepancies between actual astronomical observations and predictions derived from the theory. Astronomers responded at first by making adjustments in Ptolemy's system, but these changes, developed to correct discrepancies in one place, ended by creating discrepancies in other places. Over the centuries the theory became increasingly more complex yet no more accurate. By the sixteenth century, it was concluded that the Ptolemaic system was so complex and inaccurate that it couldn't be true of nature. Copernicus then suggested an alternative heliocentric theory that the planets revolved around the sun. This theory was simpler and more accurately accounted for a variety of astronomical phenomena. Later physicists, Sir Isaac Newton and Albert Einstein among them, so greatly modified astronomical theory that their work created a **scientific revolution**, that is, a rival tradition of scientific research.[23]

A good example of social science research that involved both induction and deduction is the work of two researchers studying news coverage and social trust.[24] For some time psychologists Stephen Holloway and Harvey Hornstein had been studying social trust by observing the rate at which people would return wallets dropped on New York City streets to the addresses of the owners identified inside. The researchers would periodically drop a number of wallets in various locations and wait and see how many were returned. Typically, half the wallets dropped were eventually returned. However, one day something happened that had never happened before: none of the wallets was returned. This unexpected result led them to search for a plausible explanation. Holloway and Hornstein set out to develop an explanation based on an observation—that is, they proceeded to the process of induction.

It so happened that this particular June 1968 day Robert Kennedy, a senator from New York and candidate for the Democratic presidential nomination, was assassinated. The investigators wondered: Could Kennedy's assassination have something to do with the failure to return any of the wallets? Perhaps the news coverage of the event made people upset, mistrustful of strangers, and unwilling to help people they did not know or had not seen. Holloway and Hornstein hypothesized that exposure to "bad" news makes people less socially trusting and cooperative.

To test this hypothesis the researchers devised a series of experiments in which people were divided into two groups and were subtly exposed to "bad" or "good" news broadcasts. Then they were asked to reveal their attitudes toward other people and to play a game with other people that allowed observation of their degree of cooperation. Holloway and Hornstein were testing a general theory with research designed to measure the occurrence of certain predicted observations—that is, they were using deduction.

The experiments demonstrated that those exposed to bad news were, indeed, less socially trusting and cooperative, confirming the researchers' hypothesis. Both induction and deduction had been involved in accumulating an empirical, verifiable, transmissible, explanatory, general (yet provisional) body of evidence regarding an important social phenomenon.

Applying an existing theory to new situations, deciding which phenomena to observe and how to measure them, and developing a theory that explains many more things than the specific observations that led to its discovery are all creative enterprises. Unfortunately, it is difficult to teach creativity. But being aware of the processes of induction and deduction, and keeping in mind the characteristics of scientific knowledge, will make your own evaluation and conduct of research more worthwhile.

Is Political Science Really "Science"?

We have implied throughout this chapter that politics can and should be studied scientifically. Some people question this position, however, because the discipline involves the study of human political behavior, and studying people raises all sorts of complexities. The search for regularities in behavior, in particular, assumes that men and women act consistently and in a discoverable manner. Moreover, if political science is a science in the same way that the natural sciences are, behavior must be describable by contingent causal laws.[25] Yet if human beings do not act predictably, or if their actions are not susceptible to description by general laws, political scientists, acting as scientists, encounter serious problems.

Even if we accept that individuals are generally predictable, some persons may deliberately act in unpredictable or misleading ways. This problem is occasionally encountered among subjects "cooperating" in a research project. For example, a subject may figure out that he or she is part of an experiment to test a theory about how people behave when put in a difficult or stressful or confusing situation. He or she may then act in a way not predicted by, or in conflict with, the theory. Or, the subject may try to conform to what he or she thinks the researcher is looking for. Similarly, people may never reveal what is really on their minds or what they have done in the past or would do in the future. In other words, our ability to observe accurately the attributes of people can at times be severely limited. It is, for instance, frequently difficult to measure and explain illegal or socially unacceptable behaviors such as drug use.

Measurement problems also arise because the concepts of interest to many political scientists are abstract and value laden. For example, one measure of unemployment takes into account persons who are out of work but actively seeking employment. An argument may be made that such a measure greatly underestimates unemployment because it does not include those who are so discouraged by their failure to find a job that they are no longer actively seeking work. Finding an adequate definition of poverty can be just as difficult because people live in different types of households and have available different kinds of support beyond just their observed income. What one scholar may feel constitutes poverty another may see as nothing more than acceptable hardship.

Furthermore, political scientists must face the fact that consistent and rational human behavior is complex, perhaps even more complex than the subject matter of other sciences (genes, subatomic particles, insects, and so on). Complexity has been a significant obstacle to the discovery of general theories that accurately explain and predict almost every kind of behavior. After all, developing a theory with broad applicability requires the identification and specification of innumerable variables and the linkages among them. Consequently, when a broad theory is proposed, it can be attacked on the grounds that it is too simple or that too many exceptions to it exist. Certainly to date no empirically verified generalizations in political science match the simplicity and explanatory power of Einstein's famous equation, $E = mc^2$.[26]

There are other practical obstacles.[27] The data needed to test explanations and theories may be extremely hard to obtain. People with the needed information may not want to release it for political or personal reasons. Or, they may not want to answer potentially embarrassing or threatening questions honestly or completely. Pollsters, for instance, find nonresponsiveness to certain questions—what they term "refusals"—such as attitudes toward ethnic groups to be a major problem in gauging public opinion. Similarly, some experiments require manipulation of people. But since humans are the subjects, the researchers must contend with ethical considerations that might preclude them from obtaining all the information they want. Asking certain question can interfere with privacy rights, and exposing subjects to certain stimuli might put the participants at physical or emotional risk. Tempting someone to commit a crime, to take an obvious case, might tell a social scientist a lot about adherence to the law but would be unacceptable nevertheless.

All of these claims about the difficulty of studying political behavior scientifically have merit. Yet they can be overstated. Consider, for example, the fact that scientists studying natural phenomena encounter many of the same problems. Paleontologists must attempt to explain events that occurred millions or even billions of years ago. Astronomers and geologists cannot mount repeated experiments on most of the phenomena of greatest interest to them. They certainly cannot visit many of the places they study most intensively, like planets or the center of the earth. And what can be more complex than organisms and their components, which consist of thousands of compounds and chemical interactions? Quite simply stated, it is in no way clear that severe practical problems distinguish political science from any of the other sciences.

Before moving on we want to emphasize that the scientific method is not the only path to knowledge. In fact, some scholars believe that because the social sciences attempt to explain human **action**—that is, physical human movement or behavior that is done for a reason—and not mere physical movement, they face problems not encountered in the natural sciences. Such concerns, however, are of a methodological nature and raise deep philosophical issues that go well beyond the task of describing the *empirical* methods that are actually used in the discipline.[28] We thus acknowledge that the scientific study of politics is controversial but nevertheless maintain that the procedures we describe in the following chapters are widely accepted and can in many circumstances lead to valuable understandings of political processes and behavior. Moreover, they have greatly shaped the research agenda and teaching of the discipline, as can be seen by looking at the evolution of the field in the last century.

A Brief History of Political Science as a Discipline

Many historians of political science divide the development of the field into two periods: traditional and behavioral. Traditional political science grew out of the study of law and ethics and dominated research and instruction until the early 1960s. Behavioral political science, which utilizes the scientific method of discovering knowledge, came of age after that time and continues today to be the dominant approach used in the study of politics, though it still arouses vigorous debate and disagreement.

Traditional Political Science

Traditional political science emphasized historical, legalistic, and institutional subjects.[29] The historical emphasis produced detailed descriptions of the developments leading to political events and practices. Legalism, on the other hand, involved the study of constitutions and legal codes, while the concentration on institutions included studies of the powers and functions of political institutions such as legislatures, bureaucracies, and courts. In general, traditional political science focused on formal governments and their legally defined powers. Legal and historical documents including laws, constitutions, proclamations, and treaties were studied to trace the development of international organizations and key concepts, such as sovereignty, the state, federalism, and imperialism. Informal political processes—the exercise of informal power and the internal dynamics of institutions, for example—were frequently ignored.

In the heyday of the traditional approach, the study of politics was usually taught in colleges and universities in history and philosophy departments. Political theories concerning human nature and politics, the purpose and most desirable form of government, and the philosophy of law were the province of philosophy departments. When separate departments did appear, they were frequently called departments of government, reflecting the emphasis on formal structures rather than on political processes and behavior. In fact, some universities still have government departments.

Traditional political science was primarily descriptive rather than explanatory because most of its practitioners did not feel a need to conduct research that had the characteristics of the "hard" sciences, which were often deemed inapplicable to social behavior and institutions. Critics were later to charge that the traditional school lacked rigor and generality and that, although theorists occasionally came up with intriguing and well-reasoned verbal theories, these discoveries were usually not subjected to rigorous and extensive empirical verification.

Modern Political Science

The emergence of the scientific study of politics in the United States can be attributed to several developments.[30] First, many of the European social scientists and theorists who emigrated to the United States in the 1930s were skilled in the use of new, scientific research methods.[31] Second, war-related social research in the following decade promoted the exchange of ideas among scientifically minded persons from the disciplines of political science, sociology, psychology, and economics. There is considerable evidence, in fact, that the U.S. government looked to colleges and universities for scientific social science research that would be of use in fighting the Cold War against the Soviet Union.[32] Systematic research was aided by two related developments: the collection of large amounts of empirical data and the development of technology to store and process this information. For example, beginning in the late 1930s Paul Lazarsfeld pioneered the use of large-scale sample surveys or polls to study voting behavior and continued to refine the technique while working for the federal government during World War II. After the war he applied survey research methods to his study of the 1948 and 1952 presidential elections.[33]

Much of the post-1950 political science research has focused on **behavioralism**, or the study of the political behavior of individuals and groups.

Unlike the traditional school, the newer political science consciously embraces scientific methods, as illustrated by David Easton's influential 1967 article, "The Current Meaning of 'Behavioralism.'"

> *There are discoverable uniformities in political behavior. These can be expressed in generalizations or theories with explanatory and predictive value. Means for acquiring and interpreting data . . . need to be examined self-consciously, refined, and validated. Precision in the recording of data and the statement of findings requires measurement and quantification. Ethical evaluation and empirical explanation involve two different kinds of propositions that, for the sake of clarity, should be kept analytically distinct. Research ought to be systematic.* [34]

Behavioral political science assumes and advocates the search for fundamental units of analysis that can provide a common base for the investigation of human behavior by all social scientists. Some political scientists, for instance, suggest that groups are an important unit on which to focus, while others are more interested in decision making and decisions.[35] There is hope that a few units of analysis will be found and focused upon in much the same way as physicists and chemists focus on atoms, molecules, and the like.

The reaction to the rise of behavioral political science has not been entirely positive. Critics of empirical political science point to the trivial nature of some of its findings and applications. Common sense would have told us the same thing, they argue. As explained earlier, however, there is a difference between intuition and scientific knowledge. To build a solid base for further research and accumulation of scientific knowledge in politics, commonsense knowledge must be empirically verified and, as is frequently the case, discarded when wrong.

Some political scientists have also been concerned about the prominence of nonpolitical factors in explanations of political behavior. Psychological explanations of political behavior stress the effect of personality on political behavior while economic explanations attempt to show how costs and benefits affect people's actions. These competing approaches to understanding political behavior sometimes disturb those used to studying political institutions or political philosophies. To them it looks like "politics" is being taken out of the study of politics.

A more serious criticism of the scientific study of politics is that it leads to a failure to focus enough scholarly research attention on important social issues and problems. In the effort to be scientific and precise, some critics contend that political science overlooks the moral and policy issues that make the discipline relevant to the real world. The implications of research findings for important public policy choices or political reform are rarely addressed. In other words, the quest for scientific knowledge of politics has led to a focus on topics that are quantifiable and relatively easy to verify empirically but that are not related to significant, practical, and relevant societal concerns.[36]

By the late 1960s the president of the American Political Science Association had declared a "postbehavioral revolution."[37] **Postbehavioralism**, as the reaction to behavioralism was termed, called for political science research to be more relevant to important current political issues and included the following tenets:

> *Substance must precede technique. If one* must *be sacrificed for the other—and this need not always be so—it is more important to be relevant and meaningful for contemporary urgent social problems than to be sophisticated in the tools of investigation.*
>
> *Behavioral science conceals an ideology of empirical conservatism. To confine oneself exclusively to the description and analysis of facts is to hamper the understanding of these same facts in their broadest context. As a result empirical political science must lend its support to the maintenance of the very factual conditions it explores. It unwittingly purveys an ideology of social conservatism tempered by modest incremental change.*
>
> *Behavioral research must lose touch with reality. The heart of behavioral inquiry is abstraction and analysis and this serves to conceal the brute realities of politics. The task of post-behavioralism is to break the barriers of silence that behavioral language necessarily has created and to help political science reach out to the real needs of mankind in time of crisis.*
>
> *Research about and constructive development of values are inextinguishable parts of the study of politics. Science cannot be and never has been evaluatively neutral despite protestations to the contrary. Hence to understand the limits of our knowledge we need to be aware of the value premises on which it stands and the alternatives for which this knowledge could be used.*
>
> *Members of a learned discipline bear the responsibilities of all intellectuals. The intellectuals' historical role has been and must be to protect the humane values of civilization. This is their unique task and obligation.*
>
> *To know is to bear the responsibility of acting and to act is to engage in reshaping society. The intellectual as scientist bears the special obligation to put his knowledge to work.*
>
> *If the intellectual has the obligation to implement his knowledge, those organizations composed of intellectuals—the professional associations—and the universities themselves, cannot stand apart from the struggles of the day. Politicization of the professions is inescapable as well as desirable.*[38]

The reaction to the emergence and domination of behavioralist perspective has brought about renewed interest in normative philosophical questions of *what ought to be* rather than *what is*.[39] Others have responded by turning their attention to public policy, the policy-making process, and policy analysis.[40] Many political scientists who study these topics apply scientific methods to socially relevant and important questions.

Postbehavioralism has certainly not silenced critical reflection upon political science as a discipline and the impact of incorporating scientific method in the study of politics.[41] New concerns continue to surface. For example, some lament the failure of government to benefit from the knowledge and perspectives of political scientists and the over-reliance on economists and econometric methods in policy making.[42]

One important challenge to research in political science (as well as in other social science disciplines such as sociology) has come from feminist social scientists. Among the criticisms that have been raised is that "the nature of political action and the scope of political research have been defined in ways that, in particular, exclude *women as women* from politics" (emphasis added).[43] Accordingly, "What a feminist political science must do is develop a new vocabulary of politics so that it can express the specific and different ways in which women have wielded power, been in authority, practiced citizenship, and understood freedom."[44] Even short of arguing that political science concepts and theories have been developed from a male-only perspective, it is all too easy to point to examples of gender bias in political science research, such as failure to focus on policy issues of importance to women, assuming that findings apply to everyone when the population studied was predominantly male, and bias in survey question wording.[45]

A related complaint is that political science in the past ignored the needs, interests, and views of the poor, the lower class, and the powerless and mainly served to reinforce the belief that existing institutions were as good as they could be. Because social scientists have insisted on studying *what is*, they have neglected to ask the all-important questions about *what should be* or *what could be*.

Conclusion

In this chapter we have described the characteristics of scientific knowledge and the scientific method. We have presented reasons why political scientists are attempting to become more scientific in their research and have discussed some of the difficulties associated with empirical political science. We have also touched on questions that exist about the value of the scientific approach to the study of politics. Despite these difficulties and uncertainties, the empirical approach is widely embraced, and students of politics need to be familiar with it. In the next chapter we shall begin to examine how to take a general topic or question about some political phenomenon and develop a strategy for investigating that topic scientifically.

Notes

1. Alan C. Isaak, *Scope and Methods of Political Science,* 4th ed. (Homewood, Ill.: Dorsey, 1985), 106.

2. Ibid., 107.

3. Ibid., 66; see also 67.

4. Ted Robert Gurr, *Why Men Rebel* (Princeton: Princeton University Press, 1970).

5. Isaak, *Scope and Methods,* 30.

6. Ibid., 31.

7. The studies are reported in H.J. Eysenck and D.K.B. Nias, *Sex, Violence and the Media* (London: Temple Smith, 1978), 103–104.

8. It may be tempting to think that historians are only interested in describing and explaining unique, one-time events, such as the outbreak of a particular war. This is not the case, however. Many historians search for generalizations that account for a number of specific events. Some even claim to have discovered the "laws of history."

9. Isaak, *Scope and Methods,* 103.

10. See, for example, R. G. Collingwood, *The Idea of History* (Oxford: Oxford University Press, 1946). A good introduction to "understanding" behavior as opposed to "explaining" it is Martin Hollis, *The Philosophy of Social Science: An Introduction* (Cambridge: Cambridge University Press, 1994), chap. 7.

11. Ibid., 167.

12. Ibid.

13. Ibid., 167, 169.

14. See Raymond E. Wolfinger and Steven J. Rosenstone, *Who Votes?* (New Haven: Yale University Press, 1980).

15. Bruce A. Williams and Albert R. Matheny, "Testing Theories of Social Regulation: Hazardous Waste Regulation in the American States," *Journal of Politics* 46 (May 1984): 428–458.

16. For discussion of the process of changing scientific knowledge, see Thomas Kuhn, *The Structure of Scientific Revolutions,* 2d ed. (Chicago: University of Chicago Press, 1971).

17. Isaak, *Scope and Methods,* 297.

18. Gurr, *Why Men Rebel,* 57.

19. Ibid., 54.

20. Ibid., 51.

21. For a discussion of the theory of imitation and its role in explaining the possible effects of viewing sex and violence on TV, see Eysenck and Nias, *Sex, Violence and the Media,* 56–59.

22. This example is based on the discussion in Kuhn, *Scientific Revolutions,* 68–69.

23. Ibid.

24. The wallet-dropping episode is described in Stephen Holloway and Harvey A. Hornstein, "How Good News Makes Us Good," *Psychology Today,* December 1976, 76–78. The results of the subsequent experiments are discussed in Stephen Holloway, Lyle Tucker, and Harvey A. Hornstein, "The Effects of Social and Nonsocial Information on Interpersonal Behavior of Males: The News Makes News," *Journal of Personality and Social Psychology* 35 (July 1977): 514–522; and in Harvey A. Hornstein, Elizabeth Lakind, Gladys Frankel, and Stella Manne, "Effects of Knowledge about Remote Social Events on Prosocial Behavior, Social Conception, and Mood," *Journal of Personality and Social Psychology* 32 (December 1975): 1038–1046.

25. See Alexander Rosenberg, *The Philosophy of Social Science,* 2d ed. (Boulder: Westview, 1998).

26. For further discussion of complete and partial explanations, see Isaak, *Scope and Methods,* 143.

27. See Charles A. McCoy and John Playford, eds., *Apolitical Politics: A Critique of Behavioralism* (New York: Thomas Y. Crowell, 1967).

28. For an excellent collection of articles about the pros and cons of studying human behavior scientifically, see Michael Martin and Lee C. Anderson, eds., *Readings in the Philosophy of Social Science* (Cambridge: MIT Press, 1996).

29. Isaak, *Scope and Methods,* 34–38.

30. Ibid., 38–39. For a history of the development of survey research, see also Earl F. Babbie, *Survey Research Methods* (Belmont, Calif.: Wadsworth, 1973), 42–45.

31. For early American sources of behavioralism, see Charles E. Merriam, *New Aspects of Politics* (Chicago: University of Chicago Press, 1924).

32. See, for example, the excellent collection of articles entitled "Science and the Cold War: A Roundtable" in *Diplomatic History* 24 (winter 2000). The essay by Jefferson P. Marquis, "Social Science and Nation Building in Vietnam," 79–105, is especially relevant.

33. Paul F. Lazarsfeld, Bernard Berelson, and Hazel Gaudet, *The People's Choice* (New York: Duell, Sloane and Pearce, 1944).

34. David B. Easton, "The Current Meaning of 'Behavioralism,'" in James C. Charlesworth, ed., *Contemporary Political Analysis* (New York: Free Press, 1967), 16–17.

35. David B. Truman, *The Governmental Process* (New York: Knopf, 1951); and Robert A. Dahl, *Who Governs? Democracy and Power in an American City* (New Haven: Yale University Press, 1961).

36. See McCoy and Playford, eds., *Apolitical Politics.*

37. David Easton, "The New Revolution in Political Science," *American Political Science Review* 63 (December 1969): 1051.

38. Ibid., 1052.

39. Isaak, *Scope and Methods,* 45.

40. Ibid., 46.

41. For example, see David M. Ricci, *The Tragedy of Political Science: Politics, Scholarship, and Democracy* (New Haven: Yale University Press, 1984).

42. See Richard P. Nathan, *Social Science in Government: Uses and Misuses* (New York: Basic Books, 1988).

43. Kathleen B. Jones and Anna G. Jonasdottir, "Introduction: Gender as an Analytic Category in Political Science," in Kathleen B. Jones and Anna G. Jonasdottir, eds., *The Political Interests of Gender* (Beverly Hills, Calif.: Sage, 1988), 2.

44. Kathleen B. Jones, "Towards the Revision of Politics," in Jones and Jonasdottir, eds., *The Political Interests of Gender,* 25.

45. Margrit Eichler, *Nonsexist Research Methods: A Practical Guide* (Boston: Allen & Unwin, 1987).

Te rms introduced

ACTION. Physical human movement or behavior done for a reason.

BEHAVIORALISM. The study of politics that focuses on political behavior and embraces the scientific method.

DEDUCTION. A process of reasoning from a theory to specific observations.

EMPIRICAL GENERALIZATION. A statement that summarizes the relationship between individual facts and that communicates general knowledge.

EMPIRICAL VERIFICATION. Characteristic of scientific knowledge; demonstration by means of objective observation that a statement is true.

Explanation. A systematic, empirically verified understanding of why a phenomenon occurs as it does.

Explanatory. Characteristic of scientific knowledge; signifies that a conclusion can be derived from a set of general propositions and specific initial considerations.

General. Characteristic of scientific knowledge; applicable to many rather than a few cases.

Induction. A process of reasoning from specific observations to general principle.

Nonnormative knowledge. Knowledge concerned not with evaluation or prescription but with factual or objective determinations.

Normative knowledge. Knowledge that is evaluative, value-laden, and concerned with prescribing what ought to be.

Postbehavioralism. The reaction to behavioralism that called for political science research to be more relevant to important current political issues.

Predictive. Characteristic of explanatory knowledge; indicates an ability to correctly anticipate future events. The application of explanation to events in the future forms a prediction.

Probabilistic explanation. An explanation that does not explain or predict events with 100-percent accuracy.

Provisional. Characteristic of scientific knowledge; subject to revision and change.

Reason. Beliefs and desires that justify or explain an action or behavior.

Scientific revolution. The rapid development of a rival tradition of scientific research; usually accompanied by conflict among scientists over the theoretical perspective that will endure.

Theory. A statement or series of statements that organize, explain, and predict knowledge.

Transmissible. Characteristic of scientific knowledge; indicates that the methods used in making scientific discoveries are made explicit.

Exercises

1. Many people make the claim, "You can't predict human behavior." In light of our discussion of the scientific approach to political science, do you find this claim valid? If we were to suppose that this claim is strictly true, what consequences for social and political life would follow?

2. Make a list of questions that arise from current events. Which, if any, of these could be addressed or studied scientifically? Which would not lend themselves to scientific analysis?

3. Read David Easton's "The New Revolution in Political Science" (*American Political Science Review* 63 [December 1969]: 1051–1061). What does Easton say is wrong with behavioral political science research?

4. Read a mass circulation newspaper such as *USA Today* or the *New York Times* or a national magazine like *Newsweek*. Can you find a study of public opinion or behavior that you think would be worth replicating? What changes in methods would you propose? What would this replication show?

5. As we noted in our discussion, some observers charge that the social sciences, especially in the past, have exhibited gender and ethnic biases. Read an article or book that studies politics empirically. Can you identify bias?

6. Make a short list of questions that the scientific study of politics might not be able to answer (for example, "Is democracy the best form of government?"). What is it about these kinds of questions that prevents us from fully answering them using the scientific method? Are there *aspects* of them that empirical research might help us understand? (Consider the discussion in Chapter 1 of the connection between human rights and democracy.)

Suggested Readings

Eichler, Margrit. *Nonsexist Research Methods: A Practical Guide.* Boston: Allen & Unwin, 1987.

Elster, Jon. *Nuts and Bolts for the Social Sciences.* Cambridge: Cambridge University Press, 1990.

Heil, John. *Philosophy of the Mind: A Contemporary Introduction.* London: Routledge, 1998.

Isaak, Alan C. *Scope and Methods of Political Science.* 4th ed. Homewood, Ill.: Dorsey, 1985.

Kuhn, Thomas. *The Structure of Scientific Revolutions.* 2d ed. Chicago: University of Chicago Press, 1971.

McCoy, Charles A., and John Playford, eds. *Apolitical Politics: A Critique of Behavioralism.* New York: Thomas Y. Crowell, 1967.

Martin, Michael, and Lee C. McIntyre, eds. *Readings in the Philosophy of the Social Sciences.* Cambridge: MIT Press, 1994.

Nielsen, Joyce McCarl, ed. *Feminist Research Methods: Exemplary Readings in the Social Sciences.* Boulder: Westview, 1990.

Rosenberg, Alexander. *The Philosophy of Social Science.* 2d ed. Boulder: Westview, 1998.

CHAPTER 3

The Building Blocks
of Social Scientific Research:
Hypotheses, Concepts, and Variables

In Chapters 1 and 2 we discussed what it means to acquire scientific knowledge and presented a number of examples of political science research intended to produce this type of knowledge. In this chapter we will begin the process of evaluating and acquiring scientific knowledge by explaining the initial steps in an empirical research project. These steps require a researcher to (1) specify the question or problem with which the research is concerned; (2) propose a suitable explanation for the phenomena under study; (3) formulate testable hypotheses; and (4) define the concepts identified in the hypotheses. Although we will discuss these steps as if they represent a logical sequence of thought, in the conduct of actual research the order may vary. They must all be accomplished eventually, however, before a research project can be completed successfully. The sooner the issues and decisions involved in each of the steps are addressed, the sooner the other portions of the research project can be completed.

Specifying the Research Question

One of the most important purposes of social scientific research is to answer questions about social phenomena. The research projects summarized in Chapter 1, for example, all attempt to answer questions about some important political behavior. Why are some political regimes more stable than others? Why do human rights violations by governments vary? Why did the welfare rolls in the United States expand in the 1960s and 1970s? Do negative campaign advertising and other campaign activities have any impact on the electorate? Why do public officials make the public policy decisions they do? Why do Supreme Court justices take the positions they take on the cases that come before them? And why do the activities of bureaucracies change? In every case the researchers identified some political phenomenon that interested them and tried to answer questions about that phenomenon. The phenomena investigated by political scientists are diverse and are limited only by whether they are significant (that is, would advance our understanding of politics and government), observable, and political. Political scientists attempt to answer questions about the political behavior of individuals (voters, citizens, residents of a particular area, Supreme Court justices, presidents), groups (political parties, interest groups, labor unions, ethnic organizations), institutions (state legislatures, city governments, bureaucracies, district courts), and nations.

The first task of a researcher is to specify the question with which the research is concerned. In doing so he or she will identify the phenomenon being investigated and will point the research project in the direction of providing an explanation for that phenomenon. Failure to specify the question clearly can lead to confused researchers as well as confused readers.

Where do the research questions of political scientists originate? There are many answers. Some researchers become interested in a topic because of personal observation or experience. For example, a researcher who works for a candidate who loses a political campaign may wonder what factors are responsible for electoral success, and a researcher who fled his country of birth during a period of civil unrest may be drawn to conducting research on the causes of political disorder. Some researchers are drawn to a topic because of the research and writing of others. A scholar familiar with studies of congressional decision making may want to investigate the reasons for the success and failure of different public policy proposals. Still others select a research topic because of their interest in some broader social theory, as in the researcher whose fascination with theories of rational decision making prompted the study of federal bureaucrats' behavior; similarly, researchers concerned in general with democratic theory often conduct research on what causes people to participate in politics. Finally, researchers select research topics for practical reasons: because grant money for a particular subject is available or because demonstrating expertise in a particular area will advance their professional career objectives.

The framing of an engaging and appropriate research question will get a research project off to a good start. Any of the following questions would probably lead to a politically significant and informative research project:

Why is the voter turnout for local elections higher in some cities than others?

Why is the rate of recycling higher in some communities than others?

Why did some members of Congress vote for the North American Free Trade Agreement while others voted against it?

Why do some states have laws strongly regulating the activities of lobbyists while other states do not?

Why do state laws concerning access to abortion vary?

Why did some voters vote for Al Gore in the 2000 presidential election while others voted for George W. Bush?

Why are some judges more protective of the rights of the accused than others?

Why do some nations spend more on weapons systems than others?

Why do some states have more extensive welfare systems than others?

Why do some nations support setting specific targets for limiting carbon dioxide emissions while others do not?

Students sometimes have difficulty formulating interesting and appropriate research questions. Researchers also occasionally pose questions that are simplistic, trivial, or impossible to answer. A research project will get off on the wrong foot if the question that shapes it is inappropriate, unduly concerned with discrete facts, or focused on reaching normative conclusions.

Political scientists seek knowledge about political phenomena. Although the definition of political phenomena is vague, it does not include the study of all human characteristics or behavior. For example, research studies guided by questions such as "Why do some people drink coffee and others do not?" or "Why do some families take camping vacations?" might be interesting studies, but they would be unlikely to yield fresh insights into political phenomena. Questions such as those would be inappropriate for the study of politics and would be better addressed by people in fields other than political science.

Research questions may also limit the significance of a research project if they are unduly focused on discrete facts. Questions such as "Who is the secretary of state?" or "Which interest groups contribute the most money to political campaigns?" or "How many nuclear warheads did the Soviet Union possess in 1980?" may yield important factual knowledge, but they will not sustain a research project of the type developed in this book. Each of them asks for one discrete piece of information or fact. While important, facts alone are not enough to yield scientific explanations. What is missing is a **relationship**—that is, the association, dependence, or covariance of the values of one variable with the values of another. The researcher is interested in how to advance and test generalizations relating one phenomenon to another. In the absence of such generalizations, factual knowledge of the type called for by the preceding research questions will be fundamentally limited in scope.

Factual information, however, may prompt a researcher to ask "why" questions. For example, if a researcher had information about the number of nuclear warheads possessed by the Soviet Union and noted that the number varied substantially over time, the research question "Why did the number of nuclear warheads vary?" forms the basis of an interesting research project.

Another type of question that is inconsistent with the research methods discussed in this book is a question calling for a normative conclusion. Questions such as "Should the United States send troops to Somalia or Bosnia-Herzegovina?" or "Is the 'actual malice test' too stringent a guideline for the resolution of libel suits?" or "Should states give tax breaks to new businesses willing to locate within their borders?" are important and suitable for the attention of political scientists (indeed, for any citizen), but they, too, are inappropriate as presently framed. They ask for a normative response, seeking an indication of what is good or of what should be done. Although scientific knowledge may be helpful in answering questions like these, it cannot provide the answers without regard for an individual's personal values or preferences. What someone ultimately likes or dislikes, values or rejects, is involved in the answers to these questions.

In general, it is useful to submit your research question to the "so what" test; will the answer to it make a significant contribution to the accumulation of our understanding of and knowledge about political phenomena? Will it be useful for practitioners and policy makers? Will it provide an interesting test of a theory?

Proposing Explanations

Once a researcher has developed a suitable research question or topic, the next step is to propose an explanation for the phenomenon the researcher is interested in understanding. Proposing an explanation involves identifying other phenomena that we think will help us account for the object of our research and then specifying how and why these two (or more) phenomena are related.

In the research examples described in Chapter 1 the researchers proposed explanations for the political phenomena they were studying. Ted Gurr thought that political violence might be affected by a population's sense of relative deprivation. Benjamin Page and Robert Shapiro wondered if public policy decisions made in the United States over a forty-year period were influenced by the amount of popular support for those decisions. Jeffrey Segal and Albert Cover tried to find out if the personal attitudes of Supreme Court justices affect their judicial decisions. Daron Shaw wondered if voters' decisions were affected by exposure to candidates' campaigns. Dan Wood and Richard Waterman investigated the activities of federal agencies to see if they changed in response to attempts by presidents and Congress to influence them. And Stephen Poe and C. Neal Tate investigated whether government violation of their citizens' human rights was related to rapid population growth, military regimes, colonial history, and level of economic development.

A phenomenon that we think will help us explain the political characteristics or behavior that interest us is called an **independent variable**. Independent variables are the measures of the phenomena that are thought to influence, affect, or cause some other phenomenon. A **dependent variable** is thought to be caused, to depend upon, or to be a function of an independent variable. Thus, if a researcher has hypothesized that acquiring more formal education will lead to increased income later on (in other words, that income may be explained by education), then years of formal education would be the independent variable and income would be the dependent variable.

Proposed explanations for political phenomena are often more complicated than the simple identification of one independent variable that is thought to explain a dependent variable. More than one phenomenon is usually needed to account adequately for most political behavior. For example, suppose a researcher proposes that state efforts to regulate pollution are related to the severity of potential harm of pollution, with the higher the threat of pollution (independent variable), the greater the effort to regulate pollution (dependent variable). The insightful researcher would realize the possibility that another phenomenon, such as the wealth of a state, might also affect a state's regulatory effort. The proposed explanation for state regulatory effort, then, would involve an alternative variable in addition to the original independent variable. As another example, remember from Chapter 1 that Richard Fording thought that state governments responded to civil unrest in the 1960s and 1970s by expanding welfare programs, but that such expansion would be affected by the proportion of African Americans in the population as well as by their ease of access to the polls.

Researchers are often interested in determining the relative effect of each independent variable on the dependent variable. This is done by "controlling for" or "holding constant" one of the independent variables so that the effect of the other may be observed. This process will be discussed in more detail in Chapter 13.

Sometimes researchers are also able to propose explanations for how the independent variables are related to each other. In particular, we might want to determine which independent variables come before other independent variables and indicate which have a more direct, as opposed to indirect, effect on the phenomenon we are trying to explain (the dependent variable). A variable that occurs prior to all other variables and that may affect other independent variables is called an **antecedent variable**. A variable that occurs closer in time to the dependent variable and is itself affected by other independent variables is called an **intervening variable**. The roles of antecedent and intervening variables in the explanation of the dependent variable differ significantly. Consider these examples.

Suppose a researcher hypothesizes that a person who favored national health insurance was more likely to have voted for Bill Clinton in 1992 than a person who did not favor national health insurance. In this case the attitude toward national health insurance would be the independent variable and the presidential vote the dependent variable. The researcher might wonder what causes the attitude toward national health insurance and might propose that those people who have inadequate medical insurance are more apt to favor national health insurance. This new variable (adequacy of a person's present medical insurance) would then be an antecedent variable since it comes before and affects (we think) the independent variable. Thinking about antecedent variables pushes our explanatory scheme further back in time and, we hope, will lead to a more complete understanding of a particular phenomenon (in this case, presidential voting). Notice how the independent variable in the original hypothesis (attitude toward national health insurance) becomes the dependent variable in the hypothesis involving the antecedent variable (adequacy of health insurance). Also notice that in this example adequacy of health insurance is thought to exert an indirect effect on the dependent variable (presidential voting) via its impact on attitudes toward national health insurance.

Now let us consider a second example. Suppose a researcher hypothesizes that the number of years of formal education had by a voter will affect that voter's propensity to vote. In this case education would be the independent variable and turnout the dependent variable. If the researcher then begins to think about what it is about formal education that has this effect, he or she has begun to identify the intervening variables between education and turnout. For example, the researcher might hypothesize that formal education causes a sense of civic duty, which in turn causes voter turnout, or that formal education causes an ability to understand the different issue positions of the candidates, which in turn causes voter turnout. Intervening variables come between an independent and dependent variable and help explain the process by which one influences the other.

Explanatory schemes that involve numerous independent, alternative, antecedent, and intervening variables can become quite complex. An **arrow diagram** is a handy device for presenting and keeping track of such complicated explanations. It specifies the phenomena of interest; indicates which variables are independent, alternative, antecedent, intervening, and dependent; and shows which variables are thought to affect which other ones. Figure 3-1 presents arrow diagrams for the two examples we just considered.

In both diagrams the dependent variable is placed at the end of the time line, with the independent, alternative, intervening, and antecedent variables

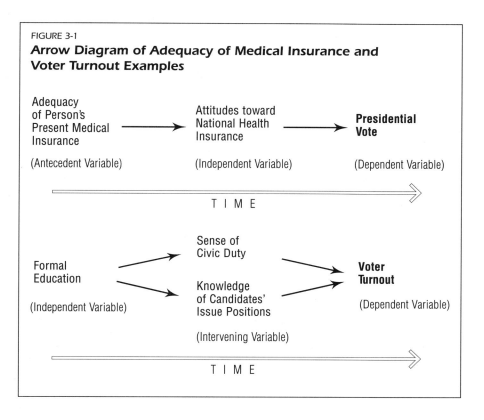

FIGURE 3-1

Arrow Diagram of Adequacy of Medical Insurance and Voter Turnout Examples

Adequacy of Person's Present Medical Insurance → Attitudes toward National Health Insurance → **Presidential Vote**

(Antecedent Variable)　　(Independent Variable)　　(Dependent Variable)

TIME

Formal Education → Sense of Civic Duty / Knowledge of Candidates' Issue Positions → **Voter Turnout**

(Independent Variable)　　(Intervening Variable)　　(Dependent Variable)

TIME

placed in their appropriate locations to indicate which ones come first. Arrows indicate that one variable is thought to explain or be related to another; the direction of the arrow indicates which variable is independent and which is dependent in that proposed relationship.

Figure 3-2 shows two examples of actual arrow diagrams that have been proposed and tested by political scientists. Both are thought to explain presidential voting behavior. In the first diagram the ultimate dependent variable is the Vote and is thought to be explained by Candidate Evaluations and Party Identification. Candidate Evaluations, in turn, is explained by Issue Losses, Party Identification, and Perceived Candidate Personalities. These, in turn, are explained by other concepts in the diagram. The variables at the top of the diagram tend to be antecedent variables (the subscript $t - 1$ denotes that these variables precede variables with subscript t, where t indicates time); the ones in the center tend to be intervening variables. Nine independent variables of one sort or another figure in the explanation of the vote.

The second diagram also has the Vote as the ultimate dependent variable, which is explained directly by only one independent variable, Comparative Candidate Evaluations. The latter variable, in turn, is dependent upon six in-

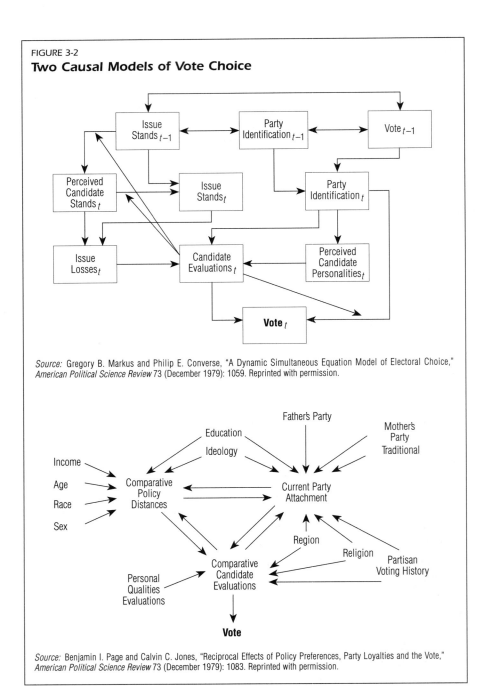

FIGURE 3-2
Two Causal Models of Vote Choice

Source: Gregory B. Markus and Philip E. Converse, "A Dynamic Simultaneous Equation Model of Electoral Choice," *American Political Science Review* 73 (December 1979): 1059. Reprinted with permission.

Source: Benjamin I. Page and Calvin C. Jones, "Reciprocal Effects of Policy Preferences, Party Loyalties and the Vote," *American Political Science Review* 73 (December 1979): 1083. Reprinted with permission.

dependent variables: Personal Qualities Evaluations, Comparative Policy Distances, Current Party Attachment, Region, Religion, and Partisan Voting History. In this diagram sixteen variables figure, either indirectly or directly, in the explanation of the vote, with the antecedent variables located around the perimeter of the diagram and the intervening variables closer to the center. Both of these diagrams clearly represent complicated and extensive attempts to explain a dependent variable.

In our discussion of developing explanations, we have talked about one phenomenon being *caused* by one or more other phenomena. It is important to recognize that when we say that something (X) is the *cause* of something else (Y), we are making three claims. One is that X and Y covary—a change in one variable is associated with a change in the other. Furthermore, we are claiming that a change in the independent variable (X) *precedes* the change in the dependent variable (Y). Finally we are claiming that the covariation we observe between X and Y is not simply a coincidence or spurious, that is, due to change in some other variable. We will have more to say about how to conduct research in order to support these claims in Chapter 5.

CONDITIONS FOR CAUSALITY (X CAUSES Y)

1. X and Y covary.
2. A change in X precedes a change in Y.
3. The covariation between X and Y is not spurious nor a coincidence.

We have discussed the first two steps in the research process—asking a question and then proposing an explanation—as occuring in this order, but quite often this is not the case. In Chapter 2 we pointed out that researchers may start out with a theory and make deductions based on it. Thus researchers often start with an explanation and look for an appropriate research question that the theory might answer. Theory is an important aspect of explanation, for in order to be able to argue effectively that something causes something else, we need to be able to supply a reason or, to use words from the natural sciences, to identify the mechanism behind the relationship. This is the role of theory.

Formulating Hypotheses

Thus far we have discussed two stages in the research process: identifying the research question and proposing explanations for the phenomena of interest. By this point, then, the researcher is ready to state what his or her hypotheses are. A **hypothesis** is an explicit statement that indicates how a researcher thinks the phenomena of interest are related. A hypothesis is a guess (but of an "educated" nature) that represents the proposed explanation for some phenomenon and that indicates how an independent variable is thought to affect, influence, or alter a dependent variable. Since hypotheses are proposed relationships, they may turn out to be incorrect.

Actually, our everyday conversation is filled with hypotheses (though they may not be properly formulated). When we suggest that the reason there are no challengers to an incumbent legislator even though there is constituent dissatisfaction with the incumbent's voting record is because the incumbent's party is the only effectively organized party in our legislative district, we are suggesting a hypothesis relating electoral competition and more than one party. We may also be suggesting a hypothesis relating party competition and official responsiveness. When we observe that a particular country is experiencing social turmoil and that its population is ethnically diverse, we are proposing a hypothesis relating ethnic homogeneity and political stability. In fact, whenever we propose an explanation for any phenomenon, we are engaging in the preliminary stages of hypothesis formulation. One of the differences between doing this in everyday conversation and doing it as part of a scientific research project is that in research, hypothesis formulation is only the beginning of a process that will include a test of our hypotheses. In everyday life we seldom test our hypotheses systematically. To test a hypothesis adequately and persuasively, it must be properly formulated.

Characteristics of Good Hypotheses

It is important to start a research project with a clearly stated hypothesis because it provides the foundation for subsequent decisions and steps in the research process. A poorly formulated hypothesis often indicates confusion about the relationship that is to be tested or can lead to mistakes that will limit the value or meaning of any findings. Our experience has shown us that many students find writing a hypothesis that precisely states the relationship to be tested is quite a challenging task. The following discussion of six characteristics of a good hypothesis will alert students to some common mistakes to avoid.

First, hypotheses should be *empirical statements*; that is, they should be educated guesses about relationships that exist in the real world, not statements about what ought to be true or about what a researcher believes should be the case. Let us return to our example of the researcher interested in democracy. If the researcher hypothesizes that "democracy is the best form of government," he or she has formulated a normative, nonempirical statement that cannot be tested in its present form. The statement states the preference of the researcher rather than an explanation for a phenomenon. By now, this researcher ought to have defined the central concept—in this case, democracy—and those concepts thought to be related to democracy (such as literacy, size of population, geographical isolation, and economic development). Therefore, to produce an acceptable hypothesis, the researcher ought to make an educated guess about the relationship between democracy and another of these concepts, for example: "Democracy is more likely to be found in countries with high literacy than in countries with low literacy." This hypothesis now proposes an explanation for a phenomenon that can be empirically observed. Whether the hypothesis is confirmed is not necessarily related to whether the researcher thinks the phenomenon (in this case democracy) is good or bad.

This does not mean, however, that empirical knowledge is completely irrelevant for normative inquiry. Often people have reached normative conclusions based on their evaluation of empirical relationships. Someone might reason, for example, that

> Some government welfare programs lead to family disintegration.
> Family disintegration is bad. Therefore, some government welfare programs are bad.

The first statement could be considered a research hypothesis and could be investigated using the techniques developed in this book. The results could then be used to evaluate the third statement. However, the second statement, which is a normative statement of preference, cannot be tested, as it stands, using these techniques.

Normative thinking is useful because it forces an individual to clarify his or her values, and it encourages research on significant empirical questions. For example, a normative distaste for crime encourages empirical research on the causes of crime. Consequently, the two modes of inquiry—normative and empirical—should be viewed as complementary rather than contradictory.

A second characteristic of a good hypothesis is *generality*. It should explain a general phenomenon rather than one particular occurrence of the phenomenon. For example, one might hypothesize that the cause of World War II was economic upheaval in Germany. If the hypothesis were confirmed, what would be the extent of our knowledge? We would know the cause of one war. This knowledge is valuable, but it would be more useful to know if economic upheaval *in general* causes wars. That would be knowledge pertaining to many occurrences of a phenomenon (in this case many wars), rather than knowledge about just one occurrence. A more general hypothesis, then, might be "countries experiencing economic upheaval are more likely to become involved in a war than countries not experiencing economic upheaval." Knowledge about the causes of particular occurrences of a phenomenon could be helpful in formulating more general guesses about the relationships between concepts, but with a general hypothesis we attempt to expand the scope of our knowledge beyond individual cases. Stating hypotheses in the plural form, rather than the singular, makes it clear that testing the hypothesis will involve more than one case.

Below are four hypotheses that are too narrow, followed by four acceptable hypotheses that are more general:

Senator X voted for a bill because it is the president's bill and they are both Democrats.	Senators are more likely to vote for bills sponsored by the president if they belong to the same political party as the president.
The United States is a democracy because its population is affluent.	Countries with high levels of affluence are more likely to be democracies than countries with low levels of affluence.
The United States has more murders than other countries because so many people own guns there.	Countries with more guns per capita will experience more murders per capita than countries with fewer guns.
Joe is a liberal because his mother is one too.	People tend to adopt political viewpoints similar to those of their parents.

A third characteristic of a good hypothesis is that it should be *plausible*; that is, there should be some logical reason for thinking that it might be confirmed. Of course, since a hypothesis is a guess about a relationship, whether it will be confirmed cannot be known for certain. Any number of hypotheses could be thought of and tested, but there are many fewer plausible ones. For example, if a researcher hypothesized that "people who eat dry cereal for breakfast are more likely to be liberal than people who eat eggs," we would question his or her logic even though the form of the hypothesis may be perfectly acceptable. It is difficult to imagine why this hypothesis would be confirmed.

But how do we make sure that a hypothesis has a good chance of being confirmed? Sometimes the justification is provided by specific instances in which the hypothesis was supported (going from specific to general knowledge in the manner discussed in Chapter 2—that is, using induction). For example, a researcher may have observed a particular election in which a hotly contested primary campaign damaged the eventual nominee's chances of winning the general election. The researcher may then have concluded that "the more difficult it is for candidates to secure their party's nomination, the more poorly those candidates will do in the general election."

And, as we pointed out earlier in our discussion of proposing explanations, a hypothesis also may be justified through the process of deduction. A researcher may deduce from more general theories that a particular hypothesis is sensible. For example, there is a general psychological theory that frustration leads to aggression. Some political scientists have adapted this general theory to the study of political violence or civil unrest and hypothesized that civil unrest occurs when a civilian population is frustrated. A population may feel frustrated when many people believe that they are economically or politically worse off than they should be, than they used to be, or than other people like themselves are. This feeling, as we now know, is called relative deprivation, and it has figured prominently in hypotheses seeking to explain civil unrest. In this way the general frustration-aggression theory led to a more specialized, deduced hypothesis for the occurrence of civil unrest.

Formulating plausible hypotheses is one of the reasons why researchers conduct a literature review early in their research projects. Literature reviews (discussed in more detail in Chapter 6) can acquaint researchers both with general theories and with specific hypotheses advanced by others. In either case, reading the literature on a subject can improve the chances that a hypothesis will be confirmed. There are no hard and fast rules to ensure plausibility, however. After all, people used to think that "germs cause diseases" was an implausible hypothesis and that "dirt may be turned into gold" was a plausible one.

The fourth characteristic of all good hypotheses is that they are *specific*. The researcher should be able to state a **directional hypothesis**—that is, he or she should be able to specify the expected relationship between two or more variables. Following are examples of directional hypotheses that specify the nature of the relationship between concepts:

> Median family income is higher in urban counties than in rural counties.

> States that are characterized by a "moralistic" political culture will have higher levels of voter turnout than states with an "individualistic" or "traditionalistic" political culture.

The first hypothesis indicates which relative values of median family income are related to which type or category of county. Similarly, the second hypothesis predicts a particular relationship between political culture (the independent variable) and voter turnout (the dependent variable).

The direction of the relationship between concepts is referred to as a **positive relationship** if the concepts are predicted to increase in size together or decrease in size together. The following are examples of hypotheses that predict positive relationships:

> As people's years of formal education increase, their income increases.

> As the percentage of a country's population that is literate increases, the country's political process becomes more democratic.

> The older people become, the more conservative they become.

People who read the newspaper more are more informed about current events than people who read the newspaper less.

The lower a state's per capita income, the less money is spent per pupil on education.

If, on the other hand, the researcher thinks that as one concept increases in size or amount another one will decrease in size or amount, then a **negative relationship** is suggested, as in the following examples:

Older people are less tolerant of social protest than younger people.

The more income a person has, the less concerned about mass transit the person will become.

More affluent countries have less property crime than less affluent countries.

In addition, the concepts used in a hypothesis should be carefully defined. For example, a hypothesis that suggests that "there is a relationship between personality and political attitudes" is far too ambiguous. What is meant by personality? Which political attitudes? A more specific reformulation of this hypothesis might be "the more self-esteem a person has, the less likely a person is to be an isolationist." Now personality has been narrowed to self-esteem, and the political attitude has been defined as isolationism, both more precise concepts. Eventually even these two terms must be given more precise definitions when it comes to measuring them. (We will return to the problem of measuring concepts in Chapter 4.) Note that as the concepts become more clearly defined, the researcher is also able to specify the direction of the hypothesized relationship.

Following are four examples of ambiguous hypotheses that have been made more specific:

How a person votes for president depends on the information he or she is exposed to.

The more information favoring candidate X a person is exposed to during a political campaign, the more likely that person is to vote for candidate X.

A country's geographical location matters for the type of political system it develops.

The more borders a country shares with other countries, the more likely that country is to have a nondemocratic political process.

A person's capabilities affect his or her political attitudes.	The more intelligent a person is, the more likely he or she is to support civil liberties.
Guns do not cause crime.	People who own guns are less likely to be the victims of crimes than persons who do not own guns.

A fifth characteristic of a good hypothesis is that it is stated in a manner that corresponds to the way in which the researcher intends to test it—that is, it should be *consistent with the data.*[1] For example, while the hypothesis "Higher levels of literacy are associated with higher levels of democracy" does state how the concepts are related, it does not indicate how the researcher plans to test the hypothesis. In contrast, the hypothesis "As the percentage of a country's population that is literate increases, the country's political process becomes more democratic" suggests that the researcher is proposing to measure the literacy rate and the amount of democracy for a country or countries at several different times to see if increases in democracy are associated with increases in literacy (i.e., that changes in one concept lead to changes in another). If, however, the researcher plans to test the hypothesis by measuring the literacy rates and levels of democracy for many countries at one point in time to see if those with higher literacy rates also have higher levels of democracy, it would be better to rephrase the hypothesis to "Countries with higher literacy rates tend to be more democratic than countries with lower literacy rates." This way of phrasing the hypothesis reflects that the researcher is planning to compare the level of democracy in countries with different literacy rates. This differs from comparing a country's level of democracy at more than one point in time to see if it changes in concert with changes in literacy.

Finally, a good hypothesis is *testable*; there must be some evidence that is obtainable and that will indicate whether the hypothesis is correct. Hypotheses for which either confirming or nonconfirming evidence is impossible to gather are untestable.

Consider this example of a promising yet untestable hypothesis: "The more supportive of political authorities a child is, the less likely that child will be to engage in political dissent as an adult." This hypothesis is general, plausible, fairly specific, and empirical, but it is currently untestable because no data exist to test the proposition. The hypothesis requires data that measure a set of attitudes for individuals when they are children and a set of behaviors when they are adults. Survey data do exist that include the political attitudes and behavior of seventeen- and eighteen-year-olds and their parents in 1965 and many of the same people in 1973.[2] These data lack childhood measures for the parents, however, and for the others there are only late adolescent and early adulthood (mid-twenties) measures. Consequently, a frustrating practical barrier prevents the testing of an otherwise acceptable hypothesis.

Students in one-semester college courses on research methods often run up against this constraint. A semester is not usually long enough to collect and analyze data, and some data may be too expensive to acquire. Many interesting hypotheses go untested simply because researchers do not have the resources to collect the data necessary to test them.

Hypotheses stated in tautological form are also untestable. A **tautology** is a statement linking two concepts that mean essentially the same thing: for example, "the less support there is for a country's political institutions, the more tenuous the stability of that country's political system." This hypothesis would be difficult to disconfirm because the two concepts are so similar. To provide a fair test one would have to measure independently—in different ways—the support for the political institutions and the stability of the political system.

Poe and Tate defined human rights abuses in their study as coercive activities (such as murder, torture, forced disappearance, and imprisonment of persons for their political views) designed to induce compliance. By defining human rights abuses in this way they were able to avoid defining human rights in terms of democratic processes or economic conditions—concepts they wanted to explore as independent variables explaining variation in human rights abuses.

There are many hypotheses, then, that are not formulated in a way that permits an informative test of them with empirical research. Readers of empirical research in political science, as well as researchers themselves, should take care that research hypotheses are empirical, general, plausible, specific, consistent with the data, and testable. Hypotheses that do not share these characteristics are likely to cause difficulty for the researcher and reader alike and make a minimal contribution to scientific knowledge.

Specifying Units of Analysis

In addition to proposing a relationship between two or more variables, a hypothesis also specifies the types or levels of political actor to which the hypothesis is thought to apply. This is called the **unit of analysis** of the hypothesis, and it also must be selected thoughtfully.

As noted in Chapter 2, political scientists are interested in understanding the behavior or properties of all sorts of political actors: individuals, groups, states, governmental agencies, regions, and nations. The particular type of actor whose political behavior is named in a hypothesis is the unit of analysis for the research project. For example, the individual member of the House of Representatives is the unit of analysis in the following hypothesis:

> Members of the House of Representatives who belong to the same party as the president are more likely to vote for legislation desired by the president than members who belong to a different party.

In the following hypothesis, the city is the unit of analysis since it is attributes of cities that are being explored:

> Northeastern cities are more likely to have mayors, while western cities have city managers.

Finally, consider this hypothesis:

> The more affluent countries are, the more likely they are to have democratic political institutions.

Here the unit of analysis is the country. It is the attributes of countries— affluence (the independent variable) and democratic political institutions (the dependent variable)—that will need to be empirically observed. In sum, the research hypothesis indicates what the researcher's unit of analysis is and what behavior or attributes must be measured for that unit.

A discrepancy between the unit of analysis specified in a hypothesis and the entities whose behavior is actually empirically observed can cause problems. For example, suppose a researcher wants to test the hypothesis "African Americans are more likely to support female candidates than are Italian Americans." He or she might select an election with a female candidate and obtain data on the voting returns in election precincts with varying proportions of African Americans and Italian Americans. If it is found that female candidates received more votes in precincts with a higher proportion of African Americans than in the precincts with a higher proportion of Italian Americans, the researcher might conclude that there was evidence in support of the hypothesis.

There is a fundamental problem with this approach, however. In the original hypothesis the unit of analysis is the individual voter, yet the data apply to election precincts, a different unit of analysis. Unless a district is 100 percent African American or 100 percent Italian American, the researcher cannot necessarily draw conclusions about the behavior of individuals from the behavior of election districts. It could be that a female candidate's support in a district with a high proportion of African American voters came mostly from non–African Americans, and that most of the female candidate's votes in the Italian American districts came from Italian Americans.

Let us take two hypothetical election precincts to illustrate this fallacy. Suppose we have Precinct 1, classified as an "African American" district, and Precinct 2, an "Italian American" district. If the African American district voted 67 percent to 33 percent in favor of the female candidate, and the Italian American district voted 53 percent to 47 percent in favor of the female candidate, we might be tempted to conclude that African Americans as individuals voted more heavily for the female candidate than did Italian Americans.

But suppose we peek inside each of the election precincts to see how individuals of different ethnicities behaved. Table 3-1 shows that in the African American district, African Americans split 25–25 for the woman, Italian Americans voted 18–2 for her, and others voted 24–6 for her. This resulted in the 67–33 edge for the woman in Precinct 1. In the Italian American district, African Americans voted 16–24 against the woman, Italian Americans split 30–20 for her, and others voted 7–3 in her favor. This resulted in the 53–47 margin for the woman in Precinct 2. When we compare the percentage of African Americans, Italian Americans, and others voting for the female candi-

TABLE 3-1
Voting by African Americans, Italian Americans, and Others for a Female Candidate

| Ethnicity | Raw Vote | | | Percent Vote | |
	Number	For Male	For Female	For Male	For Female
Precinct 1					
African Americans	50	25	25	50.0	50.0
Italian Americans	20	2	18	10.0	90.0
Other	30	6	24	20.0	80.0
Total	100	33	67	33.0	67.0
Precinct 2					
African Americans	40	24	16	60.0	40.0
Italian Americans	50	20	30	40.0	60.0
Other	10	3	7	30.0	70.0
Total	100	47	53	47.0	53.0
Voting of Individuals					
African Americans	90	49	41	54.4	45.6
Italian Americans	70	22	48	31.4	68.6
Other	40	9	31	22.5	77.5
Total	200	80	120	40.0	60.0

Note: Hypothetical data.

date, the difference in the voting behavior of the ethnic groups becomes clearer. In both precincts, the percentage of African Americans voting for the female candidate was lower than that of the two other groups of voters. In Precinct 1, 50 percent of the African Americans voted for the female candidate, compared to 90 percent of the Italian American voters and 80 percent of the others. In Precinct 2, only 40 percent of the African Americans voted for the female candidate, compared to 60 percent of the Italian Americans and 70 percent of the other voters. In other words, Italian Americans as individuals were more likely to have voted for the woman candidate than were African Americans as individuals in both precincts. Knowing only the precinct-level totals gave the opposite impression. When the results for both districts are combined and broken down by ethnicity, we see that, overall, 68.6 percent of Italian Americans and 45.6 percent of African Americans voted for the female candidate.

If a relationship is found between group indicators or characterisitics, it does not necessarily mean that there is a relationship between the characteristics for individuals in the group. Using information that shows a relationship for groups to infer that there is the same relationship for individuals when in fact there is no such relationship at the individual level is called an **ecological fallacy**. To illustrate how one can get into trouble using group information to draw conclusions about individuals within the groups, suppose a study showed that counties with high rates of driving under the influence (DUI) also had high proportions of conservative Republicans. Would it be safe to conclude that conservative Republicans drive under the influence more than people with other partisan affiliations? Perhaps liberals who live in counties with lots of conservative Republicans are driven to drink. Or, perhaps individuals who live in counties where there are high levels of DUI are more likely to become conservative Republicans.[3]

Another mistake sometimes made by researchers is to mix different units of analysis in the same hypothesis. "The more education a person has, the more democratic his country is" doesn't make much sense since it mixes the individual and country as units of analysis. However, "the smaller a government agency, the happier its workers" concerns an attribute of an agency and an attribute of individuals, but in a way that makes sense. The size of the agency in which individuals work may be an important aspect of the context or environment in which the individual phenomenon occurs and may influence the individual attribute. In this case the unit of analysis is clearly the individual, but a phenomenon that is experienced by many cases is used to explain the behavior of individuals, some of whom may well be identically situated.

In short, a researcher must be careful about the unit of analysis specified in a hypothesis and its correspondence with the unit measured. In general, a researcher should not mix units of analysis within a hypothesis.

Defining Concepts

Clear definitions of the concepts that are of interest to us are important if we are to develop specific hypotheses and avoid tautologies. Clear definitions are also important so that the knowledge we acquire from testing our hypotheses is transmissible and empirical.

Political scientists are interested in why people or social groupings (organizations, political parties, legislatures, states, countries) behave in a certain way or have particular attributes or properties. The words that we choose to describe these behaviors or attributes are called concepts. Concepts should be accurate, precise, and informative.

In our daily life we use concepts frequently to name and describe features of our environment. For example, we describe some snakes as poisonous and others as nonpoisonous, some politicians as liberal and others as conservative, some friends as shy and others as extroverted. These attributes or concepts are useful to us because they help us observe and understand aspects of our environment, and they help us communicate with others.

Concepts also contribute to the identification and delineation of the scientific disciplines within which research is conducted. In fact, to a large extent a discipline maintains its identity because different researchers within it share a concern for the same concepts. Physics, for example, is concerned with the concepts of gravity and mass (among others); sociology with social class and social mobility; psychology with personality and deviance. By contrast, political science is concerned with concepts such as democracy, power, representation, justice, and equality. The boundaries of disciplines are not well defined or rigid, however. Political scientists, developmental psychologists, sociologists, and anthropologists all share an interest in how new members of a society are "socialized" into the norms and beliefs of that society, for example. Nonetheless, because a particular discipline has some minimal level of shared consensus concerning its significant concepts, researchers can usually communicate more readily with other researchers in the same discipline than with researchers in other disciplines.

A shared consensus over those concepts thought to be significant is directly related to the development of theories. Thus, a theory of politics will identify significant concepts and suggest why they are central to an understanding of political phenomena.

Concepts are developed through a process by which some human group (tribe, nation, culture, profession) agrees to give a phenomenon or property a particular name. The process is ongoing and somewhat arbitrary and does not ensure that all peoples everywhere will give the same phenomena the same names. In some areas of the United States, for example, a "soda" is a carbonated beverage, while in other areas it is a drink with ice cream in it. Likewise, the English language has only one word for love, whereas the Greeks have three words to distinguish between romantic love, familial love, and generalized feelings of affection.[4] Concepts disappear from a group's language when they are no longer needed, and new ones are invented as new phenomena are noticed that require names (for example, computer "programs" and "software," "cultural imperialism," and "hyperkinetic" behavior).

Some concepts—such as "car," "chair," and "vote"—are fairly precise because there is considerable agreement about their meaning. Others are more abstract and lend themselves to differing definitions—for example, "liberalism," "crime," "democracy," "equal opportunity," "human rights," "social mobility," and "alienation." A similar concept is "orange." Although there is considerable agreement about it (orange is not usually confused with purple), the agreement is less than total (whether a particular object is orange or red is not always clear).

Many interesting concepts that political scientists deal with are abstract and lack a completely precise, shared meaning. This hinders communication concerning research and creates uncertainty regarding the measurement of a phenomenon. Consequently, a researcher must explain what is meant by the concept so that a measurement strategy may be developed and so that those reading and evaluating the research can decide if the meaning accords with their own understanding of the term. Although some concepts that political scientists use—such as "amount of formal education," "presidential vote," and "amount of foreign trade"—are not particularly abstract, other concepts—such as "partisan realignment," "political integration," and "regime support"—are far more abstract and need more careful consideration and definition.

Suppose, for example, that a researcher is interested in the kinds of political systems that different countries have and, in particular, why some countries are more democratic than others. "Democracy" is consequently a key concept and one that needs definition and measurement. The word contains meaning for most of us; that is, we have some idea what is democratic and what is not. But once we begin thinking about the concept, we quickly realize that it is not as clear as we thought originally. To some, a country is democratic if it has "competing political parties, operating in free elections, with some reasonable level of popular participation in the process."[5] To others, a country is democratic only if there are legal guarantees protecting free speech, press, religion, and the like. To others, a country is democratic if the political leaders make decisions that are acceptable to the populace. And to still others, democracy implies equality of economic opportunity among the citizenry. If a country has all of these attributes, it would be called a democracy by any of the criteria and there would be no problem classifying the country. But if a country possesses only one of the above attributes, its classification would be uncertain, since by some definitions it would be democratic but by others it would not. Different definitions require different measurements and may result in different research findings. Hence, defining one's concepts is important, particularly when the concept is so abstract as to make shared agreement difficult.

Concept definitions have a direct impact on the quality of knowledge produced by research studies. Suppose, for example, that a researcher is interested in the connection between economic development and democracy, the working hypothesis being that countries with a high level of economic development will be more likely to have democratic forms of government. And suppose that there are two definitions of economic development and two definitions of democracy that might be used in the research. Finally, suppose that the researcher has data on twelve countries (A–L) included in the study. Table 3-2 shows that the definition selected for each concept has a direct bearing on how different countries are categorized on each attribute. By definition 1, countries A, B, C, D, E, F are economically developed; however, by definition 2, countries A, B, C, G, H, I are. By definition 1, countries A, B, C, D, E, F are democracies; by definition 2, countries D, E, F, J, K, L are.

This is only the beginning of our troubles, however. When we look for a pattern involving the economic development and democracy of countries, we find that our answer depends mightily on how we have defined the two concepts. If we use the first definitions of the two concepts, we find that all economically developed countries are also democracies (A, B, C, D, E, F), which

TABLE 3-2

Concept Development: The Relation between Economic Development and Democracy

Is the country economically developed?

		By definition 1:	
		Yes	*No*
By definition 2:	*Yes*	A,B,C	G,H,I
	No	D,E,F	J,K,L

Is the country a democracy?

		By definition 1:	
		Yes	*No*
By definition 2:	*Yes*	D,E,F	J,K,L
	No	A,B,C	G,H,I

supports our hypothesis. If we use the first definition for economic development and the second for democracy (or vice versa), half of the economically developed nations are democracies and half are not. If we use the second definitions of both concepts, none of the economically developed countries is a democracy while all of the undeveloped countries are (D, E, F, J, K, L). In other words, because of our inability to formulate a precise definition of the two concepts, and because the two definitions of each concept yield quite different categorizations of the twelve countries, our hypothesis could be either confirmed or disconfirmed by the data at hand. Our conceptual confusion has put us in a difficult position.

Consider another example. Suppose a researcher is interested in why some people are liberal and some are not. In this case we need to define what is meant by liberal so that those who are liberal can be identified. *Liberal* is a frequently used term, but it has many different meanings: one who favors change, one who favors redistributive income or social welfare policies, one who favors increased government spending and taxation, or one who opposes government interference in the political activities of its citizens. If a person possesses all of these attributes, there is no problem deciding whether or not he or she is a liberal. A problem arises, however, when a person possesses some of these attributes but not others.

The examples above illustrate the elusive nature of concepts and the need to define them. The empirical researcher's responsibility to "define terms" is a necessary and challenging one. Unfortunately, many of the concepts used by political science researchers are fairly abstract and require careful thought and extensive elaboration.

Researchers can clarify the concept definitions they use simply by making the meanings of key concepts explicit. This requires researchers to think carefully about the concepts used in their research and to share their meanings with others. Other researchers often challenge concept definitions, requiring researchers to elaborate upon and justify their meanings.

Another way in which researchers get help in defining concepts is by reviewing the definitions used by others and revising or borrowing those definitions. This is one of the reasons why researchers conduct literature reviews of pertinent research, a task we take up in detail in Chapter 6. For example, a researcher interested in the political attitudes and behavior of the American public would find the following definitions of key concepts in the existing literature:

Political participation. Those activities by private citizens that are more or less directly aimed at influencing the selection of governmental personnel and/or the actions they take.[6]

Political violence. All collective attacks within a political community against the political regime, its actors—including competing political groups as well as incumbents—or its policies.[7]

Political efficacy. The feeling that individual political action does have, or can have, an impact upon the political processes—that it is worthwhile to perform one's civic duties.[8]

Belief system. A configuration of ideas and attitudes in which the elements are bound together by some form of constraint or functional interdependence.[9]

Each of these concepts is somewhat vague and lacks complete shared agreement about its meaning. Furthermore, it is possible to raise questions about each of these concept definitions. Notice, for example, that the definition of political participation excludes the possibility that government employees (presumably "nonprivate" citizens) engage in political activities, and the definition of political efficacy excludes the impact of collective political action on political processes. Consequently, we may find these and other concept definitions inadequate and revise them to capture more accurately what we mean by the terms.

Over time a discipline cannot proceed very far unless there is some minimal agreement about the meanings of the concepts with which scientific research is concerned. Researchers must take care to think about the phenomena named in a research project and make explicit the meanings of any problematic concepts.

Conclusion

In this chapter we have discussed the beginning stages of a scientific research project. A research project must provide—to both the producer and the consumer of social scientific knowledge—the answers to these important questions: What phenomenon is the researcher trying to understand and explain? What explanation has the researcher proposed for the political behavior or attributes in question? What are the meanings of the concepts used in this explanation? What specific hypothesis relating two or more variables will be tested? What is the unit of analysis for the observations? If all of these questions are answered adequately, then the research will have a firm foundation.

Notes

1. This term is used by Susan Ann Kay, *Introduction to the Analysis of Political Data* (Englewood Cliffs, N.J.: Prentice-Hall, 1991), 6.

2. For a description of this data set, see M. Kent Jennings and Richard G. Niemi, *Generations and Politics* (Princeton: Princeton University Press, 1981).

3. We would like to thank Paul Johnson and his students at the University of Kansas for the basis of this example.

4. Kenneth R. Hoover, *The Elements of Social Scientific Thinking* (New York: St. Martin's, 1980), 18–19.

5. W. Phillips Shively, *The Craft of Political Research* (Englewood Cliffs, N.J.: Prentice-Hall, 1980), 33.

6. Sidney Verba and Norman H. Nie, *Participation in America* (New York: Harper & Row, 1972), 2.

7. Ted Robert Gurr, *Why Men Rebel* (Princeton: Princeton University Press, 1970), 3–4.

8. Angus Campbell, Gerald Gurin, and Warren E. Miller, *The Voter Decides* (Evanston, Ill.: Row, Peterson, 1954), 187.

9. Philip E. Converse, "The Nature of Belief Systems in Mass Publics," in David E. Apter, ed., *Ideology and Discontent* (New York: Free Press, 1964), 207.

Terms introduced

ANTECEDENT VARIABLE. An independent variable that precedes other independent variables in time.

ARROW DIAGRAM. A pictorial representation of a researcher's explanatory scheme.

DEPENDENT VARIABLE. The phenomenon thought to be influenced, affected, or caused by some other phenomenon.

DIRECTIONAL HYPOTHESIS. A hypothesis that specifies the expected relationship between two or more variables.

ECOLOGICAL FALLACY. The fallacy of deducing a false relationship between the attributes or behavior of individuals based on observing that relationship for groups to which the individuals belong.

HYPOTHESIS. A statement proposing a relationship between two or more variables.

INDEPENDENT VARIABLE. The phenomenon thought to influence, affect, or cause some other phenomenon.

INTERVENING VARIABLE. A variable coming between an independent and a dependent variable in an explanatory scheme.

NEGATIVE RELATIONSHIP. A relationship in which the values of one variable increase as the values of another variable decrease.

POSITIVE RELATIONSHIP. A relationship in which the values of one variable increase as the values of another variable increase.

RELATIONSHIP. The association, dependence, or covariance of the values of one variable with the values of another variable.

TAUTOLOGY. A hypothesis in which the independent and dependent variables are identical, making it impossible to disconfirm.

UNIT OF ANALYSIS. The type of actor (individual, group, institution, nation) specified in a researcher's hypothesis.

Exercises

1. Refer to David H. Folz, "Municipal Recycling Performance: A Public Sector Environmental Success Story," *Public Administration Review* 59 (July–August 1999): 336–345.
   a. Read the section labeled "Curbside Action" on pages 138 and 139. What is the dependent variable? What are the independent variables or concepts thought to explain variation in the dependent variable? Write hypotheses relating each of the independent variables to the dependent variable. What control variable does the author use? What is the unit of analysis?
   b. Read the section labeled "Our Bins Runneth Over" on pages 139 and 140. What is the dependent variable? What are the independent variables or concepts thought to explain variation in the dependent variable? Write hypotheses relating each of the independent variables to the dependent variable. What control variable does the author use? What is the unit of analysis?

2. Read the article by Jon S.T. Quah, "Corruption in Asian Countries: Can It Be Minimized?" *Public Administration Review* 59 (November–December 1999): 482–494. What is the dependent variable? What are the independent variables? Write a hypothesis relating the independent and dependent variables. What is the unit of analysis?

3. Using the concepts listed below, develop five hypotheses. Identify the independent variable and dependent variable and unit of analysis for each hypothesis.

Region	Registration requirements
Voter registration	Gender
Voter turnout	Partisan affiliation
Age	Presidential election
Party competition	

4. Think of a political phenomenon that you are interested in understanding. Define the phenomenon as completely and carefully as possible. Now think about other phenomena or concepts that you think might help you explain the phenomenon you chose. Pick one of these concepts and state how it is related to the first phenomenon. Draw an arrow diagram to summarize your explanatory scheme.

Suggested Readings

Armstrong, R.L. "Hypotheses: Why? When? How?" *Phi Delta Kappan* 54 (1974): 213–214.

Hoover, Kenneth R. *The Elements of Social Scientific Thinking*. New York: St. Martin's, 1984.

Isaak, Alan C. *Scope and Methods of Political Science.* Homewood, Ill.: Dorsey, 1985.

Jacob, Herbert, and Robert Weissberg. *Elementary Political Analysis.* New York: McGraw-Hill, 1975.

Shively, W. Phillips. *The Craft of Political Research.* Englewood Cliffs, N.J.: Prentice-Hall, 1980.

Stock, Molly. *A Practical Guide to Graduate Research.* New York: McGraw-Hill, 1985.

CHAPTER 4

The Building Blocks
of Social Scientific Research:

Measurement

In the previous chapter we discussed the beginning stages of political science research projects: the choice of research topics, the formulation of scientific explanations, the development of testable hypotheses, and the definition of concepts. In this chapter we show how to test empirically the hypotheses we have advanced. This entails understanding a number of issues involving the **measurement**, or systematic observation and representation by scores or numerals, of the variables we have decided to investigate.

In Chapter 1 we said that scientific knowledge is based upon empirical observation. In this chapter we confront the implications of this fact. If we are to test empirically the accuracy and utility of a scientific explanation for a political phenomenon, we will have to observe and measure the presence of the concepts we are using to understand that phenomenon. Furthermore, if this test is to be an adequate one, our measurements of the political phenomena must be as accurate and precise as possible. The process of measurement is important because it provides the bridge between our proposed explanations and the empirical world they are supposed to explain.

The researchers discussed in Chapter 1 measured a variety of political phenomena. Steven Poe and C. Neal Tate measured population and economic growth as well as a number of other factors to see if they had an impact on the incidence of state terrorism.[1] Bruce Bueno de Mesquita, Randolph Siverson, and Gary Woller measured the outcomes and costs of international wars to study their post-war effects.[2]

Benjamin Page and Robert Shapiro measured the change in public opinion on more than three hundred political issues and the subsequent change, if any, in public policy on those same issues.[3] Jeffrey Segal and Albert Cover measured both the political ideologies and the written opinions of Supreme Court justices in cases involving civil rights and liberties.[4] And B. Dan Wood and Richard Waterman measured the decisions of several bureaucratic agencies to determine if they were influenced by presidential and congressional intervention.[5] Richard Fording measured growth in welfare rolls to see if it was related to the amount of civil unrest.[6] Stephen Ansolabehere, Shanto Iyengar, Adam Simon, and Nicholas Valentino measured the intention to vote reported by participants in their experiments to see if it was affected by exposure to negative campaign advertising.[7] In each case some political behavior or attribute was measured so that a scientific explanation could be tested.

Devising Measurement Strategies

As we pointed out in Chapter 3, researchers must define the concepts they use in their hypotheses. Researchers also must decide how they are actually going to measure the presence, absence, or amount of these concepts in the real world. Political scientists refer to this process as providing an **operational definition** of their concepts—in other words, deciding what kinds of empirical observations should be made to measure the occurrence of an attribute or behavior.

Let us return, for example, to the researcher trying to explain the existence of democracy in different nations. If the researcher were to hypothesize that higher rates of literacy make democracy more likely, then a definition of two concepts—literacy and democracy—would be necessary. The researcher could then develop a strategy, based on these two definitions, for measuring the existence and amount of both attributes in a number of nations.

Suppose literacy was defined as "the completion of six years of formal education," and democracy was defined as "a system of government in which public officials are selected in competitive elections." These definitions would then be used to develop operational definitions of the two concepts. These operational definitions would indicate what should be observed empirically to measure both literacy and democracy, and they would indicate specifically what data should be collected to test the researcher's hypothesis. In this example, the operational definition of literacy might be "those nations in which at least 50 percent of the population has had six years of formal education, as indicated in a publication of the United Nations," while the operational definition of democracy might be "those countries in which the second-place finisher in elections for the chief executive office has received at least 25 percent of the vote at least once in the past eight years."

When a researcher specifies the operational definition of a concept, the precise meaning of that concept in a particular research study becomes clear. In the preceding example, we now know exactly what the researcher means by literacy and democracy. Since different people often mean different things by the same concept, operational definitions are especially important. Someone might argue that defining literacy in terms of formal education ignores the possibility that people who complete six years of formal education might still be unable to read or write well. Similarly, it might be argued that defining democracy in terms of competitive elections ignores other important features of democracy such as freedom of expression and citizen involvement in government actions. In addition, the operational definition of competitive elections is clearly debatable. Is the "competitiveness" of elections based on the number of competing candidates, the size of the margin of victory, or the number of consecutive victories by a single party in a series of elections? Unfortunately, operational definitions are seldom absolutely correct or absolutely incorrect; rather, they are evaluated in terms of how well they correspond to the concepts they are meant to measure.

It is useful to think of the operational definition as the last stage in the process of defining a concept precisely. We often begin with an abstract concept (such as democracy), then attempt to define it in a meaningful way, and finally decide in specific terms how we are going to measure it. At the end of this process we hope to attain a definition that is sensible, close to our meaning of the concept, and exact in what it tells us about how to go about measuring the concept.

Let us consider another example: the researcher interested in why some individuals are more liberal than others. The concept of liberalism might be defined as "believing that government ought to pursue policies that provide benefits for the less well off." The task then is to develop an operational definition that can be used to measure whether particular individuals are liberal or not. The researcher might decide that anyone is a liberal who agrees in a public opinion poll with the following statement: "The federal government should increase the amount of money spent on food stamp and free lunch programs."

An abstract concept, liberalism has now been given an operational definition that can be used to measure the concept for individuals. This definition is also related to the original definition of the concept, and it indicates precisely what observations need to be made. It is not, however, the only operational definition possible. Others might suggest that questions regarding affirmative action, school vouchers, the death penalty, welfare benefits, and pornography could be used to measure liberalism. The important thing is to think carefully about the operational definition you choose and to try to ensure that that definition coincides closely with the meaning of the original concept.

Examples of Political Measurement

Let us take a closer look at some operational definitions used by political science researchers. Page and Shapiro's article on the relationship between public opinion and public policy contains a number of important decisions about the measurement of abstract political concepts.[8] Ever since democratic theorists first articulated the normative position that in a democracy there should be a relationship between popular preferences and the decisions made by political elites, researchers have been curious about whether such a relationship exists in modern nation-states and, if so, how strong it is. Observing the relationship requires devising proper measures of both popular preferences and public policy decisions, a requirement that effectively stymied empirical research on opinion-policy relationships until recently because of the difficulty in finding appropriate measures of popular preferences and of corresponding public policy decisions over an extensive enough period of time.

Page and Shapiro approached this problem by relying on the thousands of public opinion survey questions that have been asked of the American adult population since 1935 for their measures of popular preferences. Since they were interested in the effect of *change* in the distribution of public opinion, they decided to select those survey questions that had been asked in identical form at two or more points in time, and on which there had been at least a 6-percentage-point change in public opinion from one survey to another. This left them with 357 instances of public opinion change on public policy questions between 1935 and 1979.

To test the relationship between opinion and policy change, Page and Shapiro then had to devise measures of public policy that corresponded to the measures of public opinion. And to determine whether opinion change *precedes* policy change (recall our discussion in Chapter 3 on the importance of establishing the temporal sequence when evaluating causation), the policy measures needed to cover a period of time at least as broad as the measures of public opinion covered. So Page and Shapiro sought public policy measures that began two years before the first measure of public opinion and continued until four years after the final survey (to allow for a time lag in the policy-making process).

Developing measures of public policy that correspond with public opinion surveys is not an easy task. Suppose, for example, we decide to conduct a survey that asks whether the populace favors increasing, decreasing, or maintaining the government's defense spending. What would be an appropriate corresponding measure of public policy? Would we use the entire budget of the Defense Department? Should we include military personnel salaries, benefits, and pensions, or just expenditures on weapons systems? Should we use authorized budget figures (as a measure of willingness to spend), or the amount actually expended? Should we include expenditures on NASA, the CIA, and military foreign aid? Should we correct the measure of expenditures for inflation? Should we express expenditures as a percentage of the total budget, or as a percentage of the Gross National Product? These and other questions must be answered before we can settle on an appropriate measure of just this one public policy. Clearly, the measurement decisions required by the hypothesis relating public opinion and public policy are both numerous and difficult.

Fording's investigation of the impact of mass insurgency on welfare generosity required that he measure both welfare expansion and the extent of rioting. As a measure of welfare expansion, Fording used the annual growth in state AFDC (Aid to Families with Dependent Children) recipient rates. The AFDC program was used because data for the program were reported for each state on a regular basis. Data for another welfare program among the states, General Assistance, in contrast, were not regularly reported. Fording encountered a more complex measurement problem for the concept of mass insurgency. Previous researchers had used the number of riots as the indicator of mass insurgency, with a riot being defined as a spontaneous incident of collective violence, usually involving no less than twenty to thirty people. Fording chose to operationalize insurgency as "any act of violence on behalf of blacks or minorities, either spontaneous or planned, that is either framed as, or can be construed as politically motivated. Violent acts include rock throwing, vandalism, arson, looting, sniping, or beating of whites."[9] He used the number of incidents rather than the severity of violent incidents since previous studies had shown that measures of the severity or intensity of violence were highly correlated with the number of violent incidents. Data for violence were obtained from a variety of sources including the *New York Times*, the Kerner Report, publications from the Lemberg Center for the Study of Violence, Facts on File, and Congressional Quarterly. Fording collected data for a total of 923 events.

Because Fording also wanted to investigate whether the effect of insurgency on welfare generosity depended on the extent to which insurgent groups have effective access to electoral institutions, he needed to define and measure electoral access. Arguing that effective electoral power depends on both the acquisition of voting rights and the use of population-based districts for the election of state legislatures, he determined for each state for each year in his study whether or not the state legislature was apportioned and whether or not African Americans had access to the ballot. His measurement of ballot access was based on the passage of the Voting Rights Act of 1965 and its implementation in targeted states.

Furthermore, Fording sought to control for need for welfare, as it was possible that expanding welfare rolls merely reflected an increase in need. He measured increase in need by looking at the growth in the percentage of households in a state that were headed by females and below poverty. Fording used this measure rather than the growth in poverty among all households because AFDC was a program for families with dependent children. He also used the growth in the unemployment rate as an indicator of need. Thus, Fording developed clear definitions for the concepts in his research as he explained how he actually planned to measure each concept.

Daron Shaw's research concerned the impact of TV ads and campaign appearances on statewide presidential voting.[10] For this he needed schedules of candidate appearances, candidates' television advertising purchases by media markets, and trial ballot polling data from each state. Data to measure all three variables had previously been difficult to obtain. Shaw relied on three sources of information about campaign appearances: the *Hotline* (a daily political newsletter published in Falls Church, Virginia), the *Washington Post*, and schedules kept by the campaigns. In measuring candidate appearances, Shaw did not count visits by candidates to their hometowns, places of work, vacation destinations or debate sites unless campaign appearances were reported, nor did he weigh high-visibility appearances more than low-visibility appearances (although he did check to see if this distinction affected his results, which it did not). Data on television advertising came from the campaigns themselves and encompassed all TV advertising purchased by the campaigns between September 1 and election day. Shaw's data on television advertising represented the first time that such data were available for media markets and the states. Shaw relied on polling data from a number of public and private sources including the Republican presidential campaigns, news media consortiums, and the Republican National Committee.

Shaw confronted a number of measurement issues concerning television advertising. One problem was that his data omitted political party and independent spending, which accounted for a substantial portion of media spending, because estimates of this spending were incomplete. A second problem was related to the variability in the cost of advertising across media markets. Simply using the amount of money spent on advertising would not measure the amount of media exposure obtained. Shaw borrowed a measurement scheme called gross rating points (GRPs) used by advertising companies and communication scholars. GRPs provide a measure of the audience reached in media markets independent of markets costs. Statewide GRPs were calculated by multiplying the number of GRPs bought in a market by the percentage of the state's eligible voters in that market, repeating the procedure for all markets in a state, and then summing the results. The third issue Shaw faced was that advertising time is not always purchased in the state for which the ad is targeted. For example, ads aimed at audiences in New Jersey may be purchased in New York or Philadelphia and thus the audience exposure being purchased is not exclusively in New Jersey.

The research conducted by Segal and Cover on the behavior of U.S. Supreme Court justices is a good example of an attempt to overcome a serious measurement problem to test a scientific hypothesis.[11] Recall that Segal and Cover were interested, as many others have been before them, in the extent to which the votes cast by Supreme Court justices are dependent upon their own personal political attitudes. Measuring the justices' votes on the cases decided by the Supreme Court is no problem; the votes are public information. But measuring the personal political attitudes of judges, *independent of their votes* (remember the discussion in Chapter 3 on avoiding tautologies), is a problem. Many of the judges whose behavior is of interest have died, and it is difficult to get living Supreme Court justices to reveal their political attitudes through personal interviews or questionnaires. Furthermore, ideally one would like a measure of attitudes that is comparable across many judges and that measures attitudes related to the cases decided by the Court.

Segal and Cover decided to limit their inquiry to votes on civil liberties cases between 1953 and 1987, so they needed a measure of related political attitudes for the judges serving on the Supreme Court over that same period of time. They decided to infer each judge's attitudes from the newspaper editorials written about them in four major daily newspapers from the time each justice was appointed by the president until the justice's confirmation vote by the Senate. Trained analysts read the editorials and coded each paragraph for whether it asserted that a justice designate was liberal, moderate, or conservative (or if the paragraph was inapplicable) regarding "support for the rights of defendants in criminal cases, women and racial minorities in equality cases, and the individual against the government in privacy and First Amendment cases."[12] They selected the editorials appearing in two liberal papers and in two conservative papers to produce a more accurate measure of judicial attitudes.

Because of practical barriers to ideal measurement, then, Segal and Cover had to rely on a measure of judicial attitudes *as perceived by four newspapers* rather than on a measure of the attitudes themselves. While this approach *may* have resulted in flawed measures, it also permitted the test of an interesting hypothesis about the behavior of Supreme Court justices that had not been tested previously. If the measures that resulted were both accurate and precise then this measurement strategy would permit the empirical verification of an important hypothesis. Without such measurements, the hypothesis would have to have gone untested.

Next, let us consider the research on regime stability described briefly in Chapter 1. Recall that a common hypothesis is that the distribution of income and wealth has an impact on the tendency of populations to protest and rebel and, therefore, on the stability of governmental regimes. More specifically, it is often hypothesized that income/wealth inequality leads to political violence and instability. In many parts of the world the main form of wealth is land ownership. Consequently, researchers have been investigating the relationship between land inequality and civil unrest in places such as Latin America. Obviously the task requires an accurate measure of land inequality in a variety of nation-states.

Measuring the distribution of land ownership and especially the inequality of land ownership is not a simple matter, however. Everyone agrees that equality of land ownership would mean that every adult or family owned the same amount of land, so that 25 percent of the population owned 25 percent of the land, 75 percent of the population owned 75 percent of the land, and so on. But when the pattern of land ownership departs from this strict equality it is not altogether clear what should be measured. If a few people own most of the land and most people own little or no land, there is land inequality. But should the measure of land inequality focus on unequal land holdings throughout the range of land ownership, or on the land owned by those at both ends of the ownership range (the very rich and the very poor) and the gap between them, or on the number of people who own little or no land, regardless of how land is distributed among those who own land? The answer is not clear.

Because of this uncertainty over how best to measure land inequality, researchers have used a number of different measures. One commonly used measure is the Gini index, which attempts to take into account inequalities throughout the range of land ownership. Manus Midlarsky proposed a different measure that concentrated on the gap between the very rich and the very poor.[13]

There is some evidence that the measure of inequality used affects the conclusions reached about the relationship between land inequality and political violence. Research using the Gini index has generally found a weak relationship between land inequality and political violence and has led researchers to think about the other factors affecting regime stability. Midlarsky's research using the new measure of land inequality, however, reports a much stronger relationship with political violence, at least in Latin America. This is a good example, then, of how measurement decisions may affect substantive conclusions. Our choice of measures, especially of abstract phenomena such as land inequality, is a crucial aspect of the entire research process.

Finally, let us take a look at an innovative attempt to measure what individuals mean by that troubling concept, "democracy."[14] Given the fact that many different theorists over several centuries have written about democracy in very different ways, it is hardly surprising that the concept means different things to different people. In an attempt to understand better what citizens mean by democracy, two researchers collected roughly three hundred statements about democracy from newspapers, magazines, dictionaries, ethnographic studies, and voters' pamphlets. From these they selected sixty-four they thought best represented the domain of the concept. They then asked a group of subjects to score the statements on a scale ranging from +6 (most agree) to –6 (most disagree).

Once the sixty-four statements were scored, the researchers then looked for patterns in their subjects' responses. They discovered four different response patterns that they believe represent different meanings of democracy and developed a "discourse" to capture each one of them. The four response patterns are called contented republicanism, deferential conservatism, disaffected populism, and private liberalism, and are defined as follows:

Contented republicanism. We live in a democracy, which is fortunate because democracy is without doubt the best form of government. Democracy is a way of life, not just a political system; it is bound up with our freedoms, and, though fallible, can correct its mistakes. . . . Political equality is important and easily achieved and does not require social and economic equality. . . . Politics need not be based on greed or self-interest, for democratic debate can help establish an identity between what's good for me and what's good for society. The importance of this debate means that there should be no restraints on the availability of information; a free press is crucial, and we should not tolerate lying in politics.

Deferential conservatism. Politics is only for the few. Not everyone is capable of making good decisions, people don't know what they want, and not everyone can be represented. . . . It is undesirable for people to get any more involved in politics; citizen activism is not a good thing. Nor are the liberal values of a free press, independent judiciary, social justice rooted in basic rights, or the market very attractive. . . . There is no need to fear government; we should rely on elites to govern and hope that they are honest. Such elites will be able to look out for the long-term interest of society, which matters more than short-term economic concerns.

Disaffected populism. We do not live in a democracy, as power is in the hands of conservative, corporate elites and a government that represses the people. . . . Over time, democratic control has deteriorated, and the future of democracy is bleak unless people wake up and do something about it. The freedoms that are central to democracy have been curtailed. . . . Ordinary individuals are well motivated; and they should attend to politics, rather than be preoccupied by work and family—though politics cannot, and should not, be all-consuming. . . . One should not necessarily condemn political violence when it is undertaken by the oppressed.

Private liberalism. We do not live in an especially democratic society, and not everyone can be represented. But this is no cause for concern, for democracy is of no particular value, given that it can encompass both desirable kinds of government and undesirable forms, such as socialism. . . . Individuals should be free to pursue their own interests, but democracy will not guarantee that freedom. It is the private realm which really matters—work and family are the most important things in life, and one should rely on friends, neighbors, and the market, rather than government. . . . Government, however democratic, has intruded too far into this private realm; government should be small and subject to separation of powers and constitutional restraints.[15]

The discourses overlap some and exhibit imperfect similarities to historical/philosophical traditions, but they also reveal a good deal of variation and complexity in the meaning of democracy among the public.

The cases we have discussed here are good examples of researchers' attempts to measure important political phenomena (behaviors or attributes) in the real world. Whether the phenomenon in question was public policy decisions, judges' political attitudes, land inequality, campaign appearances and advertising by presidential candidates, mass insurgency, or democracy, the researchers devised measurement strategies that could detect and measure the presence and amount of the concept in question. These observations were then generally used as the basis for an empirical test of the researchers' hypotheses.

To be useful in providing scientific explanations for political behavior, measurements of political phenomena must correspond closely to the original meaning of a researcher's concepts. They must also provide the researcher with enough information to make valuable comparisons and contrasts. Hence the quality of measurements is judged in terms of both their *accuracy* and their *precision*.

The Accuracy of Measurements

Since we are going to use our measurements to test whether or not our explanations for political phenomena are valid, those measurements must be as accurate as possible. Inaccurate measurements may lead to erroneous conclusions since they will interfere with our ability to observe the actual relationship between two or more variables.

Suppose, for example, that you have hypothesized that "courses taught by political scientists are more worthwhile than courses taught by psychologists." During registration time you see a description for a course in the political science department that looks worthwhile, so you sign up for it. Your friend, on the other hand, signs up for a course in the psychology department. Two weeks after classes start you meet your friend in the campus dining hall and swap evaluations of your courses. Your political science course has turned out to be a dreadful experience, but your friend seems to be enjoying the psychology course.

Does your experience that semester (actually an empirical observation of two cases seemingly relevant to the hypothesis) mean that your hypothesis is wrong? Not necessarily. Suppose the course you had signed up for was not being taught by a political scientist but rather by a historian on loan to the political science department. This would mean that you had inaccurately measured the nature of the course you were taking by assuming that all courses taught in the political science department were taught by political scientists.

Thus you were being led to what might, in fact, have been an erroneous conclusion about the quality of courses taught by political scientists. Because of the inaccuracy of your measurement, the comparison you made with your friend turns out to be irrelevant to the hypothesis with which you began.

There are two major threats to the accuracy of measurements. Measures may be inaccurate because they are *unreliable* or because they are *invalid*.

Reliability

Reliability "concerns the extent to which an experiment, test, or any measuring procedure yields the same results on repeated trials. . . . The more consistent the results given by repeated measurements, the higher the reliability of the measuring procedure; conversely, the less consistent the results, the lower the reliability."[16]

Suppose, for example, you are given the responsibility of counting a stack of 1,000 paper ballots for some public office. The first time you count them, you obtain a particular result. But as you were counting the ballots you might have been interrupted, two or more ballots might have stuck together, some might have been blown onto the floor, or you might have written the totals down incorrectly. As a precaution, then, you count them five more times and get four other people to count them as well. The similarity of the results of all ten counts would be an indication of the reliability of the measure.

Or suppose you design a series of questions to measure how cynical people are and ask a group of people those questions. If a few days later you ask the same questions of the same group of people, the correspondence between the two measures would indicate the reliability of that particular measure of cynicism (assuming that the amount of cynicism has not changed). Similarly, suppose you wanted to test the hypothesis that the *New York Times* is more critical of the federal government than the *Wall Street Journal*. This would require you to measure the level of criticism found in articles in the two papers. You would need to develop criteria or instructions for identifying or measuring criticism. The reliability of your measuring scheme could be assessed by having two people read all the articles, independently rate the level of criticism in them according to your instructions, and then compare their results. Reliability would be demonstrated if both people reached similar conclusions regarding the content of the articles in question.

The reliability of political science measures can be calculated in a number of ways. The **test-retest method** involves applying the same "test" to the same observations after a period of time and then comparing the results of the different measurements. For example, if a series of questions measuring liberalism is asked of a group of respondents on two different days, a comparison of their scores at both times could be used as an indication of the reliability of the measure of liberalism. We frequently engage in test-retest behavior in our everyday lives. How often have you stepped on the bathroom scales twice or more in a matter of seconds?

The test-retest method of measuring reliability may be both difficult and problematic since one must measure the phenomenon at two different points. It is possible that two different results may be obtained because what is being measured has actually changed, not because the measure is unreliable. For example, if your bathroom scales give you two different weights within a few seconds, the scales are unreliable as your weight can not have changed. However, if you weigh yourself once a week for a month and find that you get different results each time, are the scales unreliable or has your weight changed? A further problem with the test-retest check for reliability is that the administration of the first measure may affect the second measure's results. For instance, the difference between Scholastic Aptitude Test scores the first and second times that individuals take the test may not be assumed to be a measure of the reliability of the test since test takers might alter systematically their behavior the second time as a result of taking the test the first time.

The **alternative-form method** of measuring reliability also involves measuring the same attribute more than once, but uses two different measures of the same concept rather than the same measure. For example, a researcher could devise two different sets of questions to measure the concept of liberalism, ask the two sets of questions of the same respondents at two different times, and compare the respondents' scores. Using two different forms of the measure prevents the second scores from being influenced by the first measure, but it still requires being able to measure the phenomenon twice and, depending on the length of time between the two measurements, what is being measured may change.

Going back to our bathroom scale example, if you weigh yourself on your home scales, go the the gym, weigh yourself again and get the same number, you may conclude that the scales are reliable. But, what if you get two different numbers? Assuming your weight has not changed, what is the problem? If you go back home immediately and step back on your bathroom scales and find that they give you a measurement that is different from the first, you could conclude that your scales have a faulty mechanism, are inconsistent, and therefore, unreliable. However, what if your bathroom scales give you the same weight as the first time? They would appear to be reliable. Maybe the gym scales are unreliable. You could test this out by going back to the gym and reweighing yourself. If the gym scales give a different reading than the first time, then they are unreliable. But, what if the gym scales give consistent readings? Clearly one (or both) of the scales is inaccurate and you have a measurement problem that needs to be resolved and it involves more than unreliability. Before we address this situation, let us mention one more test for reliability.

The **split-halves method** of measuring reliability involves two measures of the same concept, with both measures applied at the same time. The results of the two measures are then compared. This method avoids the problem of the change in the concept being measured. The split-halves method is often used when there is a multi-item measure that can be split into two equivalent halves. For example, one may devise a measure of liberalism consisting of the responses to ten questions on a public opinion survey. Half of these questions could be selected to represent one measure of liberalism and the other half selected to represent a second measure of liberalism. If individual scores on the two measures of liberalism are similar, then the ten-item measure may be said to be reliable by the split-halves approach.

The test-retest, alternative-form, and split-halves methods provide a basis for calculating the similarity of results of two or more applications of the same or equivalent measure. The less consistent the results are, the less reliable the measure is. Reliability of the measures used by political scientists is a serious problem. Survey researchers are often concerned about the reliability of the answers they receive. For example, respondents' answers to survey questions often vary considerably when given at two different times.[17] If respondents are not concentrating or taking the survey seriously, the answers they provide may as well have been pulled out of a hat.

Now, let us return to the problem of a measure that yields consistent results as in the case of the two scales that differed consistently in how much you weighed. Each of the scales appears to be reliable (they are not giving you different weights at random), but one or both of them is giving you a wrong measurement. That is, it is not giving you your correct weight. This problem is the type of problem one confronts in trying to assess whether or not one's measures are valid.

Validity

Essentially, a valid measure is one that measures what it is supposed to measure. Unlike reliability, which depends on whether repeated applications of the same or equivalent measure yield the same result, **validity** involves the correspondence between the measure and the concept it is thought to measure.

Let us consider first some examples of invalid measures. Suppose a researcher hypothesizes that the larger a city's police force is, the less crime that city will have. This requires the measurement of crime rates in different cities. Now also assume that some police departments systematically overrepresent the number of crimes in their cities to persuade public officials that crime is a serious problem and that the local police need more resources. Some police departments in other cities may systematically underreport crime in order to make the city appear safe. If the researcher relied on official, reported measures of crime, the measures would be invalid because they did not correspond closely to the actual amount of crime in some cities.

Or suppose you hypothesize that the more productive a scholar a faculty member is, the better a teacher he or she is. This requires measuring different faculty members' teaching abilities. The task might be accomplished by asking students to grade their instructors on teaching. But do students know a good teacher when they see one? Is it possible that students will give good grades to instructors who are personable, humorous, approachable, or easy graders, rather than to instructors who teach them something? If so, such a measurement strategy might well produce an invalid measure of good teaching.

Finally, there are many studies looking into the factors that affect voter turnout. These studies require an accurate measurement of voter turnout. One way of measuring voter turnout is to ask people if they voted in the last election. However, given the social desirability of voting in the United States, will all the people who did not vote in the previous election admit that they did not vote to an interviewer? More people might say that they voted than actually did, resulting in an invalid measure of voter turnout. In fact, this is what usually happens. Voter surveys commonly overestimate turnout by several percentage points.[18]

A measure's validity is more difficult to demonstrate empirically than its reliability because validity involves the relationship between the measurement of a concept and the actual presence or amount of the concept itself. Information regarding the correspondence is seldom abundant. Nonetheless, there are a number of ways of evaluating the validity of any particular measure.

Face validity may be asserted (not empirically demonstrated) when the measurement instrument appears to measure the concept it is supposed to measure. To assess the face validity of a measure, we need to know the meaning of the concept being measured and whether the information being collected is "germane to that concept."[19] For example, suppose you want to measure an individual's political ideology, whether someone is conservative, moderate, or liberal. It would not be a good idea to use an individual's responses to a question on party identification such as whether a person usually thinks of himself or herself as a Democrat, Republican, or Independent. It would be a mistake to assume that all Democrats are liberal, Republicans conservative, and Independents moderate. Similarly, some have argued that the results of many standard IQ tests measure intelligence *and* exposure to middle-class white culture, thus making the test results a less valid measure of intelligence.

In general, measures lack face validity when there are good reasons to question the correspondence of the measure to the concept in question. In other words, assessing face validity is essentially a matter of judgment. If there is no consensus about the meaning of the concept to be measured, the face validity of one's measure is bound to be problematic.

A second kind of validity test, **content validity**, is similar to face validity. This test (actually a logical argument rather than a test) involves determining the full domain or meaning of a particular concept and then making sure that measures of all portions of this domain are included in the measurement technique. For example, suppose you wanted to design a measure of the extent to which a nation's political system is democratic. As noted earlier, democracy means many things to many people. Ross Burkhart and Michael Lewis-Beck in their study of the relationship between economic development and democracy relied on data compiled by Raymond D. Gastil. Gastil's measure of democracy included two dimensions, political rights and civil liberties. His checklists for each dimension consisted of eleven items.[20] Political scientists are often interested in concepts with multiple dimensions or complex domains and spend quite a bit of time discussing and justifying the content of their measures. Unfortunately, many political science concepts are so abstract and ill-defined that there is little agreement about their domain. This makes content validity less useful to political scientists than to other researchers.

A third way to evaluate the validity of a measure is by empirically demonstrating **construct validity**. When a measure of a concept is related to a measure of another concept with which the original concept is thought to be related, construct validity is demonstrated. In other words, a researcher may specify, on theoretical grounds, that two concepts ought to be related (say, political efficacy with political participation, or education with income). The researcher then develops a measure of each of the concepts and examines the relationship between them. If the measures are related, then one measure has construct validity for the other measure. If the measures are unrelated, there is an absence of construct validity. In that case the theoretical relationship is in error, one or more of the measures is not an accurate representation of the concept, or the procedure used to test the relationship is inappropriate. The absence of a hypothesized relationship does not tell us for certain that the measure is invalid, but the presence of a relationship gives us some assurance of a measure's validity.

A good example of an attempt to demonstrate construct validity may be found in the Educational Testing Service's (ETS) booklet describing the Graduate Record Exam (GRE), a standardized test required for admission to most graduate schools. Since GRE test scores are supposed to measure a person's aptitude for graduate study, presumably construct validity could be demonstrated if the scores did, in fact, accurately predict the person's performance in graduate school. Over the years ETS has tested the relationships between GRE scores and first-year graduate school grade-point average. The results, shown in Table 4-1, appear to indicate that GRE scores are not very strong predictors of this measure of graduate school performance and therefore do not have construct validity. In fact, there has been much discussion in recent years about this very issue and the role that GRE scores should play in admissions decisions. But this is a good example of a situation where the absence of a strong relationship does not necessarily mean the measure lacks construct validity. Because persons with low GRE scores are generally not admitted to graduate school, we lack performance measures for them. Thus the people for whom we can test the relationship between scores and performance may be of similar ability and may not exhibit meaningful variation in their graduate school performance. Hence the test scores may be valid indicators of ability and may in fact show a stronger relationship to performance for a less selective sample of test takers (one that would include people who were not admitted to graduate school). The lack of a relationship in Table 4-1 undercuts claims of test score validity, but it does not necessarily disprove such claims.

A fourth way to demonstrate validity is through **interitem association**. This is the type of validity test most often used by political scientists. It relies

TABLE 4-1

Construct Validity of Graduate Record Examination Test Scores

Average Estimated Correlations of GRE, General Test Scores and Undergraduate Grade Point Average with Graduate First-Year Grade Point Average by Department Type

Type of Department	Number of Departments	Number of Examinees	Predictors					
			V	Q	A	U	VQA	VQAU
All Departments	1,038	12,013	.30	.29	.28	.37	.34	.46
Natural Sciences	384	4,420	.28	.27	.26	.36	.31	.44
Engineering	87	1,066	.27	.22	.24	.38	.30	.44
Social Sciences	352	4,211	.33	.32	.30	.38	.37	.48
Humanities & Arts	115	1,219	.30	.33	.27	.37	.34	.46
Education	86	901	.31	.30	.29	.35	.36	.47
Business	14	196	.28	.28	.25	.39	.31	.47

V = GRE Verbal, Q = GRE Quantitative, A = GRE Analytical, U = Undergraduate grade point average.

The departments included in these analyses participated in the GRE Validity Study Service between 1986 and 1990. A minimum of 10 departments and 100 examinees in any departmental grouping were required for inclusion in the table.

Source: Table 7, GRE ® 2000–2001 Guide to the Use of Scores, 2000, 24. Reprinted by permission of Educational Testing Services, the copyright owner.

Note: The numbers in this table are product-moment correlations—numbers that can vary between −1.0 and +1.0 and that indicate the extent to which one variable is associated with another. The closer the correlation in to ±1, the stronger the relationship between the two variables; the closer the correlation is to 0.0, the weaker the relationship. Since the correlations between VQA and graduate first-year GPA in this table are between .30 and .40, the relationships are not very strong. Notice also that undergraduate GPA is also not a very strong predictor of graduate first-year GPA, but that together GRE scores and undergraduate GPA improve predictions.

on the similarity of outcomes of more than one measure of a concept to demonstrate the validity of the entire measurement scheme.

Let us return to the researcher who wants to develop a valid measure of liberalism. First the researcher might measure people's attitudes toward (1) school vouchers, (2) welfare, (3) protection of the rights of the accused, (4) military spending, (5) affirmative action, (6) social security benefit levels, (7) abortion, and (8) a progressive income tax. Then the researcher could determine how the responses to each question relate to the responses to each of the other questions. The validity of the measurement scheme would be demonstrated if there were strong relationships among people's responses across the eight questions.

The results of such interitem association tests are often displayed in a **correlation matrix** (Table 4-2). Such a display shows how strongly related each of the items in the measurement scheme is to all of the other items. In the hypothetical data shown in Table 4-2, we can see that people's responses to six of the eight measures were strongly related to each other while responses to the questions on protection of the rights of the accused and school vouchers were not part of the general pattern. Thus the researcher would probably conclude that the first six items all measure a dimension of liberalism and that, taken together, they are a valid measurement of liberalism.

TABLE 4-2

Interitem Association Validity Test of a Measure of Liberalism

	Welfare	Military Spending	Abortion	Social Security	Affirmative Action	Income Tax	School Vouchers	Rights of Accused
Welfare	x							
Military Spending	.56	x						
Abortion	.71	.60	x					
Social Security	.80	.51	.83	x				
Affirmative Action	.63	.38	.59	.69	x			
Income Tax	.48	.67	.75	.39	.51	x		
School Vouchers	.28	.08	.19	.03	.30	−.07	x	
Rights of Accused	−.01	.14	−.12	.10	.23	.18	.45	x

Note: Hypothetical data. The figures in this table are product-moment correlations, explained in the note to Table 4-1. A high correlation indicates a strong relationship between how people answered the two different questions designed to measure liberalism. The figures in the last two rows are considerably closer to 0.0 than are the other entries, indicating that people's answers to the school vouchers and rights of the accused questions did not follow the same pattern as their answers to the other questions. Therefore, it looks like school vouchers and rights of the accused are not part of the measure of liberalism accomplished with the other questions.

Such a procedure was used by Ada Finifter and Ellen Mickiewicz in their study of popular attitudes toward political change in the Soviet Union.[21] They designed six survey questions to measure attitudes toward the pace of political change, the perceived locus of responsibility (individual or collective) for individuals' social well-being, the acceptability of differences in individual incomes and standards of living, the acceptability of unconventional forms of political expression, the importance of free speech, and the level of support for competitive elections. The questions are as follows:

1. *(Rapid vs. slow change)* *"Some people think that to solve our most pressing problems it is necessary to make decisive and rapid changes, since any delay threatens to make things worse. Others, on the other hand, think that changes should be cautious and slow, since you can never be sure that they won't cause more harm than good. Which of these points of view are you more likely to agree with?*

    "Below are some widespread but contradictory statements relating to problems of the development of our society. Which would you be most likely to agree with?"

2. *(Individual vs. state responsibility)* *"The state and government should be mainly responsible for the success and well-being of people"* or *"People should look out for themselves, decide for themselves what to do for success in life."*

3. *(Income differences)* *"The state should provide an opportunity for everyone to earn as much as he can, even if it leads to essential differences in people's standard of living and income"* or *"The state should do everything to reduce differences in people's standard of living and income, even if they won't try to work harder and earn more."*

4. *(Protest vs. traditional methods)* *"Strikes, spontaneous demonstrations, political meetings and other forms of social protest are completely acceptable methods of mass conduct and an effective means for solving social problems"* or *"These forms of protest are undesirable for society; they should be avoided in favor of more peaceful, traditional and organized methods of solving social conflicts."*

5. *(Free speech vs. order)* *"To improve things in our country people should be given the opportunity to say what they want, even if it can lead to public disorder"* or *"Keeping the peace in society should be the main effort, even if it requires limiting freedom of expression."*

6. *(Competitive elections)* *"In the coming elections for local soviets, should we elect deputies from among several candidates, as we mostly did in the spring elections? or "Is it better to avoid the conflicts these elections generated and go back to the old system of voting?"*[22]

Finifter and Mickiewicz found a pattern in Soviet citizen responses to five of the six questions. Attitudes toward the locus of responsibility for individual well-being were only weakly related to the other five questions about political change. Hence the researchers were able to combine the answers to five of the measures into an attitude scale of "support for political change" as a result of the observed interitem associations among them.

Content and face validity are difficult to assess when there is a lack of agreement on the meaning of a concept, and construct validity, which requires a well-developed theoretical perspective, usually yields a less-than-definitive result. The interitem association test requires multiple measures of the same concept. Although these validity "tests" provide important evidence, none of them is likely to support an unequivocal decision concerning the validity of particular measures.

Problems with Reliability and Validity in Political Science Measurement

An example of research performed at the Survey Research Center at the University of Michigan illustrates the numerous threats to the reliability and validity of political science measures. In 1980 the Center conducted interviews with a national sample of eligible voters and measured their income levels with the following question:

> "Please look at this page and tell me the letter of the income group that includes the income of *all members of your family living here in 1979 before taxes*. This figure should include salaries, wages, pensions, dividends, interest, and all other income."

Respondents were given the following choices:

A.	None or less than $2,000	N.	$12,000–$12,999
B.	$2,000–$2,999	P.	$13,000–$13,999
C.	$3,000–$3,999	Q.	$14,000–$14,999
D.	$4,000–$4,999	R.	$15,000–$16,999
E.	$5,000–$5,999	S.	$17,000–$19,999
F.	$6,000–$6,999	T.	$20,000–$22,999
G.	$7,000–$7,999	U.	$23,000–$24,999
H.	$8,000–$8,999	V.	$25,000–$29,999
J.	$9,000–$9,999	W.	$30,000–$34,999
K.	$10,000–$10,999	X.	$35,000–$49,999
M.	$11,000–$11,999	Y.	$50,000 and over

Both the reliability and the validity of this method of measuring income are questionable. Threats to the reliability of the measure include the following:

1. Respondents may not know how much money they make and therefore incorrectly guess their income.

2. Respondents may also not know how much money other family members make and guess incorrectly.

3. Respondents may know how much they make but carelessly select the wrong categories.

4. Interviewers may circle the wrong categories when listening to the selections of the respondents.

5. Data entry personnel may touch the wrong numbers when entering the answers into the computer.

6. Dishonest interviewers may incorrectly guess the income of a respondent who does not complete the interview.

7. Respondents may not know which family members to include in the income total; some respondents may include only a few family members while others may include even distant relations.

8. Respondents whose income is on the border between two categories may not know which one to pick. Some pick the higher category, some the lower one.

Each of these problems may introduce some error into the measurement of income, resulting in inaccurate measures that are too high for some respondents and too low for others. Therefore, if this measure were applied to the same people at two different times we could expect the results to vary.

In addition to these threats to reliability, there are numerous threats to the validity of this measure:

1. Respondents may have illegal income they do not want to reveal and, therefore, may systematically underestimate their income.

2. Respondents may try to impress the interviewer, or themselves, by systematically overestimating their income.

3. Respondents may systematically underestimate their before-tax income if they believe too much money is being withheld from their paychecks.

This long list of problems with both the reliability and the validity of this fairly straightforward measure of a relatively concrete concept is worrisome. Imagine how much more difficult it is to develop reliable and valid measures when the concept is abstract (for example, intelligence, self-esteem, or liberalism) and the measurement scheme is more complicated.

The reliability and validity of the measures used by political scientists are seldom demonstrated to everyone's satisfaction. Most measures of political phenomena are neither completely invalid or valid nor thoroughly unreliable or reliable, but rather are partially accurate. Therefore, researchers generally present the rationale and evidence that are available in support of their measures and attempt to persuade their audience that their measures are at least as accurate as alternative measures would be. Nonetheless, a skeptical stance on the part of the reader toward the reliability and validity of political science measures is often warranted.

Reliability and validity are not the same thing. A measure may be reliable without being valid. One may devise a series of questions to measure liberalism, for example, which yields the same result for the same people every time but which misidentifies individuals. A valid measure, on the other hand, will also be reliable since if it accurately measures the concept in question then it should do so consistently across measurements. It is more important, then, to demonstrate validity than reliability, but reliability is usually more easily and precisely tested.

The Precision of Measurements

Measurements should be not only accurate but also precise; that is, measurements should contain as much information as possible about the attribute or behavior being measured. The more precise our measures, the more complete and informative can be our test of the relationships between two or more variables.

Suppose, for example, that we wanted to measure the height of political candidates to see if taller candidates usually win elections. Height could be measured in many different ways. We could have two categories of the variable height, tall and short, and assign different candidates to the two categories based on whether they were of above-average or below-average height. Or we could compare the heights of candidates running for the same office and measure which candidate was the tallest, which the next tallest, and so on. Or we could take a tape measure and measure each candidate's height in inches and record that measure. Clearly, the last method of measurement captures the most information about each candidate's height and is, therefore, the most precise measure of the attribute.

When we consider the precision of our measurements, we refer to the **level of measurement**. The level of measurement involves the type of information that we think our measurements contain and the type of comparisons that can be made across a number of observations on the same variable. The level of measurement also refers to the claim we are willing to make when we assign numbers to our measurements.

There are four different levels of measurement: nominal, ordinal, interval, and ratio. Very few concepts used in political science research inherently require a particular level of measurement, so the level used in any specific research project is a function of the imagination and resources of the researcher and the decisions made when the method of measuring each of the variables is developed.

A **nominal measurement** is involved whenever the values assigned to a variable represent only different categories or classifications for that variable. In such a case, no category is more or less than another category, simply different. For example, suppose we measure the religion of individuals by asking them to indicate whether they are Protestant, Catholic, Jewish, or something else. Since the four categories or values for the variable "religion" are simply different, the measurement is at a nominal level.

Nominal level measures ought to consist of categories that are exhaustive and mutually exclusive; that is, the categories should include all of the possibilities for the measure, and they should be differentiated in such a way that a case will fit into one and only one category. For example, the categories of the measure of religion are exhaustive (because of the "something else" category) as well as mutually exclusive (since presumably an individual cannot be of more than one religion). If we attempted to measure "types of political systems" with the categories democratic, socialist, authoritarian, undeveloped, traditional, capitalist, and monarchical, however, the categories would be neither exhaustive nor mutually exclusive. (In which one category would Japan, Great Britain, and India belong?) The difficulty of deciding the category into which many countries should be put would hinder the very measurement process the variable was intended to further.

An **ordinal measurement** assumes that more or less of a variable can be measured and that a comparison can be made on which observations have more or less of a particular attribute. For example, we could create an ordinal measure of formal education completed with the following categories: "eighth grade or less," "some high school," "high school graduate," "some college," "college degree or more." Notice that we are not concerned here with the exact difference between the categories of education, but only with whether one category is more or less than another. Or suppose we ask individuals three questions designed to measure social trust, and we believe that an individual who answers all three questions a certain way has more social trust than a person who answers two of the questions a certain way, and this person has more social trust than a person who answers one of the questions a certain way. We could assign a score of 3 to the first group, 2 to the second group, 1 to the first group, and 0 to those who did not answer any of the questions in a socially trusting manner. In this case, the higher the number, the more social trust an individual has. With an ordinal measure it does not matter whether we assign to the four categories the numbers 0, 1, 2, 3; 5, 6, 7, 8; 10, 100, 1000, 10005; or 100, 101, 107, 111. The intervals between the numbers have no meaning; all that matters is that the higher numbers represent more of the attribute than do the lower numbers.

With an **interval measurement** the intervals between the categories or values assigned to the observations have meaning. For interval measures, the value of a particular observation is important not just in terms of whether it is larger or smaller than another value (as in ordinal measures), but also in terms of how much larger or smaller it is. For example, suppose we record the year in which certain events occurred. If we have three observations—1950, 1960, and 1970—we know that the event in 1950 occurred ten years before the one in 1960 and twenty years before the one in 1970. We also know that the difference between the 1950 and 1970 observations is twice the difference between the 1950 and 1960 or 1960 and 1970 observations. One-unit change (the interval) all along this measurement is identical in meaning: the passage of one year's time. This is not necessarily the case for the measure of social trust discussed earlier, since we are not certain in that example whether the difference between a score of 1 and a score of 2 is identical with the difference between a score of 2 and a score of 3.

Another characteristic of an interval level of measurement that distinguishes it from the next level of measurement (ratio) is that the zero point is arbitrarily assigned and does not represent the absence of the attribute being measured. For example, many time and temperature scales have arbitrary zero points. Thus, the year 0 A.D. does not indicate the beginning of time—if this were true, there would be no B.C. dates. Nor does 0°C indicate the absence of heat; rather, it indicates the temperature at which water freezes. For this reason, with interval level measurements we cannot calculate ratios; that is, we cannot say that 60°F is twice as warm as 30°F because it does not represent twice as much warmth.

The final level of measurement is a **ratio measurement**. This type of measurement involves the full mathematical properties of numbers. That is, the values of the categories order the categories, tell something about the intervals between the categories, and state precisely the relative amounts of the variable that the categories represent. If, for example, a researcher is willing to claim that an observation with ten units of a variable possesses exactly twice as much of that attribute as an observation with five units of that variable, then a ratio level measurement exists.

The key to making this assumption is that a value of zero on the variable actually represents the absence of that variable. Because ratio measures have a true zero point, it makes sense to say that one measurement is [×] times another. It makes sense to say a sixty-year-old person is twice the age of a thirty-year-old person (60/30 = 2), while it does not make sense to say that 60°C is twice as warm as 30°C.[23]

Identifying the level of measurement of variables is important since it affects the data analysis techniques that can be used and the conclusions that can be drawn about the relationships between variables. However, the decision is not always a straightforward one, and there is often uncertainty and disagreement among researchers concerning these decisions. Very few phenomena inherently require one particular level of measurement. Often a phenomenon can be measured with any level of measurement, depending upon the particular technique designed by the researcher and the claims that the researcher is willing to make about the resulting measure.

Political science researchers have measured many concepts at the ratio level. People's ages, unemployment rates, percent vote for a particular candidate, and crime rates are all examples of measures that contain a zero point and represent the full mathematical properties of the numbers used. However, more political science research has probably relied upon nominal and ordinal level measures than interval or ratio level measures. This has restricted the types of hypotheses and analysis techniques that political scientists have been willing and able to use.

Researchers usually try to devise as high a level of measurement for their concepts as possible (nominal being the lowest level of measurement and ratio the highest). With a higher level of measurement, more advanced data analysis techniques can be used and more precise statements about the relationships between variables can be made. Consequently, one might start with a nominal level measure and think of a way to turn it into an ordinal or interval level measure. For example, a researcher investigating the effect of campaign spending on election outcomes could devise an ordinal level measure that simply distinguished between those candidates who spent more or less than their opponent. However, more information would be preserved if a ratio level variable measuring how much more (or less) a candidate spent than the opposition were devised. Similarly, researchers measuring attitudes or personality traits also often construct a scale or index from nominal level measures that permits at least ordinal level comparisons between observations.

Multi-item Measures

Many of the measures considered so far in this chapter have consisted of a single item. Fording's measures of mass insurgency as the number of incidents and welfare generosity as the annual growth in state AFDC rates, Page and Shapiro's measures of public opinion change, and Midlarsky's measure of political violence are all based on single measures of each phenomenon in question. Often, however, researchers need to devise measures of more complicated phenomena that have more than one facet or dimension. Liberalism, democracy, access to electoral institutions and even land inequality, for example, are complex phenomena that may be measured in many different ways. In this situation, researchers often develop a measurement strategy that allows them to capture numerous aspects of a complex phenomenon while representing the existence of that phenomenon in particular cases with a single representative value. Usually this involves the construction of a multi-item index or scale representing the several dimensions of a complex phenomenon. These multi-item measures are useful because they enhance the accuracy of a measure, simplify a researcher's data by reducing it to a more manageable size, and increase the level of measurement of a phenomenon. In the remainder of this section we will describe several common types of indexes and scales.

Indexes

An **index** is a method of accumulating scores on individual items to form a composite measure of a complex phenomenon. An index is constructed by assigning a range of possible scores for a number of items, determining the score for each item for each observation, and then combining the scores for each observation across all of the items. The resulting summary score is the representative measurement of the phenomenon.

A researcher interested in measuring how much freedom there is in different countries, for example, might construct an index of political freedom by devising a list of items germane to the concept, determining where individual countries score on each of the items, and then adding these scores together to get a summary measure. In Table 4-3 such a hypothetical index is used to measure the amount of freedom in countries A through E.

The index in Table 4-3 is a simple, additive one; that is, each of the items counts equally toward the calculation of the index score, and the total score is the summation of the individual item scores. However, indexes may be constructed with more complicated aggregation procedures and by counting some items as more important than others. In the preceding example a researcher might consider some indicators of freedom more important than others and wish to have them contribute more to the calculation of the final index score. This could be done either by weighting (multiplying) some item scores by a number indicating their importance or by assigning a higher score than 1 for those attributes considered more important.

Fording's measure of access to electoral institutions included two items: whether or not a state's legislature was apportioned (representatives elected on a one person–one vote principle from equal-sized electoral districts) and

TABLE 4-3
Hypothetical Index for Measuring Freedom in Countries

	Country A	Country B	Country C	Country D	Country E
Does the country possess:					
Privately owned newspapers	1	0	0	0	1
Legal right to form political parties	1	1	0	0	0
Contested elections for significant public offices	1	1	0	0	0
Voting rights extended to most of the adult population	1	1	0	1	0
Limitations on government's ability to incarcerate citizens	1	0	0	0	1
Index Score	5	3	0	1	2

Note: Hypothetical data. The score is 1 if the answer is yes, 0 if no.

whether or not the Voting Rights Act of 1965 had been implemented within the state. Each item was scored 0 or 1 and the results of the items were multiplied. Thus only states whose legislative bodies were apportioned and complied with the Voting Rights Act received a score of 1.

Indexes are often used with public opinion surveys to measure political attitudes. This is because attitudes are complex phenomena and we usually do not know enough about them to devise single-item measures. So we often ask several questions of people about a single attitude and aggregate the answers to represent the attitude. A researcher might measure attitudes toward abortion, for example, by asking respondents to choose one of five possible responses—strongly agree, agree, undecided, disagree, and strongly disagree—to the following three statements: (1) Abortions should be permitted in the first three months of pregnancy; (2) Abortions should be permitted if the woman's life is in danger; (3) Abortions should be permitted whenever a woman wants one.

An index of attitudes toward abortion could be computed by assigning numerical values to each response (such as 1 for strongly agree, 2 for agree, 3 for undecided, and so on) and then adding the values of a respondent's answers to these three questions. (The researcher would have to decide what to do when a respondent did not answer one or more of the questions.) The lowest possible score would be a 3, indicating the most extreme pro-abortion attitude, and the highest possible score would be a 15, indicating the most extreme anti-abortion attitude. Scores in between would indicate varying degrees of approval of abortion.

Finifter and Mickiewicz, the researchers who attempted to measure attitudes toward political change in the former Soviet Union, developed this type of index of attitudes. Once they had decided that there was a pattern in the responses to five of their questionnaire items, they then assigned a score of +1 to proreform answers and a –1 to status quo (opposite) answers and summed each individual's answers to the five questions. What resulted were index scores representing individual answers to all five questions that ranged in value from +5 to –5. This single index score of attitudes toward political change was then used in further analysis.

Another example of a multi-item index appears in a study of attitudes toward feminism in Europe.[24] To determine the extent and distribution of attitudinal support for feminism across European society, Lee Ann Banaszak and Eric Plutzer constructed a measure of profeminism attitudes. Respondents were asked six questions about various aspects of a feminist belief system (e.g., achieving equality between women and men in their work and careers, fighting against people who would like to keep women in a subordinate role, achieving gender equality in responsibilities for child care) and were given scores ranging from 0 to 3 for the degree of agreement with each profeminist statement. Responses across the six items were then summed to yield a profeminism index score that varied from 0 to 18.

Indexes are typically fairly simple ways of producing single representative scores of complicated phenomena such as political attitudes. They are probably more accurate than most single-item measures, but they may also be flawed in important ways. Aggregating scores across several items assumes, for example, that each item is equally important to the summary measure of the concept and that the items used faithfully encompass the domain of the concept. Although individual item scores can be weighted to change their contribution to the summary measure, there is often little information upon which to base a weighting scheme.

Several standard indexes are often used in political science research. The FBI crime index and the consumer price index, for example, have been used by many researchers. Although simple summation indexes are generally more accurate than single-item measures of complicated phenomena would be, it is often unclear how valid they are or what level of measurement they represent.

Scales

Although indexes are often an improvement over single-item measures, there is also an element of arbitrariness in their construction. Both the selection of particular items making up the index and the way in which the scores on individual items are aggregated are based on the judgment of the researcher. Scales are also multi-item measures, but the selection and combination of items in them is more systematically accomplished than is usually the case for indexes. Over the years several different kinds of multi-item scales have been used frequently in political science research. We will discuss three of them: Likert scales, Guttman scales, and the semantic differential.

A **Likert scale** score is calculated from the scores obtained on individual items. Each item generally asks a respondent to indicate a degree of agreement or disagreement with the item, as with the abortion questions discussed earlier. A Likert scale differs from an index, however, in that once the scores on each of the items are obtained, only some of the items are selected for inclusion in the calculation of the final score. Those items that allow a researcher to distinguish most readily those scoring high on an attribute from those scoring low will be retained, and a new scale score will be calculated based only on those items.

For example, recall the researcher interested in measuring the liberalism of a group of respondents. Since definitions of liberalism vary, the researcher cannot be sure how many aspects of liberalism need to be measured. With Likert scaling the researcher would begin with a large group of questions thought to express various aspects of liberalism that respondents would be asked to agree or disagree with. A provisional Likert scale for liberalism, then, might look like this:

	Strongly Disagree (1)	Disagree (2)	Undecided (3)	Agree (4)	Strongly Agree (5)
The government should ensure that no one lives in poverty.	___	___	___	___	___
Military spending should be reduced.	___	___	___	___	___
It is more important to take care of people's needs than it is to balance the federal budget.	___	___	___	___	___
Social Security benefits should not be cut.	___	___	___	___	___
The government should spend money to improve housing and transportation in urban areas.	___	___	___	___	___

	Strongly Disagree (1)	Disagree (2)	Undecided (3)	Agree (4)	Strongly Agree (5)
Wealthy people should pay taxes at a much higher rate than poor people.	____	____	____	____	____
Busing should be used to integrate public schools.	____	____	____	____	____
The rights of persons accused of a crime must be vigorously protected.	____	____	____	____	____

In practice, a set of questions like this would be scattered throughout a questionnaire so that respondents do not see them as related. Some of the questions might also be worded in the opposite way (that is, so an "agree" response is a conservative response) to ensure genuine answers.

The respondents' answers to these eight questions would be summed to produce a provisional score. The scores in this case can range from 8 to 40. Then the responses of the most liberal and the most conservative people to each question would be compared; any questions with similar answers from the disparate respondents would be eliminated—such questions would not distinguish liberals from conservatives. A new summary scale score for all the respondents would be calculated from the questions that remained.

Likert scales are improvements over multi-item indexes because the items that make up the multi-item measure are selected in part based on the behavior of the respondents rather than on the judgment of the researcher. Likert scales suffer two of the other defects of indexes, however: the researcher cannot be sure that all of the dimensions of a concept have been measured, and the relative importance of each item is still arbitrarily determined.

The **Guttman scale** also employs a series of items to produce a scale score for respondents. Unlike the Likert scale, however, a Guttman scale is designed to present respondents with a range of attitude choices that are increasingly difficult to agree with; that is, the items composing the scale range from those easy to agree with to those difficult to agree with. Respondents who agree with one of the "more difficult" attitude items will also generally agree with the "less difficult" ones. (Guttman scales have also been used to measure attributes other than attitudes. Their main application has been in the area of attitude research, however, so an example of that type is used here.)

Let us return to the researcher interested in measuring attitudes toward abortion. He or she might devise a series of items ranging from "easy to agree with" to "difficult to agree with." Such an approach might be represented by the following items.

Do you agree or disagree that abortions should be permitted:

1. When the life of the woman is in danger.
2. In the case of incest or rape.
3. When the fetus appears to be unhealthy.
4. When the father does not want to have a baby.
5. When the woman cannot afford to have a baby.
6. Whenever the woman wants one.

This array of items seems likely to result in responses consistent with Guttman scaling. A respondent agreeing with any one of the items is likely to also agree with those items numbered lower than that one. This would result in the "stepwise" pattern of responses characteristic of a Guttman scale.

Suppose six respondents answered this series of questions, as shown in Table 4-4. Generally speaking, the pattern of responses is as expected; those who agreed with the "most difficult" questions were also likely to agree with the "less difficult" ones. However, the responses of three people (2, 4, and 5) to the question about the father's preferences do not fit the pattern. Consequently, the question about the father does not seem to fit the pattern and would be removed from the scale. Once that has been done, the stepwise pattern becomes clear.

With real data, it is unlikely that every respondent would give answers that fit the pattern perfectly. For example, in Table 4-4 respondent 6 gave an

TABLE 4-4
Guttman Scale of Attitudes toward Abortion

Respon- dent	Life of Woman	Incest or Rape	Un- healthy Fetus	Father	Afford	Any- time	No. of Agree Answers	Revised Scale Score
1	A	A	A	A	A	A	6	5
2	A	A	A	D	A	D	4	4
3	A	A	A	D	D	D	3	3
4	A	A	D	A	D	D	3	2
5	A	D	D	A	D	D	2	1
6	D	A	D	D	D	D	1	0

Note: Hypothetical data. A = Agree, D = Disagree.

"agree" response to the question about incest or rape. This response is unexpected and does not fit the pattern. Therefore, we would be making an error if we assigned a scale score of "0" to respondent 6. There are statistical procedures to calculate how well the data fit the scale pattern. When the data fit the scale pattern well (number of errors is small), researchers assume that the scale is an appropriate measure and that the respondent's "error" may be "corrected" (in this case, either the "agree" in the case of incest or rape or the "disagree" in the case of the life of the woman). There are standard procedures to follow to determine how to correct the data to make it conform to the scale pattern. We emphasize, however, that this is done only if the changes are few.

Guttman scales differ from Likert scales in that generally only one set of responses will yield a particular scale score. That is, to get a score of 3 on the abortion scale a particular pattern of responses (or something very close to it) is necessary. In the case of a Likert scale, however, many different patterns of responses can yield the same scale score. A Guttman scale is also much more difficult to achieve than a Likert scale since the items must have been ordered and be perceived by the respondents as representing increasingly more difficult responses to the same attitude.

Both Likert and Guttman scales have shortcomings in their level of measurement. The level of measurement produced by Likert scales is, at best, ordinal (since we do not know what the relative importance is of each item and so we cannot be sure that a "5" answer on one item is the same as a "5" answer on another), and the level of measurement produced by Guttman scales is usually assumed to be ordinal.

Another method of producing multi-item summary measures is a technique called the **semantic differential**. This technique presents respondents with a series of adjective pairs to bring out the ways in which people respond to some particular object. These responses may then be used to understand the dimensions or attributes of that object and/or to compare evaluations across objects.

Suppose, for example, that you were a political consultant preparing for the reelection campaign of an incumbent U.S. senator. You would probably be interested in the public's attitude toward your client so that you could identify his or her major strengths and weaknesses. If you were uncertain about the attitudes that people had toward your candidate you might use the semantic differential to explore those attitudes.

In the typical semantic differential application respondents are presented with adjective pairs (opposites) with seven response categories available for each pair, and they are asked to evaluate some object in terms of each adjective pair. For example, respondents might be asked to reveal their feelings toward a political candidate in the following way:

Listed below are several pairs of words that could be used to describe Senator X. Between the words in each pair are several blanks. Please put an X in the blank between each pair that best describes how you feel about Senator X.

Senator X

honest	___	___	___	___	___	___	___	dishonest
smart	___	___	___	___	___	___	___	dumb
sincere	___	___	___	___	___	___	___	insincere
superficial	___	___	___	___	___	___	___	profound
good	___	___	___	___	___	___	___	bad
serious	___	___	___	___	___	___	___	humorous
idealistic	___	___	___	___	___	___	___	realistic
strong	___	___	___	___	___	___	___	weak
pleasant	___	___	___	___	___	___	___	unpleasant
helpful	___	___	___	___	___	___	___	unhelpful
powerful	___	___	___	___	___	___	___	powerless
active	___	___	___	___	___	___	___	inactive
young	___	___	___	___	___	___	___	old
nice	___	___	___	___	___	___	___	awful

Research on the use of the semantic differential has discovered that there are often three primary underlying dimensions for attitudes toward most objects: an evaluative dimension (favorable versus unfavorable), a potency dimension (strong versus weak), and an activity dimension (active versus passive). Typically, responses to a set of adjective pairs are analyzed in terms of these three dimensions, allowing a researcher to infer the respondents' attitudes toward one or more objects of interest. In the example above, the adjective pairs honest-dishonest, good-bad, pleasant-unpleasant, nice-awful, helpful-unhelpful, sincere-insincere, and smart-dumb would probably capture the evaluative dimension while strong-weak, powerful-powerless, serious-humorous, and superficial-profound would represent the potency dimension. Young-old and active-inactive would measure activity. Asking citizens to indicate their perceptions about a candidate in this way would probably allow a political consultant to determine the perceived evaluation, potency, and activity of a candidate more accurately than would any single questionnaire item.

Factor Analysis

The procedures described so far for constructing multi-item measures are fairly straightforward. Sometimes, however, researchers attempt to construct measures of abstract, complicated phenomena where they are uncertain about the domain to be measured. **Factor analysis** is a statistical technique that may be used to uncover patterns across a number of measures. It is especially useful when a researcher has a large number of measures and when there is uncertainty about how the measures are interrelated. Factor analysis is often used in attitudinal research to construct a limited number of attitude scales, and corresponding scale scores, out of a much larger number of questionnaire items.

The factor analysis procedure involves calculating a statistic that measures the relationships between every pair of measures and then looking for groups of measures that are closely related to each other. These groups of closely related measures are said to *load* on a *factor,* which measures a particular aspect or dimension of the phenomenon.

Let us take a look at an example. Banaszak and Plutzer, who were interested in studying feminism among men and women in Europe, included six questions meant to measure attitudes toward feminism on their questionnaire. They did not know, however, whether the six questions measured six different attitudes, one attitude, or something in between; nor did they know if all six questions were equally effective measures of feminism. A factor analysis of people's responses to the questions revealed that all six measures were, in fact, highly interrelated; that the six measures constituted one, and only one, factor, or attitude; and that each question was an equally good measure of feminism. This information led to the decision to construct a single attitude scale utilizing the answers to all six questions.

A more complicated and abstract use of factor analysis may be found in research explaining levels of governmental welfare spending during the period between 1960 and 1982 in eighteen capitalist democracies.[25] In this study, researchers Alexander Hicks and Duane Swank measured a number of attributes of the eighteen nation-states they studied, including partisan control of the government, the amount of electoral competition and voter turnout, working class organization and interest representation, the amount of governmental centralization and bureaucratization, and the existence of welfare-related policy precedents. By employing a factor analysis, the researchers were able to identify three dimensions of a nation-state's political institutions and process. One dimension, called "left corporatism," reflects union strength, class mobilization, and left-leaning governmental control. Another dimension, called "state centralization," captures various aspects of governmental centralization. The third dimension, called "bureaucratic patrimonialism," measures such things as the extent of bureaucratic power, resistance to mass enfranchisement, and class rigidity. The researchers constructed three scale scores made up of several measures to capture each of these dimensions and demonstrate their relationships with governmental welfare spending.

Factor analysis is just one of many techniques that have been developed to explore the dimensionality of measures and to construct multi-item scales. The readings listed at the end of this chapter include some resources for students who are especially interested in this aspect of variable measurement.

Through indexes and scales, researchers attempt to enhance both the accuracy and the precision of their measures. Although these multi-item measures have received most use in attitude research, they are often useful in other endeavors as well. Both indexes and scales require researchers to make decisions regarding the selection of individual items and the way in which the scores on those items will be combined to produce more useful measures of political phenomena.

Conclusion

To a large extent, a research project is only as good as the measurements that are developed and used in it. Inaccurate measurements will interfere with the testing of scientific explanations for political phenomena and may lead to erroneous conclusions. Imprecise measurements will limit the extent of the comparisons that can be made between observations and the precision of the knowledge that results from empirical research.

Despite the importance of good measurement, political science researchers often find that their measurement schemes are of uncertain accuracy and precision. Abstract concepts are difficult to measure in a valid way, and the practical constraints of time and money often jeopardize the reliability and precision of measurements. The quality of a researcher's measurements makes an important contribution to the results of his or her empirical research and should not be lightly or routinely sacrificed.

Sometimes the accuracy of measurements may be enhanced through the use of multi-item measures. With indexes and scales, researchers select multiple indicators of a phenomenon, assign scores to each of these indicators, and combine those scores into a summary measure. While these methods have been used most frequently in attitude research, they can also be used in other situations to improve the accuracy and precision of single-item measures.

Notes

1. Stephen C. Poe and C. Neal Tate, "Repression of Human Rights to Personal Integrity in the 1980s: A Global Analysis," *American Political Science Review* 88 (December 1994): 853–872.

2. Bruce Bueno de Mesquita, Randolph M. Siverson, and Gary Woller, "War and the Fate of Regimes: A Comparative Analysis," *American Political Science Review* 86 (September 1992): 638–646.

3. Benjamin I. Page and Robert Y. Shapiro, "Effects of Public Opinion on Policy," *American Political Science Review* 77 (March 1983): 175–190.

4. Jeffrey A. Segal and Albert D. Cover, "Ideological Values and the Votes of U.S. Supreme Court Justices," *American Political Science Review* 83 (June 1989): 557–565.

5. B. Dan Wood and Richard W. Waterman, "The Dynamics of Political Control of the Bureaucracy," *American Political Science Review* 85 (September 1991): 801–828.

6. Richard C. Fording, "The Conditional Effect of Violence as a Political Tactic: Mass Insurgency, Welfare Generosity, and Electoral Context in the American States," *American Journal of Political Science* 41 (January 1997): 1–29.

7. Stephen Ansolabehere, Shanto Iyengar, Adam Simon, and Nicholas Valentino, "Does Attack Advertising Demobilize the Electorate?" *American Political Science Review* 88 (December 1994): 829–838.

8. Page and Shapiro, "Effects of Public Opinion."

9. Fording, "The Conditional Effect of Violence as a Political Tactic," 11.

10. Daron R. Shaw, "The Effect of TV Ads and Candidate Appearances on Statewide Presidential Votes, 1988–96," *American Political Science Review* 93 (June 1999): 345–362.

11. Segal and Cover, "Ideological Values."

12. Ibid., 559.

13. Manus I. Midlarsky, "Rulers and the Ruled: Patterned Inequality and the Onset of Mass Political Violence," *American Political Science Review* 82 (June 1988): 491–509.

14. John S. Dryzek and Jeffrey Berejikian, "Reconstructive Democratic Theory," *American Political Science Review* 87 (March 1993): 48–60.

15. Ibid.

16. Edward G. Carmines and Richard A. Zeller, *Reliability and Validity Assessment,* Series on Quantitative Applications in the Social Sciences, No. 07-001, Sage University Papers (Beverly Hills, Calif.: Sage, 1979).

17. Philip E. Converse, "The Nature of Belief Systems in Mass Publics," in David E. Apter, ed., *Ideology and Discontent* (New York: Free Press, 1964); D.M. Vaillancourt, "Stability of Children's Survey Responses," *Public Opinion Quarterly* 37 (fall 1973): 373–387; J. Miller McPherson, Susan Welch, and Cal Clark, "The Stability and Reliability of Political Efficacy: Using Path Analysis to Test Alternative Models," *American Political Science Review* 71 (June 1977): 509–521; and Philip E. Converse and Gregory B. Markus, "The New CPS Election Study Panel," *American Political Science Review* 73 (March 1979): 32–49.

18. Raymond E. Wolfinger and Steven J. Rosenstone, *Who Votes?* (New Haven: Yale University Press, 1980), Appendix A.

19. Kenneth D. Bailey, *Methods of Social Research* (New York: Free Press, 1978), 58.

20. Ross E. Burkhart and Michael S. Lewis-Beck, "Comparative Democracy: The Economic Development Thesis," *American Political Science Review* 88 (December 1994): Appendix A.

21. Ada W. Finifter and Ellen Mickiewicz, "Redefining the Political System of the USSR: Mass Support for Political Change," *American Political Science Review* 86 (December 1992): 857–874.

22. Ibid.

23. The distinction between an interval and a ratio level measure is not always clear, and some political science texts do not distinguish between them. Interval level measures in political science are rather rare; ratio level measures (money spent, age, number of children, years living in the same location, for example) are more common.

24. Lee Ann Banaszak and Eric Plutzer, "The Social Bases of Feminism in the European Community," *Public Opinion Quarterly* 57 (spring 1993): 29–53.

25. Alexander M. Hicks and Duane H. Swank, "Politics, Institutions and Welfare Spending in Industrialized Democracies, 1960–82," *American Political Science Review* 86 (September 1992): 658–674.

Terms introduced

ALTERNATIVE-FORM METHOD. A method of calculating reliability by repeating different but equivalent measures at two or more points in time.

CONSTRUCT VALIDITY. Validity demonstrated for a measure by showing that it is related to the measure of another concept.

CONTENT VALIDITY. Validity demonstrated by ensuring that the full domain of a concept is measured.

CORRELATION MATRIX. A table showing the relationships among a number of discrete measures.

FACE VALIDITY. Validity asserted by arguing that a measure corresponds closely to the concept it is designed to measure.

FACTOR ANALYSIS. A statistical technique useful in the construction of multiple-item scales to measure abstract concepts.

GUTTMAN SCALE. A multi-item measure in which respondents are presented with increasingly difficult measures of approval for an attitude.

INDEX. A multi-item measure in which individual scores on a set of items are combined to form a summary measure.

INTERITEM ASSOCIATION. A test of the extent to which the scores of several items, each thought to measure the same concept, are the same. Results are displayed in a correlation matrix.

INTERVAL MEASUREMENT. A measure for which a one-unit difference in scores is the same throughout the range of the measure.

LEVEL OF MEASUREMENT. An indication of what is meant by assigning scores or numerals to empirical observations.

LIKERT SCALE. A multi-item measure in which the items are selected based on their ability to discriminate between those scoring high and those scoring low on the measure.

MEASUREMENT. The process by which phenomena are observed systematically and represented by scores or numerals.

NOMINAL MEASUREMENT. A measure for which different scores represent different, but not ordered, categories.

OPERATIONAL DEFINITION. The rules by which a concept is measured and scores assigned.

ORDINAL MEASUREMENT. A measure for which the scores represent ordered categories that are not necessarily equidistant from each other.

RATIO MEASUREMENT. A measure for which the scores possess the full mathematical properties of the numbers assigned.

RELIABILITY. The extent to which a measure yields the same results on repeated trials.

SEMANTIC DIFFERENTIAL. A technique for measuring attitudes toward an object in which respondents are presented with a series of opposite adjective pairs.

SPLIT-HALVES METHOD. A method of calculating reliability by comparing the results of two equivalent measures made at the same time.

TEST-RETEST METHOD. A method of calculating reliability by repeating the same measure at two or more points in time.

VALIDITY. The correspondence between a measure and the concept it is supposed to measure.

Exercises

1. Read the article by David H. Folz, "Municipal Recycling Performance: A Public Sector Environmental Success Story," *Public Administration Review* 59 (July–August 1999): 336–345.

   a. How was the importance of problems in municipal recycling measured? What is the level of measurement for this variable?

   b. How was change in recycling participation measured? What is its level of measurement?

   c. How were recycling program costs measured? What is the level of measurement? What problems did Folz encounter in trying to measure program costs?

2. Refer to the article by Jon S.T. Quah, "Corruption in Asian Countries: Can It Be Minimized?" *Public Administration Review* 59 (November–December 1999): 482–494. Review the discussion of the measurement of political corruption on page 484. What exactly is being measured? How is it measured? And what level of measurement are the measures?

3. Read the article by Jeff Yates and Andrew Whitford, "Presidential Power and the United States Supreme Court," *Political Research Quarterly* 51 (June 1998): 539–550. How are the variables for presidential approval, judicial appointment, and policy area of cases measured and what are their levels of measurement?

4. Read the article by Stephen C. Poe and C. Neal Tate, "Repression of Human Rights to Personal Integrity in the 1980s: A Global Analysis," *American Political Science Review* 88 (December 1994): 853–872. The authors do not measure the complete domain of the concept of human rights. What components do they leave out and why do they limit their definition of human rights abuses to those which violate the "integrity of the person"? Poe and Tate also discuss their measurement of democracy. What are the limitations of the two measures of democracy that they use? Are these reliability or validity problems?

5. What would be the level of measurement of the following measures?
   a. Current marital status (married, divorced, widowed, never married)
   b. College class (freshman, sophomore, junior, senior)
   c. Percent of news time devoted to election coverage during the evening news broadcast
   d. Attitudes toward government spending on the environment (too little, just about right, too much)
   e. Partisan control of Congress (Republican, split, Democratic)
   f. Republican control of Congress (neither chamber, one chamber only, both chambers)
   g. Sales tax rates in each of the fifty American states
   h. Month in which presidential primary is held in a state
   i. Percent of eligible voters registered to vote
   j. Whether or not a state requires annual safety inspection of automobiles

Suggested Readings

Carmines, Edward G., and Richard A. Zeller. *Reliability and Validity Assessment.* Series on Quantitative Applications in the Social Sciences. No. 07-001, Sage University Papers. Beverly Hills, Calif.: Sage, 1979.

DeVellis, Robert F. *Scale Development.* Newbury Park, Calif.: Sage, 1991.

Hatry, Harry P. *Performance Measurement: Getting Results.* Washington, D.C.: Urban Institute Press, 1999.

Kerlinger, Fred N. *Behavioral Research.* New York: Holt, Rinehart & Winston, 1979.

Kim, Jae-On, and Charles W. Mueller. *Introduction to Factor Analysis.* Newbury Park, Calif.: Sage, 1978.

Lodge, Milton. *Magnitude Scaling.* Newbury Park, Calif.: Sage, 1983.

Maranell, Gary M. *Scaling: A Sourcebook for Behavioral Scientists.* 4th ed. Hawthorne, N.Y.: Longman, 1983.

Rabinowitz, George. "Nonmetric Multidimensional Scaling and Individual Difference Scaling." In William D. Berry and Michael S. Lewis-Beck, eds. *New Tools for Social Scientists,* 77–107. Beverly Hills, Calif.: Sage, 1986.

Robinson, John P., Jerrold G. Rusk, and Kendra B. Head. *Measures of Political Attitudes.* Ann Arbor, Mich.: Institute for Social Research, 1969.

Rubin, Herbert J. *Applied Social Research.* Columbus, Ohio: Merrill, 1983.

CHAPTER 5

Research Design

In the previous two chapters we discussed how to formulate a testable research hypothesis that will serve as the basis for inquiry, and how to measure the variables named in the hypothesis with accuracy and precision. In this chapter we consider how to observe the relationship between the independent and dependent variables in a manner that enables us to draw appropriate conclusions about the way, and extent to which, they are related. These decisions are what we mean when we refer to a study's research design.

In general, a **research design** is a plan that shows how a researcher intends to fulfill the goals of a proposed study. It indicates what observations will be made to provide answers to the questions posed by the researcher, how the observations will be made, and the analytical and statistical procedures to be used once the data are collected. If the goal of the research is to test hypotheses, a research design will also explain how the test is to be accomplished.

A research design has been defined as a plan that "guides the investigator in the process of collecting, analyzing, and interpreting observations. It is a model of proof that allows the researcher to draw inferences concerning causal relations among the variables under investigation. . . . Furthermore, the research design also defines the domain of generalizability; that is, whether the obtained interpretations can be generalized to a larger population or to different situations."[1]

Developing the research design is just as important as developing research questions, hypotheses, and methods of measurement. A poor research design may produce insignificant and erroneous conclusions, no matter how original and brilliant the hypothesis. In this chapter we discuss various research designs and their advantages and disadvantages and show how a poor research design can result in uninformative or misleading research.

Many factors affect the choice of a particular research design. One is the purpose of the investigation. Whether the research is intended to be exploratory, descriptive, or explanatory will most likely influence the choice of a research design. Another is the practical limitations on how researchers may test their hypotheses. Some research designs may be unethical, others impossible to implement for lack of data or sufficient time and money. Researchers frequently must balance what is humanly possible to accomplish against what would be ideally done to test a particular hypothesis. Consequently, many of the research designs that researchers actually use are unfortunate but necessary compromises. The conclusions that may be drawn from most political science research are, therefore, more tentative and incomplete than we would like.

All research designs *to test hypotheses* are attempts by researchers to (1) establish a relationship between two or more variables; (2) demonstrate that the results are generally true in the real world; (3) reveal whether one phenomenon precedes another in time; and (4) eliminate as many alternative explanations for a phenomenon as possible. In this chapter we explain how various research designs allow or do not allow researchers to accomplish these four objectives. We will discuss two different general types of designs: experimental and nonexperimental.

Experimentation

Experimentation, or research involving experimental designs, allows the researcher to have more control over the independent variable, the units of analysis, and the environment in which behavior occurs. Consequently, experimental designs allow researchers to establish causal explanations for political behavior more easily than do nonexperimental designs. Although most of the research examples we presented in Chapter 1 did not use an experimental research design, some political scientists do conduct experiments, as illustrated by the research by Stephen Ansolabehere, Shanto Iyengar, Adam Simon, and Nicholas Valentino on the effects of negative campaign advertising on intentions to vote.[2] Whether or not the political phenomena of interest to you may be studied using an experimental research design, it is important to understand how an experimental research design allows researchers to evaluate causal explanations.

An ideal experiment has the following five basic characteristics:[3]

- There is an **experimental group** that receives an experimental treatment or **test stimulus** (the independent variable in a research hypothesis) and a **control group** that does not.
- The researcher determines the composition of the experimental and control groups by choosing the subjects and assigning them to one of the groups. In other words, the researcher can control who experiences the independent variable and who does not. Exactly how subjects are assigned to experimental and control groups is critical and will be discussed further later in this chapter.

■ The researcher has control over the introduction of the experimental treatment—that is, the researcher can determine when, and under what circumstances, the experimental group is exposed to the experimental stimulus.

■ The researcher is able to measure the dependent variable both before and after the experimental stimulus is given. He or she may then identify the **experimental effect**, or the effect of the independent variable on the dependent variable, as a result.

■ The researcher is able to control the environment of the subjects to control or exclude **extraneous factors**, or factors besides the independent variable that might affect the dependent variable.

In an ideal experiment a researcher can make causal statements and rule out alternative explanations; that is, he or she can argue that manipulation of the experimental stimulus caused the experimental and control groups to differ with respect to the dependent variable. Before we examine some of the types of experimental research designs used by researchers and the advantages and limitations of each, let us consider how we might experimentally test an actual hypothesis.

Suppose you want to test the hypothesis that "watching violence on television causes people to engage in aggressive social behavior." The independent variable, or experimental stimulus, is the amount and/or type of violence watched on television, and the dependent variable is the frequency and/or severity of people's aggressive social behavior. To test this hypothesis you might ask some people to experience the experimental stimulus (watch a lot of television violence) and ask others to avoid this same stimulus. In this experiment you would want to exercise enough control over the participants' lives that you could determine who watched a lot of television violence and who did not. You would also want to control when, how often, for how long, and under what conditions those in the experimental group watched violence on television. The next step would be to observe the amount of aggressive social behavior by all participants in the experiment, both before and after the experimental group watched the violent programming. It would be important to ensure that nothing other than the difference in television viewing affected one group and not the other during the course of the experiment.

If all of these conditions could be met, an experiment could be conducted that would shed considerable light on the hypothesis. You would be particularly interested in the amount, and change in the amount, of aggressive behavior for the experimental group compared with the control group and would have some basis for concluding that any observed difference could be attributed to the experimental stimulus. In other words, if significant differences in the aggressive behavior of the two groups occurred, then you could legitimately conclude that watching television violence was a causal explanation for at least a portion of a group's aggressive behavior.

This is persuasive evidence for a researcher to have, hence the attraction of experimentation. But problems may arise with the actual conduct of experiments that will call research findings into question. These problems are often referred to as threats to the validity of the research and are discussed in terms of internal and external validity.[4]

Internal Validity

Internal validity deals with whether the manipulation or variation in the independent variable, and not change in some other factor, makes a difference in the dependent variable. That is, we attempt to establish that the relationship between variables is *nonspurious*. The internal validity of experimental research may be adversely affected by several factors.

As we have seen, one of the characteristics of experimental research is that the researcher has enough control over the environment to make sure that exposure to the experimental stimulus is the only difference between experimental and control groups. Sometimes, however, **history**, or events other than the experimental stimulus that occur between the pre-treatment and post-treatment measurements of the dependent variable, will affect the dependent variable. For example, suppose that after an automobile safety inspection program is introduced in a state, a crackdown on drunk driving also begins. A decline in the traffic fatality rate could be due to the inspection program, the drunk driving campaign, or a combination of both.

Maturation, or a change in subjects over time, may create differences between experimental and control groups. For example, subjects may grow older or become tired, confused, distracted, or bored during the course of an experiment. These changes may affect their reaction to the test stimulus and introduce an unanticipated effect on post-treatment scores.

The standard experimental research design includes a **pre-test**, or measurement of the dependent variable before the experimental stimulus, and a **post-test**, or measurement of the dependent variable after the experimental stimulus. However, **testing**, or the act of measuring the dependent variable prior to the experimental stimulus, may itself affect the post-treatment scores of subjects. For example, suppose individuals who do poorly on the Scholastic Aptitude Test enroll in a course to improve their performance (the experimental stimulus), retake the SATs, and obtain higher scores. The improvement could be due to the course, to the experience that taking the SATs earlier provided, or to a combination of the initial test and the course. Similarly, suppose a researcher wanted to see if watching a presidential debate makes viewers better informed than nonviewers. If the researcher measures the political awareness of the experimental and control groups prior to the debate, he or she runs the risk of sensitizing the subjects to certain topics or issues and contributing to a more attentive audience than would otherwise be the case. Consequently, we would not know for sure whether any increase in awareness was due to the debate, the pre-test, or a combination of both. Fortunately, some research designs have been developed to separate these various effects.

Sometimes a person is selected for participation in an experimental program because of some extreme characteristic such as a very high or low reading test score. However, this score may be a temporary deviation—due to illness, fatigue, emotional upset, or luck—from a person's average score if he or she were to take the test several times. With subsequent retesting, a person's score would be expected to be less extreme and closer to that person's average score, regardless of the impact of the person's participation in any special program. If this happens, improvements in scores may be attributed erroneously to the program. Thus, **statistical regression**, or change in a dependent variable due to the temporary nature of extreme values, might affect internal validity.

In assigning subjects to experimental and control groups, a researcher hopes that the two groups will be equivalent. If subjects drop out of the experiment, experimental and control groups that may have been the same at the start may no longer be equivalent. Thus, **experimental mortality**, or the differential loss of participants from comparison groups, may raise doubts about whether the changes and variation in the dependent variable are due to manipulation of the independent variable.

Sometimes, **instrument decay**, or change in the instrument used to measure the dependent variable, occurs during the course of an experiment so that the pre-test and post-test measures are not made in the same way. For example, a researcher may become tired and not take post-test measurements as carefully as pre-test ones. Or different persons with different biases may conduct the pre-test and post-test. Thus changes in the dependent variable may be due to measurement changes, not to the experimental stimulus.

Selection, or bias in the assigning of subjects to experimental and control groups, may also threaten internal validity. If experimental and control group subjects are not equivalent, then differences between the groups at the end of an experiment cannot be attributed conclusively to the independent variable. Bias in the selection of subjects may occur if a researcher does not control assignment of subjects to experimental and control groups or if the researcher personally assigns subjects in a biased manner. A common selection problem occurs when subjects volunteer to participate in a program. Volunteers may differ significantly from nonvolunteers; they may be more compliant and eager to please, healthier or more outgoing.

Some of the difficulties that may prevent completion of a successful experiment may be anticipated and guarded against by using particular experimental designs and by adhering to the five basic characteristics of an ideal experiment. In other cases, however, a researcher cannot rule out all possible threats to internal validity. Nevertheless, experimental research designs are better able to resist threats to internal validity than are other types of research designs.

External Validity

External validity refers to the representativeness of research findings and their "generalizability," that is, whether it is possible to generalize from them to other situations. One possible problem is that the same effects may not be found using a different population. For example, findings from an experiment investigating the effects of live television coverage on legislators' behavior in state legislatures with fewer than one hundred members may not be generalizable to larger state legislative bodies or to Congress. In general, if a study population is not representative of a larger population, the ability to generalize about the larger population will be limited.

Another question is whether slightly different experimental treatments will result in similar findings with small differences or in findings that are fundamentally different. For example, a small increase in city spending for neighborhood improvements may not result in a more positive attitude of residents toward their neighborhood or the city. A slightly larger increase, however, may have an effect, perhaps because it has resulted in more noticeable improvements.

Threats to the external validity of an experiment also may be caused if the artificiality of the experimental setting or treatments makes it hard to generalize about findings in more natural settings. For example, some experiments on the effects of televised campaign advertising have used fictitious candidates. Because these studies cannot examine relationships between voters' existing information and preferences concerning candidates, it is difficult to generalize their findings to real-world campaigns. Subjects may also react to a stimulus differently when they know they are being studied than when they are in a natural setting.

Despite these problems with experimental research designs, experiments are still attractive to researchers because they provide control over the subjects and their exposure to various levels of the independent variable.[5] The purpose of an experiment is to isolate and measure the effects of the independent variable or variables. Researchers want to be able separate the effect of the independent variables from the effect of other factors that might also influence the dependent variable. Control over the assignment of subjects to experimental and control groups by researchers is a key feature of experiments because it helps them to "exclude," rule out, or control for the effects of other factors.

Control over Assignment of Subjects

The way researchers actually assign subjects to control and experimental groups is important. The most common way is known as **assignment at random**, where the researcher assigns subjects to the groups at random under the assumption that extraneous factors will affect all groups equally. Random assignment is the practical choice when the researcher is not able to specify possible extraneous factors in advance or when there are so many that it is not possible to assign subjects to experimental and control groups in a manner that ensures the equal distribution of extraneous factors.

Even if a researcher assigns subjects at random, extraneous factors may not be randomly distributed and therefore will affect the outcome of the experiment. This is especially true if the number of subjects is small. Prudent researchers do not assume that all significant factors are randomly distributed just because subjects have been assigned at random. In addition to random assignment, researchers often use a pre-test to check to see if the control and experimental groups are, in fact, equivalent with regard to those factors that are suspected of influencing the dependent variable.

If the researcher knows ahead of time that certain factors are related to differences in the dependent variable, he or she can use **precision matching** to control for extraneous factors. This requires the researcher to match pairs of subjects who are as similar as possible and assign one to the experimental group and the other to the control group. Thus the researcher does not take the chance that random assignment will equalize the groups with respect to these factors. One problem with this method is that when there are many factors to be controlled, it becomes difficult to match subjects on all relevant characteristics and a larger pool of prospective subjects is required. A second problem is that not all extraneous factors may be known by the researcher ahead of time. To guard against bias in the assignment of pairs, members of the matched pairs should be randomly assigned to the control and experimental groups.

One of the biggest obstacles to experimentation in social science research is the inability of researchers to control assignment of subjects to experimental and control groups. This is especially true when public policies are involved. Even though the point of conducting an experiment is to test whether a treatment or program has a beneficial effect, it is often politically difficult to assign subjects to a control group; people assume that the experimental treatment must be beneficial—otherwise the treatment or program would not have been proposed as a response to a public policy problem. In setting up experimental and control groups, social scientists generally lack sufficient authority or incentives to offer subjects.

Experimental Designs

Now that we have discussed experimental research in general and some problems associated with it, let us consider some specific experimental research designs. Each one represents a different attempt by the researcher to retain experimental control while also dealing with the various threats to internal and external validity. Students may not have the immediate opportunity to employ these research designs, but knowledge of them will help in evaluating research and in determining whether the research design employed by a researcher supports the conclusions that are reached.

Simple Post-test Design

The simplest of the experimental designs, the **simple post-test design,** involves two groups and two variables, one independent and one dependent. Subjects are assigned to one or the other of the two groups. One group, the experimental group, is exposed to a treatment or stimulus that represents the independent variable. The other group, the control group, is not or it is given a placebo. Then the dependent variable is measured for each group. This design may be diagrammed as follows:

(Random Assignment)	*Treatment*	*Post-treatment Measurement of Dependent Variable*
Experimental Group	Yes	Yes
Control Group	No	Yes

A researcher using this design can make causal inferences because he or she can make sure that the treatment occurred prior to measurement of the dependent variable. Furthermore, the researcher can argue that any difference between the two groups on the measure of the dependent variable may be attributed to the difference in the treatment—in other words, to the introduction of the independent variable—between the groups. This design requires random assignment of subjects to the experimental and control groups, and therefore assumes that extraneous factors have been controlled (that is, were the same for both groups). It also assumes that prior to the application of the experimental stimulus, both groups were equivalent with respect to the dependent variable.

A simple example will illustrate this design. Suppose we wanted to test the hypothesis that watching a national nominating convention on television makes people better informed politically. Using this research design, we would take our subjects, randomly assign them to a group that will watch a convention or a group that will not, and measure how well informed the members of the two groups are after the convention is over. Any difference in the level of awareness between the two groups after the convention would be attributed to the impact of watching convention coverage.

The simple post-test experimental design assumes that the random assignment of subjects to the experimental and control groups creates two groups that are equivalent in all significant ways prior to the introduction of the experimental stimulus. If the assignment to experimental or control groups is truly random, and the size of the two groups is large, this is ordinarily a safe assumption. However, if the assignment to groups is not truly random and/or the sample size is small, then post-treatment differences between the two groups may be the result of pre-treatment differences and not the result of the independent variable. Since it is impossible with this design to tell how much of the post-treatment difference is simply a reflection of pre-treatment differences, a second experimental research design is sometimes used.

Pre-test/Post-test Design

Unlike the simplest experimental design, the **classic experimental design** provides for a measurement of the dependent variable both before and after the experimental stimulus is introduced. This design may be diagrammed as follows:

(Random Assignment)	Pre-treatment Measurement of Dependent Variable	Treatment	Post-treatment Measurement of Dependent Variable
Experimental Group	Yes	Yes	Yes
Control Group	Yes	No	Yes

In this design it is possible to determine whether the experimental and control groups are equivalent with respect to the dependent variable prior to the experimental treatment. The extra measurement of the dependent variable before the experimental stimulus strengthens the internal validity of the experiment by removing the possibility that the groups might not have been equivalent despite random assignment of subjects to groups. Furthermore, any pre-test difference between control and experimental groups can be taken into account when calculating the effect of the experimental stimulus.

For example, let's assume that a researcher wants to test the effect of a presidential candidate's televised campaign commercials on the ability of voters to identify important issues in a campaign. In a post-test-only experimental design, subjects would be randomly assigned to experimental and control groups, and one group of subjects would be shown the commercials while the other group would not. After the experimental group had seen the commercials, a test measuring ability to identify campaign issues would be given to subjects in both groups. Suppose the average score on this test was 9.5 for the experimental group and 7.5 for the control group. The effect of having seen the campaign commercials would seem to be the difference in the two scores (2).

Now suppose a pre-test of issue awareness had also been given to both groups. The experimental group might have had a mean pre-test score of 8 and the control group a mean score of 7.5. In this case the presence of a pre-test would reveal to the researcher that the random assignment to the two groups did not create perfectly equivalent groups. Furthermore, the researcher would then realize that the gain in awareness for the experimental group was 1.5 (9.5 – 8), while the gain in awareness for the control group was 0 (7.5 – 7.5). Hence the researcher could conclude that the effect of seeing the ads translated into a 1.5-point change on the average score of the experimental group, not 2 points as measured in the simple post-test only design.

Pre-test, post-test designs with a control group have another advantage as well. Sometimes a considerable amount of time elapses between the pre-test and the post-test. This increases the possibility that extraneous factors may intrude and cause the dependent variable to change. Historical events or maturation processes may take place, for example. If it can be assumed that extraneous factors affect control and experimental groups equally, then the effect of extraneous factors is measured by the change in the dependent variable for the control group. Therefore, change in the dependent variable due only to the experimental stimulus can be calculated as follows:

$$\text{Experimental effect} = \left(\begin{array}{cc} \text{Post-test} & \text{Pre-test} \\ \text{score for} & \text{score for} \\ \text{experimental} & \text{experimental} \\ \text{group} & \text{group} \end{array} \right) - \left(\begin{array}{cc} \text{Post-test} & \text{Pre-test} \\ \text{score for} & \text{score for} \\ \text{control} & \text{control} \\ \text{group} & \text{group} \end{array} \right) \quad (5.1)$$

Now assume for a moment that the post-test score for the control group was 8 instead of 7.5 (reflecting the possibility that the control group would increase its issue awareness over time during a campaign even though it did not watch any political commercials on television). The effect of seeing the campaign commercials would be only a one-point difference in awareness:

$$(9.5 - 8.0) - (8.0 - 7.5) = 1.$$

Although this classic experimental design allows researchers to assess the pre-treatment equivalence of the experimental and control groups, it, too, is vulnerable to a particular problem—namely, testing, or more specifically, **instrument reactivity**, in which the pre-test itself sensitizes or otherwise affects respondents and causes a change in the dependent variable for both control and experimental groups. For example, if you are in the control group, taking the pre-test may make you more attentive to information touched on in the test in the days and weeks that follow. To minimize the possibility of the pre-test having an enduring effect, researchers often allow a considerable amount of time to elapse between pre-test and post-test measurements. If the effect of the pre-test is equal for both control and experimental groups, any instrument reactivity caused by the pre-test would be factored out along with any other extraneous factors by Equation 5.1. The pre-test may sensitize both the control and experimental groups, but the effect may be greater for the experimental group. The pre-test may cause the experimental group to react differently to the treatment than it would have if there had been no pre-test. If the pre-test affects the experimental and control groups differently, the pre-test, post-test design does not permit precise measurement and adjustment for the effect of the pre-test.

In addition to instrument reactivity, you may be able to see the potential for another threat to internal validity of the experiment: instrument decay. Compared to the simple post-test design, there are more opportunities for instrument decay with the classical pre-test, post-test design because more measurements are taken. This is true as well for other designs involving multiple measurements of the dependent variable.[6]

A good example of utilization of the classic pre-test, post-test design may be found in a study of the impact of television news coverage on public policy agenda-setting.[7] Researchers Shanto Iyengar, Mark D. Peters, and Donald Kinder attempted to determine the extent to which exposure to televised network news coverage of particular public policy issues can increase the public's concern about those issues.

To test the effect of the hypothesized independent variable (exposure to television news), the researchers employed a classic experimental research design. First, they recruited participants for their experiments (paying each participant $20) and had them fill out a questionnaire that included measures of the importance of various national problems (the pre-test). The participants were then randomly divided into experimental and control groups and, over a four-day period, exposed to videotape recordings of the preceding evening's network newscast.

Unknown to the participants, these newscasts had been edited to include (or exclude) actual stories from previous newscasts dealing with a particular public policy issue. In one session the experimental group saw newscasts that included stories about alleged weaknesses in U.S. defense capability while the control group saw newscasts with no defense-related stories. In another session one experimental group again saw newscasts with stories about inadequacies in U.S. defense preparedness while a second experimental group saw stories about environmental pollution and a third experimental group saw stories about inflation. The day after the last viewing session participants completed a second questionnaire that again included measures of the importance of various policy issues. All groups except for one reported a significant increase in concern about an issue after they had been exposed to news stories about that issue. The exception involved concern about inflation. In that case, the level of concern about inflation was already so high (a score of 18.5 out of 20) that exposure to the newscasts about inflation did not show any appreciable effect.

The researchers conducting this experiment were sensitive to the measurement, instrument reactivity, and external validity issues discussed above. They believe that they achieved fairly natural viewing conditions (exposure to the news stories took place over several days, in small groups, in an informal setting, without any pressure to pay close attention), that the participants showed no signs of knowing what the experiment was about, and that the participants were fairly representative of a larger adult population. Consequently, they believe that their experimental results demonstrated that network news coverage can significantly alter the public's sense of the importance of different political issues.

One might argue that the second part of their experiment was not actually a classical experiment in that there was no control group, only three experimental groups using a pre-test, post-test design. The pre-test, post-test design allows the researcher to compare changes in groups receiving different treatments. Any differences in change may be attributed to differences in treatments. Without a control group, however, change between a pre-test and post-test does not absolutely establish the factors that caused the change. The researcher can never be sure what might have happened to subjects if no treatment had been given at all. Nevertheless, there may be good reasons for omitting a control group. Because the researchers had already conducted an experiment in which there was a control group and which demonstrated the impact of newscasts on issue concern, it was reasonable for them to omit a control group from their second experiment.

Time Series Design

The pre-test must come before the experimental treatment and the post-test must come afterward, but exactly how long before and how long afterward? Researchers seldom know for sure. Therefore, an experimental **times series design**, a research design that includes several pre-treatment and post-treatment measures, may be used when a researcher is uncertain exactly how quickly the effect of the independent variable should be observed or when the most reliable pre-test measurement of the dependent variable should be taken.

An example of an experimental time series design would be an attempt to test the relationship between watching a presidential debate and support for the candidates. Suppose we started out by conducting a classical experiment, randomly assigning some people to a group that watches a debate and others to a group that does not watch the debate. On the pre- and post-tests we might receive the following scores:

	Pre-debate Support for Candidate X	Treatment	Post-debate Support for Candidate X
Experimental Group	60	Yes	50
Control Group	55	No	50

These scores seem to indicate that the control group was slightly less supportive of Candidate X before the debate (that is, the random assignment did not work perfectly) and that the debate led to a decline in support for Candidate X of 5 percent $(60 - 50) - (55 - 50)$.

Suppose, however, that you had the following additional measures:

	Pre-test			Treatment	Post-test		
	First	Second	Third		First	Second	Third
Experimental Group	80	70	60	Yes	50	40	30
Control Group	65	60	55	No	50	45	40

It appears now that support for Candidate X eroded throughout the whole period for both the experimental and control groups and that the rate of decline was consistently more rapid for the experimental group (that is, the two groups were not equivalent prior to the debate). Viewed from this perspective, it seems that the debate had no effect on the experimental group since the rate of decline both before and after the debate was the same. Hence the existence of multiple measures of the dependent variable, both before and after the introduction of the independent variable, would lead in this case to a more accurate conclusion regarding the effects of the independent variable.

Multigroup Design

So far we have discussed mainly research involving one experimental and one control group, although in a previous example an experiment included three experimental groups rather than a single experimental and single control group. In a **multigroup design**, more experimental or control groups are added. This is useful if the independent variable can assume several values and if the researcher wants to see the possible effects of manipulating the independent variable in several different ways. Multigroup designs may involve a post-test only or both a pre-test and a post-test. They may also include time series component.

Suppose you were concerned with the problem of how to increase the proportion of respondents who fill out and return mail questionnaires. The proportion of respondents who return questionnaires in a mail survey is usually quite low. Consequently, investigators have attempted to increase response rates by including an incentive or token of appreciation inside the survey. Since these add to the cost of the survey, researchers like to know whether or not the incentives really do increase response rates and, if so, which ones are most effective and cost efficient.

To test the effect of various incentives, we could use a multigroup post-test design. If we wanted to test the effects of five treatments, we could randomly assign subjects to six groups. One group would receive no reward (the control group) while the other groups would each receive a different reward—for example, 25¢, 50¢, $1.00, a pen, or a key ring. Response rates (the post-treatment measure of the dependent variable) for the groups could then be compared. Table 5-1 presents a set of hypothetical results for such an experiment.

The response rates indicate that rewards increase response rates and that monetary incentives have more effect than do token gifts. Furthermore, it seems that the dollar incentive is not cost effective since it did not yield a sufficiently greater response rate than the 50¢ reward to warrant the additional expense. Other experiments of this type could be conducted to compare the effects of other aspects of mail questionnaires, such as the use of prepaid versus promised monetary rewards or the inclusion or exclusion of a pre-stamped return envelope.

An example of a multigroup time series design might consist of the following:

(Random Assignment)	Pre-test		Treatment	Post-test	
	First	Second		First	Second
Experimental Group 1	Yes	Yes	Yes	Yes	Yes
Experimental Group 2	Yes	Yes	Yes, but different	Yes	Yes
Control Group	Yes	Yes	No	Yes	Yes

One good reason to use this design is to establish pre-treatment trends in the dependent variable. Multiple measurements can be used to check for stability in the dependent variable for all groups prior to treatment. In addition, multiple measurements after treatment allow researchers to see if treatment effects are immediate or delayed and whether the effects are lasting. The issue of lasting effects is often an important one in the evaluation of programs in education, health, and criminal justice or of changes in public opinion. One drawback to this design, however, is that the possibility of instrument reactiv-

TABLE 5-1
Mail Survey Incentive Experiment

(Random Assignment)	Treatment	Response Rate (percent)
Experimental Group 1	25¢	45.0
Experimental Group 2	50¢	51.0
Experimental Group 3	$1.00	52.0
Experimental Group 4	pen	38.0
Experimental Group 5	key ring	37.0
Control Group	no reward	30.2

Note: Hypothetical data.

ity becomes greater when there are multiple measurements of the dependent variable.

Factorial Design

In experiments where researchers are interested in determining the effects of several independent variables on a dependent variable, alone and in combination, a **factorial design** is used. The simplest factorial design is the 2×2 design. In this design there are two independent variables, each of which takes on two values. However, factorial designs may involve more than two dimensions, and an independent variable may have any number of values or levels.

An example of a 2×2 factorial design is an experiment to test the effectiveness of token gifts and follow-up reminders alone and in combination on the response rate in a mail survey. Suppose that four hundred respondents were randomly assigned in equal numbers to the four treatment groups shown in Table 5-2.

To examine the effect of each independent variable singly, observe the percentages at the bottom and along the side of the table. There is a 12.5 percentage point (52.5 percent – 40 percent) increase in response rates when a token gift is included with the mail survey. Similarly, there is a 17.5 percent (55.0 percent – 37.5 percent) improvement in the response rate when a follow-up reminder is offered. Therefore, each independent variable (token gift, follow-up reminder) has a positive effect on the dependent variable (response rate) and the effect of the follow-up reminder is somewhat larger than the effect of the token gift. In addition, the measures within the four cells of the table indicate the combined effect of the two independent variables on response rate. When neither a follow-up reminder nor a token gift is employed, the response rate is 30 percent; when both are used the response rate improves to 60 percent. We can also see that the effect of the follow-up reminder

TABLE 5-2
Response Rates in Mail Survey Experiment

	No Gift		Token Gift			
No Follow Up	30.0%	(30/100)	45.0%	(45/100)	37.5%	(75/200)
Follow Up	50.0%	(50/100)	60.0%	(60/100)	55.0%	(110/200)
	40.0%	(80/200)	52.5%	(105/200)		

is greater when no token gift is used, and the effect of the token gift is greater when no follow-up reminder is used. This research design, then, yields considerable information about the effects of these two independent variables, both separately and in combination.

Solomon Four-Group Design

Earlier we discussed the problem of instrument reactivity caused by using a pre-test. A more complex pattern of reactivity, however, may also occur: the pre-test and test stimulus may interact to cause additional change in the dependent variable beyond the effects attributable to the pre-test and the test stimulus individually.

Consider this example. An experiment is designed to test the effect of a film about water use and supplies on attitudes about water conservation. Subjects are assigned at random to two groups. Both groups are given a pre-test asking them about their attitudes about water conservation. Then the test group, but not the control group, is shown the film. Sometime later both groups are retested on their attitudes toward water conservation. It is possible that the control group will show a change in attitudes if the pre-test made the subjects more aware of water conservation issues. Suppose the experimental group showed a much larger change. The difference between the control and test groups could be due to the effect of the film, but it also could be due to the combined effect of the pre-test and the film. The combination might create a much greater effect than simply the sum of the effect of the pre-test alone and the effect of the film alone. The experimental group may have watched the film differently and responded to it differently than it would have if it had not been given the pre-test. (Perhaps it is easier to understand the concept of measurement interaction by recalling how you may have felt after consuming a little too much pizza *or* beer. Now how would you have felt if you had had too much pizza *and* beer at the same sitting?)

The **Solomon four-group design** is an experimental design that allows a researcher to measure the interaction between a pre-test and an experimental treatment. The effect of the treatment, the effect of the pre-test on the post-test, and the effect of other extraneous factors can be measured as well.[8] Thus, unlike the two-group pre-test, post-test design, the Solomon four-group design permits the researcher to isolate extraneous factors from pre-test factors.

In this design one group is given the pre-test, test stimulus, and post-test. A second group is given the test stimulus and post-test, but no pre-test. A third group is given a pre-test and post-test, but no experimental stimulus. A fourth group is given only the post-test. The design can be represented as follows:

(Random Assignment)	Pre-test	Treatment	Post-test
Experimental Group 1	Yes	Yes	Yes
Experimental Group 2	No	Yes	Yes
Control Group 1	Yes	No	Yes
Control Group 2	No	No	Yes

The total change in the first experimental group can be summarized as:

$$\text{Change} = \text{Pre-test effect} + \text{treatment effect} + \text{interaction effect} + \text{effect due to other factors} \qquad (5.2)$$

Table 5-3 presents the hypothetical results of this four-group experiment. Total change in Experimental Group 1 equals 10 (20 – 10). The pre-test effect is determined by comparing the post-test scores of the two control groups, one of which had a pre-test. Subtracting the post-test of Control Group 2 from that of Control Group 1, we get (12 – 11) for a pre-test only effect of one. The treatment effect can be determined by comparing Experimental Group 2, which received no pre-test and saw only the film, and Control Group 2, which received no pre-test and did not see the film. The treatment effect equals 4 (15 – 11). To calculate the effect of other factors only, we need to compare the post-test score for Control Group 2 with the pre-test scores of the groups given a pre-test. Since subjects were assigned at random to all four groups, we can assume that the pre-test score of Control Group 2 is the average of the

TABLE 5-3
Hypothetical Water Conservation Experiment

(Random Assignment)	Pre-test	Treatment	Post-test
Experimental Group 1	10	Yes	20
Experimental Group 2		Yes	15
Control Group 1	10	No	12
Control Group 2	(Assumed to be 10)	No	11

pre-test scores of the two pre-tested groups, or 10. Thus, the effect of other factors affecting the dependent variable is 1 (11 − 10).

Substituting these numbers into Equation 5.2 and rearranging the terms to solve for the interaction effect, we find that 4 points out of the 10-point change were due to the interaction between the pre-test and the test stimulus.

$$10 = 1 + 4 + \text{interaction effect} + 1$$
$$\text{Interaction effect} = 10 - 1 - 4 - 1 = 4$$

The six experimental research designs discussed above appear here in order of increased complexity and are far more sophisticated than the experimental designs typically used in political science research. However, they illustrate the logic of making observations that may be used to evaluate hypotheses and the importance of striving for both internal and external validity in a research design. In addition to the experimental designs described here, there are many others that have been developed and employed in social scientific research. The Suggested Readings at the end of this chapter include a number of references to other types of experimental designs.

The New Jersey Income-Maintenance Field Experiment

Field experiments are experimental designs applied in a natural setting. As in any experimental research design, researchers try to control the selection of subjects, their assignment to treatment groups, and the manipulation of the independent variable. But in the field experiment the behaviors of interest are observed in a natural setting, increasing the likelihood that extraneous factors such as historical events will intrude and affect experimental results. While it is possible to choose a natural setting that is isolated in some respects (and thereby approximates a controlled environment), in general the researcher can only hope that the environment remains unchanged during the course of his or her experiment.

Field experiments should not be considered inferior to laboratory experiments. The artificial environment of a laboratory or controlled setting may seriously affect the external validity of an experiment. Something that can be demonstrated in a laboratory may have limited applicability in the real world. Therefore, a program or treatment that is effective in a controlled setting may be ineffective in a natural setting. Field experiments are likelier to produce results that reflect the real-world impact of a program or treatment than are researchers' controlled experimental manipulations.

An interesting example of a field experiment in political science was the New Jersey experiment in income maintenance funded by the Office of Economic Opportunity and conducted from 1967 to 1971.[9] This effort was the forerunner of other large-scale social experiments designed to test the effects of new social programs. The experiment is a good illustration of the difficulty of testing the effects of public policies on a large scale in a natural setting.

At the time of the experiment, dissatisfaction with the existing welfare system was high because of its cost and because it was thought to discourage the poor from lifting themselves out of poverty. The system was also blamed for discouraging marriage and breaking up families. Families headed by able-bodied men generally were excluded from welfare programs, and welfare recipients' earned income was taxed at such a rate that many thought there was little incentive for recipients to work.

In 1965 a negative income tax was proposed that provided a minimum, non-taxable allowance to all families and that attempted to maintain work incentives by allowing the poor to keep a significant fraction of their earnings. For example, a family of four might be guaranteed an income of $5,000 and be allowed to keep 50 percent of all its earnings up to a break-even point, where it could choose to remain in the program or opt out. If the break-even income was $10,000, a family earning $10,000 could receive a $5,000 guaranteed minimum plus half of $10,000 ($5,000) for a total of $10,000, or it could keep all of the $10,000 earned and choose not to receive any income from the government. Critics of the proposed program argued that a guaranteed minimum income would encourage people to reduce their work effort. Others expressed concern about how families would use their cash allowances. Numerous questions about the administration of the program were raised as well. Because of these uncertainties, researchers designed the New Jersey income-maintenance experiment to test the consequences of a guaranteed minimum income system with actual recipients in a natural setting.

The experimental design included two experimental factors. One was the income guarantee level, expressed as a percentage of the poverty line. The level is the amount of money a family received if other income was zero. The other factor was the rate at which each dollar of earned income was taxed.

Table 5-4 shows the experimental conditions of the two independent variables of interest to the researchers. Policy analysts were originally interested in income guarantee levels of 50, 75, 100, and 125 percent of the poverty level and tax rates of 30, 50, and 70 percent. The 4×3 factorial design displayed in Table 5-4 would allow researchers to examine the effect of the variation in one factor while the other was held constant and to measure the effects of different combinations of the independent variables. For example, it would allow researchers to examine the effect of varying the tax rate from 30 to 50 to 70 percent while the guarantee remained set at 75 percent of the poverty line.

Certain theoretical combinations of the experimental conditions were not chosen for study because they were unrealistic policy options or because they increased the cost of the study. Therefore, actual income-maintenance results were investigated for only eight of the twelve possible experimental condi-

TABLE 5-4

Experimental Design of New Jersey Income-Maintenance Experiment

Guarantee (percentage of poverty line)	Tax Rate		
	30%	50%	70%
125		X	
100		X	X
75	X	X	X
50	X	X	

Note: X represents experimental conditions actually tested.

tions, and families participating in the study were assigned to one of those eight conditions. In assigning families to cells representing experimental treatments, there was a trade-off between the number of families that could be included in the study and the number of families assigned to each cell since some cells were more costly than others. The cells representing the most likely national policy options (the 100–50 and 75–50 plans) were assigned more families to make sure that enough families completed the experiment. Finally, for some of the less generous treatments, the researchers experienced difficulty in finding eligible families willing to participate in the experiment. Families placed in these cells were likely to receive at most a small payment because they were near the break-even point. This situation created resentment within the community because all of the families participating in the program had hoped to gain benefits beyond the nominal payment they could expect each time they completed an income report. If the researchers had had complete control over their subjects, assignment problems would have been fewer. But in research involving human subjects, such control is understandably lacking.

Only families headed by able-bodied males were eligible for the experiment because of the great interest in the possible impact of the program on the work effort of poor families. Information about the work behavior of females with dependent children was not considered a good indicator of the work response of able-bodied males to public assistance. Very little was known about the work response of males because, as a group, able-bodied men and their families were generally not entitled to public assistance.

In the rest of this section we will explore some of the issues and problems faced by the researchers during the course of this field experiment and discuss its outcome.

Generalizability. To limit possible extraneous factors, families were originally chosen from a fairly homogeneous setting—New Jersey. Because a nationally dispersed sample was not chosen, however, the ability to generalize findings to a national program was limited. Generalizability was also affected by the three-year duration of the experiment. Families knew that the program was not permanent, and this may have affected their behavior.

Instrumentation Difficulties. The experiment also encountered problems with income measurement. Participants were asked to report their gross income, but families had trouble distinguishing between net and gross income. Families in the experimental groups learned more quickly how to fill out the reports correctly than did control group families because the experimental group families were asked to report income every month. Control group families (that is, other low-income families) were asked to report income only every three months. As a result, the accuracy of income data changed over time and differentially for experimental and control group families. This one month–three month difference arose because researchers were afraid that too much contact with control families would change their behavior (instrument reactivity) and make them less than true controls. This is an example of the trade-offs that researchers must make to avoid the numerous threats to the validity of experiments.

Uncontrolled Environment. In field experiments, unlike in laboratory experiments, researchers are not in complete control of subjects' environments. This was dramatically illustrated during the New Jersey income-maintenance experiment. In the middle of the experiment, New Jersey adopted AFDC-UP, a public assistance program. Eligible families included those with dependent children and an unemployed parent, male or female. One reason that New Jersey had been chosen as an appropriate location for the income-maintenance experiment in the first place was precisely because it did not offer AFDC-UP. When it became available, however, AFDC-UP provided an attractive alternative to some of the experimental cell conditions, and thus many families dropped out of the experiment.

Another problem arose because there were not enough eligible families in the New Jersey communities that were chosen to provide sufficient ethnic diversity. As a consequence, an urban area in northeastern Pennsylvania was included. However, the families in that area faced different conditions than the New Jersey families and varied on some important characteristics such as home ownership. One purpose of the study was to examine whether ethnic groups responded differently to the income-maintenance program. Because whites were represented mostly from one site, it became difficult to separate ethnic differences from site-induced differences.

Ethical Issues. Even though participation in the program was voluntary, the researchers were concerned about the effect of termination of the experiment on families that had been receiving payments. At the start of the experiment, families were given a card with the termination date of payments printed on it. Researchers debated tapering off payments and providing families with reminders as the end of the experiment approached. They decided to remind the families once toward the end, and research field offices remained open as referral agencies in case families needed help. But none requested help. Answers to a questionnaire three months after the last payment indicated that the experiment caused no serious adverse effects on the families that had participated.

Major Findings. Among white male heads of families receiving negative income tax payments, there was only a 5- to 6-percent reduction in average hours worked. For black male heads of families the average hours worked increased, although not significantly. For Spanish-speaking male heads of families the average hours worked decreased, but also not significantly. Researchers were unable to explain this unexpected finding, and therefore it may be unreliable. The behavior of black working wives was not affected, while Spanish-speaking and white working wives reduced their work effort considerably. Experimental families made larger investments in housing and durable goods than control families. There was also an indication that experimental families experienced increased educational attainment.

Because of the many difficulties discussed above, the income-maintenance experiment failed to provide accurate cost estimates for alternative negative income tax plans or clear findings on the work disincentive of various tax rates. Because of these shortcomings, the experiment was not able to provide conclusive evidence in favor of or against a negative income tax plan.

The New Jersey income-maintenance experiment is a good example of the difficulty of studying a significant political phenomenon both experimentally and in a natural setting. The researchers who conducted this experiment developed plausible, significant, and testable hypotheses and employed an imaginative research design to test those hypotheses. They identified the most interesting experimental treatments, attempted to assign their subjects to those treatments to accomplish pre-treatment equivalence, and conducted their experiment over a fairly lengthy period of time and in a natural setting to increase the external validity of their findings. Still, their efforts to isolate the effects of the independent variables in question were stymied by the real-world behavior of their subjects and their inability to control completely both the experimental treatment and the environment in which it was operating. Researchers with fewer resources and even less control over both their subjects and the introduction of experimental treatments find it even more difficult to conduct meaningful experimental inquiries.

We have spent a considerable amount of time describing a number of experimental research designs to illustrate how experimental designs can help researchers draw appropriate conclusions about the effects of independent variables. Experimental designs are potentially useful because they allow researchers to isolate the effects of independent variables by controlling the assignment of subjects to experimental treatments, the introduction of the experimental stimulus itself, and the presence of extraneous influences. As a result, well-conducted experiments permit the evaluation of research hypotheses and the accumulation of causal knowledge.

Unfortunately, many of the sorts of hypotheses and behavioral phenomena of interest to political scientists do not lend themselves to the use of experimental research designs. Political scientists are limited by their inability to control completely the variables or the subjects of interest. Suppose, for example, that a researcher wanted to test the hypothesis that poverty causes people to commit robberies. Following the logic of experimental research, the researcher would have to randomly assign people to two groups, measure the number of robberies committed by members of the two groups prior to the experimental treatment, force the experimental group to become poor, and then remeasure the number of robberies committed at some later date. Clearly, no researcher would be permitted to have this much control over a subject's life. While the logic of experimental research designs is compelling, many researchers interested in explaining significant political phenomena have had to develop and employ other research designs.

Nonexperimental Designs

Political scientists have developed a number of nonexperimental research designs that are more practical. A **nonexperimental design** is characterized by at least one of the following: presence of a single group, lack of researcher control over the assignment of subjects to control and experimental groups, lack of researcher control over the application of the independent variable, or inability of researcher to measure the dependent variable before and after exposure to the independent variable occurs. A few of these designs are described in the remainder of this chapter. In reviewing them, we will compare their features to the five characteristics of ideal experiments mentioned earlier.

Time Series Design

Nonexperimental time series designs are charcterized by the availability of measures of the dependent variable both before and after the introduction of the independent variable. The researcher does not control the introduction of the independent variable and usually must rely on the data collection of others to measure the dependent variable rather than personally conducting the measurements. Nonexperimental time series designs are often used by political scientists, as evidenced by several of the examples discussed in Chapter 1.

Steven Poe and C. Neal Tate measured over time a number of factors such as population and economic growth, international and civil war participation, democratic practices, and regime type to see if changes in these factors led to changes in the incidence of human rights abuses. Ross Burkhart and Michael Lewis-Beck looked at the impact of economic development on democracy in nations over time. Thomas Hartley and Bruce Russet investigated the relationship between public opinion and military spending in the United States over a period of twenty-five years. B. Dan Wood and Richard Waterman's study concerned whether agency outputs changed in response to attempts by Congress and presidents to control agency behaviors.

In one version of a nonexperimental time series design, numerous measurements of the dependent variable are taken both before and after the introduction of the independent variable. The premeasurements allow a researcher to establish trends in the dependent variable that are presumably unaffected by the independent variable so that appropriate conclusions can be drawn about post-treatment measures. These trends may be linear (either increasing or decreasing) or curvilinear, as illustrated in Figure 5-1. After the pre-test trends are established, the researcher then makes several more measurements of the dependent variable after the independent variable has occurred. A change in direction of the measures of the dependent variable away from the existing trend may indicate that the independent variable has had an effect. (In Figure 5-1 such an effect is presumably present in examples B and C, but not in A.) This assumes that nothing else changed that might have affected the dependent variable and that the trend would have continued undisturbed if not for the independent variable.

Time series designs work best when the independent variable occurs at a particular moment or during a fairly brief period of time, affects a dependent variable that is routinely measured, or is known about in advance so that appropriate pre-test measurements can be made. Consequently, this design would work well if we wished to evaluate the impact of a new program or policy initiative. For example, we might try to evaluate the impact of sobriety checks on alcohol-related traffic accidents in states by examining the number of such accidents for several years before and after the introduction of the checks. If we observed a decline in accidents we might conclude that sobriety checks have been effective; however, whether the decline is attributable to the checks alone, or even at all, would remain unclear. Some other factor may have caused the decline in accidents.

One problem with the time series design example just described is that there is no control group with which to compare the unit or units of analysis that experienced the independent variable. This problem was addressed by Robert Fording in his review of research relating to welfare and civil unrest. Fording noted that several previous studies had used time series analysis to examine variation in national measures of social welfare programs in response to rioting. These studies found that welfare programs expanded one

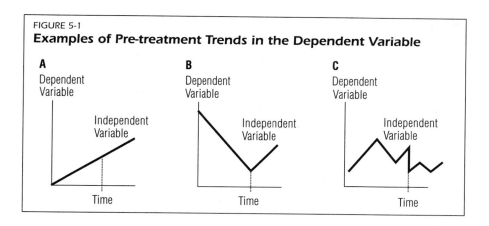

FIGURE 5-1
Examples of Pre-treatment Trends in the Dependent Variable

to two years after an increase in the number of riots. But, measurements were made on only one group (the nation) over time. Without a control group for comparison, it is impossible to rule out that time or some other factor was responsible for the expansion of welfare programs in the United States. As a result, Fording decided to look at the relationship between rioting and welfare rolls at the state level.

The results of a time series can often be improved if the researcher can identify quasi-experimental and quasi-control groups and produce a time series of measurements of the dependent variable for each. In this way the researcher can have more confidence that the observed shift in the dependent variable is the result of the introduction or presence of the independent variable. We use the word "quasi" to indicate that the researcher does not control the assignment to the experimental or control groups.

For example, some states may adopt health insurance programs for children while others do not. Researchers can compare children's health trends in both types of states using regularly collected indicators of children's health to determine whether or not the health of children in the states with insurance programs has improved relative to the health of those in states without the programs. Even though the researcher controls neither the assignment of states to the groups with or without the program nor the content or implementation of the programs, this situation is often referred to as a "natural" experiment because of the presence of before and after measurements for both quasi-experimental and quasi-control groups.

As another example, suppose that we are interested in whether or not an aggressive media campaign organized by the White House has an effect on popular support for a public policy initiative, such as mandatory, comprehensive health care coverage. We might first obtain a series of public opinion polls measuring popular support for mandatory coverage. Using a measure of overall media exposure, we could then separate the respondents into two groups: those most likely to be exposed to the media campaign and those least likely to be exposed to the media campaign. By continuing the time series of popular support for health care during and after the media campaign and comparing the entire series for the quasi-experimental and quasi-control groups, we could assess the influence of the White House's media campaign on popular support for the comprehensive health care initiative.

Figure 5-2 shows the hypothetical results of such a time-series-with-quasi-control-group design. We can see that before the introduction of the independent variable the less-exposed (quasi-control) group was more supportive of mandatory health care coverage, and that there was already in place a positive trend among the less-exposed group and a negative trend among the more-exposed group. (This could be because the less-exposed group was more Democratic and less affluent than the more-exposed group, and that both groups were already responding to Washington and interest group rhetoric before the White House campaign began.) During the White House media campaign the downward trend in support in the quasi-experimental group was reversed, and by the end of the campaign the most-exposed group was just as supportive of mandatory health care coverage as the less-exposed group. After the White House media campaign concluded, the level of support among the most-exposed group began to decline again while the level of support in the less-exposed group remained fairly constant. This is strong evidence that the White House media campaign had an effect.

Sometimes a time series analysis consists not only of measures of the dependent variable over an extended period of time, but also of measures of the independent variable over a similar period. The challenge here is to look for patterns in both series of measurements that suggest the independent and dependent variables are related.

A good example of such a study is a recent test of the hypothesis that changes in public opinion affect changes in the character of Supreme Court decisions over time.[10] Researchers William Mishler and Reginald Sheehan developed a measure of the overall ideological tenor of Court decisions (the dependent variable) for each year from 1956 through 1989. They then supplemented that time series with a similar series of measures of the ideological mood of the public each year, as derived from a number of public opinion polls. Figure 5-3 shows the results of these two time series over this thirty-three-year period.

Although there appear to be similar trends in these two time series, there are many additional questions to be answered about the time lag between the two variables; the alternate manners in which opinion can influence judicial decisions; and the possibility that other factors, such as the political composi-

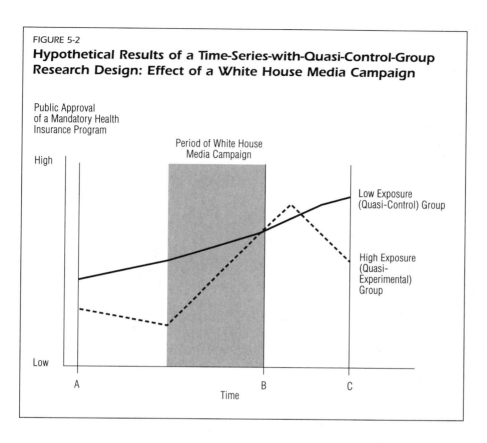

FIGURE 5-2

Hypothetical Results of a Time-Series-with-Quasi-Control-Group Research Design: Effect of a White House Media Campaign

Public Approval
of a Mandatory Health
Insurance Program

High

Period of White House
Media Campaign

Low Exposure
(Quasi-Control) Group

High Exposure
(Quasi-
Experimental)
Group

Low

A

B

C

Time

tion of the Congress and the ideology of the president, could also influence the ideological nature of Court decisions. All of these questions are explored by Mishler and Sheehan through modifications in their time series design.

Time series studies may be affected by numerous threats to internal validity. For example, instrument change may affect the measurement of the dependent variable over time. This may be a problem if the researcher has relied on existing data collected by others. For example, city crime rates may be compared for several years before and after a change in the way crime statistics are collected has been made. Achievement scores of school children may be assessed before and after a change in the school's reading program has been made. City budgets may be examined before and after a reorganization of city departments. In these instances, the researcher's conclusions may be jeopardized by the different ways of recording crimes, by the affect of the new reading program on achievement tests, or by different city accounting methods. The longer the time period under study, the more likely that instrument change has occurred.

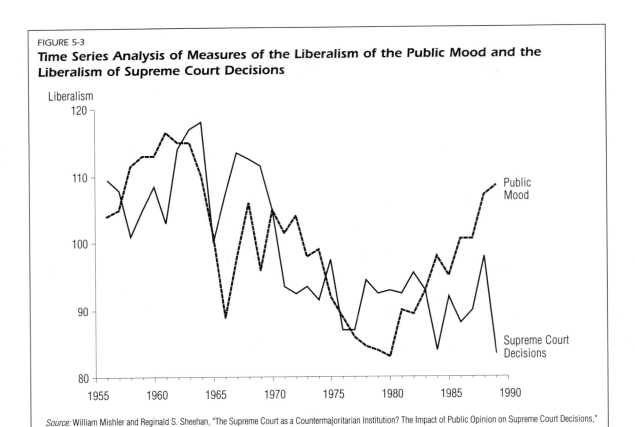

FIGURE 5-3

Time Series Analysis of Measures of the Liberalism of the Public Mood and the Liberalism of Supreme Court Decisions

Source: William Mishler and Reginald S. Sheehan, "The Supreme Court as a Countermajoritarian Institution? The Impact of Public Opinion on Supreme Court Decisions," *American Political Science Review* 87:1 (March 1993): 91. Reprinted with permission.

Cross-sectional Design

A nonexperimental research design frequently used by political scientists is the cross-sectional research design. In a **cross-sectional design**, measurements of the independent and dependent variables are taken at the same point in time, and the researcher does not have any control over the introduction of the independent variable, the assignment of subjects to treatment or control groups, or the conditions under which the independent variable is experienced. Instead, the measurements of the independent variable are used to construct, with the help of statistical methods, post-treatment quasi-experimental and quasi-control groups that have naturally occurred, and the measurements of the dependent variable are used to assess the differences between the quasi-experimental and quasi-control groups. Data analysis, rather than experimental manipulation, is then used to draw conclusions about the effect of the independent variable.

While this research design makes it far more difficult to measure the effect that can be attributed to the presence or introduction of independent variables (treatments) and to draw conclusions about causal relationships, it has the virtues of allowing observation of phenomena in more natural, realistic settings; increasing the size and representativeness of the populations studied; and allowing the testing of hypotheses that do not lend themselves to experimental manipulation. In short, cross-sectional research designs improve external validity at the expense of internal validity.

For example, to test the hypothesis "those with more formal education earn more income" using a cross-sectional design, we could survey a random sample of adults, ask them questions about their income and educational attainment, and divide them into groups based on their differing levels of formal education. In this way we can observe the quasi-control group (those with no formal education) and the quasi-experimental group (all others). (Notice that we did not control who would be in each group by forcing people to have differing amounts of formal education. The groups were simply naturally occurring and observed.) We could then measure and contrast the income levels of each of these groups to assess the impact of education on income.

If the incomes of those with greater educational attainment were higher than those with less education, we would have accumulated evidence that education and income are related. Because of our research design, however, and our inability to ensure that those with less and those with more education are alike in every other way, we could not necessarily conclude that education determines income. There may be other ways in which those with less and those with more education are different (gender, age, race, geographical location, for example) that also have an effect on income. With a cross-sectional design, we typically employ data analysis techniques to control for variables that may affect both the independent and dependent variables.

The cross-sectional design is frequently used in survey research (see Chapter 10). In a study of attitudes toward busing, for example, researchers used survey data to measure the dependent variable (support for busing) and the independent variables (racial intolerance, political conservatism, and self-interest in the busing issue—that is, whether or not the respondent had a child in school) at the same point in time.[11] They divided people into groups based on the measures of the independent variables and then observed the amount of the dependent variable in each of the groups. They found that measures of racial intolerance and political conservatism were inversely correlated with support for busing while measures of self-interest and support for busing were not related.

This study and others of the same type have several limitations. Because all measures were taken at one point in time, the researchers could not be certain that racial intolerance or political conservatism preceded attitudes toward busing. Therefore, they could not assert that racial intolerance caused attitudes toward busing, even though there was a strong relationship between the two. The respondents' attitudes toward busing, after all, may have been formed before their development of racial intolerance. Furthermore, since the subjects were not randomly assigned to treatment groups, any differences between treatment groups may have resulted from factors other than the independent variables under consideration.

Because of the limitations of the cross-sectional design—that is, lack of control over exposure to the independent variable and inability to form pure experimental and control groups—researchers have to rely on data analysis techniques to isolate the impact of the independent variables of interest. They attempt to remove the effects of other factors by controlling for them statistically. This process requires researchers to make their comparison groups equivalent by holding relevant extraneous factors constant and then observing the relationship between independent and dependent variables (we will describe this process more fully in Chapter 13). Yet holding these factors constant is problematic since it is very difficult to be sure that all relevant variables have been controlled for.

Edward Tufte's use of a cross-sectional design in his study of whether compulsory automobile safety inspection programs help reduce traffic fatalities is a good example of an attempt to control for variables that might disguise the effect of an independent variable.[12] The hypothesis Tufte tested was that "states with inspection programs have fewer automobile deaths than states without inspection programs." Tufte measured the relevant variables at the same time, even though he used the average of auto fatality rates in three years as the dependent variable. The average number of traffic fatalities per 100,000 people for states with mandatory inspections was 26.1. For states without inspections it was 31.9.

Given Tufte's data, would we be safe in concluding that inspection programs caused the lower death rate? Possibly, but there are some problems with this conclusion. First, since the study lacks a pre-test of the dependent variable, it may be that there has always been a difference in the auto death rates of these two groups of states and that the existence or absence of state inspections is irrelevant. Even before adopting inspection programs, some states may have had very low death rates for reasons that have nothing to do with car inspections. Second, because Tufte did not control the assignment of the states to the two groups, he could not be sure that all relevant extraneous factors were distributed at random. Tufte did statistically control for some relevant differences among states, yet states with inspection programs may still have differed systematically from states without programs in some other way that was related to traffic fatalities. Hence we cannot be certain that any portion of the difference in fatality rates between the two groups of states can be attributed to the effect of an automobile inspection program.

That said, the difference in average death rates between the two groups of states may in fact actually understate the benefits of inspection programs, especially if many of the inspection programs were weak or poorly implemented. This possibility is plausible since the treatment given in the states with inspection was not controlled by Tufte and could not be carefully observed. Clearly, the lack of a pre-test and of control over the assignment of cases to the quasi-experimental and quasi-control groups creates difficulties for researchers who use the cross-sectional design. One way of improving upon the cross-sectional design is by introducing a pre-test of the independent variable.

Panel Study Design

A **panel study** is a cross-sectional design that introduces a time element. In a panel study the researcher takes measurements of the variables of interest on the same units of analysis at several points in time. Panel studies may thus be used to observe changes over time and to provide a pre-test of some phenomenon prior to natural exposure to the experimental stimulus. A panel study is similar to a cross-sectional study, however, in that measurements of the independent and dependent variables are typically made at the same time, and the researcher has no control over which subjects are exposed to the experimental stimulus.

Let us return to the hypothetical example of a classic pre-test/post-test experiment described earlier in this chapter. In that example we were interested in finding out whether or not exposure to a candidate's televised campaign commercials increased voters' ability to identify the important issues in a campaign. If we used the pre-test/post-test experimental design to test this hypothesis, we would measure pre-exposure issue awareness, randomly assign people to an experimental or control group, expose only the experimental group to the commercials, and then measure post-exposure issue awareness again.

When using a panel research design, a researcher would proceed in a slightly different way. First, pre-exposure issue awareness would be measured for a group of subjects (presumably before any commercials have been broadcast). The researcher would wait for time to pass, the campaign to begin, and the commercials to be broadcast. Then the researcher would interview the same respondents again and measure both the amount of exposure to commercials and the post-exposure issue awareness for everyone. Finally, the researcher would use the measure of commercial exposure to construct quasi-experimental and quasi-control groups and compare the change in the amount of issue awareness for the two groups.

The major difference between the panel study and the classic experiment is that in the former the researcher waits for exposure to the experimental stimulus to occur naturally and then uses the amount of exposure reported by the respondents to create naturally occurring quasi-experimental and quasi-control groups. Hence, the researcher observes rather than controls exposure to the experimental stimulus.

Since the panel study has a pre-test and a quasi-control group, the researcher can claim greater confidence in his or her conclusions than is possible with the cross-sectional design. However, the lack of control over who is exposed to the independent variable and under what conditions creates the problem of nonequivalent experimental and control groups. In our example those who are naturally exposed to more commercials may be more interested in politics and hence more likely to develop issue awareness than those who are not for reasons that have nothing to do with exposure to commercials.

Panel studies are particularly useful in studies of change in individuals over time. One difficulty with panel studies, however, is that individuals may die, move away, or decide to drop out of the study—what researchers refer to as **panel mortality**. If these persons differ from those who remain in the study, study findings may become biased and unrepresentative.

Panel studies have often been used in election campaigns to investigate the changes in voter beliefs, attitudes, and behavior that may be attributed to aspects of a campaign. A panel study of opinion change during the 1980 presidential campaign, for example, relied on surveys conducted with the same national sample of voting-age citizens in January/February, June, and September of 1980.[13] Researcher Larry Bartels was interested in the effect of media exposure during a presidential campaign on "each of 37 distinct perceptions and opinions regarding the presidential candidates, their character traits, their issue positions, the respondents' own issue preferences, and (in the case of incumbent Jimmy Carter) various aspects of job performance."[14] Since Bartels had available both January/February measures of the dependent variables, which were presumably unaffected by campaign news exposure, and later measures of the same variables after four and seven months of campaign coverage, change in voter perceptions and opinions could be analyzed. Measures of exposure to television network news and daily newspapers during the campaign allowed the creation of quasi-experimental and quasi-control comparison groups, and measures of other attributes, such as party identification, permitted statistical control of other significant political factors. As a result, the researcher was able to demonstrate significant media effects during a campaign with considerable confidence, even without experimental control over the introduction of the media exposure in question.

Case Study Design

The final nonexperimental research design we will discuss is the case study. In a **case study design** the researcher examines one or a few cases of a phenomenon in considerable detail, typically using a number of data collection methods, such as personal interviews, document analysis, and observation. For many years the case study was considered to be an inferior research strategy, but it is now recognized as a "distinctive form of empirical inquiry" and an important design to use for the development and evaluation of public policies as well as for developing explanations for and testing theories of political phenomena.[15]

Robert Yin, one of the leading proponents of the case study design, defines the case study as an empirical inquiry that (1) investigates a contemporary phenomenon within its real-life context; when (2) the boundaries between phenomenon and context are not clearly evident; and in which (3) multiple sources of evidence are used.[16] Yin distinguishes between histories and case studies, reserving the term *case study* for the study of contemporary events.[17] Other researchers do not make this distinction, but the study of contemporary events does allow researchers a wider selection of data collection methods, including observation and interviewing.[18]

A case study may be used for exploratory, descriptive, or explanatory purposes. Exploratory case studies may be conducted when little is known about some political phenomenon. Researchers initially may observe only one or a few cases of that phenomenon. Careful observation of a small number of cases may suggest possible general explanations for the behavior or attributes that are observed. These explanations—in the form of hypotheses—can then be tested more systematically by observing more cases. Carefully observing the origins of political dissent within one group at one location may suggest general explanations for dissent, and observing a handful of incumbent representatives when they return to their districts may suggest hypotheses relating incumbent attributes, district settings, and incumbent-constituency relations.[19] In the descriptive case, the purpose of a case study may be to find out and describe what happened in a single or select few situations. The emphasis is not on developing general explanations for what happened.

According to Yin, case studies are most appropriately used to answer "how" or "why" questions.[20] These questions direct our attention toward *explaining* events. The strongest case studies start out with clearly identified theories that are expected to explain the events. Case studies are particularly useful for testing hypotheses deduced from existing theories of politics.

Proponents argue that the case study has some distinct advantages over experimental and cross-sectional designs for testing hypotheses under certain conditions. For example, a case study may be useful in assessing whether a statistical correlation between independent and dependent variables, discovered using a cross-sectional design with survey data, is causal.[21] By choosing a case in which the appropriate values of the independent and dependent variables are present, researchers can try to determine whether and how the independent variable actually caused the dependent variable. That is, they can learn whether there is an actual link between the variables and, therefore, can more likely offer an explanation for the statistical association. Benjamin Page and Robert Shapiro concluded their study of the statistical relationship between public opinion and public policy with a number of case studies.[22]

The case study design differs from experimental designs in that the researcher is neither able to assign subjects or cases to experimental and control groups nor to manipulate the independent variable. Furthermore, the researcher does not control the context or environment as in the case of a laboratory experiment. Yet the researcher can, through the careful selection of a case or cases, achieve a quasi-experimental situation. For example, a researcher may choose cases with different values of an independent variable, but with the same values for important control variables. Cases with similar environments can be chosen. Furthermore, lack of complete control over the environment or context of a phenomenon can be seen as useful. If it can be shown that a theory actually works and is applicable in a real situation, then the theory may more readily be accepted. This may be especially important, for example, in testing theories underlying public policies and public programs.

Like experimental and other nonexperimental research designs, the case study design has several variations. In a single case study, the researcher focuses on a single unit of analysis, such as a single group, neighborhood, bureaucracy, or program. In some situations a single case may represent a critical test of a theory.[23] For example, in a study of organization innovation, a school with a history of innovation was used to test theories that claimed "barriers to innovation" accounted for innovation failure. The researchers showed that even in the school that did not suffer from these barriers, an innovation failed. The result of this case study was to reorient innovation theory away from a focus on barriers.[24]

Another example that demonstrates the explanatory possibilities of a case study is Jeffrey Pressman and Aaron Wildavsky's study of the implementation of an economic development program in Oakland, California.[25] In contrast to earlier programs that had failed, the Oakland program lacked certain factors associated with failure: a high level of conflict, excessive publicity, political importance and sensitivity, and insufficient funds. Yet the Oakland program also failed. Pressman and Wildavsky attributed the program's failure to the fact that numerous approvals and clearances had to be obtained from a variety of participants. These "perfectly ordinary circumstances" led to the unraveling of previous agreements and ultimately the demise of the Oakland program.[26]

By choosing a case in which implementation looked as if it would be easy, Pressman and Wildavsky were able to shed considerable light on the process of implementation. This type of case study design has been called the **deviant case study**, a case that differs from what prevailing theory would lead the researcher to expect. The researcher looks for factors that may explain why the case differs. Research like this may lead to the revision or clarification of existing theories.

Another good example of a deviant case study is discussed in *Union Democracy* by Seymour Martin Lipset, Martin Trow, and James Coleman.[27] It has long been observed that voluntary organizations conform to Robert Michels's "iron law of oligarchy."[28] Lipset, however, observed that the International Typographical Union (ITU) did not conform to the normal oligarchical pattern in which one group "controls the administration, usually retains power indefinitely, rarely faces organized opposition, and when faced with such opposition often resorts to undemocratic procedures to eliminate it."[29] The ITU had an institutionalized two-party system that regularly presented candidates for chief union posts elected in biennial elections. In *Union Democracy,* the authors attempted to understand this anomaly and in doing so helped explain the workings of democratic processes in general.

Single case studies are also called for where the case represents an extreme or unique case (that is, a rarely occurring phenomenon) and when a researcher has an opportunity to study a phenomenon (not necessarily a rare one) previously inaccessible to researchers that thus serves a "revelatory" purpose.[30] In other uses of single case studies, the single case is either exploratory or otherwise considered to be one case in a multiple case study, not a complete explanatory study on its own.[31]

An embedded single case study involves studying subunits within the single case. Actually, Lipset, Trow, and Coleman's study of the ITU involved several units of analysis; the main unit was the ITU, but the researchers also investigated ITU locals, shops, and individual members.[32] Martha Weinberg's study of former Massachusetts governor Francis Sargent was a case study of gubernatorial management and decision-making style, but she investigated several state departments and agencies and their interaction with the governor in depth.[33] Researchers who use this case study design must be careful to remember their main unit of analysis. Weinberg's main unit of analysis was the governor, not the various state agencies. Her case study could have become one that focused on agencies and how and why they resisted or complied with a governor's attempts to influence their behavior. Weinberg, however, was investigating the validity of various theories of executive decision making and thus her focus appropriately remained the governor. This example shows the vital importance of clearly specifying the theory of interest and the unit or units of analysis for which the theory applies. This provides necessary direction and purpose for the investigator as he or she becomes immersed in the details of the case under study.

Case studies may involve more than one case. A multiple case study is more likely to have explanatory power than a single case study because it provides the opportunity for replication; that is, it enables a researcher to test a single theory more than once. For some cases, similar results will be predicted; for others, different results will be predicted.[34] Multiple cases should not be thought of as a "sample." Cases are not chosen using a statistical procedure to form a "representative" sample from which the frequency of a particular phenomenon will be calculated and inferences about a larger population drawn.[35] Rather, cases are chosen for the presence or absence of factors that a political theory has indicated to be important. Multiple case studies may be either holistic or embedded, as with the single case study.

Despite the important contribution to our understanding of political phenomena a researcher can make with case study research, some researchers avoid using case study designs and do not give researchers who use the case study as much recognition as those who use other research designs. Yin gives three reasons for the poor reputation of case studies.[36] One concern about case studies is the "lack of rigor" in presenting evidence and the possibility for bias in the use of evidence. Typically, researchers sift through enormous quantities of detailed information about their cases. In studying contemporary events, the researcher may be the only one to record certain behavior or phenomena. Certainly, the potential for bias is not limited to case studies. However, as Yin points out, the problems of bias have not been investigated as thoroughly for case studies as they have been for other research strategies, such as survey research (Chapter 10).

A second criticism of case studies is the inability to generalize from a single case. One response to this criticism is to use multiple case studies. In fact, as Yin points out, the same criticism can be leveled against a single experiment—scientific knowledge is usually based on multiple experiments rather than on a single experiment.[37] Yet people do not say that performing a single experiment is not worthwhile. Furthermore, Yin states: "Case studies, like experiments, are generalizable to theoretical propositions and not to populations or universes. In this sense, the case study, like the experiment, does not represent a 'sample,' and the investigator's goal is to expand and generalize theories (analytic generalization) and not to enumerate frequencies (statistical generalization)."[38]

The third criticism about case studies is that they take ages to conduct and result in lengthy, unreadable reports. This criticism confuses the case study with particular methods of data collection, such as participant observation (discussed in Chapter 8); furthermore, the evidence collected in a case study can be presented succinctly—even if long reports have been the rule.[39]

In short, the case study design can be an informative and appropriate research design in many circumstances. The design permits a deeper understanding of causal processes, the explication of general explanatory theory, and the development of hypotheses regarding difficult-to-observe phenomena. Much of our understanding of politics and political processes actually comes from case studies of individual presidents, senators, representatives, mayors, judges, statutes, campaigns, treaties, policy initiatives, and wars. The case study design should be viewed as complementary to, rather than inconsistent with, other experimental and nonexperimental designs.

Conclusion

In this chapter we have discussed why choosing a research design is an important step in the research process. A research design is a plan that enables the researcher to achieve his or her research objectives. A good research design produces definitive, informative research results.

We presented two basic types of research designs—experimental and nonexperimental—along with numerous variations of these designs (see Table 5-5). We discussed their advantages and disadvantages. Experimental designs—which allow the researcher to have control over the independent variable, the units of analysis, and their environment—are often preferred over nonexperimental designs because they enable the researcher to establish more easily causal explanations of the phenomena being studied. Therefore, experimental designs are generally stronger in internal validity than nonexperimental

TABLE 5-5

Comparison of Selected Research Designs

Type of Design	Objectives of Design			
	Establish that X and Y covary	Establish that X precedes Y	Establish nonspuriousness	Establish generalizability
Classic Experimental	yes	yes	yes	maybe
Nonexperimental Time Series	yes	yes	maybe	maybe
Cross-sectional	yes	usually not	maybe	maybe
Panel	yes	yes	maybe	maybe
Descriptive Case Study	maybe	maybe	maybe	no
Exploratory Case Study	maybe	maybe	no	no
Explanatory Case Study	yes	yes	maybe	maybe

ones. However, it may not always be possible or appropriate to use an experimental design. Thus nonexperimental observation may also be used to test hypotheses in a meaningful fashion and often in a way that increases the external validity of the results. The principles and objectives of research designs, whether experimental or nonexperimental, are the same. It is important to understand the strengths of experimental designs to choose an appropriate research design from the remaining options.

A single research design may not be able to avoid all threats to internal and external validity. Researchers often use several designs together so that the weaknesses of one can be overcome by the strengths of another. Also, findings based on research with a weak design are likely to be more readily accepted if they corroborate findings from previous research that used different designs.

In the next chapter we will discuss how to conduct background research on a topic you may be interested in studying. One purpose of this process is to discover and evaluate the research designs that other researchers have used to study the topic. Background research may suggest appropriate research designs for you to employ. You may be able to use a research design that results in an improvement over past research. In later chapters we will discuss various methods that you can use to collect the data you need to implement your design.

Notes

1. David Nachmias and Chava Nachmias, *Research Methods in the Social Sciences* (London: Edward Arnold, 1976), 29.
2. Stephen Ansolabehere, Shanto Iyengar, Adam Simon, and Nicholas Valentino, "Does Attack Advertising Demobilize the Electorate?" *American Political Science Review* 88 (December 1994): 829–838.
3. See Donald T. Campbell and Julian C. Stanley, *Experimental and Quasi-Experimental Designs for Research* (Chicago: Rand-McNally, 1966), 5–6; and Paul E. Spector, *Research Designs* (Beverly Hills, Calif.: Sage, 1981), 24–27. Four components of an ideal experiment are identified by Kenneth D. Bailey in *Methods of Social Research* (New York: Free Press, 1978), 191.
4. Spector, *Research Designs,* 22.
5. This discussion is based on Bailey, *Methods of Social Research,* 204–206; and Jarol B. Mannheim and Richard C. Rich, *Empirical Political Science* (Englewood Cliffs, N.J.: Prentice-Hall, 1981), 76–77.
6. Spector, *Research Designs,* 46–47.
7. Shanto Iyengar, Mark D. Peters, and Donald R. Kinder, "Experimental Demonstrations of the 'Not-So-Minimal' Consequences of Television News Programs," *American Political Science Review* 76 (December 1982): 848–858.
8. Spector, *Research Designs,* 60–61; and Campbell and Stanley, *Experimental and Quasi-Experimental Designs,* 24–25.
9. This discussion is based on Joseph A. Pechman and P. Michael Timpare, eds., *Work Incentives and Income Guarantees: The New Jersey Negative Income Tax Experiment* (Washington, D.C.: Brookings Institution, 1975), esp. chaps. 2 and 3.
10. William Mishler and Reginald S. Sheehan, "The Supreme Court as a Countermajoritarian Institution? The Impact of Public Opinion on Supreme Court Decisions," *American Political Science Review* 87:1 (March 1993): 87–101.

11. David O. Sears, Carl P. Hensler, and Leslie K. Speer, "Whites' Opposition to 'Busing': Self-Interest or Symbolic Politics?" *American Political Science Review* 73 (June 1979): 369–384.

12. Edward R. Tufte, *Data Analysis for Politics and Policy* (Englewood Cliffs, N.J.: Prentice-Hall, 1974), 5–17.

13. Larry M. Bartels, "Messages Received: The Political Impact of Media Exposure," *American Political Science Review* 87 (June 1993): 267–285.

14. Ibid., 269.

15. Robert K. Yin, *Case Study Research: Design and Methods,* rev. ed. (Beverly Hills, Calif.: Sage, 1989), 21.

16. Ibid., 23.

17. Ibid., 19.

18. Ibid., 19–20.

19. See Richard F. Fenno Jr., *Home Style: House Members in Their Districts* (Boston: Little, Brown, 1978).

20. Yin, *Case Study Research,* 17–19.

21. Alexander L. George, "Case Studies and Theory Development: The Method of Structured, Focused Comparison," in Paul Gordon Lauren, ed., *Diplomacy: New Approaches in History, Theory and Policy* (New York: Free Press, 1979), 46.

22. Benjamin Page and Robert Shapiro, "Effects of Public Opinion on Policy," *American Political Science Review* 77 (March 1983): 186.

23. Yin, *Case Study Research,* 47.

24. Neal Gross, Joseph B. Giacquinta, and Marilyn Bernstein, *Implementing Organizational Innovations* (New York: Basic Books, 1971). See Yin's discussion in *Case Study Research,* 47.

25. Jeffrey L. Pressman and Aaron B. Wildavsky, *Implementation* (Berkeley: University of California Press, 1973).

26. Ibid., xii.

27. Seymour Martin Lipset, Martin Trow, and James Coleman, *Union Democracy* (Garden City, N.Y.: Anchor, 1962).

28. Robert Michels, *Political Parties* (New York: Dover, 1959).

29. Lipset, Trow, and Coleman, *Union Democracy,* 1.

30. Yin, *Case Study Research,* 47–48.

31. Ibid., 49.

32. Ibid., 50.

33. Martha Wagner Weinberg, *Managing the State* (Cambridge: MIT Press, 1977).

34. Yin, *Case Study Research,* 53.

35. Ibid.

36. Ibid., 21–22.

37. Ibid., 21.

38. Ibid., 23.

39. Ibid.

Terms introduced

ASSIGNMENT AT RANDOM. Random assignment of subjects to experimental and control groups.

CASE STUDY DESIGN. A comprehensive and in-depth study of a single case or several cases. A nonexperimental design in which the investigator has little control over events.

CLASSIC EXPERIMENTAL DESIGN. An experiment with the random assignment of subjects to experimental and control groups with a pre-test and post-test for both groups.

CONTROL GROUP. A group of subjects that does not receive the experimental treatment or test stimulus.

CROSS-SECTIONAL DESIGN. A research design in which measurements of independent and dependent variables are taken at the same time; naturally occurring differences in the independent variable are used to create quasi-experimental and quasi-control groups; extraneous factors are controlled for by statistical means.

DEVIANT CASE STUDY. Study of a case that deviates from other cases and from what prevailing theory would lead the researcher to expect.

EXPERIMENTAL EFFECT. Effect of the independent variable on the dependent variable.

EXPERIMENTAL GROUP. A group of subjects that receives the experimental treatment or test stimulus.

EXPERIMENTAL MORTALITY. A differential loss of subjects from experimental and control groups that affects the equivalency of groups; threat to internal validity.

EXPERIMENTATION. Research using an experimental research design in which the researcher has control over the independent variable, the units of analysis, and their environment; used to test causal relationships.

EXTERNAL VALIDITY. The ability to generalize from one set of research findings to other situations.

EXTRANEOUS FACTORS. Factors besides the independent variable that may cause change in the dependent variable.

FACTORIAL DESIGN. Experimental design used to measure the effect of two or more independent variables singly and in combination.

FIELD EXPERIMENTS. Experimental designs applied in a natural setting.

HISTORY. A change in the dependent variable due to changes in the environment over time; threat to internal validity.

INSTRUMENT DECAY. A change in the measurement device used to measure the dependent variable, producing change in measurements; threat to internal validity.

INSTRUMENT REACTIVITY. Reaction of subjects to a pre-test.

INTERACTION EFFECT. Reaction of subjects to a combination of pre-test and experimental stimulus.

INTERNAL VALIDITY. The ability to show that manipulation or variation of the independent variable causes the dependent variable to change.

MATURATION. A change in subjects over time that affects the dependent variable; threat to internal validity.

MULTIGROUP DESIGN. Experimental design with more than one control and experimental group.

NONEXPERIMENTAL DESIGN. A research design characterized by at least one of the following: presence of a single group, lack of researcher control over the assignment of subjects to control and experimental groups, lack of researcher control over application of the independent variable, or inability of researcher to measure dependent variable before and after exposure to the independent variable occurs.

PANEL MORTALITY. Loss of participants from panel study.

PANEL STUDY. A cross-sectional study in which measurements of variables are taken on the same units of analysis at multiple points in time.

POST-TEST. Measurement of the dependent variable after manipulation of the independent variable.

PRECISION MATCHING. Matching of pairs of subjects with one of the pair assigned to the experimental group and the other to the control group.

PRE-TEST. Measurement of the dependent variable prior to the administration of the experimental treatment or manipulation of the independent variable.

RESEARCH DESIGN. A plan specifying how the researcher intends to fulfill the goals of the study; a logical plan for testing hypotheses.

SELECTION. Bias in the assignment of subjects to experimental and control groups; threat to internal validity.

SIMPLE POST-TEST DESIGN. Weak type of experimental design with control and experimental groups but no pretest.

SOLOMON FOUR-GROUP DESIGN. Type of experimental design used to measure interaction between pretest and experimental treatment.

STATISTICAL REGRESSION. Change in the dependent variable due to the temporary nature of extreme values; threat to internal validity.

TEST STIMULUS. The independent variable.

TESTING. Effect of a pre-test on the dependent variable; threat to internal validity.

TIME SERIES DESIGN. A research design featuring multiple measurements of the dependent variable before and after experimental treatment.

Exercises

1. Refer to Figure 5-2. If you had used a cross-sectional design to test for the effect of a media campaign on public opinion, at what point(s) would you have taken your measures of public opinion and media exposure? What would your conclusions be?

2. Refer to Figure 5-2. Assume that you have used a "two-wave" panel design to measure the impact of media exposure on public opinion and that you

knew when the White House media campaign was going to start. At what point (A, B, or C) would you have conducted the first wave (taken the first measurements)? What would you have measured at this time? When could you have conducted the second wave? At what point would you be able to know who was in the quasi-control group and who was in the quasi-experimental group? What would you conclude? Did exposure to the media campaign have an effect on people's opinion on health care policy?

3. What research designs are used by the researchers in the following articles? What are the key concepts being measured?

    a. Lani Lee Malysa, "A Comparative Assessment of State Planning and Management Capacity: Tidal Wetlands Protection in Virginia and Maryland," *State and Local Government Review* 28 (fall 1996): 205–218.

    b. David H. Folz, "Municipal Recycling Performance: A Public Sector Environmental Success Story," *Public Administration Review* 59 (July–August 1999): 336–345.

    c. Rebecca E. Deen and Thomas H. Little, "Getting to the Top: Factors Influencing the Selection of Women to Positions of Leadership in State Legislatures," *State and Local Government Review* 31 (spring 1999): 123–134.

    d. Jon S.T. Quah, "Corruption in Asian Countries: Can It Be Minimized?" *Public Administration Review* 59 (November–December 1999): 482–494.

    e. J. Eric Oliver, "City Size and Civic Involvement in Metropolitan America," *American Political Science Review* 94 (June 2000): 361–373.

4. What is the most appropriate research design to answer the following questions? Is another design appropriate? What control variables would you need to consider? How does your design allow for these controls?

    a. Why have some states adopted strict lobbying laws while others have not?

    b. What is the effect of a state law changing the curfew for teenage drivers from midnight to 11 p.m.?

    c. Are voters who voted for losing candidates in presidential primaries less likely to vote in the general election than voters who voted for winning primary candidates?

    d. What is the effect of an increase of the cost of a gallon of gas by 50¢ on public transit ridership?

5. Read the article by Stephen Ansolabehere, Shanto Iyengar, Adam Simon, and Nicholas Valentino, "Does Attack Advertising Demobilize the Electorate?" *American Political Science Review* 88 (December 1994): 829–838.

    a. How were subjects selected by the researchers for participation in the controlled experiment? How could this have affected the validity of the results? How did the authors respond to this problem? What was the unit of analysis?

b. How were subjects assigned to treatment groups?

c. How many treatment groups were there?

d. Why did the authors refer to real candidates in their advertisements? Produce their own advertisements rather than rely on campaign spots produced by the candidates? Conduct their experiment for several different campaigns? Vary the content of the experimental advertisements across campaigns? Identify how these features of their research design affected the internal or external validity of their experiment.

e. Review the authors' reconstruction of their experiment in the real world beginning on page 833. Why did they develop this alternative research design? What was the unit of analysis? How did the authors' design vary from the characteristics of an ideal experiment? What were two advantages of the decision to focus on the Senate campaigns in 1992?

Suggested Readings

Campbell, Donald T., and Julian C. Stanley. *Experimental and Quasi-Experimental Designs for Research.* Chicago: Rand-McNally, 1966.

Creswell, John W. *Research Design: Qualitative & Quantitative Approaches.* Thousand Oaks, Calif.: Sage, 1994.

Hakim, Catherine. *Research Design: Strategies and Choices in the Design of Social Research.* London: Allen & Unwin, 1987.

Spector, Paul E. *Research Designs.* Beverly Hills, Calif.: Sage, 1981.

Yin, Robert K. *Case Study Research: Design and Methods.* Rev. ed. Beverly Hills, Calif.: Sage, 1989.

CHAPTER 6

Conducting a Literature Review

So far we have discussed the initial stages of a typical research project: hypothesis formation, conceptualization, measurement, and the development of a suitable research design. At some point early in the process it is important to spend time reading others' reports of similar research. We refer to this enterprise as conducting background research or a literature review.

You should undertake a literature review near the outset of a research effort, if only to make sure that your research does not duplicate someone else's. More important, a literature review can help you narrow your topic and direct your investigation. In this chapter we will discuss the reasons for undertaking background research and explain how to conduct it.

For many students simply finding a research topic can be a time-consuming and frustrating experience. So while this chapter focuses on what to do once you have identified a research topic (if only in a general sense), we also make some suggestions to help you become more familiar with political issues, debates, sources, and events and to help you identify potential research topics of interest. We also demonstrate techniques for searching for information on the Internet.

Selecting A Research Topic

Potential research topics about politics come from many sources: your own life experiences and political activities and those of your family and friends; class readings, lectures, and discussions; and newspapers, television, and magazines, to name a few. Becoming aware of current or recent issues in public affairs will help you develop interesting research topics. You can start by reading a daily newspaper or issues of popular magazines that deal with government policies and politics. We have listed a few below.

Popular and Political Journals and Magazines

American Prospect. Biweekly magazine of liberal analyses and opinions.

American Spectator. Conservative weekly magazine of current events.

The Atlantic. Essays on American and world political, social, and economic events.

The Economist. Weekly newsmagazine with worldwide coverage of news related to economics. International perspective aimed at the layperson.

National Review. Biweekly newsmagazine with articles on current issues from a conservative perspective.

The New Republic. Weekly coverage of issues facing the United States, traditionally from a liberal perspective.

The New York Review of Books. A biweekly magazine that includes reviews and articles, many of which are related to government and politics.

The New Yorker. A weekly magazine that contains columns and articles relevant to domestic and international affairs.

Journals and Magazines with a Government and Policy Focus

CQ Weekly (formerly the *Congressional Quarterly Weekly Report*). A weekly report of hot topics in Congress. The information is later compiled into annual volumes called the *CQ Almanac.*

National Journal: the weekly on politics and government. Similar to the *CQ Weekly,* except the focus tends to be on the executive branch rather than Congress.

Public Perspective. Contains articles and data about public opinion toward political issues and policies.

Reasons for Conducting a Literature Review

Good research involves reviewing what has been written about a topic. Among the reasons for such a review are (1) to see what has and has not been investigated; (2) to develop general explanations for observed variations in a behavior or phenomenon; (3) to identify potential relationships between concepts and to identify researchable hypotheses; (4) to learn how others have defined and measured key concepts; (5) to identify data sources that other researchers have used; (6) to develop alternative research designs; and (7) to discover how a research project is related to the work of others. Let us examine some of these reasons more closely.

Often a beginner will start out by expressing only a general interest in a topic, such as childhood socialization or campaign advertising. At this stage the person will not have formulated a specific research question (for example, "How soon in childhood does socialization begin?" or "Do negative televised campaign advertisements sway voters?"). A review of the previous research will help sharpen a topic by identifying major research questions that have been asked by others. Note also that having a precise topic in mind greatly facilitates Internet searches.

After reading the published work in an area, a researcher may decide that previous reports do not adequately answer the question at hand. Thus a research project may be designed to answer an "old" question in a new way. Published reports are often sources of important questions and untested hypotheses that require further research. An investigation may follow up on one of these ideas.

At other times, researchers may begin a research project with a hypothesis or with a desire to explain a relationship that has already been observed. Here a literature review may reveal reports of similar observations made by others and may also help a researcher develop general explanations for the relationship by identifying theories that explain the phenomenon of interest. The value of the research will be greater if the researcher can provide a general explanation of the observed or hypothesized relationship rather than simply a report of the empirical verification of a relationship.

In addition to seeking theories that support the plausibility and increase the significance of a hypothesis, a researcher should be alert for competing or alternative hypotheses. A researcher may start out with a hypothesis specifying a simple relationship between two variables. Since it is uncommon for one political phenomenon to be related to or caused by just one other factor or variable, it is important to look for other possible causes or correlates of the dependent variable. Data collection should include measurement of these other relevant variables so that in subsequent data analysis the researcher may rule out competing explanations or at least indicate more clearly the nature of the relationship between the variables in the original hypothesis.

For example, suppose someone has hypothesized that people become active in politics because they have some serious dissatisfaction with government policy. A review of the literature on political participation would show that participation is related to years of formal education, attitudes toward citizen duty, and beliefs about one's own ability to affect political affairs. Thus it would be wise to include measures of all these variables in the research design so that the policy dissatisfaction explanation may be compared with the other explanations for political participation. In fact, without conducting a literature review the investigator might not be aware of the potential importance of these other variables.

A researcher also may compare his or her concept definitions with those of other researchers. Using the same definitions of a concept as other researchers will lead to greater comparability of research findings on the same topic. Furthermore, the validity of a researcher's measures may be improved if the literature reveals that other researchers' definitions of a concept are ambiguous or combine two or more concepts that need to be treated separately. For example, in his study of political participation of French peasants, Sidney Tarrow found that it was important to separate the concept "support for political parties" from the concept "interest in politics."[1] The concept "interest in politics" was interpreted by French peasants to include the idea of approval of existing parties. Because French peasants did not approve of the parties, they denied that they were interested in politics despite their high levels of voter turnout. Hence, in this case it was advisable to measure political interest and party support separately.

A researcher may also discover the opposite problem: he or she may be using overly narrow definitions that fail to capture important dimensions of a concept. For example, if you were conducting a survey to measure support for democratic values, you would be missing numerous definitions of this concept if you simply defined it as a belief in regular elections. A review of other studies on democratic values would alert you to other definitions such as support for political rights.

Research reports provide us with valuable information about viable research designs, measurement strategies, and data collection methods. A note of caution is necessary, however. Dead ends and "bonehead" mistakes are rarely reported. Published research reports may lead us to believe that the research process proceeds in an orderly, nonproblematical, textbook fashion. Thus some of the more obvious alternatives in research design, measurement, and data collection may have been tried by other researchers and rejected for good reasons. Sometimes, however, an author will discuss possible improvements and explain why they were not incorporated into his or her own research. Although reading previous research will not necessarily tell you everything other researchers have tried and rejected, it may suggest to you ways of improving your research design and measurements and help you turn your study into a more interesting and successful research project.

As an example of the benefits of a literature review, let us look at a review conducted by one of us, Richard Joslyn, who was interested in the impact of television news on the political opinions and behavior of the American public. In particular, he wondered whether watching the news affected people's beliefs about the utility of political participation.

Joslyn's review of the literature on political participation revealed four main considerations. First, he discovered that previous investigators had developed a concept that was relevant to his hypothesis. It was called *political efficacy* or *sense of civic competence*. This concept had been defined in a number of similar ways:

■ the feeling that political and social change is possible, and that the individual citizen can play a part in bringing about this change;[2]

■ the timeless theme of democratic theory that members of a democratic regime ought to regard those who occupy positions of political authority as responsive agents and that the members themselves ought to be disposed to participate in the honors and offices of the system;[3]

■ an individual's belief in the value of political action and the probability of success in this action;[4]

■ belief in the efficacy of one's own political action, consisting of (1) a belief that public officials can be and are influenced by ordinary citizens, (2) some knowledge about how to proceed in making this influence felt, and (3) sufficient self-confidence to try to put this knowledge to work at appropriate times and places.[5]

This looked to the author like a concept that might be influenced by watching television news shows.

Second, Joslyn discovered that political efficacy had recently been divided into two different types of belief: internal political efficacy, or "the level of perceived personal power in the political system,"[6] and external political efficacy, or "the feeling that an individual and the public can have an impact on the political process because government institutions will respond to their needs."[7] This division meant that a researcher might want to specify which aspect of political efficacy was involved in any given hypothesis.

Third, the literature review revealed ways in which both internal and external political efficacy had been measured by other researchers. A set of six to eight questions on public opinion surveys had originally been used to measure efficacy in general; later, a smaller set of questions was found to measure internal and external political efficacy separately.

Fourth, the literature review turned up numerous studies that had tested different explanations for variations in people's political efficacy (see Table 6-1). These explanations focused on individuals' personality, social status, social cohesion, and political experiences, and consequently they represented rival hypotheses for efficacy that did not depend upon television news viewing. Joslyn was able to include some of these alternative explanations in his research design so that the television news hypothesis could be evaluated more completely.

At the conclusion of this literature review, then, the researcher had become familiar with the conceptualization and measurement of a phenomenon relevant to his original hypothesis, had discovered sources of data that included at least some of the measures of interest, and had been alerted to competing hypotheses that would have to be taken into consideration in testing the link between political efficacy and television news exposure. One can readily see that literature reviews further the conceptual, empirical, and theoretical aims of most research projects.

TABLE 6-1

Explanations for Political Efficacy Concepts Used as Independent Variables

Personality

Political cynicism	Self-competence/personal efficacy
Opinion intensity	Political interest
Interpersonal trust	Cosmopolitanism

Social Status

Education	Religion
Region	Sex
Size and place of residence	Race
Age	Relative deprivation
Income	IQ
Occupation	

Social Cohesion

Marital status	Organization membership/
Number of children	leadership
Years of residence	Political, social participation
Church attendance	Size of community

Political Environment/Experiences/Interaction

Newspaper exposure	Ideology
Incumbent support	Political milieu (exposure to
Partisan domination	corrupt urban politics)
Partisan competition	Political subculture
Political success	Exposure to political agitation
Events/period/history	Attitudes of friends
Accumulation of democratic experience	Attitudes of parents
Party identification	Attitudes of teachers

Source: Richard Joslyn, "The Portrayal of Government and Nation on Television Network News: Content and Implications." (Paper delivered at the annual meeting of the Midwest Political Science Association, Cincinnati, Ohio, 1981).

Conducting a Literature Review

How you conduct a literature review depends on the main purpose of the review, the stage of development of the research topic, and available resources. If you are starting with only a general interest in a subject and not a specific hypothesis, then it might be a good idea to locate a textbook covering the subject, read the appropriate sections, and then check out the sources cited in the notes. A perusal of the subject catalog in your library will also help you identify books that broadly address your topic. From there you can begin to develop and refine a more specific research question. Another approach to get you started would be to skim the contents of a few professional journals likely to have articles in your area of interest. Any of these approaches can be done with standard library materials, however, using electronic sources such as the Internet and electronic databases often facilitates the task.

A thorough literature search includes anything published on your topic in professional journals, magazines, books, newspapers, government publications and documents, and conference proceedings. To guide you in this endeavor, we have listed later in this chapter a number of professional journals in political science, with comments on their content. Also listed are indexes and bibliographies that will help you locate materials related to your topic.[8] Several of these indexes are available as compact disc databases. Your library's reference librarian will undoubtedly be able to provide you with additional information and guidance on the particular library sources available.

PYRAMID CITATIONS

Each time you find what appears to be a useful source, look at its list of notes and references. One article, for example, may cite two more potentially useful papers. Each of these in turn may point to two or more additional ones, and so on. It is easy to see that by starting with a small list you can quickly assemble a huge list of sources. Moreover, you increase your changes of covering all of the relevant literature.

Using the Internet to Conduct a Literature Review

The Internet is a relatively new tool for conducting literature reviews. The Internet can be thought of as an enormous collection of files or documents that are stored on computers throughout the world and that can be searched for information of all kinds, including text, quantitative data, graphic images, and video and audio files. Since all of the sites where this material is stored are electronically linked, they can be accessed from a personal computer or terminal connected to a network. It is then possible to "download," or retrieve, selected information. The World Wide Web is a networked information system that makes finding and retrieving this information especially easy.[9]

A person uses a commercial browser such as Netscape or Internet Explorer or one provided by an Internet provider like America Online to visit Internet locations, look for documents or data of interest, and retrieve them. Most readers of this book have probably been surfing the web since high school, if not before.

One of the benefits of this revolution in global communications is that it places an almost limitless supply of information literally at one's fingertips. Scouring the Internet also allows one to find many kinds of documents and data that a traditional library search will not turn up or that are simply not available on many campuses.

To see the advantages—and also the problems—with using the "net" to conduct a literature search, let's suppose that you want to write a paper on some aspect of television in American presidential elections. You might think you need only access a **search engine**, a computer program that systematically visits and searches web pages, and type in your **search term** or keyword. However, the process is not always so simple. Figure 6-1 shows the results obtained from Google, a widely used search engine, when the phrase "presidential elections and television" is entered as the search term. On this particular occasion the search program returned over 30,000 sources, or "hits," many of which are not relevant. Clearly, there is a drawback to using the net *unless* careful planning and thought have preceded your search.

Your search should begin with a list of search terms. The purpose of this is to find documents and information that contain these terms. If you were writing about television and politics, for instance, keywords for your search might include, among many others, "television," "mass media," "elections," and "public opinion." When entered into your computer, the appropriate program will browse the Internet for documents that contain these words and phrases. The trick is to find as many relevant documents as possible while excluding those that contain irrelevant information.

You need to plan ahead to draw up the list. Do not even sit in front of a computer or terminal until you have a tentative search strategy in mind. At the outset list exactly what it is that you are looking for. Do you want to find

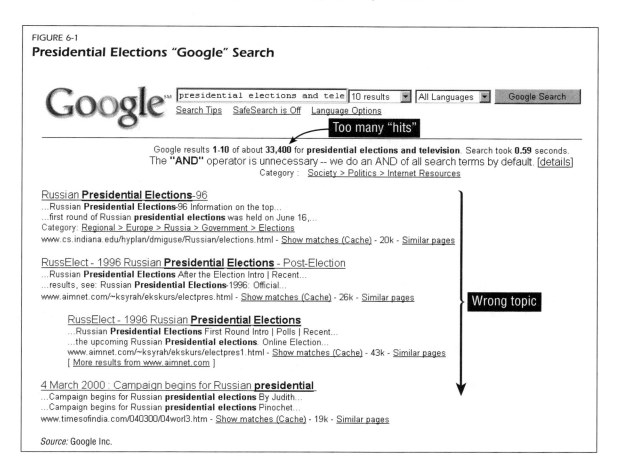

FIGURE 6-1
Presidential Elections "Google" Search

Source: Google Inc.

articles or books about the topic? What time period are you interested in? If you want articles, do you want them to come from scholarly sources like academic journals or do you want them to come from newspapers and magazines? If the latter, are you looking for general circulation publications such as *Time* and *Newsweek* or do you want to read articles from "opinion presses" like *The Progressive, American Spectator,* and *The New Republic*? Do you need political speeches and essays? Will you be analyzing "raw" data such as public opinion polls or government statistics? Answering questions like these will speed the search process.

After you clarify these matters you can then consult your hypotheses to develop a list of search terms. Presumably your research involves a few tentative hypotheses. What specific words, concepts, phrases, and ideas do those propositions contain?

Unless you have a particular source in mind it is probably easiest to go first to one of the many comprehensive electronic directories, such as Yahoo. Much like the yellow pages in a phonebook, a **directory** arranges terms in a hierarchy by subject matter, which lets the search proceed from general to specific topics. For example, the larger category "Politics" is divided into a subcategory, such as "Elections." "Elections" may then itself be reduced further, for example, into the subcategory "Campaigns." Since the directory contains lists of links to web pages, but not the pages themselves or indexes of pages, it permits a targeted or structured search of potentially relevant links.

If you wish to undertake a more comprehensive search, then you can use a full-blown search engine database. Such a site contains copies of web pages as well as exhaustive indexes of those pages (see Figure 6-1). This massive amount of material can be searched by keyword for actual web pages. However, because the material in a search engine is collected mechanically by computer programs called spiders or robots that mindlessly crawl around the Internet, the search engine database will as often as not contain a lot of information that is unneeded or irrelevant. (In Figure 6-1, for example, note that information about the *Russian* presidential election was found.)

When you begin to write your paper on the importance of television in American presidential elections—a paper that you may have initially believed already contained a specific topic—you will quickly find that it is still necessary to think clearly about what information will answer the questions posed in the research design. Searching for broad terms such as "elections," "television," or "advertisements" will lead you to so much information that you will waste time trying to sort out the useful from the irrelevant. If you look for items containing "presidential elections," you could find dozens and dozens of articles on the history of campaigns, foreign elections, electoral laws, candidate biographies, and political consultants, to name just a few. It is possible that none of these will be relevant to your topic. Indeed, with such broad searches you may not find what you're looking for at all. By using your hypotheses to develop a list of relevant search terms you will be much more efficient, saving time and avoiding frustration.

It sometimes makes sense to make a second list that contains terms that should be *excluded* from the search. If your project involves the study of televised political advertisements, for instance, you would want to eliminate documents and articles that pertained to speeches, debates, and press conferences, all of which might show up in a general search for "television and elections."

Figure 6-2 shows how narrowly defined search terms lead to more useful results. In this case the terms "negative political advertising" *and* "presidential elections" have been entered. The list of documents now totals less than three thousand, still too many perhaps, but most seem directly related to the topic.

After deriving a list of words and phrases from the hypotheses, you might then develop a list of synonyms. Once again, the clearer and more narrow a topic the easier it is to come up with synonyms. As an example, instead of a huge topic such as "the effects of television on presidential elections," you

FIGURE 6-2
Improved "Google" Search Results

Source: Google Inc.

might limit the scope of the study to a specific question: "Has negative campaign advertising increased in the past thirty years?" It should now be relatively easy to list the main concepts and some synonyms for use in an Internet search. The list might include

Term	*Synonyms*
advertisement	commercial(s), ad(s), spot(s)
negative	attack, hostile, dirty
television	mass media, media

Using the guidelines presented below, one can search for various combinations of these words and phrases, as in, for instance, "negative advertising" or "attack ads" or "political spot advertisements."

Surfing the Net

A wide variety of Internet resources exists. Besides those provided by familiar sites such as Yahoo, there are sites maintained by academic organizations, government bureaus, research firms, interest groups, media companies, and a host of other institutions that are devoted to particular topics. We discuss a few of the possibilities in this section.

Table 6-2 presents a list of search engines and directories. Although many more exist, these are probably familiar to most readers and provide a good place to start a general search. To go to one of these directories, enter the Internet address, or uniform resource locator (URL), into your browser's "go to" box.

TABLE 6-2
Popular Search Engines and Directories

Search Engine or Directory	Internet Address (URL)
AltaVista	http://altavista.com/
Excite	http://www.excite.com
Google	http://www.google.com
Hotbot	http://www.hotbot.com
Infoseek	http://guide.infoseek.com
Lycos	http://www.lycos.com
Metacrawler	http://www.metacrawler.com
Open Text Index	http://www.opentext.com/omw/f-omw.html
Search	http://www.search.com
Webcrawler	http://webcrawler.com
Yahoo	http://www.yahoo.com

Besides these comprehensive directories and search engines, electronic databases are also widely available. An **electronic database** is a collection of documents assembled by a company or organization. It usually contains specific types of information such as lists of journal articles, government documents, research reports, numerical data, or newspaper and magazine files. Although some of these are private and cannot be visited by the general public, many others can be accessed by all users. Table 6-3 lists some of the networked or electronic databases and indexes that are especially useful for the social sciences. These are becoming so widespread and popular that they have begun to replace the paper indexes listed later in this chapter. The information in these compilations can be searched for documents containing keywords. To visit one of these databases, enter its URL into your browser's "go to" box.

Figure 6-3 shows how Jstor, a repository of the back issues of scholarly journals, responds to a requested search for articles dealing with "political advertisement" in political science journals between 1980 and 1999. The results of the search appear in Figure 6-4. Entries 1, 2, and 4 appear to apply directly to the topic. The user can click on "Citation/Abstract" (or even look at the entire document) to check for relevance.

Note that Jstor was asked to look for the search terms in the full text of the articles, not just in the titles. To limit the search to citations or titles, you can choose other options. Many search programs have a list of choices that allows you to expand on or narrow a query.

TABLE 6-3
Library Sites and Networked Databases

Name	Location (URL)
Jstor	http://www.jstor.org
Lexis	http://www.lexis.com
Web of Science	http://webofscience.com
Libraries Political Science Research Guide	http://www.indiana.edu/~libpoli/RR/ps_res.html
(Indiana University, Bloomington)	
Political Science: A Net Station	http://www.library.ubc.ca/poli/
(Walter C. Koener Library, University of British Columbia)	
Documents in the News Current Events Research	http://www.lib.umich.edu/libhome/Documents.center/docnews.html
(University of Michigan)	

Note: You may have to use some or all of these databases at your library or at least be connecting to the Internet from a campus location. The reference library staff should be able to help you.

In addition to these sites, many research institutes and other organizations maintain Internet web sites that are open to the public. Most of these contain searchable files that can be retrieved. Table 6-4 lists some of the most helpful. Once you access these sites you will find that they are really lists of lists. That is, they do not contain many documents themselves but point you to places that do. For example, if you want information about campaigns, you would need to start at one of the sites devoted to political or social sciences. Once there, you will find that many of these offer connections to more specific sites, for example, sites concerned with parties, campaign headquarters, polling firms, survey research, and the like. It is at these sites that you will find the information you need.

Table 6-4 offers a list of general political science resources available on the web. To access a far larger list of sites, please go to this book's web page at http://psrm.cqpress.com where you will find a vast array of specialized web

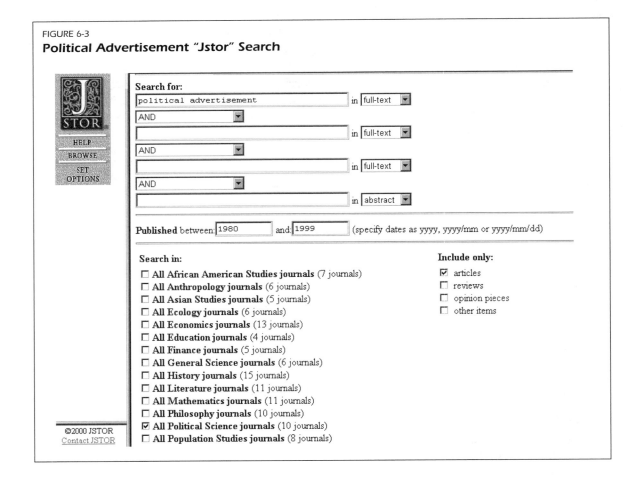

FIGURE 6-3
Political Advertisement "Jstor" Search

resources. We have opted to place them on the Internet rather than in these pages both because of the large quantity involved and because of the propensity of sites to come and go. We will update our web page as new resources become available and older ones are discontinued.

Conducting An Effective Electronic Literature Review

Carrying out an effective electronic literature review takes practice. Like many of life's activities, the more it is done, the easier it becomes. Nevertheless, following a few practical guidelines will expedite the process.

Most search engines and databases have ways to narrow a search to meet the user's specific needs. Usually a person wants to see only documents that contain all of a list of words or even a specific phrase, such as "international terrorism." Advanced search features allow you to specify exactly what words or phrases should be included in the document and which should be excluded by using connectors and modifiers. If you simply enter the desired words without adding modifiers, the program will in all likelihood look for

---

FIGURE 6-4

"Jstor" Search Results

HELP
SEARCH
BROWSE
SET
OPTIONS

You may [modify your search] if you wish.

Results 1 through 5:

1. **A Spot Check: Casting Doubt on the Demobilizing Effect of Attack Advertising**
    Steven E. Finkel, John G. Geer
    American Journal of Political Science, Vol. 42, No. 2. (Apr., 1998), pp. 573-595.
    [Citation / Abstract][Article][Page of First Match]

2. **Does Attack Advertising Demobilize the Electorate?** (in Articles)
    Stephen Ansolabehere, Shanto Iyengar, Adam Simon, Nicholas Valentino
    The American Political Science Review, Vol. 88, No. 4. (Dec., 1994), pp. 829-838.
    [Citation / Abstract][Article][Page of First Match]

3. **The Senate Judiciary Committee and Supreme Court Nominees: Measuring the Dynamics of Confirmation Criteria** (in Research Notes)
    Frank Guliuzza III, Daniel J. Reagan, David M. Barrett
    The Journal of Politics, Vol. 56, No. 3. (Aug., 1994), pp. 773-787.
    [Citation][Article][Page of First Match]

4. **Television Exposure and Attitude Change: The Impact of Political Interest**
    Thomas A. Kazee
    Public Opinion Quarterly, Vol. 45, No. 4. (Winter, 1981), pp. 507-518.
    [Citation / Abstract][Article][Page of First Match]

5. **The Levels of Conceptualization: False Measures of Ideological Sophistication**
    Eric R. A. N. Smith
    The American Political Science Review, Vol. 74, No. 3. (Sep., 1980), pp. 685-696.
    [Citation / Abstract][Article][Page of First Match]

TABLE 6-4
General Political Science Resources on the Web

Resource	Comments
Political Resources on the Net http://www.agora.stm.it/politic	Very useful general site with links to politics and political science information.
The Ultimate Political Science Links Page http://ednet.rvc.cc.il.us/~PeterR/PSLinks.htm	Another very useful general source. (Maintained by P. S. Ruckman, Jr. Rock Valley College, Rockford, Illinois.)
Political Party Materials http://www.lsu.edu/guests/poli/public_html/polpart.html	Page of links sorted by country. Good for political parties and organizations, governments, and mass media from all around the world.
Social Sciences Virtual Library http://web.clas.ufl.edu/users/gthursby/socsci/	This place "keeps track of online information as part of The World-Wide Web Virtual Library. Sites are inspected and evaluated for their adequacy as information sources."
Poly-Cy: Internet Resources for Political Science http://www.polsci.wvu.edu/polycy/	An exhaustive set of links to political science, public policy, and international relations resources.
American Government and Politics http://www.lsu.edu/guests/poli/public_html/ampols.html	Links to the political science profession as well as information and data. (Sponsored by the Department of Political Science, Louisiana State University.)
Political Science Resources http://www.psr.keele.ac.uk/	Contains links to American as well as international political resources. (Maintained by Richard Kimble, University of Keele.)
National Political Index http://www.politicalindex.com/	Connections to more than 3,500 political Web sites including current political news sources, federal elected officials, tracking congressional legislation.
ESRC: Research Guide to the Social Sciences http://www.jisc.ac.uk/subject/socsci/	This directory provides annotated links to sites sorted by subject matter.
GovSpot http://www.govspot.com/	This commercial but free site simplifies the search for government sites and documents, facts, news, and other information.
Social Science Information Gateway http://scout18.cs.wisc.edu/sosig_mirror/	You can receive via e-mail notices of web documents as they become available.
CNN/Time All Politics http://allpolitics.com/	This gateway leads to numerous public policy research organizations and journals.
Institute for the Study of Civic Values http://www.libertynet.org/~edcivic/iscvhome.html	Information made available by groups and individuals of many political persuasions.

pages that contain any of the listed words but not necessarily all of them. What you need to do is force the engine to look for all of the words or for a complete phrase, if that is what you want.

Different programs have different ways of accomplishing this task (hence the need to consult a program's "help" feature), but often one of two conventions will work. To identify only those documents that contain all of the words in your list, some programs require you to connect the words with the boolean operator AND. Other programs require you to insert a plus sign (+) between the words.

Suppose, for instance, that you want to conduct research on attack ads in recent presidential campaigns. If you type

negative advertisement elections

the retrieved documents could contain "negative" *or* "advertisement" *or* "elections" *or* any combination of these. Since any document with the word "election" could appear, you would have to wade through many more documents than are relevant to your topic. But by typing

negative AND advertisement AND elections

or

negative + advertisement + elections

(depending on the program you are using), you instruct the program to select only those documents that contain all three of these words.

If you want a specific phrase or term, you must enclose it in quotation marks. For example, by typing

"presidential election"

you instruct the program to search for the exact phrase. (Note that proper names, such as Bill Clinton, normally do not have to be included in quotes.)

If a search engine allows an AND, it will also permit the use of OR to search for lists of terms. For example, if you type

ads OR advertisement

the program will search for documents having *either* "ads" *or* "advertisement."

SEARCHING THE NET

Here are some quick tricks for surfing the Net:

- When first visiting a site, particularly one with search features, click the "help" button, which usually provides specific instructions for searching that site.

- If possible, pyramid your search by going first to a political science page and then from there looking for more specific sites.

- If you have a clear topic in mind, start with a specific Internet site such as those sponsored by research organizations or universities. Doing so will reduce the number of false hits.

- Open a simple word processing program such as Notepad or WordPad. Highlight and copy selected text from a web page to facilitate collecting information. Be sure to properly source this material. This technique is especially helpful for copying complicated and long Internet addresses (URLs).

- Take advantage of advanced search options. If possible, limit your search to specified time periods, to certain types of articles, to particular authors or subjects, and to data formats.

- Check this book's web page (http://psrm.cqpress. com) for links to specific topics.

In addition, the user can often force the program to skip pages having certain words by using NOT or, in some programs, by using the minus sign (–). For example, if you type

elections NOT Russian

the program will provide you with all documents containing the word "elections" except for those where the word "Russian" appears as well.

Taking advantage of the advanced search features of whatever search engine you are using will allow you to conduct a more thorough and efficient literature review.

Ensuring a Reliable Internet Literature Review

As in any type of research, when conducting an Internet literature review you want to be sure not just that you have found as many references as possible, but that those references are reliable. It does not follow that simply because the information appears on the World Wide Web it is good information. Some sources are patently unreliable. Virtually anyone or any group, no matter what their credentials, can create a web site. The only way to know for sure that the information you are looking at is dependable is to be familiar with the site's sponsor. In general, sites presented by individuals, even those with impressive-looking titles and qualifications, may not have the credibility or scholarly standing that your literature review requires. On the other hand, you can usually have confidence in sources that have been cited in professional publications or by established authors. Note too that dependability is not necessarily adversely impacted when it comes in the form of opinion. Many associations that hold strong political or ideological positions nevertheless offer useful information that is worth citing. If you are in doubt about the reliability of any of the sources you are thinking about using, check with your instructor or advisor. He or she should be able to help you assess whether or not accessed information is usable.

Because there is so much variation in the quality of Internet sources, and even more important, because any work consulted should be properly cited, you must be sure to properly credit your sources. In this way authors are fully credited for their data and ideas and your readers can check the accuracy of the information and the quality of your understanding of it.

At a minimum, the citation should include the page author or creator and the article title as well as the complete Internet address at which you accessed the article. Following is a generic form for citing a web page in a bibliography or note:

Author [last name, first name, or full organization name]. (Date of publication, if available) Title [Online]. Available: Full web address (Date page was accessed).

For example,

Reynolds, H. T. (1996) Power Elite Theories [Online]. Available: http://www.udel.edu/htr/American/(June 21, 2000).

indicates that your information is from a web page authored by H.T. Reynolds entitled "Power Elite Theories" that you accessed online at http://www.udel.edu/htr/American/on June 21, 2000.

The particular style you use will depend on the standards set by your institution or instructor. But you should include at least enough detail to let a reader retrieve the page and verify your interpretation of the information.

Printed Research Sources

Although the Internet provides a new and, when done properly, particularly effective method of literature review, use of printed material remains a mainstay of any research effort.

Professional Journals in Political Science and Related Fields

Any good literature review will include research reports published in professional political science journals. It is a sign of the information explosion and of academic pressures to publish that there are now an increasing number of journals with political science–related articles. While the lists presented in the next two sections are not exhaustive, they do include the major journals of general political science, a representative selection of journals that specialize in some aspect of political science, multidisciplinary journals, and some major journals in related disciplines.

While more and more journals and professional associations now have their own Internet sites, very few actually provide direct access to the full text of articles contained in their printed publications. They do, however, provide tables of contents and abstracts. Refer to this book's web site (http://www.psrm.cqpress.com) for the Internet addresses of those journals offering web pages.

Note that back issues of the entries marked with an asterisk are available in Jstor.

Journals of National and Regional Political Science Associations

American Journal of Political Science.* Primarily American government and politics articles.

American Political Science Review.* The official journal of the American Political Science Association.

British Journal of Political Science. Although emphasizing a comparative perspective, this publication contains important research on American political institutions and behavior.

Canadian Journal of Political Science/Revue Canadien de Science Politique. Focus on Canadian political matters, some articles on international affairs and political theory. Bilingual.

*Journal of Politics.** Primarily American government and politics articles.

Political Research Quarterly (formerly *Western Political Quarterly*). Broad coverage of political science and public administration.

Polity. Articles on American politics, comparative politics, international relations, and political philosophy.

Social Science Quarterly. Articles on a wide range of topics in the social sciences.

Specialized Journals and Journals from Related Disciplines

*Academy of Political Science Proceedings.** Each issue is devoted to a single theme. Presents divergent views on topics. Articles tend to be expository rather than analytical or empirical.

*American Economic Review.** The journal of the American Economics Association, the articles contained in this publication present technical research on economic topics.

*American Historical Review.** Main journal of the American Historical Association. Articles focus on recent American political history.

*American Journal of Sociology.** Wide-ranging coverage of topics in sociology and related fields.

American Politics Quarterly. Articles on American political behavior.

American Psychologist. Official journal of the American Psychological Association. Topics cover current issues in psychology.

*American Sociological Review.** Official journal of the American Sociological Association. Contains general articles in the field of sociology.

*Annals (American Academy of Political and Social Sciences).** Each issue focuses on a single topic.

The Brookings Review. Articles on public affairs research by scholars associated with the Brookings Institution.

Campaigns and Elections: The Journal of Political Action. Articles by academics and practitioners on the contemporary American political scene.

Comparative Political Studies. Interdisciplinary articles on cross-national comparative studies.

Comparative Politics. Broad coverage of comparative politics topics.

Comparative Strategy: An International Journal. Focus on international politics and strategic problems.

Congress and the Presidency (formerly *Congressional Studies; Capitol Studies*). Focus on research on the presidency and Congress.

Electoral Studies. International, interdisciplinary journal focusing on voting and elections.

Ethics.* Philosophical analysis of political and social issues such as abortion, the death penalty, and nuclear weapons.

European Journal of Political Science. Research on European political matters.

Foreign Affairs. Focus on current issues in American foreign policy, usually with policy recommendations. Articles by scholars, government officials, or journalists.

Foreign Policy. Wide-ranging coverage of foreign affairs. Articles debate current American foreign policy decisions.

Government and Opposition: A Quarterly Journal of Comparative Politics. Comparative studies of political development.

International Affairs. Emphasis on political and social aspects of international affairs.

International Organization. Focus on practical and theoretical problems of international organizations.

International Political Science Review. Official publication of the International Political Science Association. Each issue focuses on a theme.

International Studies Quarterly. Multidisciplinary articles related to transnational phenomena.

International Security. An excellent sources for articles about American foreign and military policy.

Journal of American History* (formerly *Mississippi Valley Historical Review*). Contains, among others, articles relevant to political history.

Journal of Communist Studies. Articles examine historical and current situations throughout the world that involve communism.

Journal of Conflict Resolution. Articles on international and intranational conflicts. (Some of the articles are technical or mathematical.)

Journal of Development Studies. Interdisciplinary journal with articles on economic and social development of Third World countries.

Journal of Policy Analysis and Management. Journal of the Association for Public Policy Analysis and Management.

Legislative Studies Quarterly. International journal concentrating on comparative legislative and cross-national studies.

Millennium. A journal devoted to scholarly research and theorizing about international relations.

Philosophy and Public Policy. * Long articles on the philosophical and moral aspects of political, economic, and social issues.

Political Psychology. This journal has empirical studies of political attitudes and behavior.

Policy Studies Journal. Theoretical and practical articles addressing important public policy problems.

Policy Studies Review. Articles related to current public policy issues.

Political Behavior. Interdisciplinary journal with articles on political behavior and decision making.

Political Science Quarterly. * Articles on American politics, comparative politics, and international relations.

Political Studies. The journal of the British Political Science Association. Contains some articles relevant to American government and politics and political thought.

Political Theory. International journal of political philosophy, published quarterly.

Presidential Studies Quarterly. Focus on the American presidency.

Public Administration Review. Focus on municipal, state, and federal management issues.

Public Choice. The articles in this journal apply rational choice theory and formal models to political decision making of all kinds. The papers can be quite technical.

Public Opinion Quarterly. * All aspects of public opinion and polling, including historical poll results on selected issues.

Public Policy. Articles on public policy formulation.

Publius: The Journal of Federalism. Intergovernmental relations in federal systems; multidisciplinary articles.

Review of International Studies. Discussion of research and theorizing about international relations.

Review of Politics. This publication emphasizes philosophical and historical approaches to politics.

Resources for Feminist Research. An international journal that contains research articles and substantive bibliographic information.

Science and Society. Journal of Marxist thought and analysis.

State and Local Government Review. Articles focus on applied public policies and government management.

Studies in American Political Development. Published four times a year, this journal publishes articles dealing with the historical development and current status of American political institutions.

Terrorism: An International Journal. Devoted to the study of terrorism.

Urban Affairs Quarterly. Interdisciplinary articles on urban affairs.

Women & Politics. Describes, predicts, and assesses the impact of politics on women and of women on politics.

*World Politics.** Articles contain in-depth historical or political analysis of current international affairs.

Indexes, Bibliographies, and Abstracts

A literature search will also use the information contained in indexes, bibliographies, and collections of abstracts. Besides those available online (see Table 6-3), there are numerous indexes to periodical literature, books, and government publications. Although some are quite comprehensive, many others are selective. After picking a topic and thinking about what you need, it is a good idea to check the description of a particular index—usually contained in the front of the publication—before using it.

Unfortunately, there is a time lag between publication of a periodical or book and its entry in an index. However, you may discover that articles of interest are concentrated among a few journals. To identify articles related to your topic that have not yet been indexed, skim the table of contents of the latest issues of these journals.

After you have located a number of sources pertinent to your research project, you will want to become familiar with this literature in the most efficient way possible. Each researcher develops a strategy best suited to the situation at hand, but we offer here three suggestions. First, locate the most important and relevant research

ORGANIZING REFERENCES
The first time you conduct a comprehensive literature search, you may be overwhelmed by the number of citations you discover. Managing them systematically is often quite a challenge. It may help to put each relevant citation on a separate 3 x 5 index card. If the citation proves to be useful, then complete bibliographic information can be entered later on the card in the form you will be using for your bibliography. These cards can be sorted according to various needs. This method preserves the fruits of a literature search in a form that will be useful to you, and it saves the step of writing the citation information onto a list and then transferring it to a card.

reports immediately and concentrate on them rather than trying to read all of the numerous research reports you have discovered, some of which are of only peripheral concern. Abstracts are helpful here. Abstracts are short summaries of the contents of books and articles. These will aid in identifying those sources most relevant to your topic and improve the efficiency of your literature review. Collections of abstracts are included in our list of indexes and bibliographies.

Second, start with the most recent publications. They will contain references to past literature. Even when the content of past work is not discussed, repeated reference to a work will indicate that it is considered by many to be important. Thus you should probably review the work early on in your review.

A final strategy is to collect a number of works that you know are directly related to your topic. Using the citation index of the Social Sciences Citation Index, locate the author and work. Below this entry will be a list of all subsequent publications that have referenced the work. These publications are likely to be closely related to your topic as well. The number of times a work is cited by others is a rough indication of its significance. This may guide your decisions about which works to read first.

The following is a list of indexes, bibliographies, and collections of abstracts and other sources of use to political science researchers conducting a literature search.

ABC Pol Sci: A Bibliography of Contents. Timely index with tables of contents of about 300 international journals in their original language in the fields of political science, sociology, economics, policy studies, and law. Author, title, and subject indexes. Updated quarterly.

Alternative Press Index. Index of left-of-center publications generally not indexed elsewhere. Issued quarterly.

America: History and Life. Abstracts and citations of articles on U.S. and Canadian history from prehistory to present. Volume 0 includes abstracts from *Historical Abstracts,* 1954–1965. Updated quarterly.

Combined Retrospective Index to Scholarly Journals in Political Science. An index of articles from 531 journals in history, political science, and sociology. Arranged by subject. Also includes author index.

Current Contents/Social and Behavioral Science. Weekly index with tables of contents of journals arranged by broad discipline headings. Good for searching for recent articles. Includes author and title word index.

Current Law Index. Monthly index of some 700 periodicals.

Dissertation Abstracts International: Humanities and Social Sciences. Monthly compilation of abstracts of doctoral dissertations from cooperating U.S., Canadian, and European institutions. Formerly called *Dissertation Abstracts and Microfilm Abstracts.* Change in title reflects increased coverage.

Energy Abstracts for Policy Analysis. Abstracts all types of publications on nontechnical aspects of energy. Annual index. Also available online.

Environment Abstracts Annual. Annual cumulation of Environment Abstracts. Covers a variety of publications, including journals, proceedings, newsletters, and reports, on a broad range of environmental topics. Contains a section entitled "Year in Review" that has a calendar of the year's key environmental events, a directory of agencies and conservation organizations, a list of conferences, and a legislative summary. Online version is called Enviroline.

Feminist Periodicals. Reproduces tables of contents of current issues of over 100 major feminist journals.

Index to Current Urban Documents. Quarterly index to local government documents of the 272 largest American cities, their counties and regions. Annual cumulation.

Index to Legal Periodicals. Monthly index with annual cumulation.

Index to Periodical Articles Related to Law. Quarterly index of journals not covered by *Current Law Index* or *Index to Legal Periodicals.* Therefore does not cover law journals or directly law-related publications.

Index to U.S. Government Periodicals. Quarterly index of approximately 200 out of more than 2,000 government periodicals.

International Bibliography of the Social Sciences–Political Science. Covers international journals in political science; updated yearly.

International Political Science Abstracts. Comprehensive source for abstracts for all subject areas of political science. Detailed subject and author indexes. Published bimonthly with cumulative annual index.

Legal Resources Index. Includes indexing for legal periodicals, legal newspapers, and law-related articles from business and general interest periodicals. Available in microfilm and online. Online version is updated daily, microfilm version monthly.

Magazine Index. Microfilm index, updated monthly, of approximately 400 magazine titles.

Monthly Catalog of United States Government Publications. Most complete index to U.S. government publications.

Public Affairs Information Service Bulletin. Biweekly index of policy-oriented literature. Includes periodicals, books, and government documents.

Public Affairs Information Service Bulletin: Foreign Language Index. Foreign language counterpart of *PAIS Bulletin,* updated quarterly.

Readers' Guide to Periodical Literature. Semi-monthly index of approximately 200 popular newsstand periodicals.

Sage Public Administration Abstracts. Quarterly index of articles, books, government publications, pamphlets, and so on. International in scope.

Sage Urban Studies Abstracts. Quarterly collection of articles international in scope. No cumulative indexes.

Social Sciences Citation Index. An index, updated three times a year, of 2,000 journals. Subject, source, and citation indexes.

Social Sciences Index. Quarterly index of approximately 300 frequently used journals in the social sciences.

Sociological Abstracts. Extensive coverage of publications in and related to sociology. Supplements include papers presented at sociological meetings, updated five times a year.

Women Studies Abstracts. Updated quarterly.

Women's Studies Index. Annual index. Provides the most comprehensive coverage of women's studies periodicals.

Universal Reference System: Political Science Series. Annual supplements commence in 1969. A ten-volume set arranged by broad topic headings indexes material prior to 1969. Includes abstracts.

Urban Affairs Abstracts. Updated weekly with semi-annual and annual cumulations.

USPSD, United States Political Science Documents. Indexes and abstracts articles from political science journals; updated yearly.

Compact Disc Databases

If you do not have access to the Internet but can use a library, quite a few of the indexes and abstracts described above are available in compact disc form. Below we list some of those that are most commonly available.

ABC Pol Sci. Compact disc version of index described above.

Auto-Graphics Government Documents Catalog System. An index to all government documents catalogued by the Government Printing Office since June 1976. Compact disc equivalent to Monthly Catalog.

PAIS. Compact disc incorporates the *Public Affairs Information Service Bulletin* and the *PAIS Foreign Language Index.*

Sociofile. Compact disc equivalent to *Sociological Abstracts.*

Newspaper Indexes

Newspaper articles may be a source of background information as well as of explanations and hypotheses about politics. These major newspapers have indexes:

Christian Science Monitor

New York Times

Times (London)

Wall Street Journal

Washington Post

The *National Newspaper Index* comes in microfilm and compact disc versions. The microfilm version that begins in January 1979 includes the *Christian Science Monitor,* the *New York Times,* and the *Wall Street Journal.* The *Washington Post* was added in September 1982 and the *Los Angeles Times* in October 1982. The compact disc version indexes the same newspapers from 1988 on.

Book Reviews

You may find it helpful to know how others have evaluated key books related to your research topic. Reviewers often critique the books, compare them with other works in the field, and offer interpretations and explanations that differ from those of the author. In addition, a review will often contain useful and reliable substantive information and can be used as a source just like any other.

Book Review Digest.

Book Review Index.

Combined Retrospective Index to Book Reviews in Scholarly Journals.

Current Book Review Citations. Monthly index to book reviews published in more than 1,200 periodicals.

Perspective. Monthly review of new books.

Political Science Reviewer.

Conference Proceedings

Frequently research is presented at professional conferences before it is published in a professional journal. If you want to be informed up to the minute or if a research topic is quite new, it may be worthwhile to investigate papers given at professional conferences.

The *Index to Social Sciences & Humanities Proceedings* indexes published proceedings. However, the proceedings of the annual meetings of the American Political Science Association (APSA) and regional political science associations have not been published. Summer issues of APSA's *PS* contain the preliminary program for the forthcoming annual meeting. The program lists authors and paper titles. The *International Studies Newsletter* publishes preliminary programs for International Studies Association meetings. Copies of programs for other political science and related conferences (frequently announced in *PS*) may be obtained from the sponsoring organization. Abstracts for some fields, for example *Sociological Abstracts,* include papers presented at conferences. Once promising papers presented at professional conferences have been located, copies of the papers may usually be obtained by writing to the authors directly.

Many draft manuscripts and conference papers are now available online at sites maintained by professional organizations.

Conclusion

No matter what the original purpose of your literature search, it should be thorough. In your research report you should discuss those sources that provide explanations for the phenomena you are studying and that support the plausibility of your hypotheses. You should also discuss how your research relates to other research and use the existing literature to document the significance of your research. An example of a literature review is contained in the research report in Chapter 14.

Notes

1. Sidney Tarrow, "The Urban-Rural Cleavage in Political Involvement: The Case of France," *American Political Science Review* 65 (June 1971): 341–357.
2. Angus Campbell, Gerald Gurin, and Warren E. Miller, *The Voter Decides* (Evanston, Ill.: Row, Peterson, 1959), 187.
3. David Easton and Jack Dennis, "The Child's Acquisition of Regime Norms: Political Efficacy," *American Political Science Review* 61 (March 1967): 26.
4. Robert Weissberg, *Political Learning, Political Choice and Democratic Citizenship* (Englewood Cliffs, N.J.: Prentice-Hall, 1974), 470.
5. Donald R. Matthews and James W. Prothro, *Negroes and the New Southern Politics* (New York: Harcourt, Brace & World, 1966), 276.
6. Jerome D. Becker and Ivan L. Preston, "Media Usage and Political Activity," *Journalism Quarterly* 46 (spring 1969): 130.
7. Arthur H. Miller, Edie N. Goldenberg, and Lutz Erbring, "Type-Set Politics: Impacts of Newspapers on Public Confidence," *American Political Science Review* 73 (March 1979): 67.
8. A source of much of the commentary in this chapter on journals, indexes, bibliographies, and abstracts is Bill Katz and Linda Sternberg Katz, *Magazines for Libraries,* 6th ed. (New York: R.R. Bowker, 1989).
9. The Internet and World Wide Web are really separate entities, but for simplicity we use the terms interchangeably here.

Terms introduced

DIRECTORY. A database that arranges terms in a hierarchy by subject matter, allowing a search to proceed from general to specific topics.

ELECTRONIC DATABASE. A collection of information (of any type) stored on an electromagnetic medium that can be accessed and examined by certain computer programs.

SEARCH ENGINE. A computer program that visits web pages on the Internet and looks for those containing particular directories or words.

SEARCH TERM. A word or phrase entered into a computer program (a search engine) that looks through web pages on the Internet for those that contain the word or phrase.

Exercises

1 Select a political term such as "nuclear non proliferation treaty" or "World Trade Organization." Use the search engines Altavista and Yahoo to do an electronic literature search. Do these programs generally locate the same sources, or are there important differences in what each finds? Which do you prefer? Why?

2. If available, use Jstor (www.jstor.org) to compile a bibliography of one of your favorite political scientists.

3. Use *ABC Pol Sci,* Vol. 24, no. 5 (1992), to find the year, volume, and issue number of the following periodicals: *African Studies Review, American Politics Quarterly, Policy Studies Review, World Development.* Give the name and author of the last article in each periodical.

4. Using the *Social Sciences Index,* determine the number of sources listed for the following topics: Environmental Policy–United States; Presidential elections; Kosovo; Political Science–Political Science as a Profession; State Legislatures. Give the titles of the sources listed under state legislatures.

Suggested Readings

Cooper, Harris M. *Integrating Research: A Guide for Literature Reviews.* 2d ed. Beverly Hills, Calif.: Sage, 1989.

Lester, James D. Citing Cyberspace: How to Search the Web [Online]. Available: http://longman.awl.com/englishpages (November 5, 1999).

Sarah Byrd Askew Library. Guide for Citing Electronic Information [Online]. Available: http://www.wpunj.edu/library (November 16, 2000).

CHAPTER 7
Sampling

In this and the next three chapters we address the task of making the empirical observations with which to implement research design and test hypotheses. This is what is generally called the data collection stage of a research project.

We have said that empirical observations are necessary to test hypotheses, but so far we have not explained how those observations are obtained and the implications of making them in particular ways. In this chapter we will discuss the decisions that have to be made about the number and kind of cases that will be observed. In the following three chapters we will present actual techniques for observing and measuring political phenomena.

Whatever the hypothesis under consideration, researchers must decide what observations are appropriate for testing it. Equally important, they must decide whether they will measure all or only some of the possible observations. If data are collected on only some, then care must be taken to ensure that the selection process leads to accurate and reliable conclusions. We will illustrate the need for this decision by returning to some of our examples of political science research.

Recall from Chapter 1 that Jeffrey Segal and Albert Cover were interested in the relationship between the ideological values of U.S. Supreme Court justices and their votes on cases brought before the Court. The unit of analysis was the judge and their votes on cases and their ideological outlook were the variables measured. The researchers had to decide whether to perform this measurement (that is, collect the data) for all Supreme Court justices or for only some of the justices. They chose to collect data for only some of the justices: those appointed from Earl Warren to Anthony Kennedy. They also chose to limit their analysis to the justices' votes on civil liberties cases.

Benjamin Page and Robert Shapiro, who were interested in the responsiveness of government policy to citizens' preferences, decided to observe cases of significant changes in Americans' policy preferences. They sorted through hundreds of public opinion surveys that were conducted between 1935 and 1979 by three major survey organizations using national samples. They found 609 questions that were repeated in identical form at two or more points in time and 357 instances of significant changes in citizens' policy preferences. Hence, their research was limited to these 357 cases of public opinion change.

In many cases researchers choose to collect data on only *some* of the pertinent observations instead of measuring or observing all of the possible observations covered by a hypothesis. One therefore needs to keep an important distinction in mind. A **population** is any well-defined set of units of analysis. It does not necessarily refer to people. A population might be all of the adults living in a geographical area such as a county or state or working in an organization. But it could equally well be a set of countries, corporations, government agencies, events, magazine articles, or years. What is important is that the population be carefully and fully defined and that it be relevant to the research question. A **sample**, by contrast, is any subset of units collected in some manner from the population. Here the important thing to clarify is the method of selection

KEEP TERMS STRAIGHT
Do not be confused by the term *population,* which, as the text indicates, simply means a collection of things. We could define a population as the people living in New Castle, Delaware. But a population could also consist of a set of geographical areas such as the voting districts in New Castle County. In the first case, the units of analysis are individuals; in the second case, they are aggregates of individuals.

and the number of observations to be drawn from the population. In the remainder of this chapter we discuss the differences between populations and samples and the ways in which a sample may be drawn from a specified population.

Population or Sample?

A researcher's decision whether to collect data for a population or for a sample is usually made on practical grounds. If time, money, and other costs were not considerations, it would almost always be better to collect data for a population since we would then be sure that the observed cases accurately reflect the population characteristics of interest. However, in many if not most instances it is simply not possible or feasible to study an entire population. Imagine, for instance, the difficulty of attempting to interview every adult in even a small city. Since research is costly and time consuming, researchers must weigh the advantages and disadvantages of using a population or a sample. The advantages of taking a sample are often savings in time and money. The disadvantage is that information based on a sample is usually less accurate or more subject to error than is information collected from a population.[1]

Some studies simply do not lend themselves to sampling. For example, case studies, which are often quite useful and lead to scientific understanding, involve the detailed examination of just one or a few units.[2]

Consider as an example of the choices involved in whether to use a sample versus a population a political scientist who wants to test some hypotheses regarding the content of televised political campaign commercials. The project requires an examination of the content of a number of commercials, which is the unit of analysis. Clearly, from the standpoint of accuracy, it would be preferable to have data on the total population of televised commercials (in other words, to have available for measurement every campaign commercial that ever aired). But undertaking this type of analysis is simply impossible because no such data bank exists anywhere, nor does anyone even know how many commercials have been televised across the country in the last forty years. Consequently, the researcher will have to rely on a sample of readily available commercials to test the hypotheses—a decision that is practical, necessary, and less costly, but perhaps subject to error.[3]

Thus for reasons of necessity and convenience, political science researchers often collect data on a sample of observations. In fact, public opinion and voting behavior researchers almost always rely on samples. This means, however, that they must know how to select good samples and must appreciate the implications of relying on samples for testing hypotheses if they want to be able to claim that their findings for the sample accurately reflect what they would find if they were to test the hypothesis on the whole population.

The Basics of Sampling

As noted in the previous section, a sample is simply a subset of a larger population, just as a sample of blood is a subset of all of the blood in your body at one moment in time. If the sample is selected properly, the information it yields may be used to make inferences about the whole population. Since sampling is always used in public opinion surveys, it is often thought of in connection with that activity. But sampling arises whenever a researcher takes measurements on a subset of the observations in a population, however defined, covered by the hypothesis being investigated. After all, whatever empirical findings emerge from a sample from a specified population will apply to that and only that population. It would be a mistake, for instance, to sample campaign speeches from the last four presidential elections and then generalize to *all* American presidential rhetoric.

Before proceeding further, we should note that what usually matters most is not that a sample rather than a population is analyzed, or that the sample is a tiny fraction of the population, but that the data are obtained according to well-established rules. To understand why, we need to review some terms commonly used in discussions of sampling.[4]

Social scientists are mainly interested in certain characteristics of populations, such as averages, differences between groups, and relationships among variables. If any one of these traits can be quantified as a number, we call it a **population parameter**. Population parameters are typically denoted by capital English or Greek letters. For example, the proportion of Americans registered as Democrats at a particular time can be designated P or π (the Greek letter pi). The purpose of sampling is to collect data that provide an accurate estimate of a population parameter. An **estimator** is a statistic based on sample observations that is used to estimate the numerical value of a population characteristic or parameter. The estimator of a population characteristic or attribute that is calculated from sample data is call a **sample statistic**. Like population parameters, these are typically denoted by symbols or letters. Most commonly we use a hat (ˆ) over a character as an indicator of a sample statistic that estimates a parameter. Sometimes, though, another symbol is used, as in $\overline{Y}$, which denotes a sample mean.

An **element** (sometimes called a "unit of analysis") is a single occurrence, realization, or instance of the objects or entities being studied. Elements in political science research are often individuals, but they also can be states, cities, agencies, countries, campaign advertisements, political speeches, wars, social or professional organizations, crimes, or legislatures, just to name a few.

As noted previously, a population is a collection of elements defined according to a researcher's theoretical interest. It may, for example, consist of all campaign speeches given by major candidates for president in the last four presidential elections. Or it may be all international armed conflicts that have occurred in the last two hundred years. The key is to be clear and specific. You may refer to presidential campaign speeches as the focus of your research, but at some point you should make clear which speeches in what time periods constitute the population.

DON'T BE INTIMIDATED BY SYMBOLS AND FORMULAS Empirical social scientists frequently use symbols or letters as a shorthand way to describe terms. These devices allow for greater precision in expression. But there is no need to panic when you come across them. Authors are usually very clear in describing exactly what a symbol means.

In this book, we employ capital English and Greek letters to designate population parameters (for example, the mean or proportion) and the same symbols with hats over them to denote corresponding sample statistics. Thus, P refers to population proportion, which can be estimated by drawing a sample and calculating $\hat{P}$, the sample proportion. These figures can be combined with other symbols to form useful equations. (One important exception is that in this book $\overline{Y}$ always stands for the sample mean. We do not use $\hat{\mu}$.)

For reasons that we will discuss shortly, a population may be stratified—that is, subdivided or broken up into groups of similar elements—before a sample is drawn. Each **stratum** is a subgroup of a population that shares one or more characteristics. For example, we might divide the population of campaign speeches in the last four presidential elections into four strata, each stratum containing speeches from one of the four elections. In a study of students' attitudes, particularly at a university, the student body may be stratified by academic class, major, and grade-point average. The strata that are chosen are usually characteristics or attributes thought to be related to the dependent variables under study.

The population from which a sample is *actually* drawn is called a **sampling frame**. Technically speaking, all elements that are part of the population defined to be of interest to the research question should be part of the sampling frame. If they are not, any data collected may not be representative of the population studied. Often, however, sampling frames are incomplete, as the following example illustrates.

Suppose a researcher evaluates community opinion about snow removal by interviewing every fifth adult entering a local supermarket. The sampling frame would consist of all adults entering the supermarket while the researcher was standing outside. This sampling frame could hardly be construed as including all adult members of the community unless all adult members of the community made a trip to the supermarket *when* the researcher was there. (In a few communities this might be a valid assumption.) Furthermore, use of such a sampling frame would probably introduce bias into the results. Perhaps many of the people who stayed at home rather than going to the supermarket considered the trip too hazardous because of poor snow removal. The closer the sampling frame is to the target population, the better.

Sometimes lists of elements exist that constitute the sampling frame. For example, a university may have a list of all students, or the Conference of Mayors may have a list of current mayors of cities with 500,000 residents or more. The existence of a list may be enticing to a researcher since it removes the need to create one from scratch. But lists may represent an inappropriate sampling frame if they are out of date, incorrect, or do not really correspond to the population of interest. A common example would be if a researcher used a telephone directory as the sampling frame for interviewing sample households within the service area. Households with unlisted numbers would be missed, some numbers would belong to commercial establishments or no longer be working, and recently assigned numbers would not be included. Consequently, the telephone book could constitute an inaccurate or inappropriate sampling frame for the population in that area. Researchers should carefully check their sampling frames for potential omissions or erroneously included elements. Consumers of research should also carefully examine sampling frames to see that they match the populations researchers claim to be studying.

An example of a poll that relied on an incomplete sampling frame is the infamous *Literary Digest* poll of 1936. It predicted that the winner of the presidential election would be Alf Landon, not Franklin D. Roosevelt. This poll imprudently relied on a sample drawn from telephone directories and automobile registration lists. At that time telephone and automobile ownership were not as widespread as they are today. Thus the sampling frame overrepresented wealthy individuals.[5] The problem was compounded by the fact that in the midst of the depression an unprecedented number of poor people voted, and they voted overwhelmingly for Roosevelt.

A newer problem with use of telephone directories is that so many people have unlisted numbers that reliance on a printed list will quite possibly lead to a biased sample. To deal with this problem a procedure known as **random digit dialing** has been developed. In effect, numbers are dialed randomly.[6] In this way, all telephone owners can potentially be contacted, whether they have listed numbers or not.[7] Keep in mind, however, that not all households have telephones. Hence, even a sampling frame consisting of randomly generated telephone numbers is still an incomplete listing of households. It is estimated that 90 to 98 percent of all households have telephones.[8] Therefore, if the survey population is *all* households in the United States, a telephone sample will not be entirely representative of that population.

In many instances a list of the population may not exist or it may not be feasible to create one. It may be possible, however, to make a list of groups. Then the researcher could sample this list of groups and enumerate the elements only in those groups that are selected. In this case, the initial sampling frame would consist of a list of groups, not elements.

For example, suppose you wanted to collect data on the attitudes and behavior of civic and social service volunteers in a large metropolitan area. Rather than initially developing a list of all such volunteers—a laborious and time-consuming task—you could develop a list of all organizations that are known to use volunteers. Next a subset of these organizations could be selected and then a list of volunteers secured for only this subset.

A **sampling unit** is an entity listed in a sampling frame. In simple cases the sampling unit is the same as an element. In more complicated sampling designs it may be a collection of elements. In the previous example, organizations are the sampling units.

Types of Samples

Researchers make a basic distinction among types of samples according to how the data are collected. We mentioned earlier that political scientists often select a sample, collect information about elements in the sample, and then use that data to talk about the population from which the sample was drawn. In other words, they make *inferences* about the whole population from what they know about a smaller group. If a sampling frame is incomplete or inappropriate, **sample bias** will occur. In such cases the sample will be unrepresentative of the population and inaccurate conclusions about the population may be drawn. Sample bias may also be caused by a biased selection of elements, even if the sampling frame is a complete and accurate list of the elements in the population.

This point can be described a bit more formally as follows. A political scientist may be interested in estimating the proportion of residents in a city who are registered as "independent" or "decline" rather than "Republican" or "Democrat." Let's call this *unknown* proportion P. A statistic based on a properly collected sample provides an estimator, denoted $\hat{P}$, of this quantity. What does "properly collected" mean? It means that the estimator should in some sense be a good or *unbiased* guess about the true value of P with the least error possible. We explore this topic in more detail later in the chapter, but for now consider an example.

Suppose that in the survey of opinion on snow removal mentioned above every adult in the community did enter the supermarket while the researcher was there. And suppose that instead of selecting every fifth adult who entered, the researcher avoided individuals who appeared in a hurry or in poor humor (perhaps because of snowy roads). In this case the researcher's sampling frame was fine, but the sample itself would probably be biased, and not representative of public opinion in that community. Any estimate $\hat{P}$ about the magnitude of support for snow removal P would probably be biased.

Because of the concern over sample bias it is important to distinguish between two basic types of samples: probability and nonprobability samples. A **probability sample** is simply a sample for which each element in the total population has a known probability of being included in the sample. This knowledge allows a researcher to calculate how accurately the sample reflects the population from which it is drawn. By contrast, a **nonprobability sample** is one in which each element in the population has an unknown probability of being selected. Not knowing the probabilities of inclusion rules out the use of statistical theory to make inferences, and thus whenever possible probability samples are preferred to nonprobability samples.

In the next several sections we will consider different types of probability samples: simple random samples, systematic samples, stratified samples (both proportionate and disproportionate), cluster samples, and telephone samples. We will then examine nonprobability samples and their uses.

Simple Random Samples

In a **simple random sample** each element and combination of elements have an *equal* chance of being selected. A list of all the elements in the population must be available, and a method of selecting those elements must be used that ensures that each element has an equal chance of being selected.[9] We will review two common ways of selecting a simple random sample so that you can see how elements are given an equal chance of selection.

SAMPLING

One way of selecting elements at random from a list is by assigning a number to each element in the sample frame and then using a **random numbers table**, which is simply a list of random numbers, to select a sample of numbers. A computer can also create random numbers for this purpose. However it is done, those units having the chosen numbers associated with them are included in the sample.

Suppose, for instance, we have a population of 1,507 elements and wish to draw from it a sample of 150. We first number each member of the population, 1, 2, 3, . . . and so on up to 1,507. Then we can start at a random place in a random numbers table and look across and down the columns of numbers to identify our selections. Each time a number between 0001 and 1,507 appears, that element in the population with that number is selected. If a number appears more than once, that number is ignored after the first time, and we simply go on to another number. (This is called sampling without replacement.) For example, if we combine the adjacent cells of the first two columns in Table 7-1, we would have the following, random numbers: 9852, 1180, 8345, 8868, and 9959. Because only element 1180 falls between 0001 and 1,507, it (or more precisely, the element to which it is assigned) would be included in the sample. As long as we do not deliberately look for a certain number, we may start anywhere in the table and use any system to move through it. It is not acceptable to generate four-digit numbers in one's head, however, since these are likely to be biased in some way.[10]

The second way of drawing a random sample is the by-the-lot method. In this procedure all the elements in the population are "tossed" in a hat (or some analogous procedure), and elements are randomly drawn out until the desired sample size has been reached. This procedure requires that the elements "in the hat" be continuously and thoroughly mixed so that each remaining element has an equal chance of being selected. This procedure can

TABLE 7-1
Portion of a Random Numbers Table

98	52	01	77	67
11	80	50	54	31
83	45	29	96	34
88	68	54	02	00
99	59	46	73	48
65	48	11	76	74
80	12	43	56	35
74	35	09	98	17
69	91	62	68	03
09	89	32	05	05

Source: Rand Corporation, *A Million Random Digits* (Glencoe, Ill.: Free Press, 1955), 1–3. Quoted from Hubert M. Blalock Jr., *Social Statistics*, rev. 2d ed., (New York: McGraw Hill, 1979), 598.

be quite cumbersome when the population size is large. It does, however, eliminate the necessity of assigning a number to each element in the sampling frame.

Whichever method of selection is used, simple random sampling requires a numbered list of the members of the population. For example, a random sample of members of Congress could be drawn from a list of all 100 senators and 435 representatives. A simple random sample of countries could be chosen from a list of all of the countries in the world, or a random sample of American cities with more than 50,000 people could be selected from a list of all such cities in the United States. In other words, whenever an accurate and complete list the target population is available and is of manageable size, a simple random sample can usually be drawn. The problem, as we will see, is that obtaining such a list is not always easy or even possible.

Systematic Samples

Assigning numbers to all elements in a list and then using random numbers to select elements may be a cumbersome procedure. Fortunately, a **systematic sample**, in which elements are selected from a list at predetermined intervals, provides an alternative method that is sometimes easier to apply. It too requires a list of the target population. But the elements are chosen from the list systematically rather than randomly. That is, every jth element on the list is selected where j is the number that will result in the desired number of elements being selected. This number is called the **sampling interval**, or the "space" or number between elements that are drawn.

Suppose we wanted to draw a sample of 100 names from a list of all 5,000 students attending a college. If we were going to use systematic sampling, we would first calculate the sampling interval by dividing the number of elements in the list by the desired sample size. In this case, we would divide 5,000 by the desired sample size of 100 to get a sampling interval of 50 ($j = 50$). Next we would systematically go through the list and select every fiftieth student, thereby selecting 100 names. To determine where on the list to begin, we would need to make a **random start**—that is, we would select a number at random. In our example, we would choose a number between 1 and 50 at random using a table of random digits or some other process. Thus, if we chose the number 31 at random, then students 31, 81, and 131 would be included in our sample.

Systematic sampling is very useful when dealing with a long list of population elements. It is often used in product testing. Suppose you have been given the job of ensuring that a firm's tuna fish cans are properly sealed before they are delivered to grocery stores. And assume that your resources permit you to test only a sample of tuna fish cans rather than the entire population of tuna fish cans. It would be much easier to systematically select every

300th tuna fish can as it rolls off the assembly line than to collect all the cans in one place and randomly select some of them for testing.

Despite its advantages, systematic sampling may result in a biased sample in two situations.[11] One occurs if elements on the list have been ranked according to a characteristic. In that situation the position of the random start will affect the average value of the characteristic for the sample. For example, if students were ranked from the lowest to the highest grade-point average, a systematic sample with students 1, 51, and 101 would have a lower grade-point average than a sample with students 50, 100, and 150. Each sample would yield a grade-point average that presents a biased picture of the student population.

The second situation leading to bias occurs if the list contains a pattern that corresponds to the sampling interval. Suppose you were conducting a study of the attitudes of children from large families and you were working with a list where the children in each family were listed by age. If the families included in the list all had six children and your sampling interval was 6 (or any multiple of 6), then systematic sampling would result in a sample of children who were all in the same position among their siblings. If attitudes varied with birth order, then your findings would be biased.

A survey of soldiers conducted during World War II offers a good example of a case in which a pattern in the list used as the sampling frame interfered with the selection of an unbiased systematic sample.[12] The list of soldiers was arranged by squad, with each squad roster arranged by rank. The sampling interval and squad size were both 10. Consequently, the sample consisted of all persons who held the same rank, in this case squad sergeant. Clearly, sergeants might not be representative of all soldiers serving in World War II.

Stratified Samples

A **stratified sample** is a probability sample in which elements sharing one or more characteristics are grouped, and elements are selected from each group in proportion to the group's representation in the total population. Stratified samples take advantage of the principle that the more homogeneous the population, the easier it is to select a representative sample from it. Also, if a population is relatively homogeneous, the size of the sample needed to produce a given degree of accuracy will be smaller than for a heterogeneous population. In stratified sampling, sampling units are divided into strata with each unit appearing in only one stratum. Then a simple random sample or systematic sample is taken from each stratum.

A stratified sample can be either proportionate or disproportionate. In proportionate sampling, a researcher uses a stratified sample in which each stratum is represented in proportion to its size in the population—what researchers call a **proportionate sample**. For example, let's assume we have a total population of 500 colored balls: 50 each of red, yellow, orange, and green and 100 each of blue, black, and white. We wish to draw a sample of 100 balls. To ensure a sample with each color represented in proportion to its presence in the population, we would first stratify the balls according to color. To determine the number of balls to sample from each stratum, we calculate the **sampling fraction**, which is the size of the desired sample divided by the size of the population. In this example the sampling fraction is 100/500 or one-fifth of the balls. Therefore, we must sample one-fifth of all the balls in each stratum.

Since there are 50 red balls, we want one-fifth, or 10 red balls. We could select these 10 red balls at random or select every fifth ball with a random start between 1 and 5. If we followed this procedure for each color, we would end up with a sample of 10 each of red, yellow, orange, and green balls and 20 each of blue, black, and white balls. Note that if we select a simple random sample of 100 balls, there is a finite chance (albeit slight) that all 100 balls will be blue or black or white. Stratified sampling guarantees that this cannot happen, and that is why stratified sampling results in a more representative sample.

Systematic sampling of an entire stratified list, rather than sampling from each stratum, will yield a sample in which each stratum's representation is roughly proportional to its representation in the population. Some deviation from proportional representation will occur, depending on the sampling interval, the random start, and the number of sampling units in a stratum.

In selecting characteristics on which to stratify a list, you should choose characteristics that are expected to be related to or affect the dependent variables in your study. If you are attempting to measure the average income of households in a city, for example, you might stratify the list of households by education, sex, or race of household head. Because income may vary by education, sex, or race, you would want to make sure that the sample is representative with respect to these factors. Otherwise the sample estimate of average household income might be biased.

If you were selecting a sample of members of Congress to interview, you might want to divide the list of members into strata consisting of the two major parties, or the length of congressional service, or both. This would ensure that your sample accurately reflected the distribution of party and seniority in Congress. Or if you were selecting a sample of television news stories to analyze, you might want to divide the population of news stories into four strata based on the network of origin to ensure that your sample contained an equal number of stories from NBC, CBS, CNN, and ABC.

Some lists may be inherently stratified. Telephone directories are stratified to a degree by ethnic groups since certain last names are associated with particular ethnic groups. Lists of social security numbers arranged consecutively are stratified by geographical area since numbers are assigned based on the applicant's place of residence.

In the examples of stratified sampling we have considered so far, we assured ourselves of a more representative sample in which each stratum was represented in proportion to its size in the population. There may be occasions, however, when we wish to take a **disproportionate sample**. In such case we would use a stratified sample in which elements sharing a characteristic are underrepresented or overrepresented in our sample.[13]

For example, suppose we are conducting a survey of 200 students at a college, and there are 500 liberal arts majors, 100 engineering majors, and 200 business majors, for a total of 800 students at the college. If we sampled from each major (the strata) in proportion to its size, we would have 125 liberal arts majors, 25 engineering majors, and 50 business majors. If we wished to analyze the student population as a whole, this would be an acceptable sample. But if we wished to investigate some questions by looking at students in each major separately, we would find that 25 engineering students was too small a sample with which to draw inferences about the population of engineering students.

To get around this problem we could sample disproportionately—for example, we could include 100 liberal arts majors, 50 engineering majors, and 50 business majors in our study. Then we would have enough engineering students to draw inferences about the population of engineering majors. The problem now becomes evaluating the student population as a whole since our sample is biased due to an undersampling of liberal arts majors and an oversampling of engineering majors. Suppose engineering students have high grade-point averages. Our sample estimate of the student body's grade-point average would be biased upward because we have oversampled engineering students. Therefore, when we wish to analyze the total sample, not just a major, we need some method of adjusting our sample so that each major is represented in proportion to its real representation in the total student population.[14]

Table 7-2 shows the proportion of the population of each major and the mean grade-point average (GPA) for each group in a hypothetical sample of college students. To calculate an unbiased estimate of the overall mean GPA for the college, we could use a **weighting factor**, a mathematical factor used to make a disproportionate sample representative. In this example, we would multiply the mean GPA for each major by the proportion of the population of each major (i.e., the weighting factor).[15] Thus, the mean GPA would be $.625(2.5) + .125(3.3) + .25(2.7) = 2.65$.

Disproportionate stratified samples allow a researcher to represent more accurately the elements in each stratum and ensure that the overall sample is an accurate representation of important strata within the target population. This is done by weighting the data from each stratum when the sample is

TABLE 7-2
Stratified Sample of Student Majors

	Liberal Arts	Engineering	Business	Total
Number of students	500	100	200	800
Proportion or weight	.625	.125	.25	1.00
Size of sample	100	50	50	200
Sample mean grade-point average	2.5	3.3	2.7	

Note: Hypothetical data.

used to estimate characteristics of the target population. Of course, to accomplish disproportionate stratified sampling, the proportion of each stratum in the target population must be known.

Cluster Samples

Thus far we have considered examples in which a list of elements in the sampling frame exists. There are, however, situations where a sample is needed but no list of elements exists and to create one would be prohibitively expensive. A **cluster sample** is a probability sample in which the sampling frame initially consists of clusters of elements. Cluster sampling is used to address the problem of having no list of the elements in the target population. Since only some of the elements are to be selected in a sample, it is unnecessary to be able to list all elements at the outset.

In cluster sampling, groups or clusters of elements are identified and listed as sampling units. Next a sample is drawn from this list of sampling units. Then for the sampled units only, elements are identified and sampled. For example, suppose we wanted to take an opinion poll of 1,000 persons in a city. Since there is no complete list of city residents, we might begin by obtaining a map of the city and identifying and listing all blocks. This list of blocks becomes the sampling frame from which a number of blocks are sampled at random or systematically. (The individual blocks are sometimes called the "primary sampling units.") Next we would go to the selected blocks and list all the dwelling units in those blocks. Then a sample of dwelling units would be drawn from each block. Finally, the households in the sampled dwellings would be contacted, and someone in each household would be interviewed for the opinion poll. Suppose there are 500 blocks, and from these 500 blocks 25 are chosen at random. On these 25 blocks, 4,000 dwelling units or households are identified. One-quarter of these households will be contacted because a sample of 1,000 individuals is desired. These 1,000 households could be selected with a random sample or a systematic sample.

Note that even though we did not know the number of households ahead of time, each household has an equal chance of being selected. The probability that any given household will be selected is equal to the probability of one's block being selected times the probability of one's household being selected or $25/500 \times 1000/4000 = 1/80$. Thus, cluster sampling conforms to the requirements of a probability sample.

Our example involved taking only two samples or levels (the city block and the household). Some cluster samples involve many levels or stages and thus many samples. For example, in a national opinion poll the researcher might list and sample states, list and sample counties within states, list and sample municipalities within counties, list and sample census tracts within municipalities, list and sample blocks within census tracts, and finally list and sample households—a total of six stages.

Cluster sampling allows researchers to get around the problem of acquiring a list of elements in the target population. Cluster sampling also reduces fieldwork costs for public opinion surveys because it produces respondents who are close together. For example, in a national opinion poll respondents will not come from every state. This reduces travel and administrative costs.

A drawback to cluster sampling is greater imprecision. **Sampling error**, which is the discrepancy between an observed and a true value, occurs at each stage of the cluster sample. For example, a sample of states will not be totally representative of all states, a sample of counties will not be totally representative of all counties, and so on. The sampling error at each level must be added together to arrive at the total sampling error for a cluster sample.

In cluster sampling, the researcher must decide how many elements to select from each cluster. In the previous example, the researcher could have selected two individuals from each of the 500 blocks (hence requiring no selection of blocks), or 1,000 individuals from one of the blocks (hence making the selection of the particular block terribly important), or some other combination in between (40 individuals from 25 blocks, 25 individuals from 40 blocks, and so on). But how does the researcher decide how many units to sample at each stage?

We know that samples are more accurate when drawn from homogeneous populations. Generally, elements within a group are more similar than are elements from two different groups. Thus households on the same block are more likely to resemble each other than households on different blocks. Sample size can be smaller for homogeneous populations than for heterogeneous populations and still be as accurate. (If a population is totally homogeneous, a sample of one element will be accurate.) Therefore, sampling error could be reduced by selecting many blocks but interviewing only a few households from each block. Following this reasoning to the extreme, we could select all 500 blocks and sample two households from each block. This, however, would be very expensive since every household in the city would have to be identified and listed, which defeats the purpose of a cluster sample.

The desire to maximize the accuracy of a sample must be balanced by the need to reduce the time and cost of creating a sampling frame—a major advantage of cluster sampling. Sometimes the stratification of clusters can reduce sampling error by creating more homogenous sampling units. States can be grouped by region, census tracts by average income, and so forth, before the selection of sample elements occurs.

Systematic, stratified (both proportionate and disproportionate), and cluster samples are acceptable and often more practical alternatives to the simple random sample. In each case the probability of a particular element being selected is known, and consequently the accuracy of the sample can be determined. The type of sample chosen depends upon the resources a researcher has available and the availability of an accurate and comprehensive list of the elements in a well-defined target population.

Nonprobability Samples

A **nonprobability sample** is a sample for which each element in the total population has an unknown probability of being selected. Probability samples are usually preferable to nonprobability samples because they represent fairly accurately a large population, and it is possible to calculate how close an estimated characteristic is to the population value. In some situations, however, probability sampling may be too expensive to justify (in exploratory research, for example), or the target population may be too ill-defined to permit probability sampling (this was the case with the television commercials example discussed earlier). Researchers may feel that they can learn more by studying carefully selected and perhaps unusual cases than by studying representative ones. A brief description follows of some of the types of nonprobability samples.

With a **purposive sample** a researcher exercises considerable discretion over what observations to study because the goal is typically to study a diverse and usually limited number of observations rather than to analyze a sample representative of a larger target population. Richard Fenno's *Home Style,* which describes the behavior of eighteen incumbent representatives, is an example of research based on a purposive sample.[16] Likewise, a study of journalists that concentrated on prominent journalists in Washington or New York would be a purposive rather than a representative sample of all journalists.

In a **convenience sample**, elements are included because they are convenient or easy for a researcher to select. A public opinion sample in which interviewers haphazardly select whomever they wish is an example of a convenience sample. A sample of campaign commercials that consists of those advertisements that a researcher is able to acquire and a study of the personalities of politicians dependent upon those who have sought psychoanalysis are also convenience samples, as is any public opinion survey consisting of those who volunteer their opinions. Convenience samples are most appropriate when the research is exploratory or when a target population is impossible to define or locate. But like other nonprobability samples, convenience samples provide estimates of the attributes of target populations that are of unknown accuracy.

A **quota sample** is a sample in which elements are sampled in proportion to their representation in the population. In this quota sampling is similar to proportionate stratified sampling. The difference between quota sampling and stratified sampling is that the elements in the quota sample are not chosen in a probabilistic manner. Instead, they are chosen in a purposive or convenient fashion until the appropriate number of each type of element (quota) has been found. Because of the lack of probability sampling of elements, quota samples are usually biased estimates of the target population. Even more important, it is impossible to calculate the accuracy of a quota sample.

A researcher who decided to conduct a public opinion survey of 550 women and 450 men and who instructed his interviewers to select whomever they pleased until these quotas were reached would be drawing a quota sample. A famous example of an error-ridden quota sample is the 1948 Gallup poll that predicted that Thomas Dewey would defeat Harry Truman for president.[17]

In a **snowball sample**, respondents are used to identify other persons who might qualify for inclusion in the sample.[18] These people are then interviewed and asked to supply appropriate names for further interviewing. This process is continued until enough persons are interviewed to satisfy the researcher's needs. Snowball sampling is particularly useful in studying a relatively select, rare, or difficult-to-locate population such as draft evaders, campaign contributors, political protesters, drug users, or even home gardeners who use sewage sludge on their gardens—a group estimated to constitute only 3 to 4 percent of households.[19]

We have discussed the various types of samples that political science researchers use in their data collection. Samples allow researchers to save time, money, and other costs. However, this benefit is a mixed blessing, for by avoiding these costs researchers must rely on information that is less accurate than if they had collected data on the entire target population. Now we will consider the type of information that a sample provides and the implications of using this information to make inferences about a target population.

Sample and Statistical Inference

As we noted, when a researcher measures some attribute in a sample, the result of that measurement is called a sample statistic. However, the researcher is usually not interested in the measurement of that attribute for the sample alone, but is interested in it as an estimator of the corresponding population parameter. The sample statistic, then, provides a basis for estimating the attribute of interest in the population, a process called **statistical inference**.

At best, samples provide us with estimates of attributes of, and relationships within, a target population. For example, a finding that 30 percent of a random sample of members of Congress did not accept campaign contributions from political action committees does not mean that exactly 30 percent of all members refused such contributions; it means that *approximately* 30 percent refused them. In other words, researchers sacrifice some precision of information whenever they decide to rely on samples for their empirical observations. How much precision is lost (that is, how accurate our estimate is) depends on how the sample has been drawn and the sample size or number of cases drawn.

The accuracy of the estimates gleaned from sample data can be calculated for probability samples but not for nonprobability samples. The accuracy of estimates for probability samples is expressed in terms of a **margin of error**, a range around a sample statistic within which the population parameter is likely to fall, and a **confidence level**, the probability that the population parameter actually falls within the margin of error. Both the margin of error and confidence level depend on the **sampling distribution**, that is, on a theoretical (non-observed) distribution of sample statistics calculated on samples of size N and its **standard error**, which is a number that measures the variability or dispersion of the sample statistics within the sampling distribution.

Because of the importance of inferences based on samples in empirical research, we will now explore these concepts in more detail. In later chapters on hypothesis testing we will build on them further.

Sampling Distribution

Let's start with a simple case study. A candidate for the state senate wants to know how many independents there are in her district, which has grown rapidly in the last ten years. Although the Bureau of Elections reports that 25 percent of registered voters declined to name a party, she believes that the records are badly out of date. She asks you to conduct a poll to estimate the proportion of citizens, eighteen years and older, who registered as independents rather than Democrats or Republicans.

Suppose you interview 10 randomly chosen individuals and discover that 2 of them registered to vote as an independent. Based on this finding, you could estimate that 20 percent of voters are registered as independents. Intuitively, however, you know that this estimate may be off by quite a bit because you only interviewed 10 people. The "true" proportion may be very different, either above or below that number.

Now suppose for the moment that in fact the Bureau of Elections' records are still accurate: one-fourth, or 25 percent, of the population are registered as independents, or, in more formal terms, $P = .25$, where P stands for the population or "true" proportion. (Of course, no one can know the current population value because at the time of your poll it is unobserved, but we will make this assumption to illustrate our point.) Your first estimate, .20, then, is a little bit below the true value. This difference is called sampling error, or the discrepancy between an observed and a true value that arises purely by chance or happenstance.

What you need is some way to measure the uncertainty in the estimate so that you can tell your client what the margin of error is. That is, you want to be able to say, "Yes, my estimate is probably not equal to the real value, but chances are that it is close." What exactly do words like "chances are" and "close" mean?

Imagine taking another, totally independent sample of 10 adults from the same district and calculating the proportion of independents. (We will assume that not much time has passed since the first sample, so the probability of being an independent is still 25 percent, that is, $P = .25$.) This estimate turns out to be .33. As with your first sample, such a result is possible if $P = .25$ because your data come from a small sample, and samples are unlikely to reproduce exactly the characteristics of the populations from which they are drawn.

Repeating the procedure once more you find that the next estimated proportion of independents is .42. This estimate, while quite high off the mark, is still possible. And after you take a fourth independent sample, you find that the estimated proportion, .18, is again wide of the mark. So far two of your estimates have been too large, two too low, and none exactly on target. But notice that the average of the estimates, $(.22 + .33 + .42 + .18)/4 = .29$, is not too far from the real value of .25. What would happen, you might wonder, if you repeated the process indefinitely? That is, what would happen if you took repeated independent samples of $N = 10$ and calculated the proportion of independents in each one?[20] After a while you would have a long list of sample proportions. What would their distribution look like? Figure 7-1, which is based on 1,000 repeats, provides an illustration.

The sample proportions $\hat{P}$s are spread around the true value ($P = .25$) in a bell-curve–shaped distribution. A few of the estimates are quite low, even close to zero, and a number of them are way above .25. (The frequencies can be determined by looking at the Y axis.) But the vast majority are in the range .15 to .35, and the center of the distribution (the average of the sample proportions) is near .25, the population value. This is no coincidence, as we will see.

This illustration highlights some important points about samples and the statistics that are calculated from them. First, if the samples are collected in-

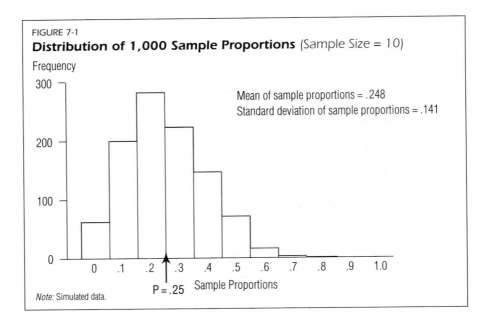

FIGURE 7-1
Distribution of 1,000 Sample Proportions (Sample Size = 10)

Frequency

Mean of sample proportions = .248
Standard deviation of sample proportions = .141

$P = .25$ Sample Proportions

Note: Simulated data.

dependently and randomly, the average or mean of many statistics—what in more technical language researchers refer to as the **expected value**—will equal the corresponding true or population value, no matter what the sample size. This idea can be stated more succinctly. Let θ represent a population parameter or characteristic such as a proportion or mean, and let $\hat{\theta}$ stand for a sample estimator of that characteristic. We can then write

$$E(\hat{\theta}) = \theta.$$

Here, $\hat{\theta}$ is the estimate based on the sample, θ is the population value, and the equation reads, "The expected (or long run) value of the estimator equals the corresponding value for the population from which the sample has been drawn."

In the case of a sample proportion based on a simple random sample, we have

$$E(\hat{P}) = P,$$

where $\hat{P}$ is the estimated proportion, and the equation reads, "The expected (or long run or average) value of the sample proportions equals the population proportion."

In plain words, while any particular estimate result may not equal the parameter value of the population from which the data come,[21] if the sampling procedure were to be repeated an infinite number of times, and a sample estimate correctly calculated each time, then the average or mean of these results would equal the true value. Figure 7-1 illustrates what can be demonstrated mathematically for many types of sample statistics such as the proportion.

Of course, knowing that your procedure (that is, taking a sample of 10 people and calculating the proportion of independents) is not biased in the long run does not help with the immediate problem of letting the candidate know the proportion of independents amongst registered voters because you have, in fact, only one sample and one estimated proportion. What you need to know, then, is how far from the true value your estimate is likely to be.

Statistical theory again comes to the rescue, for it shows that if the true proportion in a population is P, and one takes repeated samples of size N from that population, the resulting sample proportions, $\hat{P}$, will have "normal" (symmetric, bell-curve–shaped) distribution,[22] with a mean of P and a standard deviation (or standard error, signified σ) as follows:

$$\sigma_{\hat{P}} = \sqrt{\frac{P(1-P)}{N}}$$

When, for example, P equals .25 and N is 10, the standard error of the proportion is as follows:

$$\sigma_{\hat{P}} = \sqrt{P(1-P)/N} = \sqrt{(.25)(.75)/10} = .136$$

This number measures how much variation there is among the sample proportions.

In short, if a population proportion is .25 and we draw from it repeated independent samples, with each sample size equal to 10, and calculate sample proportions each time, the expected or long run value of the sample estimates will be .25, with a standard deviation of .136.

These are theoretical values. Note that even though the data shown in Figure 7-1 are based on 1,000 samples of size 10 each, their average and variation are quite close to the theoretical values: the mean of the 1,000 $\hat{P}$s is .248, and their standard deviation is .141, both of which approximate the quantities in the formulas above.

We will discuss the interpretation of the standard error in Chapter 11. For now think of it as an indicator of how much uncertainty there is in an estimate. We see from Figure 7-1, for example, that roughly two-thirds of the estimates are in the range .248 ± .141, or between .107 and .389. We might call this range a "66 percent confidence interval." Conversely, about one-third of the other estimates are either below .107 or above .389. We can tell from the frequencies that not many are greater than .5 or below .1. Nevertheless, there is quite a range of possible sample results when we draw a sample size of just

10 people. In other words, any particular sample could be quite far from the true value. So we have confidence in the method but not much confidence that any particular observed estimate equals or is even near the true value.

At this point you can tell your client that the true proportion of independents in the district is probably somewhere between 10 and 39 percent. When she asks, what do you mean by "probably," the answer is, "I am about 66 percent sure."

Needless to say, this uncertain estimate may not be too helpful to the campaign, which must decide how to target its limited resources. The senator would like you to narrow the range of uncertainty. What can you do? The answer should be obvious: take a larger sample, say 50 cases instead of 10.

This time, imagine that you draw a simple random sample that includes 50 registered voters ($N = 50$) from the population in which $P = .25$ and then note the estimated proportion. If you indefinitely drew 1,000 such independent random samples and plotted the distribution of the estimated proportions, you would get a graph similar to the one in Figure 7-2.

Note that the mean of the proportions of these 1,000 samples is .251, a value that is near the true number.[23] The figure illustrates once again what can be shown mathematically, namely that the distribution of $\hat{P}$s is approximately normal with expected or long-run value equal to the true proportion of the population from which the samples have been collected. But also notice that the distribution is not as spread out as that depicted in Figure 7-1. Using our formula for the standard error we see that

$$\sigma_{\hat{P}} = \sqrt{P(1 - P)/N} = \sqrt{(.25)(.75)/50} = .061.$$

Most of the $\hat{P}$s in Figure 7-2 lie between .20 and .30; very few fall in the tails of the distribution. This is to be expected given the formula for the standard error of the sample proportions. Recall that the standard deviation based on samples of 10 was .136, twice as large as the standard deviation based on samples of 50. This difference tells us that as sample sizes get larger, the standard deviation of the estimates—a measure of the variability of our estimates—gets smaller. You can see this by looking at the formula for the standard error: the numerator stays constant because it depends only on P. As N increases, the fraction necessarily gets smaller and smaller.

FORMULAS

As we mentioned elsewhere, there is no need to be put off by formulas no matter how complicated they look. Formulas simply define a mathematical concept or show how some calculation is to be carried out. The equation for the standard error is a good example. It just says to multiply a proportion by one minus that proportion, divide the result by N (the sample size), and then find the square root of that figure. All of this can be done on a hand calculator. What you should focus on here is the meaning of the terms. In this text we always supply a verbalization of formulas so that your introduction to their meaning and calculation is gradual. After thinking about the intuitive meaning of the terms, consider the formulas as blueprints for obtaining them.

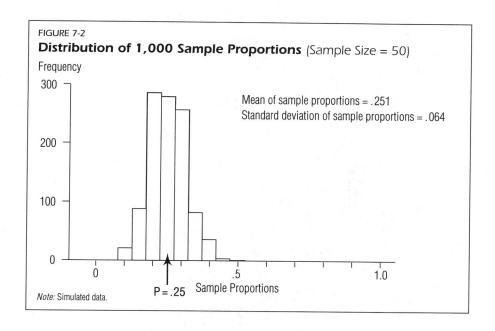

FIGURE 7-2

Distribution of 1,000 Sample Proportions (Sample Size = 50)

Frequency

Mean of sample proportions = .251
Standard deviation of sample proportions = .064

P = .25   Sample Proportions

Note: Simulated data.

Simply stated, the larger the sample size, the greater the certainty of the results. Now you can report to your client that you are 66 percent confident that your estimate doesn't differ by more than ±.06 from the true value. That is, if the sample proportion from a given sample is .31, then the real value is most likely in an interval between .31 ± .064, or between .246 and .374. This interval is smaller than the one based on samples of 10.

Figures 7-3 and 7-4 demonstrate what happens when our experiment is repeated with samples of 100 and 500, respectively. Each time we draw a large number of independent random samples from a population where *P* = .25, we find that the average of sample proportions is close to that value and that we are less and less likely to find any particular estimate very far from the mean in either direction. (Look at Figure 7-4; none of the estimates are below .22 or above .28.[24])

This intuitive discussion leads us to an important fact: *A sampling distribution of a sample statistic is a theoretical expression that describes the mean, variation, and shape of the distribution of an infinite number of occurrences of the statistic when calculated on samples of size N drawn independently and randomly from a population.* The sampling distribution can be used to find the probability that sample statistics fall within certain distances of the population parameter. The sample information cannot, of course, tell us exactly where within the range of values the population parameter lies. But it allows us to make an educated guess.

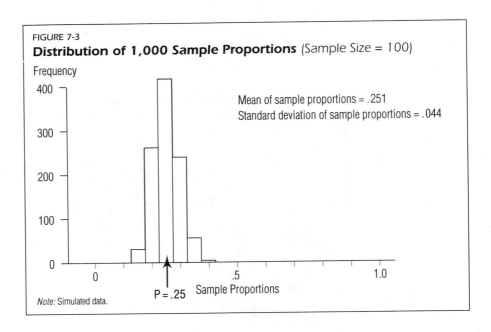

FIGURE 7-3

Distribution of 1,000 Sample Proportions (Sample Size = 100)

Frequency

Mean of sample proportions = .251
Standard deviation of sample proportions = .044

P = .25   Sample Proportions

Note: Simulated data.

A general method for making such a guess is actually quite simple. Let $\hat{\theta}$ be a sample statistic that estimates a population parameter, θ. (In the previous example we called these $\hat{P}$ and P, respectively.) Since θ is unknown we want to surround an estimate of it with a range or interval of values that with some known probability includes it. (For example: Is the population parameter "probably" between 20 and 30?) This range can be found by adding and subtracting some multiple of the standard error.

For some sample statistics obtained from random samples we can say that the interval $\hat{\theta} \pm 1.96\hat{\sigma}_{\hat{\theta}}$ has a 95 percent probability of containing the population value. Obviously, you need to know how to calculate the standard error $(\hat{\sigma}_{\hat{\theta}})$ and where numbers like "1.96" come from. We will explain this in Chapter 11. For now only the basic idea is important: by adding and subtracting some multiple of the standard error to the estimator we can obtain a confidence interval for the statistic and interpret this range to mean "there is such and such a probability that the calculated interval includes the population value."

Our brief excursion into statistical theory tells us that properly collected samples and correctly calculated statistics can be used to make systematic inferences about unknown population characteristics and that the probability of making errors can be objectively understood. This information in turn allows the researcher and the scientific community to judge the tenability of the conclusions reached.

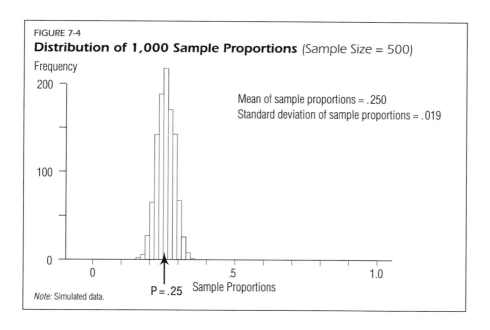

FIGURE 7-4

Distribution of 1,000 Sample Proportions (Sample Size = 500)

Frequency

Mean of sample proportions = .250
Standard deviation of sample proportions = .019

P = .25   Sample Proportions

Note: Simulated data.

The Margin of Error and Sample Size

When presenting poll results and other data based on samples, the media commonly use the term *margin of error*, as in "the estimated favorable rating for a candidate is 54 percent with a margin of error of ±3 percent," to depict uncertainty. *Margin of error* is rather imprecise, however, as a substitution for the terms *standard error* or *standard deviation* that we introduced above and will discuss further in Chapter 11. But it does capture an idea we have been stressing: a sample estimator is just that, an estimate made with more or less uncertainty.

You may occasionally see reports of sample-based information that imply that the sample results are precise estimates of the target population. During the 2000 presidential election campaign, for example, you may have seen newspaper headlines declaring: "Bush Leads Gore, 55% to 45%." Such reports are misleading. No probability sample can produce such precise estimates of the national voting-age population. Although the results may have been 55 percent for Bush to Gore's 45 percent, these estimates of presidential preferences in the voting population are subject to error. True, the calculation of these errors and related "confidence intervals" flows directly from knowledge of the sampling distribution of statistics and mathematical theory, which in many cases is well understood. But keep in mind there is always some doubt about an estimate.

Ideally, sample estimates of the target population are as accurate and precise as possible. The margin of error should be small. However, the only way to eliminate sampling error entirely is to collect data from the entire target population (in other words, not to rely on a sample at all). Since doing so is usually impractical, sampling error is the price researchers pay for reducing the costs involved in measuring some attribute of the target population.

Note too that sampling error occurs not just in public opinion polls, but whenever a researcher relies on a sample. For example, any measurements of attributes in samples of members of Congress, convention delegates, census tracts, or nation-states are estimates of the target population of members, convention delegates, census tracts, or nation-states, and therefore are subject to sampling error.

As we learned above, the most important factor in the sampling error is the sample size. Generally, the larger the sample, the smaller the sampling error. Given that the sample size figures so prominently in sampling distributions, you might think that by increasing N you can reduce uncertainty to near zero. However, there is an exponential rather than a linear relationship between sample size and sampling error. For example, to cut sampling error in half, the sample size must be quadrupled. This means that researchers must balance the costs of increasing sample size with the size of the sampling error they are willing to tolerate.

Table 7-3 shows the relationship between sample size and the margin of error for Gallup Poll–type samples.[25] In public opinion research, increasing sample size may be too costly. Survey analysts usually draw samples of 1,500 to 2,000 people (regardless of the size of the target population). This yields a margin of error (about ±3 percent) at a cost that is within reach for at least some survey organizations. But reducing the sampling error appreciably in this kind of research would mean incurring costs that are prohibitive for most researchers.

TABLE 7-3
The Relationship between Sample Size and Sampling Error

Sample Size	Confidence Interval (percent)
4,000	± 2
1,500	± 3
1,000	± 4
600	± 5
400	± 6
200	± 8
100	± 11

Source: Charles W. Roll Jr. and Albert H. Cantril, *Polls: Their Use and Misuse in Politics* (New York: Basic Books, 1972), 72. Copyright © 1972 by Basic Books, Inc. Reprinted by permission of the publisher.
Note: This table is based on a 95-percent confidence level and is derived from experience with Gallup Poll samples.

In addition the formula for the standard error given above shows that perhaps too much can be made from large samples. Suppose, for example, we draw a sample of 100 from a population where $P = .25$, as before. The standard error would be as follows:

$$\sigma_{\hat{P}} = \sqrt{\frac{(.25)(1-.75)}{100}} = .043.$$

Now suppose we increase the sample size tenfold, to 1,000. The standard error is reduced as follows:

$$\sigma_{\hat{P}} = \sqrt{\frac{(.25)(1-.75)}{1000}} = .014.$$

We have now added to our research costs dramatically, since obtaining 900 more interviews is very time consuming and expensive, but we have also cut the error by roughly two-thirds. However, if an estimated proportion is .26 ($\hat{P} = .26$), the 66 percent confidence interval is .26± .043, or .217 to .303, for the sample size of 100 ($N = 100$). If the estimated proportion was .26 ($\hat{P} = .26$) for the sample size of 1,000 ($N = 1,000$), then the interval is .26 ± .104, or .246 to .274. While the second interval is smaller, for all practical purposes the difference is unimportant. Increasing the sample size in this case has greatly increased our costs for relatively little gain.

The question of how large a sample should be thus depends not so much on bias or non-bias (after all, the expected value of a statistic based on even a very small sample is unbiased, as we saw above), rather, the determining factor is how narrow an interval a researcher needs for a given level of confidence. For exploratory projects in which a rough approximation is adequate, a sample need not be huge. But when researchers attempt to make fine distinctions it is necessary to collect more data.

We can illustrate this with another example. Assume that we want to estimate a population mean, and suppose further that we want to be 99 percent certain about our estimate. (Notice that we have established a specific level of confidence—99 percent certainty.) To achieve this level of confidence, how wide of the mark can our estimate be and still be useful? Once we answer this question we can choose an appropriate sample size. For example, if we want to say with 99 percent certainty that the interval $25,500 to $28,500 contains the true mean, then we would need a sample of a certain size (perhaps 200) to achieve this level of certainty. But if we want to be 99 percent certain that the mean lies between $26,500 and $26,600—a mere $100 difference—then we will need a much larger sample to achieve 99 percent certainty.[26]

Sampling error is also dependent on the type of sample drawn. For a given sample size, a simple random sample provides a more accurate estimate of the target (that is, a smaller margin of error) than does a cluster sample. Sampling error is also smaller for an attribute that is shared by almost all elements in the sample than for one that is distributed across only half of the sample elements.

Finally, sampling error is reduced if the sample represents a significant proportion of the target population—that is, if the sampling fraction is greater than one-fourth of the target population. Because this is unusual, however, the effect of the sampling fraction on sampling error is generally minuscule.

Conclusion

In this chapter we have discussed what it means to select a sample out of a target population, the various types of samples that political scientists use, and the kind of information that a sample yields. The following guidelines may help researchers who are deciding whether to rely on a sample and students evaluating research based on sample data.

1. If cost is not a major consideration, and the validity of one's measures will not suffer, it is generally better to collect data for one's target population than for just a sample of that population.

2. If cost or validity considerations dictate that a sample be drawn, a probability sample is usually preferable to a nonprobability sample. It is only for probability samples that the accuracy of sample estimates can be determined. If the desire to accurately represent a target population is not a major concern or is impossible to achieve, then a nonprobability sample may be used.

3. Probability samples yield *estimates* of the target population. All samples are subject to sampling error; no sample, no matter how well drawn, can provide an exact measurement of an attribute of, or relationship within, the target population.

4. The accuracy of sample estimates is expressed in terms of the margin of error and the confidence level. Sampling error is dependent mainly on sample size, but it also depends on the shape of the distribution of the attribute being measured, the type of probability sample, and the sampling fraction.

Sampling error is unavoidable whenever a researcher uses sample data, but it can be minimized with careful sampling techniques. Non-sampling error can also interfere with the ability to draw accurate conclusions from one's observations, especially when a researcher is using survey research.

We will return to this subject in Chapter 10, where we discuss the proper conduct of sample surveys.

Notes

1. The point is more subtle than it first appears. In the late 1990s Congress and President Bill Clinton debated the merits of taking a sample instead of interviewing the entire population when conducting the 2000 Census. Many members of Congress (mainly Republicans) argued that the Constitution requires a complete enumeration of the people. But Clinton and the Census Bureau argued that trying to tally everyone leads to so many errors that many groups are undercounted, in particular inhabitants of inner cities and of rural areas and undocumented aliens. It would be more accurate, they maintained, to draw careful samples of target populations and conduct quality interviews and measurements. (We should note that politics per se formed the context of this dispute; after all, innumerable government grants as well as seats in the House of Representatives are awarded according to population size.)

2. For a good discussion, see Gary King, Robert O. Keohane, and Sidney Verba, *Designing Social Inquiry* (Princeton: Princeton University Press, 1994).

3. Richard A. Joslyn, *Mass Media and Elections* (Reading, Mass.: Addison-Wesley, 1984).

4. This discussion of terms used in sampling is drawn primarily from Earl R. Babbie, *Survey Research Methods* (Belmont, Calif.: Wadsworth, 1973), 79–81.

5. Ibid., 74–75.

6. Actually, random digit dialing has become increasingly sophisticated. For more details on how it works, see Johnny Blair and others, "Sample Design for Household Telephone Surveys," Survey Research Center University of Maryland [Online], available: http://www.bsos.umd.edu/src/sampbib.html, for a list of references.

7. For various methods of RDD, see E. L. Landon Jr. and S. K. Banks, "Relative Efficiency and Bias of Plus-One Telephone Sampling," *Journal of Marketing Research* 14 (August 1977): 294–299; K. M. Cummings, "Random Digit Dialing: A Sampling Technique for Telephone Surveys," *Public Opinion Quarterly* 43 (summer 1979): 233–244; R. M. Groves and R. L. Kahn, *Surveys by Telephone* (New York: Academic Press, 1979); and J. Waksberg, "Sampling Methods for Random Digit Dialing," *Journal of the American Statistical Association* 73 (March 1978): 40–46.

8. James H. Frey, *Survey Research by Telephone* (Beverly Hills, Calif.: Sage, 1983), 22.

9. When used to describe a type of sample, "random" does not mean haphazard or casual; rather, it means that every element has an equal probability of being selected. Strictly speaking, to ensure an equal chance of selection, *replacement* is required; that is, putting each selected element back on the list before the next element is selected. In *simple* random sampling, however, elements are selected without replacement. This means that on each successive draw, the probability of an element's being selected increases because there are fewer and fewer elements remaining. But for each draw the probability of being selected is equal among the remaining elements. If the sample size is less than one-fifth the size of the population, the slight deviation from strict random sampling caused by sampling without replacement is acceptable. See Hubert M. Blalock Jr., *Social Statistics*, 2d ed. (New York: McGraw-Hill, 1972), 513–514.

10. See Exercise 10 on p. 214 for an example.

11. Blalock, *Social Statistics*, 515.

12. Babbie, *Survey Research Methods*, 93.

13. There are two reasons for using disproportionate sampling in addition to obtaining enough cases for statistical analysis of subgroups: the high cost of sampling some strata and differences in the heterogeneity of some strata that result in differences in sampling error. A researcher might want to minimize sampling where it was costly and increase sampling from heterogeneous strata while decreasing it from homogeneous strata. See Blalock, *Social Statistics*, 518–519.

14. Ibid., 521–522.

15. We could have obtained the same results by multiplying the GPA of each student by the weighting factor associated with the student's major and then calculating the mean GPA for the whole sample.

16. Richard F. Fenno Jr., *Home Style: House Members in Their Districts* (Boston: Little, Brown, 1978).

17. Babbie, *Survey Research Methods,* 75.

18. Snowball sampling is generally considered to be a nonprobability sampling technique, although strategies have been developed to achieve a probability sample with this method. See Kenneth D. Bailey, *Methods of Social Research* (New York: Free Press, 1978), 83.

19. J.W. Bergsten and S.A. Pierson, "Telephone Screening for Rare Characteristics Using Multiplicity Counting Rules," *1982 Proceedings of the American Statistical Association Section on Survey Research Methods* (Alexandria, Va.: American Statistical Association, 1982), 145–150.

20. This procedure, called "sampling with replacement," is premised on the assumption that, at least theoretically, people will sooner or later be interviewed twice or more. We will ignore this nuance since it does not affect the validity of the conclusions in this case.

21. Indeed, in all likelihood it will not exactly equal the population value.

22. Technically, the distribution of the sample estimators will be exactly *or* approximately normal depending on the shape of the population distribution from which the samples come. We will not worry about this nuance here.

23. Note, too, that it is close to the value obtained from the 1,000 samples where $N = 10$. So the average of the Ps based on samples of 10 is not much different than the average based on samples of 50.

24. Were we to repeat the process, say, 10 million or more times, we would sooner or later find one sample in which P is quite far from the true proportion. But with samples of 500 such a result will be quite rare, and we might have to repeat the process a million more times to see it again.

25. In reality, the decision about appropriate sample size is dependent upon a number of factors, including the type of sample, attributes being measured, heterogeneity of the population, and complexity of the data analysis plan. A more complete discussion of these factors may be found in Royce Singleton Jr., Bruce C. Straits, Margaret M. Straits, and Ronald J. McAllister, *Approaches to Social Research* (New York: Oxford University Press, 1988), 158–163; and Edwin Mansfield, *Basic Statistics with Applications* (New York: W. W. Norton, 1986), 287–294.

26. Note that sample size is not the only factor that affects statistical inferences. For a somewhat advanced discussion see Daniel D. Boos and Jacqueline M. Hughes-Oliver, "How Large Does *n* have to be for *Z* and *t* Intervals?" *American Statistician* 54 (May 2000): 121–128.

Terms introduced

CLUSTER SAMPLE. A probability sample that is used when no list of elements exists. The sampling frame initially consists of clusters of elements.

CONFIDENCE LEVEL. The probability that the population parameter actually falls within the margin of error of a sample statistic.

CONVENIENCE SAMPLE. A nonprobability sample in which the selection of elements is determined by the researcher's convenience.

DISPROPORTIONATE SAMPLE. A stratified sample in which elements sharing a characteristic are underrepresented or overrepresented in the sample.

ELEMENT. A particular case or entity about which information is collected; the unit of analysis.

ESTIMATOR. A statistic based on sample observations that is used to estimate the numerical value of a population characteristic or parameter.

EXPECTED VALUE. The mean or average value of a sample statistic based on repeated samples from a population.

MARGIN OF ERROR. The range around a sample statistic within which the population parameter is likely to fall.

NONPROBABILITY SAMPLE. A sample for which each element in the total population has an unknown probability of being selected.

POPULATION. All of the cases or observations covered by a hypothesis; all the units of analysis to which a hypothesis applies.

POPULATION PARAMETER. The incidence of a characteristic or attribute in a population (not a sample).

PROBABILITY SAMPLE. A sample for which each element in the total population has a known probability of being selected.

PROPORTIONATE SAMPLE. A probability sample that draws elements from a stratified population at a rate proportional to the size of the samples.

PURPOSIVE SAMPLE. A nonprobability sample in which a researcher uses discretion in selecting elements for observation.

QUOTA SAMPLE. A nonprobability sample in which elements are sampled in proportion to their representation in the population.

RANDOM DIGIT DIALING. A procedure used to improve the representativeness of telephone samples by giving both listed and unlisted numbers a chance of selection.

RANDOM NUMBERS TABLE. A list of random numbers in tabular form.

RANDOM START. Selection of a number at random to determine where to start selecting elements in a systematic sample.

SAMPLE. A subset of observations or cases drawn from a specified population.

SAMPLE BIAS. The bias that occurs whenever some elements of a population are systematically excluded from a sample. It is usually due to an incomplete sampling frame or a nonprobability method of selecting elements.

SAMPLE STATISTIC. The estimator of a population characteristic or attribute that is calculated from sample data.

SAMPLING DISTRIBUTION. A theoretical (non-observed) distribution of sample statistics calculated on samples of size N.

SAMPLING ERROR. The confidence level and the margin of error taken together.

SAMPLING FRACTION. The proportion of the population included in a sample.

SAMPLING FRAME. The population from which a sample is drawn. Ideally it is the same as the total population of interest to a study.

SAMPLING INTERVAL. The number of elements in a sampling frame divided by the desired sample size.

SAMPLING UNIT. The entity listed in a sampling frame. It may be the same as an element, or it may be a group or cluster of elements.

SIMPLE RANDOM SAMPLE. A probability sample in which each element has an equal chance of being selected.

SNOWBALL SAMPLE. A sample in which respondents are asked to identify additional members of a population.

STANDARD ERROR. The standard deviation or measure of variability or dispersion of a sampling distribution.

STATISTICAL INFERENCE. Making probability statements about population parameters and characteristics based on sample statistics and the use of statistical theory.

STRATIFIED SAMPLE. A probability sample in which elements sharing one or more characteristics are grouped, and elements are selected from each group in proportion to the group's representation in the total population.

STRATUM. A subgroup of a population that shares one or more characteristics.

SYSTEMATIC SAMPLE. A probability sample in which elements are selected from a list at predetermined intervals.

WEIGHTING FACTOR. A mathematical factor used to make a disproportionate sample representative.

Exercises

1. Evaluate a public opinion poll in a national newspaper or magazine and answer the following questions: Does the article clearly define the population? Is this target appropriate for the substantive issues under discussion? Is the sampling procedure fully explained? Can you think of biases that might affect the results despite the organization's efforts to collect a representative sample?

2. If there are 5,000 elements in a sampling frame and a simple random sample of 100 elements is taken, what is the chance of an element being included in the sample? What is this chance called?

3. If a systematic sample of 200 elements is taken from a sampling frame of 2,400 elements, what is the sampling interval? How would you decide where to start?

4. Suppose you want to send mail to U.S. military personnel stationed overseas and have obtained permission from the Department of Defense to draw a sample of names and addresses from duty rosters. The numbers of personnel stationed in the selected countries are as follows:

Bosnia and Herzegovina	8,170
Egypt	5,846
Germany	60,053
Italy	11,677
Japan	41,257
Korea, Republic of	35,663
Panama	5,400
United Kingdom	11,379

Source: U.S. Census Bureau, *Statistical Abstract of the United States: 1999* (Washington, D.C.: Government Printing Office, 1999), 376, Table 590.

Your sample is to be 1,000. How many from each country must your sample include?

5. A researcher has collected data on voter turnout rates for city council elections in a sample of cities. To analyze her data by population size, she found it necessary to oversample in some categories. Now she would like to calculate the overall mean turnout for her sample as a whole. Based on the information below, complete the table and calculate the overall mean turnout rate for the sample.

City Council Election Voter Turnout

	Small	Medium	Large	Total
Number of cities	300	600	100	1,000
Proportion	—	—	—	1.00
Size of sample	50	50	50	150
Mean percent turnout	31.0	27.0	21.0	—

6. A researcher uses cluster sampling for a survey of local libraries in a state. Out of 50 counties, a sample of 10 counties is selected. From the selected counties, a list containing 1,000 libraries is created and a sample of libraries is drawn. If the probability of a library being selected is 1/25, how many libraries were selected from the list of libraries?

7. In the wake of a severe budget shortfall, state support for social service activities has been reduced sharply. A group of civic-minded researchers wants to investigate the potential for increased support of social service activities by private voluntary service organizations. The group decides to undertake a survey of members of these organizations to determine the members' perceptions of the need for certain programs and their willingness to devote their organizations' resources to these programs. It is estimated that there are 1,000 local organizations across the state with a combined membership of about 500,000. The researchers have decided upon a sample size of 500. How should they go about selecting a probability sample? Explain your decision.

8. Try this with members of your class. Use a single coin. Ask one of your classmates to flip the coin ten times and count the number of times it comes up heads. Pass the coin to another classmate and ask him or her to do the same. Keep the process going until everyone in your class has participated. Then summarize the results by calculating the **average** number of times the coin landed heads up. It should, of course, be close to five if

each person has made ten flips. How much variation is there in your results? Do you think that flipping a coin is a fair (that is, unbiased) way of making a choice?

9. Two reporters have just called you asking about an article they read on the Internet. According to the article, eight out of ten people clicked "Do Not Favor" when asked about the death penalty. The journalists know that this finding cannot necessarily be generalized to the American population as a whole. But the web page claims that the data are a reasonable sample of Internet users. They want your opinion. What, if anything, do the poll results say about web surfers?

10. How easy is it to generate random digits? Ask your classmates to help you find out. Have each member of your class develop a list of twenty or thirty four-digit *random* numbers on a piece of paper. Work rapidly. Then compare your work by counting the frequency of digits that appear on the lists. If the numbers are random there should be as many zeroes as there are ones, twos, threes, and so forth. Look also for "runs" in which the same digits occur several times together. (A series of, say, four "ones" in a row would be unusual if numbers are random.)

11. Can you manipulate the formula for the standard error of a proportion to determine how many cases (N) would be necessary for it to equal .1 if $P = .5$?

12. Describe the "sampling" procedure used in Michael S. Kochin, "Decollectivization of Agriculture and the Planned Economy," *American Journal of Political Science* 40 (August 1996): 717–739.

13. Describe and comment on the sampling procedures used in Alan S. Gerber and Donald P. Green, "The Effect of a Nonpartisan Get-Out-the-Vote Drive: An Experimental Study of Leafletting," *Journal of Politics* 62 (August 2000): 846–847. Do the authors provide enough information for you to judge the adequacy of the design?

14. If you were to take repeated samples with a sample size of 100 from a population in which the proportion of people 50 years and older who have never voted is .10, what would be the expected value of all the sample proportions? What would be the variability or standard error of these sample proportions? Suppose one of the sample proportions turned out to be .15. Would this be an unusual result? Why? How about .5?

Suggested Readings

Govindarajulu, Zakkula. *Elements of Sampling Theory and Methods.* Upper Saddle River, N.J.: Prentice-Hall, 1999.

Levy, Paul S., and Stanley Lemeshow. *Sampling of Populations.* New York: Wiley, 1999.

Lohr, Sharon L. *Sampling.* Pacific Grove, Calif.: Brooks/Cole, 1998.

Rea, Louis M., and Richard A. Parker. *Designing and Conducting Survey Research.* San Francisco: Jossey-Bass, 1997.

Rosnow, Ralph L., and Robert Rosenthal. *Beginning Behavioral Research.* Upper Saddle River, N.J.: Prentice-Hall, 1998.

CHAPTER 8

Making Empirical Observations:
Direct and Indirect Observation

Types of Data and Collection Techniques

Political scientists tend to use three broad types of observations or data, depending on the phenomena they are interested in studying. *Interview data,* the subject of Chapter 10, are data derived from written or verbal questioning of some group of respondents. This type of data collection may involve interviewing a representative cross-section of the national adult population or a select group of political actors, such as committee chairs in Congress. It may involve face-to-face interviews or interviews conducted over the phone or through the mail. It may involve highly structured interviews in which a questionnaire is closely followed or a less structured, open-ended discussion. Regardless of the particular type of interview setting, however, the essentials of the data collection method are the same: the data come from responses to the verbal or written cues of the researcher and the respondent knows these responses are being recorded.

In addition to interview data, political scientists rely heavily on data that exist in various archival records. In this type of data collection, known as *document analysis* (the subject of Chapter 9), researchers rely on the record-keeping activities of government agencies, private institutes, interest groups, media organizations, and even private citizens. Some of this data may be based on interviews, but it is in summary form. For example, unemployment statistics are derived from the Census Bureau's *Current Population Survey*, a household survey conducted each month. What sets document analysis apart from other data collection methods is that the researcher is usually not the original collector of the data and the original reason for the collection of the data may not have been to further a scientific research project. The record keepers are usually unaware of how the data they collect will ultimately be used, and the phenomena they record are not generally the personal beliefs and attitudes collected through interviews.

Finally, data may be collected through *observation,* the subject of this chapter. In this type of data collection the researcher collects data on political behavior by observing either the behavior itself or some physical trace of the behavior. Unlike interviewing, this method of data collection does not rely on people's verbal responses to verbal stimuli presented by the researcher. Furthermore, those whose behavior is being directly observed may be unaware that they are being observed.

A political scientist's choice of a data collection method depends upon a number of factors. One important consideration is the validity of the measurements that a particular method will permit. For example, a researcher who wants to measure the crime rate of different cities may feel that the crime rates reported by local police departments to the FBI are not sufficiently accurate to support a research project. The researcher may be concerned that some departments overreport and some underreport various criminal acts or that some victims of crimes may fail to report the crimes to the police, hence rendering that method of collecting data and measuring the crime rate unacceptable. Therefore, the researcher may decide that a more accurate indication of the crime rate can be secured by interviewing a sample of citizens in different cities and asking them how much crime they have experienced themselves.

A political scientist is also influenced by the reactivity of a data collection method—the effect of the data collection itself on the phenomena being measured. When people know their behavior is being observed and know or can guess the purpose of the observation, they may alter their behavior. As a result, the observed behavior may be an unnatural reaction to the process of being observed. People may be reluctant, for example, to admit to an interviewer that they are anti-Semitic or have failed to vote in an election. For this reason many researchers prefer unobtrusive or nonreactive measures of political behavior because they believe that the resulting data are more natural or real.

The population covered by a data collection method is another important consideration for a researcher. The population determines whose behavior is observed. One type of data may be available for only a few people, while another type may permit more numerous, interesting, and worthwhile comparisons. A researcher studying the behavior of political consultants, for example, may decide that relying on the published memoirs of a handful of consultants will not adequately cover the population of consultants (not to mention the validity problems of the data) and that it would be better to seek out a broad cross-section of consultants and interview them. Or a researcher interested in political corruption might decide that interviewing a broad cross-section of politicians charged with various corrupt practices is not feasible and that data (of a different kind) could be obtained for a more diverse set of corrupt acts from accounts published in the mass media.

Additionally, cost and availability are crucial elements in the choice of a data collection technique. Some types of data collection are simply more expensive than others, and some types of observations are more readily made than others. Large-scale interviewing, for example, is very expensive and time-consuming, and the types of questions that can be asked and behaviors that can be observed are limited. Data from archival records are usually much less expensive since the record-keeping entity has borne most of the cost of collecting and publishing the data. With the increased use of computers, many organizations are systematically collecting data of interest to researchers. The disadvantage, however, is that because the data are not under the researcher's control they must be made available by the record-keeping organization, which can refuse a researcher's request or take a long time filling it. Finally, observation can be time-consuming (if the researcher does it) or expensive (if the researcher pays others to do it).

In addition to these factors, researchers must consider the ethical implications of their proposed research. In most cases, the research topics you are likely to propose will not raise serious ethical concerns, nor will your choice of method of data collection hinge on the risk it may pose to human subjects. Nevertheless, you should be aware of the ethical issues and risks to others that can result from social science research and you should be aware of the review process that researchers are required to follow when proposing research involving human subjects.

In accordance with federal regulations, universities and other research organizations require faculty and students to submit research proposals involving human subjects for review to an **institutional review board** (often called Human Subject Review Board). There may be some variation in practice concerning unfunded research, but the proper course of action is to contact your institution's research office for information regarding the human subjects review policy. There are three levels of review: some research may be exempt, some may require only expedited review, and some research will be subject to full board review. Even if your research project seems to fit one of the categories of research exempt from review, you must request and be granted an exemption.

Three ethical principles—respect for persons, beneficence, and justice— form the foundation for assessing the ethical dimensions of research involving human subjects. These principles were identified in *The Belmont Report,* a report of the National Commission for the Protection of Human Subjects in Biomedical and Behavioral Research.[1] Respect for persons requires that individuals should be treated as autonomous agents, and asserts that persons with diminished capacity are entitled to protection. Beneficence refers to protecting people from harm as well as making efforts to secure their well-being. The principle of justice requires researchers to consider the distribution of the benefits and burdens of research.

The principle of respect for persons requires that subjects be given the opportunity to choose what shall or shall not happen to them. **Informed consent** means that subjects are to be given information about the research, including the research procedure, its purposes, risks and anticipated benefits; alternative procedures (where therapy is involved); how subjects are selected; the person responsible for the research; and a statement offering the subject the opportunity to ask questions and to withdraw from the research at any time. This information should be conveyed in a manner that is comprehensible to the subject and the consent of the subject must be voluntary.

An assessment of risks and benefits relates directly to the beneficence principle by helping in determining whether risks to subjects are justified as well as providing information useful to subjects for their informed consent. The justice principle is often associated with the selection of subjects insofar as some populations may be more likely to be targeted for study.

As mentioned earlier, there are categories of research that are exempt from review:

1. *Research conducted in established or commonly accepted educational settings, involving normal educational practices, such as (a) research on regular and special education instructional strategies or (b) research on the effectiveness of or the comparison among instructional techniques, curricula, or classroom management methods.*

2. *Research involving the use of educational tests (cognitive, diagnostic, aptitude, achievement), survey procedures, interview procedures, or observation of public behavior, unless (a) information obtained is recorded in such a manner that human subjects can be identified, directly or through identifiers linked to the subjects, AND (b) any disclosure of the human subjects' responses outside the research could reasonably place the subjects at risk of criminal or civil liability or be damaging to the subjects' financial standing, employability, or reputation.*

3. *Research involving the use of education tests, survey procedures, interview procedures, or observation of public behavior that is not exempt under category 2, if (a) the human subjects are elected or appointed public officials or candidates for public office or (b) federal statute(s) requires without exception that the confidentiality of the personally identifiable information will be maintained throughout the research and thereafter.*

4. *Research involving the collection or study of existing data, documents, records, pathological specimens, or diagnostic specimens, if these sources are publicly available or if the information is recorded by the investigator in such a manner that subjects cannot be identified directly or through identifiers linked to the subjects.*

5. *Research and demonstration projects that are conducted by or subject to the approval of department or agency heads and that are designed to study, evaluate, or otherwise examine (a) public benefit or service programs, (b) procedures for obtaining benefits or services under those programs, (c) possible changes in or alternatives to those programs or procedures, or (d) possible changes in methods or levels of payment for benefits or services under those programs.*

6. *Taste and food quality evaluation and consumer acceptance studies, (a) if wholesome foods without additives are consumed or (b) if a food is consumed that contains a food ingredient at or below the level and for a use found to be safe, or agricultural chemical or environmental contaminant at or below the level found to be safe, by the Food and Drug Administration or approved by the Environmental Protection Agency or the Food Safety and Inspection Service of the U.S. Department of Agriculture.*[2]

Categories 2–4 are likely to apply to most political science research projects, especially those undertaken by students.

In this and the following chapter, the relative advantages and disadvantages of each of the major data collection methods will be examined with respect to the factors of validity, reactivity, population coverage, cost, and availability. We will also point out the ethical issues raised by some applications of these data collection methods.

Observation

Although observation is more generally a research tool of anthropologists, psychologists, and sociologists, political observation has been used by political scientists to study political campaigning, community politics, leadership and executive decision making, program implementation, judicial proceedings, the U.S. Congress, and state legislatures. In fact, any student who has had an internship, kept a daily log or diary, and written a paper based on his or her experiences has used this method of data collection.

Every day we "collect data" using observational techniques. We observe some attribute or characteristic of people and infer some behavioral trait from that observation. For example, we watch the car in front of us sway between the traffic lanes and conclude that the driver has been drinking; we observe the mannerisms, voice pitch, and facial expressions of a student making a presentation in one of our classes and decide that the person is exceptionally nervous; or we decide that most of the citizens attending a public hearing are opposed to a proposed project by listening to their comments to each other before the start of the hearing. The observational techniques used by political scientists are really only extensions of this method of data collection.

They resemble everyday observations, but are usually more self-conscious and systematic.

Observations may be classified in at least four different ways: *direct* or *indirect, participant* or *nonparticipant, overt* or *covert,* and *structured* or *unstructured.* The most basic distinction is whether an observation is direct—the actual behavior, verbal or nonverbal, is observed firsthand—or indirect—the results or physical traces of behavior are observed.[3] For example, an indirect method of observing college students' favorite studying spots in classrooms and office buildings would be to arrive on campus early in the morning before the custodial staff and measure the amount of food wrappers, soda cans, and other debris at various locations. A direct method of observing the same thing would be to go around the buildings and notice where students are.

In **participant observation**, the investigator is a regular participant in the activities or group being observed. For example, someone who studies political campaigns by becoming actively involved in them is a participant observer. A researcher does not, however, have to become a full-fledged member of group to be a participant observer; some mutually acceptable role or identity must be worked out. For example, Ruth Horowitz did not become a gang member when she studied Chicano youth in a Chicago neighborhood.[4] She hung around with gang members, but as a nonmember. She did not participate in fights and was able to decline when asked to conceal weapons for gang members. A nonparticipant observer does not participate in group activities or become a member of the group or community. For example, an investigator interested in hearings held by public departments of transportation or city council meetings could observe those proceedings without becoming a participant.

A third way to characterize observation is by noting whether it is overt or covert. In **overt observation**, those being observed are aware of the investigator's presence and intentions. In **covert observation**, the investigator's presence is hidden or undisclosed and his or her intentions are disguised. For example, a recent study involved observation to measure what percentage of people washed their hands after using the rest room. Research involving covert observation of public behavior of private individuals is not likely to raise ethical issues as long as individuals are not or cannot be identified and disclosure of individuals' behavior would not place them at risk. However, elected or appointed public officials are not shielded by these limitations. Ethical standards and their application or enforcement has changed and it is likely that a number of earlier examples of participant observation research, especially those involving covert observation, would not receive approval from human subject review boards today. For example, social scientists Mary Henle and Marian B. Hubble once hid under beds in students' rooms to study student conversations.[5]

In **structured observation**, the investigator looks for and systematically records the incidence of specific behaviors. In **unstructured observation**, all behavior is considered relevant, at least at first, and recorded. Only later, upon reflection, will the investigator distinguish between important and trivial behavior.

Direct Observation

The vast majority of observation studies conducted by political scientists involves **direct observation**, in which the researcher observes actual behavior, with the observation more likely to occur in a natural setting rather than in a laboratory. Again, observation may be structured or unstructured. The term **field study** is usually used to refer to open-ended and wide-ranging rather than structured observation in a natural setting. It is not likely that as a student you will conduct your own observation research in a laboratory.

Observation in a laboratory setting gives a researcher the advantage of control over the environment of the observed. Thus the researcher may be able to employ a more rigorous experimental design than is possible in a natural, uncontrolled setting. Also, observation may be easier and more convenient to record and preserve since one-way windows, videotape machines, and other observational aids are more readily available in a laboratory.

A disadvantage of laboratory observation is that subjects usually know they are being observed and therefore may alter their behavior, raising questions about the validity of the data collected. The use of aids that allow the observer to be physically removed from the setting and laboratories that are designed to be as inviting and as natural as possible may lead subjects to behave more naturally and less self-consciously.

An example of an attempt to create a natural-looking laboratory setting may be found in Stanley Milgram and R. Lance Shotland's book *Television and Antisocial Behavior.*[6] These researchers were interested in the impact of television programming on adult behavior, specifically in the ability of television drama to stimulate antisocial acts such as theft. They devised four versions of a program called "Medical Center," each with a different plot, and showed the versions in a theater to four different audiences. Some of the versions showed a character stealing money, and the versions differed in whether the person was punished for his theft or not. The participants in the study were then asked to go to a particular office at a particular time to pick up a free transistor radio, their payment for participating in the research study. When they arrived in the office (the laboratory), they encountered a sign that said the radios were all gone. The researchers were interested in how people would react and specifically in whether they would imitate any of the behaviors in the versions of "Medical Center" that they had seen (such as the theft of money from see-through plastic collection dishes). Their behavior was observed covertly via a one-way mirror. Once the subjects left the office, they were directed to another location where they were, in fact, given the promised radio. This experiment, reported in 1973, raises some serious ethical issues about deceiving research subjects.

Direct observation in natural settings has its own advantages. One advantage of observing people in a natural setting rather than in the artificiality of a laboratory setting is that generally people will behave as they would ordinarily. Furthermore, the investigator is able to observe people for longer periods of time than would be possible in a laboratory. In fact, one of the striking features of field studies is the considerable amount of time an investigator may spend in the field. It is not uncommon for investigators to live in the community they are observing for a year or more. William F. Whyte's classic study of life in an Italian slum, *Street Corner Society,* was based on three years of observation (1937–1940), and Marc Ross's study of political participation in Nairobi, Kenya, took more than a year of field observation.[7] To study the behavior of U.S. representatives in their districts, Richard Fenno traveled intermittently for almost seven years, making thirty-six separate visits and spending 110 working days in eighteen congressional districts.[8] Ruth Horowitz spent three years researching youth in an inner-city Chicano community in Chicago.[9]

Sometimes researchers have no choice but to observe political phenomena as they occur in their natural setting. Written records of events may not exist, or the records may not cover the behavior of interest to the researcher. Relying on personal accounts of participants may be unsatisfactory because of participants' distorted views of events, incomplete memories, or failure to observe what is of interest to the researcher.

Open-ended, flexible observation is appropriate if the research purpose is one of description and exploration. For example, Fenno's research purpose was to study "representatives' perceptions of their constituencies while they are actually in their constituencies."[10]

As Fenno explains, his visits with representatives in their districts

> *were totally open-ended and exploratory. I tried to observe and inquire into anything and everything these members did. I worried about whatever they worried about. Rather than assume that I already knew what was interesting, I remained prepared to find interesting questions emerging in the course of the experience. The same with data. The research method was largely one of soaking and poking or just hanging around.*[11]

In these kinds of field studies, researchers do not start out with particular hypotheses that they want to test. They often do not know enough about what they plan to observe to establish lists and specific categories of behaviors to look for and record systematically. The purpose of the research is to discover what these might be.

Some political scientists have used observation as a preliminary research method.[12] For example, James Robinson's work in Congress provided first-hand information for his studies of the House Rules Committee and of the role of Congress in foreign policy making.[13] Ralph Huitt's service on Lyndon B. Johnson's Senate majority leader staff gave Huitt inside access to information for his study of Democratic party leadership in the Senate.[14] And David Minar served as a school board member and used his experience to develop questionnaires in his comparative study of several school districts in the Chicago area.[15]

You may look upon an internship, volunteer work, or participation in a community or political organization as opportunities to conduct your own research using direct observation. More than likely yours will be a case study in which you are able to compare the real world to theories and general expectations suggested in course readings and lectures. If you are fortunate your case may turn out to be a critical or deviant case study.

Most field studies involve participant observation. An investigator cannot be like the proverbial fly on the wall, observing a group of people for long periods of time. Usually he or she must assume a role or identity within the group that is being studied and participate in the activities of the group. As noted earlier, many political scientists who have studied Congress have worked as staff members on committees and in congressional offices.

Acceptance by the group is necessary if the investigator is going to benefit from the naturalness of the research setting. Negotiating an appropriate role for oneself within a group may be a challenging and evolving process. As Chicago gang researcher Ruth Horowitz points out, a researcher may not wish, or be able, to assume a role as a "member" of the observed group. Personal attributes (gender, age, ethnicity) of the researcher or ethical considerations (gang violence) may prevent this.[16] The role the researcher is able to establish also depends on the setting and the members of the group.

> *I was able to negotiate multiple identities and relationships that were atypical of those generally found in the research setting, but that nonetheless allowed me to become sufficiently close to the setting members to do the research. By becoming aware of the nature, content, and consequences of these identities, I was able to use the appropriate identity to successfully collect different kinds of data and at the same time avoid some difficult situations that full participation as a member might have engendered.*[17]

Investigators using participant observation often depend on members of the group they are observing to serve as *informants,* persons who are willing to be interviewed about the activities and behavior of themselves and of the group to which they belong. An informant also helps the researcher interpret behavior. A close relationship between the researcher and informant may help the researcher gain access to other group members, not only because an informant may familiarize the researcher with community members and norms, but also because the informant, through close association with the researcher, will be able to pass on information about the researcher to the community.[18] Some participant observation studies will have one key informant; others will have several. For example, Whyte relied on the leader of a street corner gang whom he called "Doc" as his key informant, while Fenno's eighteen representatives all could be considered informants.

Although a valuable asset to researchers, informants may present problems. A researcher should not rely too much on one or a few informants since they may give a biased view of a community. And if the informant is associated with one faction in a multifaction community or is a marginal member of the community (and thus more willing to associate with the researcher), the researcher's affiliation with the informant may inhibit rather than enhance access to the community.[19]

Participant observation offers the advantages of a natural setting, the opportunity to observe people for lengthy periods of time so that interaction and changes in behavior may be studied, and a degree of accuracy or completeness impossible with documents or recall data such as that obtained in surveys. Observing a city council or school board meeting or a public hearing on the licensing of a locally undesirable land use will allow you to know and understand what happened at these events far better than reading official minutes or transcripts. However, there are some noteworthy limitations to the method as well.

The main problem with direct, participant observation as a method of empirical research for political scientists is that many significant instances of political behavior are not accessible for observation. The privacy of the voter in the voting booth is legally protected, U.S. Supreme Court conferences are not open to anyone but the justices themselves, political consultants and bureaucrats do not usually wish to have political scientists privy to their discussions and decisions, and most White House conversations and deliberations are carefully guarded. Occasionally physical traces of these private behaviors become public—such as the Watergate tapes of Richard Nixon's conversations with his aides—and disclosures are made about some aspects of government decision making, such as congressional committee hearings and Supreme Court oral arguments, but typically access is the major barrier to directly observing consequential political behavior.

Another disadvantage of participant observation is lack of control over the environment. A researcher may be unable to isolate individual factors and observe their effect on behavior. Participant observation is also limited by the small number of cases that are usually involved. For example, Fenno observed only eighteen members or would-be members of Congress—too few for any sort of statistical analysis. He chose "analytical depth" over "analytical range"; in-depth observation of eighteen cases was the limit that Fenno thought he could manage intellectually, professionally, financially, and physically.[20] Whyte observed one street-corner gang in-depth, although he did observe others less closely. Because of the small numbers of cases, the representativeness of the results of participant observation has been questioned. But, as we have tried to stress earlier in our discussion of research designs, the number of cases deemed appropriate for a research topic depends on the purpose of the research. Understanding how people function in a particular community may be the knowledge that is desired, not whether the particular community is representative of some larger number of communities.

Unstructured participant observation also has been criticized as invalid and biased. A researcher may selectively perceive behaviors, noting some, ignoring others. The interpretation of behaviors may reflect the personality and culture of the observer rather than the meaning attributed to them by the observed themselves. Moreover, the presence of the observer may alter the behavior of the observed no matter how skillfully the observer attempts to become accepted as a nonthreatening part of the community.

Fieldworkers attempt to minimize these possible threats to data validity by immersing themselves in the culture they are observing and by taking copious notes on everything going on around them no matter how seemingly trivial. Events without apparent meaning at the time of observation may become important and revealing upon later reflection. Of course, copious note taking leads to what is known as a "high dross rat"; much of what is recorded is not relevant to the research problem or question as it is finally formulated. It may be painful for the investigator to discard so much of the material that was carefully recorded, but this is a standard practice with this method.

Another way to obtain more valid data is to allow the observed to read and comment on what the investigator has written and point out events and behavior that may have been misinterpreted. This check on observations may be of limited or no value if the observed cannot read or if the written material is aimed at persons well versed in the researcher's discipline and therefore is over the observed's head.

Researchers' observations may be compromised if the researchers begin to overidentify with their subjects or informants. "Going native," as this phenomenon is known, may lead them to paint a more complimentary picture of the observed than is warranted. Researchers combat this problem by returning to their own culture to analyze their data and by asking colleagues or others to comment on their findings.

A demanding yet essential aspect of field study is note taking. Notes can be divided into three types: mental notes, jotted notes, and field notes. Mental note taking involves orienting one's consciousness to the task of remembering things one has observed, such as "who and how many were there, the physical character of the place, who said what to whom, who moved about in what way, and a general characterization of an order of events."[21] Since mental notes may fade rapidly, researchers use jotted notes to preserve them. Jotted notes consist of short phrases and key words that will activate a researcher's memory later when the full field notes are written down. Researchers may be able to use tape recorders if they have the permission of those being observed.

Taped conversations do not constitute "full" field notes, which should include a running description of conversations and events. For this aspect of field notes, John Lofland advises that researchers should be factual and concrete, avoid making inferences, and employ participants' descriptive and interpretative terms. Full field notes should include material previously forgotten and subsequently recalled. Lofland suggests that researchers distinguish between verbal material that is exact recall, paraphrased or close recall, and reasonable recall.[22]

Field notes should also include a researcher's analytic ideas and inferences, personal impressions and feelings, and notes for further information.[23] Because events and emotional states in a researcher's life may affect observation, they should be recorded. Notes for further information provide guidance for future observation, either to fill in gaps in observations, call attention to things that may happen, or test out emerging analytic themes.

Full field notes should be legible and should be reviewed periodically, since the passage of time may present past observations in a new light to the researcher or reveal a pattern worthy of attention in a series of disjointed events. Creating and reviewing field notes is an important part of the observational method. Consequently, a field worker should expect to spend as much time on field notes as he or she spends on observation in the field.

Indirect Observation

Indirect observation, the observation of physical traces of behavior, is essentially detective work.[24] Based on physical traces, inferences about people and their behavior can be drawn. An unobtrusive research method, indirect observation is nonreactive: subjects do not change their behavior because they do not know they are being studied.

Physical Trace Measures

Researchers employ two methods of measurement when undertaking indirect observation. An **erosion measure** is created by selective wear on some material. For example, campus planners at one university observed paths worn in grassy areas and then rerouted paved walkways to correspond to the most heavily trafficked routes. Other examples of natural erosion measures include wear on library books, wear and tear on selected articles within volumes, and depletion of items in stores such as sales of newspapers.

The second measurement of indirect observation is the **accretion measure**, which is created by the deposition and accumulation of materials. Archeologists and geologists commonly use accretion measures in their research by measuring, mapping, and analyzing accretion of materials. Other professions find them useful as well. Eugene Webb and his colleagues report a study in which mechanics in an automotive service department recorded radio dial settings to estimate radio station popularity.[25] This information was then used to select radio stations to carry the dealer's advertising. The popularity of television programs could be measured by recording the drop in water level while commercials are aired since viewers tend to use the toilet only during commercials when watching very popular shows. Similarly, declines in telephone usage could indicate television program popularity. The presence of fingerprints and nose prints on glass display cases may indicate interest as well as reveal information about the size and age of those attracted to the display. The effectiveness of various anti-litter policies and conservation programs could also be measured using physical trace evidence, and the amount and content of graffiti may represent an interesting measurement of the beliefs, attitudes, and mood of a population.

One of the best known examples of the use of accretion measures is W. L. Rathje's study of people's garbage.[26] He studied people's behavior based on what they discarded in their trash cans. One project involved investigating whether poor people wasted more food than those better off: they did not.

Indirect observation typically raises fewer ethical issues than direct observation since the measures of individual behavior are taken after the individuals have left the scene, thus assuring anonymity in most cases. However, Rathje's studies of garbage raised ethical concerns because some discarded items (such as letters and bills) identified the source of the garbage. Although a court ruled in Rathje's favor by declaring that when people discard their garbage they have no further legal interest in it, one might consider sorting through one's garbage an invasion of privacy. In a study in which data on households were collected, consent forms were obtained, codes were used to link household information to garbage data, and then the codes were destroyed. Rathje's assistants in another garbage study were instructed not to examine closely any material.

It is also possible that garbage may contain evidence of criminal wrongdoing. Twice during Rathje's research body parts were discovered, although not in the actual bags collected as part of the study. Rathje took the position that evidence of victimless crimes should be ignored; evidence of serious crimes should be reported. Of course, the publicity surrounding Rathje's garbage study may have deterred disposal of such evidence. This raises the problem of reactivity: to what extent might people change their garbage-disposing habits if they know there is a small chance that what they throw away will be examined?

This example also illustrates the possibility that indirect observation of physical traces of behavior may border on direct observation of subjects if the observation of physical traces quickly follows their creation. In some situations, extra measures may have to be taken to preserve the anonymity of subjects.

Another good example of the use of accretion measures is Kurt and Gladys Lang's study of the MacArthur Day parade in Chicago in 1951.[27] General Douglas MacArthur and President Harry S. Truman were locked in an important political struggle at the time, and the Langs wanted to find out how much interest there was in the parade. They used data on mass-transit passenger fares, hotel reservations, retail store and street vendor sales, parking lot usage, and the volume of tickertape on the streets to measure the size of the crowd attracted by MacArthur's appearance.

Validity Problems with Indirect Observation

Although physical trace measures generally are not subject to reactivity to the degree that participant observation and survey research are, threats to the validity of these measures do exist. Also, erosion and accretion measures may be biased. For example, certain traces are more likely to survive because the materials are more durable. Thus physical traces may provide a selective, rather than complete, picture of the past. Differential wear patterns may be due not to variation in use but to differences in material. Researchers studying garbage must be careful not to infer that garbage reflects all that is used or consumed. Someone who owns a garbage disposal, for example, will generally discard less garbage than someone who doesn't.

Researchers should exercise caution in linking changes in physical traces to particular causes. Other factors may account for variation in the measures. Webb and his colleagues suggest that several physical trace measures be used simultaneously or that alternative data collection methods be used to supplement physical trace measures.[28] For example, physical trace measures of use of recreational facilities, such as which trash cans in a park fill up the fastest, could be supplemented with questionnaires to park visitors on facility usage.

Caution should also be used in making inferences about the behavior that caused the physical traces. For example, wear around a particular museum exhibit could be indicative either of the number of people viewing the exhibit or of the amount of time people spent near the exhibit shuffling their feet. Direct observation could determine the answer; but in cases where the physical trace measures occurred in the past, this solution is not possible.

Examples of the use of indirect observation in political science research are not numerous. Nevertheless, this method has been used profitably, and you may be able to think of cases where it would be appropriate For example, you could assess the popularity of candidates by determining the number of yard signs appearing in a community. Or, you could estimate the number of visitors and level of office activity of elected representatives by noting carpet wear in office entryways. While this would not be as precise as counting visitors, it would allow you to avoid having to post observers or question office staff.

Indirect observation, when used ingeniously, can be a low-cost research method free from many of the ethical issues that surround direct observation. Let us now turn to a consideration of some of the ethical issues that develop in the course of fieldwork and in simple, nonexperimental laboratory observations.

Ethical Issues in Observation

Ethical dilemmas arise primarily when there is a potential for harm to the observed. The potential for serious harm to subjects in most observational studies is quite low. Observation generally does not entail investigation of highly sensitive, personal, or illegal behavior because people are reluctant to be observed in those circumstances and would not give their informed consent. Nor do fieldwork and simple laboratory observation typically involve experimental manipulations of subjects and exposure to risky experimental treatments. Nonetheless, harm or risks to the observed may result from observation. They include (1) negative repercussions from associating with the researcher due to the researcher's sponsors, nationality, or outsider status; (2) invasion of privacy; (3) stress during the research interaction; and (4) disclosure of behavior or information to the researcher resulting in harm to the observed during or after the study. Each of these possibilities will be considered in turn.

In some fieldwork situations, contact with outsiders may be viewed as undesirable behavior by an informant's peers. Cooperation with a researcher may violate community norms. For example, a researcher who studies a group known to shun contact with outsiders exposes informants to the risk that they will be censured by their group.

Social scientists from the United States have encountered difficulty in conducting research in countries with hostile relations with the United States.[29] Informants and researchers may be accused of being spies, and informants may be exposed to harm for appearing to sympathize with "the enemy." Harm may result even if hostile relations develop after the research has been conducted. Military, CIA, or other government sponsorship of research may particularly endanger the observed.

A second source of harm to the observed results from the invasion of privacy that observation may entail. Even though a researcher may have permission to observe, the role of observer may not always be remembered by the observed. In fact, as a researcher gains rapport, there is a greater chance that informants may view the researcher as a friend and reveal to him or her something that could prove to be damaging. A researcher does not always warn, "Remember, you're being observed!" Furthermore, if a researcher is being treated as a friend, such a warning may damage rapport. Researchers must consider how they will use the information gathered from subjects. They must judge whether use in a publication will constitute a betrayal of confidence.[30]

Much of the harm to subjects in fieldwork occurs as a result of publication. They may be upset at the way they are portrayed, subjected to unwanted publicity, or depicted in a way that embarrasses the larger group to which they belong. Carelessness in publication may result in the violation of promises of confidentiality and anonymity. And value-laden terminology may offend those being described.[31]

Carole Johnson has prepared the following guidelines for the "ethical proofreading" of manuscripts prior to publication. To diminish the potential for harm to the observed, researchers should keep in mind these nine points:

1. *Assume that both the identities of the location studied and the identities of individuals will be discovered. What would the consequences of this discovery be to the community? To the individuals? What would the consequences be both within the community and outside the community? Do you believe that the importance of what you have revealed in your publication is great enough to warrant these consequences? Could you, yourself, live with these consequences should they occur?*

2. *Look at the words used in your manuscript. Are they judgmental or descriptive? How accurate are the descriptions of the phenomena observed? A judgment, for example, would be to say that a community is backward. A description might be to say that 10% of the adult pop-*

ulation can neither read nor write. The latter is preferable both scientifically and ethically. . . .

3. *Where appropriate in describing private or unflattering characteristics, consider generalizing first and then giving specifics. . . . This tends to make research participants feel less singled out. It also adds to the educational value of the writing.*

4. *Published data may affect the community studied and similar communities in a general way even though the identities of the community and individuals may remain unknown. In James West's book* Plainville, U.S.A., *for example, people were described as backward. Some people were said to live like animals. Some men were said to be as dirty as animals. West also related that many people from Plainville left the community to seek employment in the cities. What if such descriptive information about rural communities affected individuals' opportunities for employment due to the creation of negative stereotypes about people from rural areas? Therefore, ask yourself how your information might be used in a positive way? In a negative way? And again ask if the revelations are worth the possible consequences.*

5. *Will your research site be usable again or have you destroyed this site for other researchers? Have you destroyed other similar sites? Is such destruction worth the information obtained and disseminated?*

6. *What was your perspective toward subjects? What were your biases? How did your perspective and biases, both positive and negative, affect the way you viewed your subjects and wrote about them? . . .*

7. *In what ways can research participants be educated about the role of fieldworkers and the nature of objective reporting of fieldwork? It may be advisable to caution your subjects at various stages of the research that it is not easy to read about oneself as one is described by another.*

8. *When conducting research within a larger project, know the expectations of other project members concerning what each member will be permitted to publish both in the short and long run, i.e., are there any limitations? If not, what limits ought ethically to be imposed? Who will have the final say about publication? Who will own the data? Who will have access to the data and on what terms? What will happen to the data after publication? Most important, see that agreements are set forth in writing in a legally enforceable contract.*

9. *Have several people do "ethical proofreading" of your manuscript. One or two of those people might be your subjects. They should read it for accuracy and should provide any general feedback they are inclined to offer. One or two of your colleagues should also read the manuscript. Preferably those colleagues should not be ones who are particularly supportive or sympathetic to your research but colleagues who can be constructively critical.*[32]

Ethical proofreading of manuscripts will protect informants from some of the worst examples of researcher carelessness or insensitivity, but it does not protect the observed from the harm that might arise during observation. Protecting the observed against harm and assessing the potential for harm to the observed prior to starting observation may be difficult. The risk to subjects posed by observation cannot be precisely estimated, nor may concrete measures to avoid all harm be easily specified and enforced. It is up to the researcher to behave ethically. An appropriate ethical framework for judging fieldwork should be "constructed on respect for the autonomy of individuals and groups based on the fundamental principle that persons always be treated as ends in themselves, never merely as means" to a researcher's own personal or professional goals.[33]

Conclusion

Observation is an important research method for political scientists. Observational studies may be direct or indirect. Indirect observation is less common but has the advantage of being a nonreactive research method. Direct observation of people by social scientists has produced numerous studies that have enhanced knowledge and understanding of human beings and their behavior. Fieldwork—direct observation by a participant observer in a natural setting—is the best known variety of direct observation, although direct observation may take place in a laboratory setting. Observation tends to produce data that are qualitative rather than quantitative. Because the researcher is the measuring device, this method is subject to particular questions about researcher bias and data validity. Since there is an evolving relationship between the observer and the observed, participant observation is a demanding and often unpredictable research endeavor. Part of the demanding nature of fieldwork stems from the difficult ethical dilemmas it raises.

As a student you may find yourself in the position of an observer, but it is more likely that you will be a consumer and evaluator of observational research. In this position you should base your evaluation on a number of considerations: Does it appear that the researcher influenced the behavior of the observed or was biased in his or her observation? How many informants were used? A few or only one? Does it appear likely that the observed could have withheld significant behavior of interest to the researcher? Are generalizations from the study limited because observation was made in a laboratory setting or because of the small number of cases observed? Were any ethical issues raised by the research? Could they have been avoided? What would you have done in a similar situation? These questions should help you evaluate the validity and ethics of observational research.

Notes

1. National Commission for the Protection of Human Subjects of Biomedical and Behavioral Research. (April 18, 1979) "The Belmont Report: Ethical Principles and Guidelines for the Protection of Human Subjects of Research" [Online]. Available: http://helix.nih.gov:8001/ohsr/mpa/belmont.php3 (November 15, 2000).

2. From Title 45, Code of Federal Regulation, part 46.101(b), 6/18/91. These exemptions do not apply to research involving prisoners, fetuses, pregnant women, or human in vitro fertilization. Exemption 2 does not apply to children except for research involving observations of public behavior when the investigator does not participate in the activities being observed.

3. Eugene J. Webb et al., *Nonreactive Measures in the Social Sciences,* 2d ed. (Boston: Houghton Mifflin, 1981).

4. Ruth Horowitz, "Remaining an Outsider: Membership as a Threat to Research Rapport," *Urban Life* 14 (January 1986): 409–430.

5. Mary Henle and Marian B. Hubble, "Egocentricity in Adult Conversation," *Journal of Social Psychology* 9 (May 1938): 227–234.

6. Stanley Milgram and R. Lance Shotland, *Television and Antisocial Behavior: Field Experiments* (New York: Academic Press, 1973).

7. William F. Whyte, *Street Corner Society: The Social Structure of an Italian Slum,* 3d ed. (Chicago: University of Chicago Press, 1981); and Marc H. Ross, *Grass Roots in an African City: Political Behavior in Nairobi* (Cambridge: MIT Press, 1975).

8. Richard F. Fenno Jr., *Home Style: House Members in Their Districts* (Boston: Little, Brown, 1978).

9. Ruth Horowitz, *Honor and the American Dream* (New Brunswick: Rutgers University Press, 1983).

10. Fenno, *Home Style,* xiii.

11. Ibid., xiv.

12. Jennie-Keith Ross and Marc Howard Ross, "Participant Observation in Political Research," *Political Methodology* 1 (winter 1974): 65–66.

13. James A. Robinson, *The House Rules Committee* (Indianapolis: Bobbs-Merrill, 1963); and James A. Robinson, *Congress and Foreign Policy-making* (Homewood, Ill.: Dorsey, 1962). Also, extensive firsthand observations of Congress are reported in many of the articles in Raymond E. Wolfinger, ed., *Readings on Congress* (Englewood Cliffs, N.J.: Prentice-Hall, 1971).

14. Ralph K. Huitt, "Democratic Party Leadership in the Senate," *American Political Science Review* 55 (June 1961): 333–344.

15. David W. Minar, "The Community Basis of Conflict in School System Politics," in Scott Greer et al., eds., *The New Urbanization* (New York: St. Martin's, 1968), 246–263.

16. Horowitz, "Remaining an Outsider," 412.

17. Ibid., 413.

18. Ross and Ross, "Participant Observation," 70.

19. Ibid.

20. Fenno, *Home Style,* 255.

21. John Lofland, *Analyzing Social Settings: A Guide to Qualitative Observation and Analysis* (Belmont, Calif.: Wadsworth, 1971), 102–103.

22. Ibid., 105.

23. Ibid., 106–107.

24. Webb et al., *Nonreactive Measures,* 4.

25. Ibid., 10–11.

26. See discussion of Rathje's work in ibid., 15–17.

27. Kurt Lang and Gladys Engel Lang, *Politics and Television* (Chicago: Quadrangle, 1968).

28. See Webb et al., *Nonreactive Measures,* 27–32.

29. See Myron Glazer, *The Research Adventure: Promise and Problems of Field Work* (New York: Random House, 1973), 25–48, 97–124.

30. See Fenno, *Home Style,* 272.

31. For a discussion and examples of value-laden terminology in published reports of participant observers, see ibid.

32. Carole Garr Johnson, "Risks in the Publication of Fieldwork," in J. E. Sieber, ed., *The Ethics of Social Research: Fieldwork, Regulation and Publication* (New York: Springer-Verlag, 1982), 87–88. This passage is reprinted with permission from the publisher

33. Joan Cassell, "Harms, Benefits, Wrongs and Rights in Fieldwork," in ibid., 14.

(Te)rms introduced

ACCRETION MEASURES. Measures of phenomena through indirect observation of the accumulation of materials.

COVERT OBSERVATION. Observation in which the observer's presence or purpose is kept secret from those being observed.

DIRECT OBSERVATION. Actual observation of behavior.

EROSION MEASURES. Measures of phenomena through indirect observation of selective wear of some material.

FIELD STUDY. Observation in a natural setting.

INDIRECT OBSERVATION. Observation of physical traces of behavior.

INFORMANT. Person who helps a researcher employing participant observation method interpret the activities and behavior of the informant and the group to which the informant belongs.

INFORMED CONSENT. Procedures that inform potential research subjects about the proposed research in which they are being asked to participate. Principle that researchers must obtain the freely given consent of human subjects before they participate in a research project.

INSTITUTIONAL REVIEW BOARD. Panel to which researchers must submit descriptions of proposed research involving human subjects for the purpose of ethics review.

OVERT OBSERVATION. Observation in which those being observed are informed of the observer's presence and purpose.

PARTICIPANT OBSERVATION. Observation in which the observer becomes a regular participant in the activities of those being observed.

STRUCTURED OBSERVATION. Systematic observation and recording of the incidence of specific behaviors.

UNSTRUCTURED OBSERVATION. Observation in which all behavior and activities are recorded.

Suggested Readings

Fenno, Richard F., Jr. *Home Style: House Members in Their Districts.* Boston: Little, Brown, 1978. See the Introduction and Appendix, "Notes on Method: Participant Observation."

Glazer, Myron. *The Research Adventure: Promise and Problems of Field Work.* New York: Random House, 1972.

Horowitz, Ruth. "Remaining an Outsider: Membership as a Threat to Research Rapport." *Urban Life* 14 (January 1986): 409–430.

Ross, Jennie-Keith, and Marc Howard Ross. "Participant Observation in Political Research." *Political Methodology* 1 (winter 1974): 63–88.

Shaffir, William B., Robert A. Stebbins, and Allan Turowitz, eds. *Fieldwork Experience: Qualitative Approaches to Social Research.* New York: St. Martin's, 1980.

Shrader-Frechette, Kristin. *Ethics of Scientific Research.* Lanham, Md.: Rowman & Littlefield, 1994.

Sieber, J. E. *Planning Ethically Responsible Research: A Guide for Students and Internal Review Boards.* Newbury Park, Calif.: Sage, 1992.

———, ed. *The Ethics of Social Research: Fieldwork, Regulation and Publication.* New York: Springer-Verlag, 1982.

Whyte, William F. *Street Corner Society: The Social Structure of an Italian Slum.* 3d ed. Chicago: University of Chicago Press, 1981. See Appendix A, "On the Evolution of *Street Corner Society.*"

CHAPTER 9

Document Analysis:

Using the Written Record

Political scientists have three main methods of collecting the data they need to test hypotheses: interviewing, document analysis, and observation. Of these, interviewing and document analysis are the most frequently used. In the last chapter we discussed observation techniques; here we will describe how empirical observations can be made using the **written record**, which is composed of documents, reports, statistics, manuscripts, and other written, oral, or visual materials.

Political scientists turn to the written record when the political phenomena that interest them cannot be measured through personal interviews, with questionnaires, or by direct observation. For example, interviewing and observation are of limited utility to researchers interested in large-scale collective behavior (such as civil unrest and the budget allocations of national governments), or in phenomena that are distant in time (Supreme Court decisions during the Civil War) or space (defense spending by different countries).

The political phenomena that have been observed through written records are many and varied—for example, judicial decisions concerning the free exercise of religion, voter turnout rates in gubernatorial elections, the change over time in Soviet military expenditures, and the incidence of political corruption in the People's Republic of China.[1] Of the examples of political science research described in Chapter 1 and referred to throughout this book, Steven Poe and Neal Tate's investigation of governments' violation of human rights, Manus Midlarsky's analysis of the effect of land inequality on political violence, Richard Fording's study of the relationship between the expansion of welfare rolls and civil unrest, Jeff Yates and Andrew Whitford's investigation into Supreme Court justices' decisions in cases involving presidential powers, and Jeffrey Segal and Albert Cover's investigation of the ideology of Supreme Court justices all depended upon written records for the measurement of important political concepts.[2] Not all portions of the written record are equally useful to political scientists. Hence we will discuss the major components of the written record of interest to political scientists and how they are used to measure significant political phenomena.

Generally speaking, use of the written record raises fewer ethical issues than either observation or interviewing. Research involving the collection or study of existing data, documents, or records often does not pose risks to individuals because the unit of analysis for the data is not the individual. Also, issues of risk are not likely to arise where records are for individuals, as long as individuals cannot be identified directly or though identifiers linked to them, or where the records are publicly available as in the case of the papers of public figures such as presidents and members of Congress. However, allowing researchers access to their private papers may pose some risk to private individuals. Thus, access to private papers may be subject to conditions designed to protect the individuals involved.

Types of Written Records

Some written records are ongoing and cover an extensive period of time; others are more episodic. Some are produced by public organizations at taxpayers' expense; others are produced by business concerns or by private citizens. Some are carefully preserved and indexed; other records are written and forgotten. In this section we will discuss two types of written records: the episodic record and the running record.

The Episodic Record

Records that are not part of an ongoing, systematic record-keeping program but are produced and preserved in a more casual, personal, and accidental manner are called **episodic records.** Good examples are personal diaries, memoirs, manuscripts, correspondence, and autobiographies; biographical sketches and other biographical materials; the temporary records of organizations; and media of temporary existence, such as brochures, posters, and pamphlets. The episodic record is of particular importance to political historians since much of their subject matter can be studied only through these data.

The papers and memoirs of past presidents and members of Congress could also be classified as part of the episodic record, even though considerable resources and organizational effort are invested in their preservation, insofar as the content and methods of organization of these documents varies and the papers are not available all in the same location.

To use written records, researchers must first gain access to the materials and second code and analyze them. In the case of the episodic record, gaining access is sometimes particularly difficult.[3] Locating suitable materials can easily be the most time-consuming aspect of the whole data collection exercise, as the following example illustrates.

Historian Sandra Frances Van Burkleo became interested in Kentucky politicians' response to the financial panic of 1819. In particular, she wanted to find out how the panic altered banking practices and land law, the relationship between Kentucky and Virginia, and Kentucky's view of the judiciary. Her research led her to consult historical documents in four Kentucky archives—a quest that points out the difficulties and opportunities presented by the episodic record.

> *At my first stop . . . I reviewed legislative journals and statute books while trying to learn something about the contents of several steel warehouses. A glance at the finding aids, prepared years before and patched together by untrained personnel, suggested inaccuracy—especially because so much was stacked in packing crates. Through conversations, I gradually gained familiarity with the repository's criteria for collecting materials, and gathered clues about the crates' contents. . . .*
>
> *I also discovered several hundred bound volumes of banking records—unrecorded in any manuscript guide—and was given a preliminary inventory, which was only partly accurate: size was recorded properly, while substance was not. "Record books," for example, variously meant ledgers, minute books, and miscellaneous volumes. . . .*
>
> *The staff granted me permission to photocopy. I spent two weeks reading, selecting pages, making lists and cross references, and expanding the search into hinterland branch records as clues emerged—only to learn that archival policy had changed. Photocopying of selections was disallowed. I could choose between staff microfilming of selections at a steep price, or using the cameras myself for much less cost, provided that I filmed whole volumes rather than selected pages and left the master behind. I tried to remain calm, donned a technician's coat, and found myself behind sophisticated microfilming equipment under hot floodlights in a dank warehouse. Two weeks later, I had filmed over 10,000 pages, garnered prints, finished other research, and moved on to another repository. . . .*
>
> *My second stop was a state historical society, where I was greeted by friendly volunteers, a classically southern librarian, and a small horde of genealogists. . . . At night, I studied names in local histories; by day, I searched collections. Soon, a network of kin and business associates appeared. . . .*
>
> *I gained permission to use the original governor's papers and saw that the inventory had been prepared in the 1940s by a volunteer. Nobody knew anything about her. But whole boxes were missing and the numbers of bundles inside boxes did not tally with the inventory. . . .*
>
> *Finally, I discovered, through a volunteer, that the "storeroom" held material that nobody had ever used. Why not, I asked? She didn't know. I was granted permission to roam in the mysterious "storeroom"—a place reminiscent of another small room in a Carolina library called "the coffin." There were cobwebs, boxes, and old books buried beneath boxes. I lifted, gently moved, and dug. There was an unlabeled register of monies received by the treasury, linked to landholdings in ways that*

were not clear, and the volume had not been indexed because it lacked a title page. I found five amazing minute books, kept by the Senate clerk during five sessions after 1821—but in a curious shorthand, complete with splendid caricatures of Senate speakers in the margins. . . . I quickly photocopied them. These volumes were a reasonable substitute for long-lost legislative proceedings, providing I could penetrate the shorthand system. They listed individual votes on bills; they summarized speeches. In my hotel room, I read about early American shorthand and eventually deciphered the clerk's alphabetic coding.

At a third repository, located at a state university, another two days were given over to conversation with staff and to generalized poking and digging in finding aids. Again, I wanted to learn something about criteria for collecting, the degree of bibliographic control, the quality of calendars and descriptive inventories. And I hoped to locate someone familiar with the contents of three huge family paper collections which had never been inventoried formally. I found a junior staff member who had processed two of the collections, and had been curious enough to absorb and jot down some of the contents. She was thoughtful and meticulous. I trusted her notes and memory, and eliminated considerable searching. . . .

I had been gone well over two months, and it was clear that I would not be able to visit both repositories remaining on my list. Already I was reduced to two meals a day. I aborted a plan to drive to a small western college in order to survey three family paper collections, fragments of which had been explored in the state historical society and had proved irrelevant, and decided to concentrate remaining resources upon a private historical society in Louisville. . . .

My weeks at this final archive were the most instructive of all. The society was underbudgeted and understaffed—an increasingly typical archival condition, but the staff was dedicated. And they chose to befriend me. Over lunch, I heard horror stories (very like those told elsewhere) about visiting scholars—the "loot and pillage" variety who storm a repository with pockets filled with dimes for photocopying, and who leave without acknowledging a debt; dependent scholars who expect curatorial workers to conduct research for them; lethargic historians who, when confronted with hundreds of relevant entries in a card catalog, simply leave; or gratuitous visitors who view archivists as failed historians or bright clerks. The staff habitually responded in kind, usually by refusing to volunteer information.[4]

As Van Burkleo's saga suggests, locating episodic records can be a time-consuming and frustrating task yet a rewarding one as well. Researchers generally use episodic records to illustrate phenomena rather than a basis for the generation of a large sample and numerical measures for statistical analysis. Consequently, quotations and other excerpts from research materials are often used as evidence for a thesis or hypothesis.

Over the years, social scientists have conducted some exceptionally interesting and imaginative studies of political phenomena based on the episodic record. We will describe three particular studies that used the episodic record to illuminate an important political phenomenon.

DEVIANCE IN THE MASSACHUSETTS BAY COLONY.   More than thirty years ago sociologist Kai Erikson studied deviance in the Puritans' Massachusetts Bay Colony during the seventeenth century.[5] He was interested in the process by which communities decide what constitutes deviant behavior. In particular, he wished to test the idea that communities alter their definitions of deviance over time and use deviant behavior to reaffirm and establish the boundaries of acceptable behavior. Contrary to the conventional view that deviant behavior is uniformly harmful, Erikson believed that the identification of and reaction to deviant behavior serve a useful social purpose for a community.

Obviously, no one is still alive who could be interviewed about the Puritan form of justice in the colony. Consequently, Erikson had to search existing historical documents for evidence relating to his thesis. He found two main collections germane to his inquiry: *The Records of the Governor and Company of the Massachusetts Bay in New England* and *The Records and Files of the Quarterly Courts of Essex County, Massachusetts, 1636–1682.*[6] With these documents Erikson was able to weave together a fascinating tale of crime and punishment, Puritan style, during the mid-1600s.

Erikson's primary concern was with the identification of acts judged deviant in the Massachusetts Bay Colony. From the records of the Essex County courts he was able to collect information on all 1,954 convictions reached between 1651 and 1680. These data allowed Erikson to investigate the frequency of criminal behavior and to calculate a crude crime rate for the Bay Colony during this period.

Erikson's analysis of the historical records was not altogether straightforward. For example, he discovered that the Puritans were extremely casual about how they spelled people's names. One man named Francis Usselton made many appearances before the Essex County Court, and his name was spelled at least fourteen different ways in the court's records. This did not present insurmountable difficulties in his case because his name was so distinctive. However, Erikson had a more difficult time deciding whether Edwin and Edward Batter were the same man and whether "the George Hampton who stole a chicken in 1649" was "the same man as the George Hampden who was found drunk in 1651."[7]

A second problem with the Puritans' record keeping was that they often passed the same name from generation to generation. Hence it was sometimes unclear whether two crimes twenty years apart were committed by the same person or by a father and a son. Between 1656 and 1681, for example,

John Brown was convicted of seven offenses. However, since John Brown's father and grandfather were also named John Brown, it was unclear who committed which crimes.

Despite these difficulties, Erikson's research is a testimonial to the ability of historical records to address important contemporary issues. Without the foresight of those who preserved and printed these records, an important aspect of life in Puritan New England would have been measurably more difficult to piece together.

ECONOMICS AND THE U.S. CONSTITUTION.   In 1913 historian Charles Beard published a book about the U.S. Constitution in which he made imaginative use of the episodic record.[8] Beard's thesis was that economic interests prompted the movement to frame the Constitution. He reasoned that if he could show that the framers and pro-Constitution groups were familiar with the economic benefits that would ensue upon ratification of the Constitution, then he would be able to argue that economic considerations were central to the Constitution debate. If, in addition, he could show that the framers themselves benefited economically from the system of government established by the Constitution, the case would be that much stronger. This thesis, which has stimulated a good deal of controversy, was tested by Beard with a variety of data from the episodic record.

The first body of evidence presented by Beard measured the property holdings of those present at the 1787 Constitutional Convention. These measures, which Beard admits are distressingly incomplete, are derived largely from six different types of sources: biographical materials, such as James Herring's multivolume *National Portrait Gallery* and the *National Encyclopedia of Biography;* census materials, in particular the 1790 census of heads of families, which showed the number of slaves owned by some of the framers; U.S. Treasury records, including ledger books containing lists of securities; records of individual state loan offices; records concerning the histories of certain businesses, such as the *History of the Bank of North America* and the *History of the Insurance Company of North America;* and collections of personal papers stored in the Library of Congress.

From these written records Beard was able to discover the occupations, land holdings, number of slaves, securities, and mercantile interests of the framers. This allowed him to establish a plausible case that the framers were not economically disinterested when they met in Philadelphia to "revise" the Articles of Confederation.

Beard coupled his inventory of the framers' personal wealth with a second body of evidence concerning their political views. His objective was to demonstrate that the framers realized and discussed the economic implications of the Constitution and the new system of government. By using the existing minutes of the debate at the convention, the personal correspondence and writings of some of the framers, and the *Federalist Papers* by James Madison, Alexander Hamilton, and John Jay—which were written to persuade people to vote for the Constitution—Beard was able to demonstrate that the framers were concerned about, and cognizant of, the economic implications of the Constitution they wrote.

A third body of evidence allowed Beard to analyze the distribution of the vote for and against the Constitution. Where the data permitted, Beard measured the geographical distribution of the popular vote in favor of ratification and compared this with information about the economic interests of different geographical areas in each of the states. He also attempted to measure the personal wealth of those present at the state ratification conventions and then related those measures to the vote on the Constitution. These data were gleaned from the financial records of the individual states, the U.S. Treasury Department, and historical accounts of the ratification process in the states.

Through this painstaking and time-consuming reading of the historical record, Beard constructed a persuasive (although not necessarily proven) case for his conclusion that "the movement for the Constitution of the United States was originated and carried through principally by four groups of personal interests which had been adversely affected under the Articles of Confederation: money, public securities, manufactures, and trade and shipping."[9]

PRESIDENTIAL PERSONALITY. A third example of the use of the episodic record may be found in James David Barber's *The Presidential Character.* Because of the importance of the presidency in the American political system and the extent to which that institution is shaped by its sole occupant, Barber was interested in understanding the personalities of the individuals who had occupied the office during the twentieth century. Although he undoubtedly would have preferred to observe directly the behavior of the fourteen presidents who held office between 1908 and 1984 (when he conducted his study), he was forced instead to rely on the available written materials about them.

For Barber, discerning a president's personality means understanding his style, world view, and character. Style is "the President's habitual way of performing his three political roles: rhetoric, personal relations, and homework." A president's world view is measured by his "primary, politically relevant beliefs, particularly his conceptions of social causality, human nature, and the central moral conflicts of the time." And character "is the way the President orients himself toward life." Barber believes that a president's style, character, and world view "fit together in a dynamic package understandable in psychological terms" and that this personality "is an important shaper of his Presidential behavior on nontrivial matters." But how is one to measure the style, character, and world view of presidents who are dead or who will not permit a political psychologist access to their thoughts and deeds? This is an especially troublesome question when one believes, as Barber does, that "the best way to predict a President's character, world view, and style is to see how they were put together in the first place . . . in his early life, culminating in his first independent political success."[10]

Barber's solution to this problem was to use available materials on the twentieth-century presidents he studied, including biographies, memoirs, diaries, speeches, and, in the case of Richard Nixon, tape recordings of presidential conversations. Barber did not use all the available biographical materials. For example, he "steered clear of obvious puff jobs put out in campaigns and of the quickie exposés composed to destroy reputations."[11] He quotes frequently from the biographical materials as he builds his case that a particular president was one of four basic personality types. Had these materials been unavailable or of questionable accuracy (a possibility that Barber glosses over in a single paragraph), measuring presidential personalities would have been a good deal more difficult, if not impossible.

Barber's analysis of the presidential personality is exclusively qualitative; there is not one table or graph in the book. He uses the biographical material to categorize each president as one of four personality types and to show that the presidents with similar personalities exhibited similar behavioral patterns when in office. In brief, Barber uses two dimensions—activity-passivity (how much energy does the man invest in his presidency?) and positive-negative affect (how does he feel about what he does?)—to define the four types of presidential personality (Table 9-1).

Barber's research is a provocative and imaginative example of the use of the episodic record—in this case, biographical material—as evidence for a series of generalizations about presidential personality. Although Barber does not empirically test his hypotheses in the ways that we have been discussing in this book, he does accumulate a body of evidence in support of his assertions and present his evidence in such a way that the reader can evaluate how persuasive it is.[12]

The Running Record

Unlike the episodic record, the **running record** is more likely to be produced by organizations than by private citizens; it is carefully stored and easily accessed; and it is available for long periods of time. The portion of the running record that is concerned with political phenomena is extensive and growing. The data collection and reporting efforts of the U.S. government alone are impressive, and if one adds to that the written records collected and preserved by state and local governments, interest groups, publishing houses, research institutes, and commercial concerns, the quantity of politi-

TABLE 9-1

Presidential Personality Types

Positive-Negative Affect	Activity-Passivity	
	Active	Passive
Positive	Franklin D. Roosevelt	William Howard Taft
	Harry S. Truman	Warren Harding
	John F. Kennedy	Ronald Reagan
	Gerald Ford	
	Jimmy Carter	
Negative	Woodrow Wilson	Calvin Coolidge
	Herbert Hoover	Dwight Eisenhower
	Lyndon Johnson	
	Richard Nixon	

Source: This table is based on data found in James David Barber, The Presidential Character, 3d ed. (Englewood Cliffs, N.J.: Prentice-Hall, 1985).

cally relevant written records increases quickly. Reports of the U.S. government, for example, now cover everything from electoral votes to electrical rates, taxes to taxi cabs, and, in summary form, fill one thousand pages in the *Statistical Abstract of the United States,* published annually by the U.S. Bureau of the Census. What makes the running record especially attractive as a resource is that fact that many data sets are now housed online, as we will point out from time to time. The *Statistical Abstract,* for example, can be found at http://www.census.gov/statab/www/.

In this section we will summarize the main types of running records of interest to political scientists.

ELECTION RETURNS. Election returns have been collected, tabulated, and published for almost 200 years. They are available for most federal offices and some statewide offices at the state and county levels. Commonly used sources of such data are the *America Votes* series (published biennially since 1956 by the Elections Research Center and Congressional Quarterly) and the Inter-University Consortium for Political and Social Research (ICPSR) at the University of Michigan.

CONGRESSIONAL VOTING. Votes of members of the U.S. Congress since 1789 are available from the ICPSR. Congressional roll call votes since 1945 and a plethora of other records concerning individual members of Congress (presidential support scores and party support scores, for example) are published annually in the *Congressional Quarterly Almanac. Politics in America,* published biennially by Congressional Quarterly since 1972, contains more detailed information on individual members, including data on each member's district or state, political career, and voting record, as rated by a variety of interest groups.

JUDICIAL DECISIONS.   Summaries of all state and federal judicial decisions are reported in the *Decennial Digest* (published by West Publishing Co.) and the text of all Supreme Court decisions may be found in *United States Reports,* published by the U.S. Government Printing Office. In addition, the ICPSR has information on the votes cast in the 4,573 cases decided by the U.S. Supreme Court between 1946 and 1969. The ICPSR also has more limited collections of data on topics such as civil and criminal federal court cases (1962–1963), plea bargaining in felony cases in Alaska (1974–1976), state criminal court cases (1962), and U.S. Supreme Court certiorari decisions (1947–1956).

For online collections of Supreme Court, federal courts, and state court decisions and related documents try the U.S. Supreme Court Multimedia Database (Oyez, Oyez, Oyez) at http://oyez.nwu.edu/; Cornell University Law School Legal Information Institute at http://www.law.cornell.edu/; Fedworld Supreme Court Decision 1937–1975 at http://www.fedworld.gov/supcourt/index.htm; and Washburn University School of Law, Washlaw Web, at http://www.washlaw.edu/.

GOVERNMENTAL POLICY.   For information on public policy, researchers have a wide variety of sources. The laws passed each year by the federal government are summarized in the *Congressional Quarterly Almanac* and cited in full in the *United States Statutes at Large.* Data on federal expenditures are included in the *Congressional Quarterly Almanac* as well as the *Statistical Abstract of the United States.* (For an excellent online source of federal budget data that is presented in an easily understood format, go to the Office of Budget and Management at http://www.whitehouse.gov/OMB/budget/index.html.) Measures of public policy at the state and local levels may be found in the *Book of the States* (published biennially by the Council of State Governments), the *County and City Data Book* and the *State and Metropolitan Area Data Book* (both published by the U.S. Bureau of the Census and available on the web at http://www.census.gov/statab/www/), the *Statistical Abstract of the United States* (also accessible at the Census Bureau's web site), and the U.S. Census Bureau's *Annual Survey of Governments.*

The ICPSR also has historical data describing government policy at the national, state, and local levels. *Annual Time Series Statistics for the U.S.* describes federal expenditures by various departments, agencies, and commissions from 1929 to 1968. Four separate studies contain information on state policy making and governmental expenditures; one covers 1950 to 1964, one provides data at decennial points from 1890 to 1960, one covers 1956 to 1965, and one has select data from the nineteenth and twentieth centuries. At the local level, ICPSR has data for 676 incorporated urban places with populations of 25,000 or more during the 1960s and other data since 1960 for 130 incorporated cities with populations greater than 100,000. These and many other datasets can be found at the ICPSR's vast online data archive at http://www.icpsr.umich.edu/archive1.html.

The *Statistical Abstract of the United States* is a treasure trove of data on American society. It contains summaries of all the major data collection efforts of the national government. Between its covers you will find information on health care expenditures, drug use, crime and victimization rates, numbers of arrests and prisoners, air quality, weather, environmental control expenditures, leisure time activities, state and local government finances, federal government personnel and expenditures, veterans' benefits, unemployment, occupational injury rates, the consumer price index, banking and publishing activities, number of foreign-owned U.S. firms, energy production and consumption, transportation revenues, motor vehicle accidents, crop production, housing construction, public housing, department store sales, foreign assistance, and exports and imports. Such a publication is truly an archival researcher's delight.

CRIME STATISTICS.   One particular area of American life that has generated a huge record-keeping enterprise is the criminal justice system. Many elements of these data can be retrieved from the Internet at the Department of Justice's Bureau of Justice Statistics web page (http://www.ojp.usdoj.gov/bjs/). Both the *Statistical Abstract* and the ICPSR resources cited above also offer data on many aspects of crime and the criminal justice system. A more comprehensive set of links to crime data is the Sourcebook of Criminal Justice Statistics at http://www.albany.edu/sourcebook/index.html.

CAMPAIGN SPENDING.   For decades, political scientists have been interested in the role of money in election campaigns. However, it is only within the past thirty years that reliable and comprehensive data on campaign spending have been available to researchers. As a result of the Federal Election Campaign Act of 1971, a federal agency—the Federal Election Commission (FEC)—was established and given the responsibility of collecting data on the fund-raising and campaign spending practices of candidates for federal elective office. The FEC is the source of data on check-off rates to the Presidential Election Campaign Fund among states. The online files of the Federal Election Commission are at http://www.fec.gov/. A better and easy-to-use source, however, is the Non-partisan Federal Candidate Campaign Money Page at http://www.tray.com/fecinfo/, which allows a search for specific candidates' contribution and spending records.

Of related interest are the *Encyclopedia of Third Parties in America* and *Encyclopedia of Interest Groups and Lobbyists in the United States,* the latter of which contains tables of donations to candidates.[13]

SPEECHES. There is also an ongoing written record of the public statements of politicians. Presidential campaign speeches, for example, are contained in a variety of publications, including those published by individual candidates (such as *Nixon Speaks Out,* published by the Nixon-Agnew Campaign Committee) and those published for every president (such as *Public Papers of the Presidents of the United States,* published annually by the U.S. Government Office of the Federal Register). Presidential debate transcripts since 1960 can be found at the Commission on Presidential Debates web site at http://www.debates.org/pages/sitemap.html. Vice-presidential debates are also available here. Debate transcripts and other information about presidential debates may be accessed through the Poynter Institute at http://www.poynter.org/Research/index.htm. A searchable database of speeches can be found at Douglass Archive of American Public Addresses at http://douglass.speech.nwu.edu/. Floor speeches of members of Congress are recorded in the *Congressional Record,* although since members are allowed to excise, revise, and add to what they actually said this record is not completely accurate. For a large collection of links to speech archives go to the University of Iowa Department of Communications Studies' Links to Resources at http://www.uiowa.edu/~commstud/resources/speech.html. Presidential inaugural addresses are stored at the page Inaugural Addresses of the Presidents of the United States at http://www.landmark-project.com/Inaugural_Addresses.html. and at the page INAUGURAL ADDRESSES OF THE PRESIDENTS OF THE UNITED STATES FROM GEORGE WASHINGTION 1789 TO GEORGE BUSH 1989 at http://www.agmay.com/books/TEXT/INAUG.html.

National Party Platforms, published by the University of Illinois Press, contains a collection of the documents put together every four years since 1840 by the American political parties.

MASS MEDIA MATERIALS. The output of news organizations is a running record of daily events and public affairs. The types of stories written, the political issues and personalities covered, the photographs taken, and the opinions expressed may all be considered written records of political and social life. Recall that Segal and Cover's study of the relationship between the personal ideology and judicial decisions of Supreme Court justices relied on published newspaper editorials for the measure of political ideology.[14]

In the past, the running news record was difficult to use simply because it was so massive, disorganized, and hard to retrieve, yet now with the development of newspaper and television indices a sizable portion of the news is both enduring and readily accessible. The *New York Times* has been indexed since 1851, the *Wall Street Journal* since 1957, the *Christian Science Monitor* since 1960, and the *Washington Post* since 1971. Local libraries often have extensive collections of local newspapers. The Philadelphia Free Library, for example, has preserved the *Philadelphia Inquirer* since 1860, the *Evening-Bulletin* for 1847–1982, the *Public Ledger* for 1836–1934, and the *North American* for 1839–1925 (the last three papers went out of business in 1982, 1934, and 1925, respectively). Some newspapers maintain files of articles but many charge a fee for access to them. Lexis-Nexis, however, provides a useful search and retrieval program for looking for newspaper and magazine articles (see Chapter 6).

If a researcher is interested in a phenomenon that can be measured using newspaper content, the running news record is well preserved and extensive. But the running record for broadcast news is less satisfactory. Television network news coverage has been preserved and indexed only since 1968. And, as far as we know, there is no archive or collection of radio news or local television news that can be used by researchers with the exception of National Public Radio, which archives its news programs *Morning Edition* and *All Things Considered* as well as its other programs online in audio format at http://www.npr.org. Tapes and transcripts are also available.

FOREIGN AFFAIRS.   Researchers interested in comparative politics and international relations have used a variety of data on an array of subjects, including the socioeconomic and political attributes of nations; instances of political dissent, conflicts, or violence within different nations; events of conflict and cooperation between nations; trade and arms transfers between nations; and defense expenditures and use of military force by nations. These data represent a rich and readily accessible archival source of observations that would be time consuming and difficult to collect on one's own. Midlarsky's research on the relationship between land inequality and political violence, for example, was facilitated by the availability of data on both the distribution of land ownership and the number of deaths due to political violence in a number of countries.[15]

The United Nations collects large amounts of statistical information. Students interested in the environment, natural resources, population, and human health will find the *World Resources* volumes, published biennially by the World Resources Institute in collaboration with the United Nations Environment Programme and the United Nations Development Programme, especially helpful. The data printed in the volumes are also available on diskette. *The Illustrated Book of World Rankings 2000,* published by M E. Sharpe, contains numerous country rankings, including business indicators and use of various information technologies.

BIOGRAPHICAL DATA. Biographical data are part of the running record. Using biographical publications such as *Who's Who in America* and the *Social Register,* researchers have been able to trace the origins and relationships among people in various positions of power and influence and to contrast different types of elite groups.[16] The ICPSR has biographical data on higher echelon federal executive appointees (1932–1965), arms control bureaucrats, higher civil servants in American federal agencies (1963), state and federal supreme court judges (1955), U.S. Supreme Court justices (1789–1958), members of the Congress of the Confederate States of America (1862–1865), and members of the U.S. Congress (1789–1980). Biographical data also exist on selected foreign elites. The ICPSR has data on political elites in Eastern Europe (1971), Kenya (1966–1967), Tanzania (1964–1968), the Soviet Union (1966), France and Germany (1964), Brazil (1960), and Uganda (1964–1968). As one might expect, electronic versions of these sources are appearing on the Internet at a rapid rate.

STATISTICAL INDEXES. Finally, to help in gathering statistics, there are several statistical indexes, many of which are available as compact disc databases. Some of these are listed below:

American Statistics Index. 1973–. Washington, D.C., Congressional Information Service. An annual publication with monthly supplements. A comprehensive guide and index to statistical publications of the U.S. Government. Attempts to list and index all federal government publications that contain statistical data for probable research significance. Does not contain actual data.

Statistical Reference Index. 1980–. Washington, D.C., Congressional Information Service. Also annual with monthly supplements. Indexes statistical publications published by selected state government agencies, nongovernmental organizations, businesses, and associations. Indexes publications by title, issuing agency, category (race, age, etc.), and subject. Does not include the actual data.

Index to International Statistics. 1983–. Washington, D.C., Congressional Information Service. Annual publication with monthly supplements. Indexes publications published by the United Nations, World Bank, International Monetary Fund, and other nongovernmental international organizations. Does not include the actual data.

Statistical Masterfile. 1970–. Washington, D.C., Congressional Information Service. Combines all three indexes into one compact disc index. Enables researchers to search all three indexes or search one at a time for citations to statistical data. Does not include the actual data.

FedStats. Available at http://www.fedstats.gov/, FedStats describes itself as a one-stop source for data and information from more than seventy agencies in the United States federal government. It is very easy to use and leads to a huge variety of current and historical statistics.

The Running Record and Episodic Record Compared

There are three primary advantages to using the running record over the episodic record. The first is cost, in terms of both time and money. Since the costs of collecting, tabulating, storing, and reporting the data in the running record are generally borne by the record keepers themselves, political scientists are usually able to use these data very inexpensively. In contrast to the time-consuming and expensive research of the episodic record described earlier by the historian interested in early nineteenth-century Kentucky, researchers can often use the data stored in the running record by photocopying a few pages of a reference book, purchasing a government report, or acquiring a computer printout. In fact, the continued expansion of the data collection and record-keeping activities of the national government has been a financial boon to social scientists of all types.

A second, related advantage is the accessibility of the running record. Instead of searching packing crates, deteriorated ledgers, and musty storerooms, as users of the episodic record often do, users of the running record more often handle reference books, government publications, and computer printouts. Many political science research projects have been completed with only the data stored in the reference books and government documents of a decent research library.

A third advantage of the running record is that by definition it covers a more extensive period of time than does the episodic record. This permits the type of longitudinal analysis and before-and-after research designs discussed in Chapter 5. Although the episodic record helps explain the origins of and reasons for a particular event, episode, or period, the running record allows the measurement of political phenomena over time.

The running record presents problems, however. One is that a researcher is at the mercy of the data collection practices and procedures of the record-keeping organizations themselves. Researchers are rarely in a position to influence record-keeping practices; they must rely instead on what organizations such as the U.S. Census Bureau, Federal Election Commission, and the Roper Center for Public Opinion Research decide to do. There is often a tradeoff between ease of access and researcher influence over the measurements that are made. Some organizations—some state and local governments, for example—do not maintain records as consistently as researchers may like. One colleague has found tracing the fate of proposed constitutional amendments to the Delaware State Constitution to be a difficult task.

Delaware is the only state in which voters do not ratify constitutional amendments. Instead, the state legislature must pass an amendment in two consecutive legislative sessions in between which a legislative election has occurred. Thus, constitutional amendments are treated like bills and tracking them depends on the archival practices of the state legislature. Even when clear records are kept, such as election returns for mayoral contests, researchers may still face a substantial task in collecting the data from individual cities because the returns from only the largest cities are reported in various statistical compilations.

Another related disadvantage of the running record is that some organizations are not willing to share their raw data with researchers. The processed data that they do release may reflect calculations, categorizations, and aggregations that are inaccurate or uninformative.

Finally, it is sometimes difficult for researchers to find out exactly what the record-keeping practices of some organizations are. Unless the organization publishes a description of its procedures, a researcher may not know what decisions have guided the record-keeping process. This can be a special problem when these practices change, altering in an unknown way the measurements reported.

Although the running record has its disadvantages, often political scientists must rely on it if they wish to do any empirical research on a particular topic. For years, for example, the only reasonable way of conducting research on crime in the United States was to use the *Uniform Crime Report* (UCR) of the Federal Bureau of Investigation. To illustrate some of the problems with using written records, we conclude this section with a description of the *Uniform Crime Report,* one of the longest and most often used portions of the running record.

The Uniform Crime Report

First issued in 1930, the *Uniform Crime Report* is the only enduring, national compilation of statistics on crime in the United States; consequently it has become the basis for numerous research reports on crime and police behavior. In recent years, however, the accuracy and precision of the measures reported in the UCR have been called into question and the report has been criticized by many of its users.

The FBI's measure of criminal activity is based on the reports it receives from thousands of law enforcement agencies across the country. State and local police departments voluntarily submit these reports; the FBI has never been given the power to enforce participation. Each police agency must bear the cost and responsibility of providing the information, although the FBI does provide instructions and assistance to participating police departments. The FBI's intent, then, is to produce a report representing the *population* of police departments; no sampling is done.

Police departments are asked to report two types of information: the number of criminal acts of seven different kinds that come to their attention ("Part I" crimes) and the number of arrests that they make for many other types of crimes ("Part II" crimes). Part I crimes include criminal homicide, forcible rape, robbery, aggravated assault, burglary, larceny, and auto theft. Part II crimes include other assaults; forgery and counterfeiting; embezzlement and fraud; buying, receiving, or possessing stolen property; carrying or possessing weapons; prostitution and commercialized vice; sex offenses; offenses against the family and children; violations of narcotic drug laws; violations of liquor laws; drunkenness; disorderly conduct; vagrancy; gambling; driving while intoxicated; violation of road and driving laws; parking violations; other violations of traffic and motor vehicle laws; all other offenses; and suspicion.[17] Trends in crime over time are reported, as well as rates of crimes per 100,000 people.

In this section we will discuss the flaws in the UCR that have led to questionable measures of criminal activity in the United States. The most obvious problem is that not all crimes are reported to the police and therefore some are never included in the UCR.[18] There are many reasons why victims do not report a crime: they may be unable to do so (for example, they may have been murdered), they may fear reprisal by the accused, they may think that nothing will be done by the police, they may wish to hide their own participation in criminal activity, they may consider their losses too minor to justify the inconvenience, they may be reluctant to publicize their victimization, and they may be able to secure compensation from other sources (for example, from an insurance company).[19] Many crimes are reported elsewhere: to military officials, prosecutors, and regulatory agencies with judicial power, such as the Securities and Exchange Commission. Violations of federal laws, misrepresentation in advertising, restraints of trade, and manipulation of prices and markets are not the kinds of crimes reported to state and local police forces.

Moreover, the police themselves may neglect, either by accident or intention, to report crimes to headquarters or to the FBI. Resources are often scarce, records poorly kept, and employees incompetent and inefficient. In addition, the police may try to protect the reputation of their co-workers, superiors, precincts, and municipality by failing to report criminal acts. If they know that the UCR statistics are going to be used to compare the safety of their city with that of another, they may be tempted to underreport crime.[20] Who wants to be a policeman in the city dubbed "the murder capital of the world"?

Another problem with the UCR is that Part II crimes are included only if an arrest is made. This is because it is known that many Part II crimes are never reported to the police, thus making UCR reports of these crimes even less reliable than UCR reports of Part I crimes.[21]

Just as some crimes go unreported, some crimes are reported that never took place. After all, the courts, not the victim, decide that someone is guilty of committing a crime. Yet the UCR assumes that any criminal act reported to the police did, in fact, happen, regardless of the eventual disposition of the case. Crimes may be overreported, then, as well as underreported.[22] The FBI asks that crimes be reported in one of twenty-seven categories—seven Part I crimes, twenty Part II crimes. The behavior that constitutes each of these crimes, however, varies widely across the many police departments represented in the UCR. Assault and larceny are often used as substitutes for robbery, for example, and there is tremendous variation in what constitutes drunkenness, disorderly conduct, prostitution, vagrancy, assault and battery, and aggravated assault.[23] An act committed by a minority youth in a center city precinct may be considered criminal, whereas the same act committed by a white youth in a privileged suburban community might simply engender a stern warning and a free ride home.[24] Yet there is no way that the FBI can force state and local police departments to maintain uniformity in either law or practice. As long as individual state and local legislatures are the ones defining crimes and state and local police are the ones enforcing these laws, there will be no uniformity in how criminal acts are reported.[25]

By the late 1960s, most police departments had joined the UCR system, amounting to coverage of areas containing 96 percent of the U.S. population.[26] In earlier years, however, the rate of participation was much lower, and there were no crime statistics for large areas of the country. Thus UCR measures of over-time trends, if not based on identical reporting areas, are suspect.

One criminal incident may involve the breaking of several laws. Yet the FBI has decided that the UCR should reflect only the most serious offense in a multiple-offense episode. For example, if someone breaks into a home, steals $300 worth of jewels, kills an occupant, injures a bystander, and steals a car with which to make an escape, only the murder will be recorded. Obviously this systematically underestimates the number of criminal acts committed or laws broken.[27]

Beginning in 1958, the UCR included an "index" of criminal activity calculated by summing the Part I crimes reported. The rationale for calculating such an index was that Part I crimes are the most serious and the most likely to be reported to the police.[28]

The crime index has been the subject of two major criticisms. First, by excluding Part II crimes, the index does not reflect many crimes that are serious and cause major physical harm (such as arson, kidnapping, and assault and battery) or substantial financial loss and property damage (such as embezzlement, malicious mischief, and disorderly conduct). Second, by summing the number of Part I crimes, the index effectively treats each crime, regardless of its type, equally. A murder counts the same as an auto theft in calculating the crime index. Since the FBI believes that the seven Part I crimes may be rank-ordered in terms of severity, the equally weighted index would seem to be inconsistent with the FBI's own approach to the measurement of crime.[29]

In short, one must be careful about the inferences drawn from the crime index. The index does not represent all crime, or all crimes reported to the police, or even all serious crimes reported to the police. Nor do changes in the crime index necessarily mean that crime has become any more or less serious. Since the index is composed of many very different kinds of crime but not all crimes, exactly what it does measure is unclear.

As we have seen, the validity and reliability of the *Uniform Crime Report* are jeopardized by numerous shortcomings in the FBI's record-keeping system. Nevertheless, without the UCR data it would be more difficult for researchers to conduct rigorous hypothesis-testing research about the prevalence of criminal behavior. In fact, users of the running record are often faced with the choice between using data that they know are flawed in some way and leaving a hypothesis untested because of the absence of a superior data source. Each researcher must ultimately decide whether the flaws in the written record are tolerable or not, since the running record is often a valuable source of information about political phenomena that are impossible to observe in any other way.

Content Analysis

Sometimes researchers extract excerpts, quotations, or examples from the written record to support an observation or relationship. Those who rely on the episodic record, such as Charles Beard and James David Barber, often use the written record in this way. At other times researchers use numerical measures calculated by record keepers and presented in the written record without altering these measures appreciably. Users of the *Uniform Crime Reports,* for example, often simply use the crime rates reported there as their independent and dependent variables, as do users of the Federal Election Commission's campaign spending reports. With both of these written records, very little conversion is done by the researcher.

Yet researchers may wish to extract numerical measures from an extensive written record that exists in nonnumerical form. For example, a researcher might want to study the news coverage of a presidential campaign to measure how favorable the tone of the coverage was for different candidates. This might require reducing hundreds of newspaper articles and news programs to a handful of numerical measures of the tone of news stories.

To derive numerical measures from a nonnumerical written record, researchers use a technique called **content analysis.** This procedure enables us to "take a verbal, nonquantitative document and transform it into quantitative data." A researcher "first constructs a set of mutually exclusive and exhaustive categories that can be used to analyze documents, and then records the frequency with which each of these categories is observed in the documents studied."[30] This is exactly what Segal and Cover had to do with a number of newspaper editorials to produce a quantitative measure of the political ideologies of Supreme Court justices.[31]

Content Analysis Procedures

The first step in content analysis is deciding what sample of materials to include in the analysis. If a researcher is interested in the political values of candidates for public office, a sample of political party platforms and campaign speeches might be suitable. If the level of sexism in a society is of interest, then a sample of television entertainment programs and films might be drawn. Or if a researcher is interested in what liberals are thinking about, liberal opinion magazines might be sampled. Actually, two tasks are involved at this stage: selecting materials germane to the researcher's subject (in other words, choosing the appropriate sampling frame) and sampling the actual material to be analyzed from that sampling frame. Once the appropriate sampling frame has been selected, then any of the possible types of samples described in Chapter 7—random, systematic, stratified, cluster, and non-probability—could be used.

The second task in any content analysis is to define the categories of content that are going to be measured. A study of the prevalence of crime in the news, for example, might measure the amount of news content that either deals with crime or does not. Content that deals with crime might be further subdivided into the kinds of crime covered. A study of news coverage of a presidential campaign might measure whether news content concerning a particular presidential candidate is favorable, neutral, or unfavorable. Or a study might measure the personality traits of various prime-time television characters—such as strength, warmth, integrity, humility, and wisdom—and the sex, age, race, and occupation of those characters. This process is in many respects the most important part of any content analysis because the researcher must measure the content in such a way that it relates to the research topic, and he or she must define this content so that the measures of it are both valid and reliable.

The third task is to choose the recording unit. For example, from a given document, news source, or other material, the researcher may want to code (1) each word, (2) each theme, (3) each character or actor, (4) each sentence,

(5) each paragraph, or (6) each item in its entirety. To measure concern with crime in the daily newspaper, the recording unit might be the article. To measure the favorableness of news coverage of presidential campaigns in news weeklies, the recording unit might be the paragraph. And to measure the amount of attention focused on different governmental institutions on television network news, the recording unit might be the story.

In choosing the recording unit, the researcher usually considers the ease of identifying the unit (words, sentences, and paragraphs are easier to identify than stories and themes) and the correspondence between the unit and the content categories (stories may be more appropriate than words in determining whether crime is a topic of concern, while individual words or sentences rather than larger units may be more appropriate for measuring the traits of political candidates). Generally, if the recording unit is too small, each case will be unlikely to possess any of the content categories. On the other hand, if the recording unit is too large, it will be difficult to measure the single category of a content variable that it possesses (in other words, the case will possess multiple values of a given content variable). The selection of the appropriate recording unit is often a matter of trial and error, adjustment, and compromise in the pursuit of measures that capture the content of the material being coded.

Finally, a researcher has to devise a system of enumeration for the content being coded. The presence or absence of a given content category can be measured or the "frequency with which the category appears," or the "amount of space allotted to the category," or the "strength or intensity with which the category is represented."[32] For example, suppose we were coding the presence of Hispanics in televised entertainment programming, with the program as the recording unit. For each program we could count (1) whether there was at least one Hispanic present, (2) how many Hispanics there were, (3) how much time Hispanics were on the screen, and (4) how favorable or how important the portrayal of Hispanics was for the overall story.

The validity of a content analysis can usually be enhanced with a precise explanation of the procedures followed and content categories used. Usually the best way to demonstrate the reliability of content analysis measures is to show intercoder reliability. **Intercoder reliability** simply means that two or more analysts, using the same procedures and definitions, agree on the content categories applied to the material analyzed. The more the agreement, the stronger the researcher's confidence can be that the meaning of the content is not heavily dependent on the particular person doing the analysis. If different coders disagree frequently, then the content categories have not been defined with enough clarity and precision.

The following example of a content analysis may be helpful. Suppose you were interested in studying 2000 presidential campaign coverage by *Time* and *Newsweek* (the sampling frame). You could decide to analyze every article about the campaign from September 1 to election day, taking the article as the recording unit. The content categories could be (1) the subject of the article (that is, the "who"); (2) the topic of the article (that is, the "what"); and (3) the tone of the article (was it unfavorable or favorable?). To encode the content you could devise a coding sheet like the one presented in Table 9-2. It shows the content variables, the categories for each variable, the recording unit, and the system of enumeration. This is the type of sheet that would be used to quantify the data.

Among the drawbacks of content analysis are the time involved and the need to avoid mistakes when analyzing a large collection of written records. Suppose, for example, you wanted to see how the use of political symbols had changed over the last fifty years. You might take a sample of presidential addresses or campaign speeches and simply count the number of occurrences of certain phrases, such as "it is not the role [job, responsibility, etc.] of government to . . . " You might then calculate and plot the proportion of such ideas over time. Doing so, though, requires that you—or, preferably, a coder or coders—read the material, look for phrases that meet the selection criteria, and make tallies. This is a time-consuming process; if a coder becomes fatigued he or she might overlook instances that should be recorded or count phrases twice or make other mistakes.

TABLE 9-2

Coding Sheet for Hypothetical Content Analysis of Presidential Campaign Coverage

Magazine   1. *Time* _____   2. *Newsweek* _____

Date _____

Page no. _____

No. of paragraphs _____

No. of paragraphs devoted
to each candidate: 1. Gore _____   3. Bush _____

      2. Lieberman _____   4. Cheney _____

Primary focus
of article:

      1. Candidate prospects _____   3. Policy issues _____

      2. Campaign events _____   4. Personalities _____

Overall tone
of article

For Bush/Cheney:	Negative	1	2	3	4	5	6	7	Positive
For Gore/Lieberman:	Negative	1	2	3	4	5	6	7	Positive

Today many social scientists are conducting content analyses with the help of computer programs. This software can read and store text and search for various patterns of words or even look for ideas implied by the text. Many of the programs have become quite sophisticated. Besides doing the actual content analysis they write reports and calculate summary statistics. Because there are now so many of these programs we cannot explain their operation here. But a good source for further information is *Text Analysis Resources,* compiled by Harald Klein and available at http://www.intext.de/ TEXTANAE.HTM.

Although political scientists have used content analysis relatively sparingly, it is a useful technique in some areas of inquiry. Content analysis may be used to analyze the content of a large number of lengthy, semi-structured interviews after they are transcribed. Following is an example of a content analysis performed by two political scientists.

A SIMPLE COMPUTER CONTENT ANALYSIS
You can use your Internet browser to find and analyze speeches or other printed records if you are willing to keep careful records of your work. As an example, suppose you wanted to compare how presidents have defined the role of government over time. To do this you could analyze presidential inaugural addresses. When you locate a particular address you could use the browser's "Find in page" key to look for, say, "we must" or a similar phrase. The sentence or ideas that follow may indicate the presidents' feelings about the role of government since in saying "we" the president is usually referring to government or society. You can then make a count of the types of references to see how they have changed over time.

News Coverage of Presidential Campaigns

A frequent subject of content analysis is press coverage of election campaigns. Given the importance of how candidates are presented and how the electoral process is treated in the news, political scientists have been interested for some time in accurately and systematically describing and explaining campaign news coverage. Most of these studies have investigated whether candidates receive favorable or unfavorable coverage, whether news coverage relays useful information to the American electorate, whether the press accurately presents the complex and lengthy presidential nomination process, and whether journalists are, in general, objective, accurate, fair, and informative.

One good example of a content analysis of this type is a study of presidential campaign coverage in 1980 by Michael Robinson and Margaret Sheehan.[33] We will discuss the procedures they followed and some of the strengths and weaknesses of their analysis.

At the beginning Robinson and Sheehan had to select the news coverage to be included in their study. Given the overwhelming amount of print and broadcast coverage that a presidential election campaign stimulates, there was no way that they could carefully analyze it all. In 1980 there were more than 1,000 daily newspapers and 6,000 broadcast stations in the United States.

Consequently, they had to select, or sample, a portion of the news coverage to analyze. Six different decisions were involved in choosing the sample.

First, the researchers decided what type of medium to analyze. Primarily because of their estimates of the audience reached by different media, they chose national network television and newspaper wire service copy. In the process, they decided not to select several regional daily newspapers and the news weeklies, as had been done in a study of the 1976 campaign, and not to draw a representative sample of daily newspapers, as had been done in a study of the 1974 congressional elections.[34]

Second, because Robinson and Sheehan's resources were limited, they had to decide which of the media outlets to select. In other words, which television network and which wire service would be chosen? Based again on audience size, as well as professional prestige, they selected CBS and the Associated Press (AP). But AP refused to cooperate—an example of one of those disturbing yet all too frequent developments that cause the best laid research plans to go awry. Consequently, the researchers switched reluctantly to United Press International (UPI), even though it had far fewer clients and generally placed fewer stories in daily newspapers. CBS and UPI, then, became their case studies for 1980.

What products of these two media outlets should be included in the study? This was the third decision facing Robinson and Sheehan. CBS produces several versions of the nightly news, as well as morning news shows, midday news shows, news interviews, and news specials. And UPI offers several news services, among them an "A" wire, which is the national wire; a city wire; and a radio wire. The "A" wire itself has two versions: the night cycle, which runs from noon to midnight, and the day cycle, which runs from midnight to noon. The researchers decided to use the day "A" wire, for reasons of scope of coverage as well as accessibility, and the CBS nightly news (the 7:00 p.m. Eastern Time edition), primarily for financial reasons and convenience.

Fourth, they had to decide which of the material from these news shows and wire copy to include. They decided to include only campaign or campaign-related stories. Thus they used any story that "mentioned the presidential campaign, no matter how tangentially; mentioned any presidential candidate in his campaign role; mentioned any presidential candidate or his immediate family in a noncampaign, official role (almost always a story about the president); or discussed to a substantial degree any campaign lower than the presidential level."[35] Just over 5,500 stories on UPI and CBS—22 percent of UPI and CBS total news coverage—met these selection criteria.

Fifth, Robinson and Sheehan had to decide what time period to include in their study. Although a presidential campaign has a fairly clear ending point, election day, the beginning date of the campaign is uncertain. The researchers decided to include weekday coverage throughout 1980 (that is, from January 1 to December 31). They give no justification for excluding the weekend news.

Finally, Robinson and Sheehan made an important decision to exclude some of the content of both CBS's and UPI's news coverage. They decided not to include any photographs, film, videotape, or live pictures and to rely exclusively on verbal (CBS) or written (UPI) expression. They defended this decision on the grounds that it is more difficult to interpret the meaning of visuals and that the visual message usually supports the verbal message. Moreover, they thought that comparing the visual component of CBS with that of UPI would be difficult.

Having selected the news content to be analyzed, Robinson and Sheehan then decided on the unit of analysis to use when coding news content. Generally, they analyzed the story, although at times they analyzed the content sentence by sentence and word by word. Most content analyses of this type have also used the story as the unit of analysis, but it is unfortunate that Robinson and Sheehan did not explain this choice in any detail or discuss how difficult it was to tell where one story ended and another began.

Having selected the news content to be used in the measurement of campaign news coverage, Robinson and Sheehan then had to decide the content categories to be encoded and the definitions of the values for these content categories. They coded some twenty-five different aspects of each 1980 campaign story. Some of these were straightforward, such as the story's date, length, and reporter. Other categories, which pertained to the central subject matter of the study, were not as readily defined or measured.

The researchers were primarily concerned with five characteristics: Were CBS and UPI (1) objective, (2) equitable in providing access, (3) fair, (4) serious, and (5) comprehensive? Consequently, they needed to decide how to measure each of these attributes of news coverage.

Robinson and Sheehan measured the objectivity of the press's coverage in four ways: by the number of explicit and unsupported conclusions drawn by journalists about the personal qualities of the candidates; by the number of times the journalists expressed personal opinions concerning the issues of the campaign; by counting the number of sentences that were either descriptive, analytical, or judgmental; and by counting the number of verbs used by journalists that were either descriptive, analytical, or insinuative. Clearly, each of these content categories involved judgments by the researchers concerning what constituted an explicit and unsupported conclusion, what constituted a personal opinion, and what constituted a descriptive versus an analytical sentence. The researchers provide examples of different types of coded content, and they also give some brief definitions of what each of the categories meant to them: for example, descriptive sentences "present the who, what, where, when of the day's news, without any meaningful qualification or elaboration," analytical sentences "tell us *why* something occurs or predicts as to whether it might," and judgmental sentences "tell us how something ought to be or ought not to be."[36]

To determine whether the press granted appropriate access to each of the presidential candidates, Robinson and Sheehan measured how much coverage (in terms of seconds for CBS and column inches for UPI) each of the candidates received. They do not say whether this coding procedure presented any difficulties, although they do evaluate whether the amount of access granted each candidate was justified.

Determining whether press coverage was fair was much more difficult than measuring access since an evaluation of fairness requires that the tone of campaign coverage be measured. Establishing tone in a reliable and valid way is not easy. Robinson and Sheehan define tone and fairness in these terms:

> *Tone pertains not simply to the explicit message offered by the journalist but the implicit message as well. Tone involves the overall (and admittedly subjective) assessment we made about each story: whether the story was, for the major candidates, "good press," "bad press," or something in between. "Fairness," as we define it, involves the sum total of a candidate's press tone; how far from neutrality the candidate's press score lies.*[37]

They evaluated content in terms of whether it represented good press (a story that had three times as much positive information as negative information about a candidate) or bad press (a story that had three times as much negative as positive information). But they never discuss how they determined what constituted positive and negative information. Furthermore, in their effort to restrict their analysis to the behavior of journalists, Robinson and Sheehan excluded information about political events (such as the failure of the Iranian hostage rescue mission), polls, comments made by partisans, remarks of "criminals and anti-Americans" (such as Fidel Castro and the Ayatollah Khomeini), and statements made by the candidates themselves.[38] In short, their measurement of fairness depended upon the wisdom of a number of decisions regarding the encoding of campaign stories. Some of these decisions are questionable, such as using an arbitrary 3-to-1 ratio to determine good press/bad press and excluding political events, polls, and the words of the candidates themselves from the analysis.

The seriousness of press coverage was measured by coding each story and, at times, each sentence, according to whether it represented policy issues, candidate issues, "horse-race coverage," or something else. Policy issues were ones that "involve major questions as to how the government should (or should not) proceed in some area of social life," candidate issues "concern the personal behavior of the candidate during the course of his or her campaign," and horse-race coverage focuses on "any consideration as to winning or losing." Because of difficulty in encoding entire stories into only one of these categories, the researchers shifted to the more exacting sentence-by-sentence analysis. Some sentences did not fit into one and only one of these categories, but "the majority of sentences were fairly easy to classify as one form of news or another."[39] The seriousness of UPI and CBS campaign coverage in 1980 was then measured by comparing their amount of policy issue coverage with the policy issue coverage in other media in previous presidential election years.

Finally, to evaluate how comprehensive press coverage was in 1980, Robinson and Sheehan coded campaign stories in terms of the level of office covered: presidential, vice-presidential, senatorial, congressional, and gubernatorial. More than 90 percent of both CBS and UPI campaign coverage was of the presidential and vice-presidential races.[40]

Over the Wire and on TV represents one of the most thorough content analyses ever performed by political scientists. Certainly, in terms of the time period covered and the sheer quantity of material analyzed, it is an ambitious study. The value of the study is weakened, however, by the inadequate explanation of the content analysis procedures. The definitions of the categories used are brief and the illustrative material sketchy. Furthermore, Robinson and Sheehan dispense with the issue of measurement quality in only one paragraph, where they report that intercoder reliability figures among four members of the coding team averaged about 95 percent agreement.[41] However, they fail to report any details about how this reliability was measured or about the agreement scores for different content categories. Despite these shortcomings, this study exemplifies how content analysis can reveal useful information about a significant political phenomenon. It also illustrates how practical limitations—such as AP's refusal to participate, as well as financial constraints—all too often limit what researchers can actually accomplish.

Advantages and Disadvantages of the Written Record

Using documents and records, or what we have called the written record, has several advantages for researchers. First, it allows us access to subjects that may be difficult or impossible to research through direct, personal contact, because they pertain either to the past or to phenomena that are geographically distant. For example, the record keeping of the Puritans in the Massachusetts Bay Colony during the seventeenth century allowed Erikson to study their approach to crime control, and late eighteenth-century records permitted Beard to advance and test a novel interpretation of the framing of the U.S. Constitution. Neither of these studies would have been possible had there been no records available from these periods.

A second advantage of data gleaned from archival sources is that the raw data are usually nonreactive. As we mentioned in previous chapters, human subjects often consciously or unconsciously establish expectations or other relationships with investigators, which can influence their behavior in ways that might confound the results of a study. But those writing and preserving the records are frequently unaware of any future research goal or hypothesis or, for that matter, that the fruits of their labors will be used for research purposes at all. The record keepers of the Massachusetts Bay Colony were surely unaware that their records would ever be used to study how a society defines and reacts to deviant behavior. Similarly, state loan officers during the late 1700s had no idea that two hundred years later a historian would use their records to discover why some people were in favor of revising the Articles of Confederation. This nonreactivity has the virtue of encouraging more accurate and less self-serving measures of political phenomena.

Record keeping is not always completely nonreactive, however. Record keepers are less likely to create and preserve records that are embarrassing to them, their friends, or their bosses; that reveal illegal or immoral actions; or that disclose stupidity, greed, or other unappealing attributes. Richard Nixon, for example, undoubtedly wished that he had destroyed or never made the infamous Watergate tapes that revealed the extent of his administration's knowledge of the 1972 break-in at Democratic National Committee headquarters. Today many record-keeping agencies employ paper shredders to ensure that a portion of the written record does *not* endure. Researchers must be aware of the possibility that the written record has been selectively preserved to serve the record keepers' own interests. As noted earlier, police may underreport crimes because they know that the crime statistics they report to the FBI will be used to rate the relative safety of their cities.

A third advantage of using the written record is that sometimes the record has existed long enough to permit analyses of political phenomena over time. The before-and-after research designs discussed in Chapter 5 may then be used. For example, suppose you are interested in the impact of changes in the 55-mile-per-hour speed limit (gradually adopted by the states and then later dropped by many states on large stretches of their highway systems) on the rate of traffic accidents. Assuming that the written record contains data on the incidence of traffic accidents over time in each state, you could compare the accident rate before and after changes in the speed limit in those states that changed their speed limit. These changes in the accident rate could then be compared with the changes occurring in states in which no change in the speed limit took place. The rate changes could then be "corrected" for other factors that might affect the rate of traffic accidents. In this way an interrupted time series research design could be used, a research design that has some important advantages over cross-sectional designs. Because of the importance of time, and of changes in phenomena over time, for the acquisition of causal knowledge, a data source that supports longitudinal analyses is a valuable one. The written record more readily permits longitudinal analyses than do either interview data or direct observation.

A fourth advantage to researchers of using the written record is that it often enables us to increase sample size above what would be possible through either interviews or direct observation. For example, it would be terribly expensive and time consuming to observe the level of spending by all candidates for the House of Representatives in any given year. Interviewing candidates would require either a lot of travel, long-distance phone calls, or the design of a questionnaire to secure the necessary information. Direct observation would require gaining access to many campaigns. How much easier and less expensive to contact the Federal Election Commission in Washington, D.C., and request the printout of campaign spending for all House candidates. Without this written record, resources might permit only the inclusion of a handful of campaigns in a study; with the written record, all 435 campaigns can easily be included.

This raises the fifth main advantage of using the written record: cost. Since the cost of creating, organizing, and preserving the written record is borne by the record keepers, researchers are able to conduct research projects on a much smaller budget than would be the case if they had to bear the cost themselves. In fact, one of the major beneficiaries of the record-keeping activities of the federal government and of news organizations is the research community. It would cost a prohibitive amount for a researcher to measure the amount of crime in all cities larger than 25,000 or to collect the voting returns in all 435 congressional districts. Both pieces of information are available at little or no cost, however, because of the record-keeping activities of the FBI and the Elections Research Center, respectively. Similarly, using the written record often saves a researcher considerable time. It is usually much quicker to consult printed government documents, reference materials, computerized data, and research institute reports than it is to accumulate data ourselves. The written record is a veritable treasure trove for researchers.

Collecting data in this manner, however, is not without some disadvantages. One problem mentioned earlier is selective survival. For a variety of reasons, record keepers may not preserve all pertinent materials but rather selectively save those that are the least embarrassing, controversial, or problematic. It would be surprising, for example, if political candidates, campaign consultants, and public officials saved correspondence and memoranda that cast disfavor on themselves. Obviously, whenever a person is selectively preserving portions of the written record, the accuracy of what remains is suspect. This is less of a problem when the connection between the record keeper's self-interest and the subject being examined by the researcher is minimal.

A second, related disadvantage of the written record is its incompleteness. There are large gaps in many archives due to fires, losses of other types, personnel shortages that hinder record-keeping activities, and the failure of the record maker or record keeper to regard a record as worthy of preservation. We all throw out personal records every day; political entities do the same. It is very difficult to know what kinds of records should be preserved, and it is often impossible for record keepers to bear the costs of maintaining and storing voluminous amounts of material.

Another reason why records may be incomplete is simply because no person or organization has assumed the responsibility for collecting or preserving them. For example, before 1930 national crime statistics were not collected by the FBI, and before the creation of the Federal Election Commission in 1971 records on campaign expenditures by candidates for the U.S. Congress were spotty and inaccurate.

A third disadvantage of the written record is that its content may be biased. Not only may the record be incomplete or selectively preserved, but it also may be inaccurate or falsified, either inadvertently or on purpose. For example, memoranda or copies of letters that were never sent may be filed, events may be conveniently forgotten or misrepresented, the authorship of documents may be disguised, and the dates of written records may be altered; furthermore, the content of governmental reports may tell more about political interests than empirical facts. For example, Soviet and Eastern European governments apparently released exaggerated reports of their economic performance for many years; scholars (and investigators) attempting to reconstruct the actions in the Watergate episode have been hampered by alterations of the record by those worried about the legality of their role in it. Often historical interpretations rest upon who said or did what, and when. To the extent that falsifications of the written record lead to erroneous conclusions, the problem of record-keeping accuracy can bias the results of a research project. The main safeguard against bias is the one used by responsible journalists: confirming important pieces of information through several dissimilar sources.

A fourth disadvantage is that some written records are unavailable to researchers. Documents may be classified by the federal government; they may be sealed (that is, not made public) until a legal action has ceased or the political actors involved have passed away; or they may be stored in such a way that they are difficult to use. Other written records—such as the memoranda of multinational corporations, campaign consultants, and Supreme Court justices—are seldom made public because there is no legal obligation to do so and the authors benefit from keeping them private.

Finally, the written record may lack a standard format because it is kept by different people. For example, the Chicago budget office may have different budget categories for public expenditures than the San Francisco budget office. Or the Chicago budget office may have had different budget categories before 1960 than it had after 1960. Or the French may include items in their published military defense expenditures that differ from those included by the Chileans in their published reports. Consequently, a researcher often must expend considerable effort to ensure that the formats in which records are kept by different record-keeping entities can be made comparable.

Despite these limitations, political scientists have generally found that the advantages of using the written record outweigh the disadvantages. The written record often supplements the data we collect through interviews and direct observation, and in many cases it is the only source of data on historical and cross-cultural political phenomena.

Conclusion

The written record includes personal records, archival collections, organizational statistics, and the products of the news media. Researchers interested in historical research, or in a particular event or time in the life of a polity, generally use the episodic record. Gaining access to the appropriate material is often the most resource-consuming aspect of this method of data collection, and the hypothesis testing that results is usually more qualitative and less rigorous (some would say more flexible) than with the running record.

The running record of organizations has become a rich source of political data as a result of the record-keeping activities of governments at all levels and of interest groups and research institutes concerned with public affairs. The running record is generally more quantitative than the episodic record and may be used to conduct longitudinal research. Measurements using the running record can often be obtained inexpensively, although the researcher frequently relinquishes considerable control over the data collection enterprise in exchange for this economy.

One of the ways in which a voluminous, nonnumerical written record may be turned into numerical measures and then used to test hypotheses is through a procedure called content analysis. Content analysis is most frequently used by political scientists interested in studying media content, but it has been used to advantage in studies of political speeches, statutes, and judicial decisions.

Through the written record researchers may observe political phenomena that are geographically, physically, and temporally distant from them. Without such records, our ability to record and measure historical phenomena, cross-cultural phenomena, and political behavior that does not occur in public would be seriously hampered.

Notes

1. Frank Way and Barbara J. Burt, "Religious Marginality and the Free Exercise Clause," *American Political Science Review* 77 (September 1983): 652–665; Samuel C. Patterson and Gregory A. Caldeira, "Getting Out the Vote: Participation in Gubernatorial Elections," *American Political Science Review* 77 (September 1983): 675–689; William Zimmerman and Glenn Palmer, "Words and Deeds in Soviet Foreign Policy: The Case of Soviet Military Expenditures," *American Political Science Review* 77 (June 1983): 358–367; and Alan P. L. Liu, "The Politics of Corruption in the People's Republic of China," *American Political Science Review* 77 (September 1983): 602–623.

2. Steven C. Poe and C. Neal Tate, "Repression of Human Rights to Personal Integrity in the 1980s: A Global Analysis," *American Political Science Review* 88 (December 1994): 853–872; Manus I. Midlarsky, "Rulers and the Ruled: Patterned Inequality and the Onset of Mass Political Violence," *American Political Science Review* 82 (June 1988): 491–509; Richard C. Fording, "The Conditional Effect of Violence as a Political Tactic: Mass Insurgency, Welfare Generosity, and Electoral Context in the American States," *American Journal of Political Science* 41 (January 1997): 1–29; Jeff Yates and Andrew Whitford, "Presidential Power and the United States Supreme Court," *Political Research Quarterly* 51 (June 1998): 539–550; and Jeffrey A. Segal and Albert D. Cover, "Ideological Values and the Votes of U.S. Supreme Court Justices," *American Political Science Review* 83 (June 1989): 557–565.

3. Charles Beard reports that he was able to use some records in the U.S. Treasury Department in Washington "only after a vacuum cleaner had been brought in to excavate the ruins." See Beard, *An Economic Interpretation of the Constitution of the United States* (London: Macmillan, 1913), 22.

4. Sandra Van Burkleo, "My Own 'Desperate Deeds and Desperate Motives': How the Project Evolved," in W. Phillips Shively, ed., *The Research Process in Political Science.* Copyright 1984, 214–218. Reprinted with permission of the publisher, F. E. Peacock Publishers, Itasca, Ill.

5. Kai T. Erikson, *The Wayward Puritans* (New York: Wiley, 1966).

6. The records of the governor were edited by Nathaniel B. Shurtleff and printed by order of the Massachusetts legislature in 1853–1854; the records of the courts were edited by George Francis Dow and published by the Essex Institute in Salem, Massachusetts.

7. Erikson, *The Wayward Puritans,* 209–210.

8. Beard, *An Economic Interpretation.*

9. Ibid., 324. Beard's interpretation has been challenged by several historians. Among his critics are Robert E. Brown, *Charles Beard and the Constitution* (Princeton: Princeton University Press, 1956); Forrest McDonald, *We the People: The Economic Origins of the Constitution* (Chicago: University of Chicago Press, 1958); and Gordon Wood, *The Creation of the American Republic* (New York: Norton, 1972). Although Beard's interpretation continues to be controversial, the authors of one mainstream political science textbook state, "[A]lthough historical evidence does not fully support Beard's conclusions, most historians acknowledge that economic interests were very much at issue in the framing and ratification of the Constitution" (Lewis Lipsitz and David M. Speak, *American Democracy,* 2d ed. [New York: St. Martin's, 1989], 76).

10. James David Barber, *The Presidential Character,* 3d ed. (Englewood Cliffs, N.J.: Prentice-Hall, 1985), 4, 5.

11. Ibid., 1st ed. (1972), ix.

12. A critique of Barber's analysis may be found in Garry Wills, *The Kennedy Imprisonment* (Boston: Little, Brown, 1982).

13. See Immanuel Ness and James Ciment, *The Encyclopedia of Third Parties in America* (Armonk, N.Y.: M. E. Sharpe, 1999), and Ness, *Encyclopedia of Interest Groups and Lobbyists in the United States* (Armonk, N.Y.: M. E. Sharpe, 2000).

14. Segal and Cover, "Ideological Values."

15. Midlarsky, "Rulers and the Ruled." The data on land ownership in Latin America were taken from James W. Wilkie and Adam Perkal, eds., *Statistical Abstract of Latin America,* 1985, Vol. 24 (Los Angeles: University of California Press, 1986); the data on deaths due to political violence are in Charles L. Taylor and David A. Jodice, *World Handbook of Political and Social Indicators,* Vols. 1 and 2 (New Haven: Yale University Press, 1983).

16. See C. Wright Mills, *The Power Elite* (New York: Oxford University Press, 1956); G. William Domhoff, *Who Rules America?* (Englewood Cliffs, N.J.: Prentice-Hall, 1967); and Andrew Hacker, "The Elected and the Anointed: Two American Elites," *American Political Science Review* 55 (September 1961): 539–549.

17. Marvin E. Wolfgang, "Uniform Crime Reports: A Critical Appraisal," *University of Pennsylvania Law Review* 111 (April 1963): 717–718.

18. Ibid; Sophia M. Robison, "A Critical View of the Uniform Crime Reports," *Michigan Law Review* 64 (April 1966): 1031; Marvin E. Wolfgang, "Urban Crime," in James Q. Wilson, ed., *The Metropolitan Enigma* (Garden City, N.Y.: Doubleday, 1970), 280; and U.S. President's Commission on Law Enforcement and Administration of Justice, *The Challenge of Crime in a Free Society* (New York: Dutton, 1968), 97.

19. Peter P. Lejins, "Uniform Crime Reports," *Michigan Law Review* 64 (April 1966): 1018.

20. Wolfgang, "Uniform Crime Reports," 715; Wolfgang, "Urban Crime," 280–281; President's Commission, *The Challenge,* 107–112; and Robison, "A Critical View," 1033–1037.

21. Wolfgang, "Uniform Crime Reports," 709–710.

22. Lejins, "Uniform Crime Reports," 1019–1020.

23. Wolfgang, "Uniform Crime Reports," 714, 716; and Robison, "A Critical View," 1040–1041.

24. Robison, "A Critical View," 1042.

25. Wolfgang, "Urban Crime," 279.

26. Wolfgang, "Uniform Crime Reports," 710.

27. Ibid., 721–724; and Wolfgang, "Urban Crime," 281.

28. Wolfgang, "Uniform Crime Reports," 709–710.

29. Ibid., 719–720; and Robison, "A Critical View," 1043–1045.

30. Kenneth D. Bailey, *Methods of Social Research,* 2d ed. (New York: Free Press, 1982), 312–313.

31. Segal and Cover, "Ideological Values."

32. Bailey, *Methods of Social Research,* 319.

33. Michael J. Robinson and Margaret A. Sheehan, *Over the Wire and on TV* (New York: Russell Sage, 1983). On their survey decisions, discussed in the following paragraphs, see 17–27.

34. On the 1976 campaign, see Thomas Patterson, *The Mass Media Election: How Americans Choose Their President* (New York: Praeger, 1980). On the 1974 congressional elections, see Arthur Miller, Edie Goldenberg, and Lutz Erbring, "Type-Set Politics: Impact of Newspapers on Public Confidence," *American Political Science Review* 73 (March 1979): 67–84.

35. Robinson and Sheehan, *Over the Wire,* 20.

36. Ibid., 49–50.

37. Ibid., 92.

38. Ibid., 94–95.

39. Ibid., 144, 145, 155.

40. Ibid., 173.

41. Ibid., 22.

Terms introduced

CONTENT ANALYSIS. A procedure by which verbal, nonquantitative records are transformed into quantitative data.

EPISODIC RECORD. The portion of the written record that is not part of a regular, ongoing record-keeping enterprise.

INTERCODER RELIABILITY. Demonstration that multiple analysts, following the same content analysis procedure, agree and obtain the same measurements.

RUNNING RECORD. The portion of the written record that is enduring and covers an extensive period of time.

WRITTEN RECORD. Documents, reports, statistics, manuscripts, and other written, oral, or visual materials available and useful for empirical research.

Exercises

1. Read B. Dan Wood and Richard W. Waterman, "The Dynamics of Political Control of the Bureucracy," *American Political Science Review* 85 (September 1991): 801–828. What were the independent and dependent variables in this study? How did the researchers obtain measurements for these variables? What problems associated with documents analysis did they encounter? What recommendations do they make regarding agency record keeping?

2. Using the *State and Metropolitan Data Book* or the *Statistical Abstract of the United States*, find state data on automobile insurance cost and persons not covered by health insurance. Select two other state measures that you think might be related to the first two measures and write two hypotheses describing the relationships you expect.

3. Using a statistical source of your choice, find the infant mortality rate, life expectancy, literacy rate, and per capita income for Canada, Denmark, India, Israel, Malawi, and the United States.

4. In Jeffrey A. Segal and Albert D. Cover, "Ideological Values and the Votes of U.S. Supreme Court Justices," *American Political Science Review* 83 (June 1989): 557–565, the researchers rely on content analysis of newspaper editorials to measure the ideology of Supreme Court justices. How did the researchers decide which newspapers to use? What were the content categories they developed? What level of measurement resulted? How did they assess the reliability of their content analysis measures? What documents have been used by other researchers to measure the political attitudes of justices?

Suggested Readings

Miller, Delbert C. *Handbook of Research Design and Measurement*. Beverly Hills, Calif.: Sage, 1991.

Stanley, Harold W., and Richard K. Niemi. *Vital Statistics on American Politics: 1999–2000*. Washington, D.C.: CQ Press, 2000.

Webb, Eugene J., et al. *Unobtrusive Measures*. Rev. ed. Beverly Hills, Calif.: Sage, 1999.

CHAPTER 10

Elite Interviewing and Survey Research

In addition to observation and document analysis, discussed in the preceding two chapters, political scientists use a third major method to make empirical observations: they conduct interviews—either in person or via a questionnaire—with respondents whose attitudes and behavior will help test a hypothesis. This method of collecting data may range from interviewing a handful of elite political actors, such as big city mayors, political campaign consultants, or members of Congress, to interviewing 1,000 or more adults across the United States or another country. When interviews are conducted with a small number of people they are often less formal and less structured—more in the nature of a constrained conversation. When interviews are conducted with hundreds or thousands of respondents, however, they are usually much more carefully structured or scripted.

Many of the research studies discussed in earlier chapters relied upon data collected from interviews or questionnaires. Benjamin Page and Robert Shapiro's study of change in public policy (Chapter 1) relied heavily on public opinion surveys, as did Thomas Hartley and Bruce Russett's research on popular influence on military spending (Chapter 1), William Mishler and Reginald Sheehan's study of the impact of public opinion on Supreme Court decisions (Chapter 5), Ada Finifter and Ellen Mickiewicz's study of attitudes toward political change in the former Soviet Union (Chapter 4), Lee Ann Banaszak and Eric Plutzer's study of European attitudes toward feminism (Chapter 4), and Ted Gurr's study of relative deprivation and civil unrest (Chapter 1). B. Dan Wood and Richard Waterman's analysis of the behavior of governmental bureaucracies (Chapter 1) drew upon interviews conducted with the officials of seven federal governmental agencies. And John Dryzek and Jeffrey Berejikian's study of the different meanings or discourses of democracy (Chapter 4) relied upon interviews with thirty-seven subjects.

We will begin this chapter with a brief overview of the practice of elite interviewing and then move on to an examination of the methodology of survey research.

Elite Interviewing

Elite interviewing is the process of interviewing respondents in a nonstandardized, individualized manner. It is a special form of the **personal interview**, which involves face-to-face questioning of the respondent. In his classic book *Elite and Specialized Interviewing,* Lewis Dexter defines an elite as anyone "who in terms of the current purposes of the interviewer is given special, nonstandardized treatment."[1] Elite interviews usually differ substantially from the highly structured, standardized format of survey research.[2] There are a number of reasons for this difference. First, a researcher may lack sufficient understanding of events to be able to design an effective, structured **survey instrument,** or schedule of questions, suitable for elite respondents. The only way for researchers to learn about certain events is to interview participants or eyewitnesses directly. Second, a researcher is usually especially interested in an elite interviewee's own interpretation of events or issues and does not want to lose the valuable information that an elite "insider" may possess by unduly constraining responses. As one researcher put it, "A less structured format is relatively exploratory and stresses subject rather than researcher definitions of a problem."[3]

Finally, elite interviewees may resent being asked to respond to a standardized set of questions. In her study of Nobel laureates, for example, Harriet Zuckerman found that her subjects soon detected standardized questions. Because these were people used to being treated as individuals with minds of their own, they resented "being encased in the straitjacket of standardized questions."[4] Therefore, those who interview elites often vary the order in which topics are broached and the exact form of questions asked from interview to interview.

Eliciting valid information from elites may require variability in approaches.[5] Elite interviewing is not as simple as lining up a few interviews and chatting for a while. Researchers using elite interviews must consider numerous logistical and methodological questions. Advance preparation is extremely important. The researcher should study all available documentation of events and pertinent biographical material before interviewing elites. Advance preparation serves many purposes. First, it saves the interviewee's time by eliminating questions that can be answered elsewhere. The researcher may ask the interviewee, however, to verify the accuracy of the information obtained from other sources. Second, it gives the researcher a basis for deciding what questions to ask and in what order. Third, advance preparation helps the researcher interpret and understand the significance of what is being said, to recognize a remark that sheds new light on a topic, and to catch inconsistencies between the interviewee's version and other versions of events. Fourth, it impresses the interviewee with the researcher's serious interest in the topic. At no time, however, should the researcher dominate the conversation to show off his or her knowledge. Finally, good preparation buoys the confidence of the novice researcher interviewing important people.

The ground rules that will apply to what is said in an interview should be made clear at the start.[6] When the interview is requested, and at the beginning of the interview itself, the researcher should ask whether confidentiality is desired. If he or she promises confidentiality, the researcher should be careful not to reveal a person's identity in written descriptions. A touchy problem in confidentiality may arise if questions are based on previous interviews. It may be possible for an interviewee to guess the identity of the person whose comments must have prompted a particular question.

A researcher may desire and promise confidentiality in the hope that the interviewee will be more candid.[7] Interviewees may request confidentiality if they fear they may reveal something damaging to themselves or to others. Some persons may want to approve anything written based on what they have said. In any event, it often is beneficial to the researcher to give interviewees a chance to review what has been written about them and the opportunity to clarify and expand on what they said. Sometimes a researcher and interviewee may disagree over the content or interpretation of the interview. If the researcher has agreed to let an interviewee have final say on the use of an interview, the agreement should be honored. Otherwise the decision is the researcher's—to be made in light of the need of the researcher and those who follow for future access to elites.

ASK THE RIGHT QUESTIONS
The importance of thoroughly researching a topic before conducting elite interviews cannot be stressed enough. In addition to the guidelines discussed in the text, ask yourself this question: Can the information be provided only (or at least most easily) by the person being interviewed? If you can obtain the answers to your questions from newspapers or books, for example, then it is pointless to take up someone's time going over what is (or should be) already known. If, on the other hand, the subject believes that only she or he can help you, then you are more likely to gain her or his cooperation.

Sometimes gaining access to elites is difficult. They may want further information about the purpose of the research or need to be convinced of the professionalism of the researcher. Important people often have "gatekeepers" who limit access to them. It is advisable to obtain references from people who are known to potential interviewees. Sometimes a person who has already been interviewed will assist a researcher in gaining access to other elites. Having a letter of recommendation or introduction from someone who knows the subject can be extremely helpful in this regard.

Two researchers encountered particular access problems in their study of the 1981 outbreaks of civil disorder in several British cities when they attempted to interview community activists.[8] These activists, whom the researchers termed the "counter-elite" or the "threatened elite," were reluctant to cooperate, even hostile. They feared that the findings might be abused, that the research was for the benefit of the establishment and part of a system of oppression, and that cooperation would jeopardize their standing in their community. Unlike conventional elites, they did not assume that social science research was useful.

Whom to interview first is a difficult decision for a researcher. Interviewing persons of lesser importance in an event or of lower rank in an organization first allows a researcher to become familiar with special terminology used by an elite group and more knowledgeable about a topic before interviewing key elites. It also may bolster a researcher's experience and confidence. Lower level personnel may be more candid and revealing about events because they are able to observe major participants and have less personal involvement. On the other hand, talking to superiors first may indicate to subordinates that being interviewed is permissible. Moreover, interviewing key elites first may provide a researcher with important information early on and make subsequent interviewing more efficient. Other factors, such as age of respondents, availability, and convenience, may also affect interview order.

A tape recorder or handwritten notes may be used to record an interview. There are numerous factors to consider in choosing between the two methods. Tape recording allows the researcher to think about what the interviewee is saying, to check notes, and to formulate follow-up questions. If the recording is clear, it removes the possibility of error about what is said. Disadvantages include the fact that everything is recorded. The material must then be transcribed (an expense) and read before useful data are at hand. Much of what is transcribed will not be useful—a problem of elite interviewing in general. A tape recorder may make some interviewees uncomfortable, and they may not be candid even if promised confidentiality; there can be no denying what is recorded. Sometimes the researcher will be unfamiliar with recording equipment and will appear awkward.

Many researchers rely on handwritten notes taken during an interview. It is very important to write up interviews in more complete form soon after the interview, while it is still fresh in the researcher's mind. Typically this takes much longer than the interview itself, so enough time should be allotted. Only a few interviews should be scheduled in one day; after two or three, the researcher may not be able to distinctly recollect individual conversations. How researchers go about conducting interviews will vary by topic, by researcher, and by respondent. Although elite interviews are usually not rigidly structured, researchers still may choose to exercise control and direction in an interview. Many researchers conduct a semistructured or flexible interview—what is called a **focused interview**—when questioning elites.

They prepare an interview guide, including topics, questions, and the order in which they should be raised. Sometimes alternative forms of questions may be prepared. Generally the more exploratory the purpose of the research, the less topic control exercised by the researcher. Researchers who desire information about specific topics should communicate this need to the person being interviewed and exercise enough control over the interview to keep it on track.

Elite interviewing is difficult work. A researcher must listen, observe nonverbal behavior, think, and take notes all at the same time. Maintaining appropriate interpersonal relations is also required. A good rapport between the researcher and interviewee facilitates the flow of information, although it may be difficult to establish. For example, Zuckerman relates that one Nobel laureate she interviewed sat about four feet from her in a chair with rollers. By the end of the interview he had moved an additional ten feet away.

How aggressive should a researcher be in questioning elites? This issue is often debated. Although aggressive questioning may yield more information and allow the researcher to ferret out misinformation, it also may alienate or irritate the interviewee. Zuckerman used the tactic of rephrasing the interviewee's comments in extreme form to elicit further details. In some cases the Nobel laureates expressed irritation that she had not understood what they had already said.[9]

Establishing the meaningfulness and validity of the **interview data**—those observations collected through elite interviewing—is very important. Interview data may be biased by the questions and actions of the interviewer. Interviewees may give evasive or untruthful answers. As noted earlier, advance preparation may help an interviewer recognize remarks that differ from established fact. The validity of an interviewee's statements also may be determined by examining their plausibility, checking for internal consistency, and corroborating them with other interviewees. John Dean and William Whyte argue that a researcher should understand an interviewee's mental set and how it might affect his or her perception and interpretation of events.[10] Raymond Gordon stresses the value of being able to empathize with interviewees to understand the meaning of what they are saying.[11] Lewis Dexter warns that interviewing should be used only if "interviewers have enough relevant background to be sure that they can make sense out of interview conversations or unless there is reasonable hope of being able to . . . learn what is meaningful and significant to ask."[12]

Elite interviewing is an excellent form of data collection when the behavior of interest can best be described and explained by those who are deeply involved in political processes. It often provides a more comprehensive and complicated understanding of political phenomena than other forms of data collection, and it provides researchers with a rich variety of perspectives.

Elite interviewing is not easy; it requires a great deal of background preparation, interpersonal skill, and perseverance. More than anything else, the success of elite interviewing depends upon a researcher's ability to gain access to those who can advance our understanding of politics and government.

Survey Research

Survey research is research based on the interview method of data collection. Also known as opinion polling, it is one of the most familiar political science research methods. Scarcely a day goes by in which we are not told the results of one poll or another. There are presidential performance and popularity polls. Businesses use polling to determine satisfaction with products and services. News organizations use surveys to enhance their news gathering efforts. Nonprofit organizations conduct polls to find out about their public image and how to increase contributions. Candidates for public office use polls to help map campaign strategies; polls tell them what appeals to make to constituents, what issues to stress, and which matters to avoid. Interest groups conduct public opinion polls to determine public support for their issue positions. Public officials use surveys to evaluate the effectiveness of the programs they administer or to learn more about problems in the population that need to be addressed by new or different programs. The courts may employ survey results as well. For example, surveys of community members may be conducted to determine what proportion of the community has heard about a major criminal case and has developed opinions about the defendant. This information is used by judges to determine the need for a change in venue for the trial.[13] Surveys also are used in measuring deceptive advertising and trademark infringement and in selecting juries.[14] Social scientists also use surveys to explore and test theories about human beliefs and activities.

As the use of surveys as a research method has grown, so too has the amount of research on the method itself. This research is concerned with the validity and reliability of survey results and the costs of survey research. We now know more about many aspects of survey research than was known when the method was first used, much to the benefit of researchers and consumers of survey research.

Because high-quality survey research requires an interview structure that will elicit the desired information quickly and consistently from many different kinds of respondents, much research has been conducted on the design of the survey research instrument, or questionnaire. To construct a good questionnaire, a researcher must write well-worded questions, choose the appropriate type of question (closed- or open-ended), and place questions in the appropriate order. A clearly defined research purpose and well-developed hypotheses will help eliminate unnecessary questions, thereby reducing respondent effort and survey costs. A well-constructed questionnaire is easy for both the interviewer and the respondent to follow, resulting in correctly administered and completed interviews.

We will begin our review of the survey research method by discussing how to construct a survey instrument or questionnaire. We will then discuss surveys by mail, telephone, and personal interview, rating their relative advantages and disadvantages, and review issues of particular importance to the application of each.

Question Wording

The goal of survey research is to measure accurately people's attitudes, beliefs, and behavior by asking them questions. Success greatly depends on the quality of the questions. Good questions prompt accurate answers; poor questions provide inappropriate stimuli and result in unreliable or inaccurate responses. When writing questions, researchers should avoid double-barreled, ambiguous, or leading questions and should use appropriate vocabulary. Failure to do so may result in uncompleted questionnaires by frustrated or offended respondents and meaningless data for the researcher.

A **double-barreled question** is really two questions in one, such as "Do you agree with the statement that the Soviet Union is ahead of the United States in the arms race and that the United States should increase defense spending?" How does a person who believes that the Soviets are superior in military capacity but who does not wish an increase in defense spending answer this question? And how does the researcher interpret an answer to such a question? The researcher does not know whether the respondent meant for his or her answer to apply to both components or whether one component was given precedence over the other.

Despite a conscious effort by researchers to define and clarify concepts, words with multiple meanings or interpretations may creep into questions. An **ambiguous question** is one that contains a concept that is not clearly defined. An example would be the question "What is your income?" Is the question asking for family income or just the personal income of the respondent? Is the question asking for earned income (salary or wages), or should interest and stock dividends be included? Similarly, the question "Do you prefer Brand A or Brand B?" is ambiguous. Is the respondent telling us which brand is purchased or which brand would be purchased if there were no price difference between the brands?

Ambiguity may also result from using the word *he*. Are respondents to assume that *he* is being used generically to refer both to males and females or to males only? If a respondent interprets the question as applying only to males and would respond differently for females, it would be a mistake for the researcher to conclude that the response applies to all people.[15]

After the 1976 debate between presidential contenders Jimmy Carter and Gerald Ford, respondents to one poll were asked to rate the performance of the two debaters as good, bad, or indifferent. This ambiguous question confused respondents, who then asked whether the ratings were to be made (1) by comparing the debate with other, unspecified political debates that they had witnessed; (2) by comparing the debate with the one between John F. Kennedy and Richard Nixon; (3) by comparing Carter and Ford with each other; or (4) by measuring the candidates against the respondent's predebate expectations. Respondents were also unsure whether performance meant style, substance, or something else.[16]

Researchers must also avoid asking leading questions. A **leading question** encourages respondents to choose a particular response because the question indicates that the researcher expects it. The question "Don't you think that global warming is a serious environmental problem?" implies that to think otherwise would be unusual. Choice of words may also lead respondents. Research has shown that people are more willing to help "the needy" than those "on welfare." Asking people if they favor socialized medicine rather than national health insurance is bound to decrease affirmative responses. Moreover, linking personalities or institutions to issues can affect responses. For example, whether or not a person liked the governor would affect responses to the question, "Would you say that Governor Burnett's program for promoting economic development has been very effective, fairly effective, not too effective, or not effective at all?"[17] There are numerous additional ways of leading the respondent, such as by characterizing one response as the preference of others and thereby creating an atmosphere that is anything but neutral.[18]

Polls conducted by political organizations and politicians often include leading questions. For example, a 1980 poll for the Republican National Committee asked: "Recently the Soviet armed forces openly invaded the independent country of Afghanistan. Do you think the U.S. should supply military equipment to the rebel freedom fighters?"[19] Before accepting any interpretation of survey responses, we should check the full text of a question to make sure that it is neither leading nor biased.

As Margrit Eichler demonstrates, gender bias may occur if, for example, respondents are asked to agree or disagree with the statement "It is generally better to have a man at the head of a department composed of both men and women employees." This wording does not make it possible for a respondent to indicate that a woman as head is preferable. It would be better to rephrase the statement "What do you think is generally better: To have a woman or a man at the head of a department that is composed of both men and women employees?" and to give respondents the opportunity to indicate a man is better, a woman is better, or there is no difference.[20]

Use of inappropriate wording is another mistake often made by researchers. Technical words, slang, and unusual vocabulary should be avoided since their meaning may be misinterpreted by respondents. Questions including words with several meanings will result in ambiguous answers. For example, the answer to the question "How much bread do you have?" depends on whether the respondent thinks of bread as coming in loaves or dollar bills. In cross-cultural research the use of appropriate wording is especially important. For researchers to compare answers across cultures, questions should be equivalent in meaning. For example, the question "Are you interested in politics?" may be interpreted as "Do you vote in elections?" or "Do you belong to a political party?" The interpretation would depend on the country or culture of the respondent.

Questions also should be personal and relevant to the respondent. For example, in a questionnaire on abortion, the question "Have you ever had an abortion?" could be changed to "Have you [your wife, girlfriend] ever had an abortion?" This will permit the researcher to include the responses of men as well as women.

Questions should also be worded and selected for the research purpose and survey population at hand. This does not mean, however, that every researcher must formulate questions anew, as Seymour Sudman and Norman Bradburn point out.[21] They advise researchers to review questions asked by others. Copies of questionnaires are included in book-length research reports or may be obtained by writing to the authors of journal articles. The following general sources contain dozens of examples of actual survey questions used by researchers and others:

New York Times Index (for CBS News/*New York Times* polls)

The Gallup Poll: Public Opinion, 1935–1971 (Gallup, 1972) and *The Gallup Poll: Public Opinion, 1972–1977* (Gallup, 1978) with annual updates from 1979 to the present

General Social Surveys, 1972–1990: Cumulative Codebook (National Opinion Research Center, 1990)

Index to International Public Opinion, 1978–1979 (Hastings & Hastings, 1980)

Measures of Political Attitudes (Robinson, Ruse, & Head, 1968)

Public Opinion (opinion roundup section)

Public Opinion Quarterly (polls section)

Survey Data for Trend Analysis: An Index to Repeated Questions in U.S. National Surveys (Roper Public Opinion Research Center, 1974) American National Election Studies (Online).[22]

TEST DRIVE YOUR QUESTIONNAIRE

Students frequently underestimate the time and thought required to write effective survey research questions. A good, indeed essential way to improve and test the adequacy of a questionnaire is to read it aloud first and then administer it to classmates or friends before trying it out on a trial group of subjects. In a "debriefing" period, ask the respondents if the questions' meanings were clear and if they were able to supply the information sought. Equally important, ask yourself, "Are the people providing the information I want or do I need to rewrite the questions?"

Using existing questions has numerous benefits for the researcher. Replication and the ability to compare research results with previous research is an important aspect of accumulating scientific knowledge. Repeated use of questions in similar contexts with similar results indicates reliability of measurement. Repeated use also may allow estimates of trends.[23] Before using a question in a survey, however, a researcher should find out whether permission is needed; usually it is not.

Attention to these basic guidelines for question wording increases the probability that respondents will interpret a question consistently and as intended, yielding reliable and valid responses.

Question Type

The form or type of question as well as its specific wording is important. There are two basic types of questions: closed-ended and open-ended. A **closed-ended question** provides respondents with a list of responses from which to choose. "Do you agree or disagree with the statement that the government ought to do more to help farmers?" and "Do you think that penalties for drunk driving are too severe, too lenient, or just about right?" are examples of closed-ended questions.

A variation of the closed-ended question is a question with multiple choices for the respondent to accept or reject. A question with multiple choices is really a series of closed-ended questions. Consider the following example: "Numerous strategies have been proposed concerning the federal budget deficit. Please indicate whether you find the following alternatives acceptable or unacceptable: raise income taxes, adopt a national sales tax, reduce military spending, reduce spending on domestic programs."

In an **open-ended question**, the respondent is not provided with any answers from which to choose. The respondent or interviewer writes down the answer. An example of an open-ended question is: "Now I'd like to ask you about the good and bad points of the major candidates for President. Is there anything in particular about MR. CLINTON that might make you want to vote FOR him?"[24]

CLOSED-ENDED QUESTIONS: ADVANTAGES AND DISADVANTAGES. The main advantage of a closed-ended question is that it is easy to answer and takes little time. Also, the answers can be precoded (that is, assigned a number) and the code then easily transferred from the questionnaire to a computer. Another advantage is that answers are easy to compare since all responses fall into a fixed number of predetermined categories. These advantages aid in the quick statistical analysis of data. In open-ended questions, on the other hand, the researcher must read each answer, decide which answers are equivalent, decide how many categories or different types of answers to code, and assign codes before the data can be computerized.

Another advantage of closed-ended questions over open-ended ones is that respondents are usually willing to respond on personal or sensitive topics (for example, income, age, frequency of sexual activity, or political views) by choosing a category rather than stating the actual answer. This is especially true if the answer categories include ranges. Finally, closed-ended questions may help clarify the question for the respondent, thus avoiding misinterpretations of the question and unusable answers for the researcher.

Critics of closed-ended questions charge that they force a respondent to choose an answer category that may not accurately represent his or her position. Therefore, the response has less meaning and is less useful to the researcher. Also closed-ended questions often are phrased so that a respondent must choose between two alternatives or state which one is preferred. This may result in an oversimplified and distorted picture of public opinion. A closed-ended question allowing multiple choices does not force a respondent to choose simply between alternatives. The information produced by the question indicates which choices are acceptable to a majority of respondents. This knowledge may be much more useful to policy makers in fashioning a policy that is acceptable to most people.

Just as the wording of a question may influence responses, so too may the wording of response choices. Changes in the wording of question responses can result in different response distributions. Two questions from the 1960s concerning troop withdrawal from Vietnam provide an example of this problem.[25] A June 1969 Gallup Poll question asked:

> *President Nixon has ordered the withdrawal of 25,000 United States troops from Vietnam in the next three months. How do you feel about this—do you think troops should be withdrawn at a faster rate or a slower rate?*

The answer "same as now" was not presented but was accepted if given. The response distribution was as follows: faster, 42 percent; same as now, 29 percent; slower, 16 percent; no opinion, 13 percent. Compare the responses with those to a September–October 1969 Harris Poll. Respondents were asked:

In general, do you feel the pace at which the president is withdrawing troops is too fast, too slow, or about right?

Responses to this question were as follows: too slow, 28 percent; about right, 49 percent; too fast, 6 percent; no opinion, 18 percent.

Thus, depending on the question, support for presidential plans varied from 29 percent to 49 percent. This clearly shows the effect of question wording. The difference in response is a result of whether respondents were directly given the choice of agreeing with presidential policy or had to mention such a response spontaneously.

Response categories may also contain leading or biased language and may not provide respondents with equal opportunities to agree or disagree. Response distributions may also be affected by whether the researchers asks a **single-sided question**, which is a question that asks the respondent to agree or disagree with a single substantive statement, or a **two-sided question**, which is a question that offers the respondent two substantive choices. An example of a one-sided question is:

Do you agree or disagree with the idea that the government should see to it that every person has a job and a good standard of living?

An example of a two-sided question is:

Do you think that the government should see to it that every person has a job and a good standard of living, or should it let each person get ahead on his or her own?

With a single-sided question there is a tendency for a larger percentage of respondents to agree with the statement given. Forty-four percent of the respondents to the single-sided question given above agreed that the government should guarantee employment, while only 30.3 percent of the respondents to the two-sided question chose this position.[26] It has also been found that presenting two substantive choices reduces the proportion of respondents who give no opinion.[27]

Closed-ended questions may provide inappropriate choices, thus leading many respondents not to answer or to choose the "other" category. Unless space is provided to explain "other" (which then makes the question resemble an open-ended one), it is anybody's guess what "other" means. Another problem is that errors may enter into the data if the wrong response code is marked. With no written answer, inadvertent errors cannot be checked. A problem also arises with questions having a great many possible answers. It is time consuming to have an interviewer read a long list of fixed responses that the respondent may forget. A solution to this problem is to use a response card. Responses are typed on a card that is handed to the respondent to read and choose from.

OPEN-ENDED QUESTIONS: ADVANTAGES AND DISADVANTAGES. Unstructured, free-response questions allow respondents to state what they know and think. They are not forced to choose between fixed responses that do not apply. Open-ended questions allow the respondent to tell the researcher how he or she defines a complex issue or concept. As one survey researcher in favor of open-ended questions points out, "Presumably, although this is often forgotten, the main purpose of an interview, the most important goal of the entire survey profession, is to let the respondent have his say, to let him tell the researcher what he means, not vice versa. If we do not let the respondent have his say, why bother to interview him at all?"[28]

Sometimes researchers are unable to specify in advance the likely responses to a question. In this situation, an open-ended question is appropriate. Open-ended questions are also appropriate if the researcher is trying to test the knowledge of respondents. Respondents are better able to *recognize* names of candidates in a closed-ended question (that is, pick the candidates from a list of names) than they are able to *recall* names in response to an open-ended question about candidates. Using only one question or the other would yield an incomplete picture of citizens' awareness of candidates.

Paradoxically, a disadvantage of the open-ended question is that respondents may respond too much or too little. Some may reply at great length about an issue—a time-consuming and costly problem for the researcher. If open-ended questions are included on mailed surveys, some respondents with poor writing skills may not answer. This may bias responses. Thus the use of open-ended questions depends upon the type of survey. Another problem is that interviewers may err in recording a respondent's answer. Recording answers verbatim is tedious. Furthermore, unstructured answers may be difficult to code, interpretations of answers may vary (affecting the reliability of data), and processing answers may become time consuming and costly. For these reasons, open-ended questions are often avoided—although unnecessarily, in Patricia Labaw's opinion:

> I believe that coding costs have now been transferred into data-processing costs. To substitute for open questions, researchers lengthen their questionnaires with endless lists of multiple choice and agree/disagree statements, which are then handled by sophisticated data-processing analytical techniques to try to massage some pattern or meaning out of the huge mass of precoded and punched data. I have found that a well-written open-ended question can eliminate the need for several closed questions, and that subsequent data analysis becomes clear and easy compared to the obfuscation provided by data massaging.[29]

Question Order

The order in which questions are presented to respondents may also influence the reliability and validity of answers. Researchers call this the **question order effect**. In ordering questions, the researcher should consider the impact on the respondent of the previous question, the likelihood of the respondent's completing the questionnaire, and the need to select out groups of respondents for certain questions. In many ways, answering a survey is a learning situation, and previous questions can be expected to influence subsequent answers. This presents problems as well as opportunities for the researcher.

The first several questions in a survey are usually designed to break the ice. They are general questions that are easy to answer. Complex, specific questions may cause respondents to terminate an interview or not complete a questionnaire because they think it will be too hard. Questions on personal or sensitive topics usually are left to the end. Otherwise some respondents may suspect that the purpose of the survey is to check up on them rather than to find out public attitudes and activities in general. In some cases, however, it may be important to collect demographic information first. In a study of attitudes toward abortion, one researcher used demographic information to infer the responses of those who terminated the interview. She found that older, low-income women were most likely to terminate the interview on the abortion section. Since their group matched those who completed the interviews and who were strongly opposed to abortion, she concluded that termination expressed opposition to abortion.[30]

One problem to avoid is known as a **response set**, or straight-line responding. A response set may occur when there is a series of questions with the same answer choices. A person finding himself "agreeing" with the first several statements may skim over subsequent statements and also check "agree." This is likely to happen if statements are on related topics. To avoid the response set phenomenon, statements should be worded so that the respondent may agree with the first, disagree with the second, and so on. This way the respondent is forced to read each statement carefully before responding.

Additional question-order effects include saliency, redundancy, consistency, and fatigue.[31] Saliency is the effect that specific mention of an issue in a survey may have in causing a respondent to mention the issue in connection with a later question: the earlier question brings the issue forward in the respondent's mind. For example, a researcher should not be surprised if respondents mention crime as a problem in response to a general question on problems affecting their community if the survey had earlier asked them about crime in the community. Redundancy is the reverse of saliency. Some respondents, unwilling to repeat themselves, may not say crime is a problem in response to the general query if earlier they had indicated that crime was a problem. Respondents may also strive to appear consistent. An answer to a question may be constrained by an answer given earlier. Finally, fatigue may cause respondents to give perfunctory answers to questions late in the survey. In lengthy questionnaires, response set problems often arise due to fatigue.[32]

Lee Sigelman has used survey research techniques to explore the effects of question order on the results of different presidential popularity polls.[33] He found that placing the presidential popularity item early in the survey elicited more "no opinion" answers than occurred when it was asked toward the end of the interview. This is explained by the tendency of respondents to respond in a safe or socially desirable way early in an interview before their critical faculties have been fully engaged and before they begin to trust the interviewer. Since presidential popularity is usually measured in terms of all respondents, including those with no opinions, the percentage of people approving or disapproving of a president will be deflated by early placement of the question.

Another study tested the assumption that specific questions create a saliency effect that influences answers to more general questions.[34] People were found to express significantly more interest in politics and religion when these questions followed specific questions on political and religious matters. However, respondents' evaluations of the seriousness of energy and economic problems were not affected by previous questions about these problems. Perhaps interest is more easily influenced by question order than is evaluation because evaluation questions require more discriminating, concrete responses than do interest questions. The study also suggests that if specific questions about behavior are asked first, they give respondents concrete, behavioral references for answering later on a related, more general question.[35] For example, the answer to "How actively do you engage in sports?" may depend on whether the respondent had first been asked about participation in a number of specific sporting activities.

The learning that takes place during an interview may be an important aspect of the research being conducted. The researcher may intentionally use this process to find out more about the respondent's attitudes and potential behavior. Labaw refers to this as "leading" the respondent and notes it is used "to duplicate the effects of information, communication and education on the respondent in real life."[36] The extent of a respondent's approval or opposition to an issue may be clarified as the interviewer introduces new information about the issue.

In some cases such education *must* be done to elicit needed information on public opinion. For example, one study set out to evaluate public opinion on ethical issues in biomedical research.[37] Because the public is generally uninformed about these issues, some way had to be devised to enable respondents to make meaningful judgments. The researchers developed a procedure of presenting "research vignettes." Each vignette described or illustrated a dilemma actually encountered in biomedical research. A series of questions asking respondents to make ethical judgments followed each vignette. Such a procedure was felt to provide an appropriate decision-making framework for meaningful, spontaneous answers and a standard stimulus for respondents. A majority of persons were able to express meaningful and consistent opinions, even those with less than a high school education.

If there is no specific reason for placing questions in a particular order, researchers may vary questions randomly to control question order bias. Computerized word processing of questionnaires makes this an easier task.[38]

Question order also becomes an important consideration when the researcher uses a **branching question**, which sorts respondents into subgroups and directs these subgroups to different parts of the questionnaire, or a **filter question**, which screens respondents from inappropriate questions. For example, a marketing survey on new car purchases may use a branching question to sort people into several groups: one that has bought a car in the past year, one that is contemplating buying a car in the next year, and one that is not anticipating buying a car in the foreseeable future. For each group a different set of questions about automobile purchasing may be appropriate. A filter question is typically used to prevent the uninformed from answering questions. For example, respondents in the 1980 National Election Study were given a list of presidential candidates and asked to mark those names they had never heard of or didn't know much about. Respondents were then asked questions only about those names that they hadn't marked.

Branching and filter questions increase chances for interviewer and respondent error.[39] Questions to be answered by all respondents may be missed. However, careful attention to questionnaire layout, clear instructions to interviewer and respondent, and well-ordered questions will minimize the possibility of confusion and lost or inappropriate information.

Questionnaire Design

The term **questionnaire design** refers to the physical layout and packaging of the questionnaire. An important goal of questionnaire design is to make the questionnaire attractive and easy for the interviewer and respondent to follow. Good design increases the likelihood that the questionnaire will be completed properly. Design may also make the transfer of data from the questionnaire to the computer easier.

Design considerations are most important for mailed questionnaires. First, the researcher must make a favorable impression based almost entirely on the questionnaire materials mailed to the respondent. Second, because there is no interviewer present to explain the questionnaire to the respondent, a mailed questionnaire must be self-explanatory. Poor design increases respondent error and nonresponse. Whereas telephone and personal interviewers can and should familiarize themselves with questionnaires before administering them to a respondent, the recipient of a mailed questionnaire cannot be expected to spend much time trying to figure out a poorly designed form.

Mailed Questionnaires and Telephone and Personal Interviews

Now that we have considered basic aspects of survey instrument construction, let us turn our attention to the three major ways of administering surveys. A **mailed questionnaire** is a survey instrument that is mailed to the respondent to be filled out at his or her convenience without the presence of the researcher or interviewer. Because online questionnaires are not yet commonly used for research, we are referring to regular mail rather than electronic mail in the subsequent discussion. While some points clearly will have implications for electronic mail applications, a discussion of electronic mail surveys as a distinctive type will have to wait until further research has been done. A **telephone interview** involves the questioning of the respondent via telephone, while a **personal interview** employs face-to-face questioning of the respondent. In both the telephone and personal interviews, an interviewer is present to ask the respondent questions and record answers. Until recently, survey research connoted personal interviews: telephone and mailed surveys were considered inferior. Now, however, some consider telephone and mailed surveys superior to the personal interview in certain situations.

In the following sections we will compare the three types of surveys with respect to response rate, representativeness of respondents, response quality, and cost and administrative requirements. These four factors account for much of the debate and research on the relative merits of the survey types. As Floyd Fowler points out, researchers may be able to combine mail, telephone, and personal interviews in a research project to take advantage of the particular strengths of each type.[40] Often researchers must make compromises in choosing a survey instrument. As Don Dillman notes, "The use of any of the three [types] requires accepting less of certain qualities to achieve others, the desirability of which cannot be isolated from a consideration of the survey topic and the population to be studied."[41]

RESPONSE RATE. Response rate refers to the proportion of persons selected for participation in a survey who actually participate. If this proportion is low, either because persons cannot be reached or because they refuse to participate, the ability to make statistical inferences for the population being studied may be limited. Also, those who do participate may differ systematically from those who do not, thereby biasing survey results. Increasing the size of the survey sample to compensate for low response rates may increase costs.

At one time, response rates were clearly superior for personal interview surveys of the general population than for other types of surveys. Response rates of 80 percent to 85 percent were often required for federally funded surveys.[42] Higher response rates were not uncommon. By the 1970s, however, response rates for personal interview surveys declined. In 1979, it was reported that in "the central cities of large metropolitan areas the final proportion of respondents that are located *and* consent to an interview is declining to a rate sometimes close to 50 percent."[43]

In general, the decrease in response rates for personal interview surveys has been attributed to both an increased difficulty in contacting respondents and an increased reluctance among the population to participate in surveys. There are more households now in which all adults work outside the home, which makes it difficult for interviewers to get responses. In large cities, nonresponse is due to a number of additional factors: respondents are less likely to be home and are more likely to speak foreign languages; interviewers are less likely to enter neighborhoods after dark; and security arrangements in multiple-unit apartment buildings make it difficult for interviewers to reach potential respondents. Because of poor working conditions, it is hard to find skilled and experienced interviewers to work in large cities. In smaller cities and towns, people also have shown an increased tendency to refuse to participate in surveys.[44]

Higher refusal rates may be due to greater distrust of strangers and fear of crime as well as to the increased number of polls. For example, in one study of respondents' attitudes toward surveys, about one-third did not believe that survey participation benefited the respondent or influenced government.[45] An equal number thought that too many surveys were conducted and that too many personal questions were asked. Some survey researchers feared that the National Privacy Act, which requires researchers to inform respondents that their participation is voluntary, would lead to more refusals. However, one study found that privacy concerns and past survey experience were more frequent reasons for refusals than reminders of the voluntary nature of participation.[46]

Some of these findings about why people do not participate in personal interview surveys raise the possibility that survey research of all types may become increasingly difficult. The effect of increased nonresponse has been to reduce the advantage of the personal interview over mailed and telephone surveys. In fact, response rates rivaling those for personal interviews have been achieved by Don Dillman using his "total design method" for mail and telephone surveys.[47] He concludes that the chance someone will agree to be surveyed is best for the personal interview, but that telephone interviews are now a close second, followed by mailed surveys. Other research comparing response rates of telephone and personal interview surveys have also found little difference.[48]

It is often thought that personal interviews can obtain higher response rates because the interviewer can ask neighbors the best time to contact a respondent who is not at home, thus making return visits more efficient and effective. But repeated efforts by interviewers to contact respondents in person are expensive. Much less expensive are repeated telephone calls, even long distance ones, if special telephone services like WATS lines are used.

Two norms of telephone usage have contributed to success in contacting respondents by phone and completing telephone interviews.[49] First, most people feel compelled to answer the phone if they are home when it rings. A telephone call represents the potential for a positive social exchange. With the increase in telephone solicitation and surveys, this norm may be revised, however. Caller I.D. and answering machines can be used to screen and redirect unwanted calls. Telephone surveys may increasingly become prearranged and conducted after contact has been established by some other method.

A second norm of telephone usage is that the initiator should terminate the call. This norm gives the interviewer the opportunity to introduce himself or herself. And in a telephone interview the introductory statement is crucial. Because the respondent lacks any visual cues about the caller, there is uncertainty and distrust. Unless the caller can quickly alleviate the respondent's discomfort, **termination**, in which the respondent refuses to finish the interview, occurs and the norm of caller termination is overridden. For this reason telephone interviews are more likely to be terminated before completion than are personal interviews. It is harder to ask an interviewer to leave than it is simply to hang up the phone.

One advantage of mailed surveys is that designated respondents who have changed their address may still be reached since the postal service forwards mail for about a year; it is not as easy in phone surveys to track down persons who have moved. In personal and telephone interviews it is also harder to change the minds of those who initially refuse to be interviewed since personal contact is involved and respondents may view repeated requests as harassment. Mailed recontacts are less intrusive.[50]

Because of the importance attached to high response rates, much research on how to achieve them has been conducted. For example, an introductory letter sent prior to a telephone interview has been found to reduce refusal rates.[51] In fact, as a result there may be no significant difference in response rates between telephone and personal surveys.[52] Researchers have also investigated the best times to find people at home. One study found that for telephone interviews, evening hours are best (6:00 to 6:59 especially), with little variation by day (weekends excluded).[53] Another study concluded that the best times for finding someone at home were late afternoon and early evening during weekdays; Saturday until four in the afternoon was the best day overall.[54]

Since mailed surveys usually have the poorest response rates, many researchers have investigated ways to increase responses to them.[55] Incentives (money, pens, and other token gifts) have been found to be effective, and pre-paid incentives are better than promised incentives. Follow-up, prior contact, type of postage, sponsorship, and title of the person who signs the accompanying letter are also important factors in improving response rates. A telephone call prior to mailing a survey may increase response rates by alerting a respondent to its arrival. Telephone calls also are a quick method of reminding respondents to complete and return questionnaires. Good follow-up procedures allow a researcher to distinguish between respondents who have replied and those who have not without violating the anonymity of respondents' answers.[56] Generally, mailed surveys work best when the population is highly literate and interested in the research problem.[57]

In sum, response rates are an important consideration in survey research. When evaluating research findings based on survey research, you should check the response rate and what measures, if any, were taken to increase it. Should you ever conduct a survey of your own, there is a wealth of information that will help you to achieve adequate response rates.

REPRESENTATIVENESS OF RESPONDENTS. Bias can enter survey results either through the initial selection of respondents or through incomplete participation of those selected. In each of the survey methods, these problems arise to varying degrees. If all members of a population can be listed, there is an equal opportunity for all members to be included in the sample. This is rarely the case, however. Personal interviews based on area probability sampling that gives each household an equal chance of being selected are likely to be more representative than mailed or telephone surveys based on published lists, which are often incomplete. Random digit dialing (the use of randomly generated telephone numbers instead of telephone directories, see Chapter 7) and correcting for households with more than one number have improved the representativeness of telephone samples. Thus people who have unlisted numbers or new numbers may be included in the sample. Otherwise a telephone survey may be biased by the exclusion of these households. Estimates of the number of households in the United States that do not have phones vary from 10 percent to 2 percent, while only about 5 percent of the dwelling units are missed with personal interview sampling procedures.[58]

Sometimes researchers make substitutions if respondents cannot or will not participate. Substituting another member of a household may bias results if the survey specifically asks about the respondent rather than the respondent's household. Substituting another household from the same block for personal surveys is better than substituting another telephone number since city blocks tend to be homogeneous whereas there is no way to estimate the similarity of households reached by telephone. Substitution of respondents in mailed surveys may pose a special problem. The researcher cannot control whether the intended respondent or another member of the household completed the questionnaire. The extent of bias thus introduced by substitution of respondents depends on the nature of the survey.

As mentioned earlier, one of the major reasons for concern over response rates is the possibility that those who do not respond will differ from those who do.[59] There is ample evidence that those who refuse to participate generally differ from those who respond. African Americans, for example, have been found more likely to refuse telephone interviews.[60] Refusals are also more common among older, middle-class persons, urban residents, and westerners.[61] For personal and telephone interviews, techniques to randomly select a member of the household to participate in the survey are often used. They may not result in perfect random selection of respondents, however. One method, the Troldahl-Carter method, bases selection on the number of adult males living at the address. Some females living alone feel threatened by this question, though, and refuse to participate. The next-birthday method, which selects the adult having the next birthday, results in fewer refusals and therefore less bias in selecting households.[62]

The amount of bias introduced by nonresponse due to refusal or unavailability varies depending on the purpose of the study and the explanatory factors stressed by the research. For example, if urbanization was a key explanatory variable and refusals were concentrated in urban areas, the study could misrepresent respondents from urban areas because the urban respondents who agreed to participate could differ systematically from those who refused. The personal interview provides the best direct opportunity to judge the characteristics of refusers and estimate whether their refusal will bias the survey.[63]

RESPONSE QUALITY. Response quality refers to the extent to which responses provide accurate and complete information. The opportunities to obtain quality responses differ according to the type of survey used. Mailed surveys may have an advantage in obtaining truthful answers to threatening or embarrassing questions. Anonymity can be assured and answers given in private. A mailed survey also gives the respondent enough time to finish when it is convenient; this enables the respondent to check records to provide accurate information, something that is harder to arrange in telephone and personal interviews.

Disadvantages to the mailed survey include problems with open-ended questions. Some respondents may lack writing skills or find answering at length a burden. There is no interviewer present to probe for more information or to clarify complex or confusing questions. Further drawbacks to mailed surveys include limits to their length, the researcher's inability to control the sequence in which the respondent answers questions and to motivate the respondent to answer tedious or boring questions, and the lack of control over who else may contribute to or influence answers.

Personal and telephone interviews share many advantages and disadvantages with respect to obtaining quality responses, although there are also some important differences. Several of the advantages of personal and telephone interviews over mailed surveys stem from the presence of an interviewer. As noted earlier, an interviewer may lead to better quality data by explaining questions, by probing for more information to open-ended questions, and by making observations about the respondent and his or her environment (for example, for a personal interview, quality of furnishings and housing as an indicator of income; for a telephone interview, amount of background noise that might affect the respondent's concentration). In a personal interview, the interviewer may note that another household member is influencing a respondent's answers and take steps to avoid it. Influence by others is generally not a problem with telephone interviews since only the respondent hears the questions. One response quality problem that does occur with telephone interviews is that the respondent may not be giving the interviewer his or her undivided attention. This may be difficult for the interviewer to detect and correct.

Interviewers are expected to motivate the respondents. Generally it has been thought that warm, friendly interviewers who develop a good rapport with respondents motivate them to give quality answers and to complete the survey. Yet some research has begun to question the importance of rapport.[64] Friendly, neutral, "rapport style" interviews in which interviewers give only positive feedback no matter what the response may not be good enough, especially if the questions involve difficult reporting tasks. Feedback that is both positive ("yes, that's the kind of information we want") and negative ("that's only two things") may improve response quality. Interviewers also may need to instruct respondents about how to give complete and accurate information. This more businesslike, task-oriented style has been found to lead to better reporting than the rapport-style interview.[65]

Interviewer style appears to make less difference in telephone interviews, perhaps because of the lack of visual cues for the respondent to judge the interviewer's sincerity.[66] Even something as simple as intonation, however, may affect data quality: interviewers whose voices go up rather than down at the end of a question appear to motivate a respondent's interest in reporting.[67]

Despite the advantages of using interviewers to improve response quality, the interviewer-respondent interaction may also bias a respondent's answers.

The interviewer may give a respondent the impression that certain answers are expected or are correct. For example, interviewers who anticipate difficulties in persuading respondents to respond or to report sensitive behavior have been found to obtain lower response and reporting rates.[68] The age, sex, or race of the interviewer may affect the respondent's willingness to give honest answers. For example, on racial questions, respondents interviewed by a member of another race have been found to be more deferential to the interviewer (that is, try harder not to cause offense) than those interviewed by a member of their own race.[69] Education also has an impact on race-of-interviewer effects: less educated blacks are more deferential than better educated blacks and better educated whites more deferential than less educated whites.[70]

Interviewer bias, which occurs when the interviewer influences the respondent's answers, may have a larger impact on telephone surveys than on in-person surveys.[71] The efficiency of telephone interviewing requires fewer interviewers to complete the same number of interviews as compared to personal interviews. Also, telephone interviewers, even for national surveys, do not need to be geographically dispersed, so that the same interviewers can be used for a greater number of interviews. Centralization of telephone interviewing operations, however, allows closer supervision and monitoring of interviewers, making it easier to identify and control interviewer problems. For both personal and telephone interviewers, interview training and practice is an essential part of the research process.

A number of studies have compared response quality for personal and telephone interviews. One expected difference is in answers to open-ended questions. Telephone interviewers lack visual cues for probing. Thus telephone interviews tend to be quickly paced; pausing to see if the respondent adds more to an answer is more awkward on the telephone than in person. Research findings, however, have been mixed. One study found that shorter answers were given to open-ended questions in telephone interviews, especially among respondents who typically give complete and detailed responses; another study found no differences between personal and telephone interviews in the number of responses to open-ended questions.[72] Asking an open-ended question early in a telephone survey helps to relax the respondent, reduce the pace of the interview, and ensure that the respondent is thinking about his or her answers.[73]

Response quality for telephone interviews may be lowered because of the difficulty of asking complex questions or questions with many response categories over the phone. Research has found more acquiescence, evasiveness, and extremeness in telephone survey responses than in personal survey responses. In addition, phone respondents give more contradictory answers to checklist items and are less likely to admit to problems.[74] This finding contradicts the expectation that telephone interviews result in more accurate answers to sensitive questions due to reduced personal contact.

As we mentioned earlier, one advantage attributed to mailed questionnaires is greater privacy for the respondent in answering sensitive questions. Consequently, researchers using personal and telephone interviews have developed a number of techniques to obtain more accurate data on sensitive topics.[75] Many of these techniques depend on proper wording. For example, when asking questions about socially desirable behavior, a casual approach reduces the threat by lessening the perceived importance of the topic. The question "Did you happen to read any books this past month?" will likely result in more accurate answers than "What books did you read last month?" Giving respondents reasons for not doing something perceived as socially desirable also reduces threat and may cut down on overreporting.

A very different approach to the problem of obtaining accurate answers to sensitive questions is the **randomized response technique** (RRT).[76] This technique may reduce the disadvantage of personal and telephone interviews for asking sensitive questions. RRT is designed to allow respondents to answer sensitive questions truthfully without the interviewer knowing the question being answered. For example, the interviewer gives the respondent a card with two questions, one sensitive and one nonsensitive. A device such as a coin or a box with two colors of beads is used to randomly determine which question the respondent will answer. If a coin is used, the respondent will be instructed to answer one question if the tossed coin is a heads and the other if tails shows up. The respondent flips the coin and, without showing the interviewer the outcome of the toss, answers the appropriate question.

To calculate the proportion of yes answers to the sensitive question, the expected proportion of yes answers to the nonsensitive question must be known. Thus the nonsensitive question could be "Were you born in July?" Assuming that birthdays are distributed equally among the months, one-twelfth of the respondents would be expected to say yes to the nonsensitive question. Or the proportion of persons exhibiting the nonsensitive behavior could be estimated by asking a sample population a direct question about the nonsensitive behavior.[77] The proportion of respondents answering yes to the sensitive question can be calculated using the formula

$$R_{yes} = P(S_{yes}) + (1 - P)(N_{yes})$$

Where

R_{yes} = probability of obtaining yes answer to random question
P = probability of respondent choosing sensitive question
$1 - P$ = probability of respondent choosing nonsensitive question
S_{yes} = proportion of respondents exhibiting sensitive behavior
N_{yes} = proportion of respondents exhibiting nonsensitive behavior

Therefore

$$S_{yes} = \frac{R_{yes} - (1 - P)(N_{yes})}{P}$$

Let's assume that out of 1,000 respondents, we get 500 "yes" responses and that we have estimates showing that 80 percent of our sample should answer "yes" to the nonsensitive question. If a balanced coin is used, P equals .5. Making the substitutions, we get

$$S_{yes} = \frac{500/1000 - (1 - .5)(.80)}{.5} = \frac{.5 - .5(.80)}{.5} = .20 \text{ or } 20\%$$

The accuracy of RRT depends on the assumption that a respondent will answer both the sensitive and nonsensitive questions truthfully. The success in obtaining accurate information depends on the respondent's ability to understand the method and follow instructions and his or her belief that the random-choice device is not rigged.[78] The technique seems to work better when the nonsensitive question deals with a socially positive activity, thus further reducing the stigma attached to a "yes" response.[79]

Research has found RRT superior to other methods of asking threatening questions, such as having the respondent answer a direct question and return it in a sealed envelope.[80] For example, use of RRT produced higher estimates of abortion than previous measures.[81] RRT can be used for telephone as well as personal interviews. Random-choice devices can be supplied by the respondent—thus eliminating suspicion that the device is fixed—or they can be mailed by the researcher to the respondent.[82]

COST AND ADMINISTRATIVE REQUIREMENTS. When deciding between personal interviews, telephone interviews, and mailed surveys, cost and administrative considerations are important. Among the factors determining survey costs are the amount of professional time required for questionnaire design, the length of the questionnaire, the geographic dispersion of the sample, callback procedures, respondent selection rules, and availability of trained staff.[83]

Personal interview surveys are the most expensive due to the cost of hiring experienced, well-qualified interviewers who are willing to tolerate working conditions that are becoming less attractive. National in-person surveys also incur greater administrative costs. Regional supervisory personnel must be hired and survey instruments sent back and forth between the researcher and interviewers. While mailed surveys are thought to be less expensive than telephone surveys, Fowler argues that the cost of properly executed mail surveys is likely to be very similar to that of telephone surveys.[84]

Compared with personal interview surveys, telephone surveys have numerous administrative advantages.[85] Despite the cost of long-distance calls, centralization of survey administration is advantageous. Training of telephone interviewers is easier, and flexible working hours are attractive. But the real advantages to telephone survey administration begin after interviewing starts. Greater supervision of interviewers and quick feedback to them is possible. Also interviewers can easily inform researchers of any problems they encounter with the survey. Coders can begin coding data immediately. If they discover any errors, they can inform interviewers before a large problem emerges. With proper facilities, interviewers may be able to code respondents' answers directly on computer terminals. In some cases, the whole interview schedule may be computerized, with questions and responses displayed on a screen in front of the interviewer. These are known as computer assisted telephone interviews. The development of computer and telephone technologies gives telephone surveys a significant time advantage over personal interviews and mailed surveys. Telephone interviews may be completed and data analyzed almost immediately.[86]

As researchers and research organizations gain experience with telephone surveys, further developments are likely to occur that will reduce the cost of this method. For example, advances continue to be made in improving the efficiency of random digit dialing.[87] The efficiency of telephone surveys was also improved by a study that found that almost 97 percent of households are reached with four rings and more than 99 percent with five rings; extra rings waste time and money.[88]

Telephone surveys are particularly good for situations in which statistically rare subgroups must be reached or estimated. For example, a telephone survey was used to estimate the disabled population in an area (the only problem being that the hearing impaired were underestimated).[89] A large sample was required to obtain enough disabled persons for the survey. Where large samples are required, telephone surveys are one-half to one-third the cost of personal interviews.[90] Telephone interviews cut down on the cost of screening the population. In some cases telephone surveys may be used to locate appropriate households, and then the survey itself may be completed by personal interview. Telephone surveys are also best if the research must be conducted in a short period of time. Personal surveys are not as fast, and mail surveys are quite slow.

The type of survey chosen by a researcher will depend on the population to be reached, response quality issues, representativeness of completed interviews, and cost and time factors. No one type of survey is superior in all situations. Sometimes a single factor may dictate the type of survey to be used. In other situations the choice will be less clear cut. In many situations researchers will communicate with respondents by mail, by telephone, and in person to ensure that data collection results in a high response rate and quality responses from a representative group of respondents.

Conclusion

This chapter has discussed two ways of collecting information directly from individuals—through elite interviewing and survey research. Whether data are collected over the phone, through the mail, or in person, the researcher attempts to elicit information that is consistent, complete, accurate, and informative. This goal is advanced by being attentive to how question wording, question type, question order, and questionnaire design affect the responses of those interviewed. The choice of an in-person, telephone, or mailed survey can also affect the quality of the data collected. Interviews of elite populations require attention to a special set of issues and generally result in a less structured type of interview.

Although you may never be in a position to conduct elite interviewing or a public opinion survey of your own, the information in this chapter should help you evaluate the research of others. Polls, surveys, and interview data have become so prevalent in American life that an awareness of the decisions made and problems encountered by survey researchers is necessary for rendering an independent judgment of conclusions drawn from such data.

Notes

1. Lewis Anthony Dexter, *Elite and Specialized Interviewing* (Evanston, Ill.: Northwestern University Press, 1970), 5.

2. There are exceptions to this general rule, however. See John Kessel, *The Domestic Presidency* (Belmont, Calif.: Duxbury, 1975). Kessel administered a highly structured survey instrument to Richard Nixon's Domestic Council staff.

3. Joseph A. Pika, "Interviewing Presidential Aides: A Political Scientist's Perspective," in George C. Edwards III and Stephen J. Wayne, eds., *Studying the Presidency* (Knoxville: University of Tennessee Press, 1982), 282.

4. Harriet Zuckerman, "Interviewing an Ultra-Elite," *Public Opinion Quarterly* 36 (1972): 167.

5. Raymond L. Gordon, *Interviewing: Strategy, Techniques, and Tactics* (Homewood, Ill.: Dorsey, 1969), 49–50.

6. Dom Bonafede, "Interviewing Presidential Aides: A Journalist's Perspective," in *Studying the Presidency,* ed. Edwards and Wayne, 269.

7. Richard F. Fenno Jr., *Home Style: House Members in Their Districts* (Boston: Little, Brown, 1978), 280.

8. Margaret Wagstaffe and George Moyser, "The Threatened Elite: Studying Leaders in an Urban Community," in George Moyser and Margaret Wagstaffe, eds., *Research Methods for Elite Studies* (London: Allen and Unwin, 1987), 186–188.

9. Zuckerman, "Interviewing an Ultra-Elite," 174.

10. John P. Dean and William Foote Whyte, "How Do You Know If the Informant Is Telling the Truth?" in *Elite and Specialized Interviewing,* 127.

11. Gordon, *Interviewing,* 18.

12. Dexter, *Elite and Specialized Interviewing,* 17.

13. Norman M. Bradburn and Seymour Sudman, *Polls and Surveys: Understanding What They Tell Us* (San Francisco: Jossey-Bass, 1988), 59.

14. Ibid., 60.

15. Margrit Eichler, *Nonsexist Research Methods: A Practical Guide* (Winchester, Mass: Allen and Unwin, 1988), 51–52.

16. Doris A. Graber, "Problems in Measuring Audience Effects of the 1976 Debate," in George F. Bishop, Robert G. Meadow, and Marilyn Jackson-Beeck, eds., *The Presidential Debates: Media, Electoral and Policy Perspectives* (New York: Praeger, 1978), 116.

17. Charles H. Backstrom and Gerald Hursh-Cesar, *Survey Research,* 2d ed. (New York: Wiley, 1981), 142, 146.

18. Ibid., 141.

19. Republican National Committee, *1980 Official Republican Poll on U.S. Defense and Foreign Policy.*

20. Eichler, *Nonsexist Research Methods,* 43–44.

21. Seymour Sudman and Norman M. Bradburn, *Asking Questions: A Practical Guide to Questionnaire Design* (San Francisco: Jossey-Bass, 1982), 15.

22. Ibid., 16–17; updated by the authors.

23. Ibid., 16.

24. Quoted from 1996 American National Election Study, HTML Codebook Produced March 30, 2000 [Online]. Available: http://csa.berkeley.edu:7502/archive.htm (accessed November 22, 2000).

25. Dean and Whyte, "How Do You Know If the Informant Is Telling the Truth?" 127.

26. Gordon, *Interviewing,* 18.

27. Dexter, *Elite and Specialized Interviewing,* 17.

28. Patricia J. Labaw, *Advanced Questionnaire Design* (Cambridge, Mass.: Abt Books, 1980), 132.

29. Ibid., 132–133.

30. Ibid., 117.

31. Norman M. Bradburn and W. M. Mason, "The Effect of Question Order on Responses," *Journal of Marketing Research* 1 (1964): 57–64.

32. A. Regula Herzog and Jerald G. Bachman, "Effects of Questionnaire Length on Response Quality," *Public Opinion Quarterly* 45 (1981): 549–559.

33. Lee Sigelman, "Question-Order Effects on Presidential Popularity," *Public Opinion Quarterly* 45 (1981): 199–207.

34. Sam G. MacFarland, "Effects of Question Order on Survey Responses," *Public Opinion Quarterly* 45 (1981): 208–215.

35. Ibid., 213, 214.

36. Labaw, *Advanced Questionnaire Design,* 122.

37. Glen D. Mellinger, Carol L. Huffine, and Mitchell B. Balter, "Assessing Comprehension in a Survey of Public Reactions to Complex Issues," *Public Opinion Quarterly* 46 (1982): 97–109.

38. William D. Perrault Jr., "Controlling Order-Effect Bias," *Public Opinion Quarterly* 39 (1975): 544–551.

39. Donald J. Messmer and Daniel T. Seymour, "The Effects of Branching on Item Nonresponse," *Public Opinion Quarterly* 46 (1982): 270–277.

40. Floyd J. Fowler, *Survey Research Methods,* rev. ed. (Newbury Park, Calif.: Sage, 1988), 61.

41. Don A. Dillman, *Mail and Telephone Surveys: The Total Design Method* (New York: Wiley, 1978), 40.

42. Earl R. Babbie, *Survey Research Methods* (Belmont, Calif.: Wadsworth, 1973), 171.

43. Robert M. Groves and Robert L. Kahn, *Surveys by Telephone: A National Comparison with Personal Interviews* (New York: Academic Press, 1979), 3.

44. Charlotte G. Steeh, "Trends in Nonresponse Rates, 1952–1979," *Public Opinion Quarterly* 45 (1981): 40–57.

45. Laure M. Sharp and Joanne Frankel, "Respondent Burden: A Test of Some Common Assumptions," *Public Opinion Quarterly* 47 (1983): 36–53.

46. Theresa J. DeMaio, "Refusals: Who, Where and Why," *Public Opinion Quarterly* 44 (1980): 223–233.

47. Dillman, *Mail and Telephone Surveys.*

48. See Theresa F. Rogers, "Interviews by Telephone and in Person: Quality of Responses and Field Performance," *Public Opinion Quarterly* 39 (1975): 51–64; and Groves and Kahn, *Surveys by Telephone.* Response rates are affected by different methods of calculating rates for the three types of surveys. For example, nonreachable and ineligible persons may be dropped from the total survey population for telephone and personal interviews before response rates are calculated. Response rates to mailed surveys are depressed because all nonresponses are assumed to be refusals, not ineligibles, or nonreachables. Telephone response rates may be depressed if nonworking but ringing numbers are treated as nonreachable but eligible respondents. Telephone companies vary in their willingness to identify working numbers. If noneligibility is likely to be a problem in a mailed survey, ineligibles should be asked to return the questionnaire anyway so that they can be identified and distinguished from refusals.

49. James H. Frey, *Survey Research by Telephone* (Beverly Hills, Calif.: Sage, 1983), 15–16.

50. Herschel Shosteck and William R. Fairweather, "Physician Response Rates to Mail and Personal Interview Surveys," *Public Opinion Quarterly* 43 (1979): 206–217.

51. Don A. Dillman, Jean Gorton Gallegos, and James H. Frey, "Reducing Refusal Rates for Telephone Interviews," *Public Opinion Quarterly* 40 (1976): 66–78.

52. Fowler, *Survey Research Methods,* 67.

53. Gideon Vigderhous, "Scheduling Telephone Interviews: A Study of Seasonal Patterns," *Public Opinion Quarterly* 45 (1981): 250–259.

54. M. F. Weeks et al., "Optimal Times to Contact Sample Households," *Public Opinion Quarterly* 44 (1980): 101–114.

55. See J. Scott Armstrong, "Monetary Incentive in Mail Surveys," *Public Opinion Quarterly* 39 (1975): 111–116; Arnold S. Linsky, "Stimulating Responses to Mailed Questionnaires: A Review," *Public Opinion Quarterly* 39 (1975): 82–101; James R. Chromy and Daniel G. Horvitz, "The Use of Monetary Incentives in National Assessment Households Survey," *Journal of the American Statistical Association* 73 (1978): 473–478; Thomas A. Heberlein and Robert Baumgartner, "Factors Affecting Response Rates to Mailed Questionnaires," *American Sociological Review* 43 (1978): 447–462; R. Kenneth Godwin, "The Consequences of Large Monetary Incentives in Mail Surveys of Elites," *Public Opinion Quarterly* 43 (1979): 378–387; Kent L. Tedin and C. Richard Hofstetter, "The Effect of Cost and Importance Factors on the Return Rate for Single and Multiple Mailings," *Public Opinion Quarterly* 46 (1982): 122–128; Anton J. Nederhof, "The Effects of Material Incentives in Mail Surveys: Two Studies," *Public Opinion Quarterly* 47 (1983): 103–111; Charles D. Schewe and Norman G. Cournoyer, "Prepaid vs. Promised Monetary Incentives to Questionnaire Response: Further Evidence," *Public Opinion Quarterly* 40 (1976): 105–107; James R. Henley Jr., "Response Rate to Mail Questionnaire with a Return Deadline," *Public Opinion Quarterly* 40 (1976): 374–375; Thomas A. Heberlein and Robert Baumgartner, "Is a Questionnaire Necessary in a Second Mailing?" *Public Opinion Quarterly* 45 (1981): 102–108; and Wesley H. Jones, "Generalized Mail Survey Inducement Methods: Population Interactions with Anonymity and Sponsorship," *Public Opinion Quarterly* 43 (1979): 102–111.

56. For detailed instructions on improving the response rate to mailed surveys, see Dillman, *Mail and Telephone Surveys.*

57. Fowler, *Survey Research Methods,* 63.

58. Groves and Kahn, *Surveys by Telephone,* 214; Frey, *Survey Research by Telephone,* 22.

59. For research estimating amount of bias introduced by nonresponse due to unavailability or refusal, see F. L. Filion, "Estimating Bias Due to Nonresponse in Mail Surveys," *Public Opinion Quarterly* 39 (1975): 482–492; Michael J. O'Neil, "Estimating the Nonresponse Bias Due to Refusals in Telephone Surveys," *Public Opinion Quarterly* 43 (1979): 218–232; and Arthur L. Stinchcombe, Calvin Jones, and Paul Sheatsley, "Nonresponse Bias for Attitude Questions," *Public Opinion Quarterly* 45 (1981): 359–375.

60. Carol S. Aneshensel et al., "Measuring Depression in the Community: A Comparison of Telephone and Personal Interviews," *Public Opinion Quarterly* 46 (1982): 110–121.

61. DeMaio, "Refusals," 223–233; and Steeh, "Trends in Nonresponse Rates," 40–57.

62. Charles T. Salmon and John Spicer Nichols, "The Next-Birthday Method of Respondent Selection," *Public Opinion Quarterly* 47 (1983): 270–276.

63. Dillman, *Mail and Telephone Surveys.*

64. See Willis J. Goudy and Harry R. Potter, "Interview Rapport: Demise of a Concept," *Public Opinion Quarterly* 39 (1975): 529–543; and Charles F. Cannell, Peter V. Miller, and Lois Oksenberg, "Research on Interviewing Techniques," in Samuel Leinhardt, ed., *Sociological Methodology 1981* (San Francisco: Jossey-Bass, 1981), 389–437.

65. Rogers, "Interviews by Telephone and in Person," 51–65.

66. Ibid.; and Peter V. Miller and Charles F. Cannell, "A Study of Experimental Techniques for Telephone Interviewing," *Public Opinion Quarterly* 46 (1982): 250–269.

67. Arpad Barath and Charles F. Cannell, "Effect of Interviewer's Voice Intonation," *Public Opinion Quarterly* 40 (1976): 370–373.

68. Eleanor Singer, Martin R. Frankel, and Marc B. Glassman, "The Effect of Interviewer Characteristics and Expectations on Response," *Public Opinion Quarterly* 47 (1983): 68–83; and Eleanor Singer and Luane Kohnke-Aguirre, "Interviewer Expectation Effects: A Replication and Extension," *Public Opinion Quarterly* 43 (1979): 245–260.

69. Patrick R. Cotter, Jeffrey Cohen, and Philip B. Coulter, "Race-of-Interviewer Effects in Telephone Interviews," *Public Opinion Quarterly* 46 (1982): 278–284; and Bruce A. Campbell, "Race of Interviewer Effects among Southern Adolescents," *Public Opinion Quarterly* 45 (1981): 231–244.

70. Shirley Hatchett and Howard Schuman, "White Respondents and Race-of-Interviewer Effects," *Public Opinion Quarterly* 39 (1975): 523–528; and Michael F. Weeks and R. Paul Moore, "Ethnicity of Interviewer Effects on Ethnic Respondents," *Public Opinion Quarterly* 45 (1981): 245–249.

71. See Singer, Frankel, and Glassman, "The Effect of Interviewer Characteristics and Expectations on Response"; Groves and Kahn, *Surveys by Telephone;* Dillman, *Mail and Telephone Surveys;* and John Freeman and Edgar W. Butler, "Some Sources of Interviewer Variance in Surveys," *Public Opinion Quarterly* 40 (1976): 79–91.

72. See Groves and Kahn, *Surveys by Telephone;* and Lawrence A. Jordan, Alfred C. Marcus, and Leo G. Reeder, "Response Styles in Telephone and Household Interviewing," *Public Opinion Quarterly* 44 (1980): 210–222.

73. Dillman, *Mail and Telephone Surveys.*

74. Jordan, Marcus, and Reeder, "Response Styles"; and Groves and Kahn, *Surveys by Telephone.* See also Rogers, "Interviews by Telephone and in Person."

75. For example, see Sudman and Bradburn, *Asking Questions,* 55–86; and Jerald G. Bachman and Patrick M. O'Malley, "When Four Months Equal a Year: Inconsistencies in Student Reports of Drug Use," *Public Opinion Quarterly* 45 (1981): 542.

76. RRT was first proposed by S. L. Warner in "Randomized Response," *Journal of the American Statistical Association* 60 (1965): 63–69.

77. S. M. Zdep and Isabelle N. Rhodes, "Making the Randomized Response Technique Work," *Public Opinion Quarterly* 40 (1976): 531–537.

78. Frederick Wiseman, Mark Moriarty, and Marianne Schafer, "Estimating Public Opinion with the Randomized Response Model," *Public Opinion Quarterly* 39 (1975): 507–513.

79. Zdep and Rhodes, "Making the Randomized Response Technique Work."

80. Ibid.

81. Iris M. Shimizu and Gordon Scott Bonham, "Randomized Response Technique in a National Survey," *Journal of the American Statistical Association* 73 (1978): 35–39.

82. Robert G. Orwin and Robert F. Boruch, "RRT Meets RDD: Statistical Strategies for Assuring Response Privacy in Telephone Surveys," *Public Opinion Quarterly* 46 (1982): 560–571.

83. Fowler, *Survey Research Methods,* 68.

84. Ibid.

85. Groves and Kahn, *Surveys by Telephone*; and Frey, *Survey Research by Telephone.*

86. Frey, *Survey Research by Telephone,* 24–25.

87. Joseph Waksberg, "Sampling Methods for Random Digit Dialing," *Journal of the American Statistical Association* 73 (1978): 40–46; and K. Michael Cummings, "Random Digit Dialing: A Sampling Technique for Telephone Surveys," *Public Opinion Quarterly* 43 (1979): 233–244.

88. Raymond J. Smead and James Wilcox, "Ring Policy in Telephone Surveys," *Public Opinion Quarterly* 44 (1980): 115–116.

89. Howard E. Freeman et al., "Telephone Sampling Bias in Surveying Disability," *Public Opinion Quarterly* 46 (1982): 392–407.

90. Ibid.

Te erms introduced

AMBIGUOUS QUESTION. A question containing a concept that is not clearly defined.

BRANCHING QUESTION. A question that sorts respondents into subgroups and directs these subgroups to different parts of the questionnaire.

CLOSED-ENDED QUESTION. A question with response alternatives provided.

DOUBLE-BARRELED QUESTION. A question that is really two questions in one.

ELITE INTERVIEWING. Interviewing respondents in a nonstandardized, individualized manner.

FILTER QUESTION. A question used to screen respondents so that subsequent questions will be asked only of certain respondents for whom the questions are appropriate.

FOCUSED INTERVIEW. A semistructured or flexible interview schedule used when interviewing elites.

INTERVIEW DATA. Observations derived from written or verbal questioning of the respondent by the researcher.

INTERVIEWER BIAS. The interviewer's influence on the respondent's answers; an example of reactivity.

LEADING QUESTION. A question that encourages the respondent to choose a particular response.

MAILED QUESTIONNAIRE. A survey instrument mailed to the respondent for completion and return.

OPEN-ENDED QUESTION. A question with no response alternatives provided for the respondent.

PERSONAL INTERVIEW. Face-to-face questioning of the respondent.

QUESTION ORDER EFFECT. The effect on responses of question placement within a questionnaire.

QUESTIONNAIRE DESIGN. The physical layout and packaging of a questionnaire.

RANDOMIZED RESPONSE TECHNIQUE (RRT). A method of obtaining accurate answers to sensitive questions that protects the respondent's privacy.

RESPONSE QUALITY. The extent to which responses provide accurate and complete information.

RESPONSE RATE. The proportion of respondents selected for participation in a survey who actually participate.

RESPONSE SET. The pattern of responding to a series of questions in a similar fashion without careful reading of each question.

SINGLE-SIDED QUESTION. A question with only one substantive alternative provided for the respondent.

SURVEY INSTRUMENT. The schedule of questions to be asked of the respondent.

SURVEY RESEARCH. Research based on the interview method of data collection.

TELEPHONE INTERVIEW. The questioning of the respondent via telephone.

TERMINATION. The respondent's refusal to finish the interview.

TWO-SIDED QUESTION. A question with two substantive alternatives provided for the respondent.

Exercises

1. Read John S. Dryzek and Jeffrey Berejikian, "Reconstructive Democratic Theory," *American Political Science Review* 87 (March 1993): 48–60. What justification do the authors give for relying on the responses of just 37 subjects (pp. 51–52)? How do they say that survey research could now be used to follow up on their conclusions?

2. Read Ada W. Finifter and Ellen Mickiewicz, "Redefining the Political System of the USSR: Mass Support for Political Change," *American Political Science Review* 86 (December 1992): 857–874. What precautions did the researchers take to ensure high quality responses to the personal interviews conducted (pp. 871–872)? Do you see any problems with the questions used to measure attitudes about political change (pp. 872–873)?

3. Read Lee Ann Banaszak and Eric Plutzer, "The Social Bases of Feminism in the European Community," *Public Opinion Quarterly* 57 (Spring 1993): 29–53. Who designed the questionnaire used in this survey research (p. 34)? Do you see any problems with the questions used to measure attitudes toward feminism (pp. 50–51)?

4. Read Vincent Price and John Zeller, "Who Gets the News?" *Public Opinion Quarterly* 57 (Summer 1993): 133–164. What do these researchers think is wrong with most survey questions dealing with media exposure? How do they explore the importance of different question formats? What advice do

they give to other researchers of political communication who use survey methodology (p. 160)?

5. Read Thomas Hartley and Bruce Russett, "Public Opinion and the Common Defense: Who Governs Military Spending in the United States?" *American Political Science Review* 86 (December 1992): 905–915. How do these researchers construct public opinion measures regarding military spending over a twenty-five-year period? Which polling organization's questions on military spending do you think are apt to yield the most honest and informative responses (p. 912)?

6. Suppose you want to measure opinions about two controversial issues, the death penalty and abortion. First, think very carefully about what kinds of information you want your interviewees to supply and then try to write a couple of questions that you think will obtain these attitudes. To assess the adequacy of your questionnaire, compare your questions with those framed by scholarly and commercial organizations. A good source are the questions listed in the codebooks for the General Social Survey, a series of annual polls conducted for the National Data Program for the Social Sciences at the National Opinion Research Center at the University of Chicago. See its 1972–1996 General Social Survey Cumulative File HTML Codebook Produced March 30, 2000, which is available online at the SDA: Survey Documentation and Analysis (http://csa.berkeley.edu:7502/archive.htm.). Another source is the Pew Research Center (http://www.people-press.org/), which contains dozens of polls. Using the search procedures discussed in Chapter 6, you should be able to find the text of many questions.

7. To see how question wording affects responses, join with your classmates to write two versions of a political questionnaire. Then administer them to two randomly selected sections of an introductory undergraduate course in political science. To what extent does question wording affect the interpretation of public opinion?

8. Examine how available response choices affect the distribution of opinion by joining with your classmates to write different versions of a closed-ended question dealing with an important but not widely discussed issue such as international trade or consumer protection legislation. One version might force respondents to choose only among substantive options such as "agree" or "disagree" while another may permit (even encourage) nonresponses such as "don't know," "haven't thought about it," "no opinion," and the like. Administer the questionnaire to different sections of an introductory undergraduate course. Does support for or opposition to the matter seem to decrease significantly as respondents are allowed or encouraged to say they have no opinion? To what degree can the interpretation of the results change according to the number and kind of alternatives presented?

9. Use internet resources (see Chapter 6) to find poll data on a controversial matter such as gun control. Do the poll results lead to different conclusions about what the public supports and opposes?

Suggested Readings

Aldridge, Alan, and Kenneth Levine. *Surveying the Social World.* Buckingham, England: Open University Press, 2001.

Braverman, Marc T., and Jana Kay Slater. *Advances in Survey Research.* San Francisco: Jossey-Bass, 1998.

Dillman, Don A. *Mail and Electronic Surveys.* New York: Wiley, 1999.

Frey, James H., and Sabine M. Oishi. *How to Conduct Interviews by Telephone and in Person.* Thousand Oaks, Calif.: Sage, 1995.

Nesbary, Dale. *Survey Research and the World Wide Web.* Needham Heights, Mass.: Allyn and Bacon, 1999.

Newman, Isadore, and Keith A. McNeil. *Conducting Survey Research in the Social Sciences.* Lanham, Md.: University Press of America, 1998.

Patten, Mildred L. *Questionnaire Research: A Practical Guide.* 2d ed. Los Angeles: Pyrczak, 2001.

Rea, Louis M., and Richard A. Parker. *Designing and Conducting Survey Research.* San Francisco: Jossey-Bass, 1997.

Sapsford, Roger. *Survey Research.* Thousand Oaks, Calif.: Sage, 1999.

CHAPTER 11

Univariate Data Analysis and Descriptive Statistics

The preceding chapters discussed the initial stages of an empirical research project. We have examined the nature of scientific knowledge, the formulation of testable hypotheses, the development of a suitable research design, the process of measuring variables, and the many ways in which empirical observations may be made and data collected. The remainder of this book will cover the final steps of a research project: analyzing the data that have been collected and putting together a research report.

Major purposes of empirical analysis are to search for relationships among variables and test hypotheses about political phenomena. This activity requires the systematic study of two or more variables. In addition to or as a first step in performing this sort of analysis, however, researchers often investigate the distribution of observed values for a *single* variable and then summarize those values, a process called **univariate data analysis**. The summary measurement, known as a **descriptive statistic**, helps show features of the data that are not clear from looking at the entire data set.

You are undoubtedly already familiar with quite a few instances of univariate data analysis and descriptive statistics. For example, if you make a list of all of your course grades and then group all the identical grades together (for example, 2 As, 4 A–s, 7 Bs, 3 C+s, 1 D), you are conducting a univariate data analysis of the observed values. If you then use the numerical value of each grade (for example, A = 4.0, A– = 3.7, B = 3.0, C+ = 2.3, D = 1.0) to calculate your cumulative grade-point average, you have calculated a descriptive statistic that summarizes your academic performance.

Univariate data analyses and descriptive statistics are often encountered in the daily news. Charting the unemployment rate over time to see if it is rising or falling is a case of univariate data analysis where the unemployment rate is a descriptive statistic. Or, recall the examples introduced in Chapter 1 and referred to throughout the book. In several of those cases, the researchers present information on the distribution of the observed values on a single variable before testing the hypothesized relationship between two or more

TABLE 11-1

Distributions of Political Ideology and of Civil Liberties Votes among Supreme Court Justices

Justice	Values[a]	Votes[b]
Warren	.50	78.1
Harlan	.75	41.9
Brennan	1.00	77.9
Whittaker	.00	43.4
Stewart	.50	51.5
White	.00	43.4
Goldberg	.50	89.6
Fortas	1.00	80.4
Marshall	1.00	79.7
Burger	−.77	29.7
Blackmun	−.77	42.9
Powell	−.67	37.9
Rehnquist[c]	−.91	19.5
Stevens	−.50	56.3
O'Connor	−.17	30.9
Rehnquist[d]	−.91	23.0
Scalia	−1.00	34.7
Kennedy	−.27	40.0

Source: Jeffrey A. Segal and Albert D. Cover, "Ideological Values and the Votes of U.S. Supreme Court Justices," *American Political Science Review* 83 (June 1989): 560.

[a] Derived by Segal and Cover. The range is −1.00 (extremely conservative) to 1.00 (extremely liberal).

[b] Percentage liberal in civil liberties cases, 1953–1988.

[c] Values and votes as Nixon appointee.

[d] Values and votes as Reagan appointee.

variables. For example, Jeffrey Segal and Albert Cover, in their article about the political ideology and decision making of selected Supreme Court justices, show the observed values for each justice on the authors' political ideology measure (remember that this measure was derived from their content analysis of newspaper editorials) and on their measure of support for civil liberties as reflected in the justices' case opinions (Table 11-1).[1] This type of data presentation is called an **enumerative table** since it basically lists the values of a variable for all of the cases. It does not represent a test of a hypothesis.

A similar data display may be found in one of the articles concerning the relationship between land inequality and political violence. Edward Muller, Mitchell Seligson, and Hung-der Fu, in their critique of Manus Midlarsky's analysis of the effects of land inequality, show the number of deaths due to political violence and the presence or absence of land inequality (called "patterned" inequality) for the Latin American countries included in their analysis

TABLE 11-2

Number of Deaths from Political Violence and the Presence of Patterned Land Inequality in Latin America

Mean Death Rate from Political Violence, 1948–1977	Patterned Inequality	
	Absent	Present
225.0		Bolivia
210.8	Dominican Republic	
116.5		Colombia
100.9	Cuba	
89.6	Argentina	
54.5	Nicaragua	
38.1	Venezuela	
21.4	Guatemala	
20.0	Paraguay	
17.2	Panama	
16.8	Honduras	Peru
15.3	Haiti	
12.8	Costa Rica	
12.6		Chile
6.7	Ecuador	
6.4		El Salvador
3.4	Uruguay	
3.2	Mexico	
.5	Brazil	

Source: Edward N. Muller, Mitchell A. Seligson, and Hung-der Fu, "Land Inequality and Political Violence," *American Political Science Review* 83 (June 1989): 585.

(Table 11-2).[2] This display does not indicate whether there is a relationship between the two variables, but it does familiarize the reader with the distribution of values on each variable.

These two data displays include a relatively small number of observed values. Sometimes, however, the number of cases is far too large to be listed in a table. Consequently, researchers often use a variety of graphic devices to display the form and characteristics of the variables' distribution. We also often supplement these graphs with descriptive statistics.

Frequency Distributions

For large sets of data researchers usually begin by creating frequency distributions of the variables' observed values. A **frequency distribution** is nothing more than a table that shows the number of observations for each

TABLE 11-3
Frequency Distribution of Gender

Gender	Frequency (f)	Relative Frequency (percent)
Male	1,975	43
Female	2,623	57
Totals	4,598	100

Source: General Social Surveys. Respondents from 1993 and 1994 panels.

value of a variable. The number of observations is also called the frequency, which we often represent by the small letter *f*. In addition, a frequency distribution is usually accompanied by a number called a **relative frequency**, which simply transforms the frequency into a proportion or percentage. Proportions are calculated by dividing the number of observations in each category by the total number of observations while percentages are found by multiplying the proportions by 100. Proportions and percentages communicate information that is often more meaningful and easier to remember than raw frequencies distribution.

Tables 11-3 and 11-4 show two frequency distributions. Table 11-3 displays a **dichotomous variable**: gender. A dichotomous variable has only two categories (here, male and female). Table 11-4 shows a variable (perceptions of air quality) that has four values. In both cases the frequency distribution shows the number of cases (observations) that had each value on the variable being measured.

Table 11-3 is especially straightforward because the variable has just two categories. But Table 11-4 contains a slight complication. It too displays frequencies and relative frequencies (percentages). But notice that some of the respondents in the survey were not asked to state their perceptions or did not provide a codable response. They have thus been categorized as "Missing." The question now arises: Should the relative frequencies be based on the *total* number in the survey (1,714 in this case) or on the number of "valid" or non-missing responses (1,510)? It is customary to report the valid frequencies and valid relative frequencies since most readers are interested in the percentages in just the substantive or meaningful classes. But not always. So, if you show only the valid responses, you should also tell your audience which categories have been excluded and the number of cases in each. Omission of this information commonly occurs in newspaper and magazine reports of polls or other data. But not knowing how many cases have been excluded leaves the reader wondering, for example, do 50 percent of the respondents in the total sample favor a proposition or do 50 percent of those giving a meaningful answer favor that proposition?

TABLE 11-4
Frequency Distribution of Beliefs about Air Quality

Perceived Air Quality	Frequency	Total Relative Frequency (percent)[a]	Valid Frequency	Valid Relative Frequency (percent)	Cumulative Relative Frequency (percent)
Very good	90	5	90	6	6
Fairly good	982	57	982	65	71
Fairly bad	366	21	366	24	95
Very bad	72	4	72	5	100
Missing[b]	204	12			
Totals	1,714	99	1,510	100	

Source: 1996 American National Election Study (ICPSR 6896).

[a] Percentages do not add to 100 because of rounding. Question: Overall, how would you rate the air quality in our nation? Very good, fairly good, fairly bad, or very bad?
[b] "Missing" means "don't know," "not interviewed," and "not ascertained."

Table 11-4 also provides data on the **cumulative proportion** (or percentage), which tells the reader what portion of the total is at or below a given value. For example, we see that 71 percent of the respondents giving substantive answers rate air quality as at least fairly good and 95 percent rate it as fairly bad or better. The cumulative frequencies allow the reader to see some kinds of patterns in the data, particularly if the variable is ordinal.

We should emphasize that proportions and percentages are often preferable to simple frequencies because they make it easier to compare two populations of different size. For example, Table 11-5 shows two hypothetical student populations of different size, but with the same proportions of selected majors. It would be difficult to discern this fact from the frequency distributions alone. The percentages reveal this information immediately. (After all,

TABLE 11-5
Frequency Distribution and Percentage for Student Populations

Categories (Values)	College A		College B	
	f	%	f	%
Variable: Student majors				
Political science	35	25.9	105	25.9
Biology	30	22.2	90	22.2
English	45	33.3	135	33.3
Mathematics	25	18.5	75	18.5
Total	135	99.9	405	99.9

Note: Hypothetical data. Percentages do not add to 100 because of rounding.

"percent" means "per 100," and so the percentages in the table tell us how many students per 100 in College A major in political science and how many students per 100 in College B major in political science. Note also that the percentages add to 100 across categories of the variable.) In many tables, only percentages are shown for each category. Frequency distributions are omitted, but the total number of observations is given, making it possible to recreate the frequency distribution.[3]

Computing and Understanding Percentages

Even though percentages are commonplace, people sometimes misunderstand their meaning and calculation. The word *percent* literally means "per 100." A percentage thus indicates how many cases or subjects *per 100* have a certain property.

When you see a percentage such as 25, it is important to ask, "This is a percentage of what?" Is it 25 percent of twenty men? Of twenty Democrats? Of what? It is even more important to keep this question in mind when calculating percentages or asking a computer program to do so.

Suppose, for instance, you want to compare men and women's responses to the the question, "Do you believe in God?" The correct procedure is first to find out how many women responded to the question and then determine what percentage of them answered "yes." This number can be compared to the percentage of men who also answered "yes." This is not the same as finding out, "Of all those who said 'yes,' how many, or what percentage, were women?" The table of *frequencies* below emphasizes this point.

	Women	Men	Total
Yes	100	50	150
No	100	50	150
Total	200	100	300

To compare women and men, we first have to know how many in each group answered the question. We see that there are 200 females, and of those 100, or 50 percent, answered "yes." Similarly, there are 100 males and 50 percent of them also responded "yes." This inquiry thus involves a comparison of *column* percentages:

	Women	Men
Yes	50%	50%
No	50	50
Total	100%	100%

Note that the percentages add to one hundred down the columns.

This comparison is much different than one that asks "What is the composition of 'yes' and 'no' responses in terms of gender?" For that analysis, which probably would not be of great interest, we would need *row* percentages:

	Women	Men	Total
Yes	67%	33	100%
No	67%	33	100%

Here we see that of the 150 people who responded "yes," 100, or 67 percent, were female and 33 percent were male.

For example, recall the researchers in Chapter 1 who were interested in the relationship between changes in public opinion and changes in public policy decisions.[4] They were especially interested in whether changes in policy were in the same direction as significant changes in public opinion. The first step in the presentation of their data was to display the frequency distribution of opinion-policy change in the same direction, opinion-policy change in opposite directions, no policy change, and policy change that was impossible to categorize. These results are shown in Table 11-6. There we can see that of the 357 cases the authors had to analyze, in 153 or 43 percent of the cases policy and opinion changed in the same direction. In 78 or 22 percent of

TABLE 11-6

Congruence between Changes in Public Opinion and Changes in Public Policy, 1935–1979

	Total Cases		Cases with Policy Change	
	%	f	%	f
Congruent change in opinion and policy	43	(153)	66	(153)
Noncongruent change in policy	22	(78)	34	(78)
No change in policy	33	(120)		
Uncertain	2	(6)		
	100	(357)	100	(231)

Source: Benjamin I. Page and Robert Y. Shapiro, "Effects of Public Opinion on Policy," *American Political Science Review* 77 (March 1983): 178.

Note: Each case is an instance in which public policy preferences changed significantly according to repeated administration of identical survey items.

the cases opinion and policy changed in opposite directions, and in 120 or 33 percent of the cases there was no discernible policy change. If we concentrate only on the cases in which there was policy change (the right-hand side of the table) we can see that policy was about twice as likely to change in the direction of opinion change as it was to change in the opposite direction (66 percent versus 34 percent).

Usually, researchers use computer software programs to tabulate observed values of a variable and then display a frequency distribution. Table 11-7 shows a frequency distribution that was produced by one such software program, called SPSS.[5] Here we can see the distribution of responses to a party identification question asked in the General Social Surveys. This format shows the number or "code" assigned to each response category (value), the number of observations in each of these categories (frequency), the percentage of the total number of observations in each category (percent), the percentage of observations in each category after excluding missing observations (valid percent), and the cumulative percentages. For example, 5,676 out of 35,284 total respondents identified themselves as a "Strong Democrat" (coded 0). This number constitutes 16.1 percent of the total responses and 16.2 percent of the valid responses. Other entries in the table are interpreted in the same fashion. The cumulative percentages show the percentage of cases at or below a particular category. Codes or numbers like 0 for "Strong Democrat" are used to facilitate computer analysis. Such software programs allow researchers to produce frequency distributions quickly and accurately.

Bar charts and pie diagrams are other ways of presenting the information contained in a frequency distribution. A **bar chart** is a series of bars where each bar represents the number or percentage of observations that are in a

TABLE 11-7
Frequency Distribution Created by SPSS

		Frequency	Percent	Valid Percent	Cumulative Percent
Valid	0 STRONG DEMOCRAT	5,676	16.1	16.2	16.2
	1 NOT STRONG DEMOCRAT	8,159	23.1	23.2	39.4
	2 IND. NEAR DEMOCRAT	4,232	12.0	12.1	51.5
	3 INDEPENDENT	4,405	12.5	12.6	64.0
	4 IND. NEAR REPUBLICAN	3,135	8.9	8.9	73.0
	5 NOT STRONG REPUBLICAN	5,781	16.4	16.5	89.4
	6 STRONG REPUBLICAN	3,240	9.2	9.2	98.7
	7 OTHER PARTY	467	1.3	1.3	100.0
	Total	35,095	99.5	100.0	
Missing	8 DK	10	.0		
	9 NA	179	.5		
	Total	189	.5		
Total		35,284	100.0		

Source: General Social Survey.

category. Figure 11-1 is a bar chart of student majors in College A from Table 11-5. A **pie diagram** is a circular representation of a set of observed values where the entire circle (or pie) stands for all of the observed values and where each portion of the circle (or pie slice) represents the proportion of the observed values in each category. Figure 11-2 is a pie diagram of the beliefs about air quality data shown in Table 11-4. Both a bar chart and a pie diagram are most useful when the number of categories or values for a variable is small.

An interesting example of data presented in the form of a bar chart may be found in Henry Bienen and Nicolas van de Walle's article investigating regime (actually, ruler) stability in African countries.[6] Recall from Chapter 1 that these researchers were interested in understanding the length of time that African rulers remained in power. Figure 11-3 shows how a bar chart can efficiently present the frequency distribution of African rulers' years in office. In this case, the use of the hatching technique (which creates a segmented bar chart) allows the simultaneous presen-

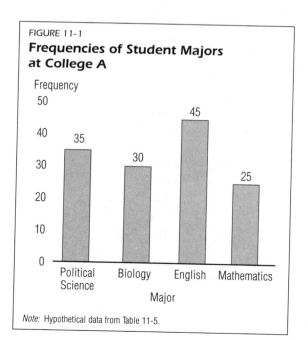

FIGURE 11-1
Frequencies of Student Majors at College A

Note: Hypothetical data from Table 11-5.

tation of two frequency distributions: one covering all 165 cases and one representing the subset of 63 cases in which a ruler died in office of natural causes or was still in office when the analysis was conducted (termed censored cases by the authors).

If graphs such as bar and pie charts are clearly drawn and fully labeled, they can help readers see patterns in data. But to be most helpful these figures should be sufficiently complete to convey all necessary information yet simple enough to be easily interpreted. There are many computer programs that create wonderful-looking graphs at the touch of a button. Unfortunately, however, this software often obscures the meaning of the data by drawing three dimensional figures and adding distracting fill patterns, colors, icons, and backgrounds. Since this pizzaz can interfere with understanding, we recommend keeping lines and areas as simple as possible and

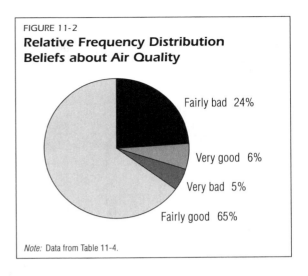

FIGURE 11-2
Relative Frequency Distribution Beliefs about Air Quality

Fairly bad 24%
Very good 6%
Very bad 5%
Fairly good 65%

Note: Data from Table 11-4.

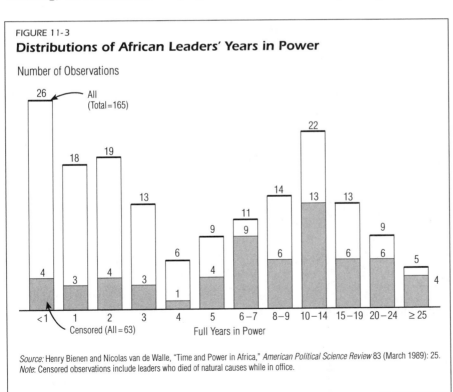

FIGURE 11-3
Distributions of African Leaders' Years in Power

Number of Observations

All (Total = 165)

Censored (All = 63)

Full Years in Power

Source: Henry Bienen and Nicolas van de Walle, "Time and Power in Africa," *American Political Science Review* 83 (March 1989): 25.
Note: Censored observations include leaders who died of natural causes while in office.

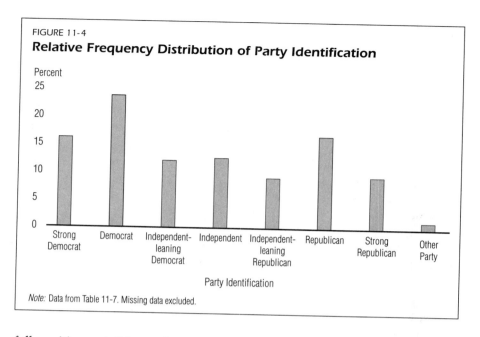

FIGURE 11-4
Relative Frequency Distribution of Party Identification

Percent

Note: Data from Table 11-7. Missing data excluded.

fully writing out titles and labels. In Edward Tufte's words, the data to ink ratio should be as high as possible.[7]

Consider Figure 11-4, which shows the distribution of party identification in the form of a bar chart. Its features include

1. a number in the title so that the graph can be referred to in the text;

2. a full title with no abbreviations;

3. a completely labeled variable name (by default, many computer programs use only an abbreviation for names such as "partyid," which makes no sense to readers, so you must be sure to change them);

4. written category labels such as "Strong Democrat" instead of "St. Dem.";

5. a description of the Y axis so that the meaning of the bars' heights is clear; and

6. a full citation of the data source and explanatory notes.

The frequency distributions and graphic displays considered so far have contained relatively few values for each of the variables presented (for example, there are eight categories of party identification in Table 11-7, four categories of beliefs about air quality in Table 11-4, and twelve categories of African leaders' duration in power in Figure 11-3). Some variables, however, are measured in such a way that the number of values is far too large to be presented in a bar chart, in a pie diagram, or even in a frequency distribution. Most such variables are interval or ratio level measures. If we prepared a frequency distribution of the ages of the respondents in a typical survey of eligible voters in the United States, for example, there might be as many as seventy age categories (Table 11-8). This is far too many to present either in a frequency distribution or in one of the graphic displays considered thus far. In such a case a line diagram or frequency curve is often used.

A **frequency curve** is simply a graph of a frequency distribution in which the values of the variable are arrayed along the X-axis and the number of observations is depicted along the Y-axis. Each data point represents the number of observations for each value, and the data points are then joined together to form a **line diagram**. This can be done for interval or ratio level measures because of the mathematical properties of the values at this level of measurement.

KEEP GRAPHS SIMPLE

Remember, a graph provides the reader with a visual description of the data. Many computer programs create wonderful-looking graphs at the touch of a button. But many of them add so many extra features such as three-dimensional bars or colorful fills that the data can get lost in the ink. It is usually best to keep lines and areas as simple as possible so that the reader can easily see what point is being conveyed. Also, be sure to thoroughly label variable and axis names and to not use abbreviations that mean nothing to a general reader.

Figure 11-5 is a line diagram of the age distribution from Table 11-8. Clearly, this way of presenting the distribution of observed values is more informative than the frequency distribution itself. Line diagrams are more often used to present the values of a variable that has been measured many different times. In Figure 11-6, for example, the responses to the Gallup poll question regarding citizen approval of presidential job performance are shown for dozens of measurements taken between January 1981 and January 1986. Each data point represents the frequency distribution for one measurement (with values of approve, disapprove, or other responses) and the data points have been connected to show the trend in Ronald Reagan's approval ratings.

Figure 11-7 is a line diagram that shows the distribution of observed values on three variables on the same graph. Each variable is a measurement of the amount of political information possessed by the American electorate, as measured in three different years. This type of graphic permits the comparison of the distribution of observed values across variables.

As one might expect, frequency curves and line diagrams come in an unlimited number of shapes. As Figure 11-8 shows, they may be symmetrical (a, b, f) or asymmetrical (c, d, e). A symmetrical distribution is the same shape on either side of the midpoint in the range of observed values. Asymmetrical distributions may be **positively skewed** (also called "skewed to the right") (c) or **negatively skewed** (also called "skewed to the left") (d). In a positively skewed distribution, there are fewer observations to the right of the midpoint,

TABLE 11-8
Frequency Distribution of the Ages of a National Sample of Americans

Value	Frequency	Percent	Cum Percent
18	2	0	0
19	20	1	1
20	23	2	3
21	37	3	6
22	29	2	8
23	50	3	11
24	47	3	14
25	39	3	17
26	32	2	19
27	44	3	22
28	37	3	25
29	33	2	27
30	28	2	29
31	28	2	31
32	37	3	33
33	39	3	36
34	31	2	38
35	37	3	40
36	41	3	43
37	38	3	46
38	31	2	48
39	24	2	50
40	28	2	51
41	25	2	53
42	21	1	55
43	25	2	56
44	23	2	58
45	20	1	59
46	18	1	60
47	19	1	62
48	22	1	63
49	21	1	65
50	8	1	65
51	16	1	66
52	21	1	68
53	14	1	69
54	17	1	70
55	19	1	71
56	19	1	72

(continued)

TABLE 11-8   (Continued)
Frequency Distribution of the Ages of a National Sample of Americans

Value	Frequency	Percent	Cum Percent
57	19	1	74
58	24	2	75
59	16	1	76
60	27	2	78
61	20	1	80
62	20	1	81
63	15	1	82
64	13	1	83
65	18	1	84
66	14	1	85
67	25	2	87
68	24	2	88
69	9	1	89
70	18	1	90
71	12	1	91
72	14	1	92
73	6	0	93
74	15	1	94
75	9	1	94
76	14	1	95
77	13	1	96
78	6	0	96
79	4	0	97
80	6	0	97
81	12	1	98
82	8	1	98
83	5	0	99
84	4	0	99
85	2	0	99
86	2	0	99
87	1	0	99
88	2	0	100
89	7	0	100

Missing Data	
Value	Frequency
99	6

Valid Cases: 1,467   Missing Cases: 6

Source: Marija J. Norusis, *SPSS/PC + Studentware* (Chicago: SPSS, Inc., 1988), 97.

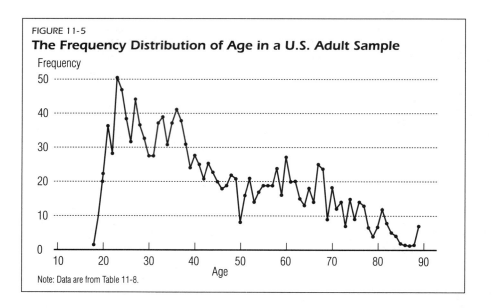

FIGURE 11-5

The Frequency Distribution of Age in a U.S. Adult Sample

Note: Data are from Table 11-8.

but those observations are farther from the midpoint. In a negatively skewed distribution, there are fewer observations on the left part of the curve.

Descriptive Statistics

As we have seen, there are a number of ways in which the information contained in a frequency distribution can be displayed and presented. Sometimes, however, the information in a frequency distribution is too extensive for a reader to understand fully. Moreover, the reader sometimes wants to compare the contents of several frequency distributions simultaneously. It would be useful to have a way of summarizing the contents of a frequency distribution so that its various aspects can be readily grasped. For example, if someone asked you to describe your academic performance in college, you could recite each course you took along with the grades you received for them. But after about ten courses, the listener might have a hard time formulating a clear understanding of your overall performance (unless you received the same grade in every course). It would be much easier if you could give the person a single number—such as your cumulative grade-point average—that summarized your academic performance.

Even the largest batch of numbers may be summarized with a few descriptive statistics. They are simply numbers that attempt to capture, precisely and efficiently, the contents of a frequency distribution. Two types are especially important: one measures **central tendency**, or what the "typical" case in the

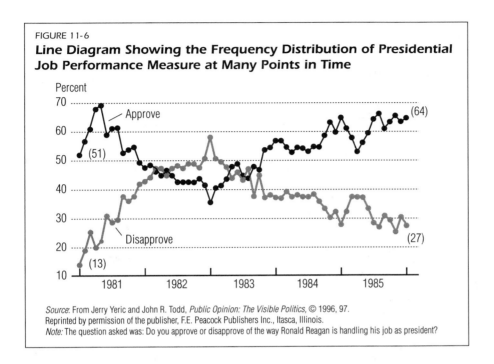

FIGURE 11-6

Line Diagram Showing the Frequency Distribution of Presidential Job Performance Measure at Many Points in Time

Source: From Jerry Yeric and John R. Todd, *Public Opinion: The Visible Politics,* © 1996, 97. Reprinted by permission of the publisher, F.E. Peacock Publishers Inc., Itasca, Illinois.
Note: The question asked was: Do you approve or disapprove of the way Ronald Reagan is handling his job as president?

distribution looks like, and the other measures **dispersion**, or how much variation occurs across the data.

Summarizing data with descriptive statistics has a disadvantage, however: information based on a single measurement is inevitably incomplete. For example, if you say you have a grade-point average of 3.0 (on a 4.0 grade scale), it is impossible to learn from that single indicator whether you have excelled in some courses and struggled in others or whether you have consistently received Bs. To minimize the loss of information, researchers often use several descriptive statistics together to summarize different aspects of their data. When used together these statistics yield a clearer picture of the individual measurements than could be obtained from a single statistic.

Since different descriptive statistics are appropriate for different levels of measurement, we will discuss in turn those that are appropriate for nominal, ordinal, and interval or ratio level measures.

Descriptive Statistics for Nominal Level Variables

A nominal level measure divides observations into two or more categories. Summarizing nominal level data is quite straightforward. A common measure of central tendency is the **mode** or modal category and is simply the category with the greatest frequency of observations. Refer to Table 11-4 or Figure

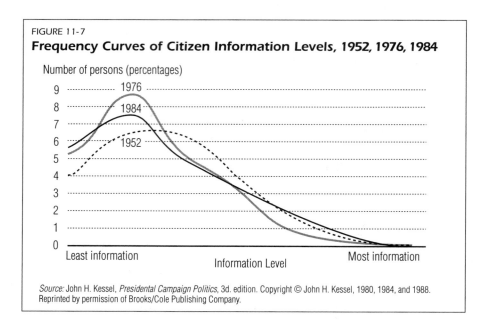

FIGURE 11-7

Frequency Curves of Citizen Information Levels, 1952, 1976, 1984

Number of persons (percentages)

Source: John H. Kessel, *Presidental Campaign Politics,* 3d. edition. Copyright © John H. Kessel, 1980, 1984, and 1988. Reprinted by permission of Brooks/Cole Publishing Company.

11-2, for example. The modal response to the question "Overall, how would you rate the quality of air in our nation?" is "Fairly good," because that is the category with the highest frequency (982) and (valid) percent (65). As another example, consider Figure 11-9, which compares two distributions. Respondents were asked a question of the form "Are we spending too much, too little, or about the right amount on . . . ?" For each item, such as "improving the nation's education system" or "military, armaments, and defense," the respondents could choose "Too much," "Too little," or "About right." Figure 11-9 shows that the modal response for education is "Too little" while the mode for defense is "About right."

Figure 11-9 demonstrates another property of distribution variation. Note that most people (about 70 percent) chose "Too little" when asked about spending on education. Almost no one (6.3 percent) picked "Too much." Compare these results with the answers to the military and defense question. In the latter case the responses are more evenly divided among the three categories. The distributions could be summarized by saying there is greater variation in responses for the defense-related question than for the one about education.

For nominal level data, the greatest dispersion occurs when the observations are distributed equally among the categories. On the other hand, a total lack of dispersion occurs if all the observations fall into one category.

A measure of dispersion for nominal level measures is the proportion of the observed values that are in the modal category. The smaller the number of observations in the modal category, the greater the dispersion.[8]

Descriptive Statistics for Ordinal Level Measures

The same descriptive statistics used to summarize nominal level data may also be used to summarize ordinal level data. Ordinal level data involve categories that are ordered from, say, lowest to highest. But there are other statistics that incorporate the ordering among the levels when summarizing the information in the data.

The **median** is widely used to indicate the central tendency of an ordinal variable. The median (frequently denoted M) is a (not necessarily unique) value that divides a distribution in half; that is, half the observations lie above the median and half below it. With grouped data, it is the category to which the middle observation belongs.[9] As an example, look at Table 11-9, which groups 729 respondents by age. To find the median we need to locate the middle of the distribution. With 729 respondents, the middle observation is 365. Since this respondent falls into the "35–44" category, the median age group is "35–44."

You can find the middle of N observations with the formula

$$mid_{obs} = \frac{N + 1}{2},$$

where mid_{obs} means "middle observation." When N is odd, as in the previous case, the middle observation is easily found. If N is even, then mid_{obs} will contain a .5, which means that you must use the observations above and below mid_{obs}. For example, if $N = 200$, then $mid_{obs} = (200 + 1) / 2 = 100.5$. The median value is the average or mean of the scores for the 100th and 101st observations.

Here is a simple example. Suppose we have six ages: 21, 23, 25, 33, 51, 60. To find the middle observation we calculate

$$mid_{obs} = \frac{6 + 1}{2} = 3.5$$

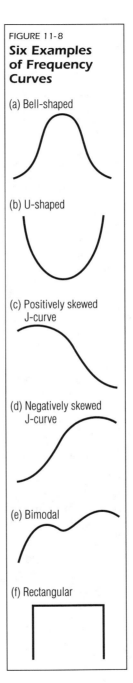

FIGURE 11-8

Six Examples of Frequency Curves

(a) Bell-shaped

(b) U-shaped

(c) Positively skewed J-curve

(d) Negatively skewed J-curve

(e) Bimodal

(f) Rectangular

321

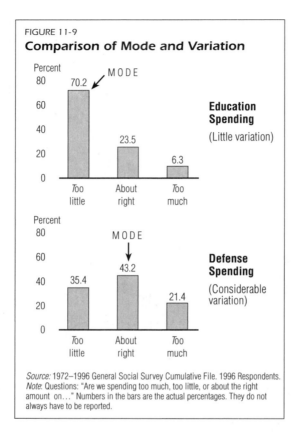

FIGURE 11-9
Comparison of Mode and Variation

Percent

Education Spending
(Little variation)

MODE — 70.2, 23.5, 6.3
(Too little / About right / Too much)

Defense Spending
(Considerable variation)

MODE — 35.4, 43.2, 21.4
(Too little / About right / Too much)

Source: 1972–1996 General Social Survey Cumulative File. 1996 Respondents.
Note: Questions: "Are we spending too much, too little, or about the right amount on..." Numbers in the bars are the actual percentages. They do not always have to be reported.

The median age is then the mean or average of the 3d and 4th observations (subtract and add .5 to find 3 and 4), or

$$M = \frac{25 + 33}{2} = \frac{58}{2} = 29$$

Dispersion for ordinal measures may be indicated by the **range**, the distance between the highest and lowest observations or the range of categories into which observations fall. The range of ages in Table 11-9 is "18–24" to "60 and over." One extreme observation may cause the range to be quite large even when most of the observations are included in only a small range of categories. For this reason, the **interquartile range**, which is not as sensitive to a few observations at the extreme ends of a distribution, is the preferred measure of dispersion. The interquartile range reflects the middle 50 percent of the observations: 25 percent are above, 25 percent are below. To calculate the interquartile range, remove the bottom quarter and the top quarter of the observations. For example, one-quarter of 729 is 182.25; removing 182.25 respondents from the low end of the age scale puts one end of the interquartile range in the "25–34" age group. Removing the same number from the high end puts the other end of the interquartile range in the "45–59" age group. Thus the interquartile range is "25–34" to "45–59."

Notice that the statistics for ordinal level measures are more informative than those for nominal level measures. For ordinal level measures, the central tendency of a frequency distribution may be judged with both the mode and the median; for nominal level measures, only the mode is appropriate. The reason is that nominal variable categories cannot necessarily be arranged from lowest to highest, whereas ordinal data are by definition ranked by magnitude. For ordinal level measures, the dispersion of a

TABLE 11-9
Ordinal Grouping of Age of Respondents

Ages	18–24	25–34	35–44	45–59	60 and over	Total
Number	91	196	128	154	160	729

Note: Hypothetical data.

frequency distribution may be indicated by the range and the interquartile range; for nominal level measures, dispersion can be judged only by the percentage of cases within the modal category.

Descriptive Statistics for Interval and Ratio Level Measures

Interval and ratio level measures can be summarized in ways that take advantage of the mathematical properties of the observed values. Measures of central tendency for interval and ratio level measures are the mode, the median, and the arithmetic mean. The **mean**, called the "average" in normal conversation, is the sum of the values of a variable divided by the number of values. This is represented symbolically as follows:

$$\bar{Y} = \frac{Y_1 + Y_2 + ... + Y_N}{N}$$

$$= \frac{\sum Y_i}{N}$$

In this equation $\bar{Y}$ is the mean and is usually read as "Y bar." (Frequently, the lowercase Greek letter "mu," μ, is used to denote a population mean, as in Chapter 7.) Y_i represents an arbitrary raw score in a set of scores; N is the number of scores, and • is the upper case Greek letter "sigma" and means "sum" or "add" the individual scores.[10] In effect, the equation simply formalizes what we do almost automatically, namely add the scores and divide by their total number.

Although the mean is widely used, it can be a misleading indicator of central tendency if there are extreme observed values in a frequency distribution. For example, the incomes in two hypothetical communities shown in Table 11-10 are identical except for the income of one person. The mean income of Community A is $37,500, of Community B, $20,500. Knowing just the mean income of the communities would give you the erroneous impression that people in Community A are much better off than people in Community B when in reality there is only one person in A who is much better off than anyone in B. In this case the median is a better indicator of central

TABLE 11-10
Hypothetical Incomes in Two Communities

Case Number	Community A	Community B
1	$ 10,000	$10,000
2	10,000	10,000
3	12,000	12,000
4	18,000	18,000
5	20,000	20,000
6	22,000	22,000
7	25,000	25,000
8	28,000	28,000
9	30,000	30,000
10	200,000	30,000
	$\bar{Y} = 37,500$	$\bar{Y} = 20,500$

tendency than the mean. The median income in both communities is the same: $21,000. Since the mean and the median are not close in value when extremely large or negative values are present, it is often safest to compute both.

Indicators of dispersion for interval and ratio level data include the range and interquartile range, discussed earlier, as well as the **mean deviation**, **standard deviation**, and **variance**. For interval and ratio level data, the range and interquartile range are represented by a single number (rather than a range of values as with ordinal data) because of the mathematical properties of the level of measurement. For example, if the highest score on a test was 100 and the lowest was 25, the range of test scores would be 100 − 25, or 75. If 25 percent of the test scores were above 80 and 25 percent were below 60, then the interquartile range would be 80 − 60, or 20. If the range of scores on another test was 90, and the interquartile range was 40, this would indicate a greater dispersion of scores on the second test. Unless the data have a few extremely large or small values, the range and interquartile range are less useful indicators of variability in scores than are the mean deviation, variance, and standard deviation. Consequently, they are used less often as indicators of dispersion with interval and ratio level measures.

The **mean deviation** (MD) is a measure of dispersion that is based on the deviation of each score from the mean. Its calculation is shown in Table 11-11. If we take each score and subtract it from the mean, we calculate the amount each score deviates from the mean (column 2). The sum of these deviations is always zero—an important mathematical property of the mean. (Check this by adding the numbers in column 2 for yourself.) Because we are interested only in the amount of deviation and not the direction or sign of the deviation,

TABLE 11-11

Distribution, Deviation, and Mean Deviation of Incomes in Community B

	Y	$Y - \bar{Y}$	$|Y - \bar{Y}|$
1.	$ 10,000	−$10,500	$10,500
2.	10,000	−10,500	10,500
3.	12,000	−8,500	8,500
4.	18,000	−2,500	2,500
5.	20,000	− 500	500
6.	22,000	1,500	1,500
7.	25,000	4,500	4,500
8.	28,000	7,500	7,500
9.	30,000	9,500	9,500
10.	30,000	9,500	9,500
	$205,000	$ 0	$65,000

$\bar{Y} = 20,500$

$\Sigma (Y - \bar{Y}) = 0$

$\Sigma |Y - \bar{Y}| = 65,000$

$MD = \dfrac{\$65,000}{10} = \$6,500$

$N = 10$

Note: Hypothetical data from Table 11-10.

we can add up the absolute values of the deviations (column 3), which is to say "ignore the minus sign if present." Then we divide this sum by the number of scores to find the mean deviation of scores from the mean. The larger the mean deviation is, the greater is the dispersion of scores around the mean.

The equation for the mean deviation is

$$MD = \frac{\Sigma |Y - \bar{Y}|}{N},$$

where $\|\ \|$ = the symbol for absolute value. In other words, carry out the subtraction and disregard the minus sign if there is one. Even though the mean deviation indicates dispersion, the standard deviation and the variance are used more often than the mean deviation. One reason for this is that the standard deviation and variance appear frequently in more advanced statistics, which we discuss later in this chapter and in Chapters 12 and 13.[11]

The *sample* standard deviation is the square root of the sum of the squared deviations from the mean divided by the number of scores minus 1:

$$\hat{\sigma} = \sqrt{\frac{\sum(Y_i - \bar{Y})^2}{N - 1}}$$

It is called the sample standard deviation and appears with a hat over the lower case Greek letter sigma (σ) because it is calculated on a sample of N observations and is usually thought of as an estimator of the corresponding population standard deviation. If we had a population, we could just use σ without a hat and divide by N instead of $N - 1$.[12] It can be interpreted as an average of squared deviations from the mean.

The (sample) variance, denoted $\hat{\sigma}^2$, is the square of the standard deviation:

$$\hat{\sigma}^2 = \frac{\sum(Y_i - \bar{Y})^2}{N - 1}$$

The greater the dispersion of data points about the mean, the higher the value of the standard deviation and, of course, the variance. If all the data points are the same, both equal zero.

Both the variance and standard deviation can be computed with a simple calculation, provided the number of cases, N, is not inordinately large. First, calculate what is called the "total sum of squares" (TSS):

$$TSS = \sum Y_i^2 - \frac{(\sum Y_i)^2}{N}$$

Note that the first term is the sum of each Y squared. The second is the square of the sum of the Ys. Many calculators have an accumulation key. Enter a Y and press the $\bullet$ + key to start the summation process. Then enter the next value, press the $\bullet$ + key, enter another number, press the $\bullet$ + key, and so on until all of the Y scores have been entered. Then the sum of the Ys squared ($\bullet$ Y^2) and the simple sum of the Ys ($\bullet$ Y) will be stored in the memory from which they can be retrieved to carry out the above calculation for TSS.

Then simply divide TSS by $N - 1$ to obtain the standard deviation. The complete formula is

$$\hat{\sigma} = \sqrt{\frac{\sum Y_i^2 - \frac{(\sum Y_i)^2}{N}}{N - 1}}$$

TABLE 11-12
Sum and Sum of Squares Used in Calculating TSS

Observation Number	Y_i	Y_i^2
1	22	484
2	33	1,089
3	15	225
4	17	289
5	29	841
6	30	900
7	11	121
$N = 7$	$\Sigma Y_i = 157$	$\Sigma Y_i^2 = 3{,}949$

Table 11-12 shows an example of the elements of this calculation. From the table, we can see that the sample standard deviation is

$$\hat{\sigma} = \sqrt{\dfrac{3{,}949 - \dfrac{(157)^2}{7}}{6}} = 8.44$$

The variance of the numbers in Table 11-12 is $(8.443)^2 = 71.29$.

Since the numerical value of the variance or standard deviation often does not have an intuitive meaning, especially since it is not as much a part of common vocabulary as are the mean or average, it is sometimes easier to explain in connection with a frequency distribution. For example, suppose the popularity of President Bush is measured with a public opinion poll and the standard deviation for the responses is 5.0. What does that tell us? It is impossible to say without further information. If presidential popularity was measured with a 10-point scale and the responses had a mean of 6.0, then a standard deviation of 5.0 indicates a great deal of dispersion or scatter in the individual answers. If, however, popularity was measured with a 100-point scale and the mean response was 65.0, then a standard deviation of 5.0 would indicate that most people's answers were similar or bunched together.

The standard deviation is an important statistic, especially in conjunction with a particular frequency distribution called a normal or bell-shaped distribution, which we discuss in the next section.

The Normal Distribution

The graph of a **normal distribution** is a symmetrical, bell-shaped curve with two interesting properties. First, the mean, the mode, and the median all

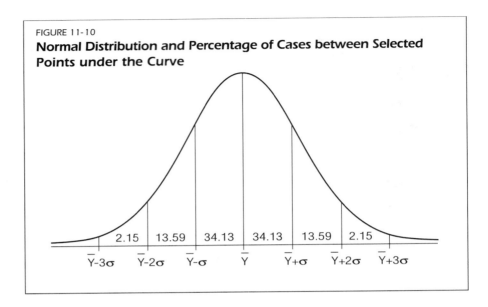

FIGURE 11-10

Normal Distribution and Percentage of Cases between Selected Points under the Curve

coincide at the peak of the curve. Second, a fixed proportion of observations or cases lies between the mean and any distance from the mean measured in terms of the standard deviation. For all normal distributions the areas between the mean and various distances above and below it are known and have been tabulated. (Appendix E contains such a table.) Figure 11-10 illustrates this information for selected distances. Consider the total area under a normal distribution to be 100 percent. Inasmuch as the curve is symmetric, and the mean divides it in half, we see that 50 percent of the area is above the mean and 50 percent is below the mean. (You can verify this by adding the segments in Figure 11-10.)

Tables of the normal curve also show, for example, that 34.13 percent of the total area lies between the mean and one standard deviation *above* the mean. And because of the symmetry, 34.13 percent of the area falls between the mean and one standard deviation *below* the mean. The area between these two points—the mean minus one standard deviation and the mean plus one standard deviation—is thus 68.26 percent of the total area. If you look at the figure and add the areas, you will find that 95.44 percent of the area lies between the mean and plus or minus *two* standard deviations. It is not necessary to use only even multiples of the standard deviation. For example, exactly 95 percent of the area lies between the mean minus 1.96 standard deviations *and* the mean plus 1.96 standard deviations. Also, 99 percent lies within plus or minus 2.58 standard deviations of the mean.

Here is a simple example. Suppose an investigator constructs a numerical ideology variable that is normally distributed with a mean score of 50 and a standard deviation of 5. Knowing these facts we can describe the distribution of ideology for the population from which the variable has been measured.

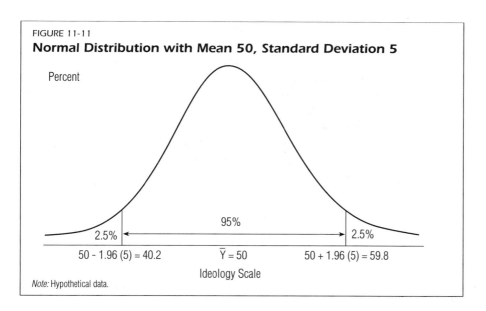

FIGURE 11-11

Normal Distribution with Mean 50, Standard Deviation 5

Percent

95%

2.5%

2.5%

50 - 1.96 (5) = 40.2 $\bar{Y}$ = 50   50 + 1.96 (5) = 59.8

Ideology Scale

Note: Hypothetical data.

We know, for instance, that 50 percent of the people have ideology scores above 50 and 50 percent have ideology scores below 50. Moreover, about 95 percent of the population lies between $50 - 1.96(5) = 40.2$ and $50 + 1.96(5) = 59.8$. Since the total area under the normal curve is 100 percent, we also know that roughly 5 percent have scores below 40.2 *or* above 59.8. Thus, someone with a value of 85 would be "extreme" compared to most population members. Figure 11-11 makes these points clear.

Because the total area can be considered 100 percent, we can also find areas above and below certain points. For example, if 34.13 percent of the area lies between the mean and one standard deviation above the mean, then $50.0 - 34.13 = 15.87$ percent of the area lies above the mean plus one standard deviation. Or, as another example, since 99 percent of the area falls between plus and minus two standard deviations of the mean, then a total of 1 percent lies beyond those points. To find these areas just draw a rough sketch of a normal distribution, mark the middle, call the total area 100, and mark off areas above and below the mean.

Note also that if we had a very large sample, many thousands for example, the previous remarks about areas could be translated into statements about the proportion of cases. For example, if a variable in a large data set has a normal distribution, we would expect to find that about 34.13 percent of the cases or observations would have scores between the mean and plus one standard deviation of the mean. As we will see below, it is also possible to interpret areas under a normal distribution as probabilities, with the total area considered 1.0.

Finally, since all normal distributions have these properties, we can use a "standard" version—called the **standard normal distribution**—to find areas between any two points by converting them to standard scores and using the standard normal distribution. A standard normal distribution has a mean of zero and a standard deviation of 1.0. This distribution is known as a z distribution. The number of standard deviations by which a score deviates from the mean score is known as the **z score**.

Suppose the mean and standard deviation of a distribution are 200 and 30, respectively. If we want to know how much area (or how many cases) fall above the value or score of 230, we could convert 230 to a z score and use a tabulated standard normal distribution to find the answer. The formula is

$$z = \frac{(Y - \bar{Y})}{\hat{\sigma}}.$$

In this case the z that corresponds to 230 is

$$z = \frac{(230 - 200)}{30} = 1.0.$$

We could then use Appendix E to figure out what proportion of the area (or percentage of cases or probability) lies above 1.0, and thus determine the corresponding proportion for the observed data. The table in Appendix E gives the proportion of the area between the midpoint of the distribution and the z score. In order to determine the proportion of cases *above* the z score, you will need to subtract the proportion you read in the table from .5 (.5 – .3413 = .1587).

Similarly, for the same case we could determine the probability or expected proportion of cases that would fall below 190 by looking up z = (190 – 200)/100 = –.10. (To do so, drop the minus sign and look for .1 because the normal distribution is symmetric, so the area above .1 will be the same as the area below –.1.) The proportion of cases falling below 190 is .4602 (.5 – .0398).

FINDING PROBABILITIES

If you are asked to find the probability that a person has a certain score or the proportion of people who fall above (or below) some value, try to convert the information to z scores by using the formula in the text. It is also helpful to draw a sketch of a normal curve and label its axis as "z" and mark the center with a zero. Then go up and down the scale as needed to mark off areas under the curve. The results can be interpreted as probabilities or proportions or percentages.

The Normal Distribution and Statistical Inference

Recall an important point from Chapter 7: we can take a large number of random samples from a population, calculate a statistic of interest each time, and examine the distribution of these sample statistics. The result is called a *sampling distribution*.

Consider what happens when the sample statistic is the mean, $\bar{Y}$. When we draw repeated samples from a population with a mean of μ and a standard deviation of σ and calculate the sample mean, $\bar{Y}$, for each one, the distribution of these sample means, called the sampling distribution of the mean, turns out to be normal with a mean of μ and a standard

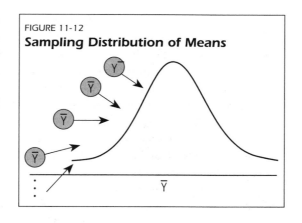

FIGURE 11-12
Sampling Distribution of Means

deviation of $\sigma_{\bar{Y}} = \sigma/\sqrt{N}$, where N is the size of the samples. In other words, most of the sample means will cluster around μ. Of course, because the individual $\bar{Y}$s are estimates most will not exactly equal the population mean but be spread around it. The variation of these estimates is given by $\sigma_{\bar{Y}}$, the standard deviation of the sampling distribution (see Figure 11-12). $\sigma_{\bar{Y}}$ is often called the standard error of the mean, or just **standard error** (S.E.). The standard error is simply a standard deviation applied to a sampling distribution. This knowledge allows us to estimate with a certain level of confidence the mean of the population based on just one sample. (For a discussion of confidence levels and margins of error, see Chapter 7.)

To estimate the mean of the population from a sample and make probability statements about it, we need to calculate the standard error of mean. For a sample of size N, this (estimated) standard error is just

$$\hat{\sigma}_{\bar{Y}} = \frac{\hat{\sigma}}{\sqrt{N}}.$$

For example, we can estimate the mean amount of financial aid received by students at a large university by taking a sample of those students. In a survey of $N = 100$ college students, let's say the mean amount of financial aid ($\bar{Y}$) is $750 and the standard deviation ($\hat{\sigma}$) is $50. What does this tell us about the mean amount of financial aid received by all students in the college? How certain are we that our sample estimate of the mean is accurate? Luckily we know that when our sample size is large, we may use the sample standard deviation ($\hat{\sigma}$) to find the standard error:

$$\hat{\sigma}_{\bar{Y}} = \frac{50}{\sqrt{100}} = 5.0.$$

Because the sampling distribution of the mean is normal, about 68 percent of the sample estimates will lie between the mean and plus or minus one standard error. (Remember that the standard error is a standard deviation, which is why we can substitute standard error for standard deviation when using a standard normal distribution.) Therefore, we can say that we are 68 percent confident that the true population mean, or average financial aid award, is $750 ± $5, or between $745 and $755. By the same token, we are about 95 percent certain that the true average financial aid award in the university population is between $740 and $760 (750 ± 2 S.E.).

To emphasize this important aspect of probability sampling, we will explain the process slightly differently. Three different distributions are involved: the distribution of a variable in a population, the distribution of the same variable in a single sample taken from the population, and the sampling distribution of a sample statistic based on that variable—that is, in the present case, the distribution of sample means.

For each distribution a standard deviation can be calculated. For the population it is σ, and normally its numerical value is unknown. For the sample it is $\hat{\sigma}$, and its value can be calculated from the N observations. And for the sampling distribution we can calculate the (estimated) standard deviation of the sample means, $\hat{\sigma}_{\bar{Y}}$.

Since the sampling distribution is normal, we can calculate the probability of obtaining a single sample mean that lies between the mean of all sample means and any number of standard errors from it. We know the value of N (the size of the sample), the sample mean, and standard deviation. And we know the properties of the normal distribution. Finally, we know from statistical theory that the sampling distribution of the means is normal with a mean μ and a standard deviation of σ. Because a probability sample can be linked to the normal distribution in this way, the characteristics of the normal distribution can be used to estimate the accuracy of a probability sample.

We can also use this information to calculate the sample size necessary to achieve a desired level of precision with a sample statistic. Suppose, for example, that we want to measure presidential popularity with a random sample. If we calculate the standard deviation of the measure in the sample, we can also calculate the sample size required for a given standard error by converting

$$\frac{\sigma}{Y} = \frac{\sigma}{\sqrt{N}}$$

to

$$N = \frac{\sigma^2}{\sigma^2_{\bar{Y}}}$$

TABLE 11-13

Standard Errors and 95 Percent Confidence Intervals for Different Sample Sizes

N	$\hat{\sigma}_{\bar{Y}}$	$(1.96)(\hat{\sigma}_{\bar{Y}})$	Intervals
36	5	9.80	55.2 – 74.8
56	4	7.84	57.2 – 72.8
100	3	5.88	59.1 – 70.9
225	2	3.92	61.1 – 68.9
900	1	1.96	63.0 – 67.0

Note: Calculations assume $\hat{\sigma} = 30$ and $\bar{Y} = 65.0$.

For example, if we measure presidential popularity with a 100 point feeling thermometer scale, with a sample mean of 65 and a standard deviation of 30, and the desired standard error is 3, then the sample size will have to be 100:

$$N = \frac{30^2}{3^2} = \frac{900}{9} = 100.$$

In short, if the sample size is $N = 100$, there is a 95 percent certainty that the population mean of presidential popularity will be within ± 1.96 (S.E.) of the sample mean, or 65 ± 5.88. If that estimate is not precise enough, or if the researcher does not have enough money to interview 100 respondents, then the sample size can be adjusted.

Table 11-13 illustrates these points. Suppose a numerical variable has a mean of $\bar{Y} = 65$ and a standard error of 30. We can use this information to calculate sampling errors of the mean ($\hat{\sigma}_{\bar{Y}}$) for different size samples and then find intervals that we are 95 percent certain include the true mean, μ. As an example, if $N = 36$, then $\hat{\sigma}_{\bar{Y}} = 30/\sqrt{36} = 5$, and the intervals are 65 ± (1.96) (5), or 55.2 to 74.8. We also see from the table that as N increases the standard errors decrease and the corresponding intervals narrow.

Finally, if we guessed ahead of time the size of the sample mean and standard deviation, we could use the formula presented above to find the number of cases (N) needed to obtain any given sized standard error.[13]

Conclusion

In this chapter we have discussed the presentation and analysis of the observed values of a single variable. A frequency distribution presents the number of observations on each value of a variable, and a variety of techniques—such as bar charts, pie diagrams, and frequency curves—are used to graphically display this information. Such graphic displays should be designed carefully to ensure that they clearly and accurately summarize the data in a frequency distribution.

Descriptive statistics are also used to summarize the observed values of a variable. Univariate descriptive statistics indicate the central tendency and the dispersion of data values for a single variable. A single number or a few numbers communicate these important characteristics and thus make the task of describing large amounts of data more manageable. Different univariate statistics are appropriate for use with nominal, ordinal, and interval or ratio level data.

Of the statistics that we discussed, the mean and the standard deviation are among the most important because they provide a foundation for more complex statistical analyses and for exploring relationships between variables. In Chapters 12 and 13 we will discuss statistical analyses that allow researchers to test for relationships between two or more variables.

Notes

1. Jeffrey A. Segal and Albert D. Cover, "Ideological Values and the Votes of U.S. Supreme Court Justices," *American Political Science Review* 83 (June 1989): 557–565.

2. Edward N. Muller, Mitchell A. Seligson, and Hung-der Fu, "Land Inequality and Political Violence," *American Political Science Review* 83 (June 1989): 577–586.

3. See Exercise 11-1.

4. Benjamin I. Page and Robert Y. Shapiro, "Effects of Public Opinion on Policy," *American Political Science Review* 77 (March 1983): 175–190.

5. SPSS, which stands for *Statistical Package for the Social Sciences,* is the trademark of a company that has developed computer software to perform data analysis. It is one of several software packages used by social scientists.

6. Henry Bienen and Nicolas van de Walle, "Time and Power in Africa," *American Political Science Review* 83 (March 1989): 19–34.

7. Edward R. Tufte, *The Visual Display of Quantitative Information* (Cheshire, Conn.: Graphics, 1983).

8. There are actually quite a few measures of variation for categorical data, many of which are used in the analysis of inequality. For a clear discussion, see Philip B. Coulter, *Measuring Inequality* (Boulder: Westview, 1989).

9. Kirk W. Elifson, Richard P. Runyon, and Audrey Haber, *Fundamentals of Social Statistics* (Reading, Mass.: Addison-Wesley, 1982), 100.

10. Ibid., 95.

11. Ibid., 118.

12. Some books show the variance calculated with an N in the denominator instead of $N - 1$. It really does not matter which is used if the data set is large, say, more than 50. (Why?) But to be precise, we use $N - 1$ since it provides an unbiased estimator of the population standard deviation.

13. As noted in Chapter 7, decisions about sample size also depend on cost, the kind of sample, and the way in which the data will be analyzed. Furthermore, sample sizes have to be acceptable for many different variables with different means and standard deviations, not just for one variable.

Terms introduced

BAR CHART. A graphic display of the data in a frequency or percentage distribution.

CENTRAL TENDENCY. The most frequent, middle, or central value in a frequency distribution.

CUMULATIVE PROPORTION. The total proportion of observations at or below a value in a frequency distribution.

DESCRIPTIVE STATISTIC. The mathematical summary of measurements for one variable.

DICHOTOMOUS VARIABLE. A variable with only two categories or values.

DISPERSION. The distribution of data values around the most frequent, middle, or central value.

ENUMERATIVE TABLE. A table listing the observed values of a variable.

FREQUENCY CURVE. A line graph summarizing a frequency distribution.

FREQUENCY DISTRIBUTION (f). The number of observations per value or category of a variable.

INTERQUARTILE RANGE. The middle 50 percent of observations.

LINE DIAGRAM. Another name for a frequency curve.

MEAN. The sum of the values of a variable divided by the number of values.

MEAN DEVIATION. A measure of dispersion of data points for interval and ratio level data.

MEDIAN. The category or value above and below which one-half of observations lie.

MODE. The category with the greatest frequency of observations.

NEGATIVELY SKEWED. A distribution of values in which fewer observations lie to the left of the middle value and those observations are fairly distant from the mean.

NORMAL DISTRIBUTION. A frequency curve showing a symmetrical, bell-shaped distribution in which the mean, mode, and median coincide and in which a fixed proportion of observations lies between the mean and any distance from the mean measured in terms of the standard deviation.

PIE DIAGRAM. A circular graphic display of a frequency distribution.

POSITIVELY SKEWED. A distribution of values in which fewer observations lie to the right of the middle value and those observations are fairly distant from the mean.

RANGE. The distance between the highest and lowest values or the range of categories into which observations fall.

RELATIVE FREQUENCY. Percent or proportion of total number of observations in a frequency distribution that have a particular value.

STANDARD DEVIATION. A measure of dispersion of data points about the mean for interval and ratio level data.

STANDARD ERROR. The standard deviation of sample means about the mean of sample means.

STANDARD NORMAL DISTRIBUTION. Normal distribution with a mean of zero and a standard deviation and variance of one.

UNIVARIATE DATA ANALYSIS. The analysis of a single variable.

VARIANCE. A measure of dispersion of data points about the mean for interval and ratio level data.

Z SCORE. The number of standard deviations by which a score deviates from the mean score.

Exercises

1. Here is a relative frequency distribution. Given the information you should be able to calculate the raw frequencies.

Marital Status	Frequency (f)	Relative Frequency
Married		52.2
Widowed		10.0
Divorced		14.7
Separated		3.2
Never married		19.9
Totals	4,598	100.0

Source: General Social Survey. Respondents are drawn from the 1993 and 1994 panels.

2. Suppose you have surveyed 1,000 people about their attitudes toward Eastern Europe. Three hundred and fifty people think that the United States should offer unilateral economic aid to the countries of Eastern Europe, 200 people think any increased aid should be part of an international aid package overseen by the United Nations, 375 people think that the United States should not offer any aid until it is certain that democratic governments have been established in Eastern Europe, and 75 people are not sure what the United States should do. Design a table showing the frequency distribution and percentage distribution of these responses. Then recalculate the percentage distribution of the responses excluding those who said "don't know" and add that information to the table. Then compute the cumulative percentages. What level of measurement does this table represent?

3. Draw a line diagram and describe the shape of the curve for the following data points: 1, 1, 2, 5, 1, 1, 6, 1, 2, 3, 1, 0, 1, 0, 1, 4, 1, 6, 1, 5.

4. Find the mean, mode, median, range, and interquartile range for the data points in exercise 3. Locate these on the line diagram. Is the mean to the left or the right of the median?

5. Calculate the mean and standard deviation for the data in exercise 3. Calculate the z score for the data point of 5. What does this tell you about the score of 5 with respect to the mean?

6. In a normally distributed population of scores with a mean of 80 and standard deviation of 5, what percentage of the scores are between 70 and 90? If a score is .5 standard deviations above the mean, what is this score?

7. Calculate the *valid* relative and cumulative frequencies for the following distribution of responses to the statement "Mothers should remain at home with young children and not work."

Agree strongly	247
Agree somewhat	386
Neither agree nor disagree	293
Disagree somewhat	277
Disagree strongly	297

Source: 1996 American Election Study.

8. In the table below are responses by whites and blacks to a statement in the 1996 American National Election Study about equality. The statement is "One of the big problems in this country is that we don't give everyone an equal chance."

	White	Black
Agree strongly	181	91
Agree somewhat	390	60
Neither agree nor disagree	224	9
Disagree somewhat	331	13
Disagree strongly	145	6

Use a computer program such as SPSS or Excel to draw two side-by-side bar or pie charts that show the distribution of responses by race. How do the distributions differ? Is there evidence of a "racial divide" on perceptions of equality in the United States?

9. Use the Survey Documentation and Analysis site at the University of California (http://css.berkeley.edu) to locate data from the 1996 American National Election Study or the 1972–1996 General Social Survey Cumulative File. Select interesting questions and variables and obtain frequency distributions. Use these data to construct relative frequency distributions and then graph them in bar or pie charts.

Suggested Readings

Blalock, Hubert M., Jr. *Social Statistics*. Rev. 2d ed. New York: McGraw-Hill, 1979.

Elifson, Kirk W., Richard P. Runyon, and Audrey Haber. *Fundamentals of Social Statistics*. Reading, Mass.: Addison-Wesley, 1982.

Tufte, Edward R. *The Visual Display of Quantitative Information*. Cheshire, Conn.: Graphics, 1983.

CHAPTER 12

Measuring Relationships and Testing Hypotheses:
Bivariate Data Analysis

In this chapter and the next we will discuss how to investigate statistically the hypotheses we advanced using the data we have collected. In testing hypotheses five general questions must be addressed: Is there a relationship between the independent and dependent variables in the hypothesis? What is the direction or shape of the relationship? How strong is the relationship? Is the relationship statistically significant? Is the relationship a causal one? Each of these questions will be considered in turn.

Generally speaking, a statistical **relationship** between two variables exists if the values of the observations for one variable are associated with or connected to the values of the other. For example, if as people get older they vote more frequently, then the values of the dependent variable (voting or not voting) are associated with values for the independent variable (age). Therefore, the observed values for the two variables are related. Knowing that two variables are related lets us make predictions because if we know the value of one variable, we can predict (subject to error) the value in the other.

Once it is established that there is a relationship between the independent and dependent variables, the nature of that association becomes important. The direction or shape of a relationship tells the researcher which values of the independent variable are associated with which values of the dependent variable, rather than simply whether the two are related. For example, if the rate at which people vote changes as their age changes, there is a relationship between age and turnout. However, the direction of the relationship tells us which values of the independent variable (age) are associated with which values of the dependent variable (turnout). A graph of the relationship may also tell us whether the relationship is linear (that is, can be roughly described by a straight line) or is non-linear. To conclude that "the younger you are, the more likely you are to vote" is quite different from concluding that "the older you are, the more likely you are to vote." In both cases there is a relationship between the two variables, but the nature of the relationship is different.

The **strength of a relationship** indicates how consistently the values of a dependent variable are associated with the values of an independent variable. A relationship is strong if most of the observed values for the independent variable are connected with values for the dependent variable. If, on the other hand, only a few of the observed values show this connection, then we refer to the relationship as "moderate" or "weak." The notion of strength, therefore, depends upon how many of the observed values of the dependent variable may be understood, accounted for, or explained with values of the independent variable. Alternatively, prediction errors are relatively small and/or few with a strong relationship whereas errors can dominate weak association.

There is always a possibility, when utilizing sample data, that the observed relationship is due only to chance and is an inaccurate indication of what we would have observed in the entire population. We test that possibility by measuring the relationship's **statistical significance**. Testing the significance of a sample result involves proposing a statistical hypothesis that states that a certain condition exists in the population—we call this the **null hypothesis**—and measuring the probability that our observed data would show the pattern they do in fact show *if our hypothesis is true*. Sometimes the sample results are so inconsistent with the hypothesis that we reject it in favor of another one. In the case of two variable relationships, hypothesis testing consists of imagining what sample data would look like if there were no relationship between the variables in a population (the null hypothesis) and then measuring the difference between those "predicted" results and the actual results in the sample. From this comparison of expected and actual results we calculate the probability that we could have observed the results we did even if there were no relationship in the population between the two variables. If the relationship observed in the sample is too weak for us to be confident that there is a relationship in the population, then we conclude that the null hypothesis cannot be rejected and we discount the importance of any relationship we observe in the sample.

That a relationship exists between independent and dependent variables does not necessarily mean that the independent variable is a cause of the dependent variable. There are a number of other possible reasons for the existence of such a relationship. For example, there is a relationship between the league of the baseball team that wins the World Series in presidential election years and the political party that wins the U.S. presidency: when National League teams win, a Democratic presidential candidate tends to win. No one seriously thinks, however, that one causes the other. The observation of a relationship, then, is really only the beginning of the search for causal knowledge, a search that is generally long and difficult. In this chapter we will show you how to answer the first four questions regarding hypotheses posed above. Observing the existence, direction, strength, and statistical significance of a relationship is a fairly objective process in which there are well-established analytical techniques and sensible conventions for evaluating evidence. Reaching conclusions about causal relationships, however, is more subjective and problematic and will be discussed in Chapter 13.

The procedure for measuring relationships and testing hypotheses depends upon the level of measurement of the independent and dependent variables. When the independent and dependent variables are both nominal or ordinal level measures, contingency table analysis (also called crosstabulation) is generally used. When one of the variables is nominal or ordinal and the other is interval or ratio, the difference of means test or analysis of variance is the preferred technique. And when both variables are interval or ratio level measures, regression analysis is often used.[1]

Crosstabulation

A **crosstabulation** (or crosstab) displays the joint distribution of values of the variables in a simple table by listing the categories for one of the variables along one side of the table and the levels for the other variable across the top. Each case is then placed in the cell of the table that represents the combination of values that corresponds to its scores on the variables.

Suppose, for example, a researcher is interested in testing the hypothesis that blondes are more likely than brunettes to vote Republican. Data are collected that measure the hair color and vote choice of a sample of voters. The first ten cases in this sample look like this:

Case Number	Hair Color	Vote
1	Blonde	Republican
2	Blonde	Democrat
3	Blonde	Republican
4	Brunette	Democrat
5	Brunette	Republican
6	Blonde	Republican
7	Brunette	Democrat
8	Brunette	Democrat
9	Brunette	Democrat
10	?	Republican

We can construct a table showing each case's value for both variables by putting the independent variable across the top and the dependent variable down the side. (This is the conventional format, but the independent variable could instead be located down the side.) In section a of Table 12-1, the cases have been placed in the appropriate box or cell in the crosstabulation.

TABLE 12-1
Relationship between Hair Color and Vote: A Simple Crosstabulation

Dependent Variable:	Independent Variable: Hair Color		
Vote	Blonde	Brunette	Total
a. Case numbers			
Republican	1, 3, 6	5	
Democrat	2	4, 7, 8, 9	
b. Number of cases			
Republican	3	1	4
Democrat	1	4	5
Total	4	5	9

Note: Hypothetical data. Case number 10 is not included because hair color is unknown.

What is important in testing the hypothesis is not which cases have particular values for the independent and dependent variables, but how many cases have each *combination* of values. The number of observations in each cell is shown in section b of Table 12-1.

How do these data help us measure a relationship and test the hypothesis? The hypothesis with which we began was that blondes vote differently from brunettes. We have separated blondes from brunettes so that we can compare their voting behavior. Our expectation is that blondes will be more likely to vote Republican than brunettes. Of the four blondes in the table, three or 75 percent voted Republican. Of the five brunettes in the table, one or 20 percent voted Republican. Therefore, a greater proportion of blondes voted Republican (75 percent) than did brunettes (20 percent), indicating that blondes and brunettes did vote differently. Therefore, the value of the independent variable matters (whether blonde or brunette) and knowing a person's hair color would help us account for that person's presidential vote.

A contingency table almost always contains many more than nine cases and often contains more than four cells. No matter what the number of cases and categories, however, the procedure remains the same: (1) separate the cases into groups based on their values for the independent variable, (2) compare the values of the dependent variable for those groups, and (3) decide whether the values for the dependent variable are different for the different groups.

Now let us take a slightly more complicated crosstabulation and see how we would use it to assess the existence, direction, and strength of the relationship between hair color and party voting. Consider Table 12-2.

The first question we need to answer is whether a relationship between hair color and presidential vote does, in fact, exist. In other words, do the votes of blondes differ from the votes of brunettes? To answer that question,

TABLE 12-2

Relationship between Hair Color and Vote: A More Complex Crosstabulation

Dependent Variable: Vote	Independent Variable: Hair Color		
	Blonde	Brunette	Total
a.			
Republican	300	400	700
Democrat	200	600	800
Total	500	1,000	1,500
b.			
Republican	60%	40%	47%
Democrat	40	60	53
Total	100	100	100

Note: Hypothetical data.

we need to calculate the percentage of people in each column who voted a particular way because each column contains people with the same hair color. Of the 500 blondes, 300 or 60 percent voted Republican; 200 or 40 percent voted Democratic. Of the 1,000 brunettes, 400 or 40 percent voted Republican; 600 or 60 percent voted Democratic. The column percentages in section b of Table 12-2 show at a glance that blondes do vote Republican more often than brunettes. Not all blondes vote Republican and not all brunettes vote Democratic, but the two groups defined by their values on the independent variable do differ. Consequently, we can conclude that there is a relationship—in this sample—between hair color and party vote.

Table 12-3 is a crosstab that shows no relationship between the independent and dependent variables. The cases in both categories of the independent variable behaved the same on the dependent variable. And the percentage of cases with a particular value of the dependent variable is the same

TABLE 12-3

A Crosstabulation Showing No Relationship between Hair Color and Vote: Column Percentages

Dependent Variable: Vote	Independent Variable: Hair Color			
	Blonde	Brunette	Total	(N)
Republican	47%	47%	47%	(700)
Democrat	53	53	53	(800)
Total	100	100	100	
(N)	(500)	(1,000)		(1,500)

Note: Hypothetical data.

TABLE 12-4

A Crosstabulation Showing No Relationship between Hair Color and Vote: Row Percentages

Independent Variable: Hair Color	Dependent Variable: Vote			
	Republican	Democrat	Total	(N)
Blonde	47%	53%	100%	(500)
Brunette	47%	53%	100%	(1,000)
Total	47%	53%	100%	
(N)	(700)	(800)		(1,500)

Note: Hypothetical data.

for both categories of the independent variable: an equal proportion of blondes and brunettes voted Republican. Consequently, the hypothesis that hair color affects voting behavior would not be supported by this evidence.

As we mentioned earlier, the categories of the independent variable may be either the rows or columns in a crosstab. The convention is to place the independent variable across the top of a crosstab, thereby creating the categories of the independent variable in the columns of the table. However, to fit a crosstabulation on one page, it sometimes will be constructed so that the variable with the most categories runs down the side of the table. It really does not matter whether a table is constructed with the independent variable across the top or down the side. Either way, the percentages in the table must be calculated for the values of the independent variable in order to test the existence of a relationship.

Table 12-4, for example, presents exactly the same information as Table 12-3, except that the independent variable runs down the side of the table rather than across the top. Therefore, the row rather than the column percentages indicate the lack of a relationship between hair color and vote. We prefer to use categories of the independent variable as column heads or labels, but others use them to label rows. The choice does not matter as long as the percentages are computed and interpreted correctly.

When constructing contingency tables make sure percentages add to 100 in each category of the *independent* variable. To avoid making mistakes, ask how many cases are in the first category of the independent variable. Then ask how many of the total are in *each* category of the dependent variable. When these numbers are converted to percentages they should add to 100. Move to the next category of independent variable and repeat the process. Continue in this fashion across all of the categories in the independent variable.

After determining whether a relationship exists between the independent and dependent variables, a researcher should investigate its "direction." The **direction of a relationship** shows which values of the independent variable

TABLE 12-5

Negative and Positive Relationships between Party Identification and Attitude toward Military Spending

Dependent Variable: Attitude toward Military Spending	Independent Variable: Party Identification				
	Democrats	Independents	Republicans	Total	(N)
a.					
Increase	20%	40%	60%	40%	(240)
Remain same	50	40	30	40	(240)
Decrease	30	20	10	20	(120)
Total	100	100	100	100	
(N)	(200)	(200)	(200)		(600)
b.					
Increase	60%	40%	20%	40%	(240)
Remain same	30	40	50	40	(240)
Decrease	10	20	30	20	(120)
Total	100	100	100	100	
(N)	(200)	(200)	(200)		(600)

Note: Hypothetical data.

are associated with which values of the dependent variable. The direction of the relationship presented in Tables 12-1 and 12-2 is that blondes, not brunettes, are more likely to vote Republican. Had we gotten different results, the direction of the relationship between hair color and party vote might have been different, with brunettes being more likely to vote Republican.

Table 12-5 displays hypothetical relationships between party identification and attitudes toward military spending. In section a of Table 12-5, the Republicans are more likely to favor increased military spending; in section b of Table 12-5, the Democrats are more likely to favor increased military spending. In both cases there is a relationship between the two variables, but the direction of the relationship differs. Since the direction of the relationship yields important information for understanding the association between the two variables, its assessment is often a crucial part of testing a hypothesis.

When low values of one variable are associated with low values of another *and* high values of the first are associated with high values of the second, a **positive relationship** exists. For example, "the more education one has, the higher one's political interest." When low values of one variable are associated with high values of another *and* high values of the first are associated with low values of the second, a **negative relationship** exists between the two variables, as in "the higher one's income, the less liberal one is." These relationships are depicted graphically in Figure 12-1. Of course, this type of statement is possible only when the variables are measured at the ordinal level or higher. Since the values of nominal level measures do not represent more or less of anything, we cannot talk about positive or negative relationships involving nominal level measures.

Most computer programs print crosstabulations with low values to the left and top of the table and high values to the right and bottom. Therefore, if the top left and bottom right corners are filled with more observations a positive relationship is indicated (as was the case in section b of Table 12-5, since 60 percent and 30 percent are higher than 20 percent and 10 percent). But if the top right and lower left corners of a table are filled with more observations, a negative relationship is generally indicated, as was the case in section a of Table 12-5. The direction of the relationship does not tell us how significant or important the relationship is, but it does tell us the nature of the relationship and it helps us test a hypothesis in which the direction has been proposed.

The *meaning* of a positive or negative relationship, however, cannot be determined without referring to how a crosstab is constructed. The meaning of the relationship in Table 12-6 is identical to the meaning of the relationship in section b of Table 12-5. The only difference is in how the values of the independent variable are displayed. Therefore, a crosstab must be inspected before the meaning of the direction of the relationship can be established.

As we noted above, the strength of a relationship refers to how different the observed values of the dependent variable are in the categories of the independent variable. If blondes are voting much differently from brunettes, then we can say that there is a strong relationship between the two variables. If they are voting only a little bit differently, a weak relationship exists.

The strongest relationship possible between two variables is one in which the value of the dependent variable for every case in one category of the independent variable differs from that of every case in another category of the independent

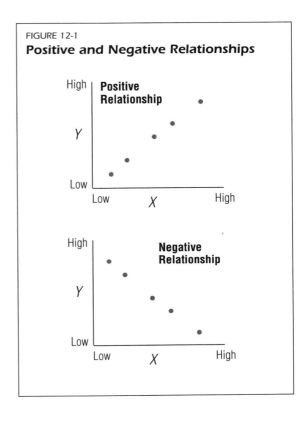

FIGURE 12-1
Positive and Negative Relationships

EXPLAIN AS MUCH AS POSSIBLE
Students frequently say one variable is related to another but do not say *how*. It is important to describe to your reader or audience generally what values of a variable are related to or connected to another variable. Simply saying age and turnout are related is not enough. Explain that older people tend to vote more regularly than younger people up to a certain age, at which point an older individual may be too infirm or immobile to get out to vote.

TABLE 12-6

Relationship between Party Identification and Attitude toward Military Spending: Different Table Construction

Dependent Variable: Attitude toward Military Spending	Independent Variable: Party Identification				
	Republicans	Independents	Democrats	Total	(N)
a.					
Increase	20%	40%	60%	40%	(240)
Remain same	50	40	30	40	(240)
Decrease	30	20	10	20	(120)
Total	100	100	100	100	
(N)	(200)	(200)	(200)		(600)

Note: Hypothetical data.

variable. We call such a relationship a *perfect relationship* because the dependent variable is perfectly associated with the independent variable; that is, there are no exceptions to the pattern. A perfect relationship between the independent and dependent variables enables a researcher to predict accurately a case's value on the dependent variable if the value on the independent variable is known. A perfect relationship for the hair color–vote example is illustrated in Table 12-7. Either a perfect positive or a perfect negative relationship between variables may exist since the direction and the strength of a relationship are two different properties.

A weak relationship would be one in which the differences in the observed values of the dependent variable for different categories of the independent variable are slight. In fact, the weakest relationship is one in which the distribution is identical for all categories of the independent variable—in other words, one in which a relationship does not exist. Table 12-3 is an example.

In reality, the strength of most relationships falls somewhere in between perfect and nonexistent. How strong a relationship is may be judged from how much the column percentages in a crosstab differ as one looks across

TABLE 12-7

Perfect Relationship between Hair Color and Vote

Dependent Variable: Vote	Independent Variable: Hair Color			
	Blonde	Brunette	Total	(N)
Republican	100%	0%	33%	(500)
Democrat	0	100	67	(1,000)
Total	100	100	100	
(N)	(500)	(1,000)		(1,500)

Note: Hypothetical data.

TABLE 12-8
A Strong but Imperfect Relationship between Hair Color and Vote

Dependent Variable:	Independent Variable: Hair Color			
Vote	Blonde	Brunette	Total	(N)
Republican	80%	10%	33%	(500)
Democrat	20	90	67	(1,000)
Total	100	100	100	
(N)	(500)	(1,000)		(1,500)

Note: Hypothetical data.

the rows (when the independent variable has been placed across the top of the table and column percentages have been calculated). In section b of Table 12-2, for example, there is a 20 percent difference in the column percentages across the rows. In Table 12-8, however, there is a 70 percent difference in the column percentages. The relationship in Table 12-8, then, is much stronger than the one in section b of Table 12-2 since the difference more closely approximates the 100 percent difference in the perfect relationship shown in Table 12-7. Essentially, the larger the differences across the rows, the stronger the relationship.

Statistical Independence

At this point it is useful to introduce a technical term that plays a large role in data analysis and that provides another way to view the strength of a relationship. Suppose we have two nominal or categorical variables, X and Y. For the sake of convenience we can label the categories of the first $a, b, c, \ldots$ and those of the second $r, s, t, \ldots$ We can then say that $X(a)$ means the ath category of X and $Y(r)$ means the rth category of Y. Let $P(X = a)$ stand for the probability that a randomly selected case has property a on variable X and $P(Y = r)$ stand for the probability that a randomly selected case has property r on Y. These two probabilities are called marginal probabilities and refer simply to the chance that an observation has a particular value (a for instance) irrespective of its value on another. And, finally, $P(X = a, Y = r)$ stands for the probability that a randomly selected observation has both property a *and* property r simultaneously. The two variables are **statistically independent** if and only if the chances of observing a combination of categories is equal to the marginal probability of one category times the marginal probability of the other:

$$P(X = a, Y = r) = [P(X = a)][P(Y = r)] \text{ for all } a \text{ and } r.$$

TABLE 12-9
Gender by Turnout

Turnout (Y)	Gender (X)		
	Male (m)	Female (f)	Total
Voted (v)	70	140	210
Did not vote (nv)	30	60	90
Total	100	200	300

Note: Hypothetical data. Cell entries are frequencies.

TABLE 12-10
Social Class by Turnout

Turnout (Y)	Social Class (X)		
	Upper (u)	Lower (l)	Total
Voted (v)	100	50	150
Did not vote (nv)	50	100	150
Total	150	150	300

Note: Hypothetical data. Cell entries are frequencies.

If, for instance, men are as likely to vote as women, then the two variables, gender and turnout, are statistically independent since, for example, the probability of observing a male non-voter in a sample is equal to the probability of observing a male times the probability of picking a non-voter.

In Table 12-9 we see that 100 out of 300 respondents are men and that 210 out of these 300 respondents said they voted. Hence, the marginal probabilities are $P(X = m) = 100/300 = .33$ and $P(Y = v) = 210/300 = .7$. The product of these marginal probabilities is $(.33)(.7) = .23$. Also, note that since there are 70 male voters, the joint probability of being male *and* voting is $70/300 = .23$, the same as the product of the marginal probabilities. Since the same relation holds for all other combinations in this data set, the two variables in Table 12-9 are statistically independent.

Now suppose we had the data shown in Table 12-10. It shows that the sample consists of 300 respondents, half of whom voted and half of whom did not. The marginal probabilities of voting and not voting are both $150/300 = .5$. It is also clear that the marginal probabilities of being upper and lower class equal .5. *If* the two variables were statistically independent, the probability that an upper class respondent voted would be $(.5)(.5) = .25$. Similarly, the probability that a lower class individual did not vote would be $(.5)(.5) = .25$. But we can see from *observed* cell frequencies that actual proportions of upper and lower class voters are .33 and .17, respectively. Since the observed joint probabilities do not equal the product of the marginal probabilities, the variables are not statistically independent. Upper class respondents are more likely to vote than are lower class individuals.

A test for statistical significance is really a test that two variables in a population are statistically independent. The hypothesis is that in the population, the variables are statistically independent and we use the observed relationship to decide whether or not this proposition is tenable in the light of the observed data. In the case of crosstabulations, the determination of statistical significance requires the calculation of a statistic called chi-square, which we discuss later in this chapter. Generally speaking, the stronger a relationship is, the more likely it is to be statistically significant because it is unlikely to arise if the variables are really independent. However, even weak relationships

TABLE 12-11
Relationship between Education and Voter Turnout (in percent)

| Independent Variable: Education | Dependent Variable: Turnout | | | |
	Voted	Did Not Vote	Total	Percent of Total
0–4 years	38	62	100	4
5–7 years	49	51	100	6
8 years	59	41	100	10
9–11 years	55	45	100	16
12 years	69	31	100	38
1–3 years college	79	21	100	14
4 years college	86	14	100	7
5+ years college	91	9	100	4

Source: Raymond E. Wolfinger and Steven J. Rosenstone, *Who Votes?* (New Haven: Yale University Press, 1980), 17. Reprinted with permission.

may turn out to be statistically significant in some situations. We will illustrate how this may be the case later in the chapter.

Example of a Crosstab Analysis

So far we have illustrated crosstabulation exclusively with hypothetical data. Let us take a look now at an example of an actual observed relationship between a nominal and an ordinal level measure.

Raymond Wolfinger and Steven Rosenstone, in their analysis of why people vote, use crosstab analysis to test their hypothesis that the more education one has, the more likely one is to vote.[2] Table 12-11 shows that only 38 percent of those with 0–4 years of formal education voted while more than 86 percent of those who completed four years of college voted, and that generally the higher a group's years of formal education, the larger the percentage of that group voting. Therefore, the relationship between education and voter turnout exists, the direction has the hypothesized shape (i.e., positive), and the strength of the relationship is fairly strong. (This is a good example of a crosstab that has the independent variable down the side because of its many categories. In this case, then, the table is percentaged across the rows, and comparisons are made down the columns.)

Researchers often use readily available computer software packages to produce the crosstabulations that will indicate relationships between nominal and ordinal level measures. Table 12-12, for example, shows a crosstab table produced by the SPSS program. There we can see that the crosstab displays the relationship between gender (the independent variable—displayed across

TABLE 12-12

Sample Crosstabulation Produced by SPSS Software Program: The Relationship between Gender and Attitudes toward Life

Count/Column Percent		Gender		Row Total
		Male	Female	
		1	2	
Exciting	1	300	384	684
		50.3	44.4	46.8
Pretty routine	2	267	437	704
		44.8	50.5	48.2
Dull	3	29	44	73
		4.9	5.1	5.0
Column total		596	865	1,461
		40.8	59.2	100.0

Number of missing observations = 12

Source: Marija J. Norusis, *SPSS/PC + Studentware* (Chicago: SPSS, Inc., 1988), 127.

Note: Question asked was: Is life exciting or dull?

the top of the table) and attitudes toward how exciting life is (the dependent variable—displayed down the side of the table). Of the 865 women in the sample 44 percent think life is exciting and 56 percent think life is pretty routine *or* dull. Of the 596 men in the sample, 50 percent think life is exciting and 49 percent think life is pretty routine *or* dull. There is a weak relationship, then, between these two variables; men are slightly more likely to think life is exciting than women are. At this point, however, we do not know whether this relationship is statistically significant.

Measures of Association

So far we have measured the relationship between two variables by inspecting a crosstabulation percentaged on the categories of the independent variable. However, if a researcher's analysis involves many crosstabs or crosstabs that are so large that a way of summarizing the information is needed, **measures of association** may be used. These measures summarize efficiently the existence, direction, and strength of a relationship between two variables in a crosstab.

Measures of association combine the data in a table arithmetically to produce a single summary number that measures the strength of a relationship according to some criterion. Some of these measures indicate both the direction and strength of a relationship and can vary from –1 to +1. Others just suggest the strength of the association. The closer the value is to 0, the weaker the relationship; the closer the value is to 1, the stronger the relationship.

TABLE 12-13

Relationship between Education and Political Interest: Concordant, Discordant, and Tied Pairs

Dependent Variable: Political Interest	Independent Variable: Education		
	Low	Medium	High
Low	1		4
Medium		2	
High	5	3	6

	Type		
	Concordant	Discordant	Tied
	1, 2	3, 4	1, 5
	1, 6	2, 4	1, 4
	1, 3	2, 5	2, 3
	2, 6	4, 5	3, 5
			3, 6
			4, 6
			5, 6

Note: Hypothetical data.

The direction of the relationship is indicated by the sign + or – that precedes the statistic.

The particular measure of association that is used to summarize a crosstab depends on the level of measurement of the variables and the intent of the researcher. When both variables in a crosstab are ordinal level measures, the most frequently used measures of association are **Kendall's tau**, **Somer's d**, and **Goodman and Kruskal's gamma**—named after the people who developed them. Most computer programs will calculate at least these statistics for any crosstab and print the value out for the researcher's use. Tau, d, and gamma are similar, but not identical, in how they summarize the contents of a crosstab. Each of them uses pairs of cases in the crosstab and measures whether those pairs are concordant, discordant, or tied.

Let us take the relationship between education and political interest. In Table 12-13 we have placed six cases in a crosstab so that we can illustrate the identification of concordant, discordant, and tied pairs. A *concordant pair* is a pair of cases in which one case is higher on both variables than the other case. The pair of observation 1 and observation 2 is concordant because 2 is higher on both education and interest than 1 is. A *discordant pair* is one in which one case is lower on one of the variables but higher on the other variable. The pair of observation 3 and observation 4 is discordant because 4 is higher on education than 3 but lower than 3 on political interest. Therefore, this pair violates the expectation that as education increases, so does political interest. A *tied pair* is a pair in which both observations are tied on at least one of the variables. The pair consisting of observations 1 and 5 is tied because both observations have the same value on education.

Tau, d, and gamma all use this evaluation of pairs to summarize the relationship in the crosstab. The basic comparison made is between the number of concordant and discordant pairs. If both types of pairs are equally numerous, the statistic will be 0, indicating no relationship. If concordant pairs are more numerous, there will be a positive statistic; if discordant pairs are more numerous, there will be a negative statistic. The degree to which one type of pair is more frequent than the other will result in the size of the statistic, which is indicative of the strength of the relationship. Hence, if only the main diagonal were filled with observations, all of the pairs would be concordant, and the statistic would be +1—a perfect, positive relationship. If only the minor diagonal were filled with observations, all of the pairs would be discordant, and the statistic would be –1—a perfect, negative relationship.

The formulas for tau, d, and gamma are as follows:

$$\text{tau b} = \frac{P - Q}{\sqrt{(P + Q + T_2)(P + Q + T_1)}}$$

$$\text{tau c} = \frac{P - Q}{1/2(n)^2\,[(m-1)/m]}$$

$$\text{asymmetric d} = \frac{P - Q}{P + Q + T_1} \quad \text{(row variable is dependent)}$$

$$= \frac{P - Q}{P + Q + T_2} \quad \text{(column variable is dependent)}$$

$$\text{symmetric d} = \frac{P - Q}{P + Q + (T_1 + T_2)/2}$$

$$\text{gamma} = \frac{P - Q}{P + Q}$$

Where

P = number of concordant pairs
Q = number of discordant pairs
T_1 = number of ties on row variables
T_2 = number of ties on column variables
m = the smaller of the number of rows and columns
n = number of cases

For all of these measures, the numerator in the equation is simply the comparison of the number of concordant and discordant pairs $(P - Q)$. The denominators differ, however, with the equation for gamma ignoring ties

TABLE 12-14
Relationship between Education and Political Interest: Calculating Measures of Association

Dependent Variable: Political Interest	Independent Variable: Education			
	Low	Medium	High	Total
Low	60	50	20	130
Medium	30	100	80	210
High	10	50	100	160
	100	200	200	500

Note: Hypothetical data.

altogether and the equations for the others taking ties into consideration in many different ways. Tau b is suitable for square tables (that is, tables with the same number of rows and columns); tau c is suitable for nonsquare tables; and Somer's d has both a symmetric and an asymmetric version, depending on which variable in the crosstab is dependent.[3]

We can illustrate the calculation of these statistics by using the data in Table 12-14. The number of concordant pairs may be found by multiplying the number of cases in each cell by the number in each cell below and to the right and summing the result:

$$P = 60(100 + 80 + 50 + 100) + 30(50 + 100) + 50(80 + 100) + 100(100)$$
$$= 43,300$$

The number of discordant pairs may be calculated by multiplying the number of cases in each cell by the number in each cell above and to the right and summing the result:

$$Q = 30(50 + 20) + 10(50 + 20 + 100 + 80) + 100(20) + 50(20 + 80)$$
$$= 11,600$$

The number of ties for the row variable may be found by multiplying the number of cases in each cell by the number of cases in the remaining cells in that row and summing the result:

$$T_1 = 60(50 + 20) + 50(20) + 30(100 + 80) + 100(80) + 10(50 + 100) + 50(100)$$
$$= 25,100$$

The number of ties for the column variable is the number of cases in each cell multiplied by the number of cases in the remaining cells in that column, added together:

$$T_2 = 60(30 + 10) + 30(10) + 50(100 + 50) + 100(50) + 20(80 + 100) + 80(100)$$
$$= 26,800$$

Once these calculations are completed, each of the measures of association can be calculated as follows:

$$\text{tau b} = \frac{43,300 - 11,600}{\sqrt{(43,300 + 11,600 + 26,800)(43,300 + 11,600 + 25,100)}}$$

$$= \frac{31,700}{80,846}$$

$$= +.39$$

$$\text{tau c} = \frac{43,300 - 11,600}{1/2(500)^2[(3-1)/3]} = \frac{31,700}{83,333}$$

$$= +.38$$

$$\text{asymmetric d} = \frac{43,300 - 11,600}{43,300 + 11,600 + 25,100} = \frac{31,700}{80,000}$$

$$= +.40$$

$$\text{symmetric d} = \frac{43,300 - 11,600}{43,300 + 11,600 + (25,100 + 26,800)/2} = \frac{31,700}{80,050}$$

$$= +.40$$

$$\text{gamma} = \frac{43,300 - 11,600}{43,300 + 11,600} = \frac{31,700}{54,900}$$

$$= +.58$$

Tau, d, and gamma will generally take on similar but not identical values for any given crosstab. They will all have a value of zero when there is no relationship between the two variables, and they will all have the same sign for a given relationship. Values of gamma, however, are higher than the other statistics and may overstate the strength of a relationship. When a researcher is uncertain about the properties of the three measures of association, tau is probably the safest measure to use.

When one or both of the variables in a crosstab is a nominal level measure, tau, d, and gamma may not be used because the identification of concordant and discordant pairs requires that the variables possess an ordering of values (one value higher than another). Hence, a different measure of association, called **Goodman and Kruskal's lambda**, is generally used.

Lambda is designed to indicate whether the values of one variable tend to cluster with certain values of the other variable so that knowing a case's value

TABLE 12-15

Relationship between Race and 1984 Democratic Primary Votes: Predicting without the Help of an Independent Variable

Dependent Variable: 1984 Democratic Primary Vote	Independent Variable: Race				
	White	Black	Hispanic	Asian	Total
Mondale					410
Hart					295
Jackson					295
Total	600	300	50	50	1,000

Note: Hypothetical data.

for the independent variable would help one predict that case's value for the dependent variable.

The formula for lambda is

$$\text{Lambda} = \frac{L - M}{L}$$

where L is the number of mistakes one would make in predicting the values of the dependent variable without taking the independent variable into consideration and M is the number of mistakes one would make in predicting values of the dependent variable when the independent variable is taken into consideration. The best prediction for values of the dependent variable without knowing the value of the independent variable is the modal value for the dependent variable. The best prediction for values of the dependent variable when taking the independent variable into consideration is the modal value for each category of the independent variable. Let us consider an example of how these calculations are performed.

Suppose we are interested in the relationship between race and primary votes for the 1984 Democratic presidential candidates. Table 12-15 shows a hypothetical crosstabulation of this relationship without any cases inside the cells. Our best prediction of how particular people voted, based only on the information in Table 12-15, would be that the cases in every category of race voted for Mondale since that is the most numerous (or modal) value on the dependent variable. Such a prediction would yield 410 correct predictions and 590 (295 + 295) errors, not a very impressive performance.

Now suppose we know something about the relationship between race and 1984 primary votes as shown in section a of Table 12-16. The primary votes of the voters in each category of race can now be predicted based on how the observations are distributed or clustered within the table. We would predict

TABLE 12-16

1984 Democratic Primary Votes: Predicting with the Help of an Independent Variable

Dependent Variable: 1984 Democratic Primary Vote	Independent Variable: Race					
	White	Black	Hispanic	Asian	Total	(N)
a.						
Mondale	50%	23%	30%	50%	41.0%	(410)
Hart	40	10	20	30	29.5	(295)
Jackson	10	67	50	20	29.5	(295)
Total	100	100	100	100	100.0	
(N)	(600)	(300)	(50)	(50)		(1,000)
b.						
Mondale	600	0	0	50	65.0%	(650)
Hart	0	0	0	0	0.0	(0)
Jackson	0	300	50	0	35.0	(350)
Total	600	300	50	50	100.0%	
c.						
Mondale	90%	80%	70%	60%	84.5%	(845)
Hart	5	0	10	40	5.5	(55)
Jackson	5	20	20	0	10.0	(100)
Total	100	100	100	100	100.0	
(N)	(600)	(300)	(50)	(50)		(1,000)

Note: Hypothetical data.

that each racial group voted for the modal value in that racial category: all 600 white voters would vote for Mondale, all 300 black voters for Jackson, all 50 Hispanic voters for Jackson, and all 50 Asian voters for Mondale. This prediction is shown in section b of Table 12-16. Since 300 white voters did vote for Mondale, 201 black voters did vote for Jackson, 25 Hispanic voters did vote for Jackson, and 25 Asian voters did vote for Mondale, this prediction would be correct in 551 of the cases (300 + 201 + 25 + 25) and incorrect in 449 of the cases. We have improved our prediction, then, from 590 incorrect predictions to 449. Consequently, lambda would be

$$\lambda = \frac{590 - 449}{590} = \frac{141}{590} = .24$$

The extent of this improvement in prediction is dependent upon the extent to which the cases in each category of the independent variable cluster within particular categories of the dependent variable. It is this improvement on the original prediction that lambda is designed to measure. If, for each category of the independent variable, all of the cases clustered one and only one category of the dependent variable, our prediction would be perfect and lambda would be 1. Since nominal measures do not have an ordering, we cannot speak of positive or negative relationships, and lambda therefore has no sign. The direction of the relationship in this case is simply which category of the dependent variable goes with which category of the independent variable.

Although lambda is the generally preferred measure of association for relationships involving nominal level measures, it yields a misleading result in two situations. First, if the best prediction (mode) for each category of the independent variable is the same as the overall mode of the dependent variable, lambda will always be 0, even if the column percentages for the categories differ markedly across the rows, as in section c of Table 12-16. In that case inspection of the column percentages would seem to indicate a relationship between the two variables even though the calculation of lambda indicates no relationship. Second, whenever there are more categories for the dependent variable than there are for the independent variable, lambda cannot take on a value of 1.0, even if the cases are clustered as much as the marginals permit. As both cases show, the result of any measure of association should not be taken at face value without inspecting the distribution of the observed values upon which that measure is based.

We should point out that more advanced techniques for analyzing categorical variables are now widely available. Since they involve somewhat more complex ideas than we have space to explain here, we suggest that the interested student explore the topic in Alan Agresti's *An Introduction to Categorical Data Analysis,* cited in Suggested Readings.

Statistical Significance

Although we may observe a relationship in sample data, we cannot be sure it arises because of sampling error or because there really is an association in the population. Finding out involves testing for statistical significance. Tests for significance involve the following general steps. Always assume that a random sample of size N has been collected.

- State a null hypothesis. This is a tentative statement about a population characteristic such as there is "no relationship between X and Y" or the "mean of a variable in one population does not differ from the mean in another."

- Select an appropriate sample test statistic. This number is calculated from the data and hence is called an observed statistic. (For example, in cross-tabulation analysis it is a chi-square statistic; for testing hypotheses about means or regression parameters it is a z or t statistic. These statistics will be discussed in detail below.)

- Identify the statistics sampling distribution. Briefly stated, a sampling distribution is a function that shows the probabilities of obtaining possible values for a statistic if a null hypothesis is true. We use it to assess the like-lihood that a *particular* sample result could have occurred by chance. A number of these sampling distributions are contained in the appendices.

■ Make a decision rule. It is necessary to decide what are probable and im-probable values of this statistic if the null hypothesis is true.

■ Define a critical region in the light of the decision rule. The logic is as fol-lows: Assume the null hypothesis is true. We draw a sample from a popula-tion and calculate a sample statistic. Given the null hypothesis we would expect to observe only a limited number of values for this statistic. (If you toss a fair coin 10 times, you expect heads to come up *about* half the time. If you see 10 heads (or 10 tails) in 10 tosses, you may suspect something is wrong.) The critical region consists of those outcomes we deem so unlikely to occur *if* the null hypothesis is true, that *if* one of them should in fact occur, then we will reject the null hypothesis.

■ Actually collect the sample and calculate the sample statistic.

■ Examine the result to see if it falls within the critical region. If the observed sample statistic is a rare event given the null hypothesis, we may decide that we have observed something so improbable that it calls into question the acceptability of this hypothesis. We would then reject it and accept an alternative. If, on the other hand, we find a result that could have happened by chance if the null hypothesis is true, then we will accept the hypothesis for the time being.

Let's state these ideas more informally. A statistical test of significance is a little like playing a game of chance with someone you don't know very well. Suppose you and an opponent agree to toss a coin. If heads comes up, your opponent wins; if tails comes up, you win. In this case the null hypothesis is that the coin is fair, which can be stated more precisely as "the probability of obtaining a head on a single flip is one-half." Your test statistic will be the number of heads, Y, that appear in, say, 20 tosses ($N = 20$). You are willing to believe that your opponent is honest and that the coin is fair if Y is less than a certain number, say 15. Hence, "15 and above "defines a critical region. If the results of the game fall in the critical region—if your opponent gets 15 or more heads—you will decide that the coin is not fair and take appropriate steps.[4] If there are 14 or fewer heads, however, you will accept the result as possible given a fair coin. Suppose your opponent obtains 20 heads in 20 tosses. Because this outcome falls within your critical region, you deem it likely that the coin is unfair and you decide not to pay.

Of course, you could be making a mistake. Maybe your opponent was lucky. This is one inescapable consequences of hypothesis testing. It is always possible to draw a mistaken conclusion.

TABLE 12-17
Relationship between Gender and Attitudes toward Nuclear Power Plants: Observed Table, Observations

Dependent Variable: Attitudes toward Nuclear Power Plants	Independent Variable: Gender			
	Male	Female	Total	(N)
Open more plants	Cell a: 200	Cell d: 100	30%	(300)
Retain status quo	Cell b: 100	Cell e: 200	30%	(300)
Close plants	Cell c: 100	Cell f: 300	40%	(400)
Total	40%	60%	100%	
(N)	(400)	(600)		(1,000)

Note: Hypothetical data.

Whether or not a relationship is statistically significant—that is, whether or not we can reject the null hypothesis that states that there is no relationship between two variables in the population based on the observed relationship in a sample—usually cannot be determined by inspecting a crosstabulation alone; instead, a statistic called **chi-square** (χ^2) must be calculated. Chi-square measures whether the observed relationship in a crosstab differs significantly from the relationship we would have observed by chance alone between the two variables. Chi-square is usually used to indicate the probability that a relationship observed among data drawn from a sample would also be observed among the target population.

Table 12-17 presents a crosstab exhibiting the observed relationship between gender and attitudes toward nuclear power plants among a sample of 1,000 people. *Among that sample* it appears that there is a relationship between gender and attitudes toward nuclear power plants, with women expressing greater opposition to the plants than men. Table 12-18, an expected values table, includes the number of cases that we would expect in each cell if the null hypothesis were true and there were no relationship between the two variables in the target population. This table has the same marginals as Table 12-17, but the cell entries will probably be different. The expected values in each cell are calculated from the marginals in Table 12-17.

Recall that no relationship is present in a crosstab when the column percentages are identical across the rows and when the column percentages are identical to the marginal percentages at the far right-hand side of the table. If there were no relationship in Table 12-18, 30 percent of both males and females would be in favor of opening more plants, 30 percent of both males and females would be in favor of retaining the status quo, and 40 percent of both males and females would be in favor of closing plants. You can verify these results by applying the formula described in the discussion of statistical

TABLE 12-18

Relationship between Gender and Attitudes toward Nuclear Power Plants: Expected Values Table, Marginals Only

Dependent Variable: Attitudes toward Nuclear Power Plants	Independent Variable: Gender			
	Male	Female	Total	(N)
Open more plants			30%	(300)
Retain status quo			30%	(300)
Close plants			40%	(400)
Total	40%	60%	100%	
(N)	(400)	(600)		(1,000)

Note: Hypothetical data.

independence. Under independence, for example, the expected properties of men who favor opening more nuclear power plants would be $(.30)(.4) = .12$. Thus, if gender and attitude were independent we would expect to find about 12 percent of the 1,000 respondents to be in the first cell of the table. The distribution of cases in the crosstab, then, would look like Table 12-19.

In general, the expected number of cases in each cell may be calculated by multiplying the marginals for each cell together and dividing by the total sample size. Hence, the expected values in Table 12-19 would be

$$\text{Cell a: } (300)(400)/1000 = 120$$
$$\text{Cell b: } (300)(400)/1000 = 120$$
$$\text{Cell c: } (400)(400)/1000 = 160$$
$$\text{Cell d: } (300)(600)/1000 = 180$$
$$\text{Cell e: } (300)(600)/1000 = 180$$
$$\text{Cell f: } (400)(600)/1000 = 240$$

TABLE 12-19

Relationship between Gender and Attitudes toward Nuclear Power Plants: Expected Values Table, Cell Frequencies

Dependent Variable: Attitudes toward Nuclear Power Plants	Independent Variable: Gender			
	Male	Female	Total	(N)
Open more plants	Cell a: 120	Cell d: 180	30%	(300)
Retain status quo	Cell b: 120	Cell e: 180	30%	(300)
Close plants	Cell c: 160	Cell f: 240	40%	(400)
Total	40%	60%	100%	
(N)	(400)	(600)		(1,000)

Note: Hypothetical data.

The next step is to calculate a test statistic, which shows how much difference there is between the observed table (Table 12-17) and the expected values table with cell frequencies consistent with the null hypothesis (Table 12-19). This will tell us how far the observed relationship is from the expected distribution if there were no relationship between the two variables in the target population. To do this, we subtract the number of cases in each cell of Table 12-19 from the number of cases in the corresponding cell of Table 12-17, square the difference, and then divide the difference by the number of cases in that cell in Table 12-19. These calculations should be done separately for each cell in the two tables and then summed across all the cells to yield the chi-square value. The formula for chi-square, then, is

$$\chi^2 = \sum_i \left(\frac{(O_i - E_i)^2}{E_i} \right)$$

where O_i is the observed frequency in the ith cell and E_i is the expected frequency in the ith cell. For Table 12-17 and Table 12-19, the calculations would look like this:

Cell	Observed Value	Expected Value	Difference	(Difference)^2	$\frac{(Difference)^2}{Expected\ Value}$
a	200	120	80	6400	53.33
b	100	120	−20	400	3.33
c	100	160	−60	3600	22.50
d	100	180	−80	6400	35.56
e	200	180	20	400	2.22
f	300	240	60	3600	15.00
				Sum	131.94

The value of chi-square in this example is 131.94. To determine whether the relationship is statistically significant, allowing us to reject the null hypothesis, we must calculate a number called the **degrees of freedom**, which is the number of columns in a table minus one (C − 1) times the number of rows in a table minus one (R − 1), or in this case (2 − 1) (3 − 1), or 2. Then we must look up the value of our chi-square on a chi-square table to determine whether it is high enough to indicate a statistically significant relationship. (See Appendix A for a chi-square table.) For a given value of chi-square and degrees of freedom, the chi-square table will indicate the probability that a χ^2 value of at least that magnitude would have been observed if there were no relationship between the two variables (or, in other words, if the null hypothesis were true). The lower this probability, the better; to reject the null hypothesis the probability that the null hypothesis is true generally must be less than .01. The value of chi-square in our example, 131.94, is well above the criterion value, 9.21, for two degrees of freedom. Therefore, the relationship is statistically significant at the .01 level and we can reject the null hypothesis. In other words, we can be quite confident that the relationship we observed in our sample also exists in the target population.

Researchers generally want their chi-square value to be large so that they can reject the null hypothesis. Large values of chi-square result when the observed and expected tables are quite different and when the sample size upon which the tables are based is large. A weak relationship among a large sample may attain statistical significance while a strong relationship within a small sample may not. In other words, statistical significance is not the same as strength or substantive significance, and chi-square values should not be used as a measure of substantive importance. Rather, chi-square values tell us the probability that an observed relationship in a sample allows us to reject the null hypothesis that there is no relationship in the target population.

Before moving on, we should note an important point about the chi-square test. First, if N (the total sample size) is large, the magnitude of the chi-square statistic will usually be large as well and we will reject the null hypothesis, even if the association is quite weak. This point can be seen by looking at Tables 12-20 and 12-21. In Table 12-20 there is virtually no relationship between the categories X and Y, as can be verified by examining the percentages and the size of the chi-square statistic, which is 1.38. In Table 12-21, which only involves a larger sample size, the same basic relationship holds. The entries in Table 12-21 have simply been multiplied by 10 so that now the sample size is 3,000 instead of 300. But even though the chi-square statistic is now statistically significant (at the .05 level), the strength of the relationship between X and Y is still the same as before, namely, quite small.

TABLE 12-20

Relationship between X and Y Based on Sample of 300

Variable Y	Variable X			
	a	b	c	Total
A	30	30	30	90
B	30	30	36	96
C	40	40	34	114
Total	100	100	100	300

$\chi^2 = 1.38$ with 4 d.f.

Note: Hypothetical data.

TABLE 12-21
Relationship between X and Y Based on Sample of 3,000

Variable Y	Variable X			
	a	b	c	Total
A	300	300	300	900
B	300	300	360	960
C	400	400	340	1,140
Total	1,000	1,000	1,000	3,000

$\chi^2 = 13.8$ with 4 d.f.

Note: Hypothetical data.

The lesson to be drawn here is that when dealing with large samples (say, N is greater than 1,500), small, inconsequential relationships can be statistically significant. As a result, we must take care to distinguish between statistical and substantive importance. The latter is better measured or assessed by a measure of association. Chi-square only refers to the evidence in support of a statistical hypothesis, not to the strength of an association.

Difference of Means Test and Analysis of Variance

Crosstabulation is the appropriate analysis technique when both variables are nominal or ordinal level measures. When the independent variable is nominal or ordinal and the dependent variable is interval or ratio, however, a crosstab would have far too many columns or rows to permit a straightforward and meaningful analysis. Therefore, two similar analysis techniques—the **difference of means test** and **analysis of variance**—are used.

Both of these techniques help test the researcher's hypothesis that the dependent variable, which is measured at the interval or ratio level, is related to the independent variable. First the cases are divided into categories based on the values of the independent variable. Then, if the values of the dependent variable are (1) less varied within each category of the independent variable than they were before *and* (2) quite different in general for different values of the independent variable, a relationship exists.

A simple example will illustrate this point. Suppose we have hypothesized that there is a relationship between gender (independent variable, X) and the amount of money contributed to political campaigns (dependent variable, Y). And suppose that we measure these two variables for a sample of ten people and receive the following results:

Gender	Money Contributed (in thousands of dollars)	Gender	Money Contributed (in thousands of dollars)
Male	10	Male	15
Female	8	Male	20
Female	5	Female	2
Male	10	Female	5
Female	10	Male	15

Now, if we ignore the independent variable, we can graph the ten observations, and calculate the mean contribution. The mean is 10 (thousand dollars) and the variation around that mean looks like this:

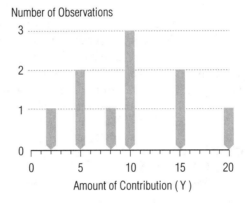

It is this variation (the actual variance is 26.8) that we are trying to explain.

Now let us consider whether the independent variable helps us account for this variation. The independent variable is clearly a nominal level measure. If we divide the cases into two groups based on this measure, we find that the original variation is distributed across the two groups in the following way:

Males	Females
10	2
10	5
15	5
15	8
20	10
Total = 70	Total = 30
$\bar{Y}$ = 14	$\bar{Y}$ = 6
$\hat{\sigma}^2$ = 14	$\hat{\sigma}^2$ = 7.6

The average amount of money contributed by the two groups is quite different, and the variation in the amount contributed is much smaller within both groups than it was originally. In other words, the independent variable has been helpful in grouping the observations into categories that are different from each other on the dependent variable and that contain observations that are similar to each other. The analysis has revealed a pattern in the data and has reduced the amount of unexplained variation.

This is the basic logic of both analysis techniques. We begin with a certain amount of so-called unexplained variance in the dependent variable. We use the measurement of the independent variable to divide the cases into analysis groups and then determine if the groups created are dissimilar from each other and more homogeneous than the original data were. The difference of means test involves comparing the means of the groups created with the independent variable to see if the difference is statistically significant and we can reject the null hypothesis. The analysis of variance, which is employed whenever there are more than two analysis groups formed by the independent variable, involves comparing the variance in each of the analysis groups with the total variance in the dependent variable to see how much variance has been explained by the independent variable.

Edward Tufte's study of the relationship between automobile inspection policy and traffic fatality rates in the states contains a good example of a hypothesis involving a nominal and a ratio level measure.[5] Tufte was interested in whether states with mandatory auto inspections experienced lower auto fatality rates than states without mandatory inspections. His initial test of this hypothesis was to measure the relationship between auto inspection policy (a nominal level independent variable with only two categories) and auto fatality rates (a ratio level dependent variable).

Tufte began with a distribution of fifty observed values (one for each state) on the dependent variable, motor vehicle deaths per 100,000 people. These observed values had a mean value of 29.8 deaths per 100,000 and a variance of 60.55. He then divided the cases (states) into two categories: states with and states without mandatory automobile inspections. This resulted in mean death rates of 26.1 for the eighteen states with inspections (with a variance of 66.07) and 31.9 for the thirty-two states without inspections (with a variance of 45.56). Therefore, the two analysis groups defined by the values of the independent variable differed somewhat. Furthermore, visual inspection of the distributions within the two categories suggested that the variation within each group was smaller than it was for the whole set of observations (see Figure 12-2). Initially, then, it appears that dividing the cases into the two analysis groups is worthwhile and that there is a relationship between the two variables.

Since the number of cases analyzed is generally larger than Tufte's fifty, visual inspection of the distribution of cases in the analysis groups is not usually adequate. Furthermore, more precise measures of the direction, strength,

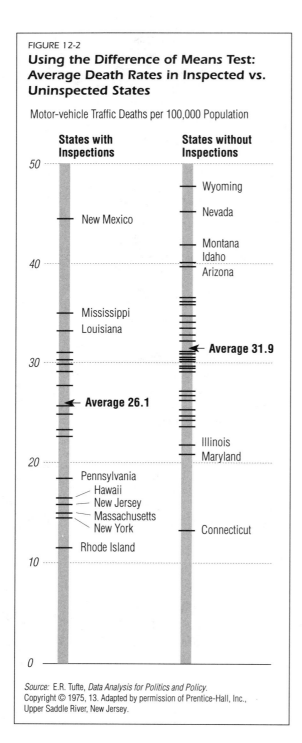

FIGURE 12-2

Using the Difference of Means Test: Average Death Rates in Inspected vs. Uninspected States

Motor-vehicle Traffic Deaths per 100,000 Population

States with Inspections — States without Inspections

- Wyoming
- Nevada
- New Mexico
- Montana
- Idaho
- Arizona
- Mississippi
- Louisiana
- ← Average 31.9
- ← Average 26.1
- Illinois
- Maryland
- Pennsylvania
- Hawaii
- New Jersey
- Massachusetts
- New York
- Connecticut
- Rhode Island

Source: E.R. Tufte, *Data Analysis for Politics and Policy.*
Copyright © 1975, 13. Adapted by permission of Prentice-Hall, Inc.,
Upper Saddle River, New Jersey.

and statistical significance of the relationships are desirable. Both the difference of means test and the analysis of variance have been developed to provide a more precise measure of relationships between variables of this type.

The initial step in both the difference of means test and the analysis of variance is to calculate the mean and variance for the cases on the dependent variable. This variance is called the **total variance**. The cases are then divided into two or more groups based on the independent variable, and the mean and variance for each group are calculated. If the means of the groups are quite different, and the statistical significance of the difference in the means can be established, then a relationship between the two variables is indicated by the difference of means test.

One can get an idea of the direction and strength of the relationship revealed by these procedures by noting which group (or groups) has the higher mean and by comparing the variances of the analysis groups with the total variance for all the observations. In Tufte's case, the direction of the relationship is that those states with mandatory auto inspections have fewer traffic fatalities, and the strength of the relationship is indicated by the variation left in the categories of the independent variable. However, a more precise measure of the relationship is given by an analysis of variance and a correlation called **eta-squared**.

Eta-squared is similar to lambda for a crosstabulation. It represents the amount of reduction that has occurred in the total variance as a result of dividing the cases into groups based on the independent variable. To calculate eta-squared, take the total variance, subtract from it a weighted sum of the variances left in the analysis groups (the **unexplained variance**), and divide this difference by the total variance. The numerator of this ratio is the **explained variance**, and the higher this number, the stronger the relationship:

$$E^2 = \frac{\text{total SS} - \text{unexplained SS}}{\text{total SS}} = \frac{\text{explained SS}}{\text{total SS}}$$

Where SS = sum of squares.

In the gender/money contributed example, the total variance was 26.8. The unexplained variance left after the cases were divided into males and females was an average of the two variances left (14 and 7.60 weighted by the number of cases in each group):

$$\frac{5(14) + 5(7.6)}{10} = \frac{70 + 38}{10} = \frac{108}{10} = 10.8$$

The unexplained variance is then subtracted from the total variance to get the explained variance, and the result is divided by the total variance:

$$\frac{26.8 - 10.8}{26.8} = \frac{16.0}{26.8} = .60$$

This value of eta-squared means that 60 percent of the variance in the dependent variable has been explained by the independent variable, indicating a fairly strong relationship in the sample data.

In Tufte's analysis of auto inspection policy the total variance with which he began was 60.55. The unexplained variance left after the states were divided into categories was

$$\frac{(45.56 \times 32) + (66.07 \times 18)}{50} = 52.94$$

The explained variance, as a proportion of the total variance, was

$$\frac{60.55 - 52.94}{60.55} = .13$$

Eta-squared was .13, indicating a weak relationship, with 13 percent of the variance in the dependent variable explained by the independent variable. Remember that the closer eta-squared is to 0 the weaker the relationship, and the closer it is to 1 the stronger the relationship.

Both a difference of means test and an analysis of variance allow us to assess the direction and strength of a relationship between a nominal or ordinal level independent variable and an interval or ratio level dependent variable. The relative means for the analysis groups tell us the direction of the relationship, while the eta-squared, derived from the comparison of the explained and unexplained variance, tells us the strength of the relationship. In an analysis of variance, the strength of the relationship is indicated by the amount of variance left in the dependent variable when the cases are divided into groups based on the independent variable.

The statistical significance of a relationship also may be determined for a difference of means test. The test involves determining when the difference in the means on the dependent variable for the analysis groups is large enough that we can reject the null hypothesis and conclude that there is also a relationship in the target population. Recall that every sample mean is an estimate of a population mean, with some associated margin of error. Therefore, the difference in two or more sample means is also an estimate of the difference in means for the corresponding groups in the target population. To reject the null hypothesis the difference in sample means must be large enough that we can be confident that a difference also exists in the population. The larger the difference in sample means relative to the variances involved and the larger the sample size, the greater the chance that a given difference will be statistically significant.

When the sample size is less than 30, we may use the **t test** to determine the statistical significance of an observed difference in means. The test statistic, *t*, effectively compares the observed difference in means with the hypothesized difference. Its general form is

$$t_{obs} = \frac{(\bar{Y}_1 - \bar{Y}_2) - (\mu_1 - \mu_2)}{\hat{\sigma}_{\bar{Y}_1 - \bar{Y}_2}}$$

Usually the hypothesized difference between means is zero (that is, $\mu_1 - \mu_2$), so the last part of the numerator drops out.

$$t_{obs} = \frac{(\bar{Y}_1 - \bar{Y}_2)}{\hat{\sigma}_{\bar{Y}_1 - \bar{Y}_2}}$$

The denominator, which is an estimate of the standard error, may be calculated in two ways, depending on what we believe or know about the population. If we assume the two population variances are equal (that is, $\sigma_1 = \sigma_2$), we can use the following formula, called the *pooled* estimate:

$$\hat{\sigma}_{\bar{Y}_1 - \bar{Y}_2} = \sqrt{\frac{N_1 \hat{\sigma}_1^2 + N_2 \hat{\sigma}_2^2}{N_1 + N_2 - 2}} \sqrt{\frac{N_1 + N_2}{N_1 N_2}}$$

If, on the other hand, there is no reason to make the assumption of equal variances (that is, $\sigma_1 \uparrow \sigma_2$), we can use the formula for the *unpooled* estimate:

$$\hat{\sigma}_{\bar{Y}_1 - \bar{Y}_2} = \sqrt{\frac{\hat{\sigma}_1^2}{N_1 - 1} + \frac{\hat{\sigma}_2^2}{N_2 - 1}}$$

Once t has been calculated it is compared with the appropriate criterion level to see if it is large enough to reject the null hypothesis (see Appendix B).

Statistical significance for an analysis of variance may be determined by calculating a statistic called the **F ratio**. Like chi-square for a crosstab, the F ratio indicates the probability that the null hypothesis is true:

$$F = \frac{\text{mean square (between groups)}}{\text{mean square (within groups)}}$$

The formula for the F ratio compares the mean square (which is the sum of squares divided by degrees of freedom) between the analysis groups with the mean square within the analysis groups. Since the sum of squares is equal to the numerator in the formula for the variance, F basically compares the variance created by the formation of the analysis groups (the effect of the independent variable) with the variance that still exists within the analysis groups. The higher this ratio, the greater is the effect of the independent variable.

The F ratio must be greater than a particular criterion level to show a statistically significant relationship between the independent and dependent variables. The criterion level depends upon the degrees of freedom (calculated from the sample size and the number of analysis groups) and the probability of rejecting the null hypothesis. Once the F ratio is calculated, then the result may be compared with an F-ratio table to decide whether to accept or reject the null hypothesis in the population (see Appendix C for an F-ratio table).[6]

Regression

Suppose we want to examine the relationship, if any, between personal income and the number of times a person contacts a public official. Both the independent (income) and the dependent (number of contacts) variables are interval or ratio level measures. **Regression analysis** is the standard procedure for exploring relationships and testing hypotheses in this circumstance. The technique has the same goals as crosstabulation analysis, the difference of means test, and the analysis of variance, although regression terms may seem at first sight different and perhaps more complicated.

TABLE 12-22

Relationship between Income and Contacts with Public Officials: A Regression Analysis

Case	Independent Variable: Income	Dependent Variable: Number of Contacts
a	$ 3,000	0
b	15,000	3
c	42,000	3
d	22,000	2
e	10,000	1
f	85,000	7
g	30,000	4
h	70,000	6
i	100,000	4
j	55,000	6

Note: Hypothetical data.

Let's investigate the proposition that there is a positive relationship between people's income and the number of times they personally contact public officials. For the moment, we will consider just the first 10 cases in a sample of 500 people. The values on the independent and dependent variables for these 10 cases are presented in Table 12-22.

Though a bit hard to tell simply by reading the numbers in the table, there does appear to be a tendency for large values of income (the independent variable) to be connected or associated with large values for number of contacts (the dependent variable). In order to see the relationship more clearly we can first display the cases in a graph called a scattergram or **scatter plot** (or, even more simply, "plot") in which the X axis (the horizontal line) represents the independent variable and the Y axis (the vertical line) is the dependent variable. (See Figure 12-3.) This is the standard arrangement of plots: they are drawn as two-axes coordinate systems with the horizontal axis representing the independent variable and the vertical axis (drawn at a right angle) representing the dependent variable. The axes scales are in units of the particular variables such as thousands of dollars. The X and Y values

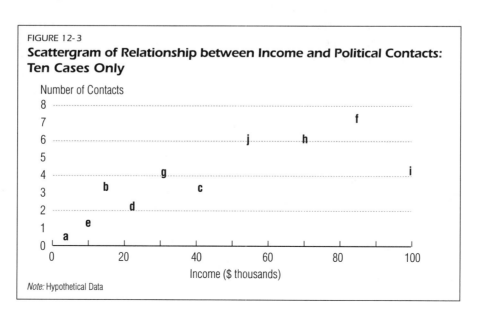

FIGURE 12-3

Scattergram of Relationship between Income and Political Contacts: Ten Cases Only

Note: Hypothetical Data

for each observation are plotted using these scales. That is, each case is placed at the point on the graph that corresponds to its values on the independent and dependent variables.

As an example, Figure 12-3 shows the plot of the ten cases in Table 12-22. The values of the independent variable are placed along the bottom of the graph on the X-axis, and the values of the dependent variable are placed along the side of the graph on the Y-axis. Each case is then located or marked at the point that corresponds to the intersection of that case's values on the independent (X-axis) and dependent (Y-axis) variables.

We can use a graphic like Figure 12-3 to make an initial guess about the type and strength of the relationship between the two variables. In the figure it appears that our hunch is correct: large values of income are associated with large values of number of contacts and small values of the independent variable are associated with small values of the dependent variable. The relationship is not perfect—look at case "i"—but there does seem to be a pattern, called a positive correlation. Moreover, most of the observations lie near a straight line that could be drawn through the center of the points. The tilt of this line will be a positive number, which means that as we go up the X scale (that is, take larger values of income) we will also go up the Y scale (that is, find larger values of number of contacts).

These ideas can be further clarified by recalling high school algebra. The equation for the graph of a straight line has the general form

$$Y = a + bX.$$

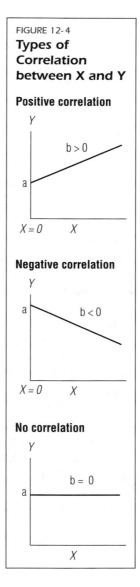

FIGURE 12-4

Types of Correlation between X and Y

Positive correlation

Negative correlation

No correlation

In the equation, X and Y are variables. The first letter is called the constant and equals the value of Y when X equals zero (just substitute 0 for X). The equation has a geometric interpretation as well. If the graph of the equation is plotted, we see that a is the point where the line crosses the Y axis (see Figure 12-4). The letter b stands for the **slope**, which indicates how much Y changes for each one-unit increase in X. In geometric terms, if we move up the X scale one unit, b indicates how much Y will change. (If we applied this type of equation to

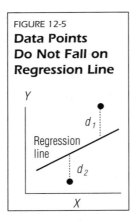

FIGURE 12-5

Data Points Do Not Fall on Regression Line

the data shown in Figure 12-3, *b* would indicate how much *Y*, the number of contacts, increased for every dollar increase in *X*, income.) Since the line slopes upward, *b* must be positive, and a positive slope means that *Y* increases as *X* increases.

If the relationship were negative—that is, if the slope were negative—the line would slant downward and increases in *X* would be associated with decreases in *Y*. If there were no (linear) relationship between the two variables, the slope of the line would be zero and its graph would be horizontal and parallel to the X axis. All of these ideas are shown in Figure 12-4.

Regression analysis can be thought of as applying these ideas to two variable relationships where both variables are numeric or quantitative. The goal is to find an equation, the graph of which "best fits" the data. If the points are approximately linearly correlated, then a straight line with a positive slope ($b > 0$) will pass through most of the points; if, on the other hand, a line with a negative slope ($b < 0$) goes through most of the data, then the correlation is negative. Finally, if the best fitting line has a slope of zero ($b = 0$), then *X* and *Y* are not linearly correlated.[7]

What exactly does "fit" mean in this context? In regression, an equation is found such that its graph is a line that *minimizes* the vertical distances between the data points and the line drawn. In Figure 12-5, for example, d_1 and d_2 represent the distances of observed data points from an estimated regression line. Regression analysis uses a mathematical procedure that finds the single line that minimizes the squared distances from the line (for instance, the line that minimizes the sum d_1^2 and d_2^2). This procedure is called least squares and regression and is often called "ordinary least squares regression," or OLS for short.

It is customary to describe the regression model or equation using Greek letters for the parameters, the constant, and the slope and to add an error term or "disturbance":

$$Y = \alpha + \beta X + \epsilon$$

The two constants are called regression parameters. The first, α, is the constant and is interpreted exactly as indicated before: it is the value of *Y* when *X* equals zero. The second, β, is the **regression coefficient** and tells how much *Y* changes if *X* changes by one unit. The regression coefficient is always measured in units of the dependent variable. So, for instance, if $\beta = .2$ in the example, then a $1,000 increase in income would lead to .2 more contacts with public officials.

The error (ϵ) indicates that observed data do not follow a neat pattern that can be summarized with a line. It suggests instead that an observation's score on Y can be broken into two parts: one that is "due to" the independent variable and is represented by the linear part of the equation, $\alpha + \beta X$, and another that is "due to" error or chance, ϵ. In other words, if we know a person's income and also know the equation that describes the relationship, we can substitute the number and obtain a predicted value of Y. This predicted value will differ from the observed value by the error

$$\text{Observed Value} = \text{Predicted Value} + \text{Error.}$$

If there are few errors, that is, if all of the data lie near the regression line, then the predicted and observed values will be very close. In that case, we would say the equation adequately explains or fits the data. On the other hand, if the observed data differ from the predicted values, then there will be considerable error and the fit will not be as good.

Figure 12-6 ties these ideas together. Suppose we consider a particular case. Its scores on X and Y (X_i and Y_i) are represented by an asterisk (*). Its score on X is denoted as X_i. If we draw a line straight up from X_i to the regression line and then draw another line to the Y axis, we find the point that represents the predicted value of Y, denoted $\hat{Y_i}$. ϵ represents the difference between the predicted score based on the **regression equation**, which is the mathematical formula describing the relationship between two interval or ratio level variables—and the observed score, Y_i. Regression estimation picks values of α and β that minimize the sum of all these squared errors. Because the regression equation gives predicted values, it is sometimes written without an error term but with a "hat" over Y to indicate that the dependent variable is not an exact function of X:

$$\hat{Y} = \hat{\alpha} + \hat{\beta} X_i$$

Although the mimimizing procedure may sound complicated, the estimated parameters can be calculated directly from the data by

$$\hat{\beta} = \frac{N\Sigma XY - (\Sigma X)(\Sigma Y)}{N\Sigma X^2 - (\Sigma X)^2}$$

Where

X = the observed values of the independent variable
Y = the observed values of the dependent variable
Σ = summation
N = the number of observed values

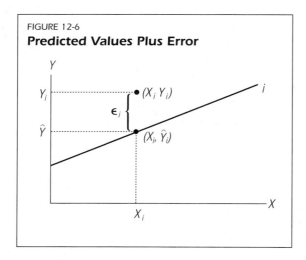

FIGURE 12-6
Predicted Values Plus Error

Once $\hat{\beta}$ has been calculated, then it is a relatively simple step to calculate α, since

$$\hat{\alpha} = \overline{Y} - \hat{\beta}\overline{X}$$

After $\hat{\beta}$ and $\hat{\alpha}$ have both been determined, the regression line that minimizes the squared distances between observed and predicted values of Y may be drawn. Computer programs designed to perform regression analysis accomplish these calculations quickly and accurately.

Let us suppose that after we have graphed all 500 data points testing the relationship between income and contacts with public officials, we end up with the regression line shown in Figure 12-7 and a regression equation of $Y = .00007X + 1$. What does this tell us about the relationship between the two variables and the hypothesis linking the two?

The slope of the line and the Y-intercept tell us the nature of the relationship between the two variables. The **Y-intercept** tells us what the value of the

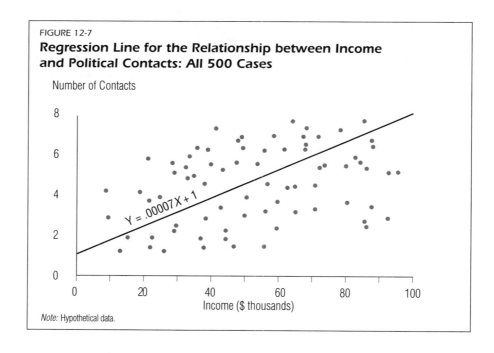

FIGURE 12-7
Regression Line for the Relationship between Income and Political Contacts: All 500 Cases

Note: Hypothetical data.

dependent variable should be when the value of the independent variable is 0. In this case, a Y-intercept of 1 tells us that when a person's income (the independent variable) is 0, that person is likely to have contacted a public official one time (that is, the dependent variable at that point on the graph is 1). This is the place at which the regression line crosses the Y-axis.

The slope of the line tells us how much the dependent variable changes when the independent variable changes or how much change will take place in values of Y for every change in X of 1 unit. In this case, the slope of .00007 tells us that for every change in X of $1, there is a change in Y, or the probability of an additional contact with a public official, of .00007. Or if we compare two people—one with $15,000 more income than the other—the expected value of Y will be different by (.00007 × 15,000) or 1.05. Therefore, we expect a difference of $15,000 in income to be associated with a difference of about one personal contact with a public official. The slope shows how responsive, in a mathematical sense, the dependent variable is to changes in the independent variable.

Finally, the sign of the slope tells us the direction of the relationship. A positive sign indicates a positive relationship: as the values of one of the variables increase, the values of the other variable increase. A negative sign indicates a negative relationship: as the values of one of the variables increase, the values of the other variable decrease. Because most graphs are drawn with the lowest values for both variables at the bottom and left-hand side, a positive relationship is usually represented by a line that rises from lower left to upper right, and a negative relationship is represented by a line that falls from upper left to lower right.

The regression equation contains a lot of useful information. It gives the expected value of the dependent variable for any value of the independent variable and the general relationship between the two variables. In this case we could substitute any value of X (income) into the equation and calculate the expected value of Y (number of personal contacts with public officials). For example, we would predict that someone who made $40,000 would have contacted a public official 3.8 times: (.00007 × 40,000) + 1.

The regression coefficient is not a good measure of the strength of the relationship between interval level measures because it is dependent upon the units in which the variables are measured. The regression coefficient in the income-political contacts example looks very small: .00007. But it is a small number because the independent variable is measured in terms of dollars, and most of the observed values of income were in the thousands of dollars range. If we measured income in thousands of dollars instead of dollars, the regression equation would change to $Y = .07X + 1$. This change in the regression coefficient does not mean that the relationship is any stronger; it means only that a unit of measurement has changed. Although the regression coefficient indicates how much change in the dependent variable is generally associated with change in the independent variable, it does not indicate how strong that association is. Correlation analysis, discussed in the next section, measures the strength of the relationships between the independent and dependent variables.

A good example of the use of regression analysis may be found in an investigation of the performance of the fifteen regional governments in Italy.[8] The researchers were interested in explaining why some of the Italian governments performed their governmental duties better than others did. First they devised a measure of institutional performance (the dependent variable) for each of the fifteen governments based on eight indicators of legislative activity, bureaucratic efficiency, programmatic innovation, and governmental stability. Then they measured the relationships between this measure and a number of possible explanations for governmental performance. One of the researchers' hypotheses was that performance would depend on socioeconomic development. Using per capita income, literacy, nonagricultural employment, and television and automobile ownership as measures of socioeconomic development, they graphed the relationship between development and performance, shown in Figure 12-8.

Clearly, a positive relationship exists between regional socioeconomic development and institutional performance. Although there are a few cases distant from the regression line, the best approximation of the data appears to be a straight line.

Since the researchers provide neither the regression equation that corresponds to the regression line nor the units of the measures along the axes, it is impossible to tell what the exact mathematical relationship is between the measures of socioeconomic development and institutional performance. (The meaning of "$r = .67$" in Figure 12-8 will be discussed below.)

Another good example of the use of regression analysis is Ted Robert Gurr's research concerning why some nations exhibit more domestic violence and turmoil than others.[9] He hypothesized that there is a relationship between the size of a country's internal security force and the amount of civil strife. Figure 12-9 indicates that a relationship exists (the data approximate a straight line), that the relationship is positive (as the size of the coercive forces increases, so does the magnitude of civil strife), and that the relationship is fairly strong (most of the data points are fairly close to the regression line).

Again, remember that the discovery of a positive relationship between the size of coercive forces and the magnitude of civil strife does not necessarily mean that one is causing the other. As Gurr himself concludes:

> *The correspondence of force size and levels of strife does not necessarily imply a simple causal connection between the two. The military establishment is relatively large in most Western countries because of*

cold-war tension, not because of the threat of internal disorder. Nonetheless, the investment of large portions of national budgets in armaments; military conscription policies; and involvement in foreign conflict have directly generated widespread popular opposition in the United States and France in the past decade, and may have provided a similar though less dramatic impetus to public protest in other Western nations.[10]

Correlation Analysis

If a straight line can be drawn through any set of data points, and as long as the slope of the line drawn is not 0, we can say that there is a relationship between the independent and dependent variables. However, that does not necessarily mean that the line is a close approximation of the data points or that the relationship is a statistically significant one. It may be that the line drawn is the best one possible, but that the data points are so scattered that no line would come close to very many of them. The test of the strength of a relationship is how close the data points are to the regression line that is drawn. The further away from the line the data points are, the weaker the relationship is. The closer to the line the data points are, the stronger the relationship is. If all of the data points are right on the regression line, then there is a perfect linear relationship between the two variables.

FIGURE 12-8

Regression Line for Relationship between Socioeconomic Development and Institutional Performance of Italian Regional Governments

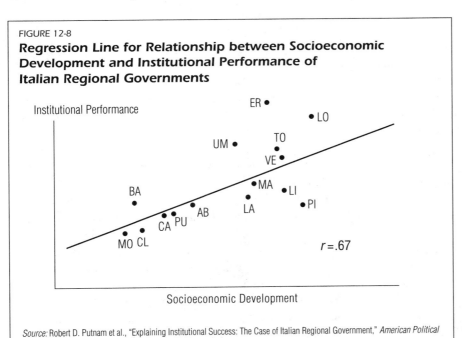

Source: Robert D. Putnam et al., "Explaining Institutional Success: The Case of Italian Regional Government," *American Political Science Review* 77 (March 1983): 64. Reprinted with permission.
Note: AB = Abruzzo, BA = Basilicata, CA = Campania, CL = Calabria, ER = Emilia-Romagna, LA = Lazio, LI - Liguria, LO = Lombardia, MA = Marche, MO = Molise, PI = Piemonte, PU = Puglia, TO = Toscana, UM = Umbria, VE = Veneto.

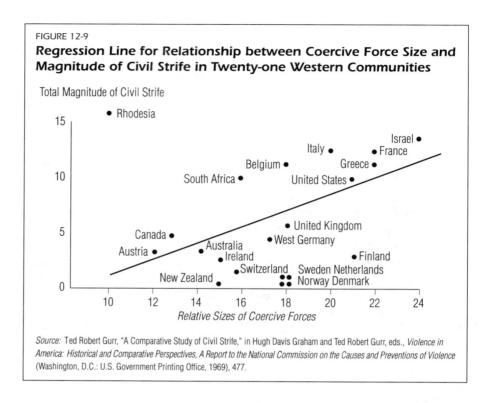

FIGURE 12-9

Regression Line for Relationship between Coercive Force Size and Magnitude of Civil Strife in Twenty-one Western Communities

Source: Ted Robert Gurr, "A Comparative Study of Civil Strife," in Hugh Davis Graham and Ted Robert Gurr, eds., *Violence in America: Historical and Comparative Perspectives, A Report to the National Commission on the Causes and Preventions of Violence* (Washington, D.C.: U.S. Government Printing Office, 1969), 477.

With hundreds of data points it is often difficult to tell visually exactly how close the regression line is to the points and how strong the relationship is between the variables. Consequently, there is a statistic, called the **Pearson product-moment correlation** (r), that may be calculated for any regression line. It tells you at a glance how good the fit is between the data points and the line. This correlation varies from 0 for no relationship to ±1 for a perfect relationship. It is calculated from the vertical distances between each of the data points and the regression line.

The product-moment correlation is very similar to eta-squared. It is based on the variance in the dependent variable (total variance) that we are trying to explain. We attempt to explain as much of the variance as possible by drawing a regression line through the points and approximating the values of the dependent variable from the values of the independent variable. The squared vertical distances from the data points to this line represent the variance in the dependent variable that is not accounted for by the regression line. The sum of these squared distances for all the data points is the unexplained variance.

The square of the product-moment correlation (r^2) shows exactly how much variance has been explained by the independent variable. Therefore, r^2

is exactly analogous to eta-squared; the closer it is to +1, the stronger the relationship is.

$$r = \sqrt{\frac{1 - \text{unexplained variance}}{\text{total variance}}} \quad \text{or} \quad \sqrt{\frac{1 - \sum_{i=1}^{N}(Y_i - \hat{Y}_i)^2}{\sum_{i=1}^{N}(Y_i - \overline{Y})^2}}$$

$$r^2 = \frac{1 - \text{unexplained variance}}{\text{total variance}} \quad \text{or} \quad \frac{1 - \sum_{i=1}^{N}(Y_i - \hat{Y}_i)^2}{\sum_{i=1}^{N}(Y_i - \overline{Y})^2}$$

Where

Y_i = actual observations

$\hat{Y}_i$ = predicted observations

$\overline{Y}$ = mean of Y

It is also possible to calculate r directly from the observed data:

$$r = \frac{N\Sigma XY - (\Sigma X)(\Sigma Y)}{[N\Sigma X^2 - (\Sigma X)^2][N\Sigma Y^2 - (\Sigma Y)^2]}$$

As we mentioned earlier, the slope of a regression line and the correlation coefficient for a regression line indicate two quite different things. The slope shows how much change in the dependent variable is associated with change in the independent variable; the correlation coefficient shows how much variance in the dependent variable is explained with the independent variable. It is quite possible to have a steep slope but a low correlation, indicating that the dependent variable changes a lot for every unit change in the independent variable but that the regression line does not approximate the data very well. It is also possible to have a very small slope but a very high correlation, indicating that the dependent variable does not change very much for every unit change in the independent variable but that the regression line is a good representation of the data.

The magnitude of the slope is heavily dependent upon the variables involved and the units of measurement being used; almost always, however, researchers hope that the correlation is high, that is, that the regression line shows a close fit with the data points.

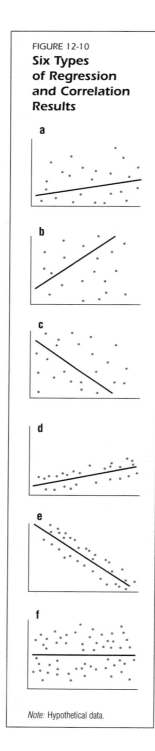

FIGURE 12-10

Six Types of Regression and Correlation Results

a

b

c

d

e

f

Note: Hypothetical data.

Figure 12-10 illustrates six different types of analytical results using regression and correlation analysis: a weak and positive relationship with a small slope (a), a weak and positive relationship with a large slope (b), a weak and negative relationship with a large slope (c), a strong and positive relationship with a small slope (d), a strong and negative relationship with a large slope (e), and no relationship between the independent and dependent variables (f). In this last example, the predicted value of the dependent variable is the same no matter what the value of the independent variable is.

A good example of the use of correlation analysis may be found in Segal and Cover's study of Supreme Court justices' votes on civil liberties cases. Recall that they were interested in the relationship between the justices' ideology, as inferred from newspaper editorials about them, and their decisions once they reached the bench. Since both variables were conceived as ratio level measures, it was possible for Segal and Cover to calculate a regression equation relating the two variables and the product-moment correlation representing the strength of the relationship. Their result was a correlation of .80 between ideological values and votes, indicating a strong relationship between the two. Figure 12-11 displays this relationship on a scattergram. Those justices positioned above the regression line had cast more liberal votes on civil liberties cases than expected based on the researchers' measure of personal ideology; those justices positioned below the line had been less liberal than expected.

The correlation coefficient (r) also may be used to indicate the statistical significance of the observed relationship. Once the coefficient has been calculated, it can be checked against the appropriate table (see Appendix D) to determine if it is above or below the criterion level of statistical significance. This criterion level is dependent upon the size of the sample from which the data are drawn, and it indicates the probability that the null hypothesis is true. Again, remember that statistical significance is not

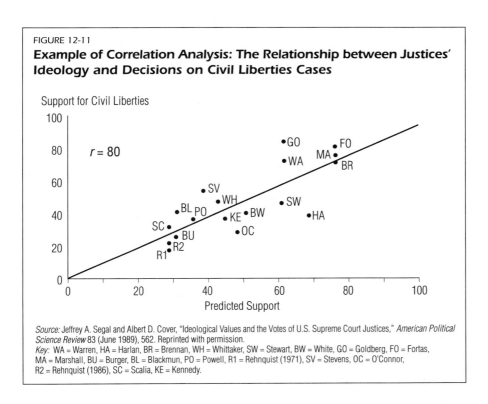

FIGURE 12-11

**Example of Correlation Analysis: The Relationship between Justices'
Ideology and Decisions on Civil Liberties Cases**

Source: Jeffrey A. Segal and Albert D. Cover, "Ideological Values and the Votes of U.S. Supreme Court Justices," *American Political Science Review* 83 (June 1989), 562. Reprinted with permission.
Key: WA = Warren, HA = Harlan, BR = Brennan, WH = Whittaker, SW = Stewart, BW = White, GO = Goldberg, FO = Fortas, MA = Marshall, BU = Burger, BL = Blackmun, PO = Powell, R1 = Rehnquist (1971), SV = Stevens, OC = O'Connor, R2 = Rehnquist (1986), SC = Scalia, KE = Kennedy.

the same as substantive importance; very weak relationships observed in very large samples readily attain statistical significance.

Researchers often use correlation analysis to determine the strength of the relationships among many different variables. In this case they are less concerned with the mathematical function associating independent and dependent variables than with how much variance in a dependent variable is explained by a number of independent variables. The results of a correlation analysis are often used to eliminate some variables from an analysis so that those most useful in accounting for the dependent variable can be studied more easily. A **correlation matrix** shows relationships *among* variables, whereas a scattergram shows only each individual relationship.

Gurr constructed a correlation matrix to test the relationship between a number of variables—such as economic deprivation, coercive force size, past strife levels, and system legitimacy—and civil strife. The matrix, presented in Table 12-23, shows the strength of the relationships among the independent variables, among the different measures of the dependent variable, and between the independent and dependent variables. Gurr then used this initial test of his hypothesis to guide him in the search for a more efficient

TABLE 12-23
Correlation Matrix Showing the Correlates of Civil Strife[a]

Variable[b]	1	2	3	4	5	6	7	8	9	10	11	12	13	14
1 Economic deprivation (+)		48	83	-02	-17	-16	-36	-09	26	32	34	31	25	44
2 Political deprivation (+)			88	08	-18	03	-37	-20	33	27	44	18	30	38
3 Short-term deprivation (+)				04	-20	-07	-42	-17	34	34	46	28	32	48
4 Persisting deprivation (+)					-04	-21	-14	-37	17	17	29	26	27	36
5 Legitimacy (-)						25	48	02	-05	-15	-29	-23	-29	-37
6 Coercive force size (±)							53	27	31	04	-23	-11	-01	-14
7 Coercive potential (-)								41	-14	-37	-44	-39	-35	-51
8 Institutionalization (-)									-19	-40	-35	-23	-26	-33
9 Past strife levels (+)										41	24	16	30	30
10 Facilitation (+)											42	57	30	67
11 Magnitude of conspiracy												30	32	59
12 Magnitude of internal war													17	79
13 Magnitude of turmoil														61
14 Total magnitude of strife														

Source: Ted Gurr, "A Causal Model of Civil Strife: A Comparative Analysis Using New Indices," *American Political Science Review* 2 (December 1968): 1117. Reprinted with permission.

[a] Product moment correlation coefficients, multiplied by 100. Underlined r's are significant, for N = 114, at the .01 level. Correlations between 18 and 23, inclusive, are significant at the .05 level.

[b] The proposed relationships between the independent variables, nos. 1 to 10, and the strife measures are shown in parentheses, the + / − for coercive force size signifying a proposed curvilinear relationship. Examination of the r's between the independent and dependent variables, in the box, shows that all are in the predicted direction with the anticipated exception of coercive force size, and that all but one are significant at the .05 level.

TABLE 12-24

Relationship between Self-Interest Measures, Racial Attitudes, and Attitudes toward Busing: Product-Moment Correlations

Independent Variable	Correlation
Parents of school-age children	.12[a]
Parents of public-school children	.10[b]
Parents of bused children	.03
Homeowner	.09[b]
Relatives in area	.04
Lived in area long time	.09[b]
Happy with neighborhood	−.06[c]
Intent to stay in area	−.01
Self interest index	.11[a]
Modern racism	.51[a]
Old-fashioned racism	.36[a]
Affect for blacks	−.15[a]

Source: John B. McConahay, "Self-Interest versus Racial Attitudes as Correlates of 'Anti-Busing' Attitudes in Louisville: Is It the Buses or the Blacks?" *Journal of Politics* 44 (August 1982): 711. Reprinted by permission of Blackwell Publishers Journals.

[a] p'' .001. This correlation indicates that parents of school-age children are slightly more likely to oppose busing than are parents without school-age children.
[b] p'' .01
[c] p'' .05

explanatory model of civil strife by eliminating from further analysis those variables weakly related to civil strife.

Another example of correlational analysis may be found in John McConahay's analysis of attitudes toward busing.[11] McConahay was interested in the relationships between a person's personal involvement in busing, racial attitudes, and attitudes toward busing. His initial analysis of these relationships involved calculating the product-moment correlation between a number of independent variables and the dependent variable (attitudes toward busing). The correlations, reported in Table 12-24, led McConahay to an initial conclusion that racial attitudes rather than personal involvement are associated with attitudes toward busing.

Other Issues

Before concluding our discussion of correlation and regression analysis, we will address two remaining issues. First, the information contained in a regression analysis may help a researcher analyze the unexplained variation in the dependent variable. Recall that the regression equation indicates the expected value of the dependent variable for each case, given that case's value on the independent variable. The difference between this expected value and the actual observed value is called the **residual** (the variation left over), and it measures how well the regression line fits the data points. Residuals also may be used to explain why the cases did not take on the value for the dependent variable that was predicted from the regression line. The researcher might be able to identify a second independent variable that could account for a portion of the unexplained variance left by the first independent variable. (We examine this procedure in more detail in Chapter 13.)

In our example of the relationship between income and personal contacts with public officials, consider the case of a person who earned $80,000 and made three contacts. According to the regression equation describing the relationship between income and personal contacts, we would expect such a person to have made 6.6 contacts. Consequently, this person made 3.6 fewer contacts than expected; –3.6 is the residual of this case. This residual might stimulate our curiosity. Why did this particular person contact public officials so many fewer times than his income alone would have predicted? This question might lead us to analyze all of those who contacted public officials fewer times than expected and to develop a hypothesis that would explain this discrepancy. In this way residuals may be used to extend a researcher's analysis and provide a more complete understanding of the phenomenon under investigation. Residual scores may themselves become dependent variables in hypotheses designed to explain the amount of discrepancy between the expected and observed values for some dependent variable.

The second issue we need to address is the deceptive simplicity of linear regression. A computer can draw a straight line through any set of data points, yielding a linear regression equation purporting to capture the relationship between two variables. However, some data points may be better described by a parabola, sine curve, U-curve, or J-curve than by a straight line. If a researcher fails to consider these other possibilities without first inspecting the graph of the data points and has a computer calculate only the best-fitting straight line, a more representative characterization of the relationship may be missed.

An actual example of a curvilinear relationship may be found in Wolfinger and Rosenstone's study of voter turnout. They hypothesized a relationship between age and voter turnout.[12] A scattergram of this relationship indicated that there was, indeed, a relationship, but that it was a curvilinear rather than a linear one, as Figure 12-12 shows. It is the middle-aged who vote most frequently, and the young and old alike who vote least frequently. Therefore, a straight line would not have been the best approximation of the relationship between age and turnout.

Like regression analysis, correlational analysis can disguise strong, non-linear relationships. All the correlation coefficient indicates is the fit between the data points and the best-fitting straight line. Drawing a straight line through a set of data points better represented with a curve will often result

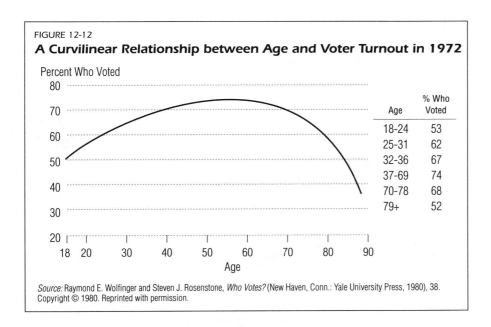

FIGURE 12-12

A Curvilinear Relationship between Age and Voter Turnout in 1972

Percent Who Voted

Age	% Who Voted
18-24	53
25-31	62
32-36	67
37-69	74
70-78	68
79+	52

Source: Raymond E. Wolfinger and Steven J. Rosenstone, *Who Votes?* (New Haven, Conn.: Yale University Press, 1980), 38. Copyright © 1980. Reprinted with permission.

in a very low product-moment correlation, perhaps leading the researcher to ignore a nonlinear relationship. Had the researcher checked the scattergram upon which the correlation coefficient was calculated, it would have become evident that a curvilinear relationship was a better representation of the data points. Researchers are well advised, therefore, to inspect the scattergrams corresponding to every regression equation and product-moment correlation that they calculate.

Conclusion

In this chapter we have shown how to measure the existence, direction, strength, and statistical significance of relationships between two variables. The particular techniques used—crosstabulation, difference of means test, analysis of variance, regression analysis, and correlation analysis—depend, in part, on the levels of measurement—nominal, ordinal, interval, or ratio—of the independent and dependent variables. Just because a relationship is present, however, does not mean that a cause of the dependent variable has been discovered. We will explain this in more detail in Chapter 13.

Notes

1. In reality, there are many techniques for analyzing relationships at a given level of measurement. The ones presented in this chapter are the most common and least complicated.

2. Raymond E. Wolfinger and Steven J. Rosenstone, *Who Votes?* (New Haven: Yale University Press, 1980).

3. For further information about the calculation of each of these statistics, see Hubert M. Blalock Jr., *Social Statistics,* rev. 2d ed. (New York: McGraw-Hill, 1979).

4. This decision rule assumes you will accept any outcome, *Y*, that is less than 15. It is the basis of what is called a one-sided test. You could establish a different decision rule by counting large values of *Y* (15 or higher) *and* low values (15 or fewer) as evidence. This would be a two-sided test.

5. Edward R. Tufte, *Data Analysis for Politics and Policy* (Upper Saddle River, N.J.: Prentice-Hall, 1975).

6. A more complete discussion of the calculation of the F ratio may be found in Blalock, *Social Statistics,* chap. 16.

7. It is important to note that two variables may be related—that is, they may not be statistically independent—but still have no linear correlation between them. In other words, it might be possible to find a line that passes through most of the data, but it will not be a *straight* line.

8. Robert D. Putnam et al., "Explaining Institutional Success: The Case of Italian Regional Government," *American Political Science Review* 77 (March 1983): 55–74.

9. Ted Robert Gurr, "A Comparative Study of Civil Strife," in Hugh Davis Graham and Ted Robert Gurr, eds., *Violence in America: Historical and Comparative Perspectives* (New York: New American Library, 1969). See also Ted Gurr, "A Causal Model of Civil Strife: A Comparative Analysis Using New Indices," *American Political Science Review* 2 (December 1968): 1104–1124.

10. Gurr, "A Comparative Study," 580–581.

11. John B. McConahay, "Self-Interest versus Racial Attitudes as Correlates of 'Anti-Busing' Attitudes in Louisville: Is It the Buses or the Blacks?" *Journal of Politics* 44 (August 1982): 692–720.

12. Wolfinger and Rosenstone, *Who Votes?*

Terms introduced

ANALYSIS OF VARIANCE. A technique for measuring the relationship between one nominal or ordinal level variable and one interval or ratio level variable.

CHI-SQUARE. A measure used with crosstabulation to determine if a relationship is statistically significant.

CORRELATION MATRIX. A table showing the correlations (usually Pearson product-moment correlations) among a number of variables.

CROSSTABULATION. A technique for measuring the relationship between nominal and ordinal level measures.

DEGREES OF FREEDOM. A measure used in conjunction with chi-square and other measures to determine if a relationship is statistically significant.

DIFFERENCE OF MEANS TEST. A technique for measuring the relationship between one nominal or ordinal level variable and one interval or ratio level variable.

DIRECTION OF A RELATIONSHIP. An indication of which values of the dependent variable are associated with which values of the independent variable.

ETA-SQUARED. A measure of association used with the analysis of variance that indicates the proportion of the variance in the dependent variable explained by the variance in the independent variable.

EXPLAINED VARIANCE. That portion of the variation in a dependent variable that is accounted for by the variation in the independent variable(s).

F RATIO. A measure used with the analysis of variance to determine if a relationship is statistically significant.

GOODMAN AND KRUSKAL'S GAMMA. A measure of association between ordinal level variables.

GOODMAN AND KRUSKAL'S LAMBDA. A measure of association between one nominal or ordinal level variable and one nominal level variable.

KENDALL'S TAU. A measure of association between ordinal level variables.

MEASURES OF ASSOCIATION. Statistics that summarize the relationship between two variables.

NEGATIVE RELATIONSHIP. A relationship in which high values of one variable are associated with low values of another variable.

NULL HYPOTHESIS. The hypothesis that there is no relationship between two variables in the target population.

PEARSON PRODUCT-MOMENT CORRELATION. The statistic computed from a regression analysis that indicates the strength of the relationship between two interval or ratio level variables.

POSITIVE RELATIONSHIP. A relationship in which high values of one variable are associated with high values of another variable.

REGRESSION ANALYSIS. A technique for measuring the relationship between two interval or ratio level variables.

REGRESSION COEFFICIENT. Another name for the slope of a regression equation.

REGRESSION EQUATION. The mathematical formula describing the relationship between two interval or ratio level variables.

RELATIONSHIP. A relationship is established when the values of one variable covary with or are dependent upon the values of another variable.

RESIDUAL. The difference between the observed and predicted values of Y (the dependent variable) in a regression analysis.

SCATTER PLOT. A technique for displaying graphically the relationship between two interval or ratio level variables.

SLOPE. The part of a regression equation that shows how much change in the value of Y (the dependent variable) corresponds to a one-unit change in the value of X (the independent variable).

SOMER'S D. A measure of association between ordinal level variables.

STATISTICAL SIGNIFICANCE. An indication of whether an observed relationship could have occurred by chance.

STATISTICALLY INDEPENDENT. Property of two variables where the probability that an observation is in a particular category of one variable *and* a particular category of the other variable equals the simple or marginal probability of being in those categories.

STRENGTH OF A RELATIONSHIP. An indication of how consistently the values of a dependent variable are associated with the values of an independent variable.

t TEST. A statistical procedure used to determine the statistical significance of a difference of means.

TOTAL VARIANCE. The variation in a dependent variable that a researcher is attempting to account for.

UNEXPLAINED VARIANCE. That portion of the variation in a dependent variable that is not accounted for by the variation in the independent variable(s).

Y-INTERCEPT. The value of Y (the dependent variable) in a regression equation when the value of X (the independent variable) is 0.

Exercises

1. A researcher interested in the relationship between city size and mass transit systems takes a random sample of 100 cities of varying sizes and finds that 20 of the small cities have transit systems and 30 do not; 12 of the mid-size cities have transit systems and 18 do not; and 8 of the large cities have transit systems and 12 do not.

   Construct a crosstabulation showing the relationship between the independent and dependent variables. Place the independent variable across the top of the table and calculate the percentages in the correct way. What do the table percentages indicate about the relationship between city size and the existence of a mass transit system?

2. Senator Blowchill, Republican from Pennsylvania, has charged that the Democratic administration is directing more federal funds to the Sunbelt states than to those in the Frostbelt. Senator Dryheat, Democrat from Alabama, disagrees and challenges Senator Blowchill to prove his claim. So Senator Blowchill tells his research assistant to select randomly ten states and analyze the relationship between the region and amount of federal funds spent. The research assistant produces the following crosstabulation and then hands it to you, a summer intern, for your interpretation. What would you say about the relationship in the table? Be sure to discuss the statistical significance, direction, and strength of the observed relationship.

	Sunbelt States	Frostbelt States
State has received an above average amount of federal funds	3	2
State has received a below average amount of federal funds	1	4

3. Suppose that you conducted a sample survey of 100 respondents and produced the following crosstabulation showing the relationship between religion and attitudes toward abortion. With 95 percent certainty, is there a relationship between the two variables? Is the relationship weak, moderate, or strong? What is the direction of the relationship? Which of the following correlation coefficients is correct for this crosstabulation: +.8, −.2, +.2, −.6? How would you express verbally the results of this crosstabulation?

	Catholic	Protestant
Oppose right to have an abortion	36	44
Favor right to have an abortion	4	16

4. What does the following crosstabulation of the relationship between education and ideology tell you about the strength, direction, and statistical significance of the relationship?

EDUCATION

	Low	Medium	High	
Liberal	20	50	80	150
Moderate	40	80	80	200
Conservative	40	70	40	150
	100	200	200	500

Which of the following correlation coefficients is the most likely: +.20, −.70, +.10, −.25? How would you express verbally the meaning of this relationship?

5. In Benjamin I. Page and Robert Y. Shapiro, "Effects of Public Opinion on Policy," *American Political Science Review* 77 (March 1983): 175–190, the authors test the relationship between the size of changes in public opinion and the congruence of opinion/policy change (Table 3). What does this crosstabulation indicate about this relationship? What measure of association is used?

6. The relationship between inequality in land ownership and political violence is tested in Manus I. Midlarsky, "Rulers and the Ruled: Patterned Inequality and the Onset of Mass Political Violence," *American Political Science Review* 82 (June 1988): 491–509. In Table 3 the relationship is displayed for twenty Latin American countries in a modified crosstabulation. What do the crosstab and the measures of association indicate about the relationship?

7. Read Ada W. Finifter and Ellen Mickiewicz, "Redefining the Political System of the USSR: Mass Support for Political Change," *American Political Science Review* 86 (December 1992): 857–874. What is the relationship between age and support for political change (Table 6)? What do the reported values of tau b and gamma indicate? Is this relationship statistically significant?

8. The relationship between family income and primary votes for the major Democratic candidates for president during the 1992 nomination campaign appears in Table 12-25. What is lambda for this crosstab? Why does it take on that value?

TABLE 12-25

Relationship between Family Income and Vote for Democratic Candidate for President, 1992

	Family Income					
Vote	Less than $15,000	$15,000–$29,999	$30,000–$49,999	$50,000–$74,999	$75,000 and over	Total
Clinton	62%	55%	48%	45%	38%	50%
Brown	17	19	23	23	23	21
Tsongas	13	18	21	25	29	20
Others	8	8	8	7	10	9
Total	100%	100%	100%	100%	100%	100%

Source: New York Times, July 12, 1992, 18.

9. Suppose you want to know if there is a relationship between the unemployment rate in cities and the number of robberies that occur within the city limits. You take a random sample of cities and plot the unemployment rates and number of robberies as shown in Figure 12-13. Answer the following questions about the graph and the regression line drawn to best approximate the data.
   a. What is the strength and direction of the relationship between the two variables? How do you know this? What does it mean?

FIGURE 12-13

Regression Line for the Relationship between Unemployment and Robberies

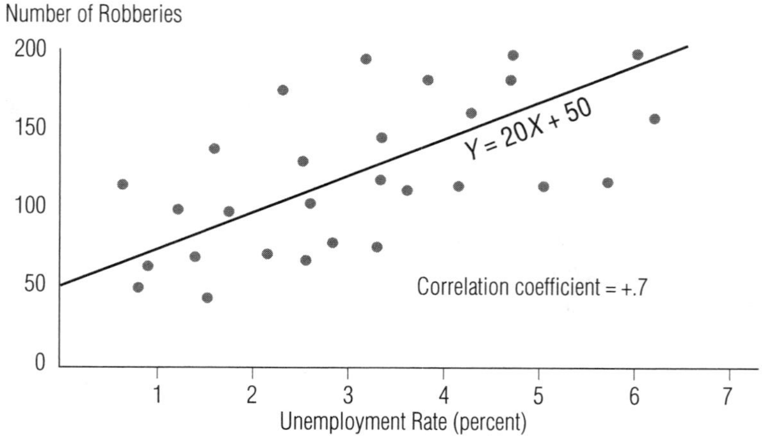

Note: Hypothetical data.

TABLE 12-26

Relationship between Gender and Political Ideology

	Male	Female	Total
Extremely liberal	10	13	23
Liberal	37	82	119
Slightly liberal	64	88	152
Moderate	167	236	403
Slightly conservative	109	102	211
Conservative	142	100	242
Extremely conservative	22	23	45
Total	551	644	1,196

Source: 1996 American National Election Study.

Note: Question: "Where would you place yourself on this scale, or haven't you thought much about this?" Only valid responses included.

b. If the unemployment rate in a given city increases by 1 percent, about how many additional robberies will occur?

c. If there were no unemployment in a city, how many robberies would you expect to occur?

d. What other factors might make a city experience more robberies or fewer robberies than you would expect based on the unemployment rate alone?

10. You observe that there is a statistically significant relationship between the amount of television Americans watch and the number of violent crimes Americans commit. Therefore, you conclude that watching television causes Americans to commit violent crimes. What is wrong with your conclusion?

11. An important issue in the study of American public opinion is the issue of a "gender gap." Do women tend to have different political attitudes and behavior than men? Table 12-26 shows a crosstab between gender and self placement on a political ideology scale. See if there is a relationship between sex and ideology by (1) constructing a table of percentages using gender as the independent variable; (2) measuring the strength of association with gamma or another measure of association described in the chapter; and (3) testing the hypothesis that the variables are statistically independent with the chi-square statistic.

Suggested Readings

Agresti, Alan. *An Introduction to Categorical Data Analysis.* New York: Wiley, 1996.

Agresti, Alan, and Barbara Finlay. *Statistical Methods for the Social Sciences.* 3d ed. Upper Saddle River, N.J.: Prentice-Hall, 1997.

Blalock, Hubert M. *Social Statistics*. 2d ed. New York: McGraw-Hill, 1972.

Elifson, Kirk W., Richard P. Runyon, and Audrey Haber. *Fundamentals of Social Statistics*. Reading, Mass.: Addison-Wesley, 1982.

Healey, Joseph F. *Statistics: A Tool for Social Research*. Belmont, Calif.: Wadsworth, 1984.

Kinnear, Paul R., and Colin D. Gray. *SPSS for Windows Made Simple Release 10*. East Sussex: Psychology Press, 2000.

Lewis-Beck, Michael S., ed. *Basic Statistics*. Vol. 1. Thousand Oaks, Calif.: Sage, 1993.

Mueller, John, Karl Schuessler, and Herbert Costner. *Statistical Reasoning in Sociology*. 2d ed. Boston: Houghton Mifflin, 1970.

Nie, Norman H., et al. *SPSS*. 2d ed. New York: McGraw-Hill, 1975.

Norusis, Marija J. *SPSS 10.0 Guide to Data Analysis*. Upper Saddle River, N.J.: Prentice-Hall, 2000.

Phillips, John L. *Statistical Thinking*. San Francisco: W. H. Freeman, 1973.

Watson, George, and Dickinson McGraw. *Statistical Inquiry*. New York: Wiley, 1980.

CHAPTER 13

Searching for Complete Explanations and Causal Knowledge:

Multivariate Data Analysis

In Chapter 12 we discussed how to measure the existence, strength, direction, and statistical significance of a relationship between two variables, one independent and one dependent, using various statistical procedures and for different types of measurement scales. Although analyzing a single relationship between two variables is fairly straightforward, most political science research involves the analysis of many independent variables. As a result, **multivariate data analysis** is required.

Many political scientists use multivariate analysis to investigate the impact of several independent variables on a dependent variable. For example, Gary Jacobson, found that the variation in votes received by candidates for the U.S. Congress could be explained in a number of ways. Although he was most interested in the impact of candidate spending on electoral outcomes, he also considered the relationships between the distribution of the vote and the challenger's party, the challenger's prior political experience, the number of years the incumbent had held office, the challenger's district party strength, and whether the candidates had run in a primary election. Only by considering the joint or simultaneous relations among these variables could he reach some firm conclusions about campaign spending and its effect on the vote for congressional candidates.[1]

Most of the research we have discussed in previous chapters also used multivariate analysis. Ted Gurr, for example, used a number of independent variables to explain cross-national variation in civil strife. Although his major independent variable was relative deprivation, he also tested the relationships between civil strife and legitimacy (the amount of popular support for and acceptance of the decisions made by the regime); coercive potential (the ability of the regime to punish those participating in civil strife); institutionalization ("the extent to which societal structures beyond the primary level are broad in scope, command substantial resources and/or personnel, and are stable and persisting"); and facilitation (the existence of social and environmental conditions that would encourage or enhance civil strife).[2] Gurr used all of these factors to account for levels of civil strife because he believed that each one would have some effect on the dependent variable. But besides looking at the individual relationships between each of the independent variables and civil strife, he also examined the *combined* relationship between all of the independent variables and civil strife. He concluded that persistent deprivation did have an impact on the magnitude of civil strife, even when other possible explanations were taken into account.

Benjamin Page and Robert Shapiro's article on the relationship between public opinion change and public policy change also concludes with a multivariate analysis designed to explain why there is more congruence between public opinion and policy in some cases than in others.[3] The authors used a variety of independent variables measuring aspects of the opinion change, the type of policy, and the political context in which the policy response occurred in an attempt to explain the variation in opinion-policy congruence.

These studies suggest that there are two reasons for analyzing relationships among more than just two variables: to provide more complete explanations for political phenomena and to make and strengthen causal inferences. For most political phenomena more than one independent variable is needed to explain the variation in a dependent variable or to make accurate predictions. Political behavior is usually so complex that one needs a number of concepts to explain it adequately.

Moreover, if a researcher is interested in acquiring causal knowledge, a number of competing possible explanations for the phenomenon must be investigated and eliminated. Simply because a factor exhibits a strong relationship with a dependent variable does not mean that the former caused the latter. Both the independent and dependent variables might be caused by a third variable, which could create the appearance of a relationship between the first two and lead to an erroneous conclusion about the effects of the independent variable. The possibility that a third variable is the real cause of both the independent and dependent variables must be considered before one makes causal claims. Only by eliminating this possibility can a researcher achieve some confidence that a relationship between an independent and dependent variable is a causal one. Figure 13-1 illustrates the problem of distinguishing possible causal explanations.

In Edward Tufte's study of automobile fatalities, to take a concrete case, a relationship between the existence of mandatory automobile inspections and

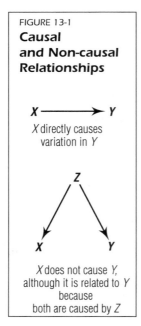

FIGURE 13-1

Causal and Non-causal Relationships

$X \longrightarrow Y$

X directly causes variation in Y

Z

X   Y

X does not cause Y, although it is related to Y because both are caused by Z lower auto fatalities was observed (see Figure 12-2 on page 366).[4] This does not necessarily mean, however, that inspections cause a decline in auto fatality rates. There may be another phenomenon related to inspections and auto deaths that is causing the relationship between the two. Tufte discovered a strong inverse relationship between population density and auto fatality rates, and he also discovered that those states with mandatory inspections tend to be more densely populated. Therefore, until population density was eliminated as a possible cause of the relationship between inspections and auto fatalities, he could not make a causal claim about the observed bivariate relationship.

In this chapter we explain how political scientists use multivariate techniques to *control for* the effects of a third variable. This means that the impact of other variables is removed or taken into account when measuring the strength and direction of the relationship between an independent and dependent variable. Generally, the impact of a third variable may be controlled either experimentally or statistically. **Experimental control** is introduced by assigning the subjects in an experiment to different groups and controlling each group's exposure to the experimental stimulus. **Statistical control**, the procedure used more frequently by political scientists, involves measuring each observation's values on the control variables and using these measures to make comparisons between observations.

Multivariate Analysis of Categorical Data

Although social scientists have very sophisticated techniques for analyzing categorical or crosstabulated data, we begin with some simple methods since they show the underlying logic. Displaying and measuring the relationship between two nominal or ordinal level variables was explained in Chapter 12. If the joint distribution of observations on the two variables is displayed in a crosstabulation table (sometimes called a contingency table), we see how the values of the dependent variable are related to the categories of the independent variable. The extent to which the cases in the different categories of the independent variable exhibit different values on the dependent variable indicates the strength and direction of the relationship.

Suppose, for example, that we have hypothesized a relationship between attitudes toward government spending and presidential voting. Our hypothesis is that "the more a person favors a decrease in government spending, the more likely she is to vote Republican." Table 13-1 seems to confirm the hypothesis, since 64 percent of those who favor decreased spending voted Republican while only 46 percent of those who favored keeping spending the same or increasing it voted Republican. This difference of 18 percentage points among a sample of 1,000 suggests that there is a weak relationship between attitudes toward government spending and presidential voting behavior.

TABLE 13-1
Relationship between Attitudes toward Government Spending and Presidential Vote

Dependent Variable: Presidential Vote	Independent Variable: Attitudes toward Government Spending		
	Decrease spending	Keep spending the same or increase it	(N)
Republican	64%	46%	(555)
Democratic	36	54	(445)
Total	100	100	
(N)	(550)	(450)	(1,000)

Note: Hypothetical data.

At this point, someone might ask, "Is there a causal relationship between opinion and vote (see the upper graph in Figure 13-1) or is there another factor, such as wealth, that creates the apparent relationship?" Or, even if one is not interested in causality, the question arises, "Can the explanation of presidential voting be increased by including another variable?" After all, 36 percent of those who favored decreased spending voted contrary to the hypothesis, as did 46 percent of those in favor of maintaining or increasing spending levels. Perhaps it would be possible to provide an explanation for those voters' behavior and hence improve the understanding of presidential voting behavior.

A second independent variable that might affect presidential voting is income. People with higher incomes might favor decreased government spending because they feel they gain little from most government programs. Those with higher incomes might also be more likely to vote Republican because they perceive the GOP to be the party that favors government policies that benefit the affluent. By the same token, people having lower incomes might feel both that increased government spending would help them *and* that Democrats generally support their interests. Therefore, income might influence both attitudes toward government spending and presidential voting and thus could create the appearance of a relationship between the two.

To consider the impact of income we need to bring it explicitly into the analysis and observe the resulting relationship between attitudes and voting. In a **multivariate crosstabulation**, we control for a third variable by holding it constant. In effect, we **control by grouping**, that is, we group the observations according to their values on the third variable and then observe the original relationship within each of these groups. In our example, each group consists of people with more or less the same income. If a relationship between opinions on spending and voting in these groups remains, it cannot be

TABLE 13-2

Spurious Relationship between Attitudes and Presidential Voting When Income is Controlled

Control Variable: Income Dependent Variable: Presidential Vote	Independent Variable: Attitudes toward Government Spending		
	Decrease spending	Keep spending the same or increase it	(N)
High income			
Republican	80%	80%	(240)
Democratic	20	20	(60)
Total	100	100	
(N)	(250)	(50)	(300)
Medium income			
Republican	60%	60%	(210)
Democratic	40	40	(140)
Total	100	100	
(N)	(200)	(150)	(350)
Low income			
Republican	30%	30%	(105)
Democratic	70	70	(245)
Total	100	100	
(N)	(100)	(250)	(350)

Note: Hypothetical data.

due to income. As an example, we can observe the relationship between government spending attitudes and vote separately among those with low, medium, and high incomes.

Table 13-2 shows what might happen were we to control for income. Notice that it actually contains three contingency tables—one for each category of income, the control variable. Within each of the categories of income there is now *no* relationship between spending attitudes and presidential voting. Regardless of their attitudes on spending, 80 percent of respondents with high incomes voted Republican, 60 percent with medium incomes voted Republican, and 30 percent with low incomes voted Republican. Once the variation in income was removed by combining those with similar incomes together, the attitude-vote relationship disappeared. Consequently, income is a possible alternative explanation for the variation in presidential voting.

The original relationship, then, was spurious. A **spurious relationship** is one in which the relationship between two variables is caused entirely by the impact of a third. In this case, attitudes cannot be a direct cause of presidential voting because they had no effect on voting once income had been taken

TABLE 13-3

Original Relationship between Attitudes and Presidential Voting Remains after Income is Controlled

Control Variable: Income	Independent Variable: Attitudes toward Government Spending		
Dependent Variable: Presidential Vote	Decrease spending	Keep spending the same or increase it	(N)
High income			
Republican	64%	64%	(192)
Democratic	36	36	(108)
Total	100	100	
(N)	(250)	(50)	(300)
Medium income			
Republican	64%	64%	(224)
Democratic	36	36	(126)
Total	100	100	
(N)	(200)	(150)	(350)
Low income			
Republican	64%	64%	(224)
Democratic	36	36	(126)
Total	100	100	
(N)	(100)	(250)	(350)

Note: Hypothetical data.

into account. Respondents did not vote the way they did because of their different attitudes toward government spending.

Note, however, that these remarks do not mean that there is *no* relationship between spending attitudes and presidential voting, for there is such a relationship, as Table 13-1 shows. But this original relationship only occurred because of the variables' relationships with a third factor, income. It also means that the original relationship was not a causal one; spending attitudes cannot possibly be a cause of presidential voting because within income groups they make no difference whatever. The only reason for the relationship between spending attitudes and presidential voting is the effect of income on both variables. (See the lower graph in Figure 13-1.)

Since we have been using hypothetical data, we can imagine other outcomes. Suppose, for instance, the control variable had absolutely no effect on the relationship between attitudes and vote. The result might look like those in Table 13-3. We now see that the strength and direction of the relationship between attitudes and voting is the same in all levels of income. In this particular situation members of the upper income group behave just like those in the lower levels. Given these data we might be tempted to support the argument that attitudes toward government spending are causally related to candidate choice.

Obviously, these hypothetical data illustrate ideal situations. Consider, then, an example of an actual multivariate crosstabulation analysis, Raymond Wolfinger and Steven Rosenstone's study of voter turnout.[5] The authors observed a positive relationship between education and turnout (the higher the education, the higher the turnout) and a curvilinear relationship between age and turnout (the older a person, up to an age of about seventy, the higher the turnout and after seventy, a decline). However, since there is also a relationship between age and educa-

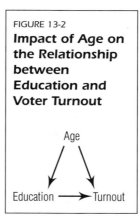

FIGURE 13-2
Impact of Age on the Relationship between Education and Voter Turnout

tion (older people tend to have fewer years of formal education since they grew up at a time when high school and college educations were rarer), the researchers wondered whether it was age, or education, or both, that affected turnout most. In other words, they were interested in testing the three-variable model presented in Figure 13-2.

The last column of Table 13-4 shows the simple bivariate relationship between education and turnout: as education increases, so too does the percentage of respondents who said they voted. Similarly, the bottom row shows the relationship between age and turnout. (Note that turnout seems to increase with age up to the 37 to 69 years old category and then declines slightly.) The relationship between education and turnout, controlling for age, may be observed in the table's body by looking *down* each column. Since each column contains observations grouped by age, age is being held constant (or nearly so). Turnout levels generally increase as one looks down each column. Thus,

TABLE 13-4
Relationship between Age, Education, and Turnout, 1972

| Education | Age | | | | | | |
	18–24	25–31	32–36	37–69	70–78	78+	Total
0–8 (grammar school)	14	26	36	56	58	44	52
9–12 (high school)	44	55	63	75	76	63	65
1–3 college	72	76	79	87	85	72	79
4 college	76	84	89	90	85	75	86
5+ college	85	86	91	93	94	80	91
Total	53	62	67	74	68	52	67

Source: Raymond E. Wolfinger and Steven J. Rosenstone, *Who Votes?* (New Haven, Conn.: Yale University Press, 1980), 47. Reprinted with permission.

Note: The entry in each cell is the percentage of people voting with the given combination of age and education. For example, 36 percent of people aged 32 to 36 who had not attended high school voted.

399

the relationship with education persists after controlling for age. In addition, the relationship between age and turnout, controlling for education, may be observed by looking *across* each row. Now education is being held approximately constant because each row contains observations grouped by education. Turnout levels increase, up to age seventy, and then decrease. Thus, the relationship with age persists after controlling for education.

In this case, then, the relationship between education and turnout is not spurious. Both independent variables exhibit relationships with turnout independent of the other. Therefore, education and age together account for more of the variation in turnout than does either variable alone.

In complex contingency tables containing more than one control factor and having variables with more than two or three response categories it is often difficult to discern changes in the magnitude and nature of the original relationships. Moreover, even in a relatively simple situation where a researcher controls for a third variable, five general results can arise. First, the original relationship may disappear entirely, indicating that it was spurious. This was the case with the government spending attitudes and presidential voting example. Second, the original relationship may decline somewhat but not completely disappear, indicating that it was partly spurious. A **partly spurious relationship** is one in which some but not all of the original relationship may be accounted for with the control variable. Third, the original relationship may remain unchanged, indicating that the third variable was not responsible for the original relationship. (See Table 13-3.) Fourth, the original relationship may increase, indicating that the control variable was disguising or deflating the true relationship between the independent and dependent variables. Fifth, the controlled relationship may be different for different categories of the control variable. This is called a **specified relationship**. It indicates that the relationship between two variables is dependent upon the values of a third. For example, the relationship between attitudes and voting may be strong only among medium income people. If the relationship between two variables differs significantly for different categories of a third, then we say that the third variable has specified the relationship, or that an "interaction" is present.

It is frequently useful to use a measure of association in addition to percentages to help see the effects of a control variable. Table 13-5 presents a summary of the possible results when a third variable is held constant. The top of each panel shows a hypothetical measure of association for the uncontrolled relationship between the independent and dependent variable. The next three lines display the same information for each *category* of the control variable. Comparing the uncontrolled results with the controlled results indicates whether the relationship is spurious (a), partially spurious (b), unchanged (c), has increased (d), or has been specified (e). (Note, for example,

TABLE 13-5
Five Results When Controlling for a Third Variable

Uncontrolled Relationship	Measure of Association	Significance Level
a.	+.35	.001
Category 1	+.05	.07
Category 2	−.03	.14
Category 3	+.01	.10
b.	+.42	.001
Category 1	+.20	.01
Category 2	+.17	.05
Category 3	+.26	.001
c.	−.28	.01
Category 1	−.30	.05
Category 2	−.35	.01
Category 3	−.27	.05
d.	−.12	.08
Category 1	−.42	.001
Category 2	−.30	.01
Category 3	−.35	.001
e.	+.31	.001
Category 1	+.55	.001
Category 2	+.37	.01
Category 3	+.16	.05

Note: Hypothetical data.

that in panel b the measure of association decreases in each level of the control variable but does not approach zero. This pattern suggests that the control factor partly but not totally explains the original relationship.)

Multivariate crosstabulation analysis, then, may be used to assess the impact of one or more control variables when those variables are measured at the nominal or ordinal level. Although this is a relatively straightforward and frequently used procedure, it has several disadvantages.

First, it is difficult to interpret the numerous crosstabs required when a researcher wishes to control for a large number of variables at once and the variables all have a large number of categories. Suppose, for example, that you wanted to observe the relationship between television news viewing and political knowledge while controlling for education (five categories), newspaper exposure (four categories), and political interest (three categories). You would need to construct sixty different groups and look at the relationship in each one!

Second, controlling by grouping similar cases together can rapidly deplete the sample size for each of the control situations, producing less accurate and statistically insignificant estimates of the relationships. Suppose that we had started out with a standard sample size of 1,500 respondents in our example of the relationship between television news exposure and political knowledge. By the time we had divided the sample into the sixty discrete control groups, each subtable measuring the relationship between news exposure and political knowledge would have, on average, only 25 people in it. In practice, many would have many fewer cases and some might not have any at all. All of these potentially sparse tables would make it virtually impossible to observe a significant relationship between news exposure and political knowledge.

A third problem is that control groups in multivariate crosstabulation analysis often disregard some of the variation in one or more of the variables. For example, to control for income in our government-spending attitude/presidential voting example, we put all those with low incomes into one group. This grouping ignored what might be important variations in actual income levels.

For these reasons social scientist are moving away from the analysis of multivariate crosstabulations with percentages and measures of association. Unfortunately, the mathematics required in the new procedures is beyond the scope of this book. (We do, however, look at the analysis of dichotomous dependent variables in a later section.) Nevertheless, the goal of the more complicated procedures is the same as that discussed here: the analysis of the effects of two or more independent variables on a dependent variable. How, for instance, does holding one or more variables constant affect the relationship between two other variables? Can one make causal inferences?

Two-Way Analysis of Variance

Two-way analysis of variance may be used to assess the extent to which two or more independent variables measured at the nominal or ordinal level can explain the variance in a quantitative or numerical dependent variable. The logic of this procedure is similar to the one-way analysis of variance described in Chapter 12. Recall that in the one-way analysis of variance, we begin with the observed variation in a dependent variable. The variance can be calculated for the full data set by subtracting the mean from each observation, squaring the difference, adding the total squared deviations, and, finally, dividing by $N - 1$. Then we divide the observations into categories based on their scores on an independent variable. Next, the mean and variance within each of these categories are calculated. If the means for the categories are quite different from one another and the variances within the categories are much smaller than the variance in the "ungrouped" dependent variable, the categorization is judged successful in accounting for variation in the dependent variable. The larger the difference in means across categories and the smaller the variances within categories of the independent variable, the stronger the relationship between independent and dependent variables.

Two-way analysis of variance proceeds in a similar fashion. Again we begin by determining the variance in the dependent variable. But now we have more than one independent variable with which to explain that variation. So it is necessary to divide the observations into categories based on combinations of values of the independent variables. The mean and variance on the dependent variable is then calculated within each of these categories.

FIGURE 13-3

Impact of State Population Density on the Relationship between State Inspection Policy and State Auto Fatality Rate

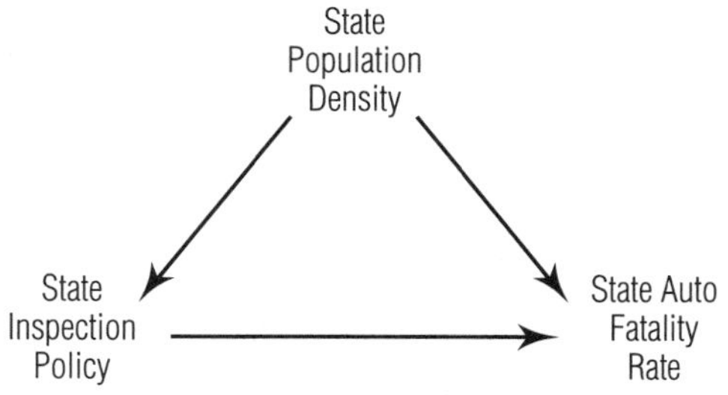

For example, recall that Tufte hypothesized that those states with mandatory automobile inspections would have fewer auto fatalities than those without them. A one-way analysis of variance showed that there was a weak relationship between the two variables. To provide a more complete explanation of auto fatalities and to confirm his suspicion that inspection policy was an important cause of variations in auto fatalities, Tufte then considered the effect of another independent variable—population density—on auto fatalities (see Figure 13-3).

Tufte argued that the population density of a state has numerous effects on behavior related to auto fatalities—such as the speed at which cars are driven, the distances they are driven, and the proximity of medical services to crash victims. When he calculated the state-level relationship between population density and auto fatality rates, he discovered a fairly strong, negative relationship; that is, as the density of a state increases, the auto fatality rate decreases. Furthermore, he found that there is a relationship between population density and the existence of auto inspection policies; eight of the nine most densely populated states had mandatory inspections. Therefore, the relationship between auto inspections and auto fatality rates may be spurious. Population density may be a much more important explanation for auto deaths than the lack of inspection policies.

We can measure the impact of both population density and auto inspection policy on auto fatality rates by dividing the fifty observations (states) into categories based on their population density and on their inspection policies. If we then calculate the mean auto fatality rate and the variance around that rate for each of the categories, we can assess the impact of the independent variables, both individually and in combination.

TABLE 13-6

Relationship between State Auto Inspection Policy and State Auto Fatality Rates: Controlling for Population Density

Auto Inspection Policy	Density			
	Thin (<25 people/ square mile)	Medium (25–125 people/ square mile)	Thick (>125 people/ square mile)	Total
States without inspections	37.4	31.6	23.6	31.9
(N)	(10)	(16)	(6)	(32)
($\hat{\sigma}^2$)	(47.0)	(11.5)	(29.5)	(31.9)
States with inspections	34.9	28.4	18.3	26.1
(N)	(3)	(9)	(6)	(18)
($\hat{\sigma}^2$)	(77.6)	(33.6)	(23.1)	(26.1)
Total	36.8	30.5	21.0	29.8
(N)	(13)	(25)	(12)	(50)
($\hat{\sigma}^2$)	(49.4)	(20.8)	(31.8)	(61.8)

Source: Adapted from Edward R. Tufte, *Data Analysis for Politics and Policy*, copyright 1974, 23. Adapted by permission of Prentice-Hall, Inc., Englewood Cliffs, New Jersey.

Note: Entries are mean auto fatality rates for each group of states in each cell. Tufte eliminates Alaska in his analysis, but it is included here in the "thin, without inspections" cell.

Table 13-6 shows the mean and variance for each of the six categories of states created by the two independent variables. An inspection of the means for those categories shows that auto fatality rates for categories of states of differing population density are still quite different even after one has controlled for inspection policies (this can be seen by looking across the rows). In addition, the fatality rates for states with auto inspections continue to be lower than those for states without inspections, even controlling for population density. The states without inspections have higher mean fatality rates by 2.5, 3.2, and 5.3 in each of the density categories, while the "uncontrolled" difference was 5.8. Therefore, although there has been some reduction in the relationship with auto inspections, the relationship has not disappeared entirely.

With the information in Table 13-6, a precise estimate of the impact of each independent variable on auto fatality rates can be calculated. A measure of the extent to which the two variables together account for the variation in auto fatality rates can also be calculated. In this case the relationship between population density and auto fatalities remains strong even when inspection policies are controlled for, and the relationship between inspection policies and auto fatality rates is diminished and becomes modest when population density is controlled for. The two variables combined account for a substantial portion (57 percent) of the variance in auto fatality rates across the fifty states.

Like multiple crosstabulation, two-way analysis of variance measures the relationship between one independent variable and a dependent variable while controlling for one or more other independent variables. Also like crosstabulation, it controls for a third variable by grouping together cases identical or similar on the control variable. The only major difference is that the dependent variable is measured at the interval or ratio level. Consequently, changes in the variance are used to measure the effect of the control variable rather than changes in the distribution of cases across categories. For the specific mathematical calculations involved in the two-way analysis of variance, consult the readings at the end of this chapter.

Multiple Regression

So far we have described how to control for a third variable by grouping cases together that have identical or similar values on it. Although this procedure works when the values of the control variable are discrete and homogeneous, control by grouping causes major problems, as we discussed earlier, because of the potential proliferation of control groups when analyzing several variables and the reduction in the sample size within each control group.

We do not face this problem with quantitative variables. When all the variables are measured at the interval or ratio level (and even sometimes when they are not), controlling may be done by statistical adjustment, using a procedure called **multiple regression analysis**. Recall from Chapter 12 that two-variable or bivariate regression analysis involves finding an equation that best fits or approximates the data and thus describes the nature of the relationship between the independent and dependent variables. Recall in addition that a regression coefficient, which lies at the core of the regression equation, tells how much the dependent variable, Y, changes for a one-unit change in the independent variable, X. Regression analysis also allows us to test various statistical hypotheses such as $\beta = 0$, which means that if true there is no relationship between an independent and a dependent variable. A regression equation moreover may be used to calculate the predicted value of Y for any given value of X. And the residuals or distances between the predicted and observed values of Y leads to a measure (R^2) of how well the equation fits the data.

As the name implies, multiple regression is simply an extension of these procedures to include more than one independent variable. The main difference—and what needs to be stressed—is that a **multiple regression coefficient** indicates how much a one-unit change in an independent variable changes the dependent variable *when all other variables in the model have been held constant or controlled*. The controlling is done by mathematical manipulation, not by literally grouping subjects together. **Control by adjustment** is a form of statistical control in which a mathematical adjustment is made to assess the impact of a third variable. That is, the values of each case are adjusted to take into account the effect of all the other variables rather than by grouping similar cases together.

The general form of a linear multiple regression equation is

$$Y = \alpha + \beta_1 X_1 + \beta_2 X_2 + ... + \beta_K X_K + \epsilon$$

Let's examine this equation piece by piece because it is actually not very complicated once the terms are understood. In general, it says that the values of a dependent variable, *Y*, are a *linear* function of (or perhaps caused by) the values of a set of independent variables. How the independent variables influence *Y* depends on the numerical values of the βs.

The parameters are denoted by lower case Greek letters. The first, alpha (α), is a **regression constant**.[6] It can be interpreted in many ways, the simplest being α is the value of *Y* when all of the independent variables have scores or values of zero. (Just substitute 0 for each *X* and note that all of the terms except the first drop out, leaving $Y = \alpha$.) As in simple regression, the βs (Greek letter beta) indicate how much *Y* changes for a one-unit change in the independent variables when the other variables are being held constant. Each β is called a **partial regression coefficient** because it indicates the relationship between a particular *X* and the *Y* after all the other independent variables have been simultaneously controlled. The presence of ϵ (epsilon), which stands for error, means that *Y* is not a perfect function of the *X*s. In other words, even if we knew the values of *X*, we could not completely or fully predict *Y*; there will be errors. (In the symbols used in Chapter 12 we denoted this idea by $Y - \hat{Y}$.) But regression proceeds on the assumption that the errors are random or cancel out and that their average value is zero. Hence we can rewrite the regression equation as

$$E(Y) = \alpha + \beta_1 X_1 + \beta_2 X_2 + ... + \beta_K X_K$$

Read this last equation as "the expected value of *Y* is a linear function of the *X*s.

Finally, predicted values of *Y* (denoted $\hat{Y}$) may be calculated by substituting any values of the various independent variables into the equation.

So important are the partial regression coefficients that we should examine their meaning carefully in the context of specific example. Table 13-7 shows the results of Jacobson's study of campaign finances. The dependent variable, labeled "CV" for "challenger's share of the vote," is modeled as a linear function of the challenger's expenditures (X_1), incumbent's expenditures (X_2), challenger's party (X_3), and challenger's district strength (X_4). (The exact meaning of the variables is not important in this context.) The

TABLE 13-7

Multivariate Explanation of Vote for Congressional Challengers: Multiple Regression Analysis, 1972–1978

	Regression Coefficient	t Ratio[a]	Standardized Regression Coefficient	(Beta)
1972				
CV^b = a	20.7			
b_1 Challenger's expenditures	.112	9.42	.51	
b_2 Incumbent's expenditures	−.002	−.14	−.01	$R^2 = .49$
b_3 Challenger's party	−.47	−.61	−.03	
b_4 Challenger's district party strength	.299	6.94	.33	
1974[c]				
CV^b = a	15.6			
b_1 Challenger's expenditures	.121	10.45	.48	
b_2 Incumbent's expenditures	−.028	−2.34	−.11	$R^2 = .65$
b_3 Challenger's party	9.78	11.19	.42	
b_4 Challenger's district party strength	.351	7.75	.28	
1976				
CV^b = a	14.8			
b_1 Challenger's expenditures	.074	9.57	.45	
b_2 Incumbent's expenditures	−.003	−.27	−.01	$R^2 = .60$
b_3 Challenger's party	.26	.32	.01	
b_4 Challenger's district party strength	.441	10.84	.48	
1978				
CV^b = a	14.8			
b_1 Challenger's expenditures	.063	11.10	.51	
b_2 Incumbent's expenditures	−.002	−.35	−.02	$R^2 = .61$
b_3 Challenger's party	−1.76	−2.15	−.08	
b_4 Challenger's district party strength	.454	9.70	.42	

Source: Gary C. Jacobson, *Money in Congressional Elections* (New Haven: Yale University Press, 1980), 42, 235. Copyright ©1980. Reprinted with permission.

[a] A t ratio of at least 1.98 is necessary for a .05 level of significance, 2.58 for .01, and 3.35 for .001.

[b] CV is challenger's share of the vote.

[c] Variables are the same as those in the 1972 analysis.

estimated values of the regression coefficients appear in the second column. As an example, for 1972 the predicted value of *CV* is

$$CV = 20.7 + .112\,CEx - .002\,IEx - .47\,CParty + .299\,CDistrict$$

where *CEx* is challenger's expenditures, *IEx* is incumbent's expenditures, *CParty* is challenger's party, and *CDistrict* is the challenger's district party strength. If a particular candidate had scores of zero on all these variables (that is, he or she spent no money, the challenger spent none, and so forth), the expected or predicted share of the vote would be 20.7 percent.

Estimation and Calculation of a Regression Equation

Where do the numerical values of the regression coefficients come from? Just as in bivariate regression, the α and βs are calculated according to the principle of *least squares*: a mathematical procedure that selects the (unique) set of coefficients that minimizes the squared distances between each data point and its predicted Y-value. Programs for performing multiple regression analysis are available in nearly every statistical software system.

Standardized Regression Coefficients

It is important to note again that the measurement scale of the independent variables affects the numerical values of the regression coefficients. Hence, one β (say for X_1) may be much larger than another β, not because that independent variable has a strong relationship to the dependent variable but because it is measured in much smaller units. If, for example, β_1 equals 10 and β_2 equals 5, the first is not twice as strongly related to Y as the second because X_1 might be measured in thousands of dollars (e.g., 1 equals 1,000) whereas X_2 is measured in years of education. Thus, it is difficult to judge the relative importance of independent variables based on the multiple regression coefficients alone.

Some social scientists try to assess the relative importance of a series of independent variables by standardizing the measurement scale of each of the independent variables. To standardize a variable we can change each of the original raw scores to a new measure by subtracting the variable mean and dividing by the standard deviation. Suppose, for example, an independent variable X has a mean of $\bar{X}$ and a standard deviation of $\hat{\sigma}$. Then x is the standardized version of X:

$$x = \frac{(X - \bar{X})}{\hat{\sigma}}$$

A regression coefficient calculated from standardized variables is called a **standardized regression coefficient**, or sometimes beta weight, and indicates the relative importance of each independent variable in explaining the variation in the dependent variable when controlling for all of the other variables. A standardized coefficient shows the "partial" effects of an X on Y in "standard" units. The larger the absolute value of a standardized coefficient, the greater the effect of a one standard-deviation change in X on the mean of Y, controlling for or holding other variables constant. Many computer programs routinely report standardized regression coefficients, and they are commonly found in scholarly articles and books. One should be careful, however, about inferring significance from the numerical magnitude of a coefficient. One reason is that standardization is affected by the variability in the sample, as can be seen by noting the presence of the standard deviation in the formula. So if one variable exhibits quite a bit of variation while another has hardly any at all, it may be wrong to say the first is a "more important" explanation than the second even if its standardized coefficient is larger.[7]

The third column in Table 13-7 lists standardized regression coefficients for Jacobson's study of campaign expenditures. In 1972, for instance, the partial standardized coefficient relating "challenger's expenditures" to "challenger's share of the vote" is .51, which means that a one standard-deviation increase in expenditures will produce about a .5 unit increase in the challenger's vote share.

Measuring the Goodness of
Fit and Testing for Significance

The overall success of a multiple regression equation in accounting for the variation in the dependent variable is indicated with the **multiple correlation coefficient**, often called the coefficient of determination, R^2. R^2 is the ratio of the explained variation in the dependent variable to the total variation in the dependent variable; hence, it equals the proportion of the variance in the dependent variable that may be explained by the independent variables acting together in the multiple regression equation:

$$R^2 = \frac{TSS - ResSS}{TSS} = \frac{RegSS}{TSS}$$

where

        TSS is the **total** sum of squares;
        $ResSS$ is the **residual** sum of squares;
        and $RegSS$ is the **regression** sum of squares.

where TSS is the total sum of squares, $ResSS$ is the residual sum of squares, and $RegSS$ is the regression sum of squares. R^2 itself can vary from 0 to 1.0, and it also has a corresponding significance test that indicates whether the entire regression equation permits a statistically significant explanation of the dependent variable.

Multiple regression is currently the preferred technique in political science for observing multivariate relationships. In fact, most of the political science researchers whose work we have been discussing used multiple regression. Jacobson, for example, used this analytical tool to determine the

TABLE 13-8
Multivariate Explanation of Civil Strife: Multiple Regression Analysis

	Regression Coefficient	Standardized Regression Coefficient (Beta)
Total magnitude of strife = a	−3.110	
b_1 Economic deprivation, short-term	1.770	.24
b_2 Political deprivation, short-term	.660	.09[a]
b_3 Persisting deprivation	.271	.39
b_4 Coercive forces loyalty	.140	−.17
b_5 Institutionalization	.056	.07[a]
b_6 Past civil strife	.024	.04[a]
b_7 Facilitation	.481	.55
b_8 Legitimacy	−.184	−.26
$R^2 = .650$		

Source: Ted Gurr, "A Causal Model of Civil Strife: A Comparative Analysis Using New Indices," *American Political Science Review* 2 (December 1968): 1119. Reprinted with permission.

[a] Not significant at the .05 level.

relationships between campaign spending, partisan strength, political party, and the vote for congressional candidates, shown in Table 13-7. He discovered that the strongest relationships are generally between challengers' expenditures and the vote, and between the challengers' district party strength and the vote, when controlling for the other variables. Incumbent spending and the challengers' party exhibit much weaker relationships with the distribution of the vote. Table 13-7 also shows that Jacobson's four-variable model generally explains over half of the variation in votes cast for challengers and that challengers have gained about 1 percent of the vote for every $5,000 to $10,000 spent (depending on the year).

Gurr used multiple regression to assess the impact of relative deprivation and other factors on cross-national measures of civil strife. The result of one of Gurr's multiple regression analyses intended to explain the variation in civil strife is shown in Table 13-8. Gurr's eight-variable equation explains 65 percent of the variation in strife, with persisting deprivation, short-term economic deprivation, social and political facilitation, and legitimacy contributing the most to the explanation. Because of the way the independent variables are measured in this case—with multimeasure scales and indices—the regression coefficients do not have a straightforward interpretation.

Page and Shapiro also employed multiple regression analysis to understand better the relationship between public opinion change and public policy change. In their analysis the presence or absence of opinion-policy congruence is the dependent variable and various measures of the opinion change,

TABLE 13-9
Multivariate Explanation of Congruence of Public Opinion with Public Policy: Multiple Regression Analysis

Variables	Bivariate Correlation[a]	Regression Standardized Beta
Size of opinion change (%)	.23	.06
No fluctuation[b]	.19	.11
How long change took (months)	.18	.01
Low salience (% DKs)	−.10	−.09
Social issues	.14	.00
Economy	.01	.03
Defense	−.09	−.03
World War II	.13	.15
Other foreign policy	−.14	−.11
Liberal opinion change	.28	.25
States' policy	.11	−.05
1969–1979 period	.14	.06
Multiple R	.40	
R^2	.16	

Source: Benjamin I. Page and Robert Y. Shapiro, "Effects of Public Opinion on Policy," American Political Science Review 77 (March 1983): 184.

Note: The dependent variable is direction of policy change from T1 to one year after T2, scored 0 (noncongruent) or 1 (congruent). Some independent variables with insignificant bivariate correlations are omitted. The excluded category of issue types consists of remaining domestic policies.

[a] Correlations with magnitudes of .11 or better are significant at the .05 level; those .07 or greater, at the .1 level.
[b] Three categories; cases with insufficient time points to detect fluctuation were coded in a middle category.

policy type, and political context of the policy response are used as independent variables. Their analysis reviewed statistically significant relationships between policy congruence and several measures of the size of opinion change, the type of issue under consideration, and the ideological direction of the opinion/policy change (Table 13-9). Fully explaining policy congruence is not an easy task, however. Page and Shapiro's multiple regression equation, employing all of the relevant independent variables, explains only 16 percent of the variation in policy congruence.

The statistical significance of a controlled relationship with an independent variable may also be derived from a multiple regression equation. The computer program that calculates a regression equation will print out the standard error of the regression coefficients. The usual test for a statement with 95 percent certainty is that the regression coefficient be at least twice its standard error. If the test is met, then the relationship is statistically significant. If it is not met, then the null hypothesis involving that relationship (controlling for the other independent variables in the equation) must be accepted.

TABLE 13-10
Raw Data

Respondent	Turnout	Race	Years of Education
1	1	1	11
2	1	0	16
3	1	1	16
4	1	1	15
5	1	1	17
6	1	1	11
7	1	1	12
8	0	1	12
9	1	1	18
10	1	1	18
11	0	1	18
12	1	1	15
13	NA	1	12
14	1	0	4
15	0	0	10

Source: General Social Survey.

Note: Data are part of a larger data set that includes 4,417 respondents interviewed in 1993 and 1994. Race coded 1 for "white" and 0 for "non-white"; turnout coded 1 for "voted in the 1992 presidential election" and 0 for "did not vote in the 1992 presidential election." NA indicates not available.

Logistic Regression

Suppose we want to explain why people in the United States do or do not vote. As we have suggested many times before, such a study should start from a theory or at least a tentative idea of political participation. We might suppose, for example, that demographic factors such as education and race are related to turnout: well-educated whites vote more frequently than do less-educated nonwhites. To test this proposition we could collect measures of education, race, and voting from a survey or poll.

Table 13-10 shows a very small portion of such data drawn from the General Social Surveys conducted by the Opinion Research Center at the University of Chicago. It contains indicators of turnout (coded 1 for "voted in the 1992 presidential election" and 0 for "did not vote in the 1992 presidential election"), race (coded 1 for "white" and 0 for "nonwhite"), and highest year of schooling completed. (In the example that follows there were actually 4,417 respondents but only the first 15 are shown here to save space.) The codes given to voting and race are admittedly arbitrary, but we will see that this scoring system has convenient properties.

One might one wonder how we could use a method like multiple regression to analyze these data since, strictly speaking, the dependent variable,

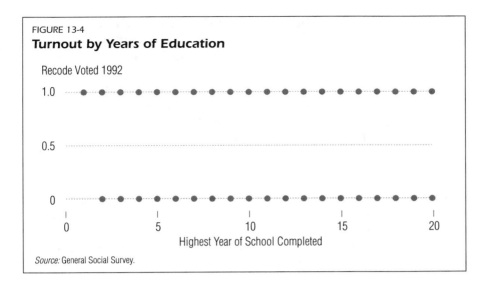

FIGURE 13-4
Turnout by Years of Education

Recode Voted 1992

Highest Year of School Completed

Source: General Social Survey.

turnout, is not numeric or quantitative. (We have already seen that categorical independent variables can be coded as dummy variables and entered into regression equations along with quantitative variables.) Indeed, a major problem for the social scientist is to explain variation in dependent variables of this type, which are often called dichotomies or binary responses. Consider, for instance, Figure 13-4, which shows the plot of turnout against number of years of schooling. We see two parallel lines of dots that do not tell us much, if anything, about the relationship between voting and education.

Nevertheless, we might conceptualize the problem this way. Denote the two outcomes of the dependent variable, Y, as 1 for "voted" and 0 for "did not vote." Each person in the study, in other words, is assigned a score on the dependent variable of 1 or 0 depending on whether or not they voted. We can then interpret the *expected value* of Y as "the probability that Y equals 1" because

$$E(Y) = [1 \times P(Y = 1)] + [0 \times (P = 0)] = P(Y = 1).$$

Note that $P(Y = 1)$ means "the probability that Y is one," which in turn is the probability that a person voted. $P(Y = 0)$ is defined similarly.[8] As noted before, the expected value of a variable can be roughly thought of as the sum of its possible values times the probability of their occurrence.[9]

We can now construct a linear regression model for the probability that Y equals 1, which we will denote simply as P. That is, for two independent variables our desired model has the general form

$$E(Y) = P = \alpha + \beta_1 X_1 + \beta_2 X_2.$$

This is called a **linear probability model** (LPM), and it means that the expected value of the binary dependent variable or (what is the same thing) the probability that Y equals 1 is a linear function of the independent variables, X_1 and X_2. The regression coefficients, the betas, simply indicate how much the predicted probability changes with a one-unit change in an independent variable, given that all the other variables in the model have been held constant.

The idea might be clarified by calculating a linear probability model for the General Social Survey data. The result is

$$\hat{Y} = .214 + .035 \, Education + .043 \, Race.$$

The parameters have the usual interpretation: when education equals zero and race is also zero (that is, nonwhite), the predicted probability of nonvoting is .214.[10] For each one-year increase in education, with race held constant, the probability of turnout increases .035. So, for example, an African American with one year of schooling completed would have a predicted vote score of

$$\hat{Y} = .214 + .035(1) + .043(0) = .249.$$

(To make sure that you understand, substitute education and race values from Tables 13-10 to get the predicted chances that various types of people will vote.)

While all of the coefficients are statistically significant by the usual standards,[11] the usual measure of goodness of fit, R^2, is quite low at .058 (as the plot of Figure 13-4 suggests). In view of this poor fit and the fact that the dependent variable is a dichotomy, it is reasonable to wonder if linear regression is in fact the right technique for analyzing dichotomous dependent variables.

The linear probability works reasonably well when all predicted values lie between .2 and .8, but statisticians still believe that it should not generally be used. One reason is that the predicted probabilities can have strange values since the linear part of the model can assume just about any value from minus to plus infinity, but a probability by definition must lie between 0 and 1. For example, a white person with 22 years of schooling would have a predicted probability of

$$\hat{P} = .214 + .035(22) + .043(1) = 1.027,$$

which is greater than 1.

In addition, the linear probability model violates certain assumptions that are necessary for valid tests of hypotheses. For example, the results of a test of the hypothesis that a β is zero in a linear probability equation might be wrong. For these and other reasons social scientists generally do not use a linear probability model to analyze dichotomous dependent variables.

So what can be done? We certainly do not want to give up because many dichotomies or binary dependent variables or responses are frequently worth investigating. A common solution is to use **logistic regression**, a non-linear model in which the log odds of one response as opposed to another is the dependent variable. The logistic regression function, which for two independent variables, X_1 and X_2, and a dichotomous dependent variable, Y, has the form

$$Prob\,(Y = 1) = P = \frac{e^{(\alpha + \beta_1 X_1 + \beta_2 X_2)}}{1 + e^{(\alpha + \beta_1 X_1 + \beta_2 X_2)}},$$

is a rather mysterious-looking formula that can actually be easily understood simply by looking at some graphics and making a few calculations. First note that e, which is often written *exp*, stands for the exponentiation function. A function can be thought of as a machine: put a number in and another, usually different number comes out. In this case, since e is a number that equals approximately 2.718218, X enters as the exponent of e and emerges as another number, 2.71828^X. For instance, if X equals 1, then e^1 is (approximately) 2.7182, and if $X = 2$, e^2 is about 7.3891. (Many hand-held calculators have an exponentiation key, usually labeled e^X or *exp(X)*. To use it just enter a number and press the key.) Although this function may seem rather abstract, it appears frequently in statistics and mathematics and is well known as the inverse function of the natural logarithm; that is, $\log(e^x) = x$. For our purposes it has a number of useful properties.

The logistic function, which uses e, can be interpreted as follows: the probability that Y equals 1 is a non-linear function of X, as shown in Figure 13-5. Curve a shows that as X increases the probability that Y equals 1 (the probability that a person votes, say) increases. But the amount or rate of the increase is not constant across the different values of X. At the lower end of the scale a one-unit change in X leads to only a small increase in the probability. For X values near the middle, however, the probability goes up quite sharply. Then, after a while, changes in X again seem to have less and less effect on the probability since a one-unit change is associated with just small increases. Depending on the substantive context, this interpretation might make a great deal of sense. Suppose, for instance, that X measures family income and Y is a dichotomous variable that represents ownership or non-ownership of a beach house. (That is, $Y = 1$ if a person owns a beach house and 0 otherwise.) Then for people who are already rich (that is, have high incomes) the probability of ownership would not be expected to change much, even if they increased their income considerably. Similarly, people at the lower end of the scale are not likely to buy a vacation cottage even if their income does increase substantially. It is only when someone reaches a threshold that a one-unit change might lead to a large change in the probability.

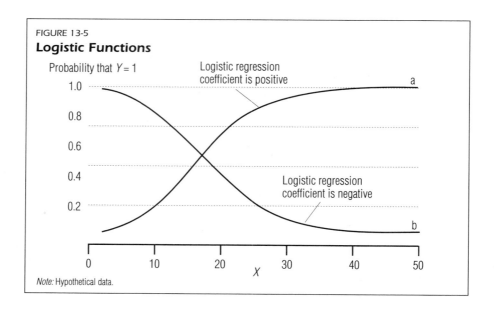

FIGURE 13-5
Logistic Functions

Note: Hypothetical data.

Curve b in Figure 13-5 can be interpreted the same way. As X increases, the probability that Y equals one decreases, but the amount of decrease depends on the magnitude of the independent variable.

The essence of non-linear models is that the effects of independent variables are not constant but depend on particular values. So the logistic regression function has a natural interpretation. It also meets the objections mentioned above, namely that predicted values will lie between 0 and 1, which are the minimums and maximums for probabilities, and that the assumptions of hypothesis testing will be met.[12]

The logistic regression can be further understood with a numerical example. Using a procedure to be described shortly, the estimated logistic regression equation for the General Social Survey voting data is

$$\hat{P} = \frac{e^{-1.593+.182\ Education+.210\ Race}}{1 + e^{-1.593+.182\ Education+.210\ Race}}$$

In this particular equation, α equals −1.593, β_1 equals .182, and β_2 equals .210. These numbers are called **logistic regression coefficients**, which are related to multiple regression coefficients in that they show how the probability of voting changes with changes in the independent variable.

It is not possible to show how the coefficients were actually calculated since the mathematics goes beyond the scope of this book. (Fortunately, computer programs for doing the work are widely available.) But we can explain their meaning by substituting some values for the independent variables into the equation. Keep in mind, however, that logistic regression coefficients are similar to regular regression coefficients: the βs indicate how much the dependent variable changes for a one-unit change in an independent variable when the other factors have been held constant. They thus show the net effect of a one-unit change in an X. But here it is important to keep in mind that the dependent variable is not a simple quantitative Y, but rather an estimated probability or (as we will see) something called a log odds. In this sense they are like regular regression coefficients, which show partial relationships, as described earlier.

An example helps clarify the meaning. Consider a person who reports zero years of schooling ($X_1 = 0$) and who is nonwhite ($X_2 = 0$). Then the equation becomes

$$\hat{P} = \frac{e^{-1.593+.182\,(\,0\,)+.210\,(\,0\,)}}{1 + e^{-1.593+.182\,(\,0\,)+.210\,(\,0\,)}}$$

$$= \frac{e^{-1.593}}{(1 + e^{-1.593})}$$

$$= .169$$

This expression means that the estimated probability of a nonwhite person with zero years of education voting is .169. (Notice that the level of education has been effectively controlled.) Consider next a white person ($X_2 = 1$) with the same amount of education ($X_1 = 0$). The predicted probability of voting is now

$$\hat{P} = \frac{e^{(-1.593+.182\,(\,0\,)+.210\,(\,1\,))}}{1 + e^{(-1.593+.182\,(\,0\,)+.210\,(\,1\,))}}$$

$$= \frac{e^{(-1.593+.210)}}{1 + e^{(-1.593+.210)}} =$$

$$= \frac{e^{(-1.488)}}{1 + e^{(-1.488)}}$$

$$= .201$$

The results show that whites with zero years of education have a slightly higher predicted probability of voting than nonwhites with zero years of education, .201 versus .169. The "effect" of race for *this* level of education is to modestly increase the chances of voting. (At different levels of education the effect will be different.)

A similar substitution shows that the probability of a nonwhite with 9 years of education voting is

$$\hat{P} = \frac{e^{-1.593+.182\,(\,9\,)+.210\,(\,0\,)}}{1 + e^{-1.593+.182\,(\,9\,)+.210\,(\,0\,)}} = \frac{e^{+.045}}{(1 + e^{+.045})} = .511.$$

Table 13-11 shows the predicted probabilities of voting for a few other combinations of education and race. Look at the entries in the first two and the last columns. (Ignore the "Odds" columns for the moment.) They show, for instance, that a nonwhite person with 20 years of schooling has an (estimated) probability of voting in the 1992 presidential election of .886 verus .896 for a white person with the same educational attainment. So, at the high end of the education scale nearly everyone votes no matter what his or her race. Now look at the middle two rows, which compare nonwhite and white people who have had 10 years of schooling. The estimated probabilities of voting are .557 and .608, respectively.

It may not be apparent, but the magnitude difference between whites and nonwhites' probabilities of voting depends on the level of education. At the lower end of the scale, for example, the differences in probabilities are noticeable, if small. But at the upper end they almost vanish. This pattern reflects the non-linear relationship between the independent variables and the dichotomous dependent variable. (Look at Curve a of Figure 13-5 again.) So we conclude that unlike ordinary regression, a one-unit change in one of the independent variables has a *variable* impact on the dependent variable. This property actually makes sense substantively. After all, a person may have so much of a property like income or education that an additional increase in it will not really affect his or her chances of voting.

Estimating the Model's Coefficients

It is natural to wonder how the coefficient estimates are derived, and it would certainly simplify things if we could provide straightforward formulas for calculating them. Unfortunately, there are no such equations. Instead, logistic

TABLE 13-11

Estimated Log Odds, Odds, and Probabilities for Voting Data

Years of Education	Race	Log Odds	Odds	Probability
0	Nonwhite (0)	−1.593	.203	.169
0	White (1)	−1.488	.226	.184
10	Nonwhite (0)	.227	1.255	.557
10	White (1)	.437	1.548	.608
20	Nonwhite (0)	2.074	7.745	.886
20	White (1)	2.152	8.602	.896

regression analysis is best performed with special computer programs. Logistic regression has become so widely used that the appropriate tools can be found in many statistical program packages such as SPSS, MINITAB, and SAS. Your instructor or computer consultant can help you find and use these programs. We recommend that if you have a dependent variable with two categories and want to perform regression, ask for a logistic regression program.[13]

If the estimated coefficients are calculated correctly and certain assumptions are met, they have desirable statistical properties. They are, for instance, unbiased estimators of corresponding population parameters and can be tested for statistical significance.

Measures of Fit

As in the case of simple and multiple regression, researchers want to know how well a proposed model "fits" data. The same is true of logistic regression. After estimating a model we want to know how well it describes or fits the observed data. Several measures of goodness of fit exist, although they have to be interpreted cautiously. In fact, there is considerable disagreement about which measure is best, and none of the alternatives has the seemingly straightforward interpretation that the multiple regression coefficient, R^2, has.

With ordinary regression analysis one way to measure the fit is to compare predicted and observed values of the dependent variable and measure the number or magnitude of the errors. Alternatively (and equivalently), we can determine what proportion of the variation in Y is statistically explained by the independent variables. We can also observe the resulting indicators such as the multiple R or coefficient of determination, R^2, which provide some useful information but can in certain circumstances be misleading.

The method used to estimate unknown logistic regression coefficients relies on a simple idea: pick those estimates that maximize the likelihood of observing the data that have in fact been observed. That is, for a certain set of coefficients, the probability or likelihood of observing a particular set of 0s and 1s might be L_1. A different set of estimates might produce a somewhat larger probability, L_2, while a third set yields an even larger probability, L_3. The set of estimated coefficients we want is the one that has the greatest or largest probability. We can call this probability the likelihood or likelihood function of the data and denote it L.

Since the maximum likelihood is a probability, which is less than or equal to 1, and the logarithm of this probability is a very large *negative* number,[14] statisticians sometimes use –2 times the logarithm of the likelihood, or $-2LL$, as the basis for assessing the fit of a model. For the sake of simplicity we will call this term the "log likelihood." A model that fits the data closely—one in which there are relatively few prediction errors, for example—has a large probability and consequently a relatively small value of $-2LL$. If the regression equation and the data agreed perfectly, the likelihood would be $L = 1$ and the -2 times the log likelihood would be 0. (Why? Because the logarithm of 1 is 0 and -2 times zero is of course 0.) Conversely, a model that does not fit the data well will have a relatively large log likelihood. So we want to find models that lead to the smallest value of $-2LL$ possible.

Most logistic regression software programs routinely report the log likelihood. As an example, log likelihood for the education and race model of the General Social Survey data is $-2LL = 5017.6$. This number looks large, but what exactly does it mean? Unfortunately, the number is not terribly informative by itself. But it can be compared with the value obtained for a model having only a constant. Doing so tells us how much adding the coefficients increases the likelihood or, what is the same, reduces $-2LL$. That is, suppose $-2LL(0)$ represents the log likelihood of a simple model with only a constant and no independent variables:

$$Prob(Y = 1) = P = \frac{e^{(\alpha)}}{1 + e^{(\alpha)}}$$

Now, let $-2LL(C)$ be the log likelihood of a model with, say, two independent variables:

$$Prob(Y = 1) = P = \frac{e^{(\alpha + \beta_1 X_1 + \beta_2 X_2)}}{1 + e^{(\alpha + \beta_1 X_1 + \beta_2 X_2)}}$$

This is, of course, just the form of the equation we have been discussing all along. A measure of "improved" fit, then, is

$$R^2_{pseudo} = \frac{(-2LL(0) - (-2LL(C)))}{(-2LL(0))}$$

The numerator of this expression shows the difference in the fit when independent variables have been added. By putting this difference over the fit of the model without variables we obtain a measure of proportional improvement. The "pseudo" in Rs subscript indicates that this statistic is not the same as the R^2 of ordinary regression, and it certainly does not represent explained variation.

For the example we have been working with, where $-2LL(0)$ for the model with no independent variables is 5279.61 and $-2LL(F)$ for the model with education and race included is 5017.64, the pseudo R^2 is

$$R^2_{\text{pseudo}} = \frac{(5279.61 - 5017.64)}{(5279.61)}$$

$$= \frac{261.97}{5279.61}$$

$$= .050.$$

The difference, 261.97, is often reported as the "improvement of goodness of fit," or the "omnibus test of model coefficients" in some software packages. It can be easily calculated because the log likelihood ($-2LL$) is routinely reported. This number suggests that the addition of two independent variables did not really improve the fit very much, for the proportional improvement is only .05 (or about 5 percent). But before rejecting the model we should keep in mind that the pseudo R^2 is not an infallible indicator of fit and that several others have been proposed.[15]

A common variant, called Snell and Cox R^2, uses the simple likelihoods (L)

$$R^2_{\text{SC}} = 1 - \left(\frac{LL(0)}{LL(C)} \right)^{\frac{2}{N}}$$

Here, N is the sample size and the squared R can be thought of as analogous to R^2 in regular regression. For the turnout data the $R_{sc}^2 = 0.58$, which also suggests that the two variables do not have much explanatory power.[16]

In addition, there is a different approach to assess goodness of fit. If our model describes the data well, then it ought to lead to accurate predictions. That is, we should be able to plug in values of the independent variables for each observation, obtain predicted probabilities for everyone, and use these predictions to predict whether or not a person has a score of 1 on Y. (For instance, we should be able to predict if a person has voted or not given the individual's scores on the independent variable.) We can then count number of observations correctly and incorrectly classified to obtain a "correct classification rate" (CCR). If a model has any explanatory power, the CCR should be relatively high, say more than 75 percent and certainly more than 50 percent. For the General Social Survey data, as an example, we use the estimated model to predict whether or not each person will vote and then compare those predictions with what the respondents actually did. Table 13-12 shows the results.

We see that the model made 3,060 + 75 = 3,135 correct predictions and 1,184 + 98 = 1,282 incorrect ones. Since there are a total of 4,417 individuals in the study, the CCR is 3,135/4,417 = .7098, or about 71 percent. (Again, many logistic regression software programs report the CCR as part of their output.) By this standard the model seems to fit modestly well.

TABLE 13-12
Crosstabulation of Predicted and Observed Votes

Actual observation	Model Prediction	
	Respondent did not vote	Respondent voted
Respondent did not vote	75	1,184
Respondent voted	98	3,060

We should note here that measuring goodness of fit in logistic regression is not as straightforward as in ordinary regression and all of the proposed methods have shortcomings as well as strengths. Moreover, perhaps because logistic regression has only been relatively recently incorporated into standard political analysis, there is no widely accepted and used list of measures. Some authors provide several indicators while others give hardly any at all. Thus, when reading articles and papers that use dichotomous dependent variables and logistic regression, you may have to reserve judgment about how solid the evidence is in favor of a particular model.[17]

Testing Hypotheses

What are more widely reported are significance tests for the individual coefficients. Recall that a statistical test of significance is a test of a null hypothesis that a population parameter equals some specific value, often zero. In the case of logistic regression we usually want to test the hypothesis that in the population a β equals zero. (Occasionally we might want to test a *set* of coefficients.[18]) In the case of the voting data we may want to use the sample data to test the proposition that the partial logistic coefficient relating education to turnout is zero. The form of this kind of test is roughly similar to the others we have described throughout the book: divide an estimated coefficient by its standard error. In this case if the sample size is large (say, greater than 200), the result gives a z statistic that has a normal distribution with a mean of zero and standard deviation. That is,

$$z = \left(\frac{\hat{\beta}}{s.e.} \right),$$

where $\hat{\beta}$ is the estimated coefficient and "s.e." is its estimated standard error. Sometimes the coefficient and standard error are squared to produce a squared z, which is called the "Wald statistic." The Wald statistic has a chi-square distribution with 1 degree of freedom and can be analyzed using the methods presented in Chapter 12. For large samples, the conclusions based on z or Wald will be equivalent.

Software invariably reports the coefficients and their standard errors and usually the z or Wald statistic as well so we need not worry about computing

TABLE 13-13
Estimated Coefficients, Standard Errors, and Tests of Significance for Voting Data

Variable	Estimated Coefficient	Standard Error	Wald Statistic	Degrees of Freedom	Probability
Constant	−1.593	.169	89.044	1	.000
Education	.182	.012	223.545	1	.000
Race	.210	.091	5.359	1	.021

them by hand. Table 13-13 shows the result for the General Social Survey data, which suggests that we can reject the hypotheses that $\beta_{education}$ and β_{race} are zero. We can thus conclude that the variables have a statistically significant effect on the probability of voting.

We conclude by pointing out that the accuracy of the Wald (or z) statistic depends on a number of factors such as the sample size. As a result, statisticians frequently advise using the difference in the log likelihoods to test the significance of one or more coefficients. Since logistic regression programs are fairly easy to use, and since they typically report log likelihoods, we can test the significance of a parameter or a group of parameters by comparing their log likelihoods. If we let $-2LL(C)$ be the log likelihood for the "complete" model—the one with all of the explanatory variables of interest included—and $-2LL(R)$ be the log likelihood for the "reduced" model—the one with one or more independent variables eliminated—then the difference between the two can be used to test the null hypothesis that a β or a set of βs is zero (or some other specific value) since this difference has a chi-square distribution with k degrees of freedom, where k is the number of variables dropped from the complete model to obtain the reduce one. This difference is sometimes called the likelihood ratio statistic, since it can be reexpressed as the log of the ratio of the two likelihoods, $L(R)$ and $L(C)$:

$$LR = -2\,LL(R) - (-2\,LL(C)) = -2\ln\left(\frac{L(R)}{L(C)}\right)$$

A small LR (i.e., near zero) means the "tested" coefficients are not statistically significant whereas a large one suggests that they are.

The likelihoods are not reported, but their two time logs are. We can thus easily make the calculation from most printouts. In fact, we actually did so earlier when we compared the reduced model with no explanatory variables in it (just the constant term) with the model having education and race. Recall that $-2LL(C)$ was 5017.64 and $-2LL(R)$ was 5279.61. The difference, 261.97, is the observed chi-square, which can be compared with a critical value from the chi-square distribution with $k = 2$ degrees of freedom ($k = 2$ because the reduced model has two fewer parameters). Since the critical value of chi-square with 2 degrees of freedom at the .001 level is 13.82, which is considerably less than the observed value, we can reject the null hypothesis that both βs equal zero.[19]

An Alternative Interpretation of Logistic Regression Coefficients

We might summarize to this point by saying that logistic regression analysis involves developing and estimating models such that the probability that Y equals 1 (or 0) is a non-linear function of the independent variable(s):

$$P(Y = 1) = \text{Non-linear function of } X$$

It is possible, though, to rewrite the logistic regression equation to create a linear relationship between the Xs and Y. Doing so provides an alternative way to interpret logistic regression results. Instead of "explaining" variation in Y with a linear probability model or P with a logistic regression, we can work with **odds**, which is the probability of one response or value of a variable over the probability of another response or value of a variable, and use it as a dependent variable.[20]

Suppose we sampled a person at random from a group of eligible voters. We could ask "what is the probability (P) that this individual actually voted?" or, a related question, "what are the *odds* that this individual voted?" Probability and odds are not the same, for the odds are the ratio of *two* probabilities, the probability of voting compared to the probability of not voting:

$$Odds = O = \frac{P_{vote}}{(1 - P_{vote})},$$

where P_{vote} is the probability of voting.

Some examples will help to illustrate the difference. Suppose the probability that a randomly selected citizen votes is .8. Then the *odds* of her doing so are $.8/(1 - .8) = .8/.2 = 4$, or, as is commonly said, 4 to 1. The person, in other words, is four times as likely to vote as not. As another example, suppose the probability of turning out is .4, then the *odds* are $.4/(1 - .4) = .4/.6 = .6667$, or about .667 to 1. In this case, the citizen is less likely to vote than not to vote. In both examples, the terms in the denominator of the fraction are just the $1 - P$, which is the probability of not voting. (Since probabilities must add to 1—either a person did or did not vote—the probability of not voting is $1 - P$.)[21] It is important not to confuse probabilities and odds; they are related, but not the same.

More generally, consider a variable, Y, that takes just two possible values, 0 and 1. Let P be the probability that $Y = 1$ and $Q = 1 - P$ be the probability that $Y = 0$. Then the odds that Y is 1 as opposed to 0 are

$$O = \frac{P}{(1 - P)} = \frac{P}{Q}.$$

The term O has intuitive appeal since it accords with common parlance. The odds, O, can vary from 0 to $+ \circ$. If $O = 1$, then the "chances" that Y equals 1 or 0 are the same, namely 1 to 1. If O is greater than 1, the probability that Y equals 1 is greater than $1/2$ and conversely if O is less than 1, the probability is less than $1/2$. Table 13-14 shows a few more examples of probabilities and odds in a case in which a random process can eventuate in just one of two possible outcomes.

TABLE 13-14
Probabilities and Odds

Probabilities	Odds
1	$\circ$
.7	2.333
.5	1
.4	.667
.1	.111
0	0

Note: Read the odds as "X to 1."

Why bother with odds? Take a look at the logistic model. It is really a formula that relates P to some Xs, so we ought to be able to rewrite it by putting 1 in front to obtain $1 - P$. Then we could put the two equations together to get an expression for P over $1 - P$. Here is how. To simplify, let $Z = \alpha + \beta_1 X_1 + \beta_2 X_2$. Now the expression for P can be written

$$\hat{P} = \frac{e^z}{1 + e^z}.$$

In the same fashion we can write $1 - P$ as

$$1 - \hat{P} = 1 - \frac{e^z}{1 + e^z}.$$

This latter expression can be simplified to

$$1 - \hat{P} = \frac{1}{1 + e^z}.$$

Now we can put the two equations for P and $1 - P$ together to obtain an expression for the odds, $O = P/(1 - P)$:

$$\hat{O} = \frac{\hat{P}}{1 - \hat{P}} = \frac{\dfrac{e^z}{1 + e^z}}{\dfrac{1}{1 + e^z}}.$$

This expression in turn simplifies to

$$\hat{O} = \frac{\hat{P}}{1 - \hat{P}} = e^{z}.$$

Remember that we let $Z = \alpha + \beta_{1}X_{1} + \beta_{2}X_{2}$, so this expression is really

$$\hat{O} = \frac{\hat{P}}{1 - \hat{P}} = e^{\alpha + \beta_{1}X_{1} + \beta_{2}X_{2}}.$$

We have thus found a simple expression for the odds. But it is still non-linear because of the exponentiation, e. But a property of the exponentiation function is that $\log(e^{Z}) = Z$, where log means the natural logarithm. So we find that the logarithm of the odds—called the log odds, or logit—can be written as a linear function of the explanatory variables:

$$\hat{Logit} = \log \hat{O} = \alpha + \beta_{1}X_{1} + \beta_{2}X_{2}.$$

This model can be interpreted in the same terms as multiple linear regression if we keep in mind that the dependent variable is the logit or log odds, not Y or probabilities. Refer for instance back to Table 13-11. The middle two columns show the predicted log odds and the odds for voting for various combinations of race and education. As an example, a non-white ($X_{2} = 0$) with no schooling ($X_{1} = 0$) has an estimated .203 to 1 chance of voting. This compares with, say, a highly educated white ($X_{1} = 20$, $X_{2} = 1$) whose odds of voting are about 86 to 1.

KEEP TERMS STRAIGHT

Note that a probability is not the same as an odds, at least in statistical analysis. A probability refers to the chances of something happening such as a person voting. Odds compare two probabilities as the probability of voting to the probability of not voting.

Also note that if we exponentiate the linear logit model we obtain an equation for the plain odds:

$$\hat{O} = e^{\alpha + \beta_{1}X_{1} + \beta_{2}X_{2}}.$$

This equation in turn can be rewritten

$$\hat{O} = e^{\alpha} e^{\beta_{1}X_{1}} e^{\beta_{2}X_{2}}.$$

This formulation shows that the logistic regression coefficients can be interpreted as the *multiplicative* effect of a one-unit increase in an X on the odds.

We should stress that these remarks are simply an alternative but equivalent way of interpreting logistic regression coefficients. Moreover, we can move from one view to the other by simply manipulating the results with a pocket calculator. Most computer programs and articles report the coefficients, along with other statistical information. To make sense of them often requires substituting actual data values into the equations and seeing what the probabilities or odds turn out to be.

A Substantive Example

To further the understanding of logistic regression parameters, we use an example from *The Bell Curve: Intelligence and Class Structure in American Life,* by Richard Herrnstein and Charles Murray. Herrnstein and Murray's work became extremely controversial because it argued that intelligence plays a larger role in economic success than does socioeconomic background and that many socially undesirable behaviors stem more from low cognitive ability than from prejudice or lack of opportunity. Many observers have tried to interpret their results as saying genes or nature are more important in explaining success and achievement than are family background and other environmental variables. If true, such findings would have enormous implications for affirmative action, head start, special education, and a host of other public policies.

We of course cannot address the correctness of Herrnstein and Murray's argument. But using this rather contentious book as an example allows us to kill two birds with one stone. Most important, the authors' use of logistic regression analysis to bolster their positions provides an interesting example of the method. But the book also shows how statistics influence policy analysis and how an understanding of statistical techniques can help one evaluate the strengths and weaknesses of substantive claims.

Table 13-15 presents a typical example of Herrnstein and Murray's results. The authors wanted to know how intelligence, which is measured by a standardized test,[22] and various demographic factors affect the probability of welfare dependency. The variables include a socioeconomic status index, age, and two additional indicators, poverty status (on or off welfare) prior to the birth of a child and marital situation at the time of the child's birth (married or unmarried). The data in Table 13-15 are based on a sample of "women with at least one child born prior to January 1, 1989."[23] The estimates in the second column of Table 13-15 are the components of a model that predicts the probability or odds that a woman is on welfare.

The model for the log odds can be read from the middle column:

$$\hat{Logit} = -1.036 - .580\,Intelligence - .061\,Social - .113\,Age - .900\,Poverty + 1.053\,Marital,$$

while the equation for the predicted probability takes the form

$$\hat{P} = \frac{e^{-1.036-.580\ Intelligence-.061\ Social-.113\ Age-.900\ Poverty+1.053\ Marital}}{1+e^{-1.036-.580\ Intelligence-.061\ Social-.113\ Age-.900\ Poverty+1.053\ Marital}}.$$

If one substitutes values for the independent variable into the equations, it is easy to find predicted log odds, odds, and probabilities for various combinations of attributes. The way Herrnstein and Murray measured the independent variables make interpretations easy because each factor is scored in standard deviation units. If, for instance, a score on intelligence is 0, then the person has the mean or average level of intelligence for the group being studied. If the score is 1, the individual is one standard deviation above the mean. Similarly, a score on intelligence of –1 indicates below-average intelligence. The socioeconomic index and age variable are interpreted in the same way. The other two factors, which need not concern us, are just dichotomous variables indicating the presence or absence of a condition. (A woman who gives birth out of wedlock, for example, receives a score of 0; otherwise the score is 1.) Putting these facts together allows us to compare women with different combinations of social background and intelligence and supposedly draw conclusions about which is the most explanatory factor.

Consider first a woman of average intelligence, socioeconomic standing, and age ($X_1 = 0$, $X_2 = 0$, $X_3 = 0$) and who has scores of zero on the two indicator variables, poverty and marital status ($X_4 = 0$, $X_5 = 0$). Then her predicted log odds of being on welfare are[24]

$$\hat{Logit} = -1.036 - .580\,(0) - .061\,(0) - .113\ Age - .900\,(0) + 1.053\,(0)$$
$$= -1.036$$

TABLE 13-15

Logistic Regression Coefficients for Log Odds of Being on Welfare

Variable	Estimate	Probability
Constant (α)	−1.036	.000
Intelligence (β_1)	−.580	.002
Socioeconomic status (β_2)	−.061	.726[c]
Age (β_3)	−.113	.439[c]
Poverty status (β_4)[a]	−.900	.000
Marital status (β^5)[b]	1.053	.000

$R_{pseudo} = .312$

Source: Adapted from Richard Herrnstein and Charles Murray, *The Bell Curve* (New York: Free Press, 1994), 607.

[a] Was woman living in poverty at the time of birth of her first child?
[b] Was woman married or not at time of birth of child?
[c] Coefficient is not significantly different from zero.

The log odds translate into estimated odds:

$$\hat{O} = e^{-1.036} = .355.$$

This number tells us that odds of a woman with mean or average characteristics has a less than even chance—.335 to 1—of being on welfare. And her estimated probability is

$$\hat{P} = \frac{e^{-1.036}}{1 + e^{-1.036}}$$

$$= \frac{.355}{(1 + .355)}$$

$$= .262$$

Now let's look at a woman who is one standard deviation above the mean on intelligence but who has the same characteristics on the other variables. The coefficient in Table 13-15 or in the equation indicates that her log odds will be decreased by .580. This effect translates into a decline in the odds and probability of being in poverty:

$$\hat{O} = e^{-1.036-.580(1)}$$

$$= .199$$

and

$$\hat{P} = \frac{e^{-1.036-.580(1)}}{1 + e^{-1.036-.580(1)}}$$

$$= \frac{.199}{(1 + .199)}$$

$$= .166$$

We can see that the data suggest being above average in intelligence seems to lower ones chances of going on public assistance. By substituting in zeros and ones for the values of other variables we can see how they affect welfare status. (Remember, the coefficients are based on Herrnstein and Murray's particular standard deviation measurement scales. In this context, letting age be 20 would not make much sense because it would mean "20 standard deviations above the average," which would perhaps be a person well over 200 years old.)

Notice that the table shows the level of significance of each variable and the pseudo R^2. The latter is .312, a value suggesting the model fits the data reasonably well. Moreover, we see from Table 13-15 that intelligence, poverty, and marital status are significant but the other variables are not. The authors take this fact as further evidence that IQ, which they believe is largely inherited, has a greater effect on the chances of being on welfare than does family background.

A last comment. The results in Table 13-15 seem to say that intelligence has a much greater impact on the chances or probability of being on welfare than does socioeconomic background because (1) the magnitude of the coefficient for IQ is about 9 times as large as the one for social and economic position and (2) it is statistically significant whereas the coefficient for socioeconomic status is not. It is, however, highly debatable whether we can draw any firm conclusions about the relative importance of variables from just these data. The size of the coefficients depends on more than just the strength of their relationships with other variables. And statistical significance, as we indicated in Chapter 12, is not always a good guide to substantive significance.

Conclusion

As we have seen, multivariate data analysis helps researchers provide more complete explanations of political phenomena and produce causal knowledge. Observing the relationship between an independent and a dependent variable while controlling for one or more control variables allows researchers to assess more precisely the effect attributable to each independent variable and to accumulate evidence in support of a causal claim. Being able to observe simultaneously the relationship between a number of independent variables and a dependent variable also helps researchers construct more parsimonious and complete explanations for political phenomena.

Multivariate data analysis techniques vary in how they control for the control variable. Multivariate crosstabulation and two-way analysis of variance control by grouping similar observations; partial correlation and multiple and logistic regression control by adjustment. Both types of procedures have their advantages and limitations. Control by grouping can result in the proliferation of analysis tables, the reduction of the number of cases within categories to a hazardous level, and the elimination of some of the variance in the control variables. Control by adjustment, on the other hand, can disguise important specified relationships; that is, relationships that are not identical across the range of values observed in the control variables.

Notes

1. Gary C. Jacobson, *Money in Congressional Elections* (New Haven: Yale University Press, 1980).

2. Ted Gurr, "A Causal Model of Civil Strife: A Comparative Analysis Using New Indices," *American Political Science Review* 2 (December 1968): 1104–1124. The quote is on 1105.

3. Benjamin I. Page and Robert Y. Shapiro, "Effects of Public Opinion on Policy," *American Political Science Review* 77 (March 1983): 175–190.

4. Edward R. Tufte, *Data Analysis for Politics and Policy* (Englewood Cliffs, N.J.: Prentice-Hall, 1974).

5. Raymond E. Wolfinger and Steven J. Rosenstone, *Who Votes?* (New Haven: Yale University Press, 1980).

6. In Chapter 12 we also called this term the "intercept" because it has a simple geometric interpretation.

7. For essentially the same reasons one might not want to compare standardized regression coefficients based on samples from two different populations.

8. If you want to clarify expressions like these, simply replace the variable's symbols and codes with substantive names. Thus, for example, $P(Y = 0)$ can in the present context be read literally as "the probability that 'turnout' equals 'did not vote.'"

9. More precisely, the expected value of a probability distribution is called the *mean* of the distribution.

10. Note that these estimates are calculated on the basis of the full sample, not just the data in Table 13-10.

11. The t statistic for education and race are 16.043 and 2.391, respectively, both of which are significant at the .05 level.

12. Of course, like any statistical technique, logistic regression analysis assumes certain conditions are true and will not lead to valid inferences if these conditions are not met.

13. Actually, there are quite a few different methods that can be used to analyze this kind of data. A related procedure, called probit analysis, is widely used, and if the data are all categorical, log-linear analysis is available.

14. For a number, x, that is less than 1 but greater than 0, the natural log of x is $-° < \log(x) < 0$.

15. See, for example, J. Scott Long, *Regression Models for Categorical and Limited Dependent Variables* (Thousand Oaks, Calif.: Sage, 1997), 104–113.

16. Snell and Cox's measure is a far from perfect indicator of fit and so other versions have been proposed. See ibid., chap. 4.

17. Actually, the same comment applies to any data analysis technique: empirical results have to be interpreted and accepted with caution.

18. Consider, for example, a model that contains two types of variables—one group measuring demographic factors and another measuring attitudes and beliefs. The investigator might want to know if the demographic variables can be dropped without significant loss of information.

19. Computer programs usually report the calculated or obtained probability of the observed chi-square so we do not even have to look up a critical value in a table.

20. Recall that odds (and odds ratios) were introduced in Chapter 12, which the reader might want quickly to review.

21. That is, $P + (1 - P) = 1$.

22. Their measure of intelligence was the Armed Forces Qualification Test, "a paper and pencil test designed for teens who have reached their late teens." See Richard Herrnstein and Charles Murray, *The Bell Curve* (New York: Free Press, 1994), 579.

23. Ibid., 607.

24. You might not get exactly these results if you repeat the calculations on your own because they were carried out to more decimal places than indicated.

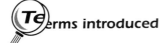

Terms introduced

CONTROL BY ADJUSTMENT. A form of statistical control in which a mathematical adjustment is made to assess the impact of a third variable.

CONTROL BY GROUPING. A form of statistical control in which observations identical or similar for the control variable are grouped together.

EXPERIMENTAL CONTROL. Manipulation of the exposure of experimental groups to experimental stimuli to assess the impact of a third variable.

LINEAR PROBABILITY MODEL. Regression model in which a dichotomous variable is treated as the dependent variable.

LOGISTIC REGRESSION. Regression model or equation in which the log odds of one response as opposed to another is the dependent variable.

LOGISTIC REGRESSION COEFFICIENT. A multiple regression coefficient based on the logistic model.

MULTIPLE REGRESSION ANALYSIS. A technique for measuring the mathematical relationships between more than one independent variable and a dependent variable, while controlling for all other independent variables in the equation.

MULTIPLE CORRELATION COEFFICIENT. A statistic varying between 0 and 1 that indicates the proportion of the total variation in Y, a dependent variable, that is statistically "explained" by the independent variables.

MULTIPLE REGRESSION COEFFICIENT. A number that tells how much Y will change for a one-unit change in a particular independent variable, if all of the other variables in the model have been held constant.

MULTIVARIATE CROSSTABULATION. A procedure by which crosstabulation is used to control for a third variable.

MULTIVARIATE DATA ANALYSIS. Data analysis techniques designed to test hypotheses involving more than two variables.

ODDS. The probability of one response or value of a variable over the probability of another response or value of a variable.

PARTLY SPURIOUS RELATIONSHIP. A relationship between two variables caused partially by the impact of a third.

PARTIAL REGRESSION COEFFICIENT. A number that indicates how much a dependent variable would change if an independent variable changed one unit and all other variables in the equation or model were held constant.

REGRESSION CONSTANT. Value of the dependent variable when all of the values of the independent variables in the equation equal zero.

SPECIFIED RELATIONSHIP. A relationship between two variables that varies with the values of a third.

SPURIOUS RELATIONSHIP. A relationship between two variables caused entirely by the impact of a third.

STANDARDIZED REGRESSION COEFFICIENT. Regression coefficient adjusted by the standard deviation of the independent and dependent variables so that its magnitude can be directly computed.

STATISTICAL CONTROL. Assessing the impact of a third variable by comparing observations across the values of a control variable.

TWO-WAY ANALYSIS OF VARIANCE. An extension of the analysis of variance procedure to allow controlling for a third variable.

Exercises

1. Refer to Table 13-9. What are the independent variables with which the authors are trying to explain opinion/policy congruence? What do the numbers in the column labeled "Bivariate Correlation" mean? Which variables are the most successful in explaining the variation in opinion/policy congruence? How much of the total variation in opinion/policy congruence is accounted for by the independent variables included in this analysis?

2. Table 13-16 shows the relationship between party and environmental support in the House for three congresses. What is the relationship in each of the congresses? How strong is the relationship? Now look at Table 13-17 in which district residential pattern has been added as a control variable. What happens to the relationship between party and environmental support?

3. Using Table 13-18, answer the following questions:
   a. For the nation, is there a difference between Democrats and Republicans in support for environmental legislation?
   b. Is this difference the same for all three congresses?
   c. Now consider what happens when region is added as a control variable. Do all regions support environmental legislation equally? What happens to the difference between Democrats and Republicans in each of the

TABLE 13-16

Relationship between Party and Environmental Support in the House, 93d (1973–74), 94th (1975–76), and 95th (1977–78) Congresses (in percentages)

	93d		94th		95th	
	Democrat	Republican	Democrat	Republican	Democrat	Republican
Environmental	42	7	42	10	37	7
Non-Environmental	58	93	58	90	63	93
(N)	(248)	(187)	(289)	(145)	(287)	(147)
gamma	.81		.73		.88	

Source: Adapted from Henry C. Kenski and Margaret C. Kenski, "Partisanship, Ideology, and Constituency Differences on Environmental Issues in the U.S. House of Representatives: 1973–1978," *Policy Studies Journal* 9 (winter 1980): Table 4, p. 334.

TABLE 13-17

Relationship between Party and Environmental Support by District Residential Pattern in the House, 93d (1973–74), 94th (1975–76), and 95th (1977–78) Congresses (in percentages)

	93d		94th		95th	
	Democrat	Repub-lican	Democrat	Repub-lican	Democrat	Repub-lican
Urban						
Environmental	64	5	52	6	44	12
Non-Environmental	36	95	48	94	56	88
(N)	(81)	(21)	(88)	(17)	(88)	(17)
Gamma		.95		.89		.71
Suburban						
Environmental	56	10	59	14	55	11
Non-Environmental	44	90	41	86	45	89
(N)	(59)	(72)	(70)	(55)	(71)	(53)
Gamma		.84		.79		.81
Rural						
Environmental	14	3	24	10	20	4
Non-Environmental	86	97	76	90	80	96
(N)	(66)	(65)	(78)	(52)	(77)	(54)
Gamma		.66		.50		.73
Mixed						
Environmental	21	10	30	5	28	5
Non-Environmental	79	90	70	95	72	95
(N)	(42)	(29)	(53)	(21)	(51)	(23)
Gamma		.40		.79		.79

Source: Henry C. Kenski and Margaret C. Kenski, "Partisanship, Ideology, and Constituency Differences on Environmental Issues in the U.S. House of Representatives: 1973–1978," *Policy Studies Journal* 9 (winter 1980): Table 4, p. 334.

regions? State whether the relationship has been stronger, weaker, or remained about the same.

4. Read pages 185–189 in Benjamin I. Page and Robert Y. Shapiro, "Effects of Public Opinion on Policy," *American Political Science Review* 77 (March 1983). What do the authors say about their evidence that changes in public opinion *cause* changes in public policy?

5. In David H. Folz and Joseph M. Hazlett, "Public Participation and Recycling Performance: Explaining Program Success," *Public Administration Review* 51 (November–December 1991): 526–532, the authors investigate what works and why in getting citizens to participate in recycling. What are the dependent variables in their study? What are the independent variables? What analysis technique is used to investigate relationships between variables? What variables are most important in explaining variation in citizen

TABLE 13-18

Mean National and Regional Percentage Support for Environmental Legislation (LCV) by Party in the House, 93d (1973–74), 94th (1975–76), and 95th (1977–78) Congresses

		LCV% All Members	(N)	LCV% Democrats	(N)	LCV% Republicans	(N)
Nation	93	46.4	(435)	57.9	(248)	39.4	(187)
	94	49.3	(434)	58.0	(289)	32.0	(145)
	95	48.1	(434)	57.2	(287)	30.3	(147)
East	93	61.0	(117)	72.3	(67)	45.8	(50)
	94	64.8	(117)	71.7	(80)	49.8	(37)
	95	64.3	(116)	70.7	(80)	49.9	(36)
South	93	28.9	(121)	32.4	(84)	20.9	(37)
	94	29.6	(120)	32.1	(89)	22.6	(31)
	95	30.8	(121)	35.0	(90)	18.8	(31)
Midwest	93	47.1	(121)	70.6	(55)	27.5	(66)
	94	51.9	(121)	69.3	(69)	28.8	(52)
	95	51.0	(121)	67.9	(67)	30.0	(54)
West	93	50.8	(76)	69.4	(42)	28.0	(34)
	94	52.2	(76)	66.2	(51)	23.6	(25)
	95	46.1	(76)	61.0	(50)	17.6	(26)

Source: Henry C. Kenski and Margaret C. Kenski, "Partisanship, Ideology, and Constituency Differences on Environmental Issues in the U.S. House of Representatives: 1973–1978," *Policy Studies Journal* 9 (winter 1980): Table 1, p. 330.

participation in mandatory recycling programs? Write a sentence summarizing the relationship between citizen participation and each of these variables. How much total variation in citizen participation is explained by these variables?

6. In Douglas A. Hibbs Jr. and Christopher Dennis, "Income Distribution in the United States," *American Political Science Review* 82 (June 1988): 467–490, the authors present an explanation for the difference in the amount of income earned by the richest 20 percent of American families and the poorest 40 percent of American families. What factors do the authors believe affect this income inequality? What hypotheses do they advance? What do their results show?

Suggested Readings

Anderson, T. W. *Introduction to Multivariate Statistical Analysis.* New York: Wiley, 1958.

Blalock, Hubert M. *Causal Inference in Non-Experimental Research.* Chapel Hill: University of North Carolina Press, 1964.

———. *Social Statistics.* 2d ed. New York: McGraw-Hill, 1972.

Draper, N. R., and H. Smith. *Applied Regression Analysis.* New York: Wiley, 1966.

Kendall, M. G., and A. Stuart. *The Advanced Theory of Statistics.* Vol 2. Griffin: London, 1961, chap. 27.

Kerlinger, F. N., and E. Pedhazer. *Multiple Regression in Behavioral Research.* New York: Holt, Rinehart & Winston, 1973.

Long, J. Scott. *Regression Models for Categorical and Limited Dependent Variables.* Thousand Oaks, Calif.: Sage, 1997.

Overall, J. E., and C. Klett. *Applied Multivariate Analysis.* New York: McGraw-Hill, 1973.

Pampel, Fred C. *Logistic Regression: A Primer.* Thousand Oaks, Calif.: Sage, 2000.

Scheffe, Henry A. *The Analysis of Variance.* New York: Wiley, 1959.

CHAPTER 14

The Research Report

An Annotated Example

In the preceding chapters we have described important stages in the process of conducting a scientific investigation of political phenomena. In this chapter we will discuss the culmination of a research project: writing a research report. A complete and well-written research report that covers each component of the research process will contribute to the researcher's goal of creating transmissible, scientific knowledge.

This chapter examines how two researchers conducted and reported their research. We will evaluate how well the authors performed each component of the research process and how adequately they described and explained the choices they made during the investigation. To help you evaluate the report, the major components of the research process and some of the criteria by which they should be analyzed are presented here as a series of numbered questions. Refer to these questions while you read the article and jot the number of the question in the margin next to the section of the article in which the question is addressed. For easier reference, the sections of the article have been assigned letters and numbers.

1. Do the researchers clearly specify the main research question or problem? What is the "why" question?

2. Have the researchers demonstrated the value and significance of their research question and indicated how their research findings will contribute to scientific knowledge about their topic?

3. Have the researchers proposed clear explanations for the political phenomena that interest them? What types of relationships are hypothesized? Do they discuss any alternative explanations?

4. Are the independent and dependent variables identified? If so, what are they? Have the authors considered any alternative or control variables? If so, identify them. Can you think of any that the researchers did not mention?

5. Are the hypotheses empirical, general, and plausible?

6. Are the concepts in the hypotheses clearly defined? Are the operational definitions given the variables valid and reasonable? What is the level of measurement for each of the variables?

7. What method of data collection is used to make the necessary observations? Are the observations valid and reliable measurements?

8. Have the researchers made empirical observations about the units of analysis specified in the hypotheses?

9. If a sample is used, what type of sample is it? Does the type of sample seriously affect the conclusions that can be drawn from the research? Do the researchers discuss this?

10. What type of research design is used? Does the research design adequately test the hypothesized relationships?

11. Are the statistics that are used appropriate for the level of measurement of the variables?

12. Are the research findings presented and discussed clearly? Is the basis for deciding whether a hypothesis is supported or refuted clearly specified?

THE EFFECTS OF STATE ABORTION POLICIES ON STATES' ABORTION RATES

A

1 Following the *Roe* decision, antiabortion activists shifted energy and resources to state legislatures, and the subsequent debate over issues such as parental involvement and Medicaid funding mobilized pro-choice activists. The stakes in this struggle increased recently when the Supreme Court in the *Webster* (1989) and *Casey* (1992) decisions permitted states to enforce more abortion restrictions.[1] As a result of these decisions, the fate of abortion policy now appears to be significantly more in the hands of state politicians. These developments highlight the importance of understanding the role of state governments in the policymaking process that influences a woman's ability to obtain an abortion.

2 In 1988 (prior to the *Webster* decision) the Supreme Court permitted state governments to regulate access to abortion only by increasing the costs of obtaining an abortion for two subgroups of women—those eligible for Medicaid and minor, unmarried women. The court has held that a state may require an unmarried minor who seeks an abortion to notify or obtain the consent of one or both of her parents, provided that if she does not wish to do so, she must also be able to obtain permission from a judge.[2] In 1980, the Supreme Court ruled in *Harris v. McRae* that the federal and state governments could exclude coverage of abortions

From "The Effects of State Abortion Policies on States' Abortion Rates," by Anita Pritchard and Sharon Kay Parsons, *State and Local Government Review* 31 (winter 1999): 43–52. Reprinted by permission of the authors and the Carl Vinson Institute of Government, University of Georgia.

from Medicaid. As a consequence of these decisions, state abortion policies necessarily involve the issue of distribution of costs among women seeking abortions.

3 However, the radical nature of state abortion politics suggests that the issue at stake is not only the fairness of imposing higher costs on some groups of women but whether or not a woman may obtain an abortion in her state of residence. Certainly the participants in the antiabortion movement indicate that their intention is to reduce the number of abortions. Thus, the public debate creates the impression that state legislatures are important sites of abortion policymaking. If this is the case, the strategy of imposing higher costs on some groups of women should succeed in regulating access to abortion, and states with more restrictive regulations should have lower abortion rates than states with less restrictive laws. The following analysis evaluates this expectation by examining whether or not the two major state abortion policies in effect in 1988—state restrictions on Medicaid financing of abortion and state requirements for parental consent/notification for minors—explain variation in state abortion rates.

4 Research to date has produced conflicting conclusions on the effectiveness of state abortion policies. For example, in a case study of the effects of Medicaid funding regulations, Trussell et al. found that "23 percent of the Medicaid-eligible women in Ohio and 18 percent in Georgia who would have obtained an abortion in 1977 before the cutoff of Medicaid funding did not do so in 1978" (1980, 127). In Michigan, the comparison state which continued to pay for abortions for Medicaid-eligible women, the proportion of pregnancies terminated by abortion declined slightly, from 38.6 to 38 percent (Trussel et al. 1980, 128). Lundberg and Plotnick (1990) showed that white women aged 14–16 in 1979 were less likely to abort in states that restricted Medicaid funding of abortions. Using time series analysis, Wetstein (1996, 5253) found that prohibitions on Medicaid-funded abortions imposed by Colorado and Pennsylvania did reduce the number of abortions obtained in those states.

5 Similarly, studies that include all states and women of all ages have failed to reach agreement. In a study using the measure of number of publicly funded abortions, Meier and McFarlane (1994) demonstrated that states that fund abortions have a significantly higher rate of abortions. Medoff (1988) predicted a 17.5 percent drop in the abortion rate if all Medicaid-financed abortions were prohibited, but Hansen (1993) found that Medicaid funding had relatively little impact on states' abortion rates.

6 Studies of the effects of parental consent and notification laws on minors' access to abortion have also reached differing conclusions. Donovan (1983, 266) reported that the number of abortions obtained by minors increased by 33 percent in Minnesota between 1980 (the last full year without a notification law) and 1982 (the first full year during which the notification law was in effect). In another study of the effects of the Minnesota notification law, Rogers et al. (1991, 296–297) found that abortion rates did drop among 15–17 year-old women, relative to older women, but birthrates also fell among 15–17 and 18–19 year-old women. Cartoof and Klerman assessed the impact of Massachusetts's parental consent law and found that the law reduced the number of adolescents obtaining in-state abortions but increased the number of adolescents obtaining abortions from out-of-state

providers: "Massachusetts minors continue to conceive, abort, and give birth in the same proportions as before the law was implemented" (1986, 400). Using abortion and pregnancy rates from all states for adolescents and adults, Ohsfeldt and Gohmann (1994) found that parental involvement laws reduced adolescent abortion rates relative to the abortion rate for older teens and adults.

B   Data and Analysis

1 The dependent variable in this study is states' abortion rates, which in 1988 ranged from 45.9 per 1,000 women in California to only 5.1 per 1,000 women in Wyoming (Table 1).[3] The question under study is whether or not state abortion regulations are responsible for a portion of the considerable variation in abortion rates.

2 To more clearly identify the effects of these regulations, two sets of controls are included in the analysis. First, a state condition that is not regulated by state governments, demand for abortion, may be responsible for the cross-state variation in abortion rates. Although there is no single satisfactory measurement for abortion demand, research has shown that abortion rates do vary among subgroups of women. Henshaw and Silverman's assessment of abortion patients (1988, 161–162) showed that nonwhite and Hispanic women, employed women, low-income women, those not enrolled in school, and women residing in a metropolitan county were more likely to have an abortion in 1987. Hansen's research (1980; 1993) also demonstrated that urbanization influences states' abortion rates. Therefore, the analysis presented here measures abortion demand using the demographic variables that are related to abortion rates in the general population. The variables are percent who live in a metropolitan area, per capita income, percent with 12 years' and 16 years' education, percent employed in white-collar occupations, percent in poverty, and percent minority (includes both Hispanics and African Americans).[4] Because of high intercorrelations, these variables were included in a factor analysis (varimax) which identified three factors. On the "professional" factor, the variables white-collar, women white-collar, and education (16 years) load highly; poverty, minority, and education (12 years) load on the "minority" factor; and urban and income load on the "urban" factor (Table 2). The "professional" factor explains approximately 52 percent of the variance; "minority," 23 percent; and "urban," 14 percent.

3 Second, a number of states have engaged in symbolic policymaking on the abortion issue (i.e., activities that concern a woman's right to an abortion but do not directly attempt to regulate access to abortion). For example, among other provisions, states have passed legislation that will prohibit abortion if *Roe* is overturned as well as antiabortion resolutions and legislation calling for a constitutional convention to propose a Human Life Amendment. This activity by state governments provides an opportunity to compare the effects of symbolic policies, which cannot influence access to abortion, with the effects of regulatory policies on states' abortion rates.[5]

4 Two indicators of symbolic policymaking by state legislatures are included in the analysis. The first reflects the level of activity by measuring the total

TABLE 1

Abortion Rates by State per 1,000 Women Aged 15–44, 1988

+	Alabama	18.7		Montana	16.5
*	Alaska	18.2		Nebraska	17.7
	Arizona	28.8	+	Nevada	40.3
	Arkansas	11.6		New Hampshire	17.5
*	California	45.9	*	New Jersey	35.1
	Colorado	22.4		New Mexico	19.1
*	Connecticut	31.2	*	New York	43.3
	Delaware	35.7	*	North Carolina	25.4
	Florida	31.5	+	North Dakota	14.9
	Georgia	23.5	+	Ohio	21.0
*	Hawaii	43.0		Oklahoma	16.2
	Idaho	8.2	*	Oregon	23.9
	Illinois	26.4		Pennsylvania	18.9
+	Indiana	11.9	+	Rhode Island	30.6
	Iowa	14.6		South Carolina	16.7
	Kansas	20.1		South Dakota	5.7
	Kentucky	13.0		Tennessee	18.9
+	Louisiana	16.3		Texas	24.8
	Maine	16.2	+	Utah	12.8
*	Maryland	28.6	*	Vermont	25.8
+*	Massachusetts	30.2		Virginia	23.7
*	Michigan	28.5	*	Washington	27.6
+	Minnesota	18.2	+*	West Virginia	7.5
	Mississippi	8.4		Wisconsin	16.0
+	Missouri	16.4		Wyoming	5.1

* Medicaid funding for abortion, FY 1987 ($N = 14$).

+ Enforced law requiring parental consent/notification 1987 ($N = 12$).

number of enactments, (including abortion restrictions and antiabortion resolutions) in each state between 1973 and 1989 (summarized by Halva-Neubauer 1990). The second indicator includes state provisions which, although unconstitutional under the *Roe* decision, will presumably regulate abortion if this decision is overruled. Included in the coding are the following: whether or not (1) a constitutional preamble exists that protects the fetus; (2) trigger laws are in effect that criminalize abortion if *Roe* is overturned; (3) restrictive pre-1973 laws have been repealed; or (4) state courts have recognized independent protection for abortion rights in the state constitution.[6] These variables are coded for the symbolic policies, "number of state enactments" and "potential restrictions," respectively.

5 The variables measuring symbolic policies and abortion demand are included in a least squares model of regression, together with the two measurements of state regulatory policy, parental consent laws and Medicaid funding regulations. As of January 1991, 41 states had laws on the books addressing the issue of parental involvement in a minor's abortion (Greenberger and Connor 1991, 32).

TABLE 2
Rotated Factor Matrix for Indicators of States' Abortion Demand

Factor Matrix

	Factor 1 ("Professional")	Factor 2 ("Minority")	Factor 3 ("Urban")
"Professional"			
White-collar workers	.91	−.04	.37
Women white-collar workers	.93	.01	.08
Education (16 years)	.77	−.37	.32
"Minority"			
Education (12 years)	.51	−.77	.07
Poverty	−.19	.80	−.51
Minority population	.14	.90	.21
"Urban"			
Urban	.15	.15	.93
Income	.37	−.24	.81

Final Statistics

Variable	Communality
Urban	.90
Income	.84
Poverty	.93
White-collar workers	.96
Women white-collar workers	.87
Minority population	.87
Education (12 years)	.85
Education (16 years)	.84

Factor	Eigenvalue	Percentage of Variance	Cumulative
1	4.14	51.7	51.7
2	1.83	22.9	74.6
3	1.10	13.7	88.4

TABLE 3

Regressions of Abortion Rate on State Variables and State Abortion Policies

	Abortion Rate 1988		
	b		t
Regulatory Policies			
Parental consent	−1.86	(2.25)	−.83
Medicaid funding	4.19	(2.48)	1.69
Symbolic Policies			
Potential restrictions	1.21	(1.25)	.97
State enactments	.09	(.27)	.35
Factors			
"Professional"	1.69	(.99)	1.71
"Minority"	.87	(.86)	1.00
"Urban"	6.13	(1.00)	6.13*
R^2	.		.68
Adjusted R^2			.62
F			12.65*

*$p < .001$.
Note: Numbers in parentheses are standard errors.

However, in 1987 only 12 states had laws that were in effect; in the other states, the statutes had been enjoined or were not enforced, or as an alternative to parental notification/consent, the law permitted counseling by the provider, a health care professional, or other qualified counselor (see Table 1).[7] The 12 states with effective parental notification/consent laws are coded 1; the remainder are coded 0.

6 In fiscal year 1987, 14 states permitted Medicaid funding for abortions: 8 states voluntarily provided Medicaid funding (Alaska, Hawaii, Maryland, New York, North Carolina, Oregon, Washington, West Virginia), and 6 states had been ordered by their state courts to pay for all medically necessary abortions (California, Connecticut, Massachusetts, Michigan, New Jersey, Vermont) (Gold and Guardado 1988, 232). Some states permitted funding in limited circumstances, such as when the pregnancy resulted from reported rape or incest. However, since the number of abortions funded in such states was very small (Meier and McFarlane 1993, 250–251), states permitting full funding are coded 1; the remainder, 0.

7 If increasing the costs of obtaining an abortion for subgroups of women effectively regulates access to abortion, the two regulations—Medicaid funding and parental consent—will have a significant effect on abortion rates in addition to any variation explained by demand for abortion. Further, the symbolic policies should not explain variation in states' abortion rates, whereas the regulations, if effective, should be responsible for some of the variation. The results of the regression analysis are presented in Table 3. As expected, the symbolic policies—"number of state enactments" and "potential restrictions"—do not have a significant effect on states' abortion rates, but neither do the two policies that are intended to regulate access to abortion. The unstandardized coefficients for the

TABLE 4

Regressions of Abortion Rate on State Variables and State Abortion Policies

	Abortion Rate 1988		
	b		t
Regulatory Policies			
Parental consent	−2.06	(2.31)	−.89
Medicaid funding[a]	.979	(.757)	1.29
Symbolic Policies			
Potential restrictions	−1.579	(1.248)	−1.27
State enactments	−3.391	(.267)	−.00
Factors			
"Professional"	1.864	(.994)	1.88
"Minority"	.961	(.886)	1.09
"Urban"	6.271	(1.004)	6.25*
R^2	.		.82
Adjusted R^2			.67
F			12.16*

*$p < .001$.

[a] Funded abortion rate, 1987 (the number of funded abortions per 1,000 female population aged 15–44 [Meier and McFarlane 1993, 250–251]). Data transformation as described in Meier and McFarlane (1993, note 7) was followed (i.e., the rate and ratio measures all had standard deviations twice the size of their respective means). All measures had a large positive slew. To avoid problems with states that funded no abortions, a constant of 1 was added to each rate and ratio before the log transformation was made. A log transformation was used in the regression analysis.

two measurements of symbolic activity and the two regulatory policies do not reach levels of significance.[8] When included in a model with variables measuring symbolic policies and demand for abortion, Medicaid funding and parental consent policies do not influence states' abortion rates.

8 These results differ from some earlier studies also based on the 50 states. Medoff (1988) and Meier and McFarlane (1993; 1994) found that Medicaid funding did have a significant effect on abortion rates. Medoff (1988) used an economic model of demand for abortion and focused primarily on the issue of explicit opportunity costs at the time of the abortion decision. Meier and McFarlane's measure of abortion funding policy (1994, 1469) is the funded abortion rate (i.e., the number of publicly funded abortions in the state per 1,000 women aged 15–44) rather than the dichotomous variable used in this study. To determine if this measure is responsible for the varying results, the analysis was repeated using the Meier and McFarlane measure. Again, however, Medicaid funding did not have a significant effect (see Table 4). The notable distinction between the two studies that did find evidence of public funding (Medoff [1988] and Meier and McFarlane [1993; 1994]) and those that did not (ours and Hansen's work [1980; 1993]) is the latter studies used urbanization rate as a control variable.

9 Ohsfeldt and Gohmann (1994) concluded that parental involvement laws reduced adolescent abortion rates relative to older teens or adults not subject to the law. Their study was based on a model including state demographic and policy

variables, parental involvement laws, the price of an abortion, and other economic factors to predict the ratios of abortion and pregnancy rates for adolescents aged 15–17, older teens 18–19, and adult women 20–44.

10 Given the differing results produced by cross-state studies, our analysis uses a second methodology to examine the effects of parental involvement laws. The abortion and birthrates in 1980 (before such laws were permitted by the Supreme Court) are compared with abortion and birthrates in 1990 in states with and without parental involvement laws. Such an approach controls for at least two objections to the cross-state approach. First, states with predominantly pro-choice attitudes or relatively high adolescent pregnancy rates may be less likely to pass parental involvement laws. Second, the contradictory results produced by this study and the Ohsfeldt and Gohmann study (1994) suggest that the results vary depending on the state variables included in the model. An across-time approach controls for all state-level variables that may affect abortion demand and birthrates. If effective, parental involvement laws should reduce abortion rates for adolescents 15–17 years but not for the 18–19 age group.

C Findings

1 The "before-and-after" analysis finds little evidence that parental involvement laws influence the decisions of underage adolescents to abort or give birth. In parental consent states, abortion and birthrates are similar for both groups of adolescents, with abortion rates falling by about 7 percent between 1980 and 1990—a significant change in both cases—and with minor and insignificant changes in birthrates (Table 5). Thus, the drop in abortion rates did not result in higher rates of births. Apparently both age groups either changed behavior, which resulted in fewer pregnancies, or sought abortions in other states. In states without parental involvement laws, the changes in abortion and birthrates are contrary to what might be expected. The birthrate among 15–17 year olds increased to a significant degree, even though adolescents did not need to involve their parents in decisions to seek abortions; the abortion rate dropped to a significant degree among 18–19 year olds who are not affected by the parental involvement laws.

2 One of the measurements for abortion demand does influence abortion rates. Urbanized states are more likely to have high abortion rates; the positive unstandardized coefficient is significant at the 0.001 level. As noted earlier, the inclusion of the measure "urban" in a regression model seems to influence whether or not Medicaid financing has a significant effect on states' abortion rates. The other two factors, "professional" and "minority," are not significant. The coefficient for the minority factor is low, even though studies at the individual level (e.g., Henshaw and Silverman 1988) have shown that abortion rates are higher among African American and Hispanic women than among non-Hispanic and white women. But this individual-level relationship does not hold for states with different proportions of minority women. As shown in Table 1, abortion rates fluctuate considerably in states with high minority populations. For example, Mississippi has a rate of 18.2 percent, whereas California's abortion rate is 45.9 percent.

TABLE 5

Average Abortions and Births among Women, by Age Group, in States with and without Parental Consent Laws in 1990

	States with Parental Consent Laws[a]		States without Parental Consent Laws[b]	
	15–17 years	18–19 years	15–17 years	18–19 years
Mean Abortions				
1980	19.2	40.1	21.7	45.7
1990	12.4	33.2	20.1	40.4
percent change	6.85	6.92	1.57	5.25
t-test	3.69*	2.26*	1.45	2.88*
Mean Births				
1980	33.8	89.2	31.9	84.2
1990	34.9	87.7	33.9	86.8
percent change	−1.16	1.52	−1.99	−2.55
t-test	−.45	.43	−2.31*	−1.57

*$p < .05$.

[a] $N = 11$ states (Arkansas, Indiana, Louisiana, Massachusetts, Missouri, Nevada, North Dakota, Ohio, Rhode Island, West Virginia, Wyoming).

[b] $N = 26$ states (Arizona, Colorado, Georgia, Hawaii, Idaho, Kansas, Kentucky, Maine, Maryland, Michigan, Mississippi, Montana, Nebraska, New Jersey, New Mexico, New York, North Carolina, Oregon, Pennsylvania, South Dakota, Tennessee, Texas, Vermont, Virginia, Washington, Wisconsin).

3 While states' abortion policies do not influence abortion rates within their borders, they may create barriers which cause residents to seek abortions in other states. Because the Alan Guttmacher Institute estimates out-of-state abortion rates using published data from the Centers for Disease Control, it is possible to explore this scenario (Henshaw, Koonin, and Smith 1991, 80). The two regulatory policies do not have a significant effect on out-of-state abortion rates (see Table 6), thus effectively eliminating the possibility that the policies force women to travel out of state to obtain abortions. Again, however, the "urban" factor has a significant effect. The coefficient is negative, which means that residents in rural states are more likely to seek abortions in other states. Since abortion facilities are located almost exclusively in urban counties, the tendency for rural residents to obtain abortions out of state is not surprising.[9]

4 Conclusions should be cautiously drawn regarding the effects of state regulatory policies, because the results seem to be sensitive to the methodology used and to the variables included in regression models. Nevertheless, according to this analysis, the major distinction between symbolic and regulatory policies seems to be that the regulatory policies impose costs on some women seeking abortions while the symbolic policies do not. Neither category of policy has a measurable effect on variation in either in-state or out-of-state abortion rates.

5 Nevertheless, regulatory policies probably do succeed in creating difficulties for many women. Medicaid-eligible women may have to divert money from rent or other essentials in order to pay for an abortion if their state Medicaid

TABLE 6

Regressions of Out-of-State Abortion Rate on State Variables and State Abortion Policies

	Out-of-State Abortion Rate 1988		
	b		t
Regulatory Policies			
Parental consent	1.46	(4.28)	.34
Medicaid funding	−.86	(4.74)	−.18
Symbolic Policies			
Potential restrictions	−.22	(2.38)	−.09
State enactments	−.09	(.52)	−.17
Factors			
"Professional"	−.99	(1.89)	−.52
"Minority"	.04	(1.65)	.02
"Urban"	−5.86	(1.99)	−3.07*
R^2			.25
Adjusted R^2			.13
F			2.05

*$p < .001$.
Note: Numbers in parentheses are standard errors.

system refuses to do so. Minors residing in states with parental consent laws must either travel to another state or deal with a private matter in a public process if they cannot turn to their parents for support. No doubt these barriers do prevent some women from obtaining abortions, but their numbers are too small to explain variation in state abortion rates. Overall, however, the strategy of imposing higher costs on subgroups of women seeking abortions does not succeed in regulating access to abortion.

6 The model does explain 63 percent of the variation in states' abortion rates. These rates vary primarily because urbanization and closely related variables vary from state to state, but the manner in which urbanization influences abortion rates appears to be complex. Studies at the individual level have shown that women residing in urban areas are more likely to obtain abortions (Henshaw and Silverman 1988, 161–162). However, "urban" is also a measurement of the availability of abortion services located almost exclusively in urban areas. It is likely that these two variables—demand for abortion and the availability of abortion facilities—interact to increase the explanatory power of urbanization.[10] Most abortions are performed in clinics established primarily for that purpose.[11] A plausible motivation for the location of such facilities is that demand for the services must be strong enough to permit the facility to be economically viable which, in turn, explains why most facilities are located in urban areas.[12] The impact of "urban" is thus increased because women must obtain abortions where a facility is available. As indicated by the analysis of out-of-state rates, women residing in rural states are more likely to travel to other states for abortions.

D   **Discussion**

1 Although state abortion politics create the impression that state governments are important sites of abortion policymaking, state abortion regulations apparently have limited influence on a woman's ability to obtain an abortion. The Supreme Court, rather than state legislatures, remains the key decision maker for abortion policy. States do not effectively regulate access to abortion because the Supreme Court has not permitted them to do so, and whether states succeed in the future depends on Supreme Court decisions. Given this situation, why do antiabortion forces organize strong offensives in several states? No doubt many involved in the struggle believe that they do succeed in influencing access to abortion. Apart from this perception, there seem to be sufficient rewards for mobilizing to oppose abortion rights at the state level.

2 First, many of these political activities promote the long-term goal of restricting access to abortion. As Laurence Tribe (1990) notes, following the *Roe* decision, antiabortion forces engaged in a "war of attrition" at the state level, which furthered the antiabortion cause by permitting the right-to-life movement to impress politicians with their political might. State legislatures also provided an arena for continually challenging Roe. Without such activities, little post-*Roe* litigation would have resulted, effectively killing the issue in the federal courts. Activity at the state level has helped antiabortion activists keep the issue alive and frame the debate in terms that are often unflattering to pro-choice activists (e.g., as members of extremist groups who would exclude parents from the abortion decisions of their minor daughters [Halva-Neubauer 1993, 174, 478]).

3 Second, the abortion issue can be used to mobilize antiabortion activists to support a broad range of issues on the conservative agenda. For example, in the 1970s opposition to abortion was on its way to becoming a main vehicle for the rise in political influence of Protestant fundamentalism. By the 1980s abortion rights was one of the potent issues (interwoven with various other issues) important to the political right (Tribe 1990, chap. 7). Leaders of the conservative movement offer antiabortion activists state policies that are symbolic while providing other individuals and groups with more substantial benefits.

4 A woman's right to an abortion may not be the issue that mobilizes many participants in the struggle. Studies of activists in both the pro-choice and antiabortion movements indicate that issues other than abortion rights often characterize the conflict. For example, Kristin Luker's study of activists in California (1984) showed how groups clash over worldviews, life expectations, and life choices. Pro-choice and antiabortion activists have conflicting views about sex roles, motherhood, family size, and careers. For participants motivated by these concerns, a symbolic ideological victory may be sufficient motivation, regardless of the practical effects of policy on womens ability to obtain abortions.

Notes

1. In *Webster v. Reproductive Health Services* (1989), the Supreme Court upheld a Missouri law banning abortions in public hospitals and the involvement of public employees in the perfor-

mance of abortions. As a consequence of this decision, states may enforce mandatory testing for viability after a specified stage in the pregnancy. In *Planned Parenthood of Southeastern Pennsylvania v. Casey* (1992), the Supreme Court ruled that state restrictions generally would be upheld unless the restrictions place "an undue burden" on women seeking abortions. As a result of this decision, states can enforce the restrictions of a 24-hour waiting period and a state-prescribed presentation on abortion.

2. *Bellotti v. Baird* 443 U.S. 622 (1979); *City of Akron v. Akron Center for Reproductive Health* 103 S.Ct. 2481 (1983); *Planned Parenthood Association of Kansas City Mo. v. Ashcroft* 103 S.Ct. 2517 (1983); *Hodgson v. Minnesota* 110 S.Ct. 2926 (1990).

3. The abortion rate is the number of abortions per 1,000 women of childbearing age. Abortion data by state is collected by the Alan Guttmacher Institute. These figures include abortions performed on out-of-state residents. The 1988 data are reported in Henshaw and Van Vort (1990, 104).

4. Sources: urban, income, minority population (*Statistical Abstract of the United States* 1988); women white-collar workers (*Geographical Profile of Employment and Unemployment* 1982); education (12 and 16 years), poverty (*County and City Data Book: A Statistical Abstract Supplement* 1988).

5. Some studies have used measurements of symbolic policymaking (e.g., the number of policy enactments) as independent variables that might explain variation in states' abortion rates (e.g., Hansen 1993; Wetstein 1996, chap. 7). However, since symbolic policies cannot influence access to abortion, they should be used as control rather than explanatory variables, which is the approach of this analysis.

6. Coding is as follows: Most restrictive 1 = the constitution has a preamble protecting the fetus and/or the state has trigger laws which mandate criminalization of abortion if *Roe* is overturned. More restrictive 2 = state has most restrictive pre-1973 laws which have not been repealed but no trigger laws or preamble protecting the fetus. Less restrictive 3 = state has some restrictions but no trigger laws and/or no preamble protecting the fetus and/or does not have most restrictive pre-1973 laws that have not been repealed. Least restrictive 4 = the state courts have recognized independent protection for abortion rights in the state constitution and/or no restriction noted.

    The distribution is as follows: most restrictive = 24 percent of states; more restrictive = 20 percent; less restrictive = 44 percent; least restrictive = 12 percent. (Source: Klassel, D. 1989. *The state your rights are in.* New York: Planned Parenthood Federation of America.)

7. Greenberg and Connor (1991) report that 17 states had parental laws in effect in January 1991. However, we did not include the three states—Connecticut, Wisconsin, and Maine—that permit counseling as an alternative to parental consent/notification. Further, three states have laws which took effect between 1987 and 1991—Arkansas, South Carolina, Wyoming. Our analysis includes Nevada, whose law had not been enjoined in 1987 but was enjoined in 1991. Information on implementation dates was obtained by calling either the state attorney general or state office for Planned Parenthood.

8. This analysis follows the conventional practice of using significance tests when the unit of analysis (the 50 states) is a population.

9. For example, no abortions were performed in 91 percent of rural counties in 1985. (Source: June 28, 1990. *News: The Alan Guttmacher Institute.* New York: The Alan Guttmacher Institute.)

10. The location of abortion facilities is not determined by public officials. While governmental entities may attempt to restrict access to abortion facilities and services by using ordinances covering zoning or public health regulations, Supreme Court decisions have overturned excessively restrictive state and local regulations. For example, regulations that singled out clinics for special controls were held to violate equal protection of the laws. A state law making it a criminal offense to perform a first trimester abortion except in a hospital or licensed health facility was invalidated in *Sendak v. Arnold* (1976). In the *City of Akron v. Akron Center for Reproductive Health* (1983), several restrictive measures imposed by the city of Akron were overturned.

11. In 1988, 86 percent of abortions were performed in clinics, with hospitals and doctors' offices accounting for the remainder (Henshaw and Van Vort 1990).

12. Some studies have used access to abortion services in the states as an independent variable to explain variation in states' abortion rates (e.g., Hansen 1980; 1993; Wetstein 1996, chap. 7). Since women cannot obtain an abortion unless facilities are available, this variable predictably has a significant effect. However, it is as plausible to argue that the abortion rate influences the location of abortion facilities as it is to argue that abortion rates are high where abortion facilities are located.

References

Cartoof, Virginia G., and Lorraine V. Klerman. 1986. Parental consent for abortion: Impact of the Massachusetts law. *American Journal of Public Health* 76:397–400.

Donovan, Patricia. 1983. Judging teenagers: How minors fare when they seek court-authorized abortions. *Family Planning Perspectives* 15: 259–67.

Gold, Rachel Benson, and Sandra Guardado. 1988. Public funding of family planning, sterilization and abortion services, 1987. *Family Planning Perspectives* 20: 228–33.

Greenberger, Marcia D., and Katherine Connor. 1991. Parental notice and consent for abortion: Out of step with family law principles and policies. *Family Planning Perspectives* 23: 31–35.

Halva-Neubauer, Glen. 1990. Abortion policy in the post-*Webster* age. *Publius* 20: 27–44.

Hansen, Susan B. 1980. State implementation of Supreme Court decisions: Abortion rates since *Roe v. Wade. Journal of Politics* 42: 372–95.

—— 1993. Differences in public policies toward abortion. In *Understanding the new politics of abortion.* Malcolm L. Goggin, ed. Newbury Park, Calif.: Sage.

Henshaw, Stanley K., Lisa M. Koonin, and Jack C. Smith. 1991. Characteristics of U.S. women having abortions, 1987. *Family Planning Perspectives* 23: 61–67.

Henshaw, Stanley K., and Jane Silverman. 1988. The characteristics and prior contraceptive use of U.S. abortion patients. *Family Planning Perspectives* 20: 160–68.

Henshaw, Stanley K., and Jennifer Van Vort. 1990. Abortion services in the United States, 1987–1988. *Family Planning Perspectives* 22: 102–9.

Luker, Kristin. 1984. *Abortion and the politics of motherhood.* Berkeley: University of California Press.

Lundberg, Shelly, and Robert D. Plotnick. 1990. Effects of state welfare, abortion, and family planning policies on premarital childbearing among white adolescents. *Family Planning Perspectives* 22: 246–51.

Medoff, Marshall H. 1988. An economic analysis of the demand for abortions. *Economic Inquiry* 26: 353–59.

Meier, Kenneth, and Deborah R. McFarlane. 1993. Abortion politics and abortion funding policy. In *Understanding the new politics of abortion.* Malcolm L. Goggin, ed. Newbury Park, Calif.: Sage.

—— 1994. State family planning and abortion expenditures: Their effect on public health. *American Journal of Public Health* 84: 1468–72.

Ohsfeldt, Robert L., and Stephen E. Gohmann. 1994. Do parental involvement laws reduce adolescent abortion rates? *Contemporary Economic Policy* 12: 65–76.

Tribe, Laurence. 1990. *Abortion: The clash of absolutes.* New York: W .W. Norton.

Trussell, James, Jane Menken, Barbara L. Lindheim, and Barbara Vaughan. 1980. The impact of restricting Medicaid financing for abortion. *Family Planning Perspectives* 12:120–30.

Wetstein, Matthew E. 1996. *Abortion rates in the United States.* Albany: State University of New York.

Now that you have read this example of a research report and noted whether and where the authors have addressed each of the twelve research questions, compare your findings with ours. The letters and numbers after each question refer to where in the article the question under discussion is addressed.

1. *Do the researchers clearly specify the main research question or problem? What is the "why" question?* (A-1, A-2, A-3, B-1)

The authors do not actually state their research question in the form of a "why" question. However, it can be stated as: "Why do abortion rates among the states vary?" Many researchers do not necessarily start out by posing a "why" question. Rather, they start out by proposing a relationship between phenomena or suggesting an explanation that they want to test. Here the authors are interested in the role of state governments in regulating access to abortion. Their research question is "Are abortion rates lower in states with more restrictive laws than in states with less restrictive laws?"

2. *Have the researchers demonstrated the value and significance of their research question* (A-1, A-3) *and indicated how their research findings will contribute to scientific knowledge about their topic?* (A-4, A-5)

Pritchard and Parson's research is expected to contribute to our understanding of the impact of state abortion policies. It is important to understand the impact of state abortion policies on a woman's ability to obtain an abortion in light of Supreme Court decisions in 1989 and 1992 that permitted states to enforce more abortion restrictions. The authors note that "public debate creates the impression that state legislatures are important sites of abortion policymaking." The actual consequences of state abortion policies are important to both antiabortion and pro-choice advocates. Both sides of the debate can be expected to want to know whether restrictive abortion laws passed by some states have reduced abortion rates. Previous research investigating the impact of restrictions on publicly funded abortions and parental consent and notification laws has produced conflicting results, and some studies have not included all states as this study proposes.

3. *Have the researchers proposed clear explanations for the political phenomena that interest them?* (A, B, C) *What types of relationships are hypothesized?* (C, E-1, E-15) *Do they discuss any alternative explanations?* (B, C, E-1, E-15)

Pritchard and Parsons are attempting to explain variation in state abortion rates. They hypothesize that states with more restrictive regulations have lower abortion rates than states with less restrictive laws. This hypothesis is directional. (A-3)

The authors consider an alternative explanation, demand for abortion, that may cause state variation in abortion rates, hypothesizing that the greater the demand, the higher the abortion rates. This hypothesis is also directional. (B-2) They also investigate whether symbolic policymaking among the states (activities that concern a woman's right to an abortion but that do not directly attempt to regulate access to abortion) have an impact on abortion rates. (B-3, B-7) They do not expect symbolic policies to have an impact on state abortion rates. Thus, they hypothesize a null relationship between symbolic policies and abortion rates.

The authors also test the hypothesis that abortion rates for adolescents in the 15–17 years age group but not for those in the 18–19 years age group should go down in states adopting parental involvement laws. (B-10)

4. *Are the independent and dependent variables identified?* (B) *If so, what are they? Have the authors considered any alternative or control variables?* (B) *If so, identify them. Can you think of any that the researchers did not mention?*

The main dependent variable is abortion rates. (B-1) The independent variable is regulation of access to abortion. (A-3) The other independent variables, demand for abortion (B-2) and symbolic policymaking (B-3), are control variables.

The authors do not initially discuss the availability of abortion facilities as a control variable, but later they note that abortion facilities are almost exclusively found in urban areas (C-3) and urbanization is included in their operationalization of demand for abortion, which they use as a control variable.

5. *Are the hypotheses empirical, general, and plausible?* (B)

The hypotheses are empirical. All hypotheses relate characteristics of states, their laws or their populations. The authors offer reasons that support the plausibility of each hypothesis. The hypotheses are general in that they apply to all states, although they are limited to the year 1988.

6. *Are the concepts in the hypotheses clearly defined? Are the operational definitions valid and reasonable? What is the level of measurement for each of the variables?*

Each of the concepts is clearly defined and the definitions appear to be reasonable. Abortion rates are defined as the number of abortions per 1,000 women of childbearing age, including abortions performed on out-of-state residents. (E-3) Because the authors also investigate whether state abortion regulations force women to travel out of state to obtain abortions, out-of-state abortion rates for each state are also measured. (C-3) These are both ratio level measures. The authors use two variables to measure restrictive state abortion policies. One is state restrictions on Medicaid financing of abortion and the other is state requirements for parental consent/notification. Each of these variables is a dichotomous nominal level variable: a state's policy is identified as restrictive or not and the coding of these variables is clearly explained. (B-5, B-6)

Demand for abortion is measured by a number of indicators because there is no single satisfactory measure of abortion demand, as the authors point out. Eight population characteristics of states are identified, each of which is measured at the ratio level. Because the characteristics are highly related to each other, the authors use factor analysis, which results in three factors that are then used as variables. (B-2) The results of the factor analysis are shown in Table 2. The factor matrix shows how the eight characteristics are related to or "load" on the three factors. The authors refer to the variance column of the final statistics half of Table 2 in their discussion when they point out that factor 1 ("professional") accounts for 51.7 percent of the variance in the eight original variables, factor 2 ("minority") for 22.9 percent, and factor 3 ("urban") for 13.7 percent.

Two indicators of symbolic policymaking are used. One measures the total number of enactments. (C-4) This a ratio level measure. The second indicator is based the content of symbolic state abortion provisions. Coding of this variable results in an ordinal level measure. (C-4, E-6)

7. *What method of data collection is used to make the necessary observations?* (D, E, F) *Are the observations valid and reliable measurements?*

The researchers use document analysis to measure most of the variables. In a few cases, the researchers called the state to determine whether the parental notification law was being implemented, which amounted to interview data collection. (E-7) The secondary sources used by the authors are clearly cited and appear to be valid and reasonable. (E)

8. *Have the researchers made empirical observations about the units of analysis specified in the hypotheses?*

The unit of analysis in this study is the state. Each variable is a characteristic of a state or its population, which can be observed empirically. (B, E)

9. *If a sample is used, what type of sample is it? Does the type of sample seriously affect the conclusions that can be drawn from the research? Is this discussed?*

The research does not use a sample; all fifty states are included in the analyses.

10. *What type of research design is used? Does the research design adequately test the hypothesized relationships?*

The research design is a cross-sectional, nonexperimental design. The researchers exercised no control over which states adopted restrictions. The researchers did not assign states at random to experimental or control groups. The authors' research design matches the way their hypothesis is formulated: they compare the abortion rates of states with restrictions to the abortion rates of states without restrictions. The goal of the research is to explain the variation in abortion rates among the states, and this research design is an appropriate test of their proposed explanation for variation in abortion rates.

Another way to test the effect of state abortion restrictions is a before-and-after test, which the authors use to look further into the impact of parental involvement laws. (C-1) Here they measure the abortion rates and birth rates in 1980 (before the adoption of such laws) and 1990 (after their adoption) and test the hypothesis that abortion rates for adolescents 15–17 years of age should be reduced and birth rates increased compared to adolescents 18–19 years of age in states with parental involvement laws. They also do the same test in states without parental involvement laws where they would not expect to see changes in the 15–17 age group compared to the 18–19 age group.

11. *Are the statistics used appropriate for the level of measurement of the variables?*

The statistics used are appropriate. It is appropriate to use multiple regression analysis because the dependent variable is a ratio level measure. The method of analysis in Table 6 is a difference of means, also appropriate as changes in the mean number of abortions and mean number of births are analyzed.

12. *Are the research findings presented and discussed clearly? Is the basis for deciding whether a hypothesis is supported or refuted clearly specified?*

The results of their analysis based on the cross-sectional research design are shown in Table 3 and Table 4 and discussed in paragraph B-7. Table 4 shows the results of the multiple regression analysis using a different measure of state abortion funding policy, but this did not alter the basic outcome of the analysis. The authors conclude that, as expected, symbolic policies have no statistically significant effect on variation in abortion rates. Contrary to their hypothesis, state restrictions on access to abortions also do not have any statistically significant effect. The only factors that did have a statistically significant effect on variation in abortion rates was the "urban" factor. If you look at the numbers in the column under *b* in Tables 3 and 4, you can see that, with the exception of "urban," the first number *(b)* is not twice the value of the number in parentheses next to it, which is the standard error. As we pointed out in Chapter 13, this means that the relationship between the independent and dependent variable is not significant at the 95 percent or $p<.05$ level. For "urban," the *b* is much more than twice the size of the standard error, thus it is statistically significant at a greater level than .05.

The total amount of variation in state abortion rates explained by all the independent and control variables is shown by the Adjusted R^2. In Table 3, 62 percent of the variation in state abortion rates was explained. The F statistic is the appropriate statistic to use for statistical significance. It shows that the explained variation is significant at the $p < .001$ level.

The results of the before-and-after analysis is shown in Table 5 and discussed in paragraph C-1. The results do not confirm the authors' expectations. Table 6 shows the result of using out-of-state abortion rates as the dependent variable. Again, state restrictions on access to abortions do not seem to cause the rate at which women seek abortions out-of-state to increase significantly.

If you look at the sign of the *b*s in Tables 3, 4, and 6, you will see that the relationship between state regulatory policies and abortion rates is in the direction hypothesized. For example, Table 3 shows that state medicaid funding is positively associated with higher state abortion rates. Table 6 shows that state medicaid funding is negatively associated with women seeking out-of-state abortions. Thus, the overall conclusion reached by the authors—that while state abortion restrictions may impose costs on some women seeking abortions, these costs do not appear to have a measureable (statistically significant) impact on state abortion rates—is supported by the data. (C-4)

Conclusion

A research report rarely answers all the questions that can be raised about a topic. But a well-written report, because it carefully explains how the researcher conducted each stage in the research process, makes it easier for other researchers to evaluate the work. Other investigators may build upon it by varying the method of data collection, the operationalization of variables, or the research design.

By now you should understand how scientific knowledge about politics is acquired. You should know how to formulate a testable hypothesis, choose valid and reliable measures for the concepts that you relate in a hypothesis, develop a research design, conduct a literature review, and make empirical observations. You should also be able to analyze data using appropriate univariate, bivariate, and multivariate statistics. Finally, you should be able to evaluate most research reports as well as write a research report yourself.

We encourage you to think up research questions of your own. Some of these may be feasible projects for a one- or two-semester course. You will learn much more about the research process by doing research than by just reading about it. We wish you success.

Exercise

For the following research article, or one assigned by your instructor, try to answer the series of questions on pages 437–438 on your own.

Rebecca E. Deen and Thomas H. Little, "Getting to the Top: Factors Influencing the Selction of Women to Positions of Leadership in State Legislatures," *State and Local Government Review* 31 (spring 1999): 123–134.

Appendix

APPENDIX A
Table of Chi-square (χ^2) Values

Degree of Freedom (df)	0.10	0.05	0.02	0.01
1	2.706	3.841	5.412	6.635
2	4.605	5.991	7.824	9.210
3	6.251	7.815	9.837	11.341
4	7.779	9.488	11.668	13.277
5	9.236	11.070	13.388	15.086
6	10.645	12.592	15.033	16.812
7	12.017	14.067	16.622	18.475
8	13.362	15.507	18.168	20.090
9	14.684	16.919	19.679	21.666
10	15.987	18.307	21.161	23.209
11	17.275	19.675	22.618	24.725
12	18.549	21.026	24.054	26.217
13	19.812	22.362	25.472	27.688
14	21.064	23.685	26.873	29.141
15	22.307	24.996	28.259	30.578
16	23.542	26.296	29.633	32.000
17	24.769	27.587	30.995	33.409
18	25.989	28.869	32.346	34.805
19	27.204	30.144	33.687	36.191
20	28.412	31.410	35.020	37.566
21	29.615	32.671	36.343	38.932
22	30.813	33.924	37.659	40.289
23	32.007	35.172	38.968	41.638
24	33.196	36.415	40.270	42.980
25	34.382	37.652	41.566	44.314
26	35.563	38.885	42.856	45.642
27	36.741	40.113	44.140	46.963
28	37.916	41.337	45.419	48.278
29	39.087	42.557	46.693	49.588
30	40.256	43.773	47.962	50.892

Source: Kirk W. Elison, Richard P. Runyon, and Audrey Haber, *Fundamentals of Social Statistics* (Reading, Mass.: Addison-Wesley, 1982), 476. Reprinted with permission of McGraw-Hill, Inc.

APPENDIX B
Critical Values from t Distribution

Degree of Freedom (df)	Alpha Level for One-Tailed Test						
	.05	.025	.01	.005	.0025	.001	.0005
	Alpha Level for Two-Tailed Test						
	.10	.05	.02	.01	.005	.002	.001
1	6.314	12.706	31.821	63.657	127.32	318.31	636.62
2	2.920	4.303	6.965	9.925	14.089	22.327	31.598
3	2.353	3.182	4.541	5.841	7.453	10.214	12.924
4	2.132	2.776	3.747	4.604	5.598	7.173	8.610
5	2.015	2.571	3.365	4.032	4.773	5.893	6.869
6	1.943	2.447	3.143	3.707	4.317	5.208	5.959
7	1.895	2.365	2.998	3.499	4.029	4.785	5.408
8	1.869	2.306	2.896	3.355	3.833	4.501	5.041
9	1.833	2.262	2.821	3.250	3.690	4.297	4.781
10	1.812	2.228	2.764	3.169	3.581	4.144	4.587
11	1.796	2.201	2.718	3.106	3.497	4.025	4.437
12	1.782	2.179	2.681	3.055	3.428	3.930	4.318
13	1.771	2.160	2.650	3.012	3.372	3.852	4.221
14	1.761	2.145	2.624	2.977	3.326	3.787	4.140
15	1.753	2.131	2.602	2.947	3.286	3.733	4.073
16	1.746	2.120	2.583	2.921	3.252	3.686	4.015
17	1.740	2.110	2.567	2.898	3.222	3.646	3.965
18	1.734	2.101	2.552	2.878	3.197	3.610	3.922
19	1.729	2.093	2.539	2.861	3.174	3.579	3.883
20	1.725	2.086	2.528	2.845	3.153	3.552	3.850
21	1.721	2.080	2.518	2.831	3.135	3.527	3.819
22	1.717	2.074	2.508	2.819	3.119	3.505	3.792
23	1.714	2.069	2.500	2.807	3.104	3.485	3.767
24	1.711	2.064	2.492	2.797	3.091	3.467	3.745
25	1.708	2.060	2.485	2.787	3.078	3.450	3.725
26	1.706	2.056	2.479	2.779	3.067	3.435	3.707
27	1.703	2.052	2.473	2.771	3.057	3.421	3.690
28	1.701	2.048	2.467	2.763	3.047	3.408	3.674
29	1.699	2.045	2.462	2.756	3.038	3.396	3.659
30	1.697	2.042	2.457	2.750	3.030	3.385	3.646
40	1.684	2.021	2.423	2.704	2.971	3.307	3.551
60	1.671	2.000	2.390	2.660	2.915	3.232	3.460
120	1.658	1.980	2.358	2.617	2.860	3.160	3.373
∞	1.645	1.960	2.326	2.576	2.807	3.090	3.291

Source: James V. Couch, *Fundamentals of Statistics for the Behavioral Sciences* (St. Paul: West, 1987), 327.

Critical Values from F Distribution ∝ = .05

Degree of freedom (df) within groups	Degree of freedom (df) between Groups																		
	1	2	3	4	5	6	7	8	9	10	12	15	20	24	30	40	60	120	∞
1	161.4	199.5	215.7	224.6	230.2	234.0	236.8	238.9	240.5	241.9	243.9	245.9	248.0	249.1	250.1	251.1	252.2	253.3	254.3
2	18.51	19.00	19.16	19.25	19.30	19.33	19.35	19.37	19.38	19.40	19.41	19.43	19.45	19.45	19.48	19.47	19.48	19.49	19.50
3	10.13	9.55	9.28	9.12	9.01	8.94	8.89	8.85	8.81	8.79	8.74	8.70	8.66	8.64	8.62	8.59	8.57	8.55	8.53
4	7.71	6.94	6.59	6.39	6.26	6.16	6.09	6.04	6.00	5.96	5.91	5.86	5.80	5.77	5.75	5.72	5.69	5.66	5.63
5	6.61	5.79	5.41	5.19	5.05	4.95	4.88	4.82	4.77	4.74	4.68	4.62	4.56	4.53	4.50	4.46	4.43	4.40	4.36
6	5.99	5.14	4.76	4.53	4.39	4.28	4.21	4.15	4.10	4.06	4.00	3.94	3.87	3.84	3.81	3.77	3.74	3.70	3.67
7	5.59	4.74	4.35	4.12	3.97	3.87	3.79	3.73	3.68	3.64	3.57	3.51	3.44	3.41	3.38	3.34	3.30	3.27	3.23
8	5.32	4.46	4.07	3.84	3.69	3.58	3.50	3.44	3.39	3.35	3.28	3.22	3.15	3.12	3.08	3.04	3.01	2.97	2.93
9	5.12	4.26	3.86	3.63	3.48	3.37	3.29	3.23	3.18	3.14	3.07	3.01	2.94	2.90	2.86	2.83	2.79	2.75	2.71
10	4.96	4.10	3.71	3.48	3.33	3.22	3.14	3.07	3.02	2.98	2.91	2.85	2.77	2.74	2.70	2.66	2.62	2.58	2.54
11	4.84	3.98	3.59	3.36	3.20	3.09	3.01	2.95	2.90	2.85	2.79	2.72	2.65	2.61	2.57	2.53	2.49	2.45	2.40
12	4.75	3.89	3.49	3.26	3.11	3.00	2.91	2.85	2.80	2.75	2.69	2.62	2.54	2.51	2.47	2.43	2.38	2.34	2.30
13	4.67	3.81	3.41	3.18	3.03	2.92	2.83	2.77	2.71	2.67	2.60	2.53	2.46	2.42	2.38	2.34	2.30	2.25	2.21
14	4.60	3.74	3.34	3.11	2.96	2.85	2.76	2.70	2.65	2.60	2.53	2.46	2.39	2.35	2.31	2.27	2.22	2.18	2.13
15	4.54	3.68	3.29	3.06	2.90	2.79	2.71	2.64	2.59	2.54	2.48	2.40	2.33	2.29	2.25	2.20	2.16	2.11	2.07
16	4.49	3.63	3.24	3.01	2.85	2.74	2.66	2.59	2.54	2.49	2.42	2.35	2.28	2.24	2.19	2.15	2.11	2.06	2.01
17	4.45	3.59	3.20	2.96	2.81	2.70	2.61	2.55	2.49	2.45	2.38	2.31	2.23	2.19	2.15	2.10	2.06	2.01	1.96

18	4.41	3.55	3.16	2.93	2.77	2.66	2.58	2.51	2.46	2.41	2.34	2.27	2.19	2.15	2.11	2.06	2.02	1.97	1.92
19	4.38	3.52	3.13	2.90	2.74	2.63	2.54	2.48	2.42	2.38	2.31	2.23	2.16	2.11	2.07	2.03	1.98	1.93	1.88
20	4.35	3.49	3.10	2.87	2.71	2.60	2.51	2.45	2.39	2.35	2.28	2.20	2.12	2.08	2.04	1.99	1.95	1.90	1.84
21	4.32	3.47	3.07	2.84	2.68	2.57	2.49	2.42	2.37	2.32	2.25	2.18	2.10	2.05	2.01	1.96	1.92	1.87	1.81
22	4.30	3.44	3.05	2.82	2.66	2.55	2.46	2.40	2.34	2.30	2.23	2.15	2.07	2.03	1.98	1.94	1.89	1.84	1.78
23	4.28	3.42	3.03	2.80	2.64	2.53	2.44	2.37	2.32	2.27	2.20	2.13	2.05	2.01	1.96	1.91	1.86	1.81	1.76
24	4.26	3.40	3.01	2.78	2.62	2.51	2.42	2.36	2.30	2.25	2.18	2.11	2.03	1.98	1.94	1.89	1.84	1.79	1.73
25	4.24	3.39	2.99	2.76	2.60	2.49	2.40	2.34	2.28	2.24	2.16	2.09	2.01	1.96	1.92	1.87	1.82	1.77	1.71
26	4.23	3.37	2.98	2.74	2.59	2.47	2.39	2.32	2.27	2.22	2.15	2.07	1.99	1.95	1.90	1.85	1.80	1.75	1.69
27	4.21	3.35	2.96	2.73	2.57	2.46	2.37	2.31	2.25	2.20	2.13	2.06	1.97	1.93	1.88	1.84	1.79	1.73	1.67
28	4.20	3.34	2.95	2.71	2.56	2.45	2.36	2.29	2.24	2.19	2.12	2.04	1.96	1.91	1.87	1.82	1.77	1.71	1.65
29	4.18	3.33	2.93	2.70	2.55	2.43	2.35	2.28	2.22	2.18	2.10	2.03	1.94	1.90	1.85	1.81	1.75	1.70	1.64
30	4.17	3.32	2.92	2.69	2.53	2.42	2.33	2.27	2.21	2.16	2.09	2.01	1.93	1.89	1.84	1.79	1.74	1.68	1.62
40	4.08	3.23	2.84	2.61	2.45	2.34	2.25	2.18	2.12	2.08	2.00	1.92	1.84	1.79	1.74	1.69	1.64	1.58	1.51
60	4.00	3.15	2.76	2.53	2.37	2.25	2.17	2.10	2.04	1.99	1.92	1.84	1.75	1.70	1.65	1.59	1.53	1.47	1.39
120	3.92	3.07	2.68	2.45	2.29	2.17	2.09	2.02	1.96	1.91	1.83	1.75	1.66	1.61	1.55	1.50	1.43	1.35	1.25
∞	3.84	3.00	2.60	2.37	2.21	2.10	2.01	1.94	1.88	1.83	1.75	1.67	1.57	1.52	1.46	1.39	1.32	1.22	1.00

APPENDIX C   Continued
Critical Values from F Distribution $\propto = .01$

Degree of freedom (df) within groups	Degree of freedom (df) between Groups																		
	1	2	3	4	5	6	7	8	9	10	12	15	20	24	30	40	60	120	∞
1	4052	4999.5	5403	5625	5764	5859	5928	5981	6022	6056	6106	6157	6209	6235	6261	6287	6313	6339	6366
2	98.58	99.00	99.17	99.25	99.30	99.33	99.36	99.37	99.39	99.40	99.42	99.43	99.45	99.46	99.47	99.47	99.48	99.49	99.50
3	34.12	30.82	29.46	28.71	28.24	27.91	27.67	27.49	27.35	27.23	27.05	26.87	26.69	26.60	26.50	26.41	26.32	26.22	26.13
4	21.20	18.00	16.69	15.98	15.52	15.21	14.98	14.80	14.66	14.55	14.37	14.20	14.02	13.93	13.64	13.75	13.65	13.56	13.46
5	16.26	13.27	12.06	11.39	10.97	10.67	10.46	10.29	10.16	10.05	9.89	9.72	9.55	9.47	9.38	9.29	9.20	9.11	9.02
6	13.75	10.92	9.78	9.15	8.75	8.47	8.26	8.10	7.98	7.87	7.72	7.56	7.40	7.31	7.23	7.14	7.06	6.97	6.88
7	12.25	9.55	8.45	7.85	7.46	7.19	6.99	6.84	6.72	6.62	6.47	6.31	6.16	6.07	5.99	5.91	5.82	5.74	5.65
8	11.26	8.65	7.59	7.01	6.63	6.37	6.18	6.03	5.91	5.81	5.67	5.52	5.36	5.28	5.20	5.12	5.03	4.95	4.86
9	10.56	8.02	6.99	6.42	6.06	5.80	5.61	5.47	5.35	5.26	5.11	4.96	4.81	4.73	4.65	4.57	4.48	4.40	4.31
10	10.04	7.56	6.55	5.99	5.64	5.39	5.20	5.06	4.94	4.85	4.71	4.56	4.41	4.33	4.25	4.17	4.08	4.00	3.91
11	9.65	7.21	6.22	5.67	5.32	5.07	4.89	4.74	4.63	4.54	4.40	4.25	4.10	4.02	3.94	3.86	3.78	3.69	3.60
12	9.33	6.93	5.95	5.41	5.06	4.82	4.64	4.50	4.39	4.30	4.16	4.01	3.86	3.78	3.70	3.62	3.54	3.45	3.36
13	9.07	6.70	5.74	5.21	4.86	4.62	4.44	4.30	4.19	4.10	3.96	3.82	3.66	3.59	3.51	3.43	3.34	3.25	3.17
14	8.86	6.51	5.56	5.04	4.69	4.46	4.28	4.14	4.03	3.94	3.80	3.66	3.51	3.43	3.35	3.27	3.18	3.09	3.00

15	8.68	6.36	5.42	4.89	4.56	4.32	4.14	4.00	3.89	3.80	3.67	3.52	3.37	3.29	3.21	3.13	3.05	2.96	2.87
16	8.53	6.23	5.29	4.77	4.44	4.20	4.03	3.89	3.78	3.69	3.55	3.41	3.26	3.18	3.10	3.02	2.93	2.84	2.75
17	8.40	6.11	5.18	4.67	4.34	4.10	3.93	3.79	3.68	3.59	3.46	3.31	3.16	3.08	3.00	2.92	2.83	2.75	2.65
18	8.29	6.01	5.09	4.58	4.25	4.01	3.84	3.71	3.60	3.51	3.37	3.23	3.08	3.00	2.92	2.84	2.75	2.66	2.57
19	8.18	5.93	5.01	4.50	4.17	3.94	3.77	3.63	3.52	3.43	3.30	3.15	3.00	2.92	2.84	2.76	2.67	2.58	2.49
20	8.10	5.85	4.94	4.43	4.10	3.87	3.70	3.56	3.46	3.37	3.23	3.09	2.94	2.86	2.78	2.69	2.61	2.52	2.42
21	8.02	5.78	4.87	4.37	4.04	3.81	3.64	3.51	3.40	3.31	3.17	3.03	2.88	2.80	2.72	2.64	2.55	2.46	2.36
22	7.95	5.72	4.82	4.31	3.99	3.76	3.59	3.45	3.35	3.26	3.12	2.98	2.83	2.75	2.67	2.58	2.50	2.40	2.31
23	7.88	5.66	4.76	4.26	3.94	3.71	3.54	3.41	3.30	3.21	3.07	2.93	2.78	2.70	2.62	2.54	2.45	2.35	2.26
24	7.82	5.61	4.72	4.22	3.90	3.67	3.50	3.36	3.26	3.17	3.03	2.89	2.74	2.66	2.58	2.49	2.40	2.31	2.21
25	7.77	5.57	4.68	4.18	3.85	3.63	3.46	3.32	3.22	3.13	2.99	2.85	2.70	2.62	2.54	2.45	2.36	2.27	2.17
26	7.72	5.53	4.64	4.14	3.82	3.59	3.42	3.29	3.18	3.09	2.96	2.81	2.66	2.58	2.50	2.42	2.33	2.23	2.13
27	7.68	5.49	4.60	4.11	3.78	3.56	3.39	3.26	3.15	3.06	2.93	2.78	2.63	2.55	2.47	2.38	2.29	2.20	2.10
28	7.64	5.45	4.57	4.07	3.75	3.53	3.36	3.23	3.12	3.03	2.90	2.75	2.60	2.52	2.44	2.35	2.26	2.17	2.06
29	7.60	5.42	4.54	4.04	3.73	3.50	3.33	3.20	3.09	3.00	2.87	2.73	2.57	2.49	2.41	2.33	2.23	2.14	2.03
30	7.56	5.39	4.51	4.02	3.70	3.47	3.30	3.17	3.07	2.98	2.84	2.70	2.55	2.47	2.39	2.30	2.21	2.11	2.01
40	7.31	5.18	4.31	3.83	3.51	3.29	3.12	2.99	2.89	2.80	2.66	2.52	2.37	2.29	2.20	2.11	2.02	1.92	1.80
60	7.08	4.98	4.13	3.65	3.34	3.12	2.95	2.82	2.72	2.63	2.50	2.35	2.20	2.12	2.03	1.94	1.84	1.73	1.60
120	6.85	4.79	3.95	3.48	3.17	2.96	2.79	2.66	2.56	2.47	2.34	2.19	2.03	1.95	1.86	1.76	1.66	1.53	1.38
∞	6.63	4.61	3.78	3.32	3.02	2.80	2.64	2.51	2.41	2.32	2.18	2.04	1.88	1.79	1.70	1.59	1.47	1.32	1.00

Source: James V. Couch, Fundamentals of Statistics for the Behavioral Sciences (St. Paul: West, 1987), 328, 330.

APPENDIX D
Critical Values for Pearson r

Degree of freedom (df) (N–2)	Alpha Level for One-Tailed Test				
	.05	.025	.01	.005	.0005
	Alpha Level for Two-Tailed Test				
	.10	.05	.02	.01	.001
1	.9877	.9969	.9995	.9999	1.0000
2	.9000	.9500	.9800	.9900	.9990
3	.8054	.8783	.9343	.9587	.9912
4	.7293	.8114	.8822	.9172	.9741
5	.6694	.7545	.8329	.8745	.9507
6	.6215	.7067	.7887	.8343	.9249
7	.5822	.6664	.7498	.7977	.8982
8	.5494	.6319	.7155	.7646	.8721
9	.5214	.6021	.6852	.7348	.8471
10	.4971	.5760	.6581	.7079	.8233
11	.4762	.5529	.6339	.6835	.8010
12	.4575	.5324	.6120	.6614	.7800
13	.4409	.5139	.5923	.6411	.7603
14	.4259	.4973	.5742	.6226	.7420
15	.4124	.4821	.5577	.6055	.7246
16	.4000	.4683	.5425	.5897	.7084
17	.3887	.4555	.5285	.5751	.6932
18	.3783	.4438	.5155	.5614	.6787
19	.3687	.4329	.5034	.5487	.6652
20	.3598	.4227	.4921	.5368	.6524
25	.3233	.3809	.4451	.4869	.5974
30	.2960	.3494	.4093	.4487	.5541
35	.2746	.3246	.3810	.4182	.5189
40	.2573	.3044	.3578	.3932	.4896
45	.2428	.2875	.3384	.3721	.4648
50	.2306	.2732	.3218	.3541	.4433
60	.2108	.2500	.2948	.3248	.4078
70	.1954	.2319	.2737	.3017	.3799
80	.1829	.2172	.2565	.2830	.3568
90	.1726	.2050	.2422	.2673	.3375
100	.1638	.1946	.2301	.2540	.3211

Source: James V. Couch, *Fundamentals of Statistics for the Behavioral Sciences* (St. Paul: West, 1987), 337.

APPENDIX E
Areas under the Standard Normal Curve

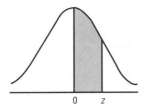

0   z

Probabilities that a random variable having the standard normal probability distribution assumes a value between 0 and z.

z	.00	.01	.02	.03	.04	.05	.06	.07	.08	.09
0.0	.0000	.0040	.0080	.0120	.0160	.0199	.0239	.0279	.0319	.0359
0.1	.0398	.0438	.0478	.0517	.0557	.0596	.0636	.0675	.0714	.0753
0.2	.0793	.0832	.0871	.0910	.0948	.0987	.1026	.1064	.1103	.1141
0.3	.1179	.1217	.1255	.1293	.1331	.1368	.1406	.1443	.1480	.1517
0.4	.1554	.1591	.1628	.1664	.1700	.1736	.1772	.1808	.1844	.1879
0.5	.1915	.1950	.1985	.2019	.2054	.2088	.2123	.2157	.2190	.2224
0.6	.2257	.2291	.2324	.2357	.2389	.2422	.2454	.2486	.2517	.2549
0.7	.2580	.2611	.2642	.2673	.2704	.2734	.2764	.2794	.2823	.2852
0.8	.2881	.2910	.2939	.2967	.2995	.3023	.3051	.3078	.3106	.3133
0.9	.3159	.3186	.3212	.3238	.3264	.3289	.3315	.3340	.3365	.3389
1.0	.3413	.3438	.3461	.3485	.3508	.3531	.3554	.3577	.3599	.3621
1.1	.3643	.3665	.3686	.3708	.3729	.3749	.3770	.3790	.3810	.3830
1.2	.3849	.3869	.3888	.3907	.3925	.3944	.3962	.3980	.3997	.4015
1.3	.4032	.4049	.4066	.4082	.4099	.4115	.4131	.4147	.4162	.4177
1.4	.4192	.4207	.4222	.4236	.4251	.4265	.4279	.4292	.4306	.4319
1.5	.4332	.4345	.4357	.4370	.4382	.4394	.4406	.4418	.4429	.4441
1.6	.4452	.4463	.4474	.4484	.4495	.4505	.4515	.4525	.4535	.4545
1.7	.4554	.4564	.4573	.4582	.4591	.4599	.4608	.4616	.4625	.4633
1.8	.4641	.4649	.4656	.4664	.4671	.4678	.4686	.4693	.4699	.4706
1.9	.4713	.4719	.4726	.4732	.4738	.4744	.4750	.4756	.4761	.4767
2.0	.4772	.4778	.4783	.4788	.4793	.4798	.4803	.4808	.4812	.4817
2.1	.4821	.4826	.4830	.4834	.4838	.4842	.4846	.4850	.4854	.4857
2.2	.4861	.4864	.4868	.4871	.4875	.4878	.4881	.4884	.4887	.4890
2.3	.4893	.4896	.4898	.4901	.4904	.4906	.4909	.4911	.4913	.4916
2.4	.4918	.4920	.4922	.4925	.4927	.4929	.4931	.4932	.4934	.4936
2.5	.4938	.4940	.4941	.4943	.4945	.4946	.4948	.4949	.4951	.4952
2.6	.4953	.4955	.4956	.4957	.4959	.4960	.4961	.4962	.4963	.4964
2.7	.4965	.4966	.4967	.4968	.4969	.4970	.4971	.4972	.4973	.4974
2.8	.4974	.4975	.4976	.4977	.4977	.4978	.4979	.4979	.4980	.4981
2.9	.4981	.4982	.4982	.4983	.4984	.4984	.4985	.4985	.4986	.4986
3.0	.4987	.4987	.4987	.4988	.4988	.4989	.4989	.4989	.4990	.4990

Source: Table II of A. Hald, *Statistical Tables and Formulas.* Copyright © 1952, John Wiley. Reprinted by permission of John Wiley & Sons, Inc.

Glossary

Accretion measures. Measures of phenomena through indirect observation of the accumulation of materials.

Action. Physical human movement or behavior done for a reason.

Alternative-form method. A method of calculating reliability by repeating different but equivalent measures at two or more points in time.

Ambiguous question. A question containing a concept that is not clearly defined.

Antecedent variable. An independent variable that precedes other independent variables in time.

Applied research. Research designed to produce knowledge useful in altering a real-world condition or situation.

Arrow diagram. A pictorial representation of a researcher's explanatory scheme.

Assignment at random. Random assignment of subjects to experimental and control groups.

Bar chart. A graphic display of the data in a frequency or percentage distribution.

Behavioralism. The study of politics that focuses on political behavior and embraces the scientific method.

Branching question. A question that sorts respondents into subgroups and directs these subgroups to different parts of the questionnaire.

Case study design. A comprehensive and in-depth study of a single case or several cases. A nonexperimental design in which the investigator has little control over events.

Central tendency. The most frequent, middle, or central value in a frequency distribution.

Chi-square. A measure used with crosstabulation to determine if a relationship is statistically significant.

Classic experimental design. An experiment with the random assignment of subjects to experimental and control groups with a pre-test and post-test for both groups.

Closed-ended question. A question with response alternatives provided.

Cluster sample. A probability sample that is used when no list of elements exists. The sampling frame initially consists of clusters of elements.

Confidence level. The probability that the population parameter actually falls within the margin of error of a sample statistic.

Construct validity. Validity demonstrated for a measure by showing that it is related to the measure of another concept.

Content analysis. A procedure by which verbal, nonquantitative records are transformed into quantitative data.

Content validity. Validity demonstrated by ensuring that the full domain of a concept is measured.

Control by adjustment. A form of statistical control in which a mathematical adjustment is made to assess the impact of a third variable.

Control by grouping. A form of statistical control in which observations identical or similar for the control variable are grouped together.

Control group. A group of subjects that does not receive the experimental treatment or test stimulus.

Convenience sample. A nonprobability sample in which the selection of elements is determined by the researcher's convenience.

Correlation matrix. A table showing the correlations (usually Pearson product-moment correlations) among a number of variables.

Covert observation. Observation in which the observer's presence or purpose is kept secret from those being observed.

Cross-sectional design. A research design in which measurements of independent and dependent variables are taken at the same time; naturally occurring differences in the independent variable are used to create quasi-experimental and quasi-control groups; extraneous factors are controlled for by statistical means.

Crosstabulation. A technique for measuring the relationship between nominal and ordinal level measures.

Cumulative proportion. The total proportion of observations at or below a value in a frequency distribution.

Deduction. A process of reasoning from a theory to specific observations.

Degrees of freedom. A measure used in conjunction with chi-square and other measures to determine if a relationship is statistically significant.

Dependent variable. The phenomenon thought to be influenced, affected, or caused by some other phenomenon.

Descriptive statistic. The mathematical summary of measurements for one variable.

Deviant case study. Study of a case that deviates from other cases and from what prevailing theory would lead the researcher to expect.

Dichotomous variable. A variable with only two categories or values.

Difference of means test. A technique for measuring the relationship between one nominal or ordinal level variable and one interval or ratio level variable.

Direction of a relationship. An indication of which values of the dependent variable are associated with which values of the independent variable.

Directional hypothesis. A hypothesis that specifies the expected relationship between two or more variables.

Direct observation. Actual observation of behavior.

Directory. A database that arranges terms in a hierarchy by subject matter, allowing a search to proceed from general to specific topics.

Dispersion. The distribution of data values around the most frequent, middle, or central value.

Disproportionate sample. A stratified sample in which elements sharing a characteristic are underrepresented or overrepresented in the sample.

Double-barreled question. A question that is really two questions in one.

Ecological fallacy. The fallacy of deducing a false relationship between the attributes or behavior of individuals based on observing that relationship for groups to which the individuals belong.

Electronic database. A collection of information (of any type) stored on an electromagnetic medium that can be accessed and examined by certain computer programs.

Element. A particular case or entity about which information is collected; the unit of analysis.

Elite interviewing. Interviewing respondents in a nonstandardized, individualized manner.

Empirical generalization. A statement that summarizes the relationship between individual facts and that communicates general knowledge.

Empirical research. Research based on actual, "objective" observation of phenomena.

Empirical verification. Characteristic of scientific knowledge; demonstration by means of objective observation that a statement is true.

Enumerative table. A table listing the observed values of a variable.

Episodic record. The portion of the written record that is not part of a regular, ongoing record-keeping enterprise.

Erosion measures. Measures of phenomena through indirect observation of selective wear of some material.

Estimator. A statistic based on sample observations that is used to estimate the numerical value of a population characteristic or parameter.

Eta-squared. A measure of association used with the analysis of variance that indicates the proportion of the variance in the dependent variable explained by the variance in the independent variable.

Expected value. The mean or average value of a sample statistic based on repeated samples from a population.

Experimental control. Manipulation of the exposure of experimental groups to experimental stimuli to assess the impact of a third variable.

Experimental effect. Effect of the independent variable on the dependent variable.

Experimental group. A group of subjects that receives the experimental treatment or test stimulus.

Experimental mortality. A differential loss of subjects from experimental and control groups that affects the equivalency of groups; threat to internal validity.

Experimentation. Research using an experimental research design in which the researcher has control over the independent variable, the units of analysis, and their environment; used to test causal relationships.

Explained variance. That portion of the variation in a dependent variable that is accounted for by the variation in the independent variable(s).

Explanation. A systematic, empirically verified understanding of why a phenomenon occurs as it does.

Explanatory. Characteristic of scientific knowledge; signifies that a conclusion can be derived from a set of general propositions and specific initial considerations.

External validity. The ability to generalize from one set of research findings to other situations.

Extraneous factors. Factors besides the independent variable that may cause change in the dependent variable.

F ratio. A measure used with the analysis of variance to determine if a relationship is statistically significant.

Face validity. Validity asserted by arguing that a measure corresponds closely to the concept it is designed to measure.

Factor analysis. A statistical technique useful in the construction of multiple-item scales to measure abstract concepts.

Factorial design. Experimental design used to measure the effect of two or more independent variables singly and in combination.

Field experiments. Experimental designs applied in a natural setting.

Field study. Observation in a natural setting.

Filter question. A question used to screen respondents so that subsequent questions will be asked only of certain respondents for whom the questions are appropriate.

Focused interview. A semistructured or flexible interview schedule used when interviewing elites.

Frequency curve. A line graph summarizing a frequency distribution.

Frequency distribution (f). The number of observations per value or category of a variable.

General. Characteristic of scientific knowledge; applicable to many rather than a few cases.

Goodman and Kruskal's gamma. A measure of association between ordinal level variables.

Goodman and Kruskal's lambda. A measure of association between one nominal or ordinal level variable and one nominal level variable.

Guttman scale. A multi-item measure in which respondents are presented with increasingly difficult measures of approval for an attitude.

History. A change in the dependent variable due to changes in the environment over time; threat to internal validity.

Hypothesis. A statement proposing a relationship between two or more variables.

Independent variable. The phenomenon thought to influence, affect, or cause some other phenomenon.

Index. A multi-item measure in which individual scores on a set of items are combined to form a summary measure.

Indirect observation. Observation of physical traces of behavior.

Induction. A process of reasoning from specific observations to general principle.

Informant. Person who helps a researcher employing participant observation method interpret the activities and behavior of him/herself and the group to which he/she belongs.

Informed consent. Procedures that inform potential research subjects about the proposed research in which they are being asked to participate. Principle that researchers must obtain the freely given consent of human subjects before they participate in a research project.

Institutional Review Board. Panel to which researchers must submit descriptions of proposed research involving human subjects for the purpose of ethics review.

Instrument decay. A change in the measurement device used to measure the dependent variable, producing change in measurements; threat to internal validity.

Instrument reactivity. Reaction of subjects to a pre-test.

Interaction effect. Reaction of subjects to a combination of pre-test and experimental stimulus.

Intercoder reliability. Demonstration that multiple analysts, following the same content analysis procedure, agree and obtain the same measurements.

Interitem association. A test of the extent to which the scores of several items, each thought to measure the same concept, are the same. Results are displayed in a correlation matrix.

Internal validity. The ability to show that manipulation or variation of the independent variable causes the dependent variable to change.

Interquartile range. The middle 50 percent of observations.

Interval measurement. A measure for which a one-unit difference in scores is the same throughout the range of the measure.

Intervening variable. A variable coming between an independent and a dependent variable in an explanatory scheme.

Interview data. Observations derived from written or verbal questioning of the respondent by the researcher.

Interviewer bias. The interviewer's influence on the respondent's answers; an example of reactivity.

Kendall's tau. A measure of association between ordinal level variables.

Leading question. A question that encourages the respondent to choose a particular response.

Level of measurement. An indication of what is meant by assigning scores or numerals to empirical observations.

Likert scale. A multi-item measure in which the items are selected based on their ability to discriminate between those scoring high and those scoring low on the measure.

Line diagram. Another name for a frequency curve.

Linear probability model. Regression model in which a dichotomous variable is treated as the dependent variable.

Logistic regression. Regression model or equation in which the log odds of one response as opposed to another is the dependent variable.

Logistic regression coefficient. A multiple regression coefficient based on the logistic model.

Mailed questionnaire. A survey instrument mailed to the respondent for completion and return.

Margin of error. The range around a sample statistic within which the population parameter is likely to fall.

Maturation. A change in subjects over time that affects the dependent variable; threat to internal validity.

Mean deviation. A measure of dispersion of data points for interval and ratio level data.

Mean. The sum of the values of a variable divided by the number of values.

Measurement. The process by which phenomena are observed systematically and represented by scores or numerals.

Measures of association. Statistics that summarize the relationship between two variables.

Median. The category or value above and below which one-half of observations lie.

Mode. The category with the greatest frequency of observations.

Multigroup design. Experimental design with more than one control and experimental group.

Multiple correlation coefficient. A statistic varying between 0 and 1 that indicates the proportion of the total variation in Y, a dependent variable, that is statistically "explained" by the independent variable.

Multiple regression analysis. A technique for measuring the mathematical relationships between more than one independent variable and a dependent variable, while controlling for all other independent variables in the equation.

Multiple regression coefficient. A number that tells how much Y will change for a one-unit change in a particular independent variable, if all of the other variables in the model have been held constant.

Multivariate crosstabulation. A procedure by which crosstabulation is used to control for a third variable.

Multivariate data analysis. Data analysis techniques designed to test hypotheses involving more than two variables.

Negative relationship. A relationship in which high values of one variable are associated with low values of another variable. Or, a relationship in which the values of one variable increase as the values of another variable decrease.

Negatively skewed. A distribution of values in which fewer observations lie to the left of the middle value and those observations are fairly distant from the mean.

Nominal measurement. A measure for which different scores represent different, but not ordered, categories.

Nonexperimental design. A research design characterized by at least one of the following: presence of a single group, lack of researcher control over the assignment of subjects to control and experimental groups, lack of researcher control over application of the independent variable, or inability of researcher to measure dependent variable before and after exposure to the independent variable occurs.

Nonnormative knowledge. Knowledge concerned not with evaluation or prescription but with factual or objective determinations.

Nonprobability sample. A sample for which each element in the total population has an unknown probability of being selected.

Normal distribution. A frequency curve showing a symmetrical, bell-shaped distribution in which the mean, mode, and median coincide and in which a fixed proportion of observations lies between the mean and any distance from the mean measured in terms of the standard deviation.

Normative knowledge. Knowledge that is evaluative, value-laden, and concerned with prescribing what ought to be.

Null hypothesis. The hypothesis that there is no relationship between two variables in the target population.

Odds. The probability of one response or value of a variable over the probability of another response or value of a variable.

Open-ended question. A question with no response alternatives provided for the respondent.

Operational definition. The rules by which a concept is measured and scores assigned.

Ordinal measurement. A measure for which the scores represent ordered categories that are not necessarily equidistant from each other.

Overt observation. Observation in which those being observed are informed of the observer's presence and purpose.

Panel mortality. Loss of participants from panel study.

Panel study. A cross-sectional study in which measurements of variables are taken on the same units of analysis at multiple points in time.

Partial regression coefficient. A number that indicates how much a dependent variable would change if an independent variable changed one unit and all other variables in the equation or model were held constant.

Participant observation. Observation in which the observer becomes a regular participant in the activities of those being observed.

Partly spurious relationship. A relationship between two variables caused partially by the impact of a third.

Pearson product-moment correlation. The statistic computed from a regression analysis that indicates the strength of the relationship between two interval or ratio level variables.

Personal interview. Face-to-face questioning of the respondent.

Pie diagram. A circular graphic display of a frequency distribution.

Political science. The application of the methods of acquiring scientific knowledge to the study of political phenomena.

Population. All of the cases or observations covered by a hypothesis; all the units of analysis to which a hypothesis applies.

Population parameter. The incidence of a characteristic or attribute in a population (not a sample).

Positive relationship. A relationship in which high values of one variable are associated with high values of another variable. Or, a relationship in which the values of one variable increase as the values of another variable increase.

Positively skewed. A distribution of values in which fewer observations lie to the right of the middle value and those observations are fairly distant from the mean.

Postbehavioralism. The reaction to behavioralism that called for political science research to be more relevant to important current political issues.

Post-test. Measurement of the dependent variable after manipulation of the independent variable.

Precision matching. Matching of pairs of subjects with one of the pair assigned to the experimental group and the other to the control group.

Predictive. Characteristic of explanatory knowledge; indicates an ability to correctly anticipate future events. The application of explanation to events in the future forms a prediction.

Pre-test. Measurement of the dependent variable prior to the administration of the experimental treatment or manipulation of the independent variable.

Probabilistic explanation. An explanation that does not explain or predict events with 100-percent accuracy.

Probability sample. A sample for which each element in the total population has a known probability of being selected.

Proportionate sample. A probability sample that draws elements from a stratified population at a rate proportional to size of the samples.

Provisional. Characteristic of scientific knowledge; subject to revision and change.

Pure, theoretical, or recreational research. Research designed to satisfy one's intellectual curiosity about some phenomenon.

Purposive sample. A nonprobability sample in which a researcher uses discretion in selecting elements for observation.

Question order effect. The effect on responses of question placement within a questionnaire.

Questionnaire design. The physical layout and packaging of a questionnaire.

Quota sample. A nonprobability sample in which elements are sampled in proportion to their representation in the population.

Random digit dialing. A procedure used to improve the representativeness of telephone samples by giving both listed and unlisted numbers a chance of selection.

Random numbers table. A list of random numbers in tabular form.

Random start. Selection of a number at random to determine where to start selecting elements in a systematic sample.

Randomized response technique (RRT). A method of obtaining accurate answers to sensitive questions that protects the respondent's privacy.

Range. The distance between the highest and lowest values or the range of categories into which observations fall.

Ratio measurement. A measure for which the scores possess the full mathematical properties of the numbers assigned.

Reason. Beliefs and desires that justify or explain an action or behavior.

Regression analysis. A technique for measuring the relationship between two interval or ratio level variables.

Regression coefficient. Another name for the slope of a regression equation.

Regression constant. Value of the dependent variable when all of the values of the independent variables in the equation equal zero.

Regression equation. The mathematical formula describing the relationship between two interval or ratio level variables.

Relationship. The association, dependence, or covariance of the values of one variable with the values of another variable.

Relative frequency. Percent or proportion of total number of observations in a frequency distribution that have a particular value.

Reliability. The extent to which a measure yields the same results on repeated trials.

Research design. A plan specifying how the researcher intends to fulfill the goals of the study; a logical plan for testing hypotheses.

Residual. The difference between the observed and predicted values of Y (the dependent variable) in a regression analysis.

Response quality. The extent to which responses provide accurate and complete information.

Response rate. The proportion of respondents selected for participation in a survey who actually participate.

Response set. The pattern of responding to a series of questions in a similar fashion without careful reading of each question.

Running record. The portion of the written record that is enduring and covers an extensive period of time.

Sample. A subset of observations or cases drawn from a specified population.

Sample bias. The bias that occurs whenever some elements of a population are systematically excluded from a sample. It is usually due to an incomplete sampling frame or a nonprobability method of selecting elements.

Sample statistic. The estimator of a population characteristic or attribute that is calculated from sample data.

Sampling distribution. A theoretical (non-observed) distribution of sample statistics calculated on samples of size N.

Sampling error. The confidence level and the margin of error taken together.

Sampling fraction. The proportion of the population included in a sample.

Sampling frame. The population from which a sample is drawn. Ideally it is the same as the total population of interest to a study.

Sampling interval. The number of elements in a sampling frame divided by the desired sample size.

Sampling unit. The entity listed in a sampling frame. It may be the same as an element, or it may be a group or cluster of elements.

Scatter plot. A technique for displaying graphically the relationship between two interval or ratio level variables.

Scientific revolution. The rapid development of a rival tradition of scientific research; usually accompanied by conflict among scientists over the theoretical perspective that will endure.

Search engine. A computer program that visits web pages on the Internet and looks for those containing particular directories or words.

Search term. A word or phrase entered into a computer program (a search engine) that looks through web pages on the Internet for those that contain the word or phrase.

Selection. Bias in the assignment of subjects to experimental and control groups; threat to internal validity.

Semantic differential. A technique for measuring attitudes toward an object in which respondents are presented with a series of opposite adjective pairs.

Simple post-test design. Weak type of experimental design with control and experimental groups but no pretest.

Simple random sample. A probability sample in which each element has an equal chance of being selected.

Single-sided question. A question with only one substantive alternative provided for the respondent.

Slope. The part of a regression equation that shows how much change in the value of Y (the dependent variable) corresponds to a one-unit change in the value of X (the independent variable).

Snowball sample. A sample in which respondents are asked to identify additional members of a population.

Solomon four-group design. Type of experimental design used to measure interaction between pretest and experimental treatment.

Somer's d. A measure of association between ordinal level variables.

Specified relationship. A relationship between two variables that varies with the values of a third.

Split-halves method. A method of calculating reliability by comparing the results of two equivalent measures made at the same time.

Spurious relationship. A relationship between two variables caused entirely by the impact of a third.

Standard deviation. A measure of dispersion of data points about the mean for interval and ratio level data.

Standard error. The standard deviation of sample statistics about the population or true value of the statistic being sampled.

Standard normal distribution. Normal distribution with a mean of zero and a standard deviation and variance of one.

Standardized regression coefficient. Regression coefficient adjusted by the standard deviation of the independent and dependent variables so that its magnitude can be directly compared.

Statistical control. Assessing the impact of a third variable by comparing observations across the values of a control variable.

Statistical inference. Making probability statements about population parameters and characteristics based on sample statistics and the use of statistical theory.

Statistical regression. Change in the dependent variable due to the temporary nature of extreme values; threat to internal validity.

Statistical significance. An indication of whether an observed relationship could have occurred by chance.

Statistically independent. Property of two variables where the probability that an observation is in a particular category of one variable *and* a particular category of the other variable equals the simple or marginal probability of being in those categories.

Stratified sample. A probability sample in which elements sharing one or more characteristics are grouped, and elements are selected from each group.

Stratum. A subgroup of a population that shares one or more characteristics.

Strength of a relationship. An indication of how consistently the values of a dependent variable are associated with the values of an independent variable.

Structured observation. Systematic observation and recording of the incidence of specific behaviors.

Survey instrument. The schedule of questions to be asked of the respondent.

Survey research. Research based on the interview method of data collection.

Systematic sample. A probability sample in which elements are selected from a list at predetermined intervals.

t test. A statistical procedure used to determine the statistical significance of a difference of means.

Tautology. A hypothesis in which the independent and dependent variables are identical, making it impossible to disconfirm.

Telephone interview. The questioning of the respondent via telephone.

Termination. The respondent's refusal to finish the interview.

Test stimulus. The independent variable.

Testing. Effect of a pre-test on the dependent variable; threat to internal validity.

Test-retest method. A method of calculating reliability by repeating the same measure at two or more points in time.

Theory. A statement or series of statements that organize, explain, and predict knowledge.

Time series design. A research design featuring multiple measurements of the dependent variable before and after experimental treatment.

Total variance. The variation in a dependent variable that a researcher is attempting to account for.

Transmissible. Characteristic of scientific knowledge; indicates that the methods used in making scientific discoveries are made explicit.

Two-sided question. A question with two substantive alternatives provided for the respondent.

Two-way analysis of variance. An extension of the analysis of variance procedure to allow controlling for a third variable.

Unexplained variance. That portion of the variation in a dependent variable that is not accounted for by the variation in the independent variable(s).

Unit of analysis. The type of actor (individual, group, institution, nation) specified in a researcher's hypothesis.

Univariate data analysis. The analysis of a single variable.

Unstructured observation. Observation in which all behavior and activities are recorded.

Validity. The correspondence between a measure and the concept it is supposed to measure.

Variance. A measure of dispersion of data points about the mean for interval and ratio level data.

Weighting factor. A mathematical factor used to make a disproportionate sample representative.

Written record. Documents, reports, statistics, manuscripts, and other written, oral, or visual materials available and useful for empirical research.

Y-intercept. The value of Y (the dependent variable) in a regression equation when the value of X (the independent variable) is 0.

Z score. The number of standard deviations by which a score deviates from the mean score.

Index

Katz, Linda Sternberg, 180 n.8
Kay, Susan Ann, 68 n.1
Kendall's tau, 351, 353
Kennedy, John F., 278
Kennedy, Robert, 33
Kentucky, 238–240
Kenya, 223
Keohane, Robert O., 209 n.2
Kessel, John, 297 n.2
Kinder, Donald, 121
King, Gary, 209 n.2
Klein, Harald, 259
Knowledge. *See also* Scientific
    knowledge
  causal, 394–395
  commonsense, 24
  explanatory, 27–28
  general, 26–27
  mystical, 23–24
  nonnormative, 25
  normative, 24–25
  provisional, 31
  transmissible, 25
Kohnke-Aguirre, Luane, 300 n.68
Kuhn, Thomas, 41 n.16

Labaw, Patricia, 283, 285
Laboratory settings, 222–223
Lakind, Elizabeth, 41 n.24
Landon, Alf, 186–187
Landon, E. L., Jr., 209 n.7
Land ownership, 5, 78–79, 237, 249,
    306–307
Lang, Gladys Engel, 229
Lang, Kurt, 229
Latin America, political violence in,
    5, 306–307
Lauren, Paul Gordon, 149 n.21
Lazarsfeld, Paul, 37
Leading questions, 278
Least squares, 408
Least squares regression, 372
Left corporatism, 104
Legalism, 36
Leinhardt, Samuel, 300 n.64
Lejins, Peter P., 269 n.19
Level of measurement, 92–95
Lewis-Beck, Michael, 10–11, 86
Lexis-Nexis, 249
Liberalism, 67, 74, 80, 88, 99–100
Likelihood, 419–420
Likelihood ratio statistic, 423
Likert scale, 99–100
Linear multiple regression equation,
    406
Linear probability model, 414, 416

Linear regression, 384–385
Line diagrams, 315–316
Linsky, Arnold S., 299 n.55
Lipset, Seymour Martin, 145
Lipsitz, Lewis, 268 n.9
Literacy, and democracy, 54–55, 59,
    73–74
Literary Digest poll, 186–187
Literature review, 154. *See also*
    Internet literature review
  benefits of, 157–158
  concept definitions and, 67–68,
    156–157
  conducting, 159–160
  on Internet, 160–171
  organizing references, 175
  printed research sources, 171–180
  purposes of, 57, 67, 155–159
  selecting a research topic,
    154–155
Liu, Alan P., 268 n.1
Lofland, John, 227
Logistic regression, 412–430
  alternative interpretation of
    logistic regression coefficients,
    424–427
  estimating the model's
    coefficients, 418–419
  measures of fit, 419–422
  substantive example, 427–430
  testing hypotheses, 422–424
Logistic regression coefficients,
    416–417, 424–427
Logistic regression function, 415
Logit, 426
Log likelihoods, 420–421, 423
Log odds, 426
Long, J. Scott, 431 n.15
Longitudinal analysis, 264–265
Lot selection method, 189–190

MacArthur, Douglas, 229
MacFarland, Sam G., 298 n.34
Madison, James, 243
Mailed questionnaires, 287–297. *See
    also* Questionnaires
  bias, 287–288, 290–291
  cost and administrative
    requirements, 295–297
  definition, 287
  incentives for return, 124
  privacy of, 294
  representativeness of
    respondents, 290–291
  response rate, 124, 125–126,
    287–290

Manne, Stella, 41 n.24
Mannheim, Jarol B., 148 n.5
Mansfield, Edwin, 210 n.25
Manuscripts, ethical proofreading
    of, 231–233
Marcus, Alfred C., 300 n.72
Marginal probabilities, 347–348
Margin of error, 198, 205–208
Market failure theory of
    government regulation, 30
Markus, Gregory B., 106 n.17
Marquis, Jefferson P., 42 n.32
Martin, Michael, 42 n.28
Mason, W. M., 298 n.31
Massachusetts Bay Colony, 241–242
Mass insurgency, 9, 75–76
Mass media. *See* Media
Matheny, Albert R., 29–30
Matthews, Donald R., 180 n.5
Maturation, 114
McAllister, Ronald J., 210 n.25
McConahay, John, 383
McCoy, Charles A., 41 n.27,
    42 n.36
McDonald, Forrest, 268 n.9
McGuire, Kevin, 14
McPherson, J. Miller, 106 n.17
Meadow, Robert G., 298 n.16
Mean, 323–324. *See also* Difference
    of means test
Mean deviation, 324–325
Measurement, 72–73. *See also*
    Reliability; Validity
  accretion measure, 228–229
  accuracy of, 81–92
  attitudes measure, 13, 97–98
  definition, 72
  erosion of, 228
  examples of political
    measurement, 74–81
  instrumentation difficulties, 131
  interval measures, 94, 323–327
  level of, 92–95
  multi-item measures, 95–105
  nominal, 93, 319–321
  ordinal, 93–94, 321–323
  physical trace, 228–229
  of political change, 89–90, 98
  of political violence, 4–6
  precision of, 92–95
  problems of, 34–35
  ratio level, 94–95, 323–327
  strategies for, 73–74
Measures of association, 350–357,
    400–401
Measures of fit, 419–422